MENTAL RETARDATION

MENTAL RETARDATION:
Nature, Cause, and Management
Third Edition

by

George S. Baroff, Ph.D.

University of North Carolina at Chapel Hill

with

J. Gregory Olley, Ph.D.

Center for the Study of Development and Learning
University of North Carolina at Chapel Hill

USA	Publishing Office:	BRUNNER/MAZEL *A member of the Taylor & Francis Group* 325 Chestnut Street Philadelphia, PA 19106 Tel: (215) 625-8900 Fax: (215) 625-2940
	Distribution Center:	BRUNNER/MAZEL *A member of the Taylor & Francis Group* 47 Runway Road, Suite G Levittown, PA 19057 Tel: (215) 269-0400 Fax: (215) 269-0363
UK		BRUNNER/MAZEL *A member of the Taylor & Francis Group* 1 Gunpowder Square London EC4A 3DE Tel: +44 171 583 0490 Fax: +44 171 583 0581

MENTAL RETARDATION: Nature, Cause, and Management, 3/E

1 2 3 4 5 6 7 8 9 0

Cover design by Nancy Abbott.

Printed by Edwards Brothers, Ann Arbor, MI, 1999.

Cover photo courtesy of National Down Syndrome Society.

A CIP catalog record for this book is available from the British Library.

⊗ The paper in this publication meets the requirements of the ANSI Standard Z39.48-1984 (Permanence of Paper).

Library of Congress Cataloging-in-Publication Data

Baroff, George S.
    Mental retardation : nature, cause, and management / George S.
Baroff with J. Gregory Olley. – 3rd ed.
        p.   cm.
    Includes bibliographical references and index.
    ISBN 1-58391-000-X (case : alk. paper). – ISBN 1-58391-001-8
(pbk. : alk. paper)
    1. Mental retardation.   2. Mentally handicapped–Care.   I. Olley,
J. Gregory.   II. Title.
    [DNLM: 1. Mental Retardation.   WS 107 B264m 1999]
RC570.B27   1999
616.85'88–dc21
DNLM/DLC
for Library of Congress   99-24045
                                                                    CIP

ISBN   1-58391-000-x   (case: alk. paper)
ISBN   1-58391-001-8   (pbk: alk. paper)

CONTENTS

6

Introduction to Services and Supports

7

Services and Supports to Children and Youth

8

Services and Supports to Adults

9

Maladaptive or "Challenging" Behavior: Its Nature and Treatment

J. Gregory Olley

10   Psychiatric Disorders in Mental Retardation

J. Gregory Olley, George S. Baroff

PREFACE

This is the third edition of a text first published in the 1970s. Like its predecessors, it aspires to comprehensiveness and readability. Targeted to upper-level undergraduate and graduate students and to professionals in the field, the book examines three aspects of the disability of mental retardation—its nature, its causes, and its management or treatment. Organized similarly to the earlier editions, the first half of the book is devoted to the nature and cause of mental retardation, and the latter half focuses on its habilitative aspect. A new feature is the inclusion of a summary and discussion questions at the end of each chapter. Certainly, the most important new dimension is the addition of a second author, Dr. J. Gregory Olley. Dr. Olley is a behaviorally-oriented clinical psychologist with a broad experience in the diagnosis and treatment of the various behavior problems seen in the disorder. Dr. Olley, Associate Director of the Clinical Center for Development and Learning, the university-affiliated mental retardation program at the University of North Carolina at Chapel Hill, is the author of the sections on the diagnosis, cause, and treatment of the major behavior and psychiatric disorders found in mental retardation.

The initial chapter of the book provides an examination of the nature of intelligence and of the disorder that represents its greatest impairment, mental retardation. The exploration of mental retardation includes an analysis of its most recent definition by the American Association on Mental Retardation, its 1992 version, which, like its immediate predecessor, has been adopted by the American Psychiatric Association. The intent of the first chapter is to convey the effects of the disability on the adaptive potential of persons with mental retardation and on their family. It is a picture that can be marked by both chronic frustration and joyous accomplishment. Perhaps most common is the achievement of goals that surprise those of us struck more by apparent deficits than by latent potential.

The second chapter deals with a topic rarely addressed in the mental retardation literature, the impact of the disability on the "personality" and emotional well-being of the affected person. The intent is to represent the individual with retardation as a person, like ourselves, although challenged by a disability that can create obstacles throughout life. The humanity of affected individuals is conveyed by first presenting a personality model useful for understanding all of us, disabled and nondisabled. The model is based on "needs," physiological and psychological, that all of us share but whose gratification is particularly threatened by disability, whatever its nature. That these needs are commonly frustrated in persons with retardation is reflected, in part, in their relatively high rate of behavioral difficulties, the nature of which is addressed in the last two chapters.

Whereas the first two chapters convey the "nature" of mental retardation, Chapters 3, 4, and 5 are concerned with its causation, biological and psychological or psychosocial. The biological contribution is divided between genetic and nongenetic causes, the former presented in Chapter 3 and the latter in Chapter 4. Chapter 3 describes the major chromosomal and genetic forms of mental retardation with special attention to Down syndrome, Prader-Willi syndrome, and fragile X syndrome. Chapter 4 reviews the various forms of retardation that can arise in a presumably genetically normal embryo or fetus because of untoward events prior to birth, at birth, and during infancy and early childhood. Much attention is given to fetal alcohol syndrome, a form of retardation caused by exposure of the fetus to high levels of alcohol and wholly preventable. The chapter also includes descriptions of two neurological conditions often accompanied by mental retardation: cerebral palsy and epilepsy.

Chapter 5 explores the role of the psychological or psychosocial environment on cognitive development. It describes current thinking about the kinds of childhood experiences that are thought to encourage healthy cognitive and emotional development and, conversely, those that inhibit it. The latter part of the chapter reviews the research in early childhood education, such as Head Start, as its effects are revealed on the biologically normal infant and young child. Apart from assuring that children are brought into this world with their capacities undamaged by prenatal insult, our society has no greater responsibility than that of providing the kind of developmental experience that enables them to fully develop those capacities.

Chapters 6 through 10 are devoted to the habilitative services and "supports" that are intended to maximize the adaptive potential of the child, youth, and adult with mental retardation and to assist his or her family. Chapter 6 introduces the habilitative aspect by describing the current beliefs and "values" that underlie these services, especially those that encourage the full integration of persons with the disability into the general community. The lessons taught by our historical separation of disabled individuals from their families and home communities were painfully revealed in the exposés of our large mental-retardation institutions in the 1960s. The ensuing scandal sparked the "deinstitutionalization" movement, one that has influenced the care of persons with psychiatric disorders as well as that of those with mental retardation.

Chapters 7 and 8 describe the services themselves. Chapter 7 presents those for children and youth, roughly divided between the preschool and school years. At the preschool level, the early childhood educational research related to children with retardation and other developmental disabilities is presented, especially with reference to its efficacy. The chapter content related to the school-aged child is organized around "special education"—its "what," "where," and "how." The "how" dimension focuses on the instructional procedures that have proved most effective for children with serious learning difficulties. Also included is a description of such noneducational services as recreation, family support, and health.

Chapter 8 is devoted to the adult, and the topics covered are educational needs; vocational, "day," and leisure services; the always vexing problem of "managing" the sexuality of persons who require varying degrees of supervision; health needs; and the special needs of older adults. With respect to the last topic mentioned, the aging of the general population is paralleled by that of those with disabilities, and increasing attention is being given to seniors with mental retardation.

The last two chapters are focused largely on the behavior problems seen in retardation. Chapter 9 describes the causation, diagnosis, and treatment of the most common challenging behaviors: aggression, repetitive movement disorder (stereotyped and self-injurious behavior), and obsessive-compulsive disorder. The chapter concludes with a brief discussion of the management of problematic sexual behavior.

The last chapter also deals with behavior problems, but here the focus is on those with formal psychiatric labels. Presented with regard to their nature and treatment are disorders of anxiety and mood, schizophrenia, Tourette syndrome, personality disorders, disorders of eating—pica and rumination—and substance abuse. The chapter also describes two other developmental disorders that include major learning difficulties: autism and the developmental learning disorders (learning disabilities). The majority of persons with autism also show mental retardation; those with learning disabilities, although grossly normal in intelligence, share with those with mental retardation academic learning problems, albeit much milder and more circumscribed.

In closing this preface, the senior author can only wonder at the enormous changes that have occurred in this field since his introduction to it in the 1950s. Perhaps most striking is the growing awareness on the part of the general population of persons with disabilities. Normally developing children have contact with their disabled peers in the classroom, and nondisabled adults meet their disabled counterparts in the workplace. The barriers between disabled and nondisabled individuals are falling, to the advantage of both groups. The Americans with Disabilities Act is clear witness to the insistence of persons with disabilities that they are no longer willing to be treated as society's stepchildren. They want the same opportunity to participate in the life of their communities as is afforded to those of us who are not disabled, and their voices increasingly are being heard.

George S. Baroff

The Nature of Mental Retardation

This is a book about *people*—children, youth, and adults who have difficulty in coping with activities of daily life because of *impaired general intelligence*. The extent of their difficulty is primarily related to the degree of intellectual impairment, although it also is much affected by both society's general attitude toward individuals with limited intelligence and the services provided to them. For those with *mild intellectual impairment*, the impact is greatest in the scholastic, vocational, and social domains. At levels of *moderate, severe,* and *profound* intellectual impairment, virtually every aspect of living is affected, the paramount consequence being to render the person incapable of assuming the degree of independence and personal responsibility expected for someone of his or her age.

The book covers each of the major dimensions of the disorder—its nature, its causes, and its treatment or management. The first two chapters examine its *nature*, the focus being on its intellectual, personality, and adaptive consequences and their impact on parents and siblings. In the next three chapters *causation* is explored, both biological and psychological. The remainder of the book is devoted to how we attempt to assist individuals with retardation[1] and their families, its *management* or treatment. This involves a description of the range of services developed for its prevention, detection, and habilitation throughout the life span—from infancy to older adulthood. The aim of habilitative services and "supports," is to enable the individual to achieve his or her[2] level of adaptive competence and life satisfaction, a goal not different from yours and mine.

In this chapter we consider the nature of intelligence (it is the impairment in this capacity that is the essence of the disorder); issues related to who is classified as mentally retarded; the prevalence and causation of retardation; the most recent definition of the disorder, the 1992 version of the American Association on Mental Retardation (Luckasson et al., 1992); the nature of intellectual functioning in mental retardation; the quality of the thinking and adaptive functioning of those with retardation; the "developmental" nature of the disorder; its impact on the family; and adaptive potential in relation to chronological age and degree of retardation.

☐ On the Nature of Intelligence

Because we all use the word "intelligence" and assume that its meaning is understood, it behooves us to consider what it really does mean to us. In a survey of the general population, three behaviors were equated with intelligence: *practical problem solving*, that is, reasoning logically, seeing all sides of a problem, keeping an open mind; *verbal ability*, that is, being a good conversationalist, enjoying good reading; and *social intelligence*, that is, being sensitive to social cues, admitting mistakes, and displaying interest in the world at large (Neisser, 1979). These popular conceptions also are shared by theorists on intelligence (e.g., Sternberg, Conway, Ketron, & Bernstein, 1981) and in varying ways are incorporated in tests of intelligence.

Underlying "Factors" and "Processes"

Intelligence is manifested in our ability to learn, in the knowledge that we come to possess, and in our everyday coping behavior. But what underlies this most valued human capacity? We now consider what are regarded as the basic building blocks of "intelligent" behavior. These can be conceptualized in terms of *basic mental capacities* and *problem-solving processes*.

Basic Mental Capacities: The "Factorial" Approach

A product of the statistical technique of factor analysis, the factorial approach seeks to isolate the fewest common denominators or *factors* that account for the correlations between measures of intelligence. Two main factorial theories can be distinguished—intelligence viewed either as a relatively unitary phenomenon or as an amalgam of relatively independent abilities.

Intelligence as Relatively Unitary.   The means by which modern researchers have sought to discover the fundamental ingredients of intelligence is through the statistical technique of factor analysis. In the

field of intelligence, it is used to isolate the fewest common denominators or factors that account for the correlations between measures of intelligence. Earlier views of intelligence tended to see it as a single or unitary phenomenon, one that manifested itself in virtually all aspects of cognition. Termed the *general* factor or *g* it was first identified by Spearman (1923, 1927) and characterized as the ability "to educe relations," that is, to engage in deductive reasoning. It is this mental process, for example, that is utilized in understanding "analogies," such as a lawyer is to a client as a doctor is to a ... (Sternberg, 1981).

The prominence of *g* lies in the finding that various measures of cognitive functions that would be regarded as forms of "intelligence" tend to correlate with each other. This is not surprising because they share a common basis for the establishment of their "validity" as tests of intelligence: academic educability. Our capacities to read, write, and calculate, traditionally have been accepted as evidence of intelligence, and our intellectual abiltiy commonly is judged by the speed and accuracy with which we perform these functions. In effect, intelligence tests share common content because they were validated on their capacity to predict school achievement.

But the significance of *g* is not limited to our academic capabilities. The capacity to reason pervades our mental lives, not only the serious work-a-day world but also in the recreational realm. The games we play, for example, commonly require the use of strategies, and in their employment we exercise the ability to reason.

In addition to *g*, Spearman recognized the existence of what he called "specific" abilities, but he left to future researchers to clarify their nature. Prominent earlier representations of specific abilities are those of the Thurstones' (1941) "primary mental abilities," Vernon's (1950) two-factor model, and Guilford's (1967) mental "operations."[3]

Intelligence as Multifactorial.   In contrast to the earlier view of intelligence as a largely unitary capacity, multifactor theories portray it as a melange of relatively independent abilities. The role of the general factor, *g*, continues to be recognized, and current models of intelligence include it as the uppermost stratum in a *hierarchy* of cognitive abilities. The general factor sits atop the hierarchy, and beneath it is nested a group of relatively unique specific or special abilities. The hierarchy of cognitive abilites, the ingredients of intelligence, may be represented at several levels of depth. Immediately below *g* are found a group of "broad" specific abilities, each of which itself subsumes more distinct or derivative abilities. This hierarchy is shown in Figures 1.1 and 1.2.

The model of intelligence shown in Figure 1.1 (Carroll, 1993) represents our current understanding of the nature of intelligence as this is revealed through factor analysis. With our cognitive abilities organized in terms of

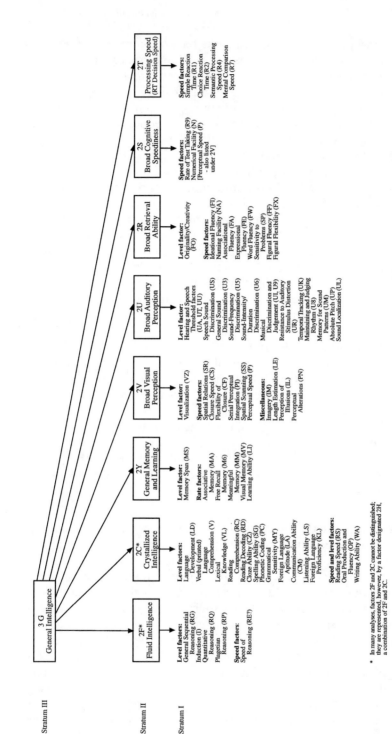

FIGURE 1.1. A three-strata hierarchical representation of cognitive abilities. (Reprinted with permission from J. B. Carroll, *Human cognitive abilities*, Cambridge University Press, 1993.)

three strata, *g* as "general intelligence" appears at the apex of the hierarchy in stratum III. At stratum II are found eight broad abilities, each receiving some contribution from *g* but also representing its own distinctive cognitive dimension.

Reading from left to right, the first two broad abilities are *fluid intelligence* and *crystallized intelligence*. The special contribution of Cattell (1971) and Horn (1968) fluid intelligence is equated with logical reasoning and crystallized intelligence with knowledge acquired through language. In its focus on logical reasoning, fluid intelligence largely would resemble *g*. Of these two forms of intelligence, the crystallized version is seen as very dependent on education; the fluid form may be more "native" or biological in its basis.

The other six broad abilities are *general learning and memory*, referring to immediate or short-term memory; *broad visual perception*, a mental ability central to spatial and mechanical understanding; *broad auditory perception*, sensitivity to various aspects of sound, such as speech sounds and rhyme; *broad retrieval ability*, the facile production of ideas, an ability pertaining to "creativity"; and two abilities related to "mental" speed—*broad cognitive speediness*, the speed of responding, and *processing speed*, reaction time and information-processing speed.

At stratum I, beneath each of the broad abilities are a large number of "narrow" or more specialized variants of the broad ability. At least 60 are now known (Carroll, 1997). Under fluid intelligence, for example, are found four kinds of reasoning—sequential, inductive, quantitative, and Piagetian. Of these, *g* was particularly associated with inductive reasoning. Crystallized intelligence encompasses a much wider number of narrow language-related abilities, such as language development, the understanding of language, knowledge of language structure, and reading decoding.

Specific Abilities and Intelligence Tests.   The measurement of specific abilities has typified tests of intelligence. The most recent version of the venerable Stanford-Binet Intelligence Scale, its fourth edition (Thorndike, Hagen, & Sattler, 1986), is organized around the assessment of crystallized and fluid intelligence and memory. Figure 1.2 shows the cognitive hierarchy with *g* at stratum III, the three broad abilities at stratum II, and components of crystallized and fluid intelligence at stratum I. In fact, the characterization of the subtests within the scale conform to stratum I—verbal reasoning and quantitative reasoning under crystallized abilities and abstract-visual reasoning under fluid-analytic abilities. Note that "reasoning" is evaluated in both crystallized and fluid forms, the distinction pertaining to language in the former and the use of visual tasks in the latter.

A very similar array of "specific" abilities is found in the Woodcock-Johnson Psycho-Educational Battery (Woodcock & Johnson, 1989), an intelligence test widely used in school settings. The Kaufman Brief Intelligence Test (K-BIT) (Kaufman & Kaufman, 1990) is organized around two broad abilities—crystallized and fluid intelligence.

Before terminating this section, it should be noted that recent researchers have expanded the array of specific abilities to include such capacities as "practical" and "social" intelligence. The former is equated with competence in the everyday world (e.g., Sternberg and Wagner, 1986), and the latter with effectiveness in social or interpersonal situations. Although both are relevant to the problems confronting people with mental retardation, impairment in social intelligence is of special interest. Lack of sophistication and social awkwardness are prominent features of mental retardation. There is a diminished awareness and sensitivity to what is appropriate in social situations. This is also characteristic of persons with the developmental disorder of autism, in whom retardation is commonly present, and is found even in those whose intellectual functions are normal. In retardation, however, it appears to be a direct consequence of intellectual impairment, and much effort is expended in attempting to "teach" more appropriate social interactions.

Information-Processing Models of Intelligence

The nature of intelligence also has been explored through a study of the mental processes that we employ in problem solving. Particular attention has been given to so-called executive functions, the processes associated with considering the nature of a given problem and the resources and strategies necessary to its solution. Parenthetically, this is another approach to intelligence that has much relevance to mental retardation. Individuals with mental retardation tend to have great difficulty in generating the kind of strategies that we commonly employ in helping us to solve problems.

An intelligence test (PASS) based on an information-processing model that incorporates an executive function seeks to assess planning (an executive function), attention, and simultaneous and successive modes of understanding information (Das, Naglieri, & Kirby, 1994). The simultaneous mode tends to be tied to understanding through vision (Carroll's broad visual perception) and the successive mode through language (broad auditory perception). Information-processing theorists have been active in mental retardation, and some of their findings related to retention of new information and to speed of responding are presented in a later section on the "quality of thinking" in persons with mental retardation.

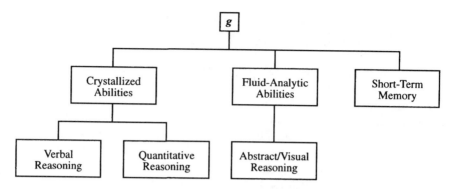

FIGURE 1.2. A hierarchical representation of the cognitive abilities measured on the Stanford-Binet Intelligence Scale: Fourth Edition. (Reprinted with permission from R. L. Thorndike, E. P. Hagen & J. M. Jattler, *The Stanford-Binet Intelligence Scale: Fourth Edition, Technical manual*, The Riverside Publishing Company, 1986.)

Relating Factors and Processes to Common Conceptions of Intelligence

Recalling popular conceptions of intelligence noted in introducing the topic, those views are a mix of process (practical problem solving), factors (crystallized intelligence), and "content" (social intelligence). The last-mentioned could be considered as the *setting* within which factors and processes operate rather than referring to a specific form of intelligence. In any case, nothing in the popular view is inconsistent with the scientific one. Perhaps implied in "problem solving," theorists have tended to equate intelligence with the ability to learn and acquire knowledge and to apply that knowledge to the solving of problems. Of the various mental abilities, special prominence has always been given to "reasoning," as that ability is manifested in crystallized and fluid forms and in g itself. Together with a motivational component, each of these elements also is found in Sternberg's (1981) definition of intelligence. Intelligence is seen as the ability to learn and to profit from experience, to acquire knowledge, to reason, to cope with changing conditions, and to motivate oneself to accomplish what needs to be done. The last-mentioned, a personality consideration, is not usually found in definitions of intelligence, although the author of the Wechsler intelligence tests observed that similar scores among individuals on those tests did not assure similar capacities to cope. Such traits as persistence and goal awareness interact with mental abilities in producing behavioral outcomes (Wechsler, 1981). We know that, too! Success in school, for example, is the product of both mental ability *and* desire.

☐ Issues Related to Classification as "Mentally Retarded"

Behavior Relevant to a Diagnosis of Retardation

Although intelligence is equated with learning ability, knowledge, reasoning, and coping with new situations, definitions of mental retardation usually refer to the adaptive problems created by intellectual limitations. Traditionally, retardation has been identified with impairment in the capacity for *personal responsibility*—that is, for assuming the degree of independence expected for one's chronological age (Benda, 1954; Doll, 1941; Luckasson et al., 1992; Tredgold, 1937). Because lack of capacity for prudent self-management also may be caused by emotional or physical problems, definitions of retardation always relate it to intellectual impairment.

Retardation and IQ

Although definitions of mental retardation are couched in terms of personal responsibility, the actual determination of retardation traditionally has been based on performance on an intelligence test. Scores on these tests commonly have been expressed in the intelligence quotient (IQ); with the IQ range representing retardation beginning at least two standard deviations below the mean or average of the general population. This is the bottom 2% to 3% of the population (Fig. 1.3).

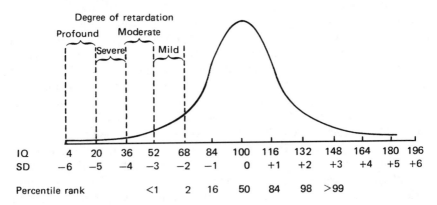

FIGURE 1.3. Distribution of measured intelligence in the normal and retarded range (based on Stanford-Binet IQs.)

The upper limit of this range typically has been set at *approximately* IQ 70[4] (Terman & Merrill, 1960; Wechsler, 1981). In 1959 the then American Association on Mental Deficiency (AAMD),[5] the main professional organization in the field, offered a definition of retardation that extended the range of retardation to within one standard deviation of the mean (Heber, 1957). Under it persons with IQs of 70 to 84 were classifiable as having "borderline" retardation. The upward extension was unwarranted, and in the 1973 revision, this category was eliminated (Grossman, 1973). In that revision, ceilings were set at IQ 68 on the Stanford-Binet and IQ 70 on the Wechsler scales. These were IQs that fell exactly two standard deviations below the mean of 100 on their respective scales. It was also in 1973 that a measure of the severity of intellectual impairment was introduced, retardation now being characterized as *mild* (IQ 52 to 69), *moderate* (IQ 36 to 54), *severe* (IQ 20 to 39), or *profound* (IQ 0 to 24) (see Fig. 1.2). In 1977, there was further softening of the ceiling criteria with the statement that "these upper limits (those modified to 67 on the Stanford-Binet and 69 on the Wechsler) are proposed as only *guidelines* rather than rigid limits" (Grossman, 1977). In the 1983 revision, there is no reference to the Stanford-Binet and Wechsler tests, as such, and the ceiling is returned to its earlier traditional upper limit of 70 although, for the first time, it is allowed to be extended beyond 70 to IQ 75 or more, depending on the statistical variability of the test used. This extension up to 75 or more, into the former borderline mental retardation range, was seen as of particular value to school settings, allowing hitherto excluded youngsters to have access to special education (Grossman, 1983). The current 1992 revision essentially continues the 1983 ceiling of 70 to 75 but now excludes the four levels of severity.

IQ and Behavior

One of the most complex issues surrounding the use of the IQ in mental retardation pertains to the distinction between performance on an intelligence test and general competency. Although subaverage intelligence unquestionably impedes school progress, it does not necessarily preclude adequate functioning in other areas of daily life. Thus, even very limited reading and arithmetic skills in and of themselves, will not, prevent an adult, for example, from achieving an independent adjustment—a level of adaptation that is attained not only by those with IQs in the 70 to 84 or "borderline" range but also by many in the below-70 range (Cobb, 1972). Is it meaningful to classify someone as retarded who, in spite of a below-70 IQ, is able to function independently?

IQ, Adaptive Behavior, and the then-AAMD Definition of Mental Retardation

In attempting to address this question, the 1959 AAMD definition of retardation specifically distinguished between IQ and overall adjustment by incorporating the concept of *adaptive behavior*. By this is meant the adjustive difficulties commonly associated with significant intellectual impairment. Classification as retarded would now require the presence of adaptive impairment as well as subaverage intelligence. The effort to link the two criteria has had only marginal success, largely because retardation traditionally has been so strongly equated with intelligence alone. Another important reason is that no measures of adaptive behavior have won the same degree of acceptance as have intelligence tests. The 1992 revision seeks to give greater emphasis to adaptive behavior and to weaken the influence of IQ, in part, by eliminating IQ levels of severity.

The Cultural Relativism of Intellectual Impairment

Nowhere is the distinction between IQ and adaptive behavior more apparent than in the effect of low measured intelligence on members of different cultural and socioeconomic groups. The impact of intellectual impairment is determined by the kinds of coping demands our culture places on us. In less technologically advanced societies, persons with some intellectual limitation can still meet cultures' criteria for a grossly normal level of adjustment. Thus, in the largely rural milieu of underdeveloped countries, the lack of good reading and arithmetic skills has a lesser impact than it does in more industrialized societies. The implication is that each culture determines which individuals are to be considered retarded. This distinction is relevant only for persons who would fall within the old "mildly retarded" IQ range because, below this, the degree of impairment ordinarily would preclude normal adaptation in any society.

The issue of cultural relativism was at the heart of criticisms of earlier intelligence testing of Mexican Americans and Black youths in California. Mercer (1973), a sociologist, has shown that the number of Mexican American children who are perceived by their community as retarded is far smaller than that so designated by intelligence tests and academic performance. Clearly, the schools and the children's community are using different criteria. The school's criteria are academic impairment and IQ, but the same youngster who fails in school may function in an essentially normal fashion outside of school. This is the origin of the earlier designation of such youngsters as "6-hour retarded children." Although we recognize the significance of this distinction, it would be the height of folly to ignore the postschool implications of poor academic achievement associated with low intelligence. As will be seen shortly, mental retardation assures poor academic achievement, and in an increasingly technological world, the lack of functional reading and arithmetic skills constitutes a severe limitation to job potential. It is, in fact, the concern for functional literacy and its occupational implications that has sparked the national quest for tying a high-school diploma to basic reading and arithmetic competencies.

Labeling

Nowhere has the controversy over who is to be classified as retarded been more evident than in issues surrounding the educational placement of poorly achieving, disadvantaged minority youth. The controversy has come to be called "labeling," and its flavor is caught in the phrase: "Label jars, not people." The storm of concern here, as previously noted, is the disproportionate representation of such youths in classes for retarded children, especially those for mildly retarded or, in educational parlance, "educable" children. The argument is made that such classes tend to stigmatize the children and, of course, the minority group they represent, and to adversely affect their self-images or self-esteem. The relevant research reveals that viewing labels and labeling as either *necessarily* bad or good represents a gross oversimplification (MacMillan, 1977).

In Chapter 2, which deals with personality factors in mental retardation, this research is presented in some detail. Here it suffices to state that, contrary to the assertions of the more impassioned opponents of labels and labeling, there is neither research evidence to support the notion that labels are the *cause* of academic difficulties nor evidence indicating that these labels in and of themselves result in either rejection by nonretarded peers or serious damage to self-esteem. This is not to say that labels have no effect, but rather that it is the *academic* and *social behaviors* of these children that call attention to them and are their primary problems.

Whether labeled or not, the difficulties are there and can neither be ignored nor wished away, as they have extraordinary consequences for future employability and economic security. Whether these children should continue to carry the label of "mental retardation" is another question. The senior author has suggested the term *general learning disorder* as an alternative (Baroff, 1999). Children and adults with general learning disorder would be viewed as having a member of a diagnostic family called *disorders of learning*. Two other learning disorders in this grouping would be *specific academic learning disorder* (the present "learning disability" category) and *broad academic learning disorder* (the present/former "slow learner" group). Many minority children formerly classified as retarded are now being termed "learning-disabled" and would be more appropriately lodged within the proposed category of *broad academic learning disorder*.

☐ Prevalence and Causation

The cultural relativism of intellectual impairment has obvious implications for who and, therefore, how many people will be considered retarded within a given population. Both age and residence influence prevalence,[6] especially in those with milder degrees of impairment. With reference to chronological age, the highest rates are at school age, when academic difficulties are certain to be evident (Kott, 1968). Both before and after the school years, the rates are lower because intellectual limitations, at least those that are not severe, are less disabling relative to the developmental expectations for those two periods of life.

The variation in prevalence associated with place of residence really relates to general economic status, as higher rates are found among rural (Reschly & Jipson, 1976) and inner-city populations. Within these sources of variation, the most widely used prevalence rate is 3% (Luckey & Neman, 1976). This is probably a good estimate within the general population of the number of persons with IQ below 70, but a much lower number necessarily would meet the dual American Association on Mental Retardation (AAMR) criteria of subaverage intelligence *and* adaptive impairment (Mercer, 1973; Tarjan, Wright, Eyman, & Keeran, 1973). The literature suggests that the proportion of persons meeting both criteria would be closer to 1% than 3% (Baroff, 1982). Indeed, a study of the Florida school population, aged 12 to 14 years, found an overall rate of 1.66%. Breaking the rate down further, 1.24% were classified as mildly retarded, 0.30% as moderately and severely retarded, and 0.12% as profoundly retarded. The mildly retarded group was 75% of the total retarded population. Moderate and severe were 18%, and profound 7%.[7] With regard to the 3% rate for IQs below 70, it is important to understand that it is a purely statistical extrapolation from the so-called normal curve. It merely roughly corresponds to that point on the curve that marks two standard deviations below the mean, and it has absolutely no behavioral correlate. Here we pick up the thread of the somewhat arbitrary nature of who is called retarded because no one would claim seriously that there is a meaningful difference in intelligence between a person with an IQ of 69 and one with an IQ of 71.

It has been common to include causation (etiology) in mental-retardation diagnostic systems, and it is clear that there are two distinct groups making up this population: relatively mildly impaired and physically grossly normal persons who come from lower socioeconomic backgrounds and families in which other members are likely to be similarly affected, and usually more severely impaired individuals who are visibly different from other family members and who are found with about equal frequency at all socioeconomic levels. In Aberdeen, Scotland, the site of long-term investigations of the intellectual status of the population, the former group, those with cultural-familial retardation, constituted 46% of all retarded individuals. The remaining 54% fell in the second category; persons in whom retardation is clearly associated with some biological abnormality (Birch, Richardson, Baird, Horobin, & Illsley, 1970). The term "cultural-familial" has fallen into disfavor because of its past association with genetic as well as environmental causation. This group had been seen as simply representing the lower end of the normal range of intelligence in the general population from a genetic standpoint, but increasing weight now is being given to environmental deprivation as an important contributor to intellectual impairment.

☐ Defining Mental Retardation

Since at least the 1950s, the AAMR has played the leading role in the field with respect to offering and periodically updating definitions of mental retardation. Its major early contribution was the inclusion of adaptive behavior as a component of the diagnosis (Heber, 1959); this was in recognition that IQ alone was not a sufficiently comprehensive measure for describing the behavior of individuals with limited cognitive development. Its definitions also have included identification of the IQ levels that would distinguish mental retardation from less impaired levels of intellectual functioning. IQ levels also were specified *within* mental retardation and were, at least, an implicit recognition that the degree of cognitive impairment was a relevant feature of the disorder. Four levels of cognitive impairment were recognized—mild, moderate, severe, and profound. Although representing only IQ *ranges*, for example, 55 to 69 for mild retardation, and not adaptive behavior per se, the IQ ranges themselves have come to be identified with the degree of retardation itself. This identification reflects the traditional equating of mental retardation with intellectual impairment, as it is through the intelligence test and its score, the IQ, that general intelligence commonly is represented.

Earlier versions of the AAMR definition were not without critics whose concerns have contributed to subsequent modification. As indicated, the IQ range within which mental retardation could be diagnosed had been elevated beyond the traditional one of 70 to include persons with IQs of 71 to 84 (Grossman, 1977). This was called *borderline retardation*, but this extension of the potential range was rescinded in 1973 because it disproportionately increased the number of minority individuals who could be classified as retarded. Although children falling in the extension of the range might exhibit major learning difficulties in school, they would not manifest the very broad adaptive problems traditionally associated with mental retardation. Also reflecting sensitivity to the impact of disproportionate minority representation in the below-70 IQ range itself, particularly in the range of mild retardation, the AAMR dropped the term *cultural-familial* as a designation for one of the causes of mental retardation and substituted for it *psychosocial* retardation. Although it was not explained why this change was made, the implication was that IQs in the retarded range, especially mild retardation, in the absence of clear biological abnormality were caused *exclusively* by adverse environmental experiences. Although it was not made explicit, the necessary implication was that genetic factors were noncontributory. By "genetic," we refer to the role of heredity in general intelligence as this is manifested in IQs of at least 50 and above. That genetic factors play some role in general intelligence seems indisputable, although the extent of their influence is controversial as, of course, are IQ findings that purport to distinguish particular population groups.

Inevitably bound up with the social and political realities of the time, as earlier implied in the discussion of prevalence and labeling, intelligence is a highly valued trait in our culture. The AAMR has walked a tightrope in its definitions and, with some exceptions, has been generally successful. The 1992 definition, however, has proven to be the most controversial of all.

The 1992 AAMR Definition of Mental Retardation

The 1992 definition (Luckasson et al., 1992) represents a multidisciplinary three-step process that is intended to broaden our conception of mental retardation, reduce reliance on IQ for measuring the severity of the cognitive disability, and relate adaptive skill deficits associated with intellectual impairment to the services and "supports" necessary to optimize the retarded person's general level of functioning (Table 1.1). The goal is to use assessment information in such a manner as to maximize the intellectually impaired individual's inclusion or integration within his or her general community and to enhance independence, productivity, and life satisfaction.

The 1992 definition has added some genuinely new features to the diagnostic process, but it also has eliminated an aspect that has been a part of the diagnostic system for many years, the recognition of degrees or severity of cognitive impairment and their respective IQ ranges. Reviewing the reaction to the 1992 definition, Vig and Jedrysek (1996) note that its

TABLE 1.1. The three-step process: diagnosis, classification, and systems of supports

Dimension I:
Intellectual
functioning
and adaptive
skills
	Step 1. Diagnosis of mental retardation
	Determines eligibility for supports
	Mental retardation is diagnosed if:
	  1. The individual's intellectual functioning
	     is approximately 70 to 75 or below.
	  2. There are significant disabilities in two
	     or more adaptive skill areas.
	  3. The age of onset is below 18 years.

Dimension II:
psychological/
emotional
considerations
Dimension III:
physical/health/
etiology
considerations
Dimension IV:
environmental
considerations
	Step 2. Classification and description
	Identifies strengths and weaknesses and the need
	for supports
	  1. Describe the individual's strengths
	     and weaknesses in reference to
	     psychological/emotional considerations.
	  2. Describe the individual's overall physical
	     health and indicate the condition's etiology.
	  3. Describe the individual's current environmental
	     placement and the optimal environment
	     that would facilitate his/her continued
	     growth and development.

	Step 3. Profile and intensities of needed supports
	Identifies needed supports
	Identify the kind and intensities of supports needed
	for each of the four dimensions.
	  1. Dimension I: Intellectual functioning and
	     adaptive skills
	  2. Dimension II: Psychological/emotional
	     considerations
	  3. Dimension III: Physical health/etiology
	     considerations
	  4. Dimension IV: Environmental considerations

Note. Reprinted from *Mental Retardation, Definition, Classification and Systems of Support* with permission of the American Association on Mental Retardation.

proponents highlight its flexibility and its focus on supports as a means of optimizing general functioning (Reiss, 1994a; Schalock et al., 1994). Critics have expressed concerns about the elimination of the IQ severity levels (Belmont & Borkowski, 1994), the potentially negative effect of loosening the IQ beyond the ceiling of 75 (Gresham, MacMillan, & Siperstein, 1995; MacMillan, Gresham, & Siperstein, 1995; Matson, 1995), the lack of empirical validation for the adaptive skill areas (Borthwick-Duffy, 1993;

MacMillan, Gresham, & Siperstein, 1995), the appropriateness of these adaptive skill areas for the preschool-aged child, and difficulties in delineating and differentiating the various levels of support (Gresham et al., 1995; Vig & Jedrysek, 1996).

Step 1: Diagnosing Mental Retardation

Mental retardation refers to *substantial limitations* in present functioning. It is characterized by *significantly subaverage intellectual functioning*, existing concurrently with related limitations in two or more of the following adaptive skill areas: communication, self-care, home living, social skills, community use, self-direction, health and safety, functional academics, leisure, and work. Mental retardation manifests before age 18 years (Luckasson, 1992, p. 5).

Similarity to Earlier Versions.   The 1992 version focuses on the same elements as its predecessors: subaverage intelligence, adaptive impairments, and onset in the developmental years. It differs from its immediate predecessor, the 1983 version, by providing a broader description of the adaptive impairments associated with retardation and in the elimination of IQ levels pertaining to the degree of intellectual impairment.

The Meaning of its Major Components.

"Substantial Limitations in Present Functioning."   Mental retardation always affects general functioning. It is certain to limit academic progress and, according to its degree, virtually all other areas of daily life as well. Apart from its educational consequences, its effects are seen in the retarded person's quality of thinking, in the managing of the practical tasks of daily living, and in the individual's social or interpersonal behavior. It is this combination of adaptive difficulties that results in a lesser level of personal independence and varying degrees of dependency on others for support in daily living. Mental retardation also has been characterized as a general impairment in personal *competence* (Greenspan, Switzky, & Granfield, 1996).

"Significantly Subaverage Intellectual Functioning."   Intellectual impairment is the hallmark of mental retardation. It is the very essence of what the disorder means and has always meant. The earlier discussion of retardation and IQ revealed something of the arbitrary nature of the cut-off point for the upper limit of the IQ range for mental retardation. But this is an inevitable consequence of the fact that intelligence (or intelligences in multifactorial terms) exists on a *continuum*, as in a color spectrum, with

one level blending imperceptibly into another. As indicated previously, IQ 70 has traditionally been the upper limit of retardation although, as noted, there was a brief expansion of that ceiling into the 70 to 84 range. The current definition again has loosened the ceiling by relaxing it to a "score of approximately 70 to 75." The 5-point range of 70 to 75 refers, in fact, to the usual standard error of IQ test scores, the error or range around which the "true" score would vary. An IQ of 70, for example, would predict that the person's "true" or most probable score would be 65 to 75, IQ 70 plus or minus 5 points. The authors of the definition refer to IQ 75 as a "flexible boundary," permitting the play of "clinical judgment" in the diagnostic process. If taken literally, and it is not clear that this was intended, it would allow for the possibility of classifying as retarded a person with an IQ score of greater than 75. A more recently proposed definition would restore the upper IQ limit to 70, although allowing for clinical judgment up to 75 (Barclay et al., 1996). We would agree that scores above 75 are not indicative of mental retardation; in the 75+ range one simply does not find the breadth of adaptive difficulties traditionally associated with mental retardation. There are academic problems, yes, but in general, we still can expect that these people are able to function reasonably independently in everyday life.

The restoration of the upper limit of 70 by Barclay et al. (1996) also includes the reinstatement of the traditional four degrees of intellectual impairment or levels of retardation. They are mild retardation, IQ 55 to 70; moderate retardation, IQ 35 to 54; severe retardation, IQ 20 to 34; and profound retardation, IQ below 20. It is also of interest that the American Psychiatric Association, although it has followed the leadership of the AAMR in adopting its definition of retardation, also has preserved the four levels of severity.[8]

The rationale for the retention of measures of the degree of intellectual impairment lies in the substantial effect of intelligence on general functioning. Studies indicate a correlation of from 0.4 to 0.6 between IQ and adaptive behavior (Kamphaus, 1987). It is the relationship of intelligence to adaptive behavior that permits us to estimate the degree of assistance or support that a person is likely to need. For example, mildly retarded individuals (IQ 55 to 70), as indicated earlier, often achieve full independence in their lives, generally functioning without any supervision although, admittedly, in need of assistance in some areas, notably money management and coping with emergencies. In contrast, adults with IQs below 55, those with moderate to profound retardation, will always need some assistance. Full personal independence is not expected. Admittedly, the AAMR definition takes into account the severity of intellectual impairment in describing the individual's cognitive characteristics and the intensity of support that is required, but the lack of a general cognitive severity measure leaves a vacuum. Its elimination makes no more sense than trying to talk about hearing loss without acknowledging the distinction between those with some useful hearing ("hard-of-hearing") and those who are deaf. Analogous to the effect of IQ on adaptive behavior, the degree of hearing loss can have profound effects on the person's language and general life experience.

"Existing Concurrently with Related Limitations" (in Adaptive Skills).
In mental retardation the intellectual limitations are associated with problems in daily living. These problems are, at least in part, attributable to cognitive impairment, although this is not made explicit in the language of the definition. These adaptive difficulties are to be distinguished from those from other causes, such as physical disability; chronic ill health; unfamiliarity with our language or culture, as in the case of a new immigrant; substance abuse; and personality disorder or mental illness. Although each of these conditions also may be present in the person with retardation, none is a necessary consequence of intellectual impairment, and they are rather to be viewed as additional disabilities.

Of these, mental illness, in particular, needs to be distinguished from retardation. Both are different forms of *"mental disorder,"* with mental illness associated with various kinds of behavioral abnormalities—psychoses, neuroses, and personality disorders. Mental retardation, on the other hand, is viewed as a *developmental disorder*; other developmental disorders include difficulties in acquiring language, reading, writing, and math skills in the presence of adequate intellectual functioning (*learning disabilities*). It is again pointed out that both mental retardation and mental illness can be found in the same individual. Referred to as persons with dual diagnosis, their difficulties are of special concern to the mental health community.

"In Two or More of the Applicable Adaptive Skill Areas."   The 1992 definition continues the requirement that problems in daily living, "adaptive behavior," must be present together with subaverage intelligence in order to justify a diagnosis of retardation. Furthermore, it spells out the nature of those adaptive difficulties and the number that must be present. A minimum of two areas of adaptive behavior must be significantly affected. The requirement of multiple areas of adaptive difficulty is intended to reflect the reality that the coping problems created by retardation are relatively broad and, unlike those of a physical disability, not necessarily limited to a single area of functioning. This distinction, for diagnostic purposes, has most relevance for school-aged youth with IQs in the 60+ range who are free of organic abnormalities. This is the minority population to whom we referred, the "6-hour retarded child" (Mercer, 1973). Although impaired academically, in other respects they may not be distinguishable from brighter peers.

In the more recently promulgated definition (Barclay et al., 1996), a distinction is made between degree of cognitive impairment and the number of adaptive areas that may be affected. Impairment in at least two domains is tied to moderate and mild retardation; at greater levels of impairment (severe and profound retardation) all adaptive areas can be affected. The adaptive-skill domains are now described.

"Communication, Self-care, Home Living, Social Skills, Community Use, Self-direction, Health and Safety, Functional Academics, Leisure, and Work." These are the ten domains relevant to a diagnosis of mental retardation. They are based on a teaching curriculum (Ford et al., 1989). Critics have pointed to the absence of a theoretical rationale for describing adaptive behavior in these particular domains (Greenspan, Switzky, & Granfield, 1996). Factor-analytic studies of adaptive behavior, the means whereby specific areas could be identified, have yielded evidence of at least four domains, labeled as motor or physical competency, competence in independent living skills, cognitive competence, and social competence (Kamphaus, 1987; Widaman & McGrew, 1996). Exemplifying the centrality of "intelligence" to adaptive behavior, Greenspan et al. view 8 of the 10 domains as examples of practical intelligence; one of them, functional academics, as reflecting conceptual intelligence; and one, social skills, as illustrative of social intelligence.

Each of the adaptive skills is characterized briefly here. Noting that impairment in at least two of them is necessary to justify a diagnosis of retardation, we would point out that because functional academics *always* are affected, the requirement might be modified to "functional academics plus one." The skill areas are as follows:

> *Communication*: understanding and using spoken language
>
> *Self-care*: capacities for feeding, dressing, toileting, grooming, and maintaining personal hygiene
>
> *Home living*: "domestic skills"—housekeeping, clothing care, cooking, budgeting, safety, property maintenance
>
> *Social skills*: initiating and terminating interpersonal interactions, understanding social cues and emotions, recognizing reciprocity, controlling impulses, understanding honesty and fairness and conforming to rules and laws, sexual impulses (This is, obviously, a very complex domain and one that clearly is separable into more than one area. With respect to honesty, for example, "con men" have superior social skills but are wanting in their morality!)

Community use: using public transportation, shopping, obtaining services

Self-direction: exercising choice, initiating activities, planning, showing appropriate assertiveness, problem solving

Health and safety: exercising caution, recognizing and responding to one's health problems, ability to protect oneself

Functional academics: reading, writing, and arithmetic skills as they are applied to activities of daily living (an area always affected by mental retardation)

Leisure: assuming some responsibility for one's leisure activities, capacity to participate in recreational activities in one's community

Work: capacity to maintain part-time or full-time employment in work settings, either sheltered or competitive, or to participate in adult day activity programs; ability to accept supervision, cooperate with coworkers, be punctual and reliable, work at an appropriate rate, and meet work-quality standards

"Mental Retardation Manifests Before Age 18."   As in the past, a ceiling is set for the age by which the disorder must be present. This element of the definition is intended to represent retardation as arising during the period of mental development and prior to the beginning of adulthood (Luckasson et al., 1992). Given the probability that many youths continue their education and postpone employment until after the teen years, Barclay et al. (1996) would extend the upper age limit to age 22 years. Age 22 years also accords with upper age limit for "developmental disabilities," a federal diagnostic category that includes mental retardation.

Step 2: Classification and Description

In step 2 we move beyond the establishment of the diagnosis based on intellectual subnormality, adaptive deficits, and onset by age 18 years, to a description of the retarded individual's strengths and weaknesses. As in the case of adaptive behavior domains, these are specified in terms of separate dimensions. They are intellectual functioning and adaptive skills; psychological and emotional considerations; health, physical, and etiological considerations; and environmental considerations.

Dimension I: Intellectual Functioning and Adaptive Skills.   This dimension calls for a description of the individual's score on the intelligence test and a characterization of the strengths and weaknesses in the 10 adaptive-skill areas. To the IQ score we would add the level of severity of cognitive impairment—mild, moderate, severe, or profound.

Dimension II: Psychological and Motivational Considerations.

The intent here is to indicate any significant behavior problems accompanying the intellectual impairment. Retardation appears to create a greater vulnerability to behavior disorders (Rojahn & Tassé, 1996). Surveys suggest that at least one-third of persons with retardation have significant behavior problems, a considerably higher risk than the 15% found in the general population. Chapters 8 and 9 provide a relatively detailed review of these disorders. From our perspective, the developers of the definition might have conceptualized "psychological and emotional" more broadly to include a recognition of our basic biological and psychological needs. These needs are tied to our emotions, and it is the frustration of these needs that is seen as a major cause of behavior problems. Discussed in the next chapter, the psychological and emotional status of persons with retardation is too narrowly framed if it is presented only in terms of psychopathology. To the credit of the definition's authors, this issue is touched on in dimension IV.

With respect to the evaluation of this dimension, a listing of psychopathology scales is found in Jacobson & Schwartz (1991).

Dimension III: Etiology Considerations.

Mental retardation, especially if biological in origin, often is associated with health problems. In cerebral palsy, for example, a neurological disorder in which retardation may be present, one can find paralyses of limbs, impairments in vision and hearing, and seizures.

"Etiology" refers to causation, always an important consideration because knowledge of causation can lead to prevention or treatment. Knowledge of the potentially adverse effects on the fetus of significant alcohol consumption during pregnancy, for example, can serve to reduce drinking during pregnancy and reduce both the frequency and severity of fetal alcohol syndrome. Chapters 3 through 5 are devoted to etiology.

Four potential causes of retardation are cited in the definition: biomedical, social, behavioral, and educational. Each is briefly described, and the chapter in this book in which each is discussed is indicated.

> *Biomedical*: This refers to retardation caused by biological conditions that affect the brain. Most often they are prenatal in origin (see Chapters 3 and 4).
>
> *Social*: The focus here is on the degree of stimulation afforded the child in infancy and early childhood (see Chapter 5).
>
> *Behavioral*: This refers to maternal behaviors that could result in retardation, such as the consumption of alcohol during pregnancy. Alcohol is the most common offender, although other substances also can pose risks (see Chapter 4). Also discussed in Chapter 4 is the perplexing social

question of how the fetus can be protected from the unintended harm of maternal substance abuse.

Educational: There is growing evidence that the contribution of a parent who provides verbal stimulation to the young child and access to a preschool experience can significantly enhance intellectual development, at least in children reared in economically disadvantaged environments (see Chapter 5). Conversely, the absence of such verbal stimulation may depress cognitive development.

Dimension IV: Environmental Considerations.   Seemingly the most complex of the four dimensions, dimension IV asks the diagnostician to assess the degree to which the retarded person is exposed to environments that meet important psychological needs. With regard to these needs, the equivalent terms in the personality model presented in Chapter 2 are shown in parentheses. The authors of the definition refer to needs for love and friendship (intimacy); for exercising choice and control (autonomy); for meeting health (survival), material, and cognitive needs; and for promoting stability (structure) (Blunden, 1988; O'Brien, 1987; Schalock & Kiernan, 1990).

Emphasis is placed on the individual's educational or habilitative program, place of residence, and vocational status. With respect to each, the diagnostician is to consider the degree to which it promotes inclusion or integration in the life of one's community rather than isolation or separation from it, the degree of choice that the individual exercises with regard to daily activity and residence, the intensity of the services and supports that are needed to optimize the person's adjustment, and the number of hours of supportive services that are needed monthly.

Reflecting the philosophical goals of its formulators and of O'Brien (1987), an optimum environment would include integration rather than exclusion, some control over one's life (autonomy), opportunities for growth in personal competence (*success* as a source of *self-esteem*), and a network of family and friends (*intimacy* and self-esteem). In the language of the personality model presented in Chapter 2, an optimum environment would provide for our basic biological needs (food, clothing, shelter, cognitive stimulation, and sexuality), and for our psychological ones (structure, self-esteem, and self-expression).

Step 3: Profile and Intensities of Needed Supports

In step 2, the person's strengths and weaknesses are described across four dimensions. The step 2 analysis reveals the kinds of needs created by the disabling aspects of mental retardation. In step 3, the focus is on the services and supports necessary to meet those needs. These supports should foster personal productivity, as in work; community integration; and general life satisfaction. In particular, supports are encouraged that enable the individual to live, work, and play in "natural environments." These are settings open to the entire community rather than separated from it. Two examples of supports intended to maximize productivity and community integration are supported employment and supported living. In the former, a job coach or tutor assists the retarded person in learning a job in a regular work setting. In the latter, a "personal aide" facilitates residence in a dwelling of one's choice by assisting in basic self-care needs for individuals with physical disabilities in addition to retardation.

Examples of supports for a preschooler (Jake) and a teenager (Alice) are shown in Table 1.2. Note that in addition to specifying the purpose of the support (*support function*) and its nature (*activities*), the diagnostician also is expected to delineate its time frame (ongoing or time-limited) and its intensity. The intensity aspect, in particular, would appear to relate to the degree or severity of the disability. Four degrees of intensity are proposed: intermittent—on an as-needed basis; limited—constant but not permanent; extensive—constant and not time-limited, but not in all environments; and pervasive—constant, not time-limited, and in all environments.

Summary

The 1992 AAMR definition of mental retardation is groundbreaking in scope. It is intended to broaden our conception of the disorder by shifting our attention away from intelligence, per se, at least as this is reflected in IQ, and directing it rather to the adaptive difficulties created by the disability and to the services and supports necessary to maximize the individual's integration, independence, productivity, and general life satisfaction. It truly provides a comprehensive guide for evaluation of the retarded person and for tying that evaluation to treatment and habilitation.

We have noted that the 1992 definition has not been without critics, and we have indicated our own concerns. They pertain primarily to the elimination of degrees of intellectual impairment as these have traditionally been expressed in IQ ranges. Our own unhappiness with their removal, presumably undertaken to reduce the general influence of IQ and intelligence in our perception of the disorder, appears to be widely shared. Because of its relevance to adaptive potential, continued use of the four levels of severity is recommended. Ideally, these four levels should pertain only to the degree of cognitive impairment. They are, after all, only IQ ranges and not measures of adaptive behavior as such. The terms *mild, moderate, severe,* and *profound intellectual impairment* would be the most accurate representations of these IQ ranges. But on its face this is absurd

TABLE 1.2a. Supports needed by Jake and his family

Dimension/Area	Support Function	Activities	Time	Intensity
I. Intellectual Functioning and Adaptive Skills				
Social skills, leisure	Befriending	Interaction with peers	Ongoing	Limited
Communication	Health assistance	Selection of communication derive	Time-limited	Extensive
	Teaching	Instruction to use	Ongoing	Extensive
Functional academics	Teaching	Ecological inventory	Ongoing	Intermittent
		Embed in adapted preschool lessons/activities	Ongoing	Extensive
	Health assistance	Material adaptations and switches	Ongoing	Limited
Home living	Health assistance	Use of switches and communication device	Ongoing	Limited
	Teaching	Participation in home living routines	Ongoing	Extensive
Self-care	Teaching	Participation in self-care routines	Ongoing	Extensive
II. Psychological/emotional considerations[a]				
III. Physical/health/etiology considerations	Health assistance	Physical therapy and related activities	Ongoing	Extensive
IV. Environmental considerations	Community/school access	Parents join support and advocate groups to prepare community for integration	Ongoing	Extensive
		Respite care and after-school care routines	Ongoing	Extensive
	Befriending	Planning for placement in kindergarden	Time-limited	Extensive

[a]None for this client.

TABLE 1.2b. Current supports needed by Alice

Dimension/Area	Support Function	Activities	Time	Intensity
I. Intellectual functioning and adaptive skills				
Work	Community access	To and from work	Ongoing	Limited
	Employee assistance	Job tasks	Ongoing	Intermittent
	Befriending	Learning interdependence with coworkers, supervisors	Ongoing	Intermittent
Home living	Teaching	Housekeeping	Ongoing	Intermittent
		Food management	Ongoing	Intermittent
		Budgeting	Ongoing	Intermittent
Community use/social skills	Community access Befriending/teaching	Leisure activities with peers, coworkers	Ongoing	Intermittent
Functional academics	Financial planning	Adjusting work benefits	Ongoing	Intermittent
II. Psychological/emotional considerations[a]				
III. Physical/health/etiology considerations	Health assistance	Eye surgery	Time-limited	Extensive
IV. Environmental considerations	Befriending	Options and choice of home, circle of friends	Time-limited	Intermittent
	Financial planning	Budgeting, advocating for benefits	Ongoing	Limited

[a]None for this client.

because mental retardation itself reflects a severe cognitive impairment. It is only *within* the mental retardation range that the terms *mild* or *moderate* make any sense. For this reason, we can continue to expect that the IQ ranges will be equated with the disorder itself. This is evident in the continued use of the terms in the Barclay et al. (1996) definition and in that of the American Psychiatric Association (1994).

☐ On the Nature of Intellectual Functioning in Mental Retardation

Thus far, the intellectual impairment in mental retardation has been characterized solely in terms of an IQ score generally below 70 and that falls approximately two standard deviations or 30 points below the mean of the general population. Although a child of 10 years, for example, with an IQ of 60 could be classified as retarded, the diagnostic term conveys little about the quality of the child's thinking. How, for example, does this thinking compare with that of the normally developing 10-year-old. To begin to understand something of the quality of that child's thinking, we need to define IQ and one of its historic features, *mental age*. The term "historic" is used because current tests, often multifactorial in nature, have abandoned mental age and even IQ as ways of describing intellectual functioning. Thus the PASS model of intelligence (Das et al., 1992) views intellectual functioning in terms of four processes and requires major impairment in all to justify a diagnosis of mental retardation. Referred to previously, those processes are planning, attention, and simultaneous and successive information processing.

Although multifactorial models of intelligence might assign single-score representations of intelligence such as the IQ to the dustbins of psychometric history, one of the constituents of IQ, mental age, *is* useful in conveying the nature of the individual's cognitive maturity. It also is helpful in describing change or growth in intellectual functioning and enables us to understand the chronicity of the disorder.

IQ and Mental Age

From the inception of intelligence testing, early in the 20th century, IQ and mental age have had a prominent role as descriptors of general intelligence. Originally conceived in connection with the Stanford-Binet intelligence test, a mental-age score was the basis for a given IQ, and "mental age" became a standard way of describing one's level of mental development. With each item on the Binet test typically carrying a weight of 2 months of mental age, the sum of all items passed was expressed in years and months of mental age. A 10-year-old with an IQ of 60, for example, would have a mental age of 6 years and 1 month. In effect, this 10-year-old is solving problems much more like a 6-year-old than like a child of his own age. The relationship between mental age and IQ is shown in the following arithmetic representation. Although the IQ shown, the "ratio IQ," was replaced by a "deviation IQ," the former is shown because of its explanatory value:

$$\frac{\text{Mental Age (MA)}}{\text{Chronological Age (CA)}} \times 100 = \text{IQ}$$

A child was considered to be of *average* intelligence if, at least during the preadolescent years, mental age and chronological age were the same.

$$\frac{\text{MA } 6}{\text{CA } 6} = 1, \quad 1 \times 100 = 100$$

A child at age 6 years with a mental age greater than 6 years would have an IQ above 100. On the other hand, a mental age of less than 6 years would yield an IQ of less than 100. We can think of mental age as a *general* measure of mental power; the IQ tells us how that power compares with that of other persons.

The interpretation of mental age is straightforward in childhood and early adolescence. Thereafter, its meaning is complicated by a slower rate of mental growth and a near cessation of growth by young adulthood. Moreover, the same mental-age score among different individuals is unlikely to reflect identical test performances because the mental-age score is a "total" score and does not depend on the specific test items answered correctly. In spite of these and other limitations (Sattler, 1974), mental age has been accepted widely as a measure of school readiness, which is not surprising if it is realized that the intelligence test originally was developed as a means of detecting children who were at risk of school failure. From a research perspective, mental age has been employed in studying the question of whether retarded and normal children of comparable mental ages are similar in their intellectual functioning. This always fascinating question speaks to whether mental retardation is simply a disorder of slower but "normal" mental development or whether it is associated with cognitive behaviors not typical of the normal child of that mental age.

Age-Equivalent Scores

With the publication of the 1986 version of the Stanford-Binet test (Thorndike et al., 1986), the traditional single mental-age score was replaced by three reasoning scores (verbal, abstract, and quantitative) and one memory score. The test does provide, however, *chronological age–equivalent* scores for each of its 15 subtests. These range from a low of 2 years to a high of 17 years. Nor is this limited to the Binet test. The more widely used Wechsler tests also offer this in the form of "test ages." Although intelligence tests can be expected to change as a reflection of better understanding of the nature of intelligence, it is important that they still allow us to translate scores into age equivalents, perhaps the most useful guide to understanding their meaning.

Let's illustrate this with Gerald, a 6-year-old first-grader who is functioning well below the level of his classmates. He seems to be well motivated, but new material causes frustration. His vision and hearing are fine, and the language of the class is his native tongue. Not only is he lagging in the acquisition of basic reading, writing, and number skills, his general behavior seems less mature than that of the other children. He has more difficulty in concentrating and is more easily distracted and frustrated.

His immaturities are not limited to academics. In the physical sphere, his motor coordination is poorer than his peers, and he needs assistance in tasks requiring dexterity. His speech, too, is noticeably different. It is simpler in structure, shorter in length, and less clearly articulated.

In his interactions with peers and teacher, he is more emotionally volatile, has greater difficulty in conforming to class rules, and appears to need more attention than the average first-grader. In his play with other children, he tends to be a follower and to be rather passive in his interactions. His play is also considerably less imaginative than that of his classmates.

His teacher, a woman who has worked with preschoolers in addition to her present assignment, is struck by his overall immaturity. She comments to another teacher that Gerald seems like a younger child, more like a 3- or 4-year-old than a child of 6 years.

Gerald is referred by his teacher for evaluation of his school difficulties; the examination is likely to include intelligence testing, and this might reveal a mental age or age-equivalent score of about 4 years. This would translate into an IQ of 67. The child's school difficulties are now more understandable. Although the same chronological age as his classmates, he is functioning developmentally more like a 4-year-old. The average 4-year-old is not expected to master material appropriate to first-graders. It is not surprising that he has been struggling, and that he is frustrated.

In a very essential way, Gerald's behavior can be characterized as immature. If one behaves in ways that are younger than that which is expected for one's age, one can be thought of as immature, and, in the child (or adult) with retardation, that immaturity is inevitable because mental development always will lag relative to the level expected for one's chronological age.

But to portray mental retardation as a condition of an ever-present lag or gap between expected and achieved mental development is a very incomplete description of the intellectual disparity. Not only is Gerald, with a mental age of 4 years, 2 years behind the average mental age of his classmates, but that gap will not diminish. On the contrary, assuming his mental development continues at the rate suggested by his IQ, the difference between his mental age and that of his classmates will grow *greater* over time.

IQ as a Measure of the Rate of Mental Growth

The IQ, in addition to providing a measure of general intelligence, also can be viewed as an indicator of the *rate* of mental growth. An IQ of 67, as in the case of Gerald, suggests a growth rate that is about two thirds (67%) of expectancy. The normally developing child, one with an with an IQ of 100, for example, would gain 12 months in mental age over the course of one year, while Gerald is gaining only two thirds as much, 8 months of mental age. If Gerald's growth rate is relatively constant, and this is actually more typical of the retarded than the normally developing child (Clarke, Clarke, & Reiman, 1958), the gap will increase cumulatively by 4 months per each year during the mental-age growth period (Fig. 1.4). At chronological age 6 years, the gap is 2 years (24 months); it increases to 4 years (48 months) at age 12, and to 5 years (60 months) by age 18. It will be noted that in

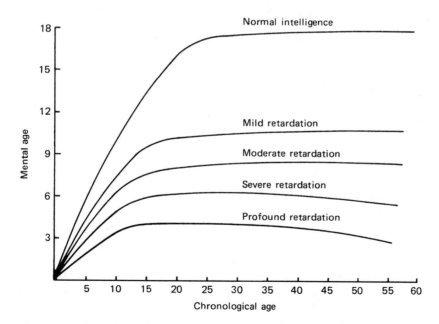

FIGURE 1.4. Mental-age growth curves corresponding to normal intelligence and to the four levels of retardation. (Adapted from Fisher & Zeaman, 1970.)

the 6-year period between ages 12 and 18, the gap grows by only 1 year (12 months) rather than 2 years (24 months). This is because of a gradual slowing in the rate of mental growth during adolescence.

The Mental-Age Growth Period

The slowing of the rate of mental-age growth and its expected cessation at about 18 years of chronological age marks the approximate upper limit of the mental-age growth period, at least as measured by the items on our intelligence tests. As indicated earlier, there is evidence of selective growth well into the adult years of some verbal abilities. Indeed, measures of practical intelligence as distinct from analytic ("academic") ones show increases into the sixth decade (Sternberg, Wagner, William, & Horrath, 1995). But the effect of this cessation or near cessation is to assure that the child with retardation, the youngster whose rate of mental growth has lagged relative to that of a normally developing child, will be at a permanent disadvantage mental age–wise because that child shares the same growth period as the normally developing one. When that period ends, whatever difference then existing will persist, because neither the retarded child nor his or her normally developing counterpart will change significantly in mental age thereafter. In this respect, mental growth parallels physical growth. We grow in height from birth into adolescence and, by late adolescence, if not earlier, our maximum height is attained. It is clear, however, that the growth limit is, to some degree, test-specific, in that on the Wechsler adult intelligence tests, scores increase up to age 26 years (Bayley, 1970). There is also some indication that the growth period in mental age actually may be shorter if the degree of intellectual impairment is more severe (see Fig. 1.4). Although scores on these tests may not increase materially after young adulthood, it also would appear that there is little general decline on into old age and, even then, there is little decline until health starts to fail (Bayley, 1970).

The Mental-Age Growth Period and Learning

Although a roughly comparable mental-age growth period for normally developing and retarded children precludes the latter's "catching up," it is important to distinguish between the mental-age growth period and our capacity to "learn." While young adulthood may see the nearly full flowering of our mental powers, whatever their extent, they can be applied to new learning throughout our lives. Lifelong learning is no less possible for persons with retardation than for ourselves. It is only that the complexity of that which can be learned does not exceed the grasp imposed by mental age.

☐ The Quality of Thinking in Persons with Mental Retardation

We now describe in greater depth the quality of thinking in individuals with retardation, both in terms of their strengths and weaknesses as shown on intelligence tests and as we "experience" their thinking in our interactions with them.

General Pattern of Strengths and Weaknesses on Intelligence Tests

On intelligence tests, individuals with retardation tend to perform at a higher level on tasks that involve the use of "visual" understanding, G_V in our factor-analytic model of intelligence (Ross et al., 1985; Silverstein, 1970). Best-known examples are reproducing block designs and putting pieces together to form a picture. No language is required for these problems, and no memory is involved because the task is always before the person. In contrast, test items demanding *both* an understanding of what is presented through language ("questions") and the ability to articulate a reply present greater difficulty. Largely falling with the domain of crystallized intelligence, examples of these language-loaded test tasks are defining words, indicating what one would do in problem situations, identifying underlying similarity between things that are different, and demonstrating factual knowledge. Similar tasks causing difficulty are arithmetic and short-term memory. The relative strength in the visual mode translates into a better performance on tasks that are "practical" and "concrete" in contrast to those that are primarily verbal or "conceptual." This pattern is seen more often in persons with mild retardation and in whom the impairment is not associated with clear organic brain abnormality (e.g., Sattler, 1974).

Specific Cognitive Difficulties

Suggestibility

Retardation increases "suggestibility"; the individual is more easily influenced by external cues (Zigler, 1966). Reflective of "preoperational" thinking in Piagetian terms, the tendency is to "center" on what is most obvious in a situation and to ignore other elements that may be affecting it.

Suggestibility is a trait that we all share, and it increases in situations in which we feel less confident. It is intensified in persons whose confidence is lessened by chronic difficulties in coping and who also have low self-esteem. Heightened suggestibility certainly contributes to parental fears of sexual exploitation of their retarded children and, in another context, to vulnerability to the criminal-justice system (Baroff, 1991b). Retarded youth and adults may be encouraged to break the law by individuals who seek to exploit their naiveté, may be left "holding the bag" if things go wrong, and, if in police custody, can be intimidated into confessing to crimes they may never have committed. In 1 year alone, the senior author, serving as a forensic psychologist and expert witness in first-degree murder and death-penalty cases involving retarded defendants, saw *two* defendants acquitted of murder charges in spite of confessions. The defendants insisted that they were innocent, regardless of earlier confessions given to the police, and, in the absence of any physical evidence connecting them to the crime, their confessions carried little weight. Indeed, in the Supreme Court Miranda decision, Miranda v. Arizona, 384 U.S. 436 (1996), the decision that set standards for the protection of the rights of persons being questioned by the police, there is reference to a man, presumably retarded, who confessed, under coercion, to *two* murders that he did not commit.

Passivity, "Strategizing," and Memory

Together with the aforementioned suggestibility, a kind of *passive* quality is seen in the retarded person's thought (e.g., Merrill & Jackson, 1992), especially evident in problem situations in which coping would be aided by initiating one or more strategies such as doing something to help one remember in a "memory" task. Retarded individuals seem to accept the tasks as presented and show less inclination to initiate strategies that could help them (Ellis, 1970; Hale & Borkowski, 1991). At its simplest level this might entail a failure to practice or to "rehearse" material one is asked to memorize.

Memory is enhanced not only by rehearsal but also by the possible reorganization or restructuring of the material such that links are created between what is to be recalled. So-called mnemonic devices are aids that we all employ, a form of mental self-help, but that seem to be less frequently employed in retardation. In part, this is a developmental phenomenon because the spontaneous use of such strategies is generally not found in normally developing children younger than 8 years. There is evidence, however, that strategies such as rehearsal can be taught to retarded youth with mental-age equivalents of at least 8 years (Justice, 1987), but there may be difficulty in generalizing or transferring the strategy to untrained settings (Hale & Borkowski, 1991). In our view, at least part of the difficulty in generalization is a lack of understanding of the abstract concept of a "strategy" itself, combined with a diminished capacity to evaluate where and how it might be employed. This kind of managerial or executive function pertains to the "planning" aspect in information-processing cognitive models. Indeed, a body of research appears to support the notion that, compared with children of the same mental age, youth with retardation have greater difficulty on tasks that involve logic, strategy, and foresight (Byrnes & Spitz, 1977). These are cognitive abilities that are the essence of planning.

Verbal Abstraction Ability, Concreteness, and Rigidity

This refers to our capacity to find similarity among nonidentical entities; to "categorize." It is illustrated in the problem, "In what way are a mouse and an elephant alike?" The task requires ignoring the perceptual or associational differences evoked by them, such as size and shape. Assuming that the individual knows that both are "animals," a category or concept, there may be failure to utilize what is known because of a centering on the obvious differences. As the difference between entities to be categorized increases, the retarded person may reject the very possibility of similarity, focusing or centering on the difference. A 16-year-old mildly retarded youth insisted that a ship and an automobile were not alike because "a ship rides on the water and an automobile rides on the land." Unaware of his use of the word "rides" in both contexts, because the word is not ordinarily applied to ships, his intent is clear. He knows that they both "ride," but it is *where* they ride that dominates his thinking and gives to it the quality of *concreteness* and rigidity.

Another aspect of concreteness, the opposite of "abstraction," is seen in a greater "literalness." Proverbs are not understood or may be interpreted literally.

Foresight and Planfulness

Retardation impairs the capacity to engage in foresight and planning (e.g., Spitz & DeRisi, 1978). Planning involves "if-then" thinking, a consideration of what *might* be rather than what *is*. It may require consideration of multiple outcomes and, in this sense, is more difficult for people who are prone to fix or center their attention on only one. It is also a process much related to strategizing.

Lack of such thinking is evident in the parenting behavior of a group of retarded women who seemed to be inflexible in dealing with problem behavior in their children (e.g., Tymchuk, Andron, & Rahbar, 1988). Conversely, these women were able to benefit from problem-solving training that consisted of breaking down problems into simpler elements,

generating alternatives, considering the consequences of each, and selecting a preferred alternative. Not only was some improvement seen in
the management of their children but, in some cases, this problem-solving
method was applied spontaneously to other situations.

In a similar vein, the senior author has observed that mildly retarded
criminal offenders are capable of considering the consequences of their
actions, although this capacity was never called on *prior* to engaging in
their offenses. In this respect, they probably do not differ from nonretarded
offenders!

Speed of Thinking.   Although characterization of persons with retardation as "slow" commonly refers to speed of learning, research actually
reveals a slower reaction time, in general. This is found even on such well-
practiced skills as simple letter discrimination in the child who can read
(Hunt, 1976) and in the speed of reading itself (Ellis, Woodley-Zanthos,
Dulaney, & Palmer, 1989; Kail, 1992). Reaction time relates to attention,
that is, preparing to respond (alertness), interpreting a sensory stimulus (encoding), activating the memory store that pertains to the stimuli-
precept, and actually responding. A related phenomenon is "inspection
time." It is defined as the time required to make a very simple discrimination accurately, such as between two lines of very different lengths.
Considered a measure of mental speed, a discrimination that can be made
without error at 0.5 seconds of visual exposure declines to only chance
accuracy at 0.2 seconds. The surprising feature of this simple task is that
performance on it correlates significantly, at least .44, with other cognitive abilities, especially the kinds of visual tasks found on the performance
scale of intelligence tests (Deary & Stough, 1996). Moreover, the speed
effect seems even stronger in the presence of intellectual impairment, as
in mental retardation (Lally & Nettelbeck, 1977) or cognitively impaired
older individuals (Deary, Hunter, Langan, & Goodwin, 1991). It is regarded
by Deary and Stough as the best simple candidate for the ability that most
regularly discriminates between people at different levels of intellectual
functioning.

We have, then, research evidence of a slowing in the information-
processing ability of persons with retardation both at the perceptual and
responding levels, a phenomenon that may be developmental in nature,
that is, tied to mental age rather than to IQ (Nugent & Mosley, 1987;
Stanovich, 1978).

Imagination and Creativity.   Although unusual cognitive and
artistic abilities are found in some persons with retardation (see Chapter 2),
the disorder does appear to generally limit imagination and creativity.

As we have seen, it unduly binds one to what *is* rather than to what *might* be. Attention is centered on what can be known through our senses as distinct from that which can only be imagined. This is evident in the difficulty of persons with retardation in generating stories from pictures whose dramatic quality usually easily evokes them. The tendency is to *describe* what is present in the picture rather than to use it as a springboard for *creating* a story.

☐ Adaptive Functioning: Problems and Potential

The second element in the 1992 definition of mental retardation refers to the impact of intellectual impairment on general adjustment. The diagnosis requires significant impairment in at least 2 of the 10 adaptive skill areas—communication, self-care, home living, social skills, community use, self-direction, health and safety, functional academics, leisure, and work. What must be stressed is that the degree of impairment is a function of not only mental development but also one's life experience. Your potential and mine are determined not only by our biologically given capacities but also by the opportunities we have had to develop them. These opportunities include being reared by parents who love, encourage, and support us and by access to experiences our society provides because it values the benefits they confer. These experiences can be thought of as services or supports, education being one with which we all are familiar.

The student who desires a professional career in mental retardation understands that its pursuit involves experiences provided by an educational institution. The existence of such institutions is taken for granted; were they not available, our career aspirations would be frustrated, and there might be resentment at a society that ignores *our* developmental needs. The intent here is to emphasize that many of the adjustment problems found in retardation are *not* intrinsic to the disability. Rather they are the *expected* emotional and behavioral consequences of the *absence* of services essential to the fulfillment of legitimate aspirations and basic psychological needs. Nor are these services a "special entitlement." All that can be reasonably expected of each of us is that we seek to maximize our potential, whatever it may be. Nor are disabled people entitled to lesser services because of a more limited potential. We all are limited to some degree—we have peers who are brighter, more attractive, more talented. Differences between us are the norm, not the exception. People with disabilities, whatever their nature, are simply part of a "capacity" continuum of which we are all a part. Given the expectation that *our* needs will be met, although we too are limited, can we justify denying that opportunity to others?

Overview of Adaptive Problems and Potential

Mental retardation interferes with the accomplishment of the behavioral goals expected for one's chronological age. It affects basic processes of maturation, learning, and social adjustment. In infancy, a slower rate of growth is seen in all phases of development—motor, language, cognitive, self-care, and social. At school age, the learning difficulty inherent in retardation is reflected in poorer academic achievement. During adolescence there is a growing awareness of self, of the nature of one's coping difficulties and the reaction of others to them, including the threat of social exclusion by peers. It is a time of increasing emotionality and this, coupled with maturing physical development, can produce behavior difficulties. Resentment may follow if one's younger siblings are accorded greater independence than oneself. The retarded youth may complain of too much control, of favoritism, of being loved less. With adolescence and the onset of sexual feelings, frightened parents further tighten controls, causing even more frustration. With the movement from school age into young adulthood, the permanence of the disability is recognized, at least by parents, and with it the understanding that there may be a lifelong need for supervision. But retardation does not preclude participation in adult roles, notably those of "worker" and "friend," and also possibly spouse or even parent.

Although any attempt to briefly characterize the adaptive effects of mental retardation cannot ignore the problems it creates, it is also true that it is a disorder of *slower* growth, not *no* growth. If achievements come at a slower pace and in smaller increments, the very difficulty of the accomplishment intensifies the gratification that accompanies them. The pleasure that we take in our child's first step may be no less than that experienced in later life at a seemingly more complex achievement. All satisfactions are relative!

Adaptive Problems in The Preschool Years

Motor Development

During the preschool years, mental retardation, especially if it is clearly organic in origin, is likely to be associated with a delay in the rate of development of gross-motor and fine-motor skills. Whereas the normally developing infant generally is sitting without support by 8 months, standing alone at 14 months, and walking alone at 15 months, the Down syndrome infant, for example, on the average does not achieve these milestones until about 12, 23, and 26 months, respectively (Dicks-Mireaux, 1972; Share, 1975). This is a rate of development of about 60% to 70% of normal. There is some indication, however, that the rate of development can be increased through programs of intensive motor training and stimulation (Ludlow & Allen, 1979; Sharav & Shlomo, 1986). After infancy, a lag in motor development is reflected in a lesser degree of hand-eye (fine-motor) and general bodily coordination.

Motor delay also can exist as a disorder unaccompanied by retardation. It is present in *hypotonia*, a muscle disorder, and in *cerebral palsy*, in movement and balance; in the latter there may be the most severe motor impairment but unaffected cognition (Kirk, 1968). Blindness, a visual rather than motor disorder, also can delay motor development. There may be fewer opportunities to move about safely, and objects in the child's environment may not evoke interest unless they emit sound (Holden, 1972). A possible motor lag in blindness illustrates how the environment can influence behavior largely governed by biological maturation.

Language Development

In the language sphere, the distinction is drawn between its understanding (receptive language) and its use (expressive language). Expressive language or "speech" deficiencies are legion in mental retardation—speech is slower to develop, tends to be less well articulated, is expressed in shorter-than-average utterances, and is more "concrete" in quality (Yoder & Miller, 1972). Apart from a general lag in speech, additional difficulties can be superimposed by specific disorders associated with retardation, notably cerebral palsy and Down syndrome. Both impair the intelligibility of utterances (Kaiser, Alpert, & Warren, 1988).

Self-Help

In retardation, delay is seen in mastery of the basic self-care skills of feeding, dressing, toileting, hygiene, and grooming. Of these, delay in bowel control can be particularly stressful. If parents or caretakers have difficulty in adjusting to the child's slower rate of training, attempts to teach can create tensions and lead to the negativism and anxiety often seen in later learning situations. Conversely, slowness to learn may cause the oversolicitous parent to make too few demands "because he's handicapped." The consequence is that the child fails to accomplish skills that are within his capability. Mental retardation inevitably increases dependency, but the oversolicitous parent, by making too *few* demands, inadvertently can add to rather than minimize the child's handicap.

Cognition

The normally developing young child has achieved much understanding by school age. The basic structure of language is present; there is understanding of concepts of color, shape, size, texture, taste, odor, space, time, and quantity, and a beginning facility in reading, writing, and arithmetic. Delay in acquiring such understanding is the hallmark of mental retardation. A 5-year-old with at least a moderate degree of mental retardation and mental development approximating that of a 2-year-old might not recognize two of something, identify the color red, or know which of two things is bigger or which shape is square. What is understood roughly corresponds to the child's mental or developmental age.

Social Skills

Perhaps the most complex of the adaptive domains, the quality of the child's relationship to adults, peers, and younger children, is affected by intellectual impairment. "Intelligence" plays a considerable role in our social behavior; we continually read cues in others that influence our interactions with them. Indeed, Greenspan and Granfield (1992) include social intelligence/competence as one of their three aspects of intelligence. The understanding of social situations is lessened, and emotional behavior is immature for the child's age. This immaturity also is expressed in the choice of playmates, often younger because they are closer to the retarded child's maturity or developmental level.

Play itself is affected. In contrast to the normal preschooler, the child who is retarded is likely to spend more time in solitary play, show less responsiveness to peers, exhibit more disruptiveness, and manifest less emotionality (Kopp, Baker, & Brown, 1992).

Apart from the effects of developmental delay on social development, parent and sibling attitudes greatly influence the quality of the child's interpersonal relationships. Out of these familial affectional experiences emerge attitudes toward the self and others that shape the child's general responsiveness to people. If the family-child interactions are positive, the child will feel wanted and loved. A sense of trust and confidence is generated that fosters receptivity to new people and experiences. On the other hand, if the child has not been adequately loved and there is the feeling of rejection, frustration of the child's unconditional need for love and for persons on whom he or she can depend, will lead to attitudes of fearfulness and antagonism.

Another determinant of the attitude toward the self and others is the degree of confidence that the child comes to have in the ability to master basic developmental skills. Retardation inevitably slows their acquisition, and, by school age, there is awareness of one's learning difficulties. "It's hard for me to learn" is an oft-heard self-appraisal in adolescence. Parenthetically, it is this acknowledgment of a slowness in learning that makes the term *general learning disorder* an apt substitute for *mental retardation*. The social implication of this view of oneself as a slow learner depends on the extent to which there is access to "significant others" who both understand the nature of the child's learning difficulties and are prepared to provide the kind of support the disability requires. Although frustration of the need to feel some competence is itself painful, it is even more so if self-esteem has been lowered by limited family acceptance. Avoiding expected criticism then becomes a means of protecting whatever self-esteem remains, and this leads to a restriction in activities to those already mastered. But the price of such self-protection is reduced opportunity for acquiring new skills and moving to higher levels of adaptation and independence.

We have introduced some important social and personality factors associated with mental retardation. Although presented in the context of the preschool years, they operate, of course, throughout life; it is only that the early years seem to be crucial in setting their direction. We return to these same personality variables in the next chapter.

Adaptive Problems in The School Years

The school years are critical in the life of the child with mental retardation because the intellectual impairment precludes normal educational progress. The acquisition of basic reading, writing, and arithmetic skills is slowed, and the degree of their ultimate attainment is closely tied to the severity of intellectual impairment. Apart from residential institutions, educational programs have been the most prominent service to children with retardation, and so-called special education has a history in American public schools that extends back into the last decade of the 19th century. Nor should the goal of educating youth with retardation in settings that most nearly approximate those of nonretarded students imply that such placement will erase the cognitive deficit and learning difficulty. The goals of mainstreaming or inclusion are at least as much social as academic, and pupils with retardation need assistance in their academic pursuits in whatever their educational setting. Indeed, within the range of retardation, it is chiefly the student with not more than mild intellectual impairment who is likely to acquire at least some functional reading and arithmetic skills. But even here the average achievement level is only about third grade (Bilsky, 1976), and this is hardly adequate for activities of daily living. Newspapers require at least a sixth-grade reading level, and at least fourth-grade arithmetic achievement is necessary for anything beyond addition and subtraction. Not surprisingly, the most common difficulty of adults with retardation who are living independently, that is, without supervision, is in managing their money.

At greater degrees of intellectual impairment, functional academic skills are less likely to be acquired, although some youth with moderate impairment may achieve some reading ability. The educational experience of students with from moderate to profound retardation tends to be nonacademic in emphasis, with stress on strengthening self-help, language, motor, and social skills (Heward & Orlansky, 1992). Ultimately, the goal for *all* students, regardless of level of retardation, is to prepare them for life in their home communities, as contrasted with institutions, and for conducting their lives as independently as possible. A taxonomy of community-living skills provides community teaching goals related to self-care, home-making, work, leisure, and travel (Dever, 1989).

The school years are also an extremely important period in social development. In the normally developing youngster they are a time of loosening ties to parents, as peer relationships assume increasing significance. Adolescence, in particular, can be as stormy for youth with retardation as for their nonretarded counterparts (Zetlin & Turner, 1985). It is a time of greater self-awareness, of beginning to recognize one's difference and what it may mean to be referred to as "retarded." At home there may be conflict with parents around the desire for greater self-determination and frustration at how one is treated in comparison with normal siblings.

The latter portion of the school period, especially for non–college-bound students, is a time of vocational preparation, and retarded youth are going to be affected in their job potential by their pronounced academic limitations. Other barriers to employment may be problems of communication, physical or motor disabilities, and emotional and behavioral difficulties. Yet, in spite of these limitations, academic and otherwise, achieving some level of employability is a realistic goal for most mildly and moderately impaired youth, in regular work settings for the former and increasingly so for the latter. The advent of "supported employment" as a vocational option has tremendously expanded their job opportunities and also opened up the possibility for employment to youth with even more severe impairment. In particular, the school years become crucial to preparing retarded youth for the world of work by inculcating in them behaviors essential to employment—reliability, persistence, accepting supervision, and cooperating with others. The fostering of these "work habits" becomes a key educational goal, as does instruction in the practical skills necessary to daily living—safety, shopping, money management, household skills, and use of public transportation and recreational resources. The school focus on preparing these students for employment has been formalized in a curriculum domain referred to as "transition" planning (e.g., Wehman, Kregel, & Barcun, 1985).

Adaptive Problems in Adulthood

Self-management and "Self-direction"

In spite of early gloomy predictions of how adults with retardation would fare in unsupervised living, numerous studies reveal that at least those with not more than mild intellectual impairment have done fairly well (Ross et al., 1985). Whether they were former pupils in "educable" classes (Baller, Charles, & Miller, 1966; Kennedy, 1966), had dwelled in institutions (Bell, 1976; Edgerton & Bercovici, 1976), or were simply identified by a citywide survey (Richardson, 1978), the evidence is overwhelming that the majority can function independently as adults. Admittedly, the quality of their adjustment can be marginal. Money-management problems have been noted (McDevitt, Smith, Schmidt, & Rosen, 1978), and there may be difficulty in finding employment (Bell, 1976) and in using leisure time. Viewed early in the 20th century as a potential criminal underclass and "reproductive menace" (Fernald, 1919; Goddard, 1912; Kostir, 1916), persons with retardation emerge from long-term studies as much more like us than different. Except for a greater dependence on nonretarded acquaintances for assistance under special circumstances, so-called benefactors (Edgerton & Bercovici, 1976), and, perhaps, being subject to greater fluctuations in their life circumstances, the overall quality of their lives seems similar to that of nonretarded persons with comparable income and education. Although work is important, so is recreation. Wishing to avoid any identification as "retarded," a stigma that may have been tied to a former institutional or special-class placement, they seek to blend in, and for the most part do, with their nonretarded counterparts. More vulnerable to misfortune because of fewer resources, they seem to have a greater stoicism but also a general satisfaction with their lives and optimism about the future (Edgerton & Bercovici, 1976; Edgerton, Bollinger, & Herr, 1984; Edgerton, 1962).

The reproductive fears early in the century related to expectations of larger-than-average families among parents who were retarded and a consequent disproportionate influence on intelligence of the *general* population! Such fear contributed to the enactment of state sterilization laws between 1910 and 1930 and to a change in the role of the then well-established state institutions (Maloney & Ward, 1979). Formerly oriented to education and training, they came to be employed as custodial settings for sexual segregation (Kanner, 1964). With the reality of the adaptation of the adult population so much at variance with earlier predictions, and with a much wider availability of services to those in need, the earlier fears are no longer heard. Nevertheless, concerns are expressed about the effectiveness of retarded adults as "parents," and this issue is addressed in several chapters.

Although an independent adjustment commonly is attained by adults with not more than mild intellectual impairment, this is not true at more severe levels of deficit. If the impairment is more than mild, some degree of dependency always will exist, although the current range of residential alternatives to the family home and institution have greatly enlarged the opportunity for a more independent community adjustment.

Employment ("Work")

As with self-management (self-direction), all levels of employability are found, with the severity of impairment influencing the nature of jobs performed (Seltzer, 1991). Adults with mild retardation are capable of regular (competitive) employment, typically in unskilled jobs (Heber & Dever, 1970). In one major long-term follow-up study, two thirds (67%) of the males were then employed full-time, a rate admittedly somewhat below those for their siblings (86%) and a control group (96%), but still clear evidence of employability (Ross et al., 1985). Although the proportion of unskilled work has declined with the growth of technology, it still represents about 15% of all employment (Bureau of Labor Statistics, 1993), chiefly in the "service" sector, for example, restaurants, motels, laundries, janitorial services.

Among the lowest paying jobs in the general economy, they provide little security, are especially vulnerable to recession, and may offer little work satisfaction (McAfee, 1988). It is the volatility of this job market that contributes to the more tenuous adjustment of persons with mild intellectual impairment. At greater levels of retardation, employment has tended to be concentrated in "sheltered" rather than in regular work settings—sheltered workshops and work-activity programs. The latter include educational as well as vocational activities. Access to regular employment has increased dramatically, however, through "supported employment," a process that places more disabled individuals directly into work settings with the aid of an on-site supervisor or teacher, a so-called job coach. In effect, the disabled person learns the job "on the job." Especially notable is the finding that even persons with severe or profound impairment can learn, over time, to perform simple assembly-type tasks consistent with employment (Bellamy, Peterson, & Close, 1975).

Fulfilling Adult Social Roles

In life we fulfill a number of social or interpersonal roles, such as child, sibling, friend, student, worker, spouse, and parent. Each role has its own culture-specific behavioral expectations, the adequate performance of which is at least partly related to general intelligence (e.g., Greenspan

& Granfield, 1992). Think of how "intelligence" influences your behavior in social situations. Why do you behave differently with peers than with a person in authority? That difference reflects your understanding of the difference between those relationships, the latter being one in which power and potential control generally are lodged on the side of authority. It is not surprising that in a study of social skills in retarded adults, their performance in "following instructions" and "accepting criticism" exceeded that in "negotiating to resolve conflicts." The last-mentioned would appear to be a much more complex skill (Sherman, Sheldon, Harchik, Edwards, & Quinn, 1992).

Persons with mild retardation function in all adult roles—they are members of families, have friends, work, marry, and have children. In general, however, they seem to be more socially isolated (e.g., Richardson, Katz, & Koller, 1993), loneliness being an oft-heard concern as fewer marry or have children. With more than mild impairment, the capacity to meet the behavioral expectation of normative adult roles is considerably diminished. Moderately retarded adults do enjoy friendships, some of which may be opposite-sex in nature, but these are not likely to lead to marriage. Frequently, with few social contacts, leisure hours may be spent in solitary activities, the television being an always convenient outlet (Stanfield, 1973). With severe or profound retardation, there may be difficulty in entering friendships, that is, relationships requiring *reciprocity*. Here one sees much solitary behavior.

Community Adjustment

The focus here is how retardation affects our capacity to conform to social mores. Two areas are of special concern—sexuality and criminality. In Chapters 5, 6, and 7, we deal in depth with sexuality and retardation; here we merely want to highlight the concerns.

Sexuality.   Given the importance of intelligence in helping us to manage our feelings and our most intimate impulses, sexual expression in persons with mental retardation has been a traditional source of anxiety. Although earlier fears of them as a "reproductive menace" were laid to rest, anxieties persist about inappropriate sexual behavior, vulnerability to exploitation, and fulfillment of "parental" roles. With respect to exploitation, parental or caregiver fears are not eased by occasional newspaper reports of young retarded women as victims of sexual assault. In Chapter 7, such vulnerability is illustrated with regard to a young woman with cerebral palsy whose various physical disabilities rendered her helpless to assault and unable to communicate it through speech.

Another concern pertains to the capacity of retarded adults to assume constructive parental roles. Although the senior author has encountered mildly retarded parents who seemed to be extremely responsible in their parental duties, the research literature indicates that they are less likely to display affection and praise, and to discipline their children appropriately (Feldman, Case, Towns, & Betel, 1985).

Another qualm in an era of free sexuality is the retarded person's capacity to protect himself or herself against AIDS (Sundram, 1992).

Criminality.   A fear of an earlier era, but less frequently heard today, is about persons with retardation who come into conflict with the law. Vulnerable to exploitation and, perhaps, unaware of the possible consequences of their actions, mildly retarded youth and young adults do commit crimes that can lead to imprisonment and even execution (Baroff, 1996). More likely to be incarcerated for offenses against persons because of a lesser participation in white collar crime, earlier surveys indicated that about 10% of the prison population was mentally retarded (Brown & Courtless, 1967). More recent studies indicate a much smaller prevalence, only about 2% (Denkowski & Denkowski, 1985; Noble, & Conley, 1992), a frequency roughly in accord with numbers in the general population.

With recognition of the need to protect the constitutional rights of persons with disabilities, there has been a surge of interest about the retarded population in the criminal-justice community. There is awareness of the need for providing education on the recognition of the retarded offender and his needs and vulnerabilities to the criminal-justice community—to policemen, prosecutors, defense lawyers, judges, probation and parole officers, and correctional staff for those incarcerated. Only recently distinguished for legal purposes from mental illness, retardation is no longer considered a form of insanity. Issues of particular importance to the retarded defendant pertain to capacities to protect constitutional rights; competence to confess, stand trial, and plead guilty; and, if convicted, the degree of culpability and appropriate punishment (Baroff, 1998, 1996; Conley, Luckasson, & Bouthilet, 1992). The senior author has served as an expert witness in criminal cases involving defendants with retardation, often capital ones (Baroff, 1991b) and has taken a special interest in how retardation affects the understanding of one's Miranda rights (Baroff & Freedman, 1988). "Miranda rights" refer to the protection accorded arrested persons at the time of their questioning by police. These consist of the rights to silence, to a lawyer, and to a refusal to speak if one fears that the answers could be used against you in a court of law. The retarded defendant is unlikely to have any understanding of these rights unless there is a previous criminal history. As such, the retarded defendant is less able to protect himself and, indeed, may be induced to admit to crimes that the person did not commit.

Another issue relates to the level of responsibility or culpability appropriate to an offender. Persons with mild retardation are commonly aware that the crimes that they commit are "wrong," but they may lack understanding of *why* they are wrong. This has to do with basic "moral" understanding. To the degree that appreciation of the significance of their offense is diminished, their level of culpability or blameworthiness is lessened, although not eliminated. Also relevant to culpability is the retarded individual's capacity to think about the consequences of actions before they are taken. At least in those with mild retardation, and this is the segment of the retarded population that is most likely to come into conflict with the law, this capacity exists, although in lesser degree. Coupled with a lack of knowledge about what those consequences might be, the "brakes" that we ordinarily apply to impulses that could get us into trouble are not applied. This gives to some of their crimes, notably those of a violent nature, an "unthinking" or impulsive quality. There is clearly need in our educational programs to acquaint students, retarded *and* nonretarded, with the *kinds* of behaviors that can get them into difficulty and *why*.

Older Adulthood

With life spans roughly comparable to our own except if there are major physical and medical disorders, the needs of older adults with mental retardation increasingly have caught our attention. For those with not more than mild impairment, the senior years may bring them back into contact with a service system that they could earlier ignore. Given the inevitable stresses of age, such as decline in health, loss of loved ones, and reduced income, they are bound to require some assistance. In contrast, the more severely impaired, not living independently and, perhaps, no longer engaged in work activities of any kind, may find themselves with "dead" time that needs to be structured. The teaching of potential sources of recreation becomes an important means of helping them to continue to experience satisfaction in their lives. In Chapter 7, a special section is devoted to the older adult and to his family. Issues of relevance here pertain to possible retirement from work and the need to make constructive use of leisure time, lesser capacities of aging parents to care for their older adult children, and the need for "permanence planning" by parents for the day when they must surrender their caregiving responsibilities. With respect to leisure time, there has been an effort to integrate the retarded older adult in general day programs for senior citizens.

Older adulthood also has special significance for persons with Down syndrome because a feature of the disorder is earlier aging. A significant decline in mental functioning is sometimes seen in the fourth decade, especially in men (Janicki, 1991; Sinex & Merrill, 1982).

☐ Mental Retardation as a "Developmental" Disorder

The third element of the 1992 retardation definition refers to the age period in which the disorder becomes manifest, and fixes age 18 years as its upper limit, the same ceiling as in earlier ones. As we have seen, it is during this period that virtually all cognitive growth occurs, and it is slowness in that growth and a permanent disparity in the ultimate level attained at the cessation of the growth period that marks both the effect and chronicity of the disorder.

A consequence of the traditional association of retardation with origin in the developmental years, generally early childhood, is to exclude from the diagnosis persons who become intellectually impaired in adulthood. This cognitive deficit, arising from head injury or illness, and following a history of normal mental development, typically has led to designation as "brain injured" rather than "retarded." In contrast to the chronicity of mental retardation, brain injury typically has an acute onset and commonly is associated with problems of cognition (memory, organization, attention span, and concentration) and personality (emotional instability). Although the brain-injured individual may come to use the same kinds of services as persons with retardation, the groups are clearly different in how they were perceived by others and by themselves during their growing-up years. Apart from the mildly retarded nonorganic segment of the retarded population, the remainder are clearly different from their parents and siblings and are so perceived by them. Their difference leads to a variety of special reactions and, sometimes, to problems of acceptance only rarely seen in nonhandicapped children. It is this aspect of the developmental period that is also highly significant. This is the time during which the basic personality characteristics of the retarded child are formed, and these have significance for future adjustment and life satisfaction. In the next chapter, a picture of personality in mental retardation is presented; here we want only to address what is probably the most important shaper of that personality: the impact, both short and long-term, of retardation on the child's parents.

☐ Impact of Mental Retardation on the Family

As a disability that can touch on all aspects of functioning and one whose effects are generally lifelong, mental retardation can be expected to significantly affect the child's family. Parents, siblings, relatives, friends—all, to varying degrees, will find themselves affected by its presence. For purposes of surveying its impact, we can distinguish between its initial effects at birth or when first diagnosed and its continuing impact through life.

Initial Impact

Shock and Grief

Whether the child is perceived as different at birth, as in Down syndrome, or the disorder is not recognized until later in childhood, typically by age 2 years; the effect on the parents is likely to be devastating (e.g., Wolfensberger & Kurtz, 1969). Unless there has been a prior abnormal birth or evidence of abnormality during the pregnancy, no parent is psychologically prepared for anything but a normal birth. For some the shock is so overwhelming that they seek immediate placement outside the home. In the past such decisions often were encouraged by health professionals who viewed the child as a prospective burden and one whose psychological disavowal was in the parents' best interest (Spock, 1961).

Such recommendations reflected our culture's negative attitude toward the disorder and the absence of any medical means of altering it. More recently, however, in view of the tremendous growth of services, from infancy to older adulthood, some moderation of this sense of despair is appropriate.

Guilt and Isolation

Apart from whatever support parents may or may not receive from those who first identify the disorder, another very stressful aspect is a frequent sense of guilt and shame (Wolfensberger & Kurtz, 1969) that restricts them from reaching out to their usual sources of emotional support. Instead of finding comfort, they seek to hide what has occurred, and this only aggravates their emotional tensions.

Continuing Impact: Unending Parental Concern

The effects of mental retardation are such as to cause adaptive difficulties throughout life (e.g., Schild, 1971). For the parent of the young child, there is a lengthening of the normal period of infancy and the intense dependency inherent in it. Later there are concerns about playmates, possibly undue pressures on siblings to assume playmate or surrogate-parent roles, and, in school, concerns about proper education, a social and recreational life, and a growing awareness of the child's developing sexuality.

A study of the most common problems experienced by families of children with developmental delays (Orr, Cameron, Dobson, & May, 1993) found that in *preschoolers* these were chiefly medical (82%), behavioral (28%), and those caused by physical disabilities (15%). In *middle childhood*, medical problems (38%), hyperactivity (38%), and severe behavior difficulties (35%) were the most frequently reported; in *adolescence* the major concerns were severe behavior problems (30%), medical disorders (27%), and hyperactivity (24%). Given stresses that typically exceed those in families with normally developing children (Dyson, 1991), the impact of these problems varies with the coping resources of the family (Crnic, Friedrich, & Greenberg, 1983; Minnes, 1988). Important contributors to effective coping include the parents' general problem-solving ability (Harris & McHale, 1989), their continued access to sources of enjoyment (Gallimore, Weisner, Kaupfman, & Bernheimer, 1989), and support from both within and outside the immediate family (Erickson & Upshur, 1989; Greenberg & Fewell, 1989).

Adding to these problems in families with retarded children can be those of the retarded adult. As parents age, they naturally become increasingly concerned about their child's welfare. When they can no longer provide a caregiving role, where will their child live? What will he or she do? Who will look after him or her? These are concerns unknown to parents of nondisabled adults.

Together with the problems associated with the rearing of a child with mental retardation, there are also special benefits, and a review of recent studies of family adjustment indicates levels of functioning not different from those of the general population (Krauss, 1993). Let us listen to some parents as they describe their experiences. In them we encounter sorrows and joys but also the emotional growth that seems often to attend this kind of family experience.

The story of Martin, now in his middle-adult years, conveys the flavor and impact of retardation on both the affected child and his family.

Martin: The Preschool Years

Martin's very early development appeared normal, although by age 6 months some parental concern was evident. He was a quiet baby but one who cried excessively at night, and some muscular weakness seemed present. For the next 18 months there was hope that his strength would increase. In comparison with his older siblings, it was clear that his rate of development was slower.

At 2 years the parents were stunned by a neurologist's opinion that there was evidence of retardation. Shocked and bewildered, they didn't know where to turn, and Martin's mother immediately began to blame herself for what happened. She felt guilty and wondered what she had done wrong. She had previously been reassured that the child was developing normally but harbored her own doubts; the diagnosis was devastating to her. Physicians are naturally protective of parents' feelings and certainly cautious about rendering such an opinion in early childhood, but parents really do want to know the truth. To live with long-term uncertainty is, ultimately, more painful than facing reality.

Martin's parents were concerned at the prospect of eventual institutional placement. Exposés of these institutions had created a public furor; this was to lead to the push for deinstitutionalization of those in both mental-retardation centers and psychiatric hospitals, and the development of community-based services.

Variable in his behavior, Martin could be bright and alert, while at other times his gaze would wander and his head droop. Speech was impaired, a very characteristic developmental problem in retardation, and his parents often could not understand his vocalizations. His developmental difficulties frustrated him too, as he tried to make himself understood.

Characteristically, the stresses of caring for Martin were largely borne by his mother. His father immersed himself in his work while his mother sought to relieve her tensions through alcohol.

The School Years

Martin initially attended a private school, but public-school placement soon followed, supplemented with private tutoring. The family tried to provide a variety of experiences to improve Martin's social skills. The intent was to create at least the outward appearance of normality. Reference to difficulties in this area are presented elsewhere in this chapter.

There were problems in school. He was teased and taunted. Other children laughed at him when he could not keep up, or they mocked his speech. Unhappily, in the service of enhancing our own self-worth, we denigrate others.

There was also a sexual assault by a male adult that Martin dealt with by calling the police. His mother was surprised that he could use the phone in that fashion. We typically underestimate what persons with disabilities can achieve.

Difficulties with peers continued and, in middle school, a gang made him sing and dance in the schoolyard to their jeers. Starved for attention from his classmates and not understanding the ridicule in their behavior, Martin thought they liked his singing! A neighborhood bully forced Martin to stand on his shoulders and knock out street lights. This illustrates how retarded individuals can be coerced into behavior that can get them into difficulty with the law. On one occasion, he was cornered at a park and made to take off his clothes.

In his teen years, Martin was a handsome youth who liked to watch movies and sports on television. He especially liked to watch golf. His mother noted that it's a game of understandable moves. He began showing interest in girls and put their pictures on the walls of his room. But he was lonely, a common problem of retarded youth.

The Postschool Years

At the age of 19, he got into difficulty when he sent a valentine to a classmate who had received an anonymous obscene letter. The police initially regarded Martin as their prime suspect because they saw him as "different." In fact, a "normal" classmate was responsible.

At age 20, Martin left the family home and moved into a "group home," a community-based residence serving other retarded youth. Although there were a variety of activities available, he eventually moved into a still smaller living unit, and then into his own apartment. Later employed and married, he far exceeded the gloomy predictions of his infancy. His comment about his life is profound in its depth of understanding: "People are retarded by what they don't know. That's why I work so hard to learn the things I don't know and become more normal." Although his life has had more than its share of stresses, he appears to have surmounted them, as have his parents. He has insight into the nature of his difficulty as does his wife, a young woman who is also mildly retarded. Asked how it is to be retarded, she replied, "How is it with us? It is no different than it is with anyone else, except we're slower."

Ben

Before ending this section there is one more parental experience that should be shared. Let us listen to a very different kind of experience, as the mother of an 8-year-old boy with Down syndrome describes her experience.

> If this turns out to be a Pollyanna-like story I hope no one reads it, or else reads it and writes a nasty letter. Being a Pollyanna can be tolerated in some instances, I suppose, but never in regard to retardation. And that's what this is about, mental retardation, or more precisely, certain feelings I have toward my eight-year-old son who is mentally retarded.

Now believe me, I have had my moments of weeping and despair. When I first learned that our baby, that rosy, dimpled infant, was retarded I almost died of agony. The doctors were wrong [grief and denial are common initial reactions to catastrophic events] . . . Our Ben couldn't be what they said, a child with Down's syndrome . . . a mongoloid. But he was, and he is, and that's a primary fact of his life and ours [ultimate acceptance of reality]. Today Ben is a sturdy eight-year-old, and I sometimes find tears in my eyes at the sight of him trying to keep up with his neighborhood peers who are so brightly normal, but I more often find myself smiling, sometimes even belly laughing at the sheer exuberance with which this child faces life. The very idea for writing this at all is that not an hour ago I witnessed the most ecstatic, uninhibited reaction to a fried chicken TV commercial that any sponsor could hope for in his wildest dreams. Who else can raise his arms in gustatory triumph over a dancing chicken and shout, "Wow!" in such a way as Ben? What an ability to translate the mundane into something terrific! It gives his life an added flavor at every turn.

He is lucky, this little boy of mine. He will not conquer the worlds of the academic, the scientific, or the great doers, but he has a unique appreciation for those ordinary rites of life that seem only dull and jaded to the rest of us. And it goes way beyond fried chicken. The neighbor's dog comes loping by covered with mud from a nearby creek and all we see is one big messy mutt. But Ben sees a friend, and they sit on the walk together, Ben's arms around the dog's neck, dog licking Ben's face; sheer joy in one another. We go to the ocean and contemplate its vast magnificence. The ocean fills a hole Ben has dug in the sand. "Beat it, ocean," says Ben. Around 3:20 every afternoon the front door bangs open and various articles are dropped on the floor. 'I'm back, Mommie,' shouts Ben and comes to give me my home again hug.

One recent Saturday morning the whole family had slept late and as my husband and I were struggling awake Ben came into our room to say good morning. He looked at his stubble-chinned, disheveled father and in the tone of a true believer announced, "Daddy is Prince Charming." At that moment I could see more of a resemblance to Godzilla but Ben saw Prince Charming. And then he turned to me—a half-unconscious Phyllis Diller—and said, "Mommie is The Sleeping Beauty." How wonderful to wake to laughter. And how wonderful to live with someone who can look at a couple of creaky parents and see a prince and a princess.

Pollyanna, go fly a kite. But, Ben, oh how I love you!

☐ Summary

In this chapter the disorder of mental retardation is introduced within the context of a consideration of the nature of intelligence. Mental retardation is the consequence of significant impairment in that valued human capacity, and its effects are felt in virtually every aspect of human endeavor. Its nature was explored in terms of its most recent definition, the 1992 version offered by the major professional organization in the field, the AAMR.

Particular attention was given to the nature of intellectual functioning in persons with the disorder, the quality of their thinking, its effect on their families, and on their general adaptation.

Possible Discussion Questions

Is "intelligence" too narrowly construed? Because intelligence tests are required to have items that lend themselves to easy administration and scoring, are some aspects of intelligence undermeasured, such as "planning" and other "executive" functions? Are the abilities to compose rhyme or to play chess cognitive capacities not measured by intelligence tests, forms of intelligence?

Mental retardation is treated as if it were a discrete entity although, in fact, it simply represents a point on a continuum of intelligence that varies from genius to retardation. When the traditional cut-off IQ score of 70 (or 75) is used as if a person scoring 71 is not retarded, the score is given an objectivity that it does not merit. In states that exclude the death penalty only for people scoring below 70, and not those scoring 71, is the state drawing a distinction that is mythical rather than real? How should a state draw such distinctions?

The presence of mental retardation in a criminal defendant can serve to lessen or mitigate the punishment for a crime. How do we balance the legitimate issue of reduced responsibility in the defendant who is retarded against society's expectation that it must protect itself against wrongdoers?

How does this society, or any society, deal with purported group and racial differences in measured intelligence? In retardation, is this reflected in differential representation in "special classes," classes for children with learning difficulties? The storm stirred by the book The Bell Curve (Herrnstein & Murray, 1994) illustrates the bedeviling aspect of suggestive group differences in a socially valued trait.

The term mental retardation is much abhorred by those so designated and aware of its negative connotation. Does the senior author's suggested redesignation of mental retardation as general learning disorder and its inclusion in a "family" of learning disorders of cognitive origin reduce its objectionability?

☐ Appendix: Adaptive Potential, Chronological Age, and Degree of Retardation

Our perspective now changes from a consideration of the adaptive *problems* associated with retardation to a focus on adaptive *potential*. What follows is a detailed description of the adaptive potential of persons with retardation from infancy into adulthood. It is presented in the form of rough norms that project behavioral expectations as a function of developmental age,[9] chronological age, and degree of cognitive impairment. The norms themselves represent an integration of earlier summarized ones (Robinson & Robinson, 1965), general developmental data (Hurlock, 1964), and those offered in the 1973 and 1977 AAMD manuals (Grossman, 1973, 1977). It should be understood that the intent is to offer a rough approximation of what may be expected consistent with chronological age and the degree of retardation. It is recognized that the child's development is much affected by environments that can encourage or discourage it, a topic addressed in depth in Chapter 5. The biologically intact child probably has a greater range of possible outcomes than the child with biological abnormality, although there is no doubt that the child with a biological basis for developmental delay can also benefit from programs designed to foster development. In Down syndrome, for example, a disorder due to an abnormal number of chromosomes, there is indication that early childhood education can slow or prevent the kind of cognitive decline typically found after age one year (Guralnick & Bricker, 1987). On the negative side, these norms may also be conceived of as creating undesirable expectancies in workers by relating behavioral expectation to degree of retardation, thus implying limitations as well as potential. It is true that we cannot know what is ultimately possible for any human being, but within the constraints of present pedagogy and medical science such limitations do exist. They're present in all of us, able as well as disabled, and awareness of them cannot be ignored in the planning of services and supports for persons with retardation.

The norms are divided into two parts—the first part covers the developmental period, the years to 18, and the second covers the adult years. The norms for the period to 18 years are organized around *cognitive or developmental age*, individuals with the same developmental age having similar behavioral expectancies although differing in chronological age and degree of retardation. The second part of the norms, those for the adult years, are organized on the basis of *degree of retardation* as changes in mental age are not expected after age 18.

Developmental Age 1 Year: Chronological Age 4 Years and Older, Profound Cognitive Impairment

Self-help: Opens mouth for feeding, drinks from cup with help; beginning attempts at finger-feeding.

Motor: Sits alone; may pull self to standing briefly; reaches for and manipulates parts of body, e.g., toes, objects; has thumb-finger grasp.

Language (expressive): Imitates sounds, laughs, or smiles in response; may say "mama" or "dada"; expressive language at a prespeech level—crying, vocalization, and gesture.

Language (receptive): Some understanding of gestures and of very familiar words, e.g., "no."

Social: Recognizes familiar persons and interacts with them, but not verbally.

Developmental Age 1 to 2 Years: Chronological Age 3 to 6 Years, Severe Cognitive Impairment; Chronological Age 8 Years and Older, Profound Cognitive Impairment

Self-help: Finger feeds, may show beginning use of spoon; passive cooperation in dressing, bathing, and toileting; may have some bowel movements when placed on toilet, may remove simple articles of clothing, e.g., hat and socks.

Motor: Stands alone; may walk though needing help; performs simple motor tasks, e.g., turning, pulling, grasping.

Language (expressive): May use one or two words, but prespeech forms continue to predominate.

Social: May respond to others in predictable fashion; plays "patty cake" or plays imitatively with others; may play by self briefly.

Developmental Age 2 to 3 Years: Chronological Age 3 to 5 Years, Mild Cognitive Impairment; Chronological Age 5 to 7 Years, Moderate Cognitive Impairment; Chronological Age 6 to 9 Years, Severe Cognitive Impairment; Chronological Age 10 Years and Older, Profound Cognitive Impairment

Self-help: Some use of spoon but with spilling; uses cup; more active cooperation in dressing and undressing; some use of toilet; may begin to indicate when pants are wet.

Motor: Walks alone steadily; may run, jump in place, and climb stairs with help; may be able to turn single pages, open boxes, unscrew lids, string beads; may be able to imitate vertical and horizontal lines.

Language (expressive): May use several words; if pronouns are used they often are used incorrectly; still using gestures.

Cognitive: May recognize different shapes; possibly beginning number concepts, e.g., distinguishing between "one" and "many."

Social: May play with others for short periods but play is "parallel" rather than interactive; recognizes other people and shows preferences.

Developmental Age 3 to 4 Years: Chronological Age 5 to 7 Years, Mild Cognitive Impairment; Chronological Age 7 to 10 Years, Moderate Cognitive Impairment; Chronological Age 9 to 12 Years, Severe Cognitive Impairment; Chronological Age 12 to 16 Years; Profound Cognitive Impairment

Self-help: Uses spoon with little spilling; beginning use of fork; can remove some clothing, e.g., coat or dress, can partially dress self; attempts to help in bathing and in washing hands; may indicate toilet accidents and need to use toilet.

Motor: Can go up and down stairs; can run, jump, and balance on one foot; can pass a ball, transfer objects; will need much assistance in "fine-motor" activities, e.g., buttoning, using zipper.

Language (expressive): May use two- and three-word phrases, e.g., "where daddy?" "mommy go bye-bye," beginning to use pronouns correctly and to refer to self by pronoun rather than by name; pronunciation usually is correct on beginning and ending consonants, e.g., mom, bib; beginning to use "what," "where," and "who."

Cognitive: Can identify own sex, recognize primary colors; beginning "time" concepts, e.g., today, tomorrow, yesterday; beginning "position" concepts, e.g., on top of, under, inside; number concepts through "two"; simple size concepts; may be able to print a few capital letters.

Social: Can spontaneously engage with others in interactive play, usually with only one or two others; can be guided into play with larger groups; shows preferences among children.

Developmental Age 4 to 5 Years: Chronological Age 6 to 9 Years, Mild Cognitive Impairment; Chronological Age 10 to 12 Years, Moderate Cognitive Impairment; Chronological Age 12 to 15 Years, Severe Cognitive Impairment; Chronological Age 16 Years and Older, Profound Cognitive Impairment

Self-help: Can feed self with spoon and fork; beginning to use knife for spreading; gets drink unassisted; can undress self; can put on clothing but needs help with zippers and small buttons; attempts to bathe self but needs assistance; washes and dries hands but not carefully; usually uses toilet if placed on it but may still have accidents (daytime training precedes nighttime control).

Motor (gross-motor skills): Can climb stairs in alternating fashion; can hop, skip, balance on toes, walk balance boards, ride tricycle (over 8 years—bicycle); may climb trees or jungle gym; can play dance games; can throw ball at target.

Motor (fine-motor skills): Can grasp pencil in manner resembling adult position; can button and lace.

Language (expressive): May have considerable speaking vocabulary, although speech will be particularly impaired in youngsters with more than mild retardation—if nonverbal, as in severely and profoundly retarded youth, there may be use of gestures to communicate needs.

Language (receptive): Understands simple verbal communications, e.g., following directions, responding to questions.

Cognitive-academic: Has size concepts, can match pictures of identical objects, can answer simple "why" questions; beginning to be able to match geometric forms; some elementary reading skills—may recognize common printed words, e.g., stop, go, boy, girl.

Social: Can engage in simple play with other children, e.g., "store," "house."

Developmental Age 5 to 6 Years: Chronological Age 8 to 10 Years, Mild Cognitive Impairment; Chronological Age 11 to 13 Years, Moderate Cognitive Impairment; Chronological Age 13 to 15 Years, Severe Cognitive Impairment

Self-help: Adequate use of spoon and fork; can use knife for buttering though needs assistance with knife in cutting; can dress self including buttoning and zipping; may tie shoes; bathes self with supervision; washes and dries hands and face; brushes teeth; toilet-trained although there may be bladder accidents at night.

Motor: Can run, hop, skip, and dance, can use skates, sled, or jump rope, can march to music.

Language (expressive): Mildly cognitively impaired child may be using fairly normal sentence structure and have speech of good intelligibility; at more severe levels of impairment, language may be at the phrase or single-word level and also be indistinct in pronunciation.

Cognitive-academic: Can match geometric forms; has concepts of texture and weight; some idea of beauty, beginning concept of laterality, right-left; able to give differences between some common objects; may have number concepts up to "thirteen"; may be able to print name in large letters; may show frequent letter reversals; can print some numbers.

Social: May participate spontaneously in group activities; can engage in simple competitive games, e.g., tag, races, dodgeball; may have true friendships (more likely in children who are not more than moderately impaired).

Community: May be able to perform simple errands, make purchases with a note; understands that money has value but does not know how to use it (except in coin machines).

Household: May prepare simple foods (sandwiches); perform simple household tasks, e.g., bed making, sweeping, vacuuming; can set and clear tables.

Self-direction: May seek things to do; can pay attention to a task for at least 10 minutes; attempts to be dependable and to carry out responsibilities (more likely of mildly impaired youth).

Developmental Age 6 to 7 Years: Chronological Age 10 to 12 Years, Mild Cognitive Impairment; Chronological Age 14 Years and Older, Moderate Cognitive Impairment

Self-help: Can feed, dress, and bath self; may choose daily clothing, combs and brushes hair; may shampoo and roll hair; may wash and iron.

Motor: Adequate motor skills especially in mildly impaired youth.

Language (expressive): May be able to carry on simple conversation and use complex sentences (more true of mildly than of moderately impaired youth).

Cognitive-academic: Beginning reading skills, can recognize simple words or read brief sentences (reading skills are likely to lag relative to mental age and its equivalent grade-age expectancy).

Social: May interact cooperatively.

Community: May be able to perform simple shopping errands without notes; can make small purchases, some beginning money skills— understands values of coins; can do simple coin counting; can add and subtract up to 10.

Household: Can prepare simple foods, e.g., sandwiches; perform simple household chores, e.g., dusting, dish washing, garbage.

Self-direction: May initiate many of own activities; can attend to tasks for at least 10 minutes; may be conscientious in assuming responsibility.

Developmental Age 7 to 11 Years: Chronological Age 13 to 18 Years, Mild Cognitive Impairment

Self-help: Cares for self in feeding, dressing, toileting, bathing, and grooming; may need health or personal-care reminders; may need some assistance in selection and purchase of clothing.

Motor: Essentially normal motor skills in "cultural-familial" (psychosocial) retarded adolescent; may be some impairment in motor skills in adolescent with "organic" retardation.

Language (expressive): Essentially normal fluency, although pronunciation problems may persist.

Cognitive-academic: Reading and arithmetic achievement will closely correspond to mental age although often lag behind it somewhat; range in reading and number skills will be from first to fourth grade.

Social: Can relate as "friend" to same sex and opposite sex; can participate in recreational activities enjoyed by adolescents but may have problems in complex games of competitive sports.

Community: Some mobility in community, able to use public transportation; may drive; can do some independent shopping; can handle simple change making but has difficulty in money management; number skills ordinarily limited to addition and subtraction.

Household: Can perform most routine household chores.

Self-direction: Initiates most of own activity; relatively normal attention span; can perform routine tasks with only nominal supervision.

The Adult with Mental Retardation

Mildly Retarded: IQ Range 55 to 70,[10] Mental-age Range 8 to 11 Years

Self-help: Full self-help skills; may function independently in the community; benefits from someone who can serve as an advisor.

Language: Adequate for ordinary purposes of communication.

Academic: May be able to read simple materials for information; unlikely to read for pleasure; number skills tend to be limited to simple addition and subtraction, and much assistance is needed in budgeting and general money management.

Vocational status: Capable of regular employment in unskilled jobs although some can achieve "helper" status in trades.

Social roles: Can fulfill all adult social roles: have friends, marry, and become parent; role as "parent" is controversial.

Community adjustment: Some potential for delinquency in young adults from disadvantaged backgrounds.

Moderately Retarded: IQ Range 35 to 54, Mental-age Range 6 to 8 Years

Self-help: Has basic self-care skills but do not achieve an independent adjustment; will always require some degree of supervision.

Language: Language is generally functional for purposes of communication but intelligibility of speech may be much impaired.

Academic: Generally does not achieve functional reading and money skills.

Vocational status: With "supported employment" services can function in regular employment and can work productively in sheltered workshops.

Social roles: Usually does not fulfill roles of spouse and parent, although capable of friendships with same and opposite sex.

Community adjustment: Does not fulfill ordinary "citizen" functions and unlikely to get into difficulties with the law.

Severely Retarded: IQ Range 20 to 35, Mental-age Range 4 to 6 Years

Self-help: Does not function independently although can acquire some self-help skills, e.g., feeding, dressing, and toileting; needs assistance in complex acts of grooming and personal hygiene.

Language: Understanding of language is likely to be much better than the ability to express it; speech may be very poorly articulated and difficult to understand.

Academic: No functional reading or number skills for activities of daily living.

Vocational status: May be capable of performing some useful work at either the sheltered-workshop or work-activity levels of productivity; more likely to be attending an activity center.

Social roles: Does not fulfill adult social roles; can have some peer relationships; relates to adults in childlike fashion.

Community adjustment: Performs no "citizen" roles; does not get into difficulties with the law.

Profoundly Retarded: IQ Range 0 to 19, Mental-age Range 0 to 4 Years

Self-help: Will always require much supervision, although some self-help skills may be acquired.

Motor: Mobility may be impaired because of physical or sensory problems; a large proportion of so-called nonambulatory retarded persons fall in this range of retardation.

Language: Ability to understand is likely to far exceed ability to speak; there may be little or no speech; capable of following simple directions.

Academic: No academic skills.

Vocational status: May be unable to perform any useful work, although with training in an activity center may achieve a work-activity level of productivity.

Social roles: Fulfills no adult social roles; may appear as a social isolate, paying little attention to others except as it relates to own needs; commonly shows "stereotyped" behavior.

Community adjustment: Fulfills no community roles; commonly in institutional or medical-like setting.

☐ Notes

1. In order to convey the idea that retardation is only an aspect of the person, not the whole person, terms such as *retarded person* or *retarded individual* are avoided in favor of such usages as *persons* or *individuals with mental retardation*, but "readability" demands variation in how things are expressed and, in its service, all forms of describing this population are employed.

2. Both sexes are affected by mental retardation, but future usage will be limited largely to forms of the personal pronoun "he," the standard substitute for antecedents whose genders are mixed or irrelevant.

3. Primary mental abilities—verbal comprehension, number, space, memory, reasoning; two-factor model—verbal-educational and practical-mechanical; operations—cognition (knowing or grasping items of information), memory, divergent production (generating alternatives), convergent production (identifying a best single choice among options), evaluation (reaching judgments based on some standard).

4. The upper limit of 68 shown in Figure 1.3 accords with the IQ range for retardation on the Stanford-Binet Intelligence Test, fourth edition, 1986.

5. Now the American Association on Mental Retardation.

6. *Prevalence* refers to the frequency of a condition either at a given moment in time or over a period of time. *Incidence*, another commonly used term, refers to the number of new cases per unit of time.

7. Personal communication, Keith Scott, 1997.

8. It is recognized that IQ is only one aspect, albeit a major one, of the person who is "retarded." Throughout this book, references to levels of severity vary among *cognitive impairment, intellectual impairment*, and *retardation*.

9. It is now common to characterize a child's developmental level in terms of one or more "age-equivalent" scores. The focus here is on the child's cognitive development or "cognitive age"; this is similar to the previously used "mental age."

10. IQ ranges in the "Manual of Diagnosis and Professional Practice in Mental Retardation" (J.W. Jacobson & J.E. Mulick, Eds.). In the presentation of these IQ ranges, the author refer to them in their traditional designation as levels of "retardation" rather than as levels of "cognitive impairment."

CHAPTER 2

Personality and Mental Retardation

☐ Overview

In Chapter 1, the topic of mental retardation was introduced with emphasis on its *cognitive* side—that is, the nature of the intellectual disability and its effect on general adjustment. Our direction now shifts to the *affective* or *emotional* side as we look at the person with retardation as an "individual" who, like ourselves, can be understood in terms of the experiences that produce happiness or unhappiness. A study of formerly institutionalized adults now living in the community (Edgerton & Bercovici, 1976) revealed that their primary interest was, not surprisingly, "enjoying life." For some, work had declined in importance, but there was widespread desire for recreation, hobbies, good times, friends, and family. These desires echo our own and speak to the nature of the human condition—of what it means to be a person. Our portrayal of the personality of the individual who is mentally retarded is conveyed through a model that describes the basic physical and psychological *needs* of all of us, nondisabled as well as disabled, and examines how the gratification of these needs is affected by the disability. Borrowing from the works of personality theorists particularly interested in the self and human motivation (Deci & Ryan, 1991; Epstein, 1973; Maslow, 1954), the personality model gives special attention to self-esteem as a motivator of behavior. This chapter offers a "need-driven" personality model and a discussion of how these needs are affected by mental retardation.

61

☐ On Personality Itself

A Rationale for Presenting a Personality Model

Why should a book on mental retardation include a personality model? The answer lies in its usefulness for understanding the behavior of persons with the disorder and, in particular, their behavior problems. These are dealt with in depth in the last two chapters; it suffices here to recognize that their behavioral difficulties, like our own, are commonly the result of chronic frustration of basic biological and psychological needs. Although behavior-oriented personality theory, the focus of our treatment approach, sensitizes us to *how* such dimensions as antecedents and consequences influence behavior, it does not seek to explain *why* these elements are so important. The *why* is to be found, ultimately, in their *rewarding* or *punishing* nature. To understand why certain consequences or contingencies are rewarding, punishing, or without effect is to begin to comprehend what motivates us. It is to begin to grasp something of our fundamental nature as human beings. Although no single theory of personality has been viewed as the sole possessor of "the truth" (Hall & Lindzey, 1970), at least some systematic way of conceptualizing behavior is preferable to none at all. Even a partial truth contributes to our understanding of ourselves and others. That partial truth serves as a *filter* that directs attention and illuminates the factors that motivate our behavior. It is in the spirit of increasing understanding of behavior in all of us, retarded and nonretarded, that the following conception of personality is offered.

Its Basic Elements

The personality model views humankind in terms of three dimensions—*resources*, *needs*, and *values*. Each is defined, illustrated, and then integrated in a summary paragraph.

Resources

"Resources" refer to our capacities or abilities and are grouped into five categories. They are intelligence; communication skills; health, sensory, and physical skills; personality—temperament, emotions, and character; and esthetic appreciation and spirituality.

Intelligence.   As elaborated in Chapter 1, intelligence is equated with learning ability, reasoning, knowledge, and problem solving.

Communication Skills. This refers to our ability to make ourselves understood, most often through speech, but also through the written word, gesture, sign language, and the artistic modes of literature, poetry, art, dance, and music.

Health, Sensory, and Physical Skills. This refers to our "physical" self—our state of health; the intactness of our senses, chiefly vision and hearing; the functionality of our limbs—arms, hands, and legs; and such characteristics as strength, endurance, speed, and coordination.

Personality—Temperament, Emotions, and Character. Temperament, emotions, and character are seen as central ingredients of what we call "personality." We can conceptualize personality as a resource, as a capacity or adaptive style that is brought to bear in our daily lives and always in our social interactions. In this sense one can think of a "good" or adaptive personality and a "bad" or maladaptive one. The ingredients of personality as a resource are now described.

Temperament. This has come to refer to behaviors seen in infants and young children. Presumed to be biological in origin, they are thought to be relatively independent of parental child-rearing style. Babies and young children appear to differ from the very beginning of life in their degrees of motor activity, irritability, distractibility, patterns of sleep and alertness, and response to new situations (Chess & Korn, 1977; Kagan, 1981; Thomas & Chess, 1977). Based on these dimensions, broad distinctions are drawn between fussy or difficult and easy babies. "Easy" babies from the first weeks of life are cheerful, relaxed, and predictable in feeding and sleeping. "Difficult" ones are more irritable, intense, and unpredictable (Thomas & Chess, 1986). In later childhood, temperament is seen as explaining differences in the response to new situations, with children characterized as shy and inhibited or spontaneous and uninhibited. It also appears to affect problem-solving styles—from the impulsive child to the reflective one (Kagan, 1966).

Emotions. Emotions are affective or feeling states, feelings that generally can be classified as pleasant (positive) or unpleasant (negative). Emotions are expressions of the interpretation that we place on events that are perceived as relevant to our welfare and self-esteem. Experiences to which we apply an emotional interpretation are not "neutral"; rather they are potential sources of benefit or threat, of happiness or unhappiness. Experiences perceived as potentially threatening or harmful evoke such emotions as anger, anxiety, fear, guilt, shame, sadness, envy, jealousy, and disgust. Experiences seen as potentially beneficial create such feelings as joy, pride, gratitude, and love (Lazarus, 1991).

Character. "Character" refers to consistent "patterns of behaviors" as these are expressed in a wide variety of situations (Cofer & Appley, 1967). Factor-analytic approaches have identified five major personality factors— emotional stability, extroversion, openness, agreeableness, and conscientiousness (McRae & Costa, 1986). Each is briefly illustrated in the form of pairs of opposite qualities.

> *Emotional stability*: calm versus anxious, secure versus insecure, self-satisfied versus self-pitying
> *Extraversion*: sociable versus retiring, fun-loving versus sober, affectionate versus reserved
> *Openness*: imaginative versus practical, preference for variety versus routine, independent versus conforming
> *Agreeableness*: soft-hearted versus ruthless, trusting versus suspicious, helpful versus uncooperative
> *Conscientiousness (the will to achieve)*: organized versus disorganized, careful versus careless, self-disciplined versus weak-willed

Esthetic Appreciation.

This refers to our capacity to experience beauty in all its manifold forms—nature, art, music, dance, literature, and poetry.

Spirituality.

Together with our esthetic capacities, we have spiritual ones. Along with language these, perhaps, are the dimensions that most distinguish us from other forms of life. Our spiritual resources include the capacity to experience awe, our moral sensibilities, and, of course, our religious interests.

Needs

Constituting the second major component of the personality model, "needs" are equated with the forces or drives that give direction and intensity to our behavior. They are the motivators of behavior. Theorists have generally agreed that *behavior is governed by an underlying fundamental motive: the desire to avoid or terminate unpleasant states and to seek pleasurable ones.* The behavioral principles presented later in this book in relation to the education of retarded youth and the management of their behavior problems rest on this precept. Pleasurable or rewarding outcomes for engaging in desired behavior are called "positive reinforcers"; unwanted behaviors evoke unpleasant, unwanted, or punishing outcomes—"negative reinforcers."

In the personality model, pleasurable and unpleasurable states are tied to the degree to which needs—biological and psychological—are met. If needs are met (gratified, satisfied), we experience a reduction in tension and increased feelings of comfort, pleasure, or well-being. If needs are unmet (frustrated), we experience unpleasant emotions, such as tension, anxiety, anger, sadness, and fear. It is in this sense that *emotions* are related directly to our basic sources of motivation.

In offering the particular group of "psychological" needs presented here, it is recognized that other "need" models exist (e.g., Alderfer, 1969; Atkinson, 1964; Herzberg, Mausner, & Snyderman, 1959; McClelland, 1961; Murray, 1938), but those represented here give special prominence to self-esteem—a need that seems to be particularly powerful in our culture. The needs posited, four in number, are viewed as either physiological/biological or psychological, an admittedly artificial distinction. Only one biological need is shown, subsuming all our specific physiological ones, while the remaining three needs are psychological in nature.

Survival.   This refers to our physiological or biological needs. To the old stand-bys of food, clothing, and shelter, we can add needs for stimulation of our five senses, and sex.

The need for stimulation of our senses, at some optimum level of intensity, is tied to the reticular activating system in the brain (Zuckerman, Buchsbaum, & Murphy, 1980). When awake, we receive both external stimulation from our environment and internal stimulation from within the brain, such as daydreams, memories, thoughts. When asleep, stimulation continues in the form of dreams. Given too little sensory stimulation while awake, typically of a visual or auditory nature, we experience boredom, restlessness, and increased tension. Chronic understimulation produces adverse cognitive and emotional effects, and one of the concerns about our earlier pattern of institutionalizing infants and young children who were not developing normally was the fear of causing additional damage because of a lack of stimulation (Thompson & Grusec, 1970).

Sex, too, is an obvious biological need; this is equally true of disabled as well as nondisabled persons. This is addressed in later chapters on adolescent and adult concerns; suffice it to say here that people with mental retardation experience sexual feelings, and these can create difficulties because their lives include varying degrees of dependency on and control by others. Privacy itself may be in short supply.

Structure. The first of the "psychological" needs, structure refers to our need for *predictability*, for congruence and consistency between what is experienced and what one expects to experience (Festinger & Bramel, 1962). It is the need for the familiar as distinct from the strange. In child rearing, it is expressed in the limits we set, and in the consistency of our discipline. These expectancies inform the child as to how the parents will respond to a given situation and enable the child to regulate his or her behavior accordingly (Coopersmith, 1967). In the games we play, it refers to the rules. To the degree that there is adequate structure, events have predictable cause-and-effect relationships; things make sense to us.

The need to make sense of or to "explain" what we experience is so powerful that under common conditions of uncertainty such as, for example, being able to specify the precise cause of a child's developmental delay, some parents inappropriately blame themselves rather than accept the reality of just "not knowing." Uncertainty or ambiguity creates a vacuum that we try to fill.

Self-esteem. A core dimension in personality theory (e.g., Coopersmith, 1967; Deci & Ryan, 1990; Epstein, 1973; Maslow, 1954; Rogers, 1951), self-esteem refers to our sense of worth, value, or "goodness." The fulfillment of this need, as reflected in a generally positive view of oneself, is regarded as essential to mental health, and much of our happiness, pleasure rather than pain, is tied to efforts to defend, maintain, or enhance it. A "cultural" preoccupation since the 1960s, self-esteem is a derivative of at least three ingredients—intimacy, success, and autonomy.

The term *self-esteem* is being used as if there is only *one* self. But we have many selves, each a reflection of important roles that we play, such as the reader as "student," as "child," as "friend," as "worker," and so forth. Somehow these various selves are integrated into a kind of "core" self. Indeed, its fragmentation is associated with serious mental disorder, as in the case of individuals with multiple personalities. This core self can be construed as an emotionally laden belief system about our "worth"; we are not *neutral* about ourselves. It is also a belief system or scheme that is highly resistive to change (e.g., Bednar, Wells, & Peterson, 1989). Indeed, our so-called defensive behavior is simply the way that we protect ourselves from experiences that would lower self-esteem. The ingredients of self-esteem—intimacy, success, and autonomy—apply to all of our valued roles or selves though their involvement will tend to be more relevant to one role than to another. Intimacy, for example, is related to our interpersonal experiences, our "social" selves.

Intimacy.   As just noted, intimacy refers to our social or affiliative behavior, a need for relatedness to other human beings (Deci & Ryan, 1990; Murray, 1938). A product of our early childhood experiences in which there was a parent-child "affectional reward system," intimacy can be fed only by other people (Severy, Brigham, & Schlenker, 1976). The infant or young child is totally dependent on his or her caregivers for sustenance, pleasures, and the relief of discomforts. This extraordinary dependency means that our caregivers are crucial to us, and we learn early that we must please them if our own needs are to be met. Our caregivers, then, typically our parents, literally control our states of happiness and unhappiness. Although as infants and children we are not *consciously* aware of this connection, it influences our behavior as a "conditioned response." In our early years we learn the importance of pleasing those who have "power" over us, a lesson that is carried through life, sometimes to our detriment.

Intimacy is the need to receive and give love and nurturing. It includes all experiences that provide mutually rewarding social interactions. At the "receiving" end, it involves attention from others, recognition, acceptance, approval, and love. At the "giving" end, it refers to the expressions of these behaviors toward others. Of the three ingredients of self-esteem, it may be the most important. To the degree that our need for intimacy is met, we feel secure, protected, loved. To the degree that it is lacking, we are subject to a wide range of painful feelings—sadness, loneliness, anxiety, anger, jealousy, and depression.

Success.   This second ingredient of self-esteem refers to the sense of accomplishment that is felt if we successfully tackle the significant challenges in our daily lives. Other terms are *achievement* (McClelland, 1961), *effectance* and *competence* (White, 1959), and *self-efficacy* (Bandura, 1977). In a book on self-esteem (Bednar et al., 1989), special prominence is given to the willingness to face rather than to avoid situations that involve personal conflict. "Coping" rather than "avoiding" is seen as bolstering self-esteem.

Autonomy.   This is the need to feel some degree of control or power over our lives. Although none of us can expect to wield total control, we do not want to feel as though we have no influence over what happens to us. Concerns with the absence of reasonable control over their lives underlie efforts in the 1990s to "empower" disabled people and their families. Given that the disability-service systems on which they depend are not always going to be responsive to their individual wants, the goal is to reduce that dependency by encouraging the recipients of services to take greater responsibility for their lives. It is not to provide them with fewer services, but rather to encourage them to choose the kinds of services that *they* want rather than always having the decision made by someone else. In fact, as is seen in other chapters dealing with services for persons with mental retardation and their families, choice has become a central ingredient. Recipients of services are now viewed as consumers and are encouraged to indicate *their* wants and desires as to the types of services or supports offered to them. They are no longer regarded as merely passive recipients of services recommended by others. An important element in fostering this greater autonomy is teaching people who have not exercised choice before to begin to make choices.

Self-expression.   This, the last of our major psychological needs, refers to our desire to engage in activities purely for the pleasure they provide. These are the activities that make up our leisure or recreational lives, although, if we are very fortunate, they may also be pursued vocationally.

Values

This is the third component of the personality model. It refers to that which we consider to be important to us—people, things, activities, ideas. We value them because they are the means through which our needs are met. We value medical services, for example, because our health or "survival" is important to us. When traveling, a map may be prized because it provides a guide to unfamiliar territory (structure). In the realm of self-esteem, parents, friends, and loved ones are prized because they are our chief sources of intimacy. Activities in which we excel are prized because they meet our need for success. Experiences that reflect higher levels of independence are valued, especially in adolescence and young adulthood, because they mean we can have greater autonomy (personal freedom). And all of the activities that we enjoy in our recreational lives are prized because of our need for self-expression.

Because values are tied to needs, like the needs themselves, they give direction and specificity to our behaviors. This is particularly apparent in our recreational activities wherein we each have our own preferences.

Integrating the Components of the Personality Model

Tendered as a vehicle for increasing understanding of ourselves and other people, notably those with mental retardation, the personality model consists of three elements—resources, needs, and values. Our *resources* are not employed randomly; rather they are directed toward activities that are *valued* because they meet biological and psychological *needs*. Indeed, the choice of the term *resources* to refer to capacities reflects awareness that they are our "tools" for coping with the activities of daily living and meeting needs.

Four major needs are recognized—survival, structure, self-esteem, and self-expression. These needs are tied to our emotions, feeling states that can be located on a pleasure-pain continuum, from extreme pleasure to extreme pain. Unmet needs evoke states of physical or psychological discomfort. If needs are met, we experience states of pleasure, from simple relief of tension to utter joy. Our needs and the emotions they create are viewed as the fundamental motivators of behavior, or "reinforcers" in behavioral parlance, because we are ultimately driven to avoid or minimize unpleasant feelings and to maximize pleasurable ones.

Managing Our Emotions

Given that our resources are channeled into meeting needs and fostering pleasurable outcomes, the effectiveness of our adaptation or adjustment is reflected in our typical emotional states and the actions they impel. This particularly relates to unpleasant feelings. We seek to rid ourselves of unwanted feelings and restore ourselves to relatively tension-free states. One of the unpleasant feelings important to adjustment is anger. Because anger seeks its own discharge and can lend itself to various forms of aggression, its means of expression or "management" is important to the quality of our adjustment. Parenthetically, problems of controlling anger and expressing it in socially acceptable means often create adaptive problems for persons with mental retardation.

With regard to anger, or to any of the other unpleasant emotions, two factors are particularly important to its effective management—awareness of the *consequences* of actions taken to relieve it and its *intensity*. In the senior author's work with offenders who are mentally retarded, he has encountered individuals who, under the pressure of needs, seem to have given little thought to the consequences of the actions taken to gratify them. But helping people to understand and to consider the consequences of their actions is not enough to assure adaptive functioning. If needs are chronically unmet, their pressure increases and can lead to tensions that exceed capacities to control them. Hence, there must be opportunities for need fulfillment, a core reality in understanding the behavior problems of all of us, normal or disabled.

A Disclaimer

Admittedly, not every human act can be traced to pain avoidance or plea-sure seeking. Some altruistic behaviors, such as "instinctively" reaching out to someone, a stranger, for example, who is about to fall, do not re-flect any form of self-interest. There is no apparent gain to the helper. Why do we do it? The answer appears to lie in an underlying *identification* with other living creatures, animal as well as human. Similarly, the war hero who throws himself on a hand grenade to protect his buddies clearly is not acting out of self-interest. Rather should these selfless acts be seen as conditioned responses to emotional ties that social experience engenders. We become connected with others through our experiences of intimacy with them. These experiences cause us to reach out not only to those with whom we are "intimate" but also to others, even strangers, and to plants and animals as well as humans; to all we identify with because they are "alive."

☐ Applying the Personality Model to Persons Who Are Retarded

"Resources" and Mental Retardation

Defining "Disability"

Within this personality model, handicapping or disabling conditions are viewed as limitations in resources of such magnitude as to interfere with the accomplishment of age-appropriate developmental tasks. Because we all are "limited" to varying degrees, and perfection is not in the nature of the human experience, we acknowledge those whose gifts far exceed our own, whether a brilliant student in the classroom or a Michael Jordan on the basketball court. Given that limitation in resources or abilities is the norm, by "disability" we refer only to resources that, even with training or correction (e.g., eyeglasses), are inadequate to the developmental tasks toward which they are generally applied.[1]

The Effect of Mental Retardation on Resources

Intelligence.   As noted in the first chapter, it is impairment in this resource that is the essence of the disability called mental retardation. Difficulties in learning, in applying existing knowledge, in evaluating and judging are always present and, in the young child, also commonly accompanied by problems of attention and concentration. Verbal skills tend to be more severely affected than visual ones, and both the processing of information and decision making are slowed.

Although educational programs have focused largely on the child's resources irrespective of the cause of retardation, there is evidence for cognitive difficulties that tend to be specific to particular biological syndromes (Hodapp & Dykens, 1994). If these disorders are present, the teacher can be alerted to their presence. In the domain of intelligence, males with fragile X syndrome, the sex-linked hereditary form of retardation (described in Chapter 3), for example, show a special weakness in the recall of visual information in the *sequence* or *order* in which it was presented (Dykens, Hodapp, & Leckman, 1987; Kemper, Hagerman, & Altshul-Stark, 1988). And in Down syndrome, the individual generally processes visual information more readily than that presented "verbally" (e.g., Elliott, Weeks, & Gray, 1990).

Communication Skill.   Language problems are legion in mental retardation at both the receptive and expressive levels. In general, speech tends to be simpler in structure, less clearly articulated, and, if the degree of intellectual impairment is either severe or profound, limited to brief phrases or single words. In many who are profoundly impaired, there is no speech at all.

Within retardation, speech difficulties are especially prominent in Down syndrome (e.g., Dykens, Hodapp, & Evans, 1994).

Health, Sensory, and Physical Skills.   To the degree that intellectual impairment is associated with a clear biological abnormality affecting the brain, there may be accompanying physical problems. The most common associated medical disorders are epilepsy and cerebral palsy, both found in from 15% to 30% of persons with retardation. Sensory deficits also frequently are present, visual and hearing impairments occurring in about 10% to 20% (McLaren & Bryson, 1987). Significant medical problems tend to be associated with the severity of cognitive impairment and are common in those with at least moderate retardation (Payne, 1971).

Temperament, Emotions, and Character

Temperament: Activity Level and Attention Span.   Retardation often is associated with high levels of motor activity, especially in the young child and in the school-aged population (Koller, Richardson, Katz, & McLaren, 1983). The so-called hyperactive child is one who seems to be in perpetual motion—always getting into things, restless, and fidgety. He or she tends to be impulsive, seemingly acting without thinking (Mulick, Hammer, & Dura, 1991; Rapport, 1989). This behavior commonly is associated with attention-deficit disorder and is often seen in children with "learning disabilities." Learning-disabled children, like those with mental retardation, have academic difficulties, but unlike children with retardation theirs are both more circumscribed and less severe. Problems in learning to read in the presence of normal intellectual potential are particularly common, although special difficulties in mathematics also are seen.

Although hyperactivity is assumed to have some biological basis, it is greatly affected by psychological factors. Under exposure to conditions of stress, too little structure, or high levels of stimulation, the behavior worsens. Conversely, hyperactivity is reduced with routine and firm limits, both means of increasing structure, and by lessening stimulation. Stimulant drugs, such as Ritalin, commonly are employed to reduce hyperactivity and are best used in combination with the aforementioned behavioral strategies (Mulick et al., 1991).

Some of the other behaviors of hyperactive children, with or without mental retardation, relate to several other aspects of temperament—distractibility, attention span, and persistence (Lerner, 1971; Van Osdol & Carlson, 1972). Like hyperactivity, these behaviors are subject to psychological influence. The retarded or even normally developing youth who seems to be unable to concentrate and to stick to a task can show surprising persistence if given activities within his ken or field of interest. Thus the adolescent with retardation, for example, who reads at a third-grade level but evinces little interest in the subject matter of a third-grade reader is likely to exhibit much greater motivation if offered materials appropriate to both his or her reading level and chronological-age interests. Such educational materials are widely available. Hyperactivity tends to diminish with age, especially in children who are less severely impaired (Koller et al., 1983), but the related problems of inattention and impulsivity may persist (Mulick et al., 1991).

Emotions.   Do individuals with mental retardation have the same emotions as we do? This question is not always posed, it being assumed that we need not underscore the obvious—that they are "people" and people have emotions. But in the senior author's experience with college students, he has been struck by the importance they place on recognizing that retarded children and youth do have feelings. Prior to their contact with them, they carry the stereotypes that our culture teaches about people who are mentally retarded, and this tends to create psychological distance between them and the person who is cognitively (or physically) disabled.

Children, youth, and adults with mental retardation or with other major disabilities are seen as "different," almost as if they were members of a different species. It is likely that much of society's treatment of persons with retardation reflects this kind of "subhuman" perception of them. One of the keys to recognizing their humanness is to discover that they, like you and I, also have feelings. This is a very powerful means of reducing psychological distance, achieving some degree of identification, and developing compassion for those who, on initial encounter, may appear to be very different from us. The Nazis understood this and sought to deprive the people that they slaughtered of their humanity. Their Jewish victims, for example, were to be regarded as "less than human." This lesson is also the theme of Shylock's assertion of his own humanity in Shakespeare's *Merchant of Venice*. Scorned as a Jew in a largely Christian world, his words could be spoken equally for those with retardation or on behalf of any other group scorned and perceived as different. They are quoted here substituting only "retarded" or "retarded person" for "Jew."

> I am retarded. Hath not a retarded person eyes? Hath not a retarded person hands, organs, dimensions, senses, affections, passions; fed with the same food, hurt with the same weapons, subject to the same desires, healed by the same means, warmed and cooled by the same winter and summer ... If you prick us, do we not bleed? If you tickle us, do we not laugh? If you poison us, do we not die?

Yes, persons with retardation know love, anger, fear, and joy. They know the same hungers, feel the same pains, and share the same longings. The experiences of Martin and Ben, described in Chapter 1, make this poignantly clear.

Character.   Much research indicates that mental retardation frequently is accompanied by personality disorder, notably problems of aggression (Mulick et al., 1991), anxiety, and fears (McNally, 1991). Perhaps the most striking evidence of the vulnerability to personality disorders in retardation is found in the previously mentioned study of the retarded population in a British city (Koller et al., 1983). Table 2.1 presents the percentages of preadolescents (ages 8–10 years) and young adults (average age 22 years) with behavior disorders. Of the children, almost two thirds (61%) showed some kind of behavior disorder, with more than half (59%) so characterized as adults. Problems of aggression, antisocial behavior, and emotional disturbance predominate; note also the presence of hyperactive behavior. Of these behavior disorders, only the frequency of hyperactivity changes from childhood to adult, its rate diminishing four-fold. It should be noted that in childhood, "aggressive conduct disorder" was most prevalent in boys with IQs of less than 50, the more severely impaired of the

TABLE 2.1. The frequency of types of behavior disorders in children and young adults with mental retardation (in %)

Type of Disorder	Childhood	Postschool
Emotional disturbance	29	31
Hyperactive behavior	12	3
Aggressive conduct disorder	33	33
Antisocial behavior	27	32
No behavior disturbance	39	41

Note. The sum of the percentages in each age group exceed 100 as the types of behavior disturbance are not mutually exclusive. From Koller et al., 1983 (Reprinted with permission of the American Association on Mental Retardation).

population. On the other hand, in young adulthood, it was the least intellectually impaired who were so affected. This accords with the senior author's experience with retarded young adults who get into difficulty with the law. They are virtually all male and, typically, not more than mildly retarded.

But aggressive conduct disorders are not gender-specific. They also are seen in females and, again, more prominently in those falling in the below-50 IQ range. Unlike the males, however, the more severely impaired female population continued to show this behavior in young adulthood.

The high rates of emotional and behavioral disorder reported in the British study parallel American findings (Jacobson, 1982; Reiss, 1990). These indicate that at least one-third of children and adults with retardation can be expected to manifest significant personality problems. These frequencies are about twice those in the nonretarded population and are viewed here as the result of the stresses that retardation imposes on the meeting of basic biological and psychological needs. These stresses, present throughout the life span, are attributed both to the adaptive problems created by the disability and to limitations in the supports that we provide. How the gratification of basic needs, especially self-esteem, is made more difficult in retardation is illustrated shortly. It must be observed, however, that about 40% of the children and young adults in the British study were *free* of personality disorder. The disability of mental retardation is *not* incompatible with the development of a healthy personality and an adaptive lifestyle. Modern television has provided examples of such individuals (McNally, 1991), for example, the actor Chris Burke, a young man with Down syndrome, in the former television series *Life Goes On.*

Esthetic Appreciation

Mental retardation in and of itself does not preclude the possibility of enjoying a variety of esthetic experiences, although the specific nature of what is enjoyed generally relates to the level of cognitive maturity (Van Osdol, 1972). Music, dancing, singing, drawing, poetry, painting, and arts and crafts all can be sources of pleasure. Indeed, teaching situations often are enhanced in their appeal to individuals with learning difficulties by incorporating activities that are inherently pleasurable, for example, teaching "following directions" by playing musical chairs or number recognition through bingo.

Unusual Esthetic and Cognitive Abilities: The "Savant"

Of special interest are persons with retardation who possess unexpected gifts in a particular artistic or even cognitive mode. The term *savant* has been applied to individuals who, except for one ability, function in the retarded range. These abilities are not merely exceptional in comparison with their other skills; they are exceptional in terms of the general population!

Art. Among individuals with retardation are those who also possess unusual painting, drawing, and sculpting abilities. A prominent painter of children and animals had retardation that had been caused by congenital hypothyroidism (cretinism) (Hill, 1974). Unusual painting and drawing talent has been found in two Japanese youths, one of whom is autistic as well as retarded (Morishima & Brown, 1976, 1977). Broadly developmentally delayed, apparently associated with hydrocephaly (see Chapter 4), this youth has superb *visual* ability. His talent was unrecognized until the seventh grade, when he showed the ability to represent straight lines. Subsequent systematic tutoring helped him develop his artistic talent.

Alonzo Clemmons, a severely retarded young Black male, attracted national attention for extraordinarily beautiful sculpture, mostly of animals (Rimland & Fein, 1988). His sculpting ability was discovered by an institutional worker who chanced upon tiny sculptures of various animals constructed with tar he had dug from a parking lot with his fingernails! Bronze copies of his work sell for thousands of dollars.

Among the most common areas of cognitive distinction are mathematics and calendar calculating (Smith, 1988), and memory (Waterhouse, 1988). Ericcson and Faivre (1988) have reviewed the relevant literature in memory, mathematics, and calendar calculating in an effort to understand how individuals with seemingly very limited intellectual abilities can perform these mental feats.

Music.   Less common among savants is musical ability, but a severely retarded and blind 36-year-old reveals such talent (Charness, Clifton, & MacDonald, 1988). With a history of developmental delay since birth, lifelong epilepsy, and paralysis of the right side of his body (spastic hemiplegia), there is unequivocal evidence of neurological damage to the left side of his brain. Cognitive functioning is extremely impaired, and his overall development is estimated at the 2-year-old level. In spite of these limitations, he began playing the piano at around age 3 years. His family members were all very musical, and although not given any formal instruction he was encouraged to practice and did so for many hours, even getting up in the middle of the night to play! He was also very interested in *listening* to music, of all kinds. He listened to the radio a great deal, and although his playing was not, initially, very skillful, he improved tremendously over the years. And all of this, it should be noted, playing with only one hand! Nor is his musical talent limited to the piano. He also plays the organ, melodica, harmonica, and guitar! He has absolute pitch and is sensitive to the musical qualities present in skilled musicians—tonal features such as scale, and temporal ones such as rhythmic grouping. Miller (1987) found similar musical abilities in another multihandicapped child, interestingly also one with visual impairment.

Given some evidence that musical ability is more dependent on the right hemisphere of the brain than on the left (Miller, 1991), his apparently intact right hemisphere, combined with a family musical heritage and an early fascination with music, produced a degree of accomplishment far exceeding his functioning in other areas.

Memory.   Some individuals with mental retardation show surprising ability to memorize apparently unrelated bits of information. This includes extraordinary recall of dates, names of people and geographic places, and numbers of objects. These memory feats appear to reflect areas of special interest, even preoccupations. On measures of memory unrelated to their special interests, performance is not remarkable. Thus a 38-year-old man who performed on stage to demonstrate his memory for the population of towns in the United States could not recall more than six digits presented at a rate of one per second, a level below that of the average adult (Jones, 1926).

Requisite to these mnemonic feats is a zeal for acquiring specific kinds of information and the ability to use memory aids to facilitate recall. Zeal, practice, and the use of associational strategies seem to be crucial, but *how* these associational strategies are acquired is puzzling given the person's overall level of impairment. This question also pertains to "calendar calculators."

Mental Calculation. Unlike those savants whose mental feats are exceptional under any circumstance, the abilities of "calculators" who are retarded seem unusual only in comparison with their other functions. An individual with a reported IQ of 50 could rapidly add a series of two-digit numbers; another could mentally multiply any two-digit numbers. Using a special kind of multiplication, the senior author taught himself to do this fairly quickly.

Calendar Calculating. "Calendar calculators" are a special breed! They can identify the day of the week for dates past and future or give the date for any given day, such as the first Wednesday in February in the year 2024. Victoria, a young woman with an IQ of 65, could correctly identify days or dates within 5 seconds! She had extensive knowledge of the relationship between months that start with the same day of the week in a given year and, unlike other savants with retardation, was able to explain something of her ability. Asked in 1934, "Which day of the week is August 5th?" she replied, "Sunday," within 2 seconds. Her explanation was as follows:

> Because August begins with the same weekday as November (at least in 1934) and I know that November begins on Wednesday and July ends on Tuesday because it begins on Sunday (Tuesday plus 5 days equals Sunday). Moreover, I know it because this year (1935), the 5th of August fell on a Saturday. And that I remember. (Lafora, 1934)

Confusing as her "explanation" is, it reveals that she knew how to derive the desired day of the week from the week of the same day in the preceding year (for years that are not leap years!). She also could determine the day of the week in any given month from the first day of that month.

Perhaps the most remarkable of the calendar calculators is a pair of autistic and retarded identical twins who, in recent decades, have received much media attention, notably on television's *60 Minutes* and in *Life* magazine. In generally less than 6 seconds, one of the twins could name the day of the week for any year, including one as distant as 132,470! The system used to perform this seemingly incredible feat involves an understanding of the regularities in our calendar, one of which is that it repeats itself every 400 years.[2]

Addis (1968) used a method of adding whole numbers that corresponded to the century, year, month, and day of the month. Their sum enabled him to derive the day of the week. He taught the method to a graduate student who, eventually, learned to do the calculations almost as rapidly as the twins. But how did twins who could not solve simple arithmetic problems learn to do this? Unlike Victoria, they could not tell us, but the utterance of the number 4 in their problem solving suggests, at least, how they might have gotten to the year equivalent.

The most revealing study of calendar calculators is that of four males whose IQs varied from 65 to 76. All were familiar with the calendar and, in particular, with a system that divides all years into 14 categories. Their interest in the calendar appeared spontaneously at age 6 or 7 years; their families knew of no experiences that influenced this interest. This appears to support the view that this ability depends on an *unlearned* or *innate* capacity (Jensen, 1990). Analysis of their methods of solution indicate memorization of the year-category association, presumably in the same way as we learn the multiplication tables. Given their interest in the calendar and the learning of the 14 year-categories, identifying dates becomes almost as automatic as answering questions based on the multiplication tables! The findings of this study support the proposition that calendar calculating involves automatic responses that are, to a limited extent, rule-based and reflect *rote learning* of those rules along with intense practice (Young & Nettelbeck, 1994).

Spirituality

Religious institutions have had some interest in the spiritual needs of persons with retardation. Given the range of complexity associated with formal religions, they can be experienced at many levels of abstraction, although intellectual impairment will narrow the range within which such appreciation is possible. One aspect of the religious experience, its emphasis on ethics and morality, is certainly a teachable dimension and important to an understanding of the reasons for the social rules that apply to us all—retarded and nonretarded (Dykeman & Levy, 1991). Moreover, the clergy certainly has important pastoral roles—as influencers of their congregations and in supporting the spiritual needs of persons with retardation and their families (Heifetz, 1987). Certainly, the presence of disability itself, for the affected person and his family, creates the same kind of challenge to beliefs in an omnipotent, just, and loving God as do other unwanted events that are beyond our control.

"Needs" and Mental Retardation

We have described the impact of mental retardation on our resources; attention now shifts to its effect on the meeting of our basic needs—survival, structure, self-esteem, and self-expression.

Survival

Multiple Disabilities and Survival. Although mental retardation is usually not a life-threatening disorder, it can be. As earlier noted, persons with the severest degrees of mental retardation often have accompanying physical problems—seizures, multiple joint contractions, feeding difficulties, and respiratory problems (Rubin, 1987). A generation ago, the average life span of profoundly retarded persons in North Carolina's institutions was less than 30 years (Baroff, 1974), but health care for this population appears to have improved, as has its average life span.

Down syndrome (mongolism), the best known of the biological forms of mental retardation, carries a survival risk in its frequent association with congenital heart abnormalities. The risk is particularly high in the first year of life.

Child Abuse. An especially grim note pertains to the vulnerability of disabled children to physical abuse. In 1993, newspapers reported that a study of the National Center on Child Abuse and Neglect found that the risk of maltreatment of children with physical, mental, and emotional disability was twice the rate for nondisabled children, and the risk of "emotional neglect" was almost three times as great.

And who commits the abuse? In the great majority of cases (86%), it was the child's primary caretaker, usually the mother! In nearly half of the cases, the child's disability was seen as a cause of the abuse. It can be assumed that we often are dealing with parents for whom the demands of caring for a disabled child, in addition to other life stresses, exceed their capacity to cope. Behavior problems associated with hyperactivity and the presence of multiple disabilities are two common sources of stress (Orr et al., 1993).

Structure

The need for structure is magnified in retardation. We "structure" our experience by automatically imposing on it expectations and meaning that derive from earlier encounters with like events. But the cognitive impairment in retardation unduly limits the capacity to transfer what has been learned in one setting to comparable new ones. The effect of this diminished ability to generalize is to create stress if the individual with retardation is confronted with what is perceived as a new and potentially challenging situation and to cause a more zealous clinging to that which is familiar and "mastered." This cognitive vulnerability leads to a greater tendency to seek guidance and direction, the quality of suggestibility described in Chapter 1. Its most general consequence is to foster a greater degree of *dependency* than is typical of nonretarded individuals of the same age. Paralleling the dependency is a greater caution and apprehension if placed in unfamiliar surroundings.

There are two important consequences of this intensified need for structure. First, it is necessary to make *explicit* ordinarily implicit expectations; it cannot be assumed that the person with retardation has the same understanding of a given situation that we do. Second, it is important to reduce anxiety likely to be evoked by unfamiliar settings or situations by building "bridges," that is, by providing for gradual movement from the *known* (mastered) to the *unknown* (unmastered). Parents apply this principle if they accompany their child to school on their first day, easing the encounter with a new environment. In adulthood, this principle is applied if we are provided with a job description in connection with a job for which we might apply. The job description makes clear to us what is expected; it provides structure.

Self-Esteem

Because self-esteem is tied to three ingredients—intimacy, success, and autonomy—the effect of mental retardation on each is treated separately.

Intimacy

Society's Attitudes Toward Persons with Disabilities.   Perhaps the most important of the three contributors to self-esteem, our desire for intimacy is reflected in the extraordinary intensity and pervasiveness of our need to be accepted, liked, respected, admired, and loved. The primary obstacle to gratification of the need for intimacy in people with disabilities is our culture's view of them as "abnormal" (Liveneh, 1988). We see them in a negative light. Their mental or physical abnormalities can evoke fear, derision, and repulsion. Recall the teasing of Martin and our own teasing and ridicule of others who are "different." Often, the most positive feeling we can engender is pity. Their unwanted mental and physical characteristics create in us attitudes of avoidance and rejection, as though they were contagious, although over the past two decades a greater degree of societal acceptance may have arisen (Rees, Spreen, & Harnadek, 1991). There is much greater awareness of disability in the public mind, itself a product of major federal legislation, notably, the Americans with Disabilities Act of 1990. *Positive* representations of disabled persons are presented in the media; public awareness campaigns abound, and there is greater visibility in the general community, especially in the schools.

Parent and Sibling Attitudes.   The unwanted characteristics of persons with retardation not only create distance between them and the general society, they can also affect bonding with parents and siblings. We have made reference to some of the problems associated with retardation that are potential sources of stress to parents; now we specifically consider the psychological consequences of being either the parent or sibling of a child with retardation.

To parents, their children are seen as psychological extensions of themselves (Ryckman & Henderson, 1965). Siblings also view their brothers and sisters in a similar vein, although perhaps to a lesser degree (Grossman, 1972; Kaplan, 1969). *Our* self-esteem, yours and mine, is affected by how *our* family members are perceived by those whose opinions we value. Children of whom parents can be proud because they possess culturally valued characteristics enhance parental pride (self-esteem).

Conversely, if one's child or sibling has unwanted characteristics, parents and siblings cannot avoid viewing, at least initially, their disabled family member as an unfavorable reflection of themselves. They react with painful feelings of shame, hostility, and then guilt at these feelings, all contributing to a diminished sense of self-worth (Roos, 1963). In a study of the adaptation of parents to children born with significant disabilities, parents have characterized the experience as "a series of assaults" to their self-esteem, assaults that interfered with parenting (Mintzer, Als, Tronick, & Brazelton, 1985). The birth itself, a source of shock and disappointment, produced severe injury to their self-worth. The period following birth was one of disequilibrium and continued low self-esteem, with more positive feelings emerging only as the parents began to view the child as a separate person rather than as simply an extension of themselves.

Apart from the crisis occasioned by the occurrence of an event for which parents are typically unprepared, the disability itself can threaten parental attachment and intimacy because the usual elicitors of parental attention may be lacking. The child may be less responsive to parental expressions of love, may smile less, may have feeding difficulties, or may show less eye contact. All of this can constrain "bonding" in an already stressed and psychologically wounded parent. The adaptive task for parents is seen as coming to view the child as separate from themselves, as a new human being with both positive and problematic aspects (Mintzer et al., 1985). It is only as the infant is psychologically separated from themselves that the caregivers can begin to recognize the *child's* needs, and not only their *own* hurt, and begin to respond to them. In so doing, the sense of worth is gradually restored.

But parental adaptation to the disabled child is not limited to infancy. The presence of what will ultimately be recognized as permanent impairment, and the child's behavior itself, can continue to stress and threaten self-esteem. This is especially true of parents whose sense of worth was low prior to the birth of the child or whose parental expectations much exceed the child's abilities. These continued threats to self-esteem lead to "defensive" behavior. Indeed, defensive behavior, as noted earlier, is simply the way you and I protect ourselves from acknowledging realities about ourselves that would produce anxiety and a fall in self-esteem. Threats to parental self-worth can lead to such maladaptive behavior as the actual *denial* of the reality of the disability ("He's only a little slow or lazy"), *zealous overprotection* (a possible response to guilt feelings over hostility to the child), or *rejection*. Whether rejection is subtle or overt, the child's need for intimacy is unmet. The child feels unloved and, later, unlovable (a chronic state of low self-esteem), and this produces emotional states of anxiety, hostility, and sadness. Such children are driven to seek attention and approval (intimacy) and are very sensitive to criticism. Criticism is such a painful experience for all of us because it directly attacks our self-worth!

Siblings, too, may harbor negative as well as positive feelings toward a brother or sister whose "difference" is, by association, experienced as a threat to *their* need for peer acceptance and self-esteem. This is especially true in adolescence when there may be a strong need to *avoid* being identified with a sibling who is retarded (Kaplan, 1969).

Other sibling concerns also can affect attitudes. Older sisters often are placed in caregiver roles (Harris, Alessandri, & Gill, 1991), and this can be experienced as intrusive. Other issues include the *degree* to which the sibling with retardation understands his or her own impairment, appropriate methods of discipline if the normal sibling is in a parental role, and the freedom to talk with parents about their brother or sister's disability.

Both positive and negative effects have been found in normal siblings (Grossman, 1972). The positive experiences involve greater tolerance, compassion, and sensitivity to prejudice. Negative ones include hostility, guilt over the hostility, and fears that they themselves are somehow "tainted." A key to understanding sibling attitudes is those of the parents. In families in which parents are accepting of the child, siblings themselves are more comfortable.

Peer Attitudes. Based largely on studies of school children, attitudes toward peers with retardation are affected by a number of determinants— the degree of impairment, the presence of additional disabilities, how the children are described or "labeled," how well they function academically, and their general behavior.

Although attitudes tend to be unfavorable, primarily related to academic and social inadequacies, more favorable ones are elicited by examples of social and academic *competence* (Bak & Siperstein, 1987; Budoff &

Siperstein, 1978; Gottlieb, 1974; Siperstein & Bak, 1985). Strengthening the skills of children with retardation so that they can compete more successfully can enhance their image. The domains of motor skills and play may particularly lend themselves to this kind of influence (Bak & Siperstein, 1987).

Another vehicle for both strengthening skills *and* creating more positive images is the use of nondisabled children as tutors to their disabled peers. In one study (Cooke, Heron, Heward, & Test, 1982), a child with Down syndrome was integrated in a second-grade class ("mainstreamed") and was tutored in "sight word" reading by a classmate. Both children benefited from the experience.

Admittedly, the inclusion of children with retardation in a regular class can challenge the teacher (Heward & Orlansky, 1992). Given a child with a level of academic development significantly below that of the average student, the teacher is expected to reach that child through individualized instruction while simultaneously providing instruction for the rest of the class and encouraging the child's social acceptance. "In-class" tutoring makes it possible to individualize instruction for learning-handicapped students without removal from the regular classroom. Peers, older students, and adult volunteers (e.g., retired persons) all can serve in this role. The senior author has long been enthusiastic about the use of tutors and regarded this as a crucial educational experience for his college students in a course on "exceptional children." As tutors, they have the opportunity to develop personal relationships with retarded children within a "constructive" context.

"Mainstreaming" and "Full Inclusion."   A central goal of the movement for integration, inclusion, or "mainstreaming" of children with retardation and other disabilities into regular classes has been to reduce the social distance between disabled and nondisabled children. One of its justifications was the apparent lack of academic benefits to children served in the traditional "self-contained" or "special" class (e.g., Goldstein, Moss, & Jordan, 1965). One could argue that the special class was not intended originally to compensate for the child's academic limitations but rather to provide a *setting* in which the disabled child could experience success. In a class with other children all functioning at comparable developmental and academic levels, the disabled child would not be presented with a learning situation in which the material presented would be beyond his level of understanding. But the presumed social and psychological effects of an educational experience that involved separation from the nondisabled student population, a kind of educational apartheid, came to be seen as an evil in and of itself, an evil paralleled by the widely reported abuses associated with institutional care. Whether in a special class or in an institution, the child

or adult with retardation was separated physically or "segregated" from other children or adults and, in that separation, either vulnerable to abuse as in institutional settings or deprived of opportunities to benefit from exposure to normally developing children: "Out of sight, out of mind!"

Within the school setting, it is hoped that both disabled and nondisabled children benefit from mutual exposure. For the disabled child, there is contact with nondisabled peers and exposure to more age-appropriate behavioral models. For the nonhandicapped child, there is the possibility of learning about peers with whom there ordinarily would be little contact, and the altering of whatever stereotypes about disability their culture teaches.

Within the school-aged population of children with retardation, it is the youngster with not more than mild intellectual impairment, the "educable mentally handicapped child" in school parlance, who has been the main target for mainstreaming, although advocates for what is called full inclusion would insist that *all* children, irrespective of the degree of disability, ought to be served in regular classes (e.g., Stainback & Stainback, 1992). The retarded or otherwise disabled child would, from the very outset of his educational experience, be a member of a regular class of same-age peers, although needing whatever special services and supports are appropriate to the child's disabilities. Just as a family may have a disabled member who, because of the disability, is no less a member of that family, so might a class have a similar composition.

Given that the bases for inclusion are presumed social and attitudinal benefits, what does the relevant research on these effects reveal? It appears that mere *placement* within regular classes for at least some part of the school day generally has had little effect on the social acceptance and academic achievement of the child with retardation (Gottlieb & Gottlieb, 1991). There do appear, however, to be behavioral benefits to the retarded child in the form of more mature or age-appropriate social behavior (Gampel, Gottlieb, & Harrison, 1974). Nonhandicapped classmates, apparently, can serve as positive behavioral models to their disabled peers.

The modest social gains of the mainstreamed child, as well as common complaints of loneliness in adulthood, ultimately must be attributed to the factors that influence friendship among children and adults. Paramount to the establishment of friendship, enduring relationships, and the experience of intimacy is a sharing of personal *thoughts* and *feelings* and, through empathy, the promotion of others' *welfare* (Myers, 1989; Zetlin & Murtaugh, 1988). But one effect of intellectual impairment is to reduce the capacity for age-appropriate *reciprocity*. There is a lesser degree of cognitive and emotional *understanding* of peers and, perhaps, capacity to communicate that which is understood.

Retardation also affects interests. The youngster with retardation generally has interests that are appropriate to a younger age than that of his classmates. The difference in interests is, in part, a reflection of the difference in cognitive maturity or mental age of the retarded child. He is functioning at a younger developmental level than age-mates, and this difference in social maturity and interests increases over time with age because of different rates of cognitive growth in the two populations. The effect of ever-widening disparity in social maturity and interests makes more difficult the creation of genuinely reciprocal relationships. Those that do exist are likely to involve a kind of older-brother or older-sister role for the nondisabled partner. Indeed, in efforts to integrate more severely impaired students with peers, it is the responsiveness and initiative of the nondisabled partner that is the key to establishing even a brief relationship (Brinker & Thorpe, 1986). The effect of the experience of potential social isolation, loneliness, and lack of intimacy is to add special stress to adaptation in adolescence (Luftig, 1988) and adulthood.

Although the risk of peer isolation and lesser friendships is inherent in the mainstreaming experience, it is precisely such placement that is the preference among youth with retardation. To the degree that one is a member of a regular class, there is at least the partial sense that one is "like everyone else," a yearning certainly shared by those whose disability has singled them out for unwanted attention.

In summary, the presence of a disability that carries a heavily negative attitudinal burden can threaten the meeting of intimacy needs in persons with retardation, with consequent unhappiness and damage to self-esteem. In the years of childhood and adolescence, parents, siblings, and classmates all are potential sources of intimacy. Movement out of school and into adult roles may be associated with fewer "group" experiences and opportunities for intimacy. In the encouragement of more independent living arrangements for adults with retardation, there needs to be special sensitivity to the possible loss of longstanding relationships and to insuring continued access to people with whom such relationships can be established. Sensitivity to the social needs of the adult with retardation is growing (e.g., Newton, Horner, Ard, LeBaron, & Sappington, 1994).

Success

Because mental retardation affects the capacity to meet the developmental expectations appropriate to one's chronological age, it can be expected that persons with retardation, children or adults, will have more than their share of "failure" experiences. In the educational sphere we have noted that special classes originally were created to *lessen* the certainty of failure by providing a learning environment different from that of the classes serving normally developing children. But to the degree that the more protected learning setting of the special class was seen as "stigmatizing," it was viewed as one that would damage the self-esteem of the child placed in it.

However, as in the case of attitudes of school children toward their disabled peers, the effect of special-class placement on self-esteem is not necessarily stigmatizing. Elementary school–aged children with mental retardation do not appear to experience their special-class placement as stigmatizing (Warner, Thrapp, & Walsh, 1973) although older children do (Gozali, 1972). Clearly the age of the child and his or her level of cognitive development affects the capacity to see oneself as others do. Children who have moved from special classes into integrated ones tend to prefer their regular-class placement (Gottlieb & Budoff, 1972), but this does not necessarily imply dissatisfaction with their earlier special-class experience.

A review of the effects of the type of class placement on self-concept (self-esteem) reveals a fascinating picture! As noted by Widaman, MacMillan, Helmsley, and Balow (1992), placement of children with retardation can lead variously to an elevation in self-esteem (Calhoun & Elliott, 1977; Meyerowitz, 1962), to a fall in self-esteem (Battle, 1979; Schurr, Towne, & Joiner, 1972), or to no change at all (Beck, Roblee, & Hanson, 1981; Mayer, 1966). How are we to understand the variable effect of type of class placement on self-esteem? The answer lies in one of the important processes that affects our *perception* of self-worth. In part, self-worth is a reflection of *comparisons* between ourselves and those with whom we compare ourselves (Festinger, 1957). To choose an athletic analogy, the college athlete derives his or her athletic self-image and self-esteem by comparing himself or herself with other college athletes, those against whom one competes, not with professionals. The college athlete recognizes that his or her skill is at a different level than that of professional counterparts, accepts that difference as a *natural* consequence of age and experience, and chooses those who are competing at similar levels for self-comparison.

The specificity with which we choose the frame of reference for self-comparison is evident in a group of mildly retarded 9- to 12-year-olds who were either mainstreamed or in a self-contained special class (Silon & Harter, 1985). There were no differences in their self-evaluations as a function of class placement because they were comparing themselves with other *learning-impaired* children in *both* settings. The special-class children had, of course, only other special-class children with whom they could compare themselves, but the mainstreamed children, those in a class with largely normal learners, took as their framework for comparison their mainstreamed counterparts. Although class placement does not seem to significantly affect self-esteem in the young or elementary-school child, it does for the older school-aged child or adolescent, especially those with not more than mild retardation. Given a choice, they prefer to be part of a class with "normal" children. Of course, such placement can only meet the retarded youth's learning needs if special assistance is provided either within the classroom or through a "resource" program.

Success and Motivation. Although the educational setting has been the primary context for the study of self-esteem, the occurrence of failure experiences in other areas of functioning also can be expected to affect personal expectancies of effectiveness. As a consequence of pervasive adaptive difficulties, individuals with retardation are viewed as tending to distrust their own judgment (Zigler, 1966), as having a lesser *expectancy* of success in new situations (Heber, 1957; Jordan & DeCharms, 1959), and as avoiding situations in which there is the possibility of failure (Moss, 1958). It should be added that such behavior is not limited to persons with retardation; we all engage in it! With regard to the avoiding of situations with the risk of failure, a distinction has been drawn between two types of achievement or success motivation—motivation to achieve based on "success striving" versus motivation to achieve based on "failure avoiding." It is the latter that is regarded as particularly relevant to retardation (Moss, 1958) and, in some cases, to the senior author as well! It is to be hoped that with the growth of services to all age groups "success striving" will become a more salient motivator to persons with retardation.

Given the significance of success and failure in retardation, we are not surprised at retarded persons' greater sensitivity to these experiences (Bialer, 1970). Conversely, one finds a more intense reaction to success than in nonretarded individuals (Gardner, 1958; Miller, 1991; Ringelheim, 1958)! Still another effect of a greater failure expectancy is a diminished willingness to persist under conditions of frustration. The student with retardation is more likely to give up in the face of failure (Heber, 1964), and this has encouraged teaching methods that seek to minimize error.

The importance of success experiences in the cognitively disabled learner cannot be minimized. Students who have largely tasted failure, *for whatever reason*, tend to resist instruction but can show dramatic reversals in their motivation if they begin to experience success. Nothing succeeds like success!

Autonomy. The ability and opportunity to exercise some degree of "control" over our daily lives is much valued in our culture. For children and youth especially, the freedom to make choices, to make decisions, is equated with being "grown up" and is perceived as the privilege that attends maturity. But people with disabilities, particularly those of a cognitive nature, often are denied this kind of autonomy or self-determination (O'Brien, 1994). Admittedly, major disability can create varying degrees of dependency, and with dependency there is an inevitable surrender of at least some measure of control or personal responsibility to those on whom one depends.

Mental retardation always has been recognized as an impediment to the exercise of age-appropriate decision making. This is most apparent in those with more than mild retardation; individuals with moderate to profound retardation are unable to assume the kind of personal responsibility that is the hallmark of the nonretarded person. If the impairment is not more than mild, however, full independence is attainable, although, as indicated in Chapter 1, these individuals can benefit from relationships with persons who can offer problem-solving assistance as the need arises—so-called benefactors.

But retardation-related obstacles to personal responsibility do not mean the total abdication of *choice* and *decision making*. The opportunity to choose and to make decisions begins as early as the second year of life, as reflected in the toddler's toy or play references. It is not the *right* to make choices that is challenged in the child; it is only *which* choices the child or otherwise intellectually and emotionally immature individual is allowed to make. Although the 2-year-old can choose what to play with, he is not free to choose when to cross a street! So it is that the individual with retardation also can exercise choice and should be encouraged to do so to reduce unnecessary dependency and to maximize the sense of personal control, the only constraint being the nature or complexity of the decisions to be made. This is very much an issue with adults who are sensitive to their own limitations and the tendency to be treated in child-like fashion.

A group of physically disabled young adults with cerebral palsy, some of whom also had retardation, has been described; they were incensed at the restrictions imposed on them by their parents (Mowatt, 1970). They wanted greater freedom (autonomy)—to ride buses, to visit friends, to date, and to try to live away from home. Only one member of the group had experienced a nonrestrictive upbringing. This was a young woman with mild retardation whose father had sought to prepare her to live as independently as her disabilities would permit. She had learned to cook, keep house, and to use the local bus system. Then living in her own apartment, presumably one that offered access to assistance as needed, she expressed gratitude for what her father had taught her.

These disabled adults felt much more confident in handling themselves than did their parents. Recall Martin's mother's surprise when he dialed the police following the attempted sexual assault. She did not think he knew how! The parents of these young adults with cerebral palsy were viewed as too protective, especially the mothers. As one wheelchair-bound member thoughtfully phrased it, "It's harder for us to get along by ourselves, so we need *more* not fewer chances to learn." Martin expressed the same insightful thought when he said, "People are retarded by what they don't know. That's why I work so hard to learn the things I don't know and become more normal."

Overprotection and Excessive Control.   Overprotection or excessive control by parents is common in mental retardation, typically arising out of fears for the safety of the cognitively disabled person. Parents or other caregivers rush in and make decisions for their charges. Although such concerns may be altogether reasonable under certain circumstances, what is termed "overprotection" is the failure of the parent or caregiver to allow the child to make decisions within the child's competence or restricting the child from experiences that could teach greater *self-determination*. The effect of excessive control is only to maintain the child's level of immaturity and dependence, not only continuing an undue degree of burden on caregivers but also sustaining an unnecessarily immature self-image.

Is there merit in encouraging greater decision making in persons who may never achieve a fully independent adult status? Of course there is! As we grant normally developing children greater responsibility, a natural consequence of "growing up," our focus is not on their future adulthood but rather on their "here and now." We want our children to be as independent as possible within the bounds set by age and cognitive and emotional maturity. As the child assumes increasing personal responsibility, the safety concerns of parents are eased, and the child feels good about his or her growing sense of "power." The point is that the sense of personal control (*autonomy*) is not limited to the adult. It is experienced through life, even in early childhood in which the "terrible twos" signifies the common battle for self-assertion by the 2-year-old. If our goal for *all* people is to maximize developmental potentials, a prudent objective because we *all* are "limited" to varying degrees, we should not restrict opportunities for growth at any level of disability.

A prominent focus in the 1990s has been the "empowerment" of people with disabilities and their families. The intent is to shift power and control from those who provide services to those who *receive* them, to encourage and foster greater self-determination. In 1992, federal legislation pertaining to vocational services gave a central role to the disabled person in decisions regarding the development and implementation of job-related activities (The Rehabilitation Act Amendments of 1992). The accomplishment of a change in power involves not only the freedom to make decisions but also *learning* how to do it. Many disabled people need to learn how to exercise choice. Individuals whose developmental histories have lacked opportunities for exercising choice may be reluctant to engage in such behavior, always expecting others to decide for them. But the power of what is termed the "self-advocacy" movement among people with disabilities reveals that the desire for some measure of personal control is not erased even with serious disability, although it may lie dormant until encouraged to be expressed. Teaching individuals with intellectual impairment to make choices—from the most mundane, such as choosing what clothes to wear, to the more complex, as in learning how to use unstructured or "leisure" hours—becomes an important goal for parents, teachers, and caregivers and has the potential for not only reducing the level of dependence but also enhancing self-esteem.

Encouraging More Age-appropriate Interests.   Apart from perpetuating undue dependency, overprotection can encourage the persistence into adulthood of behaviors and interests that are more appropriate to children. This can be expected if the adult with retardation continues to be perceived as a child. Pearl Buck, the famous novelist, saw her retarded daughter as an "eternal child." Although some of this childishness or immaturity is tied to mental age, the mental age of a child in an adult body, more age-appropriate interests *can* be encouraged. This is especially relevant at lesser levels of intellectual impairment at which, for example, a retarded adult with an IQ of 60 and an equivalent mental age of 10 years can be encouraged to participate in such non–10-year-old activities as working or as socializing with the opposite sex.

Autonomy, Overprotection, and Sex.   With regard to the sexual interests of persons with retardation, recall that one of the areas in which there was the desire for greater freedom was that of dating. We now speak to the sexual needs of retarded persons, a domain in which demands for greater autonomy are certain to produce the stiffest resistance. It is a fact that retarded youth and adults, like you and I, are sexual beings, although their parents or caregivers may prefer not to think so. The freedom to express one's sexuality is going to be constrained if those responsible for your care fear that you may be exploited, as in the case of Martin; be subjected to unwanted pregnancy, AIDS, or venereal disease; or behave in a socially unacceptable manner, such as public masturbation. Because marriage has been the traditional vehicle for full sexuality, parents or caregivers are unlikely to be sympathetic to manifestations of sexual interest in adults who are viewed as too "immature" to fulfill spousal roles. But parent or caregiver wishes notwithstanding, sexual feelings are experienced and require assistance to be expressed in socially acceptable fashion. This involves the teaching of the what, when, and how of sexuality; the relationship between sex and pregnancy and methods of contraception; and, most importantly, how to protect oneself from unwanted advances. The level of cognitive impairment, of course, determines the degree to which this can be absorbed. Mildly impaired adults can participate in dating and assume marital relationships, although parental ones are very problematic. Although persons with lesser degrees of retardation may be able to fulfill the affective side of parenting, its "teaching" or cognitive component is difficult for them. Issues pertaining to sexuality are addressed in Chapters 5, 6, and 7.

Self-esteem: A Summary.   Much attention has been given to the effect of mental retardation on our need for self-esteem, a need which is considered crucial to mental health and a core "value" in our culture. The disability of mental retardation can frustrate needs for intimacy, success, and autonomy, the ingredients of self-esteem. Threats to self-esteem, especially intimacy, are tied largely to societal attitudes toward persons with disabilities, especially those of a cognitive nature, mental illness as well as mental retardation. Potentially affecting bonding with parents and siblings, the disability can produce varying degrees of social isolation and, particularly in the postschool years, lead to loneliness. A primary goal of the normalization, mainstreaming, and full-inclusion movements has been to reduce that social isolation and encourage greater interaction with the general community. Both the disabled and nondisabled segments are seen as beneficiaries of such integration. The former are exposed to more normative models, the latter to the opportunity to examine stereotypes and to recognize the humanness in us all.

Apart from intimacy, the need for success is especially threatened at school age. There is need for an educational experience that is "functional" or life-relevant for the disabled learner in his or her home community and is presented in a manner that facilitates learning. Nothing "turns us off" like failure and nothing "turns us on" like success! The "inclusion" challenge to our schools is to address adequately the educational needs of students with retardation and simultaneously offer regular social contact with nondisabled peers.

Self-expression

Interestingly, mental retardation also affects "leisure" time, the period during which we are free to choose activities in which to engage solely for the pleasure that they bring. Because of its associated cognitive and, often, motor disabilities, retardation narrows the range of possible leisure pursuits, a narrowing that can be further constrained by the aforementioned patterns of dependency. Nondisabled individuals are much freer to seek out the variety of leisure activities our culture offers and, in so doing, broaden the possible range of satisfactions. But although more limited, the range of leisure or recreational options for retarded children and adults is still very large (Wehman & Schleien, 1981). Indoor and outdoor games, arts and crafts, movies, radio, friends, and the omnipresent television all can offer opportunities for pleasure. Some of these activities also can provide educational benefits, such as, for example, bowling (Fitzsimmons, 1970). Not only does bowling offer a pleasant physical and often social outlet, but aspects of the sport and the setting in which it occurs can provide a variety of cognitive and social learning experiences. The bowling alley milieu provides opportunities for simple shopping and money-management experiences, and the presence of nondisabled bowlers and spectators can offer appropriate social models. Recreation in settings shared with nondisabled people ("integrated" settings), as in the case of school inclusion, offers the possibility for fostering more positive attitudes toward people with disabilities (Dattilo & Schleien, 1994).

Bowling is an excellent example of "therapeutic recreation"—participating in an activity that is inherently pleasurable and also provides a host of learning opportunities. Indeed, for the learner with retardation, the embedding of learning in activities that are enjoyed for their own sake becomes an ideal means of creating enthusiasm for learning itself. Think of how the simple game of bingo can be used to teach number recognition!

We have dealt in depth with the effect of mental retardation on the meeting of our basic needs as these were spelled out in our personality model. It is self-esteem that is particularly threatened, and efforts to preserve it and to discharge the emotion tied to its frustration contribute to the behavior problems seen in retarded children and adults. In the last two chapters of the book, the nature and treatment of those disorders is presented.

☐ **Summary**

The focus of this chapter is an exploration of what it means to be a "person," child, youth, and adult, with mental retardation. In order to examine this issue we need some common understanding of what it means to be a person. A model of personhood is presented that views human beings in terms of three dimensions—their basic capacities or *resources*; their *needs*, biological and psychological; and their *values*. Particular attention is devoted to resources and needs because these are fundamentally affected by the disorder. After careful description of their nature, the effects of mental retardation on them is detailed. With regard to the need for self-esteem, emphasis is placed on the threat to its fulfillment by both the impairment of resources and the negative way in which the disability of mental retardation is viewed in the general society. This perception is most strikingly evident in the common use of the epithet "retard" as a term of denigration. It is, often, the negative effect of our view of this disability that leads to the frustration of basic needs and a high frequency of behavior problems.

But apart from the limitations imposed by the disability, there are, nonetheless, individuals who show unusual gifts. These may be in the artistic, musical, memory, or "calendar calculating" realms—so-called savants. Examples of each are described along with an effort to explain calendar-calculating ability in individuals in whom, paradoxically, arithmetic abilities are consistent with their general intellectual impairment.

Possible Discussion Questions

The term "disability" evokes unwanted connotations in the public mind. Because of its presumed "stigmatic" nature, terms such as "challenged" have been in vogue, e.g., intellectually or physically "challenged." How do I view persons with disabilities? Do I perceive them as truly different from myself, that is, from nondisabled persons? Are they less "human?" Does the personality model presented in the chapter help me to view disabled individuals, especially those with mental retardation, in a different light? How does my individual view of retardation affect my possible interactions with such persons?

How am I to view individuals whose retardation is so severe as to raise the question of whether they actually have a "concept" of themselves. Such "self-awareness" is not present in infancy, or if it is, infants do not indicate it to us. Does the degree of retardation challenge our concept of what it means to be human? Must we ultimately fall back on religious beliefs, e.g., the soul, to acknowledge the humanity of individuals whose functioning may appear to us to be largely "vegetative" in nature?

What does the presence of unusual gifts in persons with mental retardation suggest about the nature of brain functioning? Can it be that areas of the brain can have relatively independent development?

☐ Notes

1. In the Americans With Disabilities Act of 1990, a disability is defined as a physical or mental impairment that substantially limits one or more major life activities. The disability exists even if it is wholly corrected. Thus a person who uses a hearing aid that restores hearing to normal still is considered disabled. In the author's frame of reference, one could characterize that person as "disabled" but not "handicapped," the latter term referring to the effects of the disability.

2. Thus, for example, mastery of the calendar for the years 1600 to 2000 permits extrapolation to all other years. Multiplying by 4 (400) enables one to relate any number year to the familiar range of 1600 to 2000. For the year 3126, as an example, the nearest 1600 equivalent would be the year 2800 (1600 + 400 + 400 + 400). Adding 326 to get 3126 from 2800 gives us the equivalent year in our 1600 to 2000 range of 1926. Multiples of 4 will give all years equivalent to 1600 (16[00] = 4 × 4), and then one adds or subtracts to reach the correct year in the 1600–2000 range. Now all one has to know to be a calendar calculator is the 400-year calendar!

Biological Factors in Mental Retardation: Chromosomal and Genetic

☐ Overview

In the next three chapters, we explore the causes of mental retardation. The disorder may arise from biological factors, either operating fairly independently as in Down syndrome, a chromosomal disorder, or interacting with the psychological environment as in what earlier was called "cultural-familial" mental retardation, now dubbed "psychosocial disadvantage." Biological determinants are presented in Chapters 3 and 4, and psychological ones in Chapter 5.

The current chapter describes disorders created at conception—chromosomal and genetic. The topics covered are some basic biological concepts necessary to the understanding of chromosomal and genetic abnormalities, disorders of the nonsex chromosomes (autosomes), disorders of the sex chromosomes, and gene-determined conditions.

☐ Some Basic Biological Concepts

About 15% of mental retardation is attributable to events that occur at conception (Crocker, 1992). These involve abnormalities of the chromosomes (10%), as in Down syndrome, or of the genes as in phenylketonuria

95

(PKU) (5%). The genes, the units of heredity, are carriers of biochemical information to the cell, instructing it as to the kinds of proteins it will produce. Proteins serve as enzymes or catalysts of the body's biochemical reactions. A genetic disorder is, in essence, a biochemical *error* attributable to a deficiency in the enzyme necessary to a particular biochemical reaction. This is later illustrated with reference to PKU. It is first necessary to review some basic biological concepts so that we can have at least a general understanding of chromosomes and genes.

Chromosomes

Chromosomes are thread-like structures on which the genes are linearly arrayed. Chromosomes exist in pairs, with each pair structurally and genetically distinct from all other pairs (Fig. 3.1). Our chromosomes literally are given to us by our parents through their sperm and egg cells; thus there is a maternal and paternal chromosome for each chromosome pair. All human cells except the sperm and egg contain 23 pairs of chromosomes, or 46 chromosomes in all. The sperm and egg cells, however, as a result of "reduction division," contain only 23 chromosomes, with each chromosome as the sole representative of each of the original 23 pairs. In human reproduction the union of sperm and egg creates a new cell, a fertilized egg or zygote, which, combining the 23 chromosomes of the father with the 23 chromosomes of the mother, produces the correct human chromosomal complement of 46. Chromosomes determine gender. Females have two of the so-called X chromosome, males have one X and one Y chromosome.

Genes

We already have referred to the genes as the basic units of heredity. Because of their extraordinary importance in life processes and the remarkable knowledge about them gained in our own generation, some additional description of their two primary functions, self-replication and protein synthesis, is appropriate (Dobzhansky, 1962).

Self-replication

This property refers to the capacity of the gene to organize the materials around it so as to duplicate its chemical structure. This capacity for self-copying, unique in living matter, is unaffected by changes that may occur in the gene, and future "copies" incorporate these changes (*mutations*).

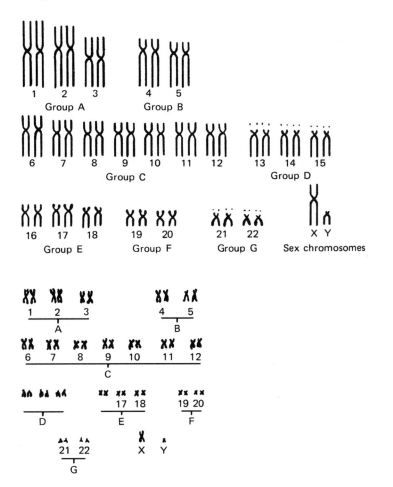

FIGURE 3.1. Schematic and actual representation of human chromosomes. Each chromosome pair has its own numerical designation as well as a letter designation for the structural group of which it is a member. The seven "groups" are arranged in order of decreasing length.

Gene Structure

The biochemical "instructions" on protein synthesis are encoded in chain molecules of nucleic acids, DNA (deoxyribonucleic acid) and RNA (ribonucleic acid). Each chain of DNA is a double spiral strand (helix) of four chemical substances called *nucleotides* (Fig. 3.2). Thousands of these nucleotides are joined end to end to form these chains. Each nucleotide itself consists of several other chemicals, a phosphate, a sugar, and a nitrogenous base; it is the last-mentioned that represents the genetic code. In

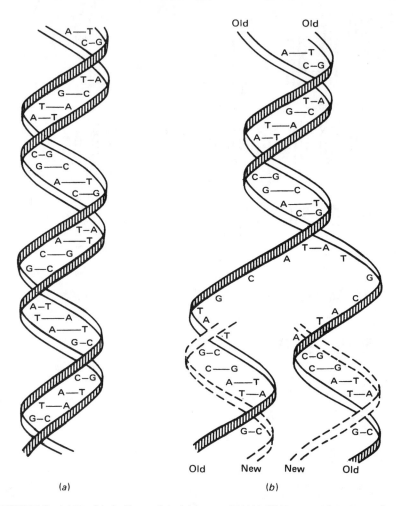

FIGURE 3.2. (a) Double helix model of the gene (DNA). (b) Presumed manner of gene replication. Strands separate in zipperlike fashion, and old strands serve as templates for new ones. (Adapted from Watson, 1968.)

DNA, four of these bases are commonly found: adenine, guanine, thymine, and cytosine. The two chains or strands can be conceptualized as a coiled ladder with the rungs of the ladder connecting the bases. The essential point is that an adenine base on one strand is always bonded to thymine on the other, and, similarly, guanine is always bonded to cytosine. The two chains are exact complements of each other. When they separate into two single strands during cell division, each separate strand can form an exact copy of the original double structure by the proper coupling of the four bases—adenine to thymine and guanine to cytosine.

Genetic Code

The genetic code can be regarded as a four-letter "alphabet," each letter standing for one of the bases—A (adenine), T (thymine), G (guanine), and C (cytosine). Just as an enormous number of words can be made up from the 26 letters of our alphabet or even just the two "letters" of the Morse code, so these four letters are capable of representing endless combinations. If we think of a gene as a "word" of n letters, the number of possible permutations of four letters in a word of n letters is four^n. If, for example, a particular gene is a section of the double helix that contains 10 base pairs, the number of possible sequences for the four "letters" is 4^{10} or 1,048,576. Thus within only 10 base pairs, more than a million genes are possible. Although it is improbable that just any sequence of bases will make a functional gene, virtually an infinity of gene structures is possible if a gene contains hundreds of thousands of bases.

Protein Synthesis

The protein code originates in the nucleus of the cell, but protein synthesis occurs in the cytoplasm. The code is transferred from the nucleus to the cytoplasm by RNA. In the cytoplasm, RNA organizes amino acids, the chemical substrate of proteins. The genetic code determines the positions in the protein of each of the approximately 20 kinds of amino acids. For example, a molecule of insulin contains a total of 51 amino acids, comprising 15 of the 20 different kinds. The insulin of different animals (e.g., cattle, sheep, and pigs) differs slightly but significantly by the substitution of only one or two amino acids. The importance of even one difference with regard to health or illness is illustrated in another protein, the oxygen-carrying component in our red blood cells, hemoglobin. In sickle-cell anemia, hemoglobin is abnormal because of the substitution of only *one* amino acid out of the approximately 300 of which hemoglobin is composed!

How Heredity Works

Sickle-cell anemia, a common disease in blacks, is an inherited disorder caused by a single gene. It is inherited as a "recessive," meaning that both parents are carriers of one normal and one abnormal gene but that the affected child receives only the abnormal gene from each parent (this mechanism is spelled out later in connection with PKU). The effect of the two recessive genes is to cause the child to be able to manufacture hemoglobin with only the one *wrong* kind of amino acid. The consequence is severe anemia, with death often occurring by adolescence.

Within-Species Sources of Genetic Variation

A general understanding of the genetic mechanism requires awareness of its role in causing diversity among living things. It influences the three known sources of variation among members of the same species—*mutation in genes* and *crossing over* and *random assortment* of chromosomes. Each of these is briefly described, although random assortment is treated in greater detail because a grasp of it is necessary to an understanding of the genetic risks borne by families in which hereditary forms of retardation have a high probability of occurrence.

Mutation

Mutation refers to a change in the biochemical structure of a gene resulting in a new or mutant gene. The mutant gene alters metabolic functioning, with major changes usually undesirable. All genes mutate, but at a very slow rate, thus ensuring biochemical stability within a population. Radioactivity increases the rate of mutation and is one of the reasons that the level of radioactivity to which we are exposed should be kept at a minimum.

Crossing Over

Crossing over refers to an exchange of chromosomal material (genes) between corresponding parts of a particular chromosome pair, resulting in the creation of two new modified members of that pair.

Random Assortment

Random or independent assortment is nature's chief means of generating diversity within sexually reproducing species by creating *variety* among the sperm or egg cells carried by each individual within that species. In humans, there is an extraordinarily high probability that no two sperm or egg cells of the same person will be identical. "Identical" means that the sperm or egg cells carry the same maternal or paternal chromosome for each of the 23 chromosome pairs. Recall that reduction division is the process by which sex cells are formed. In humans, for example, from an original 46 chromosomes (23 pairs), an egg or sperm is produced with 23 chromosomes, one member or representative from each of the 23 pairs. Each sperm or egg cell is likely to have a mix of maternal and paternal representatives of each of the 23 pairs that differs from the mix of other sperm or egg cells. The number of possible mixes or combinations that can be randomly drawn from 23 pairs is huge—2^{23} or 8,388,608. But within this diversity there is also similarity. On the average, sperm or egg cells are identical with respect to one half of the 23 chromosomes, and this is what accounts for the similarities among siblings.

The concept of random assortment can be confusing, but its understanding will be helpful when dominant and recessive forms of mental retardation are presented. Figure 3.3 illustrates the number of possible sperm cell combinations that could be generated from a cell that originally had three pairs of chromosomes. Because there are two possibilities for each chromosome pair, either drawing the maternal or paternal member of that pair, the total number of possible combinations for a cell that contains three pairs of chromosomes is 2^3 or 8. Because the maternal and paternal chromosomes within a given pair are structurally indistinguishable, for purposes of diagrammatic illustration the maternal member is denoted by *m* and the paternal member by *p*.

Summary

This survey of some basic biological concepts serves as backdrop for the presentation of major chromosomal and genetic disorders associated with mental retardation. Human life begins with the union of egg and sperm cells, creating a fertilized egg to which both parents are equal contributors. The vital material of the fertilized egg is its 46 chromosomes and the genes they carry. The human "genome" contains from 50,000 to 100,000 genes (Leroy, 1992), and it is the "mapping" of these genes that is one of the major biological goals of the 21st century.

☐ Chromosomes and Mental Retardation

A Little History

The basic principles of heredity were first enunciated by the Austrian monk Gregor Mendel in 1866. His work was lost temporarily to science but was rediscovered and confirmed in about 1900. Lacking modern laboratory technology, Mendel never saw a gene, but he hypothesized their existence on the basis of plant experiments. Human chromosome counts began in the 1920s, and into the early 1950s it was believed that we had 48 chromosomes. With improvements in laboratory technology, the scientific world was startled to learn that the correct number of human chromosomes was 46 rather than 48 (Ford & Hamerton, 1956). Shortly thereafter, it was found that several major disorders were traceable to abnormalities of the chromosomes.

Chromosomal abnormalities are not rare, but most are incompatible with life and, typically, lead to spontaneous abortion early in pregnancy (Hagerman, 1992). The chromosomal abnormalities compatible with life

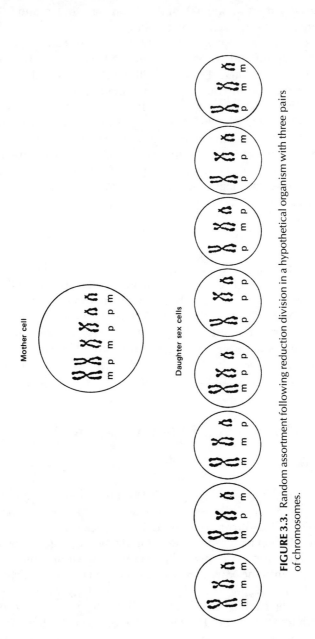

FIGURE 3.3. Random assortment following reduction division in a hypothetical organism with three pairs of chromosomes.

are those with extra numbers of chromosomes, as in Down syndrome, or the absence of part of a chromosome, a so-called deletion as in Prader-Willi syndrome. The additions or deletions can involve either the autosomes, the 22 pairs of nonsex chromosomes, or the X sex chromosome. Common additions consist of a third chromosome rather than just two, so-called trisomy, and the best known are trisomy 21 (Down syndrome or mongolism), trisomy 18 (Edward syndrome), and trisomy 13 (Patau syndrome). Trisomies 13 and 18 are associated with severe congenital malformations and usually are incompatible with life after one year of age. Examples of deletions are Prader-Willi and cri du chat (cat-cry) syndromes.

The aforementioned are all examples of autosomal abnormalities, but the sex-chromosome pair, X and Y, also can be affected, especially X. There may be extra X chromosomes (e.g., Klinefelter syndrome), an X chromosome missing (Turner syndrome), or a part of the X chromosome lost (fragile X syndrome).

Chromosomal abnormalities can be extremely variable in their effect, producing a wide range of developmental disorders and structural defects. One may find profound retardation and severe physical malformations, or only minor learning disabilities and subtle physical manifestations.

Down Syndrome (Trisomy 21)

Best known of the chromosomal disorders causing mental retardation, Down syndrome results from the presence of a third chromosome 21. The affected person has 47 chromosomes instead of 46. Older mothers, women in their late 30s and 40s, are at highest risk for the condition. Because of the association with maternal age and because females are born with all the ova they will ever have, these ova being vulnerable to adverse influences both prior to and after birth, it was thought that the chromosomal abnormality must always lie in the egg. This is largely true although in about 5% the abnormality is traceable to the sperm cell (Antonaraknis & the Down Syndrome Collaborative Group, 1991).

Historical Aspects

First described in 1886 by a London physician, Langdon Down, the disorder was called mongolism because of a superficial facial similarity to Asians of Mongolian extraction. Prior to 1959 its cause was unknown. On the basis of twin studies, it was concluded that causation must lie early in pregnancy (Allen & Baroff, 1955; Baroff, 1958), a conclusion confirmed in 1959 with the discovery of the extra chromosome 21. Vulnerability was

FIGURE 3.4. A child with Down syndrome. (Courtesy of Kaplan, Lewisville, NC.)

set at conception itself. The union of sperm and egg cell at fertilization involves an egg cell with two 21 chromosomes instead of just one and, when fertilized by a sperm carrying one chromosome 21, the resultant fertilized egg has three 21 chromosomes instead of two, or 47 chromosomes in all.

Clinical Features

The physical manifestations of the disorder (Fig. 3.4) are well known and include a variety of skeletal, joint, muscle, and organ abnormalities. Facial features and the tongue have been targets for cosmetic plastic surgery but, although parents and surgeons have tended to view the results in a positive light, systematic observation by neutral observers has failed to reveal the purported effects (Katz & Kravetz, 1989). No consistent benefits have been found in speech clarity or general appearance. Katz and Kravetz (1989) see no scientific basis for recommending the procedure, but those plastic surgeons who have performed it continue to be positive about it (May & Turnbull, 1992). Presumably, like the parents, they see what they want to see!

Apart from the head and facial features, the hand is characterized by a shortened and curved little finger, muscle tone generally is reduced, and head and thyroid abnormalities are common.

Medical Management

A number of medical approaches to treatment of Down syndrome have been employed, but without success. Effective treatment ultimately will depend on understanding the physiological consequences of the extra chromosome and extra genes (Pueschel, 1992). There are, however, medical problems that do require attention. Hearing and visual difficulties are common, as is congenital heart disease. In fact, nearly one half of newborns with Down syndrome have congenital heart disease, a major cause of death prior to age 10 years (Baird & Sadovnick, 1987). Hypothyroidism invites early recognition so as to not further compromise mental functioning, and there is a tendency to obesity in adolescence and early adulthood.

Early Aging and Alzheimer's Disease

An interesting aspect is the association of Down syndrome with Alzheimer's disease (Thase, 1988). Numerous studies have documented an earlier age-related decline in older persons with Down syndrome than in a comparable non–Down syndrome population, especially after age 50 years. The rate of clinical dementia is reported at 9% in the fourth decade, increasing to 55% by the sixth (Prasher & Krivhnan, 1993). Recent work suggests that within a picture of general neurological abnormality, dementia itself is tied to a very specific neuritic plaque abnormality as well as to neurofibrillary tangles. Two types of neuritic plaques exist, fibrillary and neurofibrillary, and it is only the former that is thought to cause dementia (Wisniewski & Silverman, 1996). The clinical picture of early dementia seen in Down syndrome differs from that of a non–Down syndrome population with Alzheimer's disease in terms of emotional manifestations. Depression is common in the general Alzheimer's disease population but is less frequent in older persons with Down syndrome. In the latter, cognitive decline seems rather to be associated with reduced general responsiveness, apathy, and withdrawal (Nelson, Lott, Touchette, Satz, & D'Elia, 1995). In addition to behavior decline, there is also a generally reduced life expectancy, again after age 50 years (Thase, 1988).

The link between Down syndrome and Alzheimer's disease is genetic. There is a clearly inherited form of Alzheimer's disease, and it is associated with genes on several chromosomes, including chromosome 21, the same chromosome associated with Down syndrome (Selkoe, 1991). The genetic link between the two disorders also is reflected in a risk for Down syndrome in relatives of persons with Alzheimer's disease that is twice as great as that found in the general population (Heston, 1982).

Maternal Age

Reference has been made to the well-established relationships between Down syndrome and maternal age. The increased frequency in children born to women over 35 years of age is simply part of a broader risk for *all* chromosomal abnormalities in babies born to older mothers. In the age range from 35 to 40 years, the general risk is 1.5%, increasing to 3.4% at 40 years old and to as much as 10% at 45 years (Milunsky, 1975; Sells & Bennett, 1977). For Down syndrome itself, the current overall incidence is about 1 in 1000 births, but after age 40 it rises to about 10 per 1000 births. Although the risk in children born to older women is much higher, that risk is tempered by access to prenatal diagnosis and the option of terminating the pregnancy. In fact, fewer than 20% of children with Down syndrome are born to women over age 35 years (Pueschel, 1992).

Forms of Down Syndrome

There are three chromosomal variants of the disorder—*trisomy, transloca-tion*, and *mosaicism*. In trisomy, each cell contains an extra chromosome 21. In translocation, the extra 21 is physically attached to another chromosome, and in mosaicism only *some* cells have the extra chromosome, the remainder being normal. Of the three variants, trisomy is by far the most common, accounting for better than 90% of all cases. The remainder are divided nearly equally between translocation and mosaicism (Pueschel & Thuline, 1991).

Prenatal Detection of Down Syndrome

Down syndrome was formerly detectable prenatally through either amniocentesis or chorion biopsy; a screening blood test now permits the identification of several developmental disorders, including Down syndrome. The test is offered routinely to pregnant women younger than 35 years old, women who are at a low risk for disorder. If the test indicates a Down syndrome pregnancy, it is followed by either amniocentesis or chorion biopsy. Because the blood test misses about 20% of women with a Down syndrome pregnancy, amniocentesis or chorion biopsy is offered to *all* women 35 years old or older, those at higher risk.

After prenatal detection, prospective mothers tend to be much more positive about carrying through the pregnancy than medical personnel and genetic counselors (Helm, Miranda, & Chedd, 1998). Professionals are strongly encouraged to provide options to parents within a *nonjudgmental* context. Prospective parents should understand that they have three options. The first of these is to carry through the pregnancy and to assume a normal parental role. The second also involves carrying through the pregnancy, but then the infant is placed for adoption. The third, of course, is to terminate the pregnancy.

Prospective parents are urged to acquaint themselves with up-to-date literature on the disorder, avoid rushing to judgement, contact parents of children with Down syndrome, and discuss their feelings with family members and other sources of support.

Developmental Aspects

Speech and Cognition. Numerous studies reveal a pattern of developmental delay already evident in the first year of life.[1] Down syndrome babies learn (condition) more slowly and lag in showing normal infantile preference for novel stimulation (Ohr & Fagen, 1991). The latter is also apparent in their later toy play, as they tend to play longer with a particular object and show a lesser interest in novel ones (Kassari, Mundy, Yirmiya, & Sigman, 1990). As early as 3 months, some developmental lag is discernible, with one study of mental and motor development in children with Down syndrome reporting developmental quotients of 88 and 87, respectively, in contrast to quotients of 119 and 115 in normally developing infants (Ohr & Fagen, 1991).

This relatively modest developmental lag is not maintained, and the rate of development progressively slows, especially after the first year (Carr, 1989; Dicks-Mireaux, 1972; Melyn & White, 1973). Most prominent is the delay in speech (Fowler, 1988). Two-word phrases, commonly used by normal children by age 2 years, often do not appear until 3 or 4 years of age, and in some not until 8 years. A group of 12-year-old children, for example, with mental ages of 5 to 6 years were speaking more like normal 2-year-olds (Fowler, Gelman, & Gleitman, 1980).

In infancy, speech delay is presaged by a later onset and reduced frequency of vocalizations, and by a lesser use of gestures, a common pre-speech communicative mode. Of particular significance as a predictor of future speech difficulties is impairment in verbal imitation.

Although the child with Down syndrome passes through the same sequence of cognitive development as the normal child, some irregularity in the *continuity* of growth is apparent. Although retardation is anticipated to be reflected in a generalized slowing of development, it is not expected that the child would show periods of no growth, literally plateaus. Such plateaus have been reported for both general intellectual development (Gibson, 1966) and in speech (Fowler, 1988). In the speech domain, in particular, the middle-childhood years of ages 8 to 11 are likely to be a time of little or no growth in the *complexity of speech*. This is followed by a period of relatively modest growth in the age range of 13 to 17 years (Dykens et al., 1994; Fowler, 1988). The lack of growth is most evident in grammatical development and is illustrated by such inappropriate usage as "what's you want?" and in the substitution of "what" for "where" and "when" (e.g., "what's you gonna bring it down?" for "when").

Together with grammatical misuse, speech is often impaired in clarity. Words may be poorly articulated and consist only of their initial sound. Short sentences are run together like a single word, and voice quality is harsh. The child's speech is most intelligible if the listener knows what the child is talking about or is familiar with the child's vocabulary. Older children, especially the brighter ones, recognize their difficulties and may complement their speech with gestures, a means of communication prominent in children who are deaf. The use of gesture or a speech supplement also reveals one of the areas of relative developmental strength in Down syndrome, the *visual* mode.

What we have in Down syndrome is a significant disparity between the ability to understand language and to express it. Speculation as to its cause involves *brain-related* language functions. In virtually all right-handed people and a sizable proportion of left-handers, both receptive and expressive language are governed by the same cerebral hemisphere, the left hemisphere. But in Down syndrome there is less localization (lateralization) of language in the left hemisphere, there being a tendency to use the right hemisphere rather than the left for understanding speech, if not for producing it (Elliott, Weeks, & Elliott, 1987). In so doing, however, the individual is using a brain hemisphere that is less biologically programmed for language; its specialty is the interpretation of *visual* experience. More specifically, the right hemisphere is less effective in interpreting serial or sequential events, the essence of both the understanding and production of speech. Speech is, after all, a *series* of sounds. Although children with Down syndrome appear unimpaired in the imitation of movement sequences, sequences presented visually, it is in the imitation of movement sequences conveyed verbally that they experience special difficulty (Elliott et al., 1990; Elliott, personal communication, 1995). It is this kind of impairment that may contribute to their well-established difficulties in verbal imitation. In effect, they are processing serial verbal requests with the hemisphere that is less biologically programmed for this kind of sensory stimulus.

With respect to general cognitive development, it has been noted that the rate of growth tends to slow especially after the first year, when intellectual functioning is already in the retarded range, albeit at the level of mild retardation. Relatively little change in intellectual status is evident through age 3 years (Peuschel, 1984), but by age 4 years IQs decline into the moderately retarded range and, by the end of the mental-age growth period, they commonly are in the range of severe retardation. It needs to be emphasized that the decline in IQ does not represent a *loss* of previously acquired abilities; rather it relates to the slowness with which new ones are being acquired. In one large-scale study of Down syndrome children, ages 6 months to 13.5 years, the mean IQ at 6 months was 58, but it had declined to 38 at 13.5 years (Melyn & White, 1973). Within individuals with Down syndrome, however, there is tremendous variation in intellectual development, at least some of which is attributable to the nature of the chromosomal anomaly. The translocation form appears to be associated with higher IQs than is true of trisomy (Shipe et al., 1968), and the mosaic type is associated with the highest IQs of all (Fishler, 1975). Mean IQs in mosaicism fall in the mildly retarded range, 57 to 67, and as many as 15% to 20% have little or no impairment, with IQs ranging from 80 to 100.

Curiously, there is no relationship between the proportion of abnormal cells and IQ. A correlational analysis of a series of 30 individuals described by Fishler and Koch (1991) found a correlation of .03, essentially zero. Complicating what is already a puzzling biological phenomenon is that the proportion of abnormal cells may change over time, either increasing or decreasing. Because the nature of mosaicism is such that not all tissues are affected, we can only speculate that it is the proportion of brain tissue that is abnormal that ultimately affects intellectual development. Parenthetically, the range of percentages of abnormal cells in the Fishler and Koch series, ages 2 to 19 years, was from a low of 8% in a 13.5-year-old girl with an IQ of 53 to a high of 89% in a 9-year-old girl with an IQ of 63.

Returning to our picture of cognitive development, the reason for the slowing in growth rate remains unexplained. The language deficit may contribute, given that thinking is a form of inner "speech." In any case, the speech domain has been one of the targets of efforts to stimulate development. One of its indirect benefits has been to heighten maternal responsiveness. Parenting cannot be a one-way experience; there must be some reciprocation to maintain caregiver responsiveness. At least *some* infants with Down syndrome show a diminished social responsiveness, a behavior that can aggravate an already potentially stressed parent-child relationship. In this regard, parents of infants with Down syndrome, as well as with other developmental disorders, are in special need of emotional support and accurate information about their children's developmental needs. Physician attitudes toward the birth of a child with Down syndrome are more positive, especially with the growth of services specifically designed to assist parents and infants (Springer & Stiele, 1980), but association with a group of other parents seems to provide the greatest support (Spiker, 1982).

Motor Development. Among the developmental domains, the motor area is one of relative strength. By age 5 years these children can walk, run, and negotiate stairs, and their hand-eye coordination is adequate for such play activities as stacking blocks and stringing large beads. The motor domain also allows us to see the previously mentioned contrast between imitating a sequence of movements presented visually and one presented orally.

Self-Help Skills. A potentially stressful aspect of rearing a child whose development lags is the slowness in acquiring the basic self-help skills of feeding, dressing, and toileting. In comparison with the normally developing child, the attainment of these skills is commonly delayed by from 1 to 2 years (Share, 1975), especially toilet training and dressing (Peuschel, 1992). Although delay in bladder and bowel control may be the most onerous, parents can anticipate that toileting skills generally will be achieved by age 1 to 4, although some assistance in dressing still will be needed. It should be recognized that unusually intensive training may speed the process, as in the 24-hour toilet-training program popularized in the 1970s (Azrin & Foxx, 1971).

Efforts to speed the rate of development have been legion, with gains particularly found in physically healthier children—those with better muscle tone and no major heart disease (Cullen, Cronk, Peuschel, Schnell, & Reed, 1981).

Efforts to stimulate development also is a rationale for encouraging the rearing of developmentally delayed children in their own homes rather than in institutions. It is presumed that being reared by one's own parents generally results in more individualized care than could be obtained in large group care settings, and that there are higher levels of stimulation. This is a topic to which we return in Chapter 5.

There is, in fact, much early research that supports the developmental advantage of being reared in one's own home (e.g., Carr, 1970). Reference already has been made to speech and mother-child benefits. Indeed, a review of major "early intervention" programs with infants and young children with Down syndrome indicates that the clearest benefits accrued to *parents* in the form of assistance, comfort, and renewed motivation.

General Development. Our focus has been on the effects of Down syndrome on general intelligence (IQ), speech, motor skills, and self-help skills. Each of these domains is assessed in measures of adaptive behavior, and data from one of these, the Vineland Adaptive Behavior Scale (Sparrow, Balla, & Cicchetti, 1984), offers a picture of the kind of abilities we can expect to see in these children. Incorporating such broad adaptive areas as communication (receptive, expressive, and written language), daily living (personal, domestic, and community skills), and socialization (interpersonal relationships, play and leisure, and coping skills), the Vineland Adaptive Behavior Scale and its predecessor, the Vineland Social Maturity Scale (Doll, 1964) were developed because individuals with the same IQs could show very different levels of adjustment (adaptive behavior), generally attributable to differences in "personality" and, presumably, most apparent in those with severe degrees of psychopathology, such as psychoses. As in the case of nonretarded individuals, IQ alone may not convey the extent of adaptive difficulties.

Earlier studies of adaptive behavior in Down syndrome, as measured by the Vineland Social Maturity Scale, had shown a picture of decline in the rate of the acquisition of new skills comparable to that seen in intelligence, but to a lesser degree (Cornwell & Birch, 1969; Melyn & White, 1973; Morgan, 1979). More recent studies, using different instruments, have found virtually no decline (Loveland & Kelley, 1988, 1991; Silverstein et al., 1988; Zigman, Schupf, Lubin, & Silverman, 1987). Rather is there a pattern of slow but steady *growth* and *maintenance* of adaptive skills on into the 40s. It is not until the 50s that significant declines appear, and these typically involve motor functioning, self-help, and cognitive skills (Silverstein et al., 1988; Zigman et al., 1987). Zigman et al. (1987) also noted that when age-related decline appears, again after age 50 years, it is much more rapid than in non–Down syndrome individuals of comparable age.

Some Adult Adaptations.

Although the picture conveyed is one of general *maintenance* of skills in the adult years, it does not provide a sense of just how these individuals *function*. Earlier studies leaned heavily on institutionalized populations, a group less likely to achieve the adaptive skills of those reared at home and living in the community. Indeed, Silverstein et al. (1988) found their community-based population to be consistently functioning at higher adaptive levels than those who were in institutional settings.

Although the degree of intellectual development and health certainly affects the level of independence achieved, and a completely independent adjustment is not ordinarily expected, varying degrees of self-sufficiency are found. Except for those with the most severe impairment, one can anticipate full self-care in dressing, grooming, and toileting. At higher ability levels, adults can learn to independently use local forms of transportation, perform household chores, and, with assistance, become employable.

Lisa, a 23-year-old woman, illustrates how skills can be acquired if parents support the goal of maximizing independence in their disabled children. As a young adult, she wanted to leave the family home and live in a residence with other adults, a "group home." Although the family was apprehensive about her capacity to function outside the home, they had offered her training that would foster it. In the family home she had learned to operate the washing machine, prepare her own lunches, get her clothes ready for the next day, and make purchases at the local grocery store (Pendler, 1979).

In the realm of employment, formerly limited to jobs in "sheltered" work settings, sheltered workshops, or day activity programs, the effect of "job coaching" and its individualized preparation for employment in regular work settings has dramatically broadened employment opportunities. From an earlier restriction to simple service and janitorial tasks, opportunities have been opened in the clerical sector. Although many adults lack functional reading and arithmetic skills, limitations related to their cognitive impairment, some possess abilities that can be applied to such office tasks as filing, sorting mail, and operating office machines.

The level of educability in Down syndrome has been controversial. The earlier tendency was to view these youth as incapable of acquiring functional reading skills; they traditionally were characterized in school parlance as "trainable" rather than "educable." We now have clear evidence that at least some youth can achieve functional reading and writing skills. This may be those with the mosaic form of the disorder. In any event, it has been suggested that continued access to reading opportunities be given to adolescents with Down syndrome who read at least at a second-grade level (Rynders & Horrobin, 1990).

The diary of Nigel Hunt (1967), an Englishman with Down syndrome, reveals his not inconsiderable writing abilities as well as his joyful view of many of his experiences. The publication of a book by someone with Down syndrome was itself a major news event. Here is an excerpt:

> I am Nigel Hunt and I live at 26 Church Avenue, Pinner, England with my parents. They are very nice indeed. I was born at Edgeware in 1947. I have never been to America yet. The lady who advised me to write this was Mrs. Eileen J. Garrett and she says that I shall be very busy.
>
> I have my own typewriter and I taught myself to type. When I went to London many years ago I made a film with professor Penrose looking at my palms. [Lionel Penrose, a major British worker in retardation, was looking for the characteristic palmar crease found in the hands of persons with Down syndrome.] I also smiled at the camera, and he says it will go to America, and I hope you have seen. (pp. 45–46)

Although the writing has an unmistakably childlike quality, both in sentence length and content, it more than demonstrates the educability of some individuals with the disorder.

Mark, a 19-year-old man, writes of his visit to the state of Israel:

Dear Mrs. Frank,
I received your letter and I thought your letter was very nice. I liked the trip very much and I thought it was very educational, I learned a lot from it. I liked the Western Wall a lot and was impressed when the enemies tried to destroy the wall, it would not fall. It felt like it was my home and my temple it made me feel like I was near God. I am also thinking about it right now. I felt bad when I left, I really miss Israel. (Frank, 1975)

Marc, at 19 years old, was living in the family home and had a job. He paid for the trip with money he had earned. He is described as a curious, courteous, and helpful young man, eager for acceptance and recognition (what we all want!).

Other Behavioral Characteristics

Typically viewed in positive behavioral terms, á la Nigel Hunt, children with the disorder have been described as affectionate, sociable, amiable, outgoing, and controllable (Gibbs & Thorpe, 1983; Gunn & Berry, 1985). Although some children can show stubborness, conduct disorder, and attention deficit (Gath & Gumley, 1986; Meyers & Pueschel, 1991), especially early in life, youngsters with Down syndrome appear to be less prone to serious behavior problems. In the sexual sphere, a generally diminished drive is noted, especially in males. Genital abnormalities are found in both sexes, and the male is considered sterile (Scola, 1982), Nevertheless, some sexual activity, often of a masturbatory nature, is found, and there may be need for sex education (Putnam & Rynders, 1982). Sex education is discussed in Chapters 6 and 7.

Other Autosomal Chromosomal Abnormalities

We have dealt at some length with Down syndrome, the best known of the chromosomal anomalies associated with mental retardation; now we briefly describe three additional ones, trisomies 18, 13, and 8.

Trisomy 18 (Edward Syndrome)

Second most common of the trisomies, trisomy 18 occurs in about 1 in 8000 live births, primarily in females (Smith, 1982). Associated with multiple physical abnormalities, its symptoms consist of abnormalities of the skull, heart, kidneys, and nervous system. Appearing feeble and undernourished at birth, newborns may require resuscitation, and later there may be episodes of cessation of breathing (apnea). There is a general "failure to thrive," and about half succumb by age 2 months. Survivors are severely retarded. Interestingly, the occurrence of trisomy 18 seems to increase the likelihood of future trisomic births in these families, especially Down syndrome (Hecht, Bryant, Gauber, & Townes, 1964).

Trisomy 13 (Patau Syndrome)

Associated with major physical anomalies—absence of eyes, cleft lip, and palate, extra (supernumerary) fingers and toes (polydactyly), and cerebral malformations (Patau, Smith, Therman, Inhorn, & Wagner, 1960), trisomy 13 is the rarest of the trisomies, with an incidence of about 1 in 20,000 births. Death usually occurs by age 3 months (Hagerman, 1992). About 8% of those affected survive the first year; they show severe retardation, seizures, and impaired growth (Smith, 1970). Some instances of the disorder are caused by translocation and, because of the much increased risk associated with that form of chromosomal anomaly, determination of the nature of the chromosomal variant is important.

Trisomy 8 Syndrome

Caused by mosaicism of chromosome 8, this trisomy is associated with thick lips, deep-set eyes, prominent ears, and bent fingers. Intellectual impairment can vary from mild to severe, with IQ usually between 50 and 80 (Hagerman, 1992). Coordination also may be affected. Children born with full trisomy 8 generally do not survive (Smith, 1982).

Partial Trisomies

Partial trisomies occur; indeed, they are more common than full ones (Hagerman, 1992). Among these are partial trisomies of chromosomes 4p, 6p, and 20p. (The p means that the extra chromosomal material comes from the short arms of a chromosome, the part that is found above the centromere, the "waist" of the chromosome. References to q in connection with a chromosome refer to genetic material on the long arms of the chromosome, that below the centromere.)

The main clinical features of some partial trisomies are listed (after Hagerman, 1992):

4p: Abnormally small head (microcephaly), excessive growth and fusion of eyebrows (synophrys), flat nasal bridge, bent fingers (campodactyly), underdeveloped nails (hypoplastic), abnormally small penis (micropenis), severe retardation, motor skills less impaired than language ones

6p: Microcephaly, small mouth, abnormal closeness of the eyes (hypotelorism), failure to thrive, mental retardation, autism

9p: Abnormally large head (macrocephaly), abnormally large distance between the eyes (hypertelorism), short fingers and toes, skeletal anomalies, cupped ears, retardation of moderate to severe degree

20p: Reduced muscle tone (hypotonia), tremor, excessive shortness of the head (brachycephaly), hypotelorism, large ears, undescended testicles (cryptoorchidism), mild to severe retardation

Autosomal Chromosomal Deletions

In this section, disorders are described in which the loss (deletion) of part of one of the nonsex chromosomes is associated with mental retardation. Loss of chromosomal (genetic) material leads to dysmorphic facial features, malformed organs, and intellectual impairment (Hagerman, 1992). Six disorders are presented. They are described in terms of their physical, cognitive, and behavioral aspects. One of them, Prader-Willi syndrome is discussed in greater detail because of both its general prominence and its unique management features. All of the deletions involve the *p* portion of a chromosome, its short arm. A minus sign indicates deletion.

4p— (Wolf-Hirschorn Syndrome)

Effects of this syndrome include failure of midline fusion of mouth, nose, lips, and penis; growth deficiency; seizures; and profound retardation.

5p— (Cri Du Chat [Cat-Cry] Syndrome)

This syndrome is characterized by a high-pitched cat-like cry, growth retardation, hypertelorism, eye abnormalities, epicanthal folds and downward slanting eyelids, severe lag in speech and language, and moderate mental retardation.

11p— (Wilms Tumor–Anaridia)

This deletion causes anaridia (absence of the iris), maldeveloped (ambiguous) genitals, and mental retardation.

11p— Interstitial

Interstitial (refers to loss of material that does not involve the terminal portion of the chromosome). There is a disproportionate shortness of the head (brachycephaly), a broad nasal bridge, short broad hands, severe hyperactivity, self-injurious behavior (described in Chapter 8), hearing loss, mental retardation, and autism.

17p— (Terminal Deletion, Miller-Diecker Syndrome)

This is characterized by a small head (microcephaly), a lack of a convolutional pattern in the cerebral cortex (abnormal smoothness or lissencephally), growth impairment, seizures, and severe mental retardation.

15q— (Either Prader-Willi or Angelman Syndrome)

If the abnormal chromosome was inherited from the father, this is Prader-Willi syndrome; from the mother, Angelman syndrome. The chromosomal abnormality is not actually present in either parent but rather arises in the sperm or egg at conception, a so-called de novo deletion. Its risk for occurrence is less than 1 in 1000 (Bruno, Loveman, & Pfadt, 1993).

15q— (Prader-Willi Syndrome)

Charles Dickens in *The Pickwick Papers* refers to "a fat and red-faced boy in a state of somnolence." Coupled with other characteristics, his description may fit a child with Prader-Willi syndrome (Smith, 1982). A rare condition, occurring in about 1 in 10,000 births (Holm & Pipes, 1981), its main symptoms are intellectual impairment of varying degree; delayed motor development (severe hypotonia) (Curfs, 1997); small stature; obesity; dysmorphic facial features; almond-shaped eyes; a narrow bifrontal skull; and small, finely shaped hands, feet, and genitalia. The small genitalia (hypogonadism) are associated with a lack of a pubertal growth spurt and generally delayed sexual development. With regard to causation, clear evidence of a deletion in chromosome 15 is found in about 60% of affected persons (Hagerman, 1992). The chromosomal deletion appears to cause an abnormality in the hypothalamus, a brain structure whose functions include the control of appetite and the producing of feelings of fullness after eating (Swaab, Puarba, & Hofman, 1995).

The disorder has two distinct stages. The first, present in infancy, is associated with muscle weakness (hypotonia) and difficulty in sucking. The second stage, beginning at about age 2 years, finds a strengthening of muscle tone but the onset of obesity. Henceforth, throughout life, there is

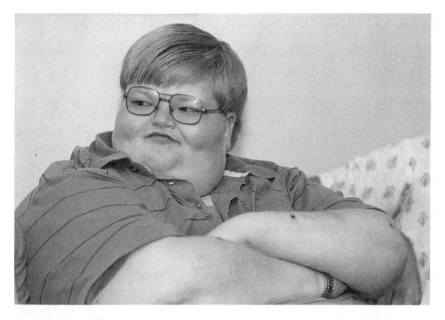

FIGURE 3.5. Geral at 18 years old is gaining 2.5 lb per day. "I'm not at all sure that they feel hunger, but they think about food all the time," says a leading researcher. If not controlled, they will literally eat themselves to death.

an all-consuming (no pun intended) passion for food. The appetite seems insatiable and can even lead to death.

Figure 3.5 shows Geral, an 18-year-old man with Prader-Willi syndrome. Living at home, he was gaining 2.5 lb per day. If not controlled, the disorder eventually may kill him.

> Geral's parents had prepared chili. Each had had a normal bowl, but Geral, eating out of quart-sized container, demanded more even before finishing his initial serving. His mother urged him to stop, but she knew he could not and that if he was refused, there would be a temper outburst. On the previous day he had found ice cream bars in the freezer intended for the family and consumed them all. On one occasion, children on his school bus "baited" him by unwrapping several candy bars and grinding them in the dirt on the school bus floor. He took the bait!

First diagnosed with Prader-Willi syndrome at age 7 years, Geral's parents were told that all they could do was to put him on a diet and prevent access to food. This meant literally locking up refrigerator, freezer, and pantry. And this remains the only way that the behavior can be controlled.

Curiously, weight gain can continue even with calorie control. In order to prevent additional weight gain, calorie consumption is further reduced to about 60% of normal—1200 to 1500 calories per day.

General Behavior. Apart from their eating obsession, one finds a mix of positive and negative personality characteristics in those with Prader-Willi syndrome. Friendly, talkative, cheerful, and good-natured, they also can be stubborn, quick to anger, and given to temper tantrums. Temper outbursts are especially notable after age 4 years (Curfs, 1997). The tantrums, typically tied to food refusal, tend to persist or even increase in intensity because, in behavioral terms, they eventually are reinforced. The tantrum ultimately is rewarded because the child gets what he or she wants—food! The obsession with food leads to foraging, eating uncooked foods, consuming enormous quantities (e.g., 10 pies at a sitting!), and, along with eating food that is unclean, even eating dog food. Another prominent characteristic, and one that is shared with autistic children, is a strong need for structure and predictability, "routine." Individuals with Prader-Willi syndrome are upset by change and benefit from firm limits.

Other problem behaviors are habitual skin picking and scratching; compulsions (other than eating), such as collecting or hoarding; rage reactions—not always about food; depression; and even psychosis. Psychotic behavior consisting of either visual or auditory hallucinations was observed in a 41-year-old woman who was apprehensive about a forthcoming minor surgery. Although she benefited from counseling, her hallucinations persisted, the surgery was withheld, and she became increasingly paranoid (Goldman, 1988).

The management of even the young child is complicated as the youngster moves into nonfamily settings such as day care or school, in which other children have ready access to food. In adolescence, "crises" can be precipitated by tantrums in food stores or by actual theft of money for food, or food itself. Local merchants, neighbors, and even strangers may be victimized (Sulzbacher, 1988). Because the behavior of affected individuals can get the attention of the police, it is suggested that contact with local merchants and the police be made to advise them of the child's disorder.

Intellectual Functioning. Virtually everyone with Prader-Willi syndrome has some cognitive impairment. Although IQs can vary from 20 to 90, from profound retardation to average intelligence, most have IQs in the borderline (70 to 79) or mildly retarded (IQ 55 to 69) ranges (Greenswag, 1987; Holm, 1981; Sulzbacher, 1988). Summarizing data from a large series of studies, IQ proportions were as follows: 86 or higher 5%, borderline 27%, mild retardation 34%, moderate retardation 27%, severe retardation 5%, and profound retardation less than 1% (Curfs, 1997; Curfs & Fryns, 1992).

The school-aged child has been described as talkative, concrete, and argumentative. Often clever and devious in hatching schemes to get food, his or her general judgment is said to be poor, even relative to IQ (Sulzbacher, 1988).

Educational Needs.   Given the prominence of some degree of cognitive impairment, difficulties in learning are present, often the kinds of developmental learning disorders described in Chapter 10 ("learning disabilities") rather than those caused by mental retardation itself. Math is likely to be a problem area (Cassidy, 1984), along with attention deficit. In contrast, long-term memory along with reading appear to be relative strengths.

Youths with Prader-Willi syndrome also appear resistant to physical activities, weight aside, and are not well coordinated (Lupi, 1988).

The most challenging aspect of meeting the educational needs as well as the general health of the affected child is controlling access to food in the school setting (Lupi & Porcella, 1987). A series of recommendations (Inwood, 1986) stress the need to provide food only at a *specific* time; to avoid punishing for taking food, because it is involuntary, or withdrawing food as a form of punishment, as it may lead only to increased upset; and to remove the child from the eating area after the meal is completed. The stringency of these recommendations is reflected in another guideline that would not allow the child to be alone in a setting in which food is available or even move about the school unescorted (Lupi & Porcella, 1985).

On the positive side, the child with Prader-Willi syndrome is to be complimented and otherwise "reinforced" for controlling his or her weight. Reinforcers might include access to activities of special interest (obviously this is not the place for M&Ms!).

Another potential problem in school is the tendency to sleepiness, Dickens's "somnolence." The teacher is encouraged to avoid activities that require long periods of "in-seat" behavior. A mix of in-seat and out-of-seat activities is recommended (Lupi, 1988).

It is clear that the individualized education plan for the Prader-Willi child must include careful management procedures in addition to purely academic goals!

Developmental Course.   A survey of parents and other caregivers of adults with Prader-Willi syndrome includes a picture of their early development (Greenswag, 1987). Major delays in infancy and early childhood were noted in both motor and language skills. In the motor area, the average age for sitting was 12 months (7 months in the normally developed infant), and walking was not accomplished until 27 months (13 months in the normal child). Single words, first heard in the nondelayed child at about 10 months, did not appear until 28 months, and two- to four-word phrases, commonly present by age 24 months, did not arise until almost age 3 years (35 months). The great majority were in special education during the school years, with particular difficulties in arithmetic. As noted previously, reading was less impaired.

Sexual development was much affected. Together with genital underdevelopment, 60% of the males had surgery for undescended testicles, and only 10% of the females had any menstrual history. If menses were present, the average age at onset was 17 years. Sex-hormone therapy was tried with both sexes, more so with males (Rubin & Cassidy, 1988). There has been some ambivalence about hormone treatment for males, fearing increased aggressiveness, but youth who have experienced greater virilization report a greater sense of well-being.

Not surprisingly, the disorder creates family stress. By young adulthood, about half of individuals with the syndrome have moved from the family residence to either special group homes for Prader-Willi adults or other residential settings for retarded adults. In their daily activity, a fair proportion (46%) is employed in sheltered workshops, but more than one third (35%) is in no day program at all!

Treatment. In spite of seemingly formidable odds, control of weight and avoidance of obesity has been achieved in some children and youth. On special diets, preferably begun in early childhood but sometimes not until adolescence, weight control is achievable, sometimes with startling effects (Holm, Sulzbacher, & Pipes, 1981). In the medical area, appetite suppressants generally have been ineffective. In an effort to decrease the proportion of fat to muscle as well as to increase stature itself, growth hormone has been tried (e.g., Pfadt & Angulo, 1991), but its use is controversial.

A number of states have created special residential programs. Group homes, serving perhaps six or fewer individuals and providing strict control of food access have proven effective. Group homes serving a mix of Prader-Willi and non–Prader-Willi individuals have been less successful (Thompson, Greenswag, & Eleazer, 1988). There are also some adults who can live independently, but this is generally not feasible over a long period of time. An effective treatment program produces measurable weight loss, is sensitive to the emotional and behavioral problems encountered, assures access to appropriate educational and vocational services, and encourages participation in community-based jobs and recreation. Central to any program is the need for "total, consistent, 24-hour supervision with a minimum of change and few surprises" (Thompson et al., 1988). Moreover, such dietary restriction must be lifelong as, for example, in the case of diabetes (Dykens et al., 1997). Apparently, it can be done!

15q– (Angelman or Happy Puppet Syndrome)

This disorder is the chromosomal obverse of Prader-Willi syndrome, as indicated in the introduction to this section on deletion. The loss of chromosomal material is on the same chromosome as in Prader-Willi, but here the deletion occurs on the 15 chromosome contributed by the mother. Again, as in the case of Prader-Willi, the chromosomal abnormality is present only in the maternal egg cell; all other maternal cells are normal. As noted by Hagerman (1992) in his description of Prader-Willi and Angelman syndromes, the gender of the transmitting parent somehow "imprints" the genetic information, allowing a unique contribution.

The major symptoms of Angelman syndrome are a large mouth, widely spaced teeth, an abnormal projection of the jaw (prognathism), abrupt inappropriate laughter, lack of motor coordination and jerky moments, absence of speech, and mental retardation.

The developmental picture is one of generalized delay, especially notable in the motor sphere. The motor abnormality ultimately can lead to a wheelchair-bound state. Leg contractures and spinal curvature (scoliosis) also are found. Seizures are particularly common.

The cognitive effect is one of severe to profound retardation. In a study of 17 children and youth, ages 5 to 20 years (Clayton-Smith, 1992), self-help skills were extremely limited. Although most could self-feed using utensils, all needed aid with dressing and most were only "day" trained, toilet-wise. Speech was much impaired. Although some words might be present, signs and gestures were the most common forms of communication.

A characteristic of the disorder is a highly affectionate nature. Although appropriate in childhood, its immature persistence into adulthood can create problems.

Dividers of the Sex Chromosomes

Klinefelter Syndrome (XXY)

This is a disorder affecting males caused by the presence of an extra X chromosome. Instead of single X and Y chromosome being present, males have a second X chromosome, or 47 chromosomes in all. Occurring in about 1 in 1000 births (Hagerman, 1992), the condition is so variant in its manifestation that its diagnosis may not be made before late adolescence or young adulthood, and then only because of an infertility problem.

Arising from a deficiency in testosterone, the male hormone, its chief symptoms are underdeveloped genitalia (hypogonadism), infertility, and some degree of cognitive impairment. The preadolescent youth is slim and has relatively long limbs and small testes. Treatment for the hypogonadism consists of testosterone replacement, beginning at 11 or 12 years old (Mandoki, Sumner, Hoffman, & Riconda, 1991).

Cognitive development is extraordinarily variable, from essentially normal intelligence to mental retardation. The majority of affected individuals are in the average or above intelligence ranges, with about one fifth (19%) with IQs below 90 (Hagerman, 1992; Mandoki et al., 1991). Of those with retardation, the majority are not more than mildly impaired. Interestingly, the disorder selectively affects intellectual development, more severely impairing language-related functions. Speech and reading difficulties are prominent. In its milder form, reading problems may present as a "specific learning disability" as distinct from mental retardation.

The reciprocal relationship between Angelman and Prader-Willi syndromes also appears to exist in the cognitive domain. In Angelman there is a greater impairment in language than in mathematics; the converse is true in Prader-Willi. In addition to the variable intellectual impairment, motor skills also are affected. Impairments are present in both gross- and fine-motor skills, and in speed, dexterity, and strength.

Not surprisingly in a hormone-related disorder, there is some effect on personality and, of course, on sexual interest. Affected individuals tend to be introverted, quiet, passive, and immature and show less interest in sex (Mandoki et al., 1991).

The genetics of Klinefelter syndrome merit further comment. Although affected males usually have only one additional X chromosome, in some cases two or even three additional X chromosomes are found. Mosaicism is common, with males showing cell lines of XY or XX, in addition to XXY. The mosaic form is associated with less severe physical effects (Hagerman, 1992). As in the case of Down syndrome, the presence of normal cells in the mosaic variant appears to reduce the degree of abnormality.

Klinefelter syndrome also reveals the central role of the Y chromosome in the sex determination. If a Y chromosome is present, the person is biologically male irrespective of the number of X chromosomes. It is the Y chromosome that causes an initially undifferentiated embryonic gonad to differentiate into testes and maleness.

XYY Males

A sensationalized chromosomal anomaly when first described in the 1970s, this is a disorder in which the male has an extra Y chromosome. Compared with a general frequency of about 1 in 700 male births (Leonard, Landy, Ruddle, & Lubs, 1974), a much higher prevalence was found in prison populations (Nyhan & Sakati, 1970). It is important to understand, however, that only 1% of males with XYY are incarcerated. Thus, virtually all XYY males are free of antisocial behavior. There are no typical physical manifestations, but some motor problems are seen (Hagerman, 1992). Intellect is grossly unimpaired, although an average reduction of 10 IQ points is indicated (Baker, Telfer, Richardson, & Clark, 1970; Nielsen, 1970).

Although the finding of an increased frequency of XYY males in a prison population suggested a relationship between the extra Y chromosome and antisocial or aggressive behavior, the chief behavioral characteristic associated with the disorder is not criminality but rather increased impulsivity (Hook, 1973; Noel, Duport, Revil, Dussuyer, & Quach, 1974). Other behaviors noted are hyperactivity, interpersonal difficulties, and, in fact, some aggression (Hagerman, 1992).

Turner Syndrome (XO)

Affecting only females, this is a condition in which the female has only one X chromosome, apparently the only chromosome for which complete absence of a chromosome is compatible with life. This may relate to the lyonization phenomenon. In the normal female cell with two X chromosomes, only one of the two is functional at any given time. Parenthetically, in Turner syndrome, it is usually the paternal X chromosome that is missing (Smith, 1982). The absence of the X chromosome, however, is not without its price. Virtually all XO conceptions are not viable (Hecht & MacFarlane, 1969). Less severe are mosaic forms (XO/XX), the same phenomenon noted earlier in Down and Klinefelter syndromes.

Variable prevalences have been reported, the most recent being 1 in 1000 (Hagerman, 1992). Variable in its symptomatology, Turner syndrome's most consistent features are small stature, sexual infantilism (because of incomplete ovarian development) (Smith, 1982), and absence of an adolescent growth spurt. Treatment consists of cyclic estrogen replacement in adolescence. Because of the ovarian dysgenesis, affected women usually are unable to conceive (Smith, 1982).

Intelligence is typically in the normal range, although some visual-spatial cognitive difficulties are seen. There are special problems in understanding spatial relationships and in visual-motor representation (Alexander, Ehrhardt, & Money, 1966; Alexander & Money, 1965). Difficulties are encountered in drawing, copying designs, handwriting, map reading, and finding one's way in unfamiliar settings (Hagerman, 1992).

Motor difficulties are very common, including hypotonia (Salbenblatt, Meyer, Bender, Linden, & Robinson, 1987). Less frequently, about one third (30%) show attention-deficit disorder with hyperactivity and may benefit from the use of medication (Hagerman, 1992).

47 XXX, 48 XXXX, 49 XXXXX (Penta X Syndrome)

In Turner syndrome we have females with a missing chromosome; in these disorders females may have one or more extra X chromosomes. The three variants, each affecting the *total* number of chromosomes, vary considerably from each other.

47 XXX.   Occurring in about 1 in 850 births, the single additional X chromosome produces no specific physical abnormality. Some cognitive problems are found, notably in receptive and expressive language. Speech difficulties are especially prominent, from severe articulation problems to the absence of speech itself. Poor motor coordination, shyness, and immaturity also have been noted (Linden, Bender, Harmon, Mrazek, & Robinson, 1988).

48 XXXX.   Here there are two additional X chromosomes. As in the case of 47 XXX, there are no particular physical abnormalities but the cognitive effects are much greater (Smith, 1982). Retardation, usually mild to moderate in degree, is generally present, although IQs may range from 30 to 80.

49 XXXXX (Penta X Syndrome).   First described in 1963 (Kesaree & Wooley, 1963), in this syndrome females are found who actually have three extra X chromosomes, or 49 chromosomes in all. In this, the most extreme of the X-chromosome variants, there are significant physical abnormalities; growth is impaired and retardation, moderate to severe in degree, is present (Smith, 1982).

☐ Genetic Disorders: Genes and Mental Retardation

Our focus now shifts from the *chromosomes* to the *genes*. Although the chromosomes actually are made up of genes, the chromosomal disorders, apart from translocations, are not heritable in the usual meaning of that term. Rather it is disorders attributable to single genes and transmitted from parents to children that largely constitute what we mean by "inherited" disorders. Three kinds of gene mechanisms are illustrated, two of which, dominant and recessive, are associated with specific disorders associated with mental retardation. The third, multifactor or polygenic inheritance, is presented because of its possible role in what used to be called "cultural-familial" retardation, now termed "psychosocial" retardation. The latter designation has been retained in the 1992 AAMR definition of mental retardation and, unlike its progenitor, implies a totally nongenetic causation. In contrast, it is our view that heredity plays *some* role in general intelligence, and that role is discussed in terms of polygenic inheritance.

Dominant Inheritance

Conditions inherited through a dominant gene are those that are likely to recur in successive generations. Typically, one of the parents is a carrier of the dominant gene, and each child has a 50% probability of inheriting that

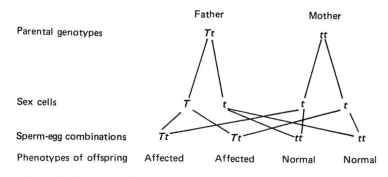

FIGURE 3.6. Mechanism of dominant inheritance.

gene. This gene mechanism is illustrated in Figure 3.6, in connection with tuberous sclerosis. Dominantly inherited conditions that include mental retardation are relatively rare because retardation itself reduces the likelihood of parenting.

Tuberous Sclerosis

This syndrome is caused by just one member of a pair of genes. To illustrate the genetic mechanism (see Fig. 3.6), let each gene be designated by the letter standing for the name of the disease and let that letter also be capital or lower-case depending on whether the gene is dominant or recessive. Thus the dominant gene causing tuberous sclerosis is shown as *T* and the recessive gene, here the gene for "health," as *t*. Located on corresponding parts of a pair of chromosomes, there are two dominant genes connected with the disorder, one on chromosome 9 and one on 16. Either gene can cause the disorder.

Each of us has some combination of these genes, referred to as our *genotype*. The possible gene combinations and their significance for tuberous sclerosis are *TT*—the person has two dominant genes and is affected; *Tt*—the person has one dominant gene and one recessive and also is affected; and *tt*—the person has two recessive genes and is unaffected.

The Tt genotype in which there is one gene for tuberous sclerosis and one for "health" illustrates the meaning of "dominant" inheritance. The two genes do not have equal weight. The mutant or "bad" gene masks the effect of the "good" gene; thus it is designated as *dominant* and the other as *recessive*.

Virtually all readers of these lines, but not all, are tt; that is, free of this disease. Some of us actually may be carriers, Tt, but only marginally affected because of the disorder's wide variability. Let us now see how the gene is transmitted from parent to child. (Parenthetically, it also should be noted that in many families *neither* parent is a carrier and the disorder arises in the child as a new mutation.) Let us assume that one of the parents is a carrier, here the father, but he is only affected to a mild degree. The father is married, works, and has raised a family. His genotype is Tt (TT would be much less probable) and his wife, who is free of the disease, is tt. Figure 3.6 shows the parental genotypes, the sperm and egg cells formed by reduction (meiotic) division, the possible combination of sperm and egg cell at fertilization, and the phenotypes of the children. Those phenotypes show half affected and half unaffected. It should be understood, however, that the 50% risk for each child is only a statement of statistical *probability*. By chance all children could be affected or none. The probability of each of these outcomes is the same, that probability being expressed as $1/2^4$ or $1/2 \times 1/2 \times 1/2 \times 1/2 = 1/16$. Note that the probabilities of occurrence for dominantly inherited disorders are the same as those for the sex of a child. At conception, with the egg fertilized by either an X- or Y-bearing sperm cell, the probability of male or female is a one in two probability that is represented in the general population! Roughly half of us are male and half female. But your family may have equal numbers of sons and daughters or more of one gender than the other. Thus, in a family of four, all children may be male or female, a probability of 1 in 16. By way of prediction, what can be said in a dominant disorder is that each child has a 50% risk of inheriting it.

Now to the disorder itself. With a prevalence of 1 in 9500 in the general population (Gomez, 1988), tuberous sclerosis has three main symptoms—seizures (epilepsy), facial angiofibroma (a nonmalignant vascular fibrous tumor appearing on the face in the form of a butterfly-shaped rash), and mental retardation. Other areas affected are the eyes, heart, kidney and lungs. Tumors in these organs can be life-threatening. Tuberous sclerosis is actually one of a group of diseases associated with abnormalities of the skin and nervous system (de la Cruz & LaVeck, 1962). The complete triad of seizures, retardation, and facial angiofibroma is present in only about 30% of affected individuals; 6% have none of the main features (Gomez, 1988).

The disorder may arise in a seemingly normal infant, seizures being its initial manifestation. These usually take the form of *infantile spasms* and generally are present by age 17 months. Lasting only seconds, this form of epileptic seizure involves the sudden flexion of the upper body and the drawing up of the knees (the so-called salaam posture). These seizures can be repetitive and physically dangerous to the child if they occur when the child is standing. Protective head gear commonly is worn. With the onset of seizures, development slows or may even regress. But the regression is only temporary, and the condition eventually stabilizes. Tuberous sclerosis is not a degenerative neurological disorder.

This is a condition in which the seizures, a result of calcifications in the brain, are thought to adversely affect mental development, their severity related to the extent of calcification. Although anticonvulsants are the primary means of trying to control seizures, psychological procedures also can be helpful. A 3-year-old girl was taught to alert herself to an impending seizure, instructed to "stop" the seizure, and rewarded with hugs and praise when she was successful. She was able to reduce the frequency of seizures and at age 7 years, with the aid of an anticonvulsant (Tegretal), achieved full control. Her intellectual functioning was unimpaired, and she was making normal school progress (Lane & Samples, 1984).

Variability of the effects of the disorder also is seen in the cognitive realm, apparently much related to the presence of seizures and, particularly, their time of onset (Gomez, 1988). Retardation is almost always present (91%) if seizures originate in the first year of life. Later seizure onset, on the other hand, does not necessarily result in retardation. Among a series of 59 patients with tuberous sclerosis who were of an average intelligence, no less than two thirds also had seizures. It is seizure onset in infancy that poses the greatest risk.

Estimates of the overall rate of retardation vary with the age groups studied. In children, some 80% show retardation (Hunt & Dennis, 1987). If the population includes adults as well as children, and adults who may be asymptomatic, the rate of retardation falls to about 50% (Gomez, 1988).

A 14-year-old girl illustrates those individuals with significant cognitive impairment but not mental retardation. Reportedly normal in achieving her early developmental milestones, difficulties were encountered in first grade. With an IQ of 81 she functions in the "low average" intelligence range and needs special assistance in school (Miller & Bigler, 1982).

The language area seems to be particularly at risk. Parents often report "communication" problems. Emily, a bright and friendly 4-year-old, is normal in her physical development but is totally lacking in speech. She can produce sounds but not words. We can assume that calcifications exist in the brain areas involved with the production of speech.

Behavior problems also often are present. Hyperactivity and aggression are seen and, in children with infantile spasms, one may observe autism (Hunt & Dennis, 1987). A major impairment in interpersonal behavior is one of the hallmarks of autism (see Chapter 10), and the onset of seizures may see a change in social relatedness, from normal responsiveness to withdrawal.

A Family with Tuberous Sclerosis.   Wallace and Jean, a rural couple, have four children. Wallace is 27 years old, is poorly educated, and works as a farm laborer. He is in good health. His wife Jean is 25 years old;

she also has a very limited education and is a housewife. Her general health is also good. Their eldest child, Martha, at age 5 years is severely retarded and has no speech, although her hearing is intact. Martha developed normally until the age of 18 months when seizures began. They were of the grand mal variety. Her seizures have been fairly well controlled through medication, but continuing seizures threaten further intellectual decline. At age 5 years she shows the standard symptom triad—facial angioma on cheeks, chin, and forehead; seizures; and mental retardation. The three other children are ages 4 years, 2 years, and 5 months. Four-year-old John is in good health, but 2-year-old Stanley began to have seizures and his development has slowed. The youngest child is only 5 months, too young to know whether she is affected.

In addition to at least two of the four children having the condition, the father has the facial angioma. He has never had seizures and, although slow, he is not retarded. Given the risks for each child, it was recommended to the parents that they consider avoiding future pregnancies, an option with which they agreed.

Neurofibromatosis (Recklinghausen Disease)

Another of the dominantly inherited skin disorders, neurofibromatosis' main symptoms are areas of abnormal skin pigmentation (café-au-lait spots), nonmalignant tumors (neurofibromas) of the nervous system, bone changes, and endocrine and growth disturbances. It also is variable in its clinical manifestation; the neurofibromas are generally just a cosmetic problem (Leroy, 1983). The disease occurs in about 1 in 3000 births and, as in tuberous sclerosis, in only about half the cases does one find affected relatives. Nevertheless, inheritance through at least four generations has been observed repeatedly (Borberg, 1951). Intellectual impairment, attributable to tumors in the brain, is present but only in a minority—some 10% to 25%. The degree of deficit is usually not more than mild (Borberg, 1951; Crowe, Schull, & Neel, 1956).

Rett Syndrome

Rett syndrome first was reported in 1965 by an Austrian physician who noticed two girls in his waiting room who were exhibiting identical hand-wringing movements. Other children in his practice were identified, all girls, and in 1966 he described a syndrome consisting of stereotyped hand movements, dementia, autistic behavior, lack of facial expression, ataxic gait, cortical brain atrophy, and hyperammonemia (Rett, 1966). Hyperammonemia generally has not been found (Menkes, 1995). Unaware of Rett's work, Hagberg (1980), a Swedish physician, reported on a group of girls who he said showed "infantile autistic disorder" and loss of hand use. When familiarized with Rett's work, he termed the disorder *Rett syndrome* (Hagberg, 1985).

Prevalence and Causation. A generally rare disorder, in the Swedish population Rett syndrome is found in about 1 in 15,000 girls (Menkes, 1995). Speculation as to its cause centers on a dominant gene present on the X chromosome. The gene is presumed to be lethal to boys, male conceptions not surviving (Hagberg, Aicardi, Dias, & Ramos, 1983).

Clinical Picture. The clinical picture is one of grossly normal development during the first 5 or 6 months of life followed by developmental arrest and then regression. The child comes to show an acquired microcephaly (because of atrophy of the cerebrum); impairment in motor coordination, movement, and balance; and autistic-like behavior (Menkes, 1995). Purposeful hand use is lost, usually by 6 to 8 months of age, although sometimes not until age 3 or 4 years. The distinctive hand mannerisms, hand wringing or hand-to-mouth movements, appear shortly thereafter and occupy much of the child's waking time. They are considered the most diagnostic feature (Trevanthan & Naidu, 1988).

Four stages in the disorder have been identified: stage I, early onset (stagnation in development)—onset in the age range of 6 to 18 months and lasting only months; stage II, rapid destructive—onset 1 to 3 years, duration weeks to months; stage III, pseudostationary—onset 2 to 10 years, duration months to years; and stage IV, late motor deterioration—onset age 10 years or older, duration years (Hagberg & Witt-Engerstrom, 1986; Trevanthan & Naidu, 1988). Some question has arisen regarding the labeling of these stages, but the stages themselves are recognized.

The cognitive, linguistic, and adaptive abilities of these children are very limited. Infants who had begun to develop speech lose their words and, generally, have little expressive or receptive language. Cognitive ability usually does not exceed the 1-year developmental level, although somewhat greater ability may be achieved in simple self-care skills (Fontanesi & Haas, 1988).

The motor abnormalities involve poor muscle coordination (apraxia) of the trunk and limbs. Movements may be jerky, balance is poor, and there may be tremors. Especially characteristic is walking gait, in those who can walk. Gait is broad-based with a jerky unbalanced quality, legs are stiff, and there is lateral swaying. Toe-walking also may be seen.

Other prominent features consist of seizures, irregularities in breathing, and spinal curvature (scoliosis). Another interesting feature, one noted in the course of an intensive behavior treatment program of three children who were originally diagnosed as autistic, is a striking variation in the child's attention and general responsiveness (Smith, Klevstrand, & Lovaas, 1995). The three children each had periods of almost complete unresponsiveness to social and sensory stimuli. These often lasted for several days, and no medical basis for them was found. Parenthetically, in spite of a treatment effort that exceeded 2 years, no significant improvement was attained with reference to unresponsiveness. Menkes (1995) suggests that the use of carbamazepine, an anticonvulsant, can improve alertness and can be helpful even in the absence of seizures.

In spite of the severity of the disorder and its very early onset, children with Rett syndrome can live on into adulthood. In one study of a mentally retarded institutional adult population, 1 in 46 females were viewed as meeting the diagnostic criteria for the condition (Burd, Randall, Martsolf, & Kerbeshian, 1991).

No treatment for the disorder currently exists.

Rubinstein-Taybi Syndrome

First described in 1963 (Rubinstein & Taybi, 1963), this disorder is characterized by anatomic abnormalities of the face, thumb, and big toe. Affecting equally both sexes, the nose is beaked, and the thumb and big toe are broadened and flattened and deviate laterally. Other facial anomalies consist of a downward slant of the palpebral fissures, a small mouth, a high-arched palate, and a "pouting" lower lip (Hennekam et al., 1992; Rubinstein, 1969; Stevens, Carey, & Blackburn, 1990).

Health problems abound (Stevens et al., 1990). They include feeding difficulties and poor weight gain in the newborn, and eye, ear, head, respiratory, urinary, and dental problems. Individuals tend to be short in stature, and head circumference may be much reduced (microcephaly). The thumb and toe deformities have been treated by surgery and, although commonly improved, may recur.

Prevalence and Causation.   A rare condition, Rubinstein-Taybi syndrome has an incidence estimated at 1 in 125,000 births. Its cause is unknown, but it is thought to be due to the mutation of an autosomal dominant gene (Hennekam et al., 1992).

Behavioral Aspects.   Studies of intellectual functioning have found IQ varying from profound retardation to the borderline intelligence range. Two of the larger studies reported mean IQs of 51 (range 30 to 79) and 36 (range 25 to 79), the former based on children living at home, average age 8 years (Stevens et al., 1990), and the latter on an older group, average age 18 years, some of whom were institutionalized (Hannekam, 1992).

All developmental milestones are much delayed, for example, not walking until an average of 2.5 years or producing first words until 2 years.

Of particular interest in older children is some tendency to perform better on nonverbal measures of intelligence. The disorder does produce language and speech difficulties, and speech therapy is common; the children often use signs to complement their spoken language (Stevens et al., 1990). Nevertheless, Hennekam et al. (1992) see these children as making good use of the communication skills that they do have. In fact, they are described quite positively in behavioral terms. They are viewed as loving, friendly, and generally happy children. Serious behavior problems are rare. They do appear to have particularly short attention spans, commonly engage in stereotyped self-stimulating movements, and may be disturbed by loud sounds.

Williams (Elfin-Facies) Syndrome

This syndrome is of special interest because of the presence of unusual speech fluency in the presence of mental retardation. Originally attributed to hypercalcemia, elevated blood calcium, this metabolic abnormality usually is not found (Menkes, 1995).

Clinical Features.   The disorder is characterized by an unusual facial appearance, an elfin-like facies. Finger nails are underdeveloped and deep-set, more than half of the children have a star-like pattern in their irises, and teeth are widely spaced. The brain is underdeveloped, and its specific abnormalities indicate developmental disruption occurring either late in pregnancy or during early infancy (Menkes, 1995). Other common features are a heart murmur and reduced height. Feeding difficulties are present in infancy, along with a hoarse cry. In some children there is a period of normal development with the initial symptoms in the form of a sudden failure to thrive (major eating difficulties) (Bennett, LaVeck, & Selms, 1978).

Prevalence and Causation.   A relatively rare disorder, its estimated incidence is 1 in 10,000 births. It is thought to be genetic in origin, inherited as an autosomal dominant trait; presumably the *mutation* of a dominant gene, because parents and siblings are commonly unaffected.

Cognitive Aspects.   On intelligence tests children show a fairly specific pattern of strengths and weaknesses. With IQs in the mid-50s, but ranging from 30 to 80 (Bennett et al., 1978; Jones & Smith, 1975), they show relatively good function in verbal, memory, and quantitative abilities, but much impaired ability in visual-spatial understanding. Their motor ability is also poor, with difficulties in balance and coordination.

Speech.   Within the context of an undoubted picture of mental retardation, speech fluency of children with Williams syndrome is notable. They are described as "talkative"; their speech gives the impression of a greater intelligence than is actually present (Bennett et al., 1978; Von Arnim & Engel, 1964). The flow of speech is captured in one child who responded to a question with a series of statements in which each thought provided the stimulus for the next one—a kind of uninhibited associational flight of ideas. There is a sense on the part of the listener that the children enjoy talking. Other children have been characterized as "eloquent" or "loquacious." The adolescent has been described as having a rich and colorful vocabulary, a sense of grammar, but severe spatial deficits.

Social Skills.   Along with their chattiness, the children are portrayed as outgoing and lively but relating much better to adults than to peers. Although earlier described as "happy" and generally free of serious behavior problems (Jones & Smith, 1975), more recent studies indicate the common presence of significant behavior disorder (Einfeld, Tonge, & Florio, 1997; Gosch & Pankau, 1994; Udwin & Yule, 1991).

General Behavioral Picture.   A behavioral picture emerges of overly affectionate, attention-seeking children who prefer the company of adults to that of peers. Although often described as anxious and tense, euphoric mood states also are found. These children tend to fixate on an idea or an activity and to show heightened sensitivity to sound (hyperacusis). Although some of these behaviors are autistic-like, their great social need and often good verbal skills distinguish them from those with autism. The authors of a carefully researched study consider that the behavior problems associated with the disorder are sufficiently characteristic to warrant the designation of *Williams syndrome behavior disorder* in the psychiatric nomenclature (Einfeld et al., 1997).

Etiology Obscure but with an Occasional Dominant Mode of Inheritance

Sturge-Weber Syndrome

A disorder involving the skin and the central nervous system, its three chief manifestations are facial angioma (a port wine–colored nevus), seizures (caused by brain calcifications, as in tuberous sclerosis), and mental retardation of varying degrees. Less often found are hemiparesis and glaucoma. Familial occurrence is rare (Warkany, 1971).

Craniostenosis

Premature closure of the sutures of the skull results in deformities of the head and also may lead to damage to the brain and eyes. The most severe abnormalities occur if the closure *precedes* birth. If growth is constrained, usually in the lateral direction, the head tends to be elevated vertically. Cerebral convolutions are flattened, meaning an absolute reduction in the volume of brain tissue, and there may be hydrocephaly, optic neuritis, and brain atrophy. To allow for growth of the expanding brain (in infancy), the prematurely closed skull is opened surgically in the first few months of life (Graham, 1983). Of the craniostenoses, two are sometimes associated with mental retardation—Crouzon syndrome (craniofacial dysostosis) and Apert syndrome (acrocephalosyndactyly). In Apert syndrome, skull and facial deformity is combined with fusion of the fingers. In Crouzon syndrome, dominant inheritance usually is seen, whereas inheritance is rarely found in Apert syndrome. As in tuberous sclerosis, in the absence of a family history, it is presumed that the condition arises from a new mutation (Smith, 1982). In keeping with other disorders of this type, cognitive effects are extremely variable (Blank, 1960).

Recessive Inheritance

Here we study genetic disorders that are not present in the parents. In recessively inherited conditions, parents are typically *carriers* of the recessive gene but unaffected by it because the gene for health carries greater weight. Figure 3.7 illustrates recessive inheritance. Denoting the recessive gene as *p* (for the condition PKU) and the dominant gene as *P*, the figure shows the parental genotypes (both parents are carriers), the kind of sperm and egg cells that can be formed from the genotypes, the

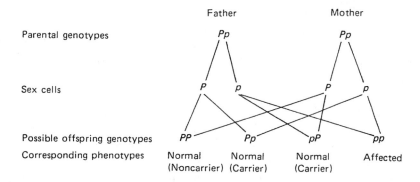

FIGURE 3.7. Mechanism of recessive inheritance.

possible sperm-egg combinations at conception, and the phenotypes of the children. The possible phenotypes show three children as normal and one affected. This illustrates the Mendelian 3:1 ratio associated with recessive inheritance. Once again it should be understood that a 3:1 distribution of unaffected to affected children is only a statement of *probability* and, as in dominant inheritance, any combination is possible. The probability of two consecutive affected children in a condition that has a probability of 1 in 4 is $1/4^2$ or 1 in 16. For three consecutive affected children it is $1/4^3$ or 1 in 64, and for four consecutive affected pregnancies it is $1/4^4$ or 1 in 256. It is this kind of information that can be communicated to carrier parents as they consider their childbearing risk.

Recessive disorders are best understood as "inborn errors of metabolism." The mutant or recessive genes cause the absence or deficiency of an enzyme, a biochemical substance necessary to proper metabolism. A large number of recessive disorders are known; in Table 3.1 we list some of the variably treatable ones associated with mental retardation. Well-known recessive disorders that do not produce retardation include cystic fibrosis and muscular dystrophy. The latter is caused by a recessive gene on the X chromosome. An example of a sex-linked recessive disorder sometimes associated with mental retardation is fragile X syndrome; it is discussed subsequently.

Phenylketonuria

This is a recessively inherited disorder, recognizable at birth, and preventable through a special diet. If untreated, it leads to severe mental retardation. One of the "inborn errors of metabolism," the recessive gene in double dose interferes with the production of an enzyme, tyrosine. Tyrosine maintains the proper blood concentration of a substance called phenylalanine. In PKU and its numerous lesser variants (e.g., mild hypephenylalanenemia), the level of phenylalanine is elevated and can be toxic to the brain.

The nature of the biochemical deficiency is shown at point A in Figure 3.8. Also illustrated are three other recessive conditions related to tyrosine metabolism. One of them, albinism, a condition of reduced pigmentation, is well known to all of us. None of the other of these disorders is associated with mental retardation.

Prevalence. Phenylketonuria occurs in about 1 in 8000 US births (DiLella, Marvit, Lidsky, Güttler, & Woo, 1986). Approximately 1 in 50 in the general population is a carrier of the recessive gene.

Clinical Features. Prior to the advent of the early diagnosis and dietary treatment of the disorder, the clinical picture was of a normal

TABLE 3.1. Some variably treatable recessively inherited disorders associated with mental retardation

Disorder	Clinical features	Prenatal detection	Treatment
Argininemia	Spastic diplegia, seizures	No	Substances with a beneficial metabolic effect
Galactosemia (classic)	Symptoms follow milk feedings: anorexia, vomiting, liver disease; later onset of cataracts, and physical retardation	Yes	Special diet; neurological damage and ovarian failure can occur despite treatment; nonclassic forms of the disorder are galactokinase and epimerase deficiency
Homocystinuria (classic)	Lens dislocation, elongation of legs, feet, and fingers; blood vessel disease, fair hair and skin	Yes	Special diet
Lesch-Nyhan disease (sex-linked)	Appearing normal in infancy, motor symptoms arise with loss of head and trunk control; variable degrees of retardation, though some are unimpaired; prominent self-injurious behavior	No	Substances with a beneficial metabolic effect
Maple-syrup urine disease	Appears normal at birth; sucking and swallowing difficulties; seizures, urine disorder of maple syrup; if untreated, severe retardation	Yes	Special diet; this is a transient form with only episodic needs for treatment
Phenylketonuria (classic)	Appears normal at birth; if untreated—hyperactivity, irritability, musty urine odor; severe retardation, lighter skin coloring (decreased skin pigmentation); eczema; seizures; reduced stature and head size	No	Special diet; there are milder forms that may not require dietary restriction
Tyrosinemia (type 1)	Early enlargement of liver and spleen; vitamin D–resistant rickets, liver disease	No	Special diet can slow but not prevent liver disease; liver transplantation has been successful in some children

Note. After Howard-Teplansky, 1992; and Leroy, 1983.

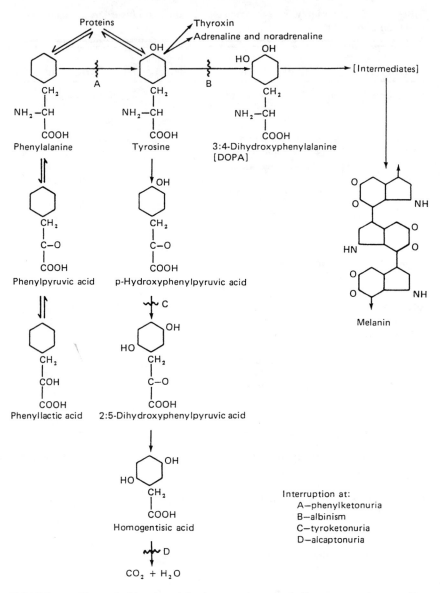

FIGURE 3.8. The probable phenylalanine-tyrosine metabolic sequence in man. The points at which this sequence appears to be interrupted by known inherited metabolic defects in man are indicated by wavy lines. The key to the specific defect involved is given in the lower right-hand corner of the figure. (With modifications after Crowe and Schull, Folia hered. et path., 1:259, 1952, and reprinted from Neel and Schull, 1954. Copyright 1954 by The University of Chicago. All rights reserved.)

appearing infant who later began to show hyperactivity, irritability, eczema, and, eventually, severe mental retardation (Howard-Teplansky, 1992). All newborns are now screened for PKU, as well as for other inborn metabolic errors, and, if detected, the affected infant is placed on a special low-phenylalanine diet. Indeed, the classic full-blown disorder is now no longer seen. The early-treated child generally functions intelligence-wise in the "average" range with IQs commonly varying between 90 and 99 (Dobson, Kushida, Williamson, & Friedman, 1977; Holtzman, Kronmal, Van Doorninck, Azen, & Koch, 1986; Koch, Azen, Friedman, & Williamson, 1984). It also appears that prior to age 10 years, adverse effects also can follow either too-low levels of phenylalanine caused by excessive treatment or untreated major rises in phenylalanine (Scriver, Kaufman, Eisensmith, & Woo, 1995). Lower IQs, typically in the 80 to 89 or "low average" range, are found in children who did not begin the diet for several months.

Although there is no question about the benefits of early diagnosis and dietary treatment, there tends to be *some* difference between even early-treated PKU children and their unaffected siblings in terms of IQ, school achievement, and general behavior. IQ-wise, the PKU child functions, on the average, some 6 to 7 points below his unaffected siblings, and also tends to perform at a lesser level in arithmetic (Berry, O'Grady, Perlmutter, & Botinger, 1979). In comparison with siblings, the PKU child also may show a slower reaction time (Krause et al., 1985); and neuropsychological studies indicate difficulties in the visuospatial, visual-motor, and conceptual spheres (Brunner, Jordan, & Berry, 1983; Pennington, van Doornick, McCabe, & McCabe, 1985). Mathematical and spatial abilities appear to go together.

The research of Diamond and her colleagues (Diamond, Prevor, Callender, & Davis, 1997) helps to explain the persistent difference between children on the diet and their unaffected siblings. She has shown that phenylalanine levels hitherto thought safe (6–10 mg/ml), or three to five times the normal level, are associated with mild impairments in immediate memory and response inhibition. These are cognitive functions specific to the *prefrontal* cortex; no other cortical area seems to be adversely affected at this level. Moreover, at levels less than three times greater than normal, these effects are not found.

There have been modifications in the low-phenylalanine diet since its inception. Initially it was extremely unpalatable, and it was difficult to restrict children to the diet after infancy. Because of the vulnerability of the developing brain to high phenylalanine levels, the goal was to keep the child on the diet at least until school age. By that time brain development was largely completed and it was thought that the child would no longer be vulnerable to the effects of a return to high phenylalanine levels. But a number of studies indicated that discontinuing the diet before age 6 years resulted in a small but significant decline in IQ.

Current recommendations in the United States and Great Britain call for maintaining the diet until at least age 10 years (Griffiths, Smith, & Harvie, 1997). After age 10, exposure to higher levels of phenylalanine during adolescence and adulthood do not appear to have any major cognitive consequences (Griffiths et al., 1997; Schmidt, Mahle, Michel, & Pietz, 1987).

Given the special needs of females with PKU, it is now recommended that they remain on a low-phenylalanine diet throughout life (Scriver, Kaufman, Eisensmith, & Woo, 1995). Women with phenylketonuria are at special risk during pregnancy because of the toxic effects of high phenylalanine levels on the developing fetus.

Apart from the previously mentioned cognitive problems seen in even those PKU children whose intellectual functioning is grossly unimpaired, a special psychological problem has been described in adults that follows termination of the diet. They are said to be prone to experiencing the condition *agoraphobia*, a fear of being in unfamiliar settings (Waisbren & Levy, 1991).

Maternal-induced Phenylketonuria.   The special risk during pregnancy of the phenylketonuric woman has been noted. Having discontinued the diet after childhood, she can now tolerate levels of phenylalanine that would have been damaging in the early developmental years. But these high levels place her baby at risk. In one family of four women with PKU, 9 of their 12 children were cognitively impaired (Farquhar, 1974). A large-scale survey of the children of normal mothers with PKU revealed a symptom picture of mental retardation, microcephaly, congenital heart disease, and low birth weight (Lenke & Levy, 1980). Exposure of the fetus to high maternal phenylalanine levels during the first 3 months of pregnancy accounts for both heart abnormalities and microcephaly, the latter reflecting small brain size. Fortunately, return to low maternal phenylalanine levels prior to and during pregnancy can protect the fetus from such damage (Krywawych, Haseler, & Brenton, 1991).

Thus, in the prevention of mental retardation in genetically vulnerable females through early dietary intervention, we inadvertently have exposed their offspring to retardation, even though these children would likely be not more than carriers of the recessive gene. Assuming that the child is born of a PKU mother who carries only recessive genes, and a noncarrier father who carries only two normal (dominant) genes, all of the children would be carriers (Pp). Not fated for PKU, their early prenatal experience can be just as threatening. Hence the need for dietary precautions on the part of the would-be phenylketonuric mother.

Galactosemia

A particularly rare disorder occurring in about 1 in 60,000 births (Howard-Teplansky, 1992), galactosemia is a potentially fatal disease in which the child lacks the enzyme necessary to metabolize galactose, a constituent of milk. Genetic variations of galactosemia include galactokinase and epimerase deficiency.

The galactosemic infant appears normal at birth, but symptoms follow milk consumption. Like PKU, the full-blown syndrome is rarely seen because of widespread neonatal screening programs and, with its detection, the immediate initiation of a milk-restricted diet. Prior to the development of a special diet, the galactosemic infant suffered severe gastric symptoms, kidney and liver damage, and eventual death. With the diet, however, initial failure-to-thrive symptoms quickly disappear and a state of health is achieved. Given the severity of the disease's symptoms, no less than lifelong adherence to a lactose-restricted diet is necessary.

With the introduction of the special diet, it was thought that major developmental problems could be avoided but, unlike the phenylketonuric diet, this has not proved to be the case. It is now well established that, in spite of early diagnosis and diet initiation, the majority of galactosemic children will show physical and behavioral abnormalities (Holton, 1991; Segal & Berry, 1995). Some degree of cognitive impairment is common, although most function in the low to average intelligence range (IQ 80–89). About one third actually show retardation (Fishler, Donnell, & Wenz, 1980; Komrower & Lee, 1970; Schweitzer, Shin, Jakobs, & Brodehl, 1993; Waggoner, Buist, & Donnell, 1990). There is also indication of some intellectual decline over time, from early childhood through adolescence (Waggoner et al., 1990).

Tay-Sachs Disease

This is an extraordinarily lethal disorder resulting from inability of the infant to metabolize fats (lipids). In the first 6 months of life, there is motor weakness (poor head control) and exaggerated startle to sharp sounds. The motor weakness (hypotonia) progresses, and there is failure to acquire gross-motor milestones (e.g., crawling and sitting unsupported). The accumulation of lipids in the retina and the brain leads to early blindness and spasticity. By the latter part of the first year, there is rapid deterioration, and death occurs between the ages of 2 and 4 years (Gravel et al., 1995).

A very rare disorder with an incidence of only about 1 in 300,000 births, the condition is notable for a particularly high frequency in Jews of Eastern European extraction. Fortunately, the carrier state can be detected in prospective parents and the disorder itself diagnosed prenatally via amniocentesis. This allows for exercise of the option of therapeutic abortion.

Sex-Linked Disorders

Certain diseases are attributable to mutant genes on the X chromosome. Sex-linked conditions disproportionately affect males because males have only one X chromosome. If the X chromosome is abnormal, unlike the female, there is no potentially normal X chromosome to counterbalance it. The "counterbalancing" phenomenon relates to the fact that, within a cell, only one of the two X chromosomes is "activated" during the life of that cell. If it is the healthy one, the abnormal one is effectively "silenced" (the *lyonization* phenomenon).

There are a number of sex-linked disorders associated with retardation (McKusick, 1990), about one third of which also include the major motor abnormalities found in cerebral palsy—spastic paraplegia and ataxia (Stevenson et al., 1990). Two of the best-known are fragile X syndrome, a dominantly inherited sex-linked disorder, and Lesch-Nyhan disease, a recessively inherited one.

Fragile X

The most common of the clearly inherited forms of mental retardation, the disorder takes its name from the so-called fragile site on one of the long arms of the X chromosome (Fig. 3.9). Inheritable fragile sites are regions of a chromosome that are prone to breakage and loss (Laird, 1987). In this condition, the fragile site is caused by a specific dominant gene on the X chromosome. The disorder occurs in 1 in 1350 males and in 1 in 2033 females (Webb, 1986).

Given the nature of the disorder and its mode of inheritance, early identification in affected children is important because their mothers and female relatives (e.g., aunts) are at high risk of having other fragile X children. Affected males (carriers of the dominant gene on their X chromosome) can only pass the gene on to their daughters because their sons necessarily receive their father's Y chromosome. On the other hand, female carriers have a one in two risk of transmitting the abnormal X chromosome to each of their children, irrespective of gender.

Clinical Features.   Disproportionately affecting males, the syndrome is characterized by retardation and enlargement of the testes (macrorchidism), the latter especially recognizable at puberty. Other common features are a narrowing of the face, protruding ears, and hyperextensible

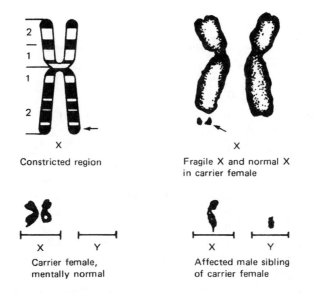

X
Constricted region

X
Fragile X and normal X
in carrier female

X   Y
Carrier female,
mentally normal

X   Y
Affected male sibling
of carrier female

FIGURE 3.9. Fragile X chromosome. Adapted from Hecht, Hecht, and Glover (1981).

joints (Lachiewicz, Harrison, Spiridigliozzi, Callahan, & Livermore, 1988). Apart from retardation, males often also show attention deficit, hyperactivity, impulsivity, and difficulty in dealing with change (Lachiewicz et al., 1988).

Affected females are free of physical abnormalities but may show some intellectual impairment, usually mild, or a specific learning disability. Whereas about 80% of males have some level of intellectual disability, in females about one third are without any effects at all. The remaining females are about equally divided among those with mild retardation, learning disabilities, and personality disorder.

Developmental Aspects.   The fragile X infant is hypotonic and delayed in language. There is often attention deficit and, in the males, also hyperactivity. Indeed, hyperactivity is frequently the initial concern. The majority of boys also exhibit autistic-like behaviors—poor eye contact or gaze avoidance; unusual hand movements; special sensitivities to touch (tactile defensiveness), noise, and lights; impulsivity; and the aforementioned language delay. Although sharing these behaviors with autistic children, the child with fragile X syndrome is more sociable and eager for intimacy. Of the autistic population itself, about 7% show the fragile X abnormality.

There is also distinction between the two disorders in language. Although children with either disorder can show perseverative questioning, their rates of speech tend to differ. The fragile X child tends to have rapid speech. Autistic children, on the other hand, may be totally bereft of speech, or their "language" may be noncommunicative in nature (e.g., echolalic or parroted speech).

Intellectual Development.   The variable picture with regard to mental development has been noted. Even though they carry the abnormal gene, some males appear to be unaffected (Lachiewicz et al., 1988). The typical picture, however, is one of some cognitive impairment, in the early years reflected in "borderline" intelligence or mild retardation. A slowing in the rate of mental development is evident by age 5 years and, in one group of 21 children, an average loss of 12 IQ points was seen between ages 5 and 12 (Lachiewicz, Gullion, Spiridigliozzi, & Aylsworth, 1987). This study also included two children who did not decline in intelligence. Most striking was the finding that although there were four children who at age 5 years were in the average to borderline ranges, all were functioning at a retarded level by age 12 years. The 21 children were at varying levels of retardation—mild (7), moderate (10), and severe (4).

In another study (Dykens et al., 1989), mean IQs fell successively from 54 during the 5- to 10-year-old age period to 44 in the 10- to 15-year-old age range, and to 38 in the period of 15 to 20 years old. Thereafter, test scores showed no further decline until age 35 years.

Although the fall in IQ in the preadult years appears to represent a slowing in the rate of acquisition of new abilities, as in Down syndrome, in young adulthood there may actually be a loss of previous skills.

Numerous studies have documented this intellectual decline, with eventual IQs in the ranges of moderate to severe retardation (Dykens et al., 1989; Dykens, Hodapp, Ort, & Leckman, 1993; Lachiewicz et al., 1987; Rogers & Simensen, 1987). One can only speculate that lifelong exposure to whatever debilitating effects are associated with gene-caused metabolic abnormalities take a toll on brain functioning. The gene for fragile X has been cloned; it is called *FMR-1*, a designation leaving open the possibility of finding additional genes causing the disorder.

Apart from the intellectual decline, affected males exhibit a cognitive pattern of particular weakness in short-term memory and relative strength in tasks tapping general alertness and visual understanding (Dykens, Hodapp, & Leckman, 1987). The memory difficulty may relate to the previously noted common problems of attention deficit and hyperactivity. A similar pattern also may be seen in affected females.

Educational Considerations.   Lachiewicz et al. (1988) have noted the special educational needs of fragle X children. Typically better "visual" learners, as with most retarded children, higher functioning males often do well in reading and spelling. The children also tend to be more comfortable in smaller classes, settings in which noise and change can be minimized.

Speech and language therapy is viewed as essential. Although vocabulary and the *understanding* of language may be a strength, it is in the speech domain that problems exist. The severity of speech disorder may be such as to warrant early instruction in sign language, a nonverbal form of communication.

Other therapies recommended are sensory integration—to help the child deal with excessive sensory stimulation; physical therapy—for the child with poor muscle tone and motor difficulties; music—it can calm the child, and many fragile X children are said to show musical talent; and counseling to families and to affected persons themselves—to help them understand the nature of their disorder.

Medical Treatment. Medical treatment is commonly directed toward reducing hyperactivity and involves the standard drugs used to treat this behavior along with the vitamin folic acid. The latter has shown some benefits in reducing hyperactivity and irritability, particularly in very young children (Lachiewicz et al., 1988).

Another medical concern is epilepsy (Hagerman, 1992). About one fifth of the children have seizures, most often of the complex partial or temporal lobe form. Their symptoms include episodes of staring, arm- and face-jerking, and unusual sensory experiences. Grand mal seizures also occur. Finally, otitis media, a chronic ear infection, is seen in fragile X males.

Cautioning Parents. Given the pattern of decline in intellectual functioning, especially in later adolescence, a finding that is particularly evident in children with initially higher levels of ability (Dykens et al., 1989; Lachiewicz et al., 1987), parents need to be cautioned with regard to future expectations regarding cognition and educability.

Adaptive Behavior. The pattern of intellectual decline is paralleled, not surprisingly, in adaptive behavior. In a study of 17 fragile X males (Dykens et al., 1993), assessment with the Vineland Adaptive Behavior Scale found steady growth in skills until adolescence. Thereafter, absolute declines were found primarily in the Vineland domains of communication and socialization. In contrast, daily living skills were relatively well preserved. Including such self-care activities as feeding, dressing, and toileting, these are skills acquired relatively early in development and daily practiced.

A Girl with Fragile X Syndrome.   The birth of Jenny was the usual joyous event. Developmental milestones were slightly delayed, and their significance minimized. She did well in a preschool program and appeared "ready" for kindergarten at age 5 years. But problems were quickly noted. She had difficulty paying attention (attention deficit), and her handwriting was poor (motor problem). Although her parents considered having her repeat kindergarden, they were advised to send her to first grade. "She is a young 5, she'll outgrow it," they were reassured.

In first grade difficulties with reading and arithmetic surfaced. Math was especially difficult, and although in second grade reading was much improved, math continued to be a major stumbling block. There were also attentional problems—she asked to be moved to a quieter corner of the classroom.

Still being assured by the school that her difficulties were caused by her just being "young" or developmentally immature for her age, her parents sought private psychological assessment. The findings were of "learning disabilities" and diminished self-esteem, the latter attributed to her perception of being disliked by her peers. (It should be noted that chronic school failure is going to frustrate the self-esteem–related need for "success" and add to the intimacy frustration caused by poor interpersonal relationships.) Evaluation also revealed an attention deficit and poor abstractive abilities. It was suggested that she receive remedial assistance in a learning disabilities "resource room," tutoring two to three times a week, occupational therapy (presumably in relation to motor problems), language therapy, and counseling.

Sometime thereafter the parents learned that a retarded uncle on the mother's side had a disorder associated with a fragile site on the X chromosome, and that this condition was hereditary. The nature of their daughter's problem soon was clarified.

Jenny's social history helps to explain her poor relationship with other children. Initially not a cuddly baby, a characteristic shared with autistic infants, she also did not respond to her name. A failure to understand language is also a common aspect of autism. In school she failed to grasp the spoken and unspoken rules that govern children's games and was excluded from them. Again, this has autistic overtones. Autistic children are especially deficient in understanding the social "rules" that govern our conduct. But unlike the typical autistic child who appears indifferent to opportunities for friendship, Jenny's heart would break as one friend after another would eventually seek other children's friendship.

Her lack of social awareness led to increasing isolation by her peers. Immature, and with interests appropriate to a younger child, she remains easily hurt but unbending in her efforts to try to win social acceptance. Her mother takes inspiration from Jenny's resilience. She notes that Jenny is not bitter nor has she lost hope, and that her personal strength and fortitude offer an example that no sermon could teach!

Lesch-Nyhan Disease

This is an extremely rare disorder caused by a recessive gene on the X chromosome. An enzyme deficiency is present that results in an excess of uric acid and produces symptoms of gout, kidney dysfunction, motor spasticity, and most notably, compulsive forms of self-mutilation.

Physical Symptoms.   Affected children initially appear normal, but by the latter half of the first year motor symptoms arise in the form of a loss of previously acquired head and trunk control. A spasticity develops that prevents unassisted sitting or standing and ultimately may require the prosthetic assistance of a form-fitting wheelchair (Nyhan, 1994).

Behavioral Aspects.   Although retardation is a prominent feature, cognition may not be as impaired as physical limitations might suggest (Anderson, Ernst, & Davis, 1992; Nyhan, 1994). A survey of caregivers of a population largely living at home revealed abilities to communicate needs in speech, the desire to interact, and age-appropriate interests (Anderson et al., 1992). School-wise, math problems were widespread but a small proportion, some 15%, were said to be achieving at grade level. More than half had some reading ability, and nearly one third enjoyed reading. Although this population is not a random sample of persons with the disorder, the survey did appear to confirm earlier reports of individuals with Lesch-Nyhan disease with little or no cognitive impairment.

Self-injurious Behavior.   The self-mutilative aspect of Lesch-Nyhan disease causes affected individuals to be seen as bizarre and aggressive (Nyhan & Sakati, 1976). Indeed, although described as generally friendly, loving, and lovable, they often behave aggressively (Nyhan, 1994). Their self-biting can cause tissue loss, including the actual partial amputation of fingers and tongue! In spite of such extraordinary trauma, there is no indication of diminished pain perception, because apparent screaming in pain may accompany self-biting. In this respect, persons with the disorder differ from other individuals who engage in self-injury, typically severely or profoundly retarded children. The latter show no discomfort; their self-hitting is likely to take the form of headbanging, and they are generally free of major motor abnormality. Extremely resistant to control by either behavioral or medical means (Nyhan, 1994), the management of this extraordinary behavior is discussed in Chapter 8. Caregivers report the common use of physical restraints to prevent self-hitting. Curiously, the removal of restraints, as during bathing, can actually lead to an increase in self-hitting. Other factors causing an intensification of self-injurious behavior were various forms of stress including illness and the facing of an unfamiliar situation. With reference to an increase in self-hitting following the removal of arm and hand restraints, the senior author has described an autistic youth with such behavior who would extend his arms to a caregiver in order to be restrained when his restraints had come loose (Baroff & Tate, 1968). It is as if he were seeking protection against a painful behavior over which he had little control.

Apart from physical restraints, the self-injurious behavior in Lesch-Nyhan disease tends to be manageable by reducing stress and being attentive to individual needs. Interventions that involve varying degrees of punishment, long a controversial issue in the treatment of such behavior, are viewed as less effective.

In addition to the self-injury, these children also show some tendencies to external aggression (Nyhan, 1994). The behavior may have a compulsive aspect, with the individual referring to an "inner urge" to act aggressively. The eyeglasses of others are a frequent target, and outbursts often are followed by remorse. The children also can be aggressive in their speech and in manipulating situations.

Prevention.   This strange disorder is detectable in unaffected "carrier" females in the form of an elevated level of uric acid (Hyman, 1996). Nevertheless, the carrier female is unaffected because the recessive mutant gene is present in only one of her two X chromosomes. The "normal" X chromosome carries the healthy gene, that gene being dominant to the one for illness. As in the case of fragile X disorder, it is the male who is affected, because if he inherits from his mother an X chromosome with the abnormal gene, he has no second X chromosome with which to offset it.

Disorders of Multiple Etiology, Including a Recessive Form

Congenital Hypothyroidism (Cretinism)

An endocrine disorder caused by deficienct thyroid functioning, this condition, like Down syndrome, has a special place in the history of mental retardation. The first formal programs for retarded children were developed in Switzerland for youth with this disorder. Earlier present in geographic areas lacking in iodine, and still endemic in some remote mountainous areas, such as Western China, with the development of iodized salt the endemic form is now wholly preventable. The nonendemic or sporadic form occurs in about 1 in 3000 births (Addison, 1988; Mengreli &

Pantelakis, 1988) and may be caused variously by failure of development of the thyroid gland, a genetic enzyme error, or maternal ingestion of antithyroid drugs during pregnancy (Warkany, 1971). The genetic form has several variants and is associated with a goiter (enlargement of the thyroid gland, present at birth or developing in childhood).

The main symptoms of the disorder are stunted growth (dwarfism) and mental retardation. There are characteristic facial features, and the child seems dull and apathetic and has a hoarse cry (Villee, 1975). The disorder now is detectable at birth through blood screening, and treatment consists of thyroid-hormone replacement.

With early treatment, mental retardation is prevented, although some impairment is found in those with skeletal abnormality (Farriaux, Dhondt, & Lebecq, 1988; Glorieux, 1988; Klees, 1988). Cognitive impairment tends to be mild and limited to language-related skills. Evaluation of intellectual functioning in later childhood on the Wechsler Intelligence Scale for Children-Revised, has found verbal IQs in the 85 to 95 range, as compared with performance IQs of 100.

Microcephaly

A condition of abnormally small skull and brain size, microcephaly can result from genetic or nongenetic causes (Smith, 1982). The genetic form is inherited in a simple autosomal recessive manner; nongenetic causation relates to any of the disease processes that arrest brain development. Parenthetically, the small skull is the effect, not the cause, of diminished brain size. The size of the skull is determined by the brain mass it contains. The microcephalic head is conical in appearance, an effect that increases with age. There is impairment in cognitive, motor, and speech functions and, often, stunting of growth and diminished weight. Retardation is likely to be severe or profound (Warkany, 1971) although normal intelligence is found; here one is likely to see learning disabilities (Martin, 1970).

Macrocephaly

Macrocephaly refers to an abnormally large head (more than two standard deviations above the mean for one's age). The enlargement may be caused by either increased cerebrospinal fluid in the brain (hydrocephaly) or an enlarged brain mass itself (megalencephaly).

Hydrocephaly.   Occurring in about 1 in 1000 births, and more often in males (Laurence, 1993), this condition also includes both genetic and nongenetic forms. It may be present at birth (congenital hydrocephaly) in association with a number of malformations of the brain and spinal cord, most notably spina bifida (gaps in the spine). It is also found in the chromosomal disorders trisomy 13 and 18. Congenital hydrocephaly is seldom compatible with a normal birth delivery and later survival. In hydrocephaly arising postnatally, one often sees other malformations, such as spina bifida, harelip, and cleft palate. It also can be found in infectious diseases of prenatal origin—congenital syphilis and congenital toxoplasmosis. The symptoms of the disorder usually result from a blockage in the circulation of cerebrospinal fluid in the ventricles of the brain, but they also can arise from an overproduction of cerebrospinal fluid or its defective absorption (Laurence, 1993). Vision is much affected by the disorder.

Ultimate physical and mental development depends on several factors—rapidity of onset, intracranial pressure, compensatory head growth, and the progress or arrest of the disease process. Treatment takes the form of installing a shunt in the brain that allows for the release of the excess fluid. In spina bifida (mylomeningocele), for example, some 70% of affected children have hydrocephalus, with the majority (50%–80%) requiring shunting. Hydrocephalus and its treatment complications are a major cause of death in infancy and in the preschool years (Nelson & Crocker, 1992).

The effect of the disorder on intellectual functioning is quite variable. All levels of intelligence are found—from superior intellect to severe retardation. The most frequently seen picture is of at least some impairment, with about half of affected persons functioning in the below-80 IQ range (Simpson & Hemmer, 1993). Children whose hydrocephaly is associated with spina bifida generally are less impaired than others with the disorder. The severest impairment is found if hydrocephalus follows a brain infection (e.g., meningitis) or traumatic brain injury.

Apart from general intelligence, special problems in speech and language are found (Hendrick, 1993). Speech may be fluent but lack substance and include inappropriate word usage. And even in those with grossly normal intellect, difficulties in concentration and memory may be present.

Withal, a substantial proportion of individuals with surgically treated hydrocephalus (shunting) are free of major intellectual impairment. They are neither handicapped in school nor in employment and can lead normal lives (Hemmer & Boehm, 1976).

Megalencephaly.   A very rare condition caused by excessive brain size (Sarnat, 1992), megalencephaly may be associated with normal as well as abnormal mental development. If present in the absence of any underlying disease, primary megalencephaly, the head is large at birth and grows rapidly but may not be distorted in shape. Although intellect may be unimpaired, more often retardation is present. Megalencephaly is obscure in origin; some instances appear to be genetic and inherited in an autosomal dominant manner. Symptomatic or secondary megalencephaly also is seen in some of the recessively inherited metabolic disorders, such as Sanfilippo's syndrome (Leroy, 1992) and in brain tumors.

Polygenic Inheritance

In our review of inherited forms of mental retardation, we have been looking at conditions caused by single genes, either dominant or recessive, and autosomal or sex-linked. The accompanying retardation is attributed to mutant genes, genes that exert their influence by interfering with normal brain-cell biochemistry. But heredity also plays a role in "ordinary" development as it influences variations in traits and characteristics that fall within the normal range. Unlike the relatively all-or-nothing or discrete quality of gene-caused disease (you either have Tay-Sachs disease or you do not), other human characteristics exist in degree and distribute themselves along a continuum, any point of which is considered normal.

Height is such a trait, as it exists in degree. People vary in height and except for the most extreme variations, especially in a downward direction, the variations are not perceived as pathological. You may be short or tall, but neither variation is viewed as a form of disease. To the degree that genetic factors contribute to such variation, as in the case of height, the genetic contribution is attributable to the action of many genes, rather than just one, each of which exerts a small effect. Such traits also are viewed as "multifactorial" in their expression in that they are influenced by nongenetic factors as well. Height, for example, is dependent on diet as well as genes. Under different diets the same genetic contribution (genotype) can lead to different heights. This heredity-environment interaction is looked at again as we consider the role of environmental influences on intelligence in Chapter 5.

Intelligence, like height, is a trait that varies along a continuum that we think of as the "normal range." Like height, it exists in degree, from extraordinarily superior intellect (genius) to mental retardation, and except for those forms of retardation that are clearly caused by biological abnormality, variation within the range is thought to be caused by both genetic and environmental factors. It has been presumed that both heredity and environment play a role in those with mild mental retardation who are biologically "normal" and who have parents or siblings who are similarly affected. Referred to in the first chapter, and previously known as "cultural-familial" retardation, this is now termed *psychosocial* retardation, a designation that appears to reject the premise of a genetic influence. Apart from retardation itself, the possible role of genetic factors in intelligence of course has been extremely controversial because it conjures up a view of differences in intelligence between different racial and ethnic groups as biologically influenced.

Granted that both heredity and environment play a role in intelligence, it is the respective contribution of each that remains to be clarified. Leroy (1992) has called attention to elements that obscure effects to divide out their respective roles. He points out the environment itself can affect biology, gene action being affected by as well as affecting phenyotypic outcomes. He also notes that although statistical correlations in family studies of intelligence are consistent with polygenic inheritance (Bouchard & McGue, 1981), they also could reflect the effects of family-influenced environmental similarity (Lewontin, 1975). Plomin and his colleagues (e.g., Plomin & Petrill, 1997) have been particulary interested in teasing out the relative contributions of genetic and environmental contributions to intelligence, and their work is cited in Chapter 5 as we examine the nature-nurture phenomenon.

The senior author has been particularly impressed with studies on the intellectual similarities of identical twins reared apart. Although the settings in which the twin partners are raised are unlikely to reflect the full range of possible childrearing environments (Lewontin, 1975), these studies certainly suggest that both heredity and environment contribute to intellectual variation within the normal IQ range. And to the degree that a genetic contribution exists within the normal range of intellectual variation, its mode of influence is polygenic in nature.

☐ Summary

This is the first of three chapters that are devoted to etiology, to the *causes* of mental retardation. Roughly divided into biological and psychological causation, in this chapter we look at biological disorders of a genetic or hereditary nature. A brief introduction to genetics is followed by a description of mental-retardation syndromes associated with chromosomal and gene abnormalities. In the chromosomal realm, particular attention is given to Down syndrome and Prader-Willi syndrome, two of the best known chromosomal abnormalities. After this, genetic disorders caused by "dominant" and "recessive" genes then are described with some emphasis on the recessive conditions PKU and fragile X. In addition to syndromes whose etiology is clear, the chapter also includes disorders that can arise from either genetic or nongenetic causes, such as congenital hypthyroidism or cretinism. The chapter concludes with a brief explanation of the role of heredity in conditions in which both heredity *and* environment play major roles, polygenic inheritance. Here the genetic influence is attributed to the effect of *multiple* genes.

Possible Discussion Questions

Down syndrome is a chromosomal disorder that can be detected prenatally. Prospective parents have the option of terminating or aborting the pregnancy. Their decision is based on a variety of influences—personal, family, and non-family. How do parents address the dilemma of the prospective birth of a child who can be expected to have significant disabilities? This dilemma arises from our desire for "normal healthy children." How do we juxtapose this preference against the reality of children born with major abnormalities? For some of us, only religion may provide a basis for the valuing of every human being. It offers the belief that we *all* are God's creatures. This is expressed beautifully by the poet Coleridge in a closing stanza of his "Rime of the Ancient Mariner."

> He prayeth best, who loveth best
> All things both great and small;
> For the dear God who loveth us
> He made and loveth all.

The Prader-Willi syndrome introduces us to a disorder in which people literally can "eat themselves to death." In this respect it does not differ from other conditions in which, unless declared "incompetent," we are free to engage in self-destructive behavior, such as drug abuse. Of course the "cause" of Prader-Willi syndrome lies "inside" the person, a gene-determined condition, but whether the cause is inside or outside, the question in a "free" society is to what extent, if any, do we have the right to interfere with such behavior. Can we, should we, seek to *compel* people who are neither legally incompetent nor dangerous to others to refrain from such behavior? How do we reconcile the "claims of society" against fundamental individual freedoms?

☐ Note

1. *Average* normative expectations in Down syndrome for motor development, speech, and self-help skills have been offered by Pueschel (1992). They are as follows: smiling 2 months, rolling over 6 months, sitting 9 months, crawling 11 months, creeping 13 months, standing 10 months, walking 20 months, using words 14 months, using sentences/phrases 24 months; eating: finger feeding 12 months, using spoon/fork 20 months; toilet training: bladder 48 months, bowel 42 months; dressing: undressing 40 months, dressing 58 months. (These are all *averages* and children will commonly vary from these averages in terms of either slower or more rapid development).

Nongenetic Biological Factors: Prenatal, Perinatal, and Postnatal

☐ Overview

The previous chapter was devoted to chromosomal and genetic determinants of mental retardation, events occurring at conception. We now move forward time-wise to biological causes arising after conception: during prenatal life, at or around the time of birth (perinatal-neonatal), and postnatally (Table 4.1). Nearly one half (47%) of retardation is attributed to events occurring during this time frame—32% to the prenatal period, 11% to the perinatal period, and 4% to the postnatal period (Crocker, 1992). It should be noted that, apart from the role of the young child's psychological environment as a contributor to mental retardation, discussed in the next chapter, nearly one third (30%) of retardation is of unknown origin (Crocker, 1992). The chapter concludes with a description of two major disorders often associated with mental retardation, cerebral palsy and epilepsy, and with a brief treatment of spina bifida, a condition that typically produces some degree of cognitive impairment.

☐ Prenatal Causes

Prenatal factors account for about one third of all cases of retardation (32%), and they are especially prominent in more severe degrees of intellectual impairment. Although, the role of a number of adverse prenatal events in causing retardation is relatively well understood, their specific

---

TABLE 4.1. Nongenetic biological causes of mental retardation

---

Prenatal
 Infection: rubella, toxoplasmosis, syphilis, cytomegalovirus, HIV
 Maternal-fetal blood incompatibilities: Rh and ABO
 Drugs and alcohol: cocaine, heroin, methadone, alcohol, therapeutic drugs
 Maternal-fetal irradiation
 Chronic maternal health problems: hypertension, diabetes

Perinatal
 Prematurity
 Asphyxia (hypoxemia): intracranial hemorrhage
 Head trauma: hemorrhage, infection
 Infection: HIV, herpes
 Kernicteris

Postnatal
 Infection: encephalitis, meningitis, brain abscess, postimmunization
  encephalopathy
 Cerebral trauma: head injury, cerebrovascular accidents, brain tumor,
  hemorrhage from coagulation defects, thromboses, ruptured aneurysm
 Poisons and environmental toxins: lead, mercury
 Anoxia: cardiac arrest, hypoglycemia, respiratory distress syndrome
 Hormonal deficiency: hypothyroidism
 Metabolic: hypernatremia, hypoglycemia
 Epilepsy
 Severe malnutrition

Note. From Milunsky, 1975; Taft and Cohen, 1977.

impact is complicated by the time period that may intervene between the precipitating event and its actual detection (e.g., alcohol consumption in the first trimester of pregnancy and some later postnatal manifestations of fetal alcohol syndrome), and a likely interplay of individually adverse effects (Masland, 1958). The latter is illustrated in such conditions as hemorrhage during pregnancy and low birth weight (prematurity), each of which increases the risk for abnormality.

Embryological/Fetal Timetables

Among the guides that assist in determining the significance of prenatal events are embryological-fetal timetables. The anatomical growth of the embryo and fetus is fixed in sequence and time, and specific anatomic abnormalities offer clues as to the time period during which the biological insult occurred. Cleft palate, for example, typically results from adverse fetal exposure occurring between the 6th and the 9th weeks of gestation.

It does not arise from an insult after the 11th week because by that time the palate has closed. Parenthetically, the embryonic period refers to the 3rd through the 8th week of life, the fetal period follows (Moore, 1977). Interestingly, in some respects the embryo-fetus is less vulnerable to environmental adversity during the first 2 weeks of development than it will be later on. During the first 2 weeks of prenatal life, exposure to a *teratogen* (any drug or agent that can cause an abnormality) either damages enough cells to cause death or only a few cells, allowing the embryo to fully recover (Moore, 1977).

Erroneous application of organ-growth timetables was reflected in speculations as to the cause of Down syndrome prior to the discovery of chromosomal abnormality as its cause. Some of its anatomical defects are tied to growth processes that are completed by the 8th to 12th weeks of life (Graham, 1992). This led to the presumption that the condition could be attributed to noxious events occurring during this particular time period. In fact, the disorder was determined at conception when an egg was fertilized that came to possess a third chromosome 21. Timetables are more useful for estimating the *latest* date at which an insult might have occurred, a date tied to time periods that come *after* organs are expected to have completed their formation.

Attempts at retrospective dating also are bedeviled by potential differences in how individual embryo-fetuses might respond to the same insult. A woman who had taken the later-banned pregnancy antinauseant drug thalidomide gave birth to fraternal twins, only one of whom showed the typical clinical picture of malformed hands and arms. The other twin had only minor abnormalities. Fraternal twins being no more alike genetically than single-born siblings, the difference in their response to the same teratogen can be viewed as an illustration of a heredity-environment interaction. Exposed to the same intrauterine stress, two different genotypes responded in two different ways.

Intrauterine Vulnerability

Prior to the 1940s, it was believed that the fetus[1] was protected from conditions affecting the pregnant woman (Golbus, 1980). But in the 1940s an association was recognized between the infection of pregnant women with the rubella virus and later delivery of a baby with serious sensory, motor, and neurological abnormalities. In the 1960s, the adverse effect of thalidomide, the drug used during pregnancy, was recognized. We now know that maternal illness during pregnancy and the ingestion of drugs both "recreational" and therapeutic can impair fetal development. Although the great majority of developmental abnormalities are of unknown origin, and only a small percentage are clearly traceable to maternal illness, drug consumption, or environmental chemicals (Wilson, 1972), the large "unknown" category should make us wary about what we put into our bodies during pregnancy. In the material that follows we look at a number of teratogens. These are drugs or other agents that interfere with normal growth processes and lead to various kinds of fetal malformation. The teratogens to be described consist of maternal infection during pregnancy, fetal exposure to drugs and alcohol, and fetal exposure to some chronic maternal illnesses.

Prenatal Infection

Infections of the nervous system of the fetus differ in their consequences from corresponding infections in children or adults (Menkes, 1995). Prenatal infection interfering with the developmental process can lead to multiple defects. The immature brain lacks the ability to repair damage, remove abnormal cells, and compensate for missing tissue. Its period of greatest vulnerability is in the first 3 months (first trimester) of pregnancy. The most common prenatal infections causing mental retardation are rubella, toxoplasmosis, syphilis, cytomegalovirus, and human immunodeficiency virus (HIV).

Congenital Rubella

The result of viral[2] infection during the first trimester, congenital rubella may produce few symptoms in the mother but be potentially devastating to the fetus. Abortions, spontaneous or selective, are common outcomes of its diagnosis (Cooper, 1977). Fetal infection occurs in about half of the mothers who contract rubella and, of those fetuses affected during the first trimester, about half do not survive. Of the survivors, about half are born with serious abnormalities. Infection of the fetus during the third and fourth months, in the second trimester, does not cause death, and the incidence of congenital anomalies drops to 20%.

The symptom picture in survivors of congenital rubella is both varied and unpredictable and includes a live birth with one or more abnormalities (about 25% having multiple abnormalities) or a perfectly normal infant (Cooper, 1968, 1977).

The rubella virus, having crossed the placenta from the maternal circulation, has an affinity for the developing brain and cardiovascular system (Graham, 1992). Primarily affecting gray matter, the nerve-cell bodies, it can stunt brain development, leaving an abnormally small brain (microcephaly) together with cognitive effects ranging from specific learning disabilities to profound retardation. Intellectual impairment is found in about half of the affected children (Chess, Korn, & Fernandez, 1971; Cooper et al., 1969). Vision, hearing, and the heart also commonly are affected—all organs whose growth occurs during the first 3 months of life. Heart disease and deafness is found in almost all infants infected prior to the 11th week. In contrast, later infection, between the 13th and 16th weeks, damages only about one third of fetuses, and here the problem is limited to hearing loss (Miller, Craddock-Watson, & Pollock, 1982).

Apart from its more dramatic effects, the rubella virus can create minor motor difficulties, feeding problems, learning deficits, and behavior disorders (Graham, 1972; Hanshaw & Dudgeon, 1978). Language problems are a special risk. They are tied to either the aforementioned hearing loss or to an incapacity to process language even with intact hearing, so-called central auditory deafness (Ames, Plotkin, Winchester, & Atkins, 1970).

The relatively destructive impact of the rubella virus on the fetus, in contrast to its generally mild effect on the pregnant woman, illustrates both "critical periods" of developmental vulnerability and the body's immunologic response to infection. With reference to the latter, postnatal rubella infection of either child or adult leads to the production of antibodies that will be available to attack and destroy the rubella virus at a future infection. The fetus, however, is vulnerable in terms of both developmental state and a lack of antibodies to fight the virus.

Congenital rubella is a largely preventable disease; immunization has been widely available since the 1960s, and children are expected to have been immunized when they begin school. The purpose of immunization is both to protect the children from future infection and to prevent their spreading the disease to adolescent girls and women of childbearing age. Some states require evidence of immunization in premarital blood tests (Graham, 1992).

Congenital Toxoplasmosis

This is a protozoan infection that, like rubella, is generally noninjurious to the pregnant woman but devastating to the fetus. Prenatal vulnerability is largely limited to the first trimester, and the severely affected infant is born with microcephaly, hydrocephalus, retinal inflammation (chorioretinitis), deafness, psychomotor retardation, and brain calcification (Menkes, 1995). At birth, less involved infants (fewer than 25% are severely affected) may be asymptomatic and either remain so or later develop usual symptoms, seizures, or psychomotor retardation. The disease is treatable, its long-term effects depending on the severity of central nervous system involvement (Graham, 1992).

The protozoan parasite that transmits the infection is found in raw meat and cat feces. The newly pregnant woman should avoid eating uncooked meats and contact with sources of cat-feces contamination, such as litter boxes and flower beds (Krick & Remington, 1978).

Congenital Syphilis

After many years of major control, syphilis has made a "comeback" via women who exchange sex for drugs. The disease is transmitted through bacteria[3] at any time during pregnancy but usually in the 4th through the 7th months (Menkes, 1995). Treatment of the pregnant woman prior to the 18th week of gestation prevents fetal infection, and treatment thereafter can cure both mother and unborn child. At high risk for stillbirth or early neonatal death, affected newborns can show meningitis, seizures, and hydrocephalus. In less severely involved infants, one sees enlargement of the liver and spleen (hepatosplenomegaly) and bone changes. Neurological symptoms may not be observable in infancy, but intellectual impairment eventually becomes evident in childhood (Finberg, 1977).

Congenital Cytomegalovirus

The most common fetal infection, only about 5% to 10% of affected newborns show symptoms of the disease (Graham, 1992). Unlike rubella, fetal infection usually occurs during the second and third trimesters (Menkes, 1995). Severely affected infants show a wide range of symptoms—liver and spleen enlargement, jaundice, diminished levels of blood platelets (thrombocytopenia), heart disease, microcephaly, brain calcifications, retinal inflammation (choreoretinitis), deafness, seizures, and mental retardation (Graham, 1992; Menkes, 1995).

Of the 90% of previously infected infants who are without symptoms at birth, some 10% to 16% eventually show effects in the late preschool or early school years (Graham, 1992; Menkes, 1995).

At present no effective treatment exists (Menkes, 1995).

Human Immunodeficiency Virus and AIDS

Initially a disease limited to homosexual males, the HIV virus has spread to women who are either intravenous drug users or sexual partners of such men and to persons receiving blood transfusions or other blood products (Crocker, 1992). There are three forms or stages of the condition: *AIDS* or acquired immunodeficiency syndrome, referring to the most advanced stage, one associated with "opportunistic infections" or tumors; *symptomatic HIV infection*, an earlier and milder form; and *asymptomatic*

HIV infection, in which the virus is present but in a latent form. The last-mentioned includes some infants who are not truly infected with the HIV virus but who temporarily show antibodies that were "passively" transferred prenatally from their HIV-infected mothers.

Unknown before 1981, 10 years later AIDS was the ninth leading cause of death in children (Fletcher et al., 1991), with the number of affected infants quadrupling every 3 years!

Like their adult counterparts, children with AIDS are disproportionately found in the large metropolitan areas—New York, Miami, Newark, San Juan, Los Angeles, and Washington, DC. They make a very small proportion, only 2%, of all AIDS cases, and the great majority (over 80%) are younger than 5 years old (Crocker, 1992). Pediatric AIDS is largely acquired prenatally (83%) from HIV-infected mothers, with the remaining cases caused by accidental exposure to HIV-infected blood, usually via transfusions (Crocker, 1992).

Fortunately, only about one third of the children with prenatally acquired HIV infection actually develop AIDS. The remainder show a gradual reduction of HIV antibody levels during the first years of life, with the expectation that all traces of the disease will vanish by 15 months (Crocker, 1992).

Whereas in adults the duration of a symptom-free or latent period following infection averages 7 years, in children the onset of symptoms following infection is much briefer. Of the one third who become symptomatic, more than half (50% to 60%) show manifestations by age 12 months, usually in the latter part of the first year. The great majority is symptomatic by age 3 years—78% by 2 years, and 83% by 3 years (Civitello, 1991–1992).

Just as the length of time between exposure and symptoms varies between children and adults, so do the symptoms themselves. In adults the manifestations are commonly a general malaise, weight loss, and so-called opportunistic infections (e.g., pneumonia and lymph-gland enlargement). Pulmonary infections also may be seen in children, but more often there is failure to thrive, diarrhea, recurrent bacterial infections, and developmental delay (Crocker, 1992).

The brain is a major target of the HIV virus, and almost all (90%) of the children who are symptomatic show brain-related neurological abnormalities (Belman et al., 1988). The disease eventually produces a progressive encephalopathy expressed in a loss of developmental milestones (regression) or arrest in attaining new ones; impaired growth of the brain itself, often with microcephaly; and motor abnormalities—weakness, poor muscle coordination (ataxia), and spasticity. Seizures also may occur (Diamond, 1989).

The course of the disease is variable. In 20% of children it follows a progressive neurological course, with death usually occurring about 8 months after initial symptom onset ("subacute progression"). In another approximately one third (30%), there is a "plateau" and a longer survival time, some 2 years after symptom onset. There is still a third group that maintains a fairly normal rate of development in the childhood years ("static" course), but their long-term survival is much in jeopardy. All told, some 60% of children die by age 5 years (Crocker, 1992). Drugs used to treat adults also have proved beneficial to children, with some surviving into early adolescence (Crocker, 1992).

Special problems are seen in the visual-perceptual and language spheres. In a small group of 4- to 8-year-olds with relatively stable disease, visual-perception problems were similar to those seen in cerebral palsy, with difficulties of organization and integration (Diamond et al., 1987). In the language area, there are problems with prelinguistic skills (Nozyce et al., 1989) and in general fluency (Epstein et al., 1986).

The management of the social, educational, and treatment needs of children with HIV infection is of special concern. Needs may change dramatically as symptoms erupt. Sudden losses of motor and language skills can signal such changes. It is necessary to recognize that the HIV-AIDS child is still a child and in need of those experiences appropriate to all children at his or her developmental level. Intimacy with family, play and stimulation, and exposure to other children and adults all need to be incorporated in the child's experience, albeit recognizing the need to assure the safety of those coming into contact with the child (Crocker, 1992).

The reality of acquired HIV infection in mentally-retarded youth and adults presents special problems. The right to sexual experience must be balanced against the need to protect vulnerable individuals against possible infection. Educational programs have been developed for at-risk youth and adults, and caregivers in programs serving them need to be aware of how they can minimized their charges' risk.

Toxins

The focus here is on the exposure of the fetus to substances consumed by the mother during pregnancy that can damage the brain. They include drugs used "recreationally," alcohol, and medicines used therapeutically. Given the high prevalence of drug and alcohol use in contemporary Western societies, it is important to be aware of the risks that they can pose during pregnancy.

Cocaine

With the dramatic rise in the late 1980s in the use of crack cocaine and its appearance in the newborn "crack babies," concern is with its effect on the fetus. A distinction is drawn between short-term effects, those found in the addicted neonate, and long-term ones, those seen in later childhood and, possibly, permanent in their consequences. During pregnancy, cocaine is passed to the fetus via the maternal blood circulation. It also can be transmitted postnatally through breast-feeding. Cocaine is a stimulant that induces constriction in blood vessels and reduces circulation to the brain (Menkes, 1995). It particularly increases fetal susceptibility to damage in the cerebral cortex blood circulation and to cerebral bleeding itself. Cocaine also poses a serious health risk to the fetus by increasing the probability of a premature separation of the placenta from the uterine wall (abruptio placentae). This literally cuts off fetal access to the maternal circulation and can be life-threatening.

At birth, the prototypic crack baby is reduced in size and small for its gestation age, particularly with regard to head circumference—typically below the 10th percentile. About 25% also have low birth weight (Chasnoff, Griffin, Freier, & Murray, 1992), a birth weight of less than 2500 g (5.5 lb). A birth weight of less than 2500 g is one of the criteria for "prematurity," and premature delivery is especially common in women who use cocaine throughout their pregnancy. Almost one third of their babies (31%) are premature. In contrast, the prematurity rate in women who stop using cocaine in the first trimester is about one half (15%) (Chasnoff et al., 1992).

After the fetus is addicted prenatally by maternal cocaine ingestion, at birth the infant's access to the drug is literally cut off with the severance of the umbilical cord, and this precipitates drug-withdrawal symptoms. These include rapid heartbeat, tremors, heightened irritability, difficulty in feeding, and, later, deviant sleep patterns (Doberczak, 1988; Oro & Dixon, 1987). There is also a high risk of seizures both immediately postnatally and later (Kramer, Locke, Ogunyemi, & Nelson, 1990). Except for those infants in whom seizures persist, these abnormalities tend to disappear after age 3 weeks.

Given the burden of commencing life with a drug addiction, the eventual developmental outcome of crack babies seems to have exceeded expectations. Like other premature infants, they tend to catch up in weight and height, and the effect on head circumference (brain size) steadily diminishes (Chasnoff et al., 1992). Studies indicate that by 2 years of age, two thirds are developing normally. The other one third show difficulties in maintaining attention, interacting with other children, and adapting to change. What is not clear is whether these behaviors are cocaine-specific. Although there is no doubt that these infants are at increased risk for developmental and behavioral problems (Zuckerman & Bresnahan, 1991), attributing their difficulties to cocaine is confounded by likely maternal use of other potentially toxic substances during pregnancy, and, possibly, a later inability to give to the child the desired level of attention. Apart from these considerations, the intelligence of the mother itself is an important determinant of the child's ultimate level of intellectual development. This is discussed in the next chapter.

Opiates: Heroin and Methadone

The impact of these two opiates on the fetus and newborn is well established, with effects generally more severe than those resulting from cocaine (Menkes, 1995). As in the case of cocaine and other toxins, growth is stunted. Infants tend to be small for their gestational age, and about half have low birth weight. Head circumference is also reduced; a little less than half (40%) have a head circumference below the 10th percentile (Vargas, Pildes, Vidiyasagar, & Keith, 1975). About two thirds of babies born to heroin-addicted mothers show postnatal symptoms of drug withdrawal (Zelson, Rubio, & Wasserman, 1971), which, if untreated, can lead to death (Menkes, 1995). Unlike cocaine, however, seizures are relatively rare. For unknown reasons, prenatal exposure to opiates seems to reduce the risk of cerebral bleeding (intraventricular hemorrhage) relative to babies of comparable weight born to nonaddicted mothers (Cepeda, Lee, Mehdizadeh, 1987).

Again, as with cocaine and crack babies, follow-up studies of babies born with the stunting effects of heroin and methadone indicate a catch-up effect by age 2 years; later development and IQs are grossly normal. These children do appear, however, to be at greater risk of behavior problems, notably temper tantrums and impulsiveness (Kaltenbach & Finnegan, 1987; Wilson, McCreary, Kean, & Baxter, 1979). And, as with cocaine, maternal use of other drugs obscures the specific role of heroin and methadone (Menkes, 1995).

Marijuana

Widely used, especially among youth (Millman & Botwin, 1992), marijuana causes few prenatal adverse effects. Marijuana does cross the placenta and can reduce muscle mass, a growth effect consistent with a diminished level of fetal oxygenation (Zuckerman & Bresnahan, 1991). Although smoking marijuana usually is associated with reduced birth weight, heavy smokers (at least five joints per week) appear to have larger babies, in weight and in height (Fried & O'Connell, 1987). This effect is attributed to a tendency of these women to consume more calories and protein. Reported neonatal drug effects—tremors and increased startle— disappear by age 1 month.

Developmental studies generally have found no effects at 12 and 24 months (Fried & Watkinson, 1988). In one study, however, 4-year-old children of heavy users during pregnancy (more than six joints per week) performed at a lesser level on memory and language skills than a control group of nonexposed children. It is suggested that there may be subtle effects of prenatal exposure, not evident until later in childhood (Zuckerman & Bresnahan, 1991) and that caution in marijuana use during pregnancy is in order (Golbus, 1980).

Alcohol and Fetal Alcohol Syndrome

Nature and Diagnostic Features.   In contrast to uncertainties of the effects of prenatal exposure to the aforementioned drugs, those related to alcohol are, at least, relatively well understood. Concerns about the consequences of maternal alcohol consumption during pregnancy have a long history. The effects of drinking in one generation on the next were noted as long ago as in ancient Greece and Rome, and an 1851 review of then-current data (Carpenter) led to the conclusion that children could suffer both mental and behavioral disabilities (Menkes, 1995). In the 1960s and 1970s, French and American researchers described symptoms seen in children exposed to alcohol prenatally, symptoms ultimately labeled fetal alcohol syndrome" (FAS) (Jones, Smith, & Ulleland, 1973). FAS is variable in its manifestations, probably because of such prenatal factors as fetal age at the time of exposure and the length and intensity of exposure; a diagnostic distinction is drawn between the full-blown disorder (FAS) and its lesser version, fetal alcohol effects (FAE). FAS is viewed as the extreme end of continuum of effects of prenatal alcohol exposure (Streissguth, Aase, et al., 1991).

FAS is diagnosed under the following conditions: (a) maternal alcohol abuse during pregnancy—consumption of at least four drinks (2 oz) per day (Streissguth, Barr, Martin, & Herman, 1980); (b) a length or weight growth deficiency of prenatal origin—below the 10th percentile; (c) a characteristic facial appearance—short palpebral fissures (narrow eye lengths), flattened midface and philtrum (the groove in the middle of the upper lip), and thin upper lips; and (d) a variety of abnormalities associated with the central nervous system, including microcephaly, a history of delayed development, and mental retardation (Streissguth, Randels, & Smith, 1991). Mental handicap and hyperactivity are viewed as the most debilitating aspects of the disorder (National Institute on Alcohol Abuse and Alcoholism [NIAAA], 1991). Individuals exposed to alcohol in utero who show only *some* of these features are characterized as "possible FAE." In addition to its main symptoms, FAS also is associated with sensorineural hearing loss and abnormalities of the heart, joints, skeleton, and genitals. These effects tend to be limited to heavy alcohol consumption during the first and second trimester (Autti-Ramo, Gaily, & Granstrom, 1992).

Incidence and Prevalence.   Determining the incidence and prevalence of FAS is complicated by the fact that the characteristic facial
features are difficult to recognize in the neonatal period and the central
nervous system abnormalities may not be evident for several years. Only
the most severely affected children are recognized at birth, thus reducing
the apparent incidence (number of new cases per live births). Moreover,
FAS facial abnormalities may "normalize" over time.

The disorder varies in frequency with ethnic drinking patterns and with
race. With an overall incidence of about 3 per 10,000 births (Abel & Sokol,
1991), variation among populations is huge; Asians, 3 per 10,000; Hispan-
ics and Whites, 1 per 10,000; and Blacks 6 per 10,000 (NIAAA, 1991). The
increased risk in blacks appears to represent a particular biological susceptibility, because risk remains high even when controlling for maternal
intake (Sokol et al., 1986). There is some indication of a genetic contribution to vulnerability (U.S. Department of Health and Human Services,
1993). FAS has been particularly prevalent in some Native American and
Canadian populations, varying from 10 per 10,000 in American Indians of
the Southwest (May, Hymbaugh, Aase, & Samet, 1989) to 120 per 10,000
in an isolated Canadian Indian population in British Colombia (Robinson,
Conry, & Conry, 1987). Variation is huge even among already high-risk
populations. The prevalence of FAS in Navajo and Pueblo Indians is about
1 in 10,000, essentially the same as the White population and one tenth
the rate in Southwestern Indians (May et al., 1989). Among women who
consume at least 4 oz of alcohol per day throughout pregnancy (8 or more
drinks per day), the incidence of FAS is about 250 per 10,000 births. In
other words, 2.5% of their offspring show the full-blown syndrome. At
greater risk are women who are single and under 25 years old, smoke
during pregnancy, and have little education.

The Effects of Alcohol on the Fetus.   The adverse effects of
alcohol on the fetus are attributed to a transient impairment in umbilical blood circulation that leads to deficient fetal oxygenation (hypoxia)
(Menkes, 1995). Acetaldehyde, the major oxidative product of ethanol,
also is deemed a contributor. Nevertheless, questions abound. We lack a biological marker to measure alcohol intake (NIAAA, 1991) and self reports
of maternal consumption during pregnancy appear to be very unreliable—
underreporting is the rule (Morrow-Tlucak, Ernhart, Sokol, Martier, &
Ager, 1989). Nor do we know how much alcohol is too much or when the
fetus is at greatest risk (NIAAA, 1991). Although FAS is associated with
chronic heavy drinking throughout pregnancy (4 oz/8 drinks per day),
even "moderate" daily consumption (two or four drinks per day) can produce abnormality (FAE). For most of "moderate drinkers," the weekly
average included heavier drinking on weekends. Under these conditions

the embryo has periodic increased exposure, and animal studies suggest that binge-like exposure is more harmful than the same level of alcohol spread evenly over time (Bonthius & West, 1990). The risk appears to be especially high in the earliest part of pregnancy, indeed before the pregnancy is even recognized (Hanson, Streissguth, & Smith, 1978; Russell & Skinner, 1988). Exposure of the embryo to at least three drinks per day (1.5 oz of alcohol) in the period prior to awareness of pregnancy clearly places it at risk for FAS (Ernhart, Sokol, Ager, Marrow-Tlucak, & Martier, 1989). In another study, drinking during the first and second months also was associated with increased risk of low birth weight (Day et al., 1991).

Admittedly, even with the existing guidelines for assessing exposure, the *specific* role of alcohol, as in the case of other drugs, is obscured by the possible contribution of other potential prenatal hazards—nutritional and vitamin deficiencies, "binge" drinking, smoking, the use of other drugs, low plasma zinc levels, and the stages of pregnancy at which exposure occurred (Assadi & Zai, 1986; Day & Richardson, 1991; Forrest & du V. Florey, 1991; Zuckerman & Bresnahan, 1991).

Developmental Aspects.   Given that FAS is viewed as the extreme of a continuum of alcohol effects on the fetus, overlap is seen in symptoms of FAS and FAE. Studies of children, adolescents, and adults indicate major problems in a number of developmental domains—physical, cognitive, educational, and behavioral (Spohr & Steinhausen, 1984; Streissguth Aase et al., 1991; Streissguth, Barr, & Martin, 1984; Streissguth et al., 1994). A description of the early development of the typical FAS child is offered by Streissguth, La Due, and Randels (1988). Presumably, this picture, in a milder degree would be seen in the FAE child.

Infancy.   At birth, the FAS infant is small in length and scrawny. Stunting of growth is one of the persisting physical consequences of high-level prenatal exposure to alcohol, and to other toxic substances as well. It is a hallmark of fetal teratogenic exposure. Growth is impaired in both height and head circumference. Given the relationship between head/skull size and brain mass, prenatal alcohol exposure appears to reduce brain mass itself.

The FAS newborn is often tremulous and irritable and has a weak sucking reflex and poor muscle tone (hypotonic). There may be lack of expected weight gain (failure to thrive) and the need for extended neonatal hospital care. Hospital readmission is common for such problems as failure to thrive, pneumonia, and heart and hip defects. Feeding difficulties may persist, with complaints of poor appetite.

Early Childhood. Motor development and speech are delayed. When speech finally appears, it can assume a superficially fluent quality. The child is perceived as talkative, but speech content is seen as lacking in age-expected complexity. Short and elf-like in appearance, the FAS child is said to "flit about with butterfly-like movements." Seemingly alert, and friendly to the extreme, the child seems to be more interested in people than in objects. A strong need for body contact is reported: They like to touch, fondle, pet, and kiss.

Hyperactivity is especially pronounced in early childhood and is one of the persisting features of the disorder (Spohr & Steinhausen, 1984). The child is into everything and unable to sit still, leading to problems in adapting to preschool (nursery, day-care) programs. Careful supervision is warranted for these children; they may lack appropriate fearfulness, have a tendency to wander, and be unresponsive to verbal restrictions. The FAS child may be especially difficult to recognize after puberty because of a change in facial features (Streissguth, Moon-Jordan, & Clarren, 1995).

During early childhood, prenatal alcohol-related effects on facial appearance and neurological status may diminish (Spohr & Steinhausen, 1984). In a large-scale follow-up study of birth weight and size effects related to level of prenatal alcohol exposure in a largely non-FAS population, birth weight and size effects present at birth were no longer observable at age 8 months, the catch-up phenomenon in children malnourished in pregnancy (Sampson, Bookstein, Barr, & Streissguth, 1994). In conjunction with an earlier study (Coles et al., 1991), the most probably persisting size effect is diminished head circumference. Interestingly, in the Sampson et al. study (1994), binge drinking (five or more drinks on at least one occasion) prior to pregnancy recognition was most predictive of some head-circumference effect.

The point here is that it is the FAS child, in particular, in whom the most persistent physical effects of alcohol exposure are found. In the absence of FAS, whatever alcohol-related physical effects were detectable at birth tend to disappear (see also O'Connor, Brill, & Sigman, 1986; Fried & O'Connell, 1987; Greene et al., 1991).

School Age. The cognitive difficulties associated with FAS and FAE are another of its continuing aspects. The several degrees of FAS are associated with outright mental retardation and its attendant learning problems. In a follow-up study of 40 children (27 FAS, 13 FAE) at average ages of 8 and 16 years, the mean IQ of FAS children was 66 S.D. 18 (range 29–105) at 8 and 67 S.D. 16 (range 20–91) at 16 (Streissguth, Aase et al., 1991). Given these standard deviations, we can estimate that about two thirds were functioning in the IQ range from 48 to 84, from moderate retardation to low-average intelligence. But the IQ ranges at both ages showed that the scores varied from profound retardation to average intelligence. Clearly, FAS is not *always* reflected in mental retardation!

A similar although less impaired picture emerges in the FAE children. Initially tested at an average age of 7 years and again at 16, their average IQ at 7 years of age was 80 S.D. 16 (range 58–101), and it was 82 S.D. 15 (range 65–114) at 16 years. With similar standard deviations at both ages, we can estimate that about two thirds were in the IQ range from 64 to 97, from mild retardation to "average" intelligence. Their range of scores varied from 52 to 114, from upper moderate retardation to "bright normal" intelligence. Although on the average, the FAE group is clearly less impaired, its mean IQ was in the low average range, albeit at its lowest extreme. Some overlap with the FAS youth is evident.

With reference to the nature of their intellect as measured by the Wechsler intelligence tests, both FAS and FAE youth functioned at a higher level on the Performance Scale than on the Verbal Scale. The difference between the two scales for both groups was 10 points. Both FAS and FAE youth perform at a higher level on tasks presented through a visual mode as compared to a language one.

Given significant degrees of intellectual impairment in both FAS and FAE children, major educational problems are inevitable. Apart from the obvious ones associated with retardation itself, the nonretarded FAE child is also at academic risk (Streissguth, Aase, et al., 1991; Streissguth, Randels, & Smith, 1991). With typical IQs in the low 80 range, the FAE youngster is going to encounter difficulties in all academic areas, and even those least affected seem to have special problems with arithmetic. Coupled with the prominence of attention deficits in both groups, we can anticipate that many FAE (and FAS) children will be served in programs for students labeled "learning disability." It also is noted that the previously mentioned superficial verbal fluency can give the impression of greater ability than is possessed and tend to create inappropriately high school expectations.

The alcohol-related learning difficulties of these children is further clarified in an evaluation of the word-attack and arithmetic skills at age 14 years of a large series of children followed since birth (Streissguth et al., 1994). In an analysis that separated the effects of drinking and smoking during the first 5 months of pregnancy, the amount of alcohol exposure was negatively related to word attack and arithmetic skills at 14 years of age. Although the actual correlations were modest, −.15 for word attack and arithmetic in relation to the average number of drinks in the earliest part of pregnancy, they reveal an enduring effect of early alcohol exposure on later academic performance. "Massed" or binge drinking, again, appears to be more heavily correlated with these effects, especially in relation to arithmetic. In comparison with children of women who abstained from alcohol during at least the first 5 months of pregnancy, higher

TABLE 4.2. Relation of prenatal alcohol exposure and arithmetic functioning at age 14 years

Parental Alcohol Exposure	N	Low Arithmetic Skills at 14 Years Old, %
Abstainer	55	45
Average 1–3 drinks per occasion	106	67
Average 3+ drinks per occasion	19	91

Note. Modified from Streissguth et al., 1994.

proportions of the children of drinkers were performing poorly in arithmetic at 14 years old. The respective proportions as a function of the amount of alcohol consumed are shown in Table 4.2.

With 45% of the children of abstaining mothers scoring below average on arithmetic at 14, it is clear that problems with arithmetic are not confined only to children of mothers who drink!

Returning now to the general FAS and FAE populations, behavior problems are common. The hyperactivity and attention problems seen in early childhood carry into school age. There they are expressed in difficulties in concentrating and impulsitivity, both problems that can presage later aggressive and antisocial human behavior. Difficulties in forming friendships are also noted.

Young Adulthood. The effects of prenatal alcohol exposure appear to persist into adult life. In the Streissguth, Aase, et al. (1991) follow-up study of adolescents and young adults, none was functioning at the expected level of personal independence. Given a background of alcoholism in one or both parents and often raised in multiple foster homes, the meeting of basic psychological needs for structure, self-esteem, and self-expression is seriously jeopardized. The great tragedy of FAS and FAE is that they are totally preventable.

We also have the picture of the FAS child who later becomes an alcoholic (Streissguth et al., 1995). Alcohol-related cognitive problems are seen in memory, in orientation to time (keeping appointments) and space, and in general judgment. With some genetic contribution to the vulnerability to alcoholism, the children of alcoholics are at special risk.

Treatment. In the absence of any direct medical treatment for the effects of prenatal alcohol exposure, treatment is largely educational in nature. It involves identifying women at risk and informing them of the potential hazards of drinking during pregnancy and providing assistance to those who are heavy drinkers. Counseling directed toward reduced drinking during pregnancy has shown that it can be helpful. In one study, women who reduced their drinking had babies with more normal growth than did those of mothers who continued their level of alcohol consumption (Quellette, Weiner, & Owens, 1978).

Nicotine

Prenatal exposure to nicotine appears to reduce birth weight. In one study women who smoked a pack a day had babies whose birth weight averaged about 5 oz less than those of nonsmokers (Fried & O'Connell, 1987). Interestingly, smoking during the third trimester had a greater effect than smoking during the first trimester. In any case, assessment of these infants at 12 and 24 months revealed normal weights. Indeed, in another study, one dealing with the effects of prenatal exposure to alcohol and caffeine as well as nicotine, no effects were evident at age 8 months (Streissguth, Barr, Martin, & Herman, 1980). In fact, women who discontinue smoking before the third trimester have babies whose weights are comparable with those of babies whose mothers never smoked (Graham, 1992). Finally, although the weight effects of prenatal nicotine exposure are short-lived, smokers are at a greater risk for pregnancy complications (Graham, 1992). Indeed, women who smoke during pregnancy are reported to be at greater risk for having a child with retardation, presumably due to pregnancy.

Caffeine

Except for extremely high levels of consumption, 300 mg or about three times average consumption, caffeine appears to have no effect on development (Fried & O'Connell, 1987; Streissguth et al., 1980). At extreme levels, effects have been seen on birth weight and head circumference.

Other Teratogenic Substances

Therapeutic Medications

Ironically, drugs used for therapeutic purposes can have teratogenic effects (Graham, 1992; Menkes, 1995). Reference was made previously to the antinauseant thalidomide. Drugs used in the treatment of epilepsy are of special concern. To prevent seizures, so-called anticonvulsant medications are employed, sometimes singly but often in combination. One of the best-known phenytoin anticonvulsants, Dilantin, is a teratogen. Indeed, its effect on the fetus is called the "fetal hydantoin syndrome." It affects intrauterine growth and causes abnormalities of the face and nails and retardation (Hanson, Myriathopoulous, Harvey, & Smith, 1976). The medical dilemma of the pregnant women with epilepsy is eased with careful monitoring of her phenytoin blood level. An earlier 11% risk has now been reduced to only 1% to 2% (Gaily & Granstrom, 1988). It is the current view that other anticonvulsants taken during pregnancy can increase fetal risk—other hydantoins as well as phenobarbitol, valproate, and carbamazepine. These drugs pose a greater risk if used in combination with each other (Delgado-Escueta & Janz, 1992).

Other therapeutic drugs that are teratogenic and can cause retardation are Warfarin (coumadin), an anticoagulant (Hall, Pauli, & Wilson, 1980), and Accutane (isotretinoin), a popular acne-fighting drug (Benke, 1984). With regard to Accutane, the one effective treatment for disfiguring acne, it is only its ingestion that poses a fetal hazard. Less severe forms of acne are treated externally by rubbing the medication on the skin, and this does not appear to be teratogenic. The effects of fetal exposure to Accutane used internally include a much increased risk of spontaneous abortion and a variety of physical anomalies, commonly hydrocephalus and microcephaly. Prior to pregnancy, discontinuation of oral Accutane is advised. Accutane is a vitamin A–like substance, and caution in the use of high doses of vitamin A during pregnancy is also appropriate.

Radiation

The teratogenic effects of radiation are well established (Menkes, 1995). Studies had found that women who received pelvic radiation for cancer early in their pregnancy bore an increased risk of a child with much reduced brain size (microcephaly) and mental retardation (Rugh, 1958). The risk is greatest during the first two trimesters of pregnancy, from the 4th week to the 20th week (Dekaban, 1968; Miller & Blot, 1972). Within this time frame, the earlier the radiation, the greater the hazard (Menkes, 1995). Maternal exposure within 1 mile of the epicenter of the Hiroshima atomic bomb explosion resulted in microcephaly when the fetus was 15 weeks of age or less (Wood, Johnson, & Omori, 1967). The Chernobyl nuclear accident in Russia in the 1980s is a more recent example of a radioactive event that is expected to increase the frequency of retardation in children born to pregnant women who were exposed at that time.

Current medical procedures limit the risk to therapeutic radiation. The level of radiation in diagnostic procedures appears to pose little hazard (Menkes, 1995).

Chronic Maternal Health Problems

Earlier in the chapter, we described a number of infectious diseases that are transmittable to the fetus. But there are also two noninfectious diseases of pregnant women that can adversely affect the fetus—hypertension and diabetes.

Hypertension

In hypertension, elevated blood pressure interferes with circulation to the uterus and can either disrupt normal development of the placenta or cause it to undergo degenerative change. In either case, the fetus is deprived of a normal blood supply, and this leads to either a general impairment in growth and development or to in utero death (Redman, 1989). A particular problem in the third trimester of pregnancy, hypertensive disease is a major threat to the mother as well as to the fetus.

Diabetes

The pregnant woman with diabetes is at increased risk of fetal abnormality (Brudnell, 1989). Typically associated with the hypertension and placental circulatory problems (preeclampsia), about 7% of diabetic pregnancies result in fetal anomalies. The most common involve the central nervous system, the skeleton, and the heart. Impairment in placental circulation is also a major cause of intrauterine growth retardation and perinatal death. Although problems tend to be limited to the more severe forms of diabetes, even insulin-dependent women whose conditions are well controlled are at risk (Fuhrmann, Reiher, Semmler, Fischer, & Glockner, 1983).

☐ Perinatal Causes

Referring to the time frame immediately before, during, and after birth, the perinatal period and, later, the first month of life (neonatal period) is a crucial time, health-wise, in the life of a child. Within this time frame, the birth process itself and then the transition from intrauterine dependence on the mother to independent extrauterine life, carries the greatest risk and vulnerability (Rubin, 1992).

Advances in the care of the pregnant woman and her newborn have greatly reduced risks for abnormality so that the likelihood of a pregnancy resulting in a normal healthy event is unprecedented (Rubin, 1992). This is especially reflected in the survival rates of babies born with low birth weights (Menkes, 1995).

Our particular concern is injury to the brain during labor or delivery or neonatally. It is this injury that causes a major proportion of the neurological problems that later manifest themselves as cerebral palsy, deafness, and mental retardation (Rubin, 1992).

Prematurity

Of the factors posing special risk of either neonatal death or brain injury, low birth weight and reduced gestation age are of particular importance. Prematurity traditionally has been defined as either a birth weight of less than 5.5 lb (2500 g) or a gestational age of less than 38 weeks. Of all births, 7% to 10% are premature, with the incidence varying with the gender and race of the child and the socioeconomic status of the mother. Prematurity is twice as frequent in nonwhites as in whites—14% to 7%, an effect largely attributed to difference in the quality of prenatal care. Among women with inadequate care,[4] the risk of a premature infant is increased threefold. Lack of adequate prenatal care is a particular problem in economically disadvantaged women, especially unwed teenagers. Their higher prematurity rates are paralleled by increased risks of perinatal and infant death (Wise, Kotelchyck, Wilson, & Mills, 1985). Because inadequate prenatal care can include exposure of the fetus to the kinds of drug effects previously discussed, the infant is put at risk of permanent brain damage by a *combination* of prenatal insult and prematurity.

We have noted the dramatic changes in the survival rate of premature infants. Neonatal distinctions are now drawn among three levels of prematurity (as defined by low birth weight). These are low birth weight—3.3 to 5.5 lb (1500 to 2500 g); very low birth weight—2.2 to 3.3 lb (1000 to 1500 g); and extremely low birth weight—less than 2.2. lb or 1000 g. Survival itself is much affected by birth weight. At present, in low birth weight babies it is 70%, in very low birth weight it is 50%, and in extremely low birth weight only 20% (Rubin, 1992). A metaanalysis of 80 outcome studies (Aylward, Pfeiffer, Wright, & Verholst, 1989) of surviving infants revealed that in *all* three groups, about 63% of the infants were normal. The remainder were divided into two groups, "suspect" and "abnormal." In the two "higher" groups, low birth weight and very low birth weight, there were comparable outcomes; 15% and 14% of the babies were abnormal. In the lowest birth weight group, extremely low birth weight, that proportion increased to 19%. But caution with regard to the *ultimate* status of the extremely low birth weight babies is in order, as there is some indication of the development of abnormalities later in infancy (Collin, Halsey, & Anderson, 1991). It also should be noted that the low birth weight babies with brain abnormalities are at particular risk of cerebral palsy (Tores, Vandenberg, Oechsli, & Cummins, 1990).

Retardation-related Disorders of the Perinatal Period

Hypoxic-Ischemic Encephalopathy

Hypoxic-ischemic encephalopathy refers to brain injury during delivery caused by prolonged deprivation of fetal oxygen (perinatal asphyxia). In its severest degree, it results in coma at birth, lack of muscle tone (hypotonia), and seizures. The rapidity of recovery predicts later outcome. Recovery from coma and seizures within 3 to 5 days is associated with a favorable outcome. Permanent central nervous system effects, if present, commonly involved motor disabilities of the types seen in cerebral palsy, most often involving the legs (spastic diplegia) (Menkes, 1995; Rubin, 1992).

Intracranial Hemorrhage

Bleeding in the brain caused by birth trauma is now more common in children born in underdeveloped nations with limited obstetric care. Its occurence can result in permanent central nervous system damage. Severity of the brain hemorrhage is crucial to outcome. Some bleeding is common in very low birth weight babies and does not necessarily lead to permanent damage. Nonetheless, even in babies experiencing "mild" hemorrhage, nearly one third (29%) show some eventual cognitive impairment, a rate that doubles to 50% if the bleeding is "severe" (Rubin, 1992).

Hyaline Membrane Disease (Idiopathic Respiratory Distress Syndrome)

Premature newborns are vulnerable to lung disorder (pulmonary insufficiency) and a resultant hypoxia (Rubin, 1992). The hypoxic state itself can produce abnormalities in cerebral blood flow and set the stage for cerebral hemorrhage. Brain circulation also can be compromised by an associated head abnormality. Further complicating the newborn's medical status is a need for a greater percentage of its oxygen to be delivered at higher pressures and for lengthy periods. This can damage the lungs (bronchopulmonary dysplasia).

Hearing Impairment

Up to 10% of babies weighing less than 3.3 lb (1500 g) experience hearing loss (Rubin, 1992). If these very low birth weight babies also suffer either a hypoxic-ischemic insult to the brain or intracranial bleeding, cognitive or motor impairment ensues. Hearing loss may be the only disability in a low birth weight baby, and because it is "invisible" it is important to check the hearing of *all* low birth weight babies in their first year (Bergman et al., 1985).

HIV Infection

HIV infection, a condition described previously as a prenatal infection, also can be acquired at birth. No distinction is drawn between the disorder with regard to its time of origin. Its nature and course are described elsewhere in some detail.

Herpes Simplex

A viral infection of the maternal genitalia, herpes simplex can be transmitted to the newborn at birth. Often following a fatal course, its symptoms include microcephaly, brain calcifications, brain inflammation (meningioencephalitis), and lesions to the eye (Rubin, 1992; Sells & Bennett, 1977). Common sequelae are retardation and blindness.

Kernicterus

Kernicterus is a condition of severe neonate jaundice that arises in the first week of life (Menkes, 1995), most often because of an incompatibility in blood types between mother and baby, such as Rh and ABO incompatibilities. The newborn nurses poorly, develops fever, and has a monotonous cry. Eventually the infant shows abnormal motor behavior—athetosis (slow writhing involuntary movements) and often dystonia (abnormal muscle tone), rigidity (muscle stiffness), and tremors. (These motor symptoms are described in the section on cerebral palsy.)

Other symptoms include hearing loss or receptive aphasia (hearing speech sounds but unable to interpret their meaning) and cognitive impairment. Retardation, if present, usually is not severe. In a study of children whose cerebral palsy was caused by kernicterus, nearly half (47%) had normal intelligence (IQs in the 90 to 110 range), about one quarter had low average to borderline intelligence (27%), and the remainder (26%) fell in the retarded range (Byers, Paine, & Crothers, 1955). Determination of intellectual level in these children can be difficult because of the hearing and language impairment and a paralysis of gaze.

Treatment involves first the prevention of the condition that leads to jaundice (hyperbilirubinemia) and includes blood exchange transfusions, in utero in some instances, and phototherapy (Menkes, 1995).

☐ **Postnatal Causes**

Postnatal factors that can cause mental retardation are infectious diseases of the brain; cerebral trauma (head injury); cerebrovascular accidents, most often from head injury; brain tumors, poison, and environmental toxins; and severe dietary protein deficiency.

Infectious Diseases

There are two brain infections that can result in permanent neurological damage and mental retardation—meningitis and encephalitis.

Meningitis

Meningitis is an inflammation of the membranes that line the brain, the meninges. Usually of bacterial origin, there are three forms of the disease—bacterial, neonatal, and tuberculosis.

Bacterial Meningitis.   This is the most common brain infection. It not only is life-threatening but also has permanent neurological sequelae. In the infant one sees fever, poor feeding, irritability, lethargy, and fullness of the fontanel. Seizures may also occur. The more severe degrees involve coma. Its mortality rate is from 1% to 5%, with as many as 50% showing some permanent effects. These include motor, sensory, and cognitive impairments (Abroms & Durbin, 1992).

Neonatal Meningitis.   Although the pathological features of neonatol meningitis resemble those of meningitis in infants, the site of bacterial invasion is different. It usually occurs at the base of the brain, and all degrees of severity are seen. With severe brain damage, there is mental retardation, paralysis of the limbs (spastic quadriplegia), seizures, blindness, and deafness. Failure of further brain growth leads to microcephaly. In less severely affected neonates, later development may be associated with hyperactivity, attention deficit, and learning disabilities (Abroms & Durbin, 1992).

Tuberculosis Meningitis.   A complication of tuberculosis, it is usually seen in the preschool-aged child (Rubin, 1992). Its major neurological sequelae include paralysis of the limbs (spastic quadriplegia),[5] partial paralysis (hemiplegia),[6] seizures, and visual impairment. About 50% of children have some degree of intellectual impairment, ranging from severe retardation to more subtle cognitive deficits, attention deficit, and hyperactivity (Abroms & Durbin, 1992).

Encephalitis

An inflammation of the brain itself as, distinct from its meninges, encephalitis arises from either a direct invasion of the brain by an infectious organism, such as a virus, or as complication of the infection of another organ. The major sources of primary encephalitis are the viruses that cause measles, mumps, herpes simplex, and infectious mononucleosis. The symptoms of these diseases, such as measles encephalitis, include hearing loss, motor impairment, seizures, and retardation. The most common of these infections is herpes simplex, previously described in connection with its occurrence at birth. Antiviral treatment has reduced its mortality rate and its residual neurological consequences, but long-term effects include motor and sensory deficits, seizures, speech and memory impairment, and retardation (Abroms & Durbin, 1992).

Cerebral Trauma (Head Injury)

After the neonatal period (the first 28 days), the leading cause of injury and death in children is accidents, especially involving automobiles. Fully one quarter of children in such accidents sustain head injuries (Abroms & Durbin, 1992). In the United States, about 200,000 children are hospitalized each year because of head injuries, with a death rate of 1 in 10,000. Sadly, second only to accidental head injury is child abuse, especially in children younger than 2 years of age. In one study of head injuries in children younger than age 1, child abuse accounted for almost one third (32%), the remainder being accidental in origin (Abroms & Durbin, 1992). Most injuries of the head are simple concussions or mild contusions, and there usually is complete recovery (Hammill, 1977). The head injuries of special concern involve intracranial bleeding, especially in children younger than age 5 years (Abroms & Durbin, 1992).

If head injury results in unconsciousness and coma (a profound state of unconsciousness from which one cannot be aroused), the length of the coma is a good predictor of long-range outcome. In a study of children who had been unconscious for at least 24 hours, about half made a complete recovery, with the remainder experiencing such sequelae as limb paralysis and seizures (Heiskanen & Kaste, 1974). If coma persists for more than 3 weeks, some degree of permanent cognitive impairment is to be expected. Depth of coma as well as length is an important indicator of eventual outcome. The Glasgow Coma Scale, a widely used measure for evaluating

TABLE 4.3. Glasgow coma scale

Characteristic	Score
Eye opening	
Spontaneous	4
To speech	3
To pain	2
Lacking	1
Best motor response	
Obeys	6
Localizes	5
Withdraws	4
Abnormal flexion	3
Extensor response	2
No response	1
Verbal responses	
Oriented	5
Confused conversation	4
Inappropriate words	3
Incomprehensible sounds	2
No response	1
Coma score	$(E + M + V) = 3$ to 15

Note. From Jennett B, Teasdale G: Management of Head Injuries. Philadelphia, FA Davis, 1981, p. 78. (Reprinted with permission).

coma in children and adults, is shown in Table 4.3. The Glasgow Scale assesses opening of the eyes, motor, and verbal responses.

In general, head injury associated with intracranial bleeding (hematoma) places the child at greater risk of death or future cognitive and neurological problems (Jennett et al., 1979). With reference to the ultimate functional status of children and adults with head injury, a five-step classification is used. Category I refers to a "vegetative state"; category II to independence in daily living activities; category III to independence in daily living and capable of sheltered employment; category IV to ability to perform simple work under normal conditions; and category V to performing at a professional level (Najensen et al., 1978).

There is the need for comprehensive rehabilitation programs for children and adults with head injuries. Under the auspices of a special branch of medicine, physical medicine, and commonly incorporating services of physical, occupational, and speech therapy, together with psychology and psychiatry, rehabilitation programs for head-injured individuals have mushroomed in recent years. Although our focus here has been on children, it is the young adult, commonly the victim of a motorcycle accident, who is most often a head-injury victim.

Cerebrovascular Disorders

Cerebrovascular disorders are much less common in children than adults (Menkes, 1995). Although congenital head defects are a predisposing factor, trauma is the most common cause of intracranial bleeding. Bleeding also may follow the rupture of a malformed blood vessel or as result of infections, toxins, metabolic disorder, and tumors (Gold, Hammill, & Carter, 1977).

Brain Tumor

Brain tumors are the second most common form of cancer in children, leukemia being the first; brain tumors account for about 20% of childhood cancers (Menkes & Till, 1995). Their frequency is greater in children aged 5 to 10 years. The clinical picture is of increased intracranial pressure (caused by space-taking mass) expressed in headaches, vomiting, impaired vision, and changes in consciousness. If the tumor is present prior to the fusing of the sutures in the skull, there is enlargement of the head. Seizures also may occur. Treatment can involve surgery, radiation, and chemotherapy. Radiation, as therapy, can create difficulties by damaging brain tissue, and neurological consequences of radiation may be delayed in appearance by months and even years. The most common cognitive sequelae are problems with attention and memory (Duffner & Cohen, 1991). Evident by age 7 years, they tend to be progressive. The greatest intellectual deficits attributable to radiation therapy are found in children who were treated before age 3 years. Radiation therapy also can affect growth, and recent treatment trends involve trying to delay radiotherapy in favor of chemotherapy in children younger than 3 years old (Duffner et al., 1993).

The diagnosis of the brain tumor in children has been underdiagnosed in the past in children under age 2 years because tumor-caused visual and motor (e.g., gait) problems were attributed to general development delay (Fessard, 1968). This has changed dramatically with the advent of neuroimaging technology in the form of magnetic resonance imaging and computed tomographic scans.

Poisons and Environmental Toxins

Lead

As a result of industrialization, lead is omnipresent in our environment. Lead has no known physiological value, and children are particularly susceptible to its toxic effects. Lead produces its destructive effects silently—most poisoned children have no symptoms. The vast majority of affected children are undiagnosed and, of course, untreated. Lead poisoning is widespread and is the most common and preventable pediatric health problem today (Roper, Houk, Falk, & Binder, 1991).

The adverse effects of lead on physical and cognitive development are well established, although what is considered a "safe" level of exposure remains to be determined. In earlier times lead water pipes were recognized as a source of lead poisoning and, later, lead in house paint was identified as a potential hazard to infants. The most serious form of lead disease, lead encephalitis, as seen in infants and young children, is typically the result of prolonged ingestion of flaking leaded paint, the kind of paint found in older and often dilapidated housing. Daily consumption by the young child of only a few chips can produce lead poisoning.

Dramatic in its clinical picture, the symptoms of acute lead encephalitis are stupor, coma, and seizures. Survivors are at risk for both cognitive impairment and stunted growth (Henretig, 1992). To protect children from lead exposure, federal legislation was enacted (Lead-Base Paint Poisoning Act of 1971) that set new standards for the amount of lead permissible in toys and paints.

Concerns about exposure to lead resulted in dramatically reducing the lead content in our gasoline. Its virtual elimination has been associated with an average decline in blood lead levels in children and adults that precisely parallels its reduction in gasoline (Annest, 1983). With the general awareness of the hazards of lead exposure, and the implementation of public-health programs of prevention and childhood screening, lead encephalitis, as such, is now rare. Nevertheless, our urban environment still contains much lead, with the main sources of exposure apart from lead paint being lead-contaminated soil and dust, drinking water via lead in pipe fittings, and proximity to lead storage batteries (Roper et al., 1991).

As in all else, children of the poor are at greater risk. They are three times more likely to have high blood lead levels. Although children in families receiving Medicaid make up only one third of American children aged 1 to 5 years, they represent a whopping 60% of children with elevated levels of lead in their blood (U.S. Government General Accounting Office, 1997).

Public health standards for what is considered a safe blood lead level have been reduced steadily as adverse effects have been documented at levels earlier thought to be safe, such as 10 μg/dl of whole blood (Roper et al., 1991). Before the 1960s only a level above 60 μg/dl was considered toxic; by 1978 that level had declined by 50% to 30 μg/dl, and now it is at 10 μg/dl. Nor is it clear that there are no adverse effects at even lesser levels but, given the industrialized nature of our world, some level of lead exposure may be unavoidable. To provide a perspective on the significance of the various lead levels, a level of 70 μg/dl is a medical emergency; 45 to 69 μg/dl requires both medical and environmental (preventive) measures, including chelation therapy; 20 to 44 μg/dl indicates the need for environmental and medical evaluation; and at 15 to 19 μg/dl there is need for nutritional and educational intervention along with more frequent screening. If a community has many children in the range from 10 to 15 μg/dl, this should trigger community-wide preventive measures. In effect, only children with blood lead levels of 9 μg/dl are to be considered as without significant risk (Roper et al., 1991). With reference to these levels, children who live in close proximity to sources of lead, such as lead storage batteries, may have blood lead levels in the range of 40 to 80 μg/dl and would require medical intervention even when they are without symptoms.

Lead and Intelligence. The insidious effect of lead on cognitive functioning has been indicated in a large number of studies conducted both in America and abroad (e.g., New Zealand). Although not all studies have shown the same picture, reviewers of this body of research conclude that "the weight of the evidence clearly supports the hypothesis that decrements in children's cognition are evident at blood lead levels well below 25 μg/dl. No minimum threshold for the lead-IQ relationship is discernible from these data" (Roper et al., 1991, p. 9). A British study (Popcok, Ashby, & Smith, 1987) of children with lead levels largely below 8 μg/dl, that is, in the desired range, also showed a lead-level effect. The IQ-lead correlation was −.16, but this correlation was largely attributed to social factors affecting intelligence, notably the mothers' IQ, rather than to lead. The role of social factors in lead studies has been noted, children with higher lead levels tending to come from lower socioeconomic backgrounds. Recent studies employing statistical techniques that can control for nonlead influences have been able to tease out the independent contribution of lead (e.g., Hawk et al., 1986).

Figure 4.1 shows the inverse relationship between IQ and blood lead levels in children whose lead levels ranged from 6 μg/dl to 47 μg/dl (Hawk et al., 1986). The population consisted of 80 children, aged 3 to 7 years, whose neighborhoods were at high risk because of leaded paint in older run-down housing. Their mean blood level was 20.8 μg/dl. The study is viewed as particularly significant because the depressing effect of lead on IQ was present in children who, for the most part, were not then seen as at risk. Almost three quarters of the children (72%) had blood levels that were then regarded as safe. It is out of these kind of findings that the safe lead level was dropped subsequently to its present one of 10 μg/dl.

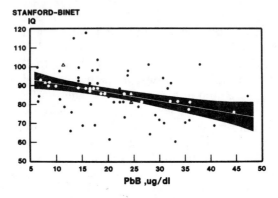

FIGURE 4.1. Child IQ (Stanford-Binet) as a function of blood lead levels. The shaded area indicates the confidence interval. Triangles indicate double values; circles, single values. (Reprinted with permission from Hawks et al., 1986.)

Although the negative effect of lead on IQ seems well established, it is also important to translate that effect in points of IQ. The various studies have found average IQ effects of from 4 to 7 points in children with lead levels of from 10 to 25 μg/dl (e.g., Milar & Schroeder, 1983). In Figure 4.1, the mean IQ at 10 μg/dl is estimated at 92, as contrasted with an estimated mean of 87 at 25 μg/dl. At the 35 μg/dl level, the mean is about 80, but there are relatively few children at this level. These IQ effects, although modest in absolute terms, are not necessarily without academic significance. In a study that looked at the educational status of children whose lead levels were determined at 6 and 7 years of age and then again at 19 years old, dose-related effects were present in their educational achievement (Needleman, Schell, Bellinger, Leviton, & Allred, 1990).

In keeping with the National Center for Disease Control and Prevention intervention guidelines (Roper et al., 1991), medical treatment generally is recommended for children who, although asymptomatic, have lead levels greater than 55 μg/dl (Henretig, 1992). Treatment can include a diet that is low in fat and rich in iron and has calcium and vitamin C. This diet can reduce the amount of lead that the body actually absorbs.

Mercury

Mercury, like lead, has neurotoxic properties. Although mercury long has been known as an occupational hazard ("mad as a hatter"), severe poisoning is rare. The more general concern is with exposure of pregnant women and of the general population to mercury-contaminated food (Henretig,

1992). Poisoning by organic mercury compounds, chiefly methylmercury, produced epidemics in Japan and Iraq. In Japan, a community was poisoned by eating shellfish exposed to mercury following a factory discharge into a local bay. In Iraq, it resulted from eating bread whose grain had been treated with a methylmercury fungicide. The neurologic picture in affected children included tingling and other sensory disturbances, progressive visual loss, motor problems of gait (ataxia) and tremor, impaired hearing, and mental retardation (Menkes, 1995). The teratogenic potential of mercury is revealed in the finding that almost one third (30%) of the children born to women in the Japanese exposure had serious developmental abnormalities (Henretig, 1992).

Malnutrition

The role of diet in intellectual development has been of special interest as it pertains to "third world" countries. Because of inadequate diet, malnutrition is humankind's most pervasive problem; it is estimated that at least half of the children in underdeveloped or third-world countries are moderately to severely undernourished. Apart from a general concern about inadequate calories in the diet of impoverished children (and adults), there is a special concern about protein, a foodstuff vital to normal growth and development. In recent years there also has been recognition of the role of "micronutrients," iron and zinc, as contributors to a healthy diet (Pollitt, Gorman, Engle, Martorell, & Rivera, 1993).

Degrees of Malnutrition

Of special concern is *severe* malnutrition. Two forms are recognized—*marasmus*, a general calorie deficit, and *kwashiorkor*, a protein deficit. Marasmus results in the wasting away of tissues and extreme stunting of growth. Kwashiorkor usually is manifest after weaning when mother's milk, a food high in protein, is replaced by a diet high in starch but low in protein. The physical effects of kwashiorkor are impaired growth, edema (accumulation of water in the tissues), skin sores, and diminished hair pigmentation. The term *kwashiorkor* is from the African country of Ghana, where it was commonly seen in children aged 1 to 3 years.

Malnutrition of a lesser severity, *moderate* malnutrition, also is associated with some degree of growth stunting. In the United States, severe malnutrition in the form of marasmus and kwashiorkor is rare, although many low income children are undernourished. School feeding programs were a response to children who came to school hungry. Importantly, virtually all children, even those who are somewhat undernourished, get adequate protein. Of all of the foodstuffs, protein is the one that is most closely linked to brain growth and cognitive development (National Institute of Child Health and Human Development, 1976).

Brain Development

There are two growth spurts in the development of the human brain. The first occurs in the second trimester of pregnancy and is marked by an increase in the number of neurons. The second spurt begins in the third trimester and continues postnatally on through about age 6 months. During this latter spurt the "supporting" cells of the brain (glia) multiply, and also branches from the neurons (dendrites) reach out and form connections with other neurons (synapses). This period of glial cell division is viewed as a time of the developing brain's greatest vulnerability to malnutrition (Kinsbourne, 1995).

Animal studies often have been cited as revealing how nutritional deficits can interfere with brain growth and produce mental retardation. But in the rat, for example, a degree of nutritional deprivation equivalent to a 40% weight reduction in humans is necessary before permanent neurological symptoms arise. Such weight deficiency rarely is seen in humans. On the other hand, iodine deficiency in the human diet can lead to mental retardation. An iodine-deficient diet can cause abnormal thyroid-gland function and the symptoms of the previously described classical form of mental retardation—cretinism.

Nutrition can affect brain size. In one study, children of severely malnourished mothers had smaller brains than well-nourished peers (Monckberg, 1968). For the brain to catch up, the malnutrition must be corrected by age 2 years (Pollitt, 1994). This "catch-up" phenomenon, one we have seen earlier in the discussion of prenatal drug exposure, also is illustrated in a study of the effects of severe prenatal malnutrition on intellectual development in young adults (age 19 years), resulting from a brief period of famine in Holland during World War II. No effects on cognitive functioning were seen in survivors; the impact of the malnutrition was modified by later access to an adequate diet (Stein, Susser, Saenger, & Marolla, 1975).

Research efforts to identify the specific role of nutrition in mental development have been confounded by the fact that malnutrition typically is accompanied by other biological and psychological hazards to normal development (e.g., Ricciuti, 1993). Infectious disorders, for example, can lead to malnutrition by increasing caloric requirements in the already chronically undernourished child (Birch & Cravioto, 1966).

Children with Severe Malnutrition. Two early studies of children who experienced severe malnutrition in the first 2 years of life found a lag in cognitive development relative to better-nourished siblings (Birch, Pinuro, Atcalde, Toca, & Cravioto, 1971; Hertzig, Birch, Richardson, & Tizard, 1972). It is the current view that severe malnutrition in infancy adversely affects intellectual functioning (Pollitt et al., 1993), *but* improvement in functioning can be brought about by a combination of nutritional replacement and general stimulation (Grantham-McGregor, Powell, Walker, & Himes, 1991). In the next chapter, we address the role of "general stimulation" on mental development.

Children with Moderate to Mild Malnutrition. Given the focus on protein as important to development, studies have been conducted on the effects of both prenatal and postnatal dietary protein supplement on physical and cognitive functioning. Chiefly directed toward chronically undernourished children in Latin America (Colombia and Guatemala), but also in American cities as well, such as New York, a protein supplement in infancy does appear to produce some enduring benefits in cognition, for example, IQ gains of about 7 points. In the physical domain, protein supplementation actually appears to speed motor development. The physical and cognitive benefits are achieved primarily by the most poorly nourished children, those in the lowest socioeconomic strata (Pollitt et al., 1994).

Prenatal protein supplement also is credited with positively influencing visual stimuli "habituation" rates in infants. The rate of visual habituation might be thought of as a "boredom threshold," with more rapid habituation said to be predictive of better cognitive functioning (Columbo, 1993).

☐ Major Neurological Disorders Often Associated with Mental Retardation: Cerebral Palsy and Epilepsy

Cerebral Palsy

Example: Paul

Paul is 12 years old and has some paralysis of his left arm and leg (left spastic hemiplegia). He walks with a marked limp. Small and underdeveloped for his age, his general development has been slower than that of an older brother. He did not begin to speak until about 2.5 years of age, but by 4 years old he was reasonably fluent and his speech could be understood easily. As a child he was hyperactive and had a short attention span. Loved and enjoyed by his parents, he did not play well with other children; they tended to overexcite him. By 7 years old his hyperactivity had diminished, but his attention span was still short. Apart from a reduced ability to attend in class, he had particular difficulty in understanding visual forms and spatial relationships, an area of expected impairment in light of motor problems indicating damage to the right cerebral hemisphere. He has been in a special class for 3 years, enjoys school and his teacher, but continues to have difficulty with other children. They tease him, and he becomes angry and strikes out. At 12 years of age he cannot read, although he has learned some street and bus signs.

His poor reading achievement may relate to his general visual-perceptual problems. These are common in children with cerebral palsy. In spite of his many disabilities, his parents take pride in Paul. His father is a carpenter, and Paul has learned a little about tools and tries to be helpful. Their main concern in his "emotionality." They feel that he could get along better if he had more control of his feelings. Apart from his emotional outbursts, he's seen as a gentle and sensitive youngster who is easily handled if one avoids direct confrontation (Baroff, 1991a).

Description

Cerebral palsy is a disorder of movement, balance, and posture that results from a nonprogressive lesion in brain areas that control muscles and maintenance of posture (Taft & Matthews, 1992). In addition to its motor manifestations, also commonly present are cognitive impairments, seizures, and sensory loss. With an incidence of about 1 to 2 per 1000 births, improvements in neonatal care have had the effect of increasing the survival rate of very low birth weight babies, infants particularly susceptible to cerebral palsy (Menkes, 1995; Taft & Matthews, 1992).

Causation

Most often attributed to perinatal brain injury, cerebral palsy also can originate prenatally or in early childhood. Prenatal causes include the kinds of hazards described earlier—infections (e.g., cytomegalovirus), exposure to teratogens and radiation, and maternal-fetal blood incompatibility. In the perinatal period, asphyxia and intracranial bleeding are the primary causes, with the low birth weight (premature) infant at particular risk. About half of all cases of cerebral palsy are found in infants whose weight at birth is less than 5.5 lb (2500 g) (Cummins, Nelson, & Grether, 1993). Following birth, cerebral palsy can result from infections (meningitis and encephalitis), brain abscess, or head trauma occurring during infancy or early childhood (Inge, 1992). Sadly, with respect to trauma, in one study

TABLE 4.4. Forms of cerebral palsy

Spastic	Extrapyramidal	Ataxic	Atonic	Mixed
Spastic quadriplegia	Athetoid	Ataxia	Atonic	Spastic-athetoid
Spastic diplegia			Hypotonic	Rigid-spastic
Spastic hemiparesis	Rigid			Spastic-Ataxic
Spastic monoplegia	Tremor			
Spastic triplegia	Dystonia			

Note. From Alexander & Baver, 1988; Menkes, 1995; Taft & Matthews, 1992.

(Cohen & Warren, 1987) no less than one third of the brain traumas were the product of physical abuse.

Forms of Cerebral Palsy

Table 4.4 lists a common grouping of the variety of motor disorders seen. They include such difficulties as weakness and paralysis of the arms and legs, poor coordination, involuntary movements, and lack of balance.

Spastic Cerebral Palsy. The most common variant, spastic cerebral palsy accounts for about half of all cases (e.g., Grether, Cummins, & Nelson, 1992). Indeed, the term is sometimes synonymous with cerebral palsy itself (e.g., The Spastics Society). In spasticity, movement is slow, effortful, and restricted in range, although it is occasionally jerky and explosive. Movement is difficult because of the tendency of muscles to contract (flex) if an "extending" motion is attempted (Denhoff, 1976). In effect, the muscle inhibits the very move intended.

Spasticity can affect all four limbs (quadriplegia), all limbs but primarily the legs (diplegia), three limbs (triplegia), only the legs (paraplegia), only the limbs on one side of the body with the arm usually more affected than the leg (hemiplegia), or only one limb (monoplegia). In a recent series (Grether et al., 1992) diplegia predominated and was especially frequent in low birth weight infants.

In addition to the nature of limb involvement, spasticity also is characterized by its severity—from mild to severe. In its *mild* form there may be only a lack of precision in fine-motor movements (Denhoff, 1976) and an awkward gait, walking with arms extended for balance (Thompson, Rubin, & Bilenker, 1983). At the *moderate* level, problems are encountered with both gross- and fine-motor movements, and there is also interference with speech. The characteristic body posture in children is shown in Figure 4.2. This degree of severity does not interfere with the performance of most activities of daily living. If spasticity is *severe*, however, there is inability to

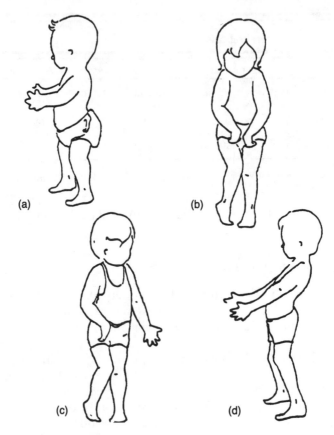

FIGURE 4.2. Postures in cerebral palsy. (*a*) *Normal* year-old child standing. (*b*) The young *spastic diplegic* child standing. This posture is one of flexion. His head "pokes" forward and up to compensate for the lack of extension in his trunk and hips. His arms are usually bent and press down and forward at the shoulders. His legs turn in and are held together; his standing base is very narrow, making balance difficult and in many cases impossible. Some children do manage to get the foot of one leg flat on the floor as illustrated, but in doing so they bend the hips even more and the whole of the pelvis is pulled back on that side. (*c*) The young *hemiplegic* child standing. His posture is asymmetrical; all his weight is on his good leg. The affected arm bends and turns in at the shoulder, which presses down, and his trunk bends on that side. The leg is stiff and turns in at the hip, the pelvis is pulled up and back; his foot is stiff, and the ankle does not bend, so that he takes weight only on the toes and ball of his foot. In some cases, the head is also pulled towards the affected side. (*d*) Typical position adopted by the *athetoid* child. His arms are held forward to overcome the extension of his hips and to prevent him falling backwards. (From *Handling the Young Cerebral Palsied Child at Home, 2nd ed.*, by Nancie R. Finnie. Copyright 1974 by Nancie R. Finnie, F.C.S.P. Reprinted by permission of the publisher, E. P. Dutton, a division of Penguin Books USA Inc.)

walk, to use hands, and to articulate intelligible speech (Denhoff, 1976). At its greatest level of severity, one may be unable to sit without support or even to hold up one's head. It is the severe degree of cerebral palsy that requires the use of assistive or prosthetic devices—braces for legs, crutches, and wheelchairs. There is also the need for assistance with the most basic activities of daily living (e.g., bathing and toileting).

Extrapyramidal Cerebral Palsy.   Referring to one of the two nerve tracts in the brain that control movement pyramidal and extrapyramidal, lesions in the extrapyramidal system lead to impairment in muscle tone (tightness) and to a variety of abnormal motor patterns and postures (Menkes, 1995). Formerly termed "dyskinesias," they include movements that are uncontrolled and without purpose. These movements disappear during sleep and intensify under stress (Shapiro, Palmer, Wachtel, & Capute, 1983). Three types of movements occur: *athetoses, rigidity,* and *tremor.* Also included in this form is *dystonia,* a postural abnormality.

Athetoid.   The most common subtype, athetoid refers to movements that are relatively slow, wormlike, and writhing. If the movements are jerky, they are called *choreic* and *choreoathetoid.* Athetoid movements are prominent in the fingers and wrist but also are seen in the face. In walking, gait is lurching and stumbling. The typical standing posture is shown in Figure 4.2*d.*

Rigid.   As in spasticity, movement is impeded. Unlike spasticity, however, in which relaxation of the muscle releases movement like the springing free of a jackknife blade, in rigidity resistance to movement is continuous and "lead pipe" in quality.

Tremor.   Tremor refers to a movement that is rhythmic and pendulum-like. Distinctions are drawn among tremor occurring with movements that are intended, unintended, and constrained (Denhoff, 1976).

Dystonia.   Dystonia is a postural abnormality that involves prolonged retention of an athetoid position (Melyn & Grossman, 1976).

Ataxic Cerebral Palsy.   Primarily a disorder of balance, ataxic cerebral palsy also includes some general incoordination (Denhoff, 1976). Gait is unsteady; one walks with high steps as if on stilts. Hand movements are awkward with a tendency to either under- or overreach (Levitt, 1982). Accounting for about 7% of cerebral palsy, this special subtype is no longer distinguished by some neurologists (Menkes, 1995).

Atonic (Hypotonic) Cerebral Palsy.   In cerebral palsy, the infant is usually hypotonic at birth (too little muscle tone) and then gradually develops spasticity (excessive tone). In atonic cerebral palsy, however, a hypotonic state persists beyond ages 2 or 3 years (Lesny, 1979). A common pattern is the eventual development of incoordination, ataxia, and difficulty with rapid successive movements. Cognitive impairment can be severe, with about one third of those affected showing mental retardation. Atonic cerebral palsy also can be a forerunner of the athetoid form, with athetoid movements present by age 3 years (Menkes, 1995; Paine, 1964).

Mixed Forms of Cerebral Palsy.   The frequently diffuse nature of brain damage results in combinations of movement disorders—a mixture of spasticity and other forms (Menkes, 1995; Taft & Matthews, 1992). This combination is illustrated in some children with spastic hemiplegia who also show athetoid posturing. Other mixes include spasticity with ataxia, rigidity, or dystonia.

Associated Disorders

Speech.   Impaired speech is characteristic and can be the most disabling aspect of cerebral palsy (Shapiro et al., 1983). Better than two thirds are so affected (68%), including virtually all with the athetoid form and about half of those with spasticity (Hopkins, Bice, & Colton, 1954). Especially prominent are difficulties in articulation, but there also can be omission of sounds or the substitution of one sound for another (Irwin, 1972) and difficulties of breath control.

Intelligence.   The assessment of intelligence in cerebral palsy is made more difficult by the impairment in speech and movement. Given these limitations and the use of tests designed to circumvent them, studies typically have found retardation in about half of the population (Stephen & Hawks, 1974; Taft & Matthews, 1992). Although better than one quarter (28%) has average to above-average intelligence, disproportionate numbers fall in the low average and below ranges. Within retardation itself, the proportions at each level of severity are estimated as mild (IQ 55 to 69), 34%; moderate (IQ 40 to 54), 28%; severe (IQ 25 to 39); and profound (IQ 0 to 24), 17%.

There is some indication that IQs tend to increase over time in children with IQs in the 51 to 89 range (Klapper & Birch, 1967). On the other hand, IQs in the below-50 and over-90 ranges tend to remain fairly constant. It is speculated that one effect of reduced mobility is a restriction in the general level of stimulation, and, with increasing experience, the child's basic potential is more fully realized.

Among the several forms, the risk of cognitive impairment is greatest in ataxia and rigidity. Between the two most frequent forms, spasticity and athetosis, there is little difference although, as previously noted, the risk of retardation is heightened in those with severe motor impairment—spastic quadriplegia—and in atonic and dystonic cerebral palsy. Within the spastic group, those with diplegia are the least affected (Ingraham, 1964).

Caution is particularly appropriate in predicting later intellectual functioning in children with the athetoid form. Delay in language and gross-motor development can lead to an underestimation of their intelligence (Crothers & Paine, 1959). In the experience of Crothers and Paine, almost two thirds (65%) of these children had IQs over 70, with nearly half (45%) with IQs of at least 90. In a later study, 78% of children with athetoid cerebral palsy had IQs of 90 or better (Kyllerman et al., 1982).

Given the widespread nature of cognitive impairment, school learning problems can be anticipated with educational needs complicated by the simultaneous presence of motor problems.

Perceptual Difficulties.   Perceptual disorders are found in a number of sensory modalities—visual, visual-motor, tactile, and auditory (Cruickshank, Bice, & Wallen, 1957; Menkes, 1995). Attention-deficit disorder—limited attention span and easy distractibility—also is found, sometimes accompanied by hyperactivity (e.g. Alexander & Bauer, 1988). Visual and visual-motor disturbances are particularly common in spasticity, although occasionally they are seen in the athetoid form. In nonretarded children with cerebral palsy, these perceptual disorders are likely to be reflected in "learning disabilities."

These perceptual problems do not refer to sensory *acuity*; rather they are impairments in the understanding (perception) of what is being experienced in a particular sensory mode. In the visual-motor realm there is difficulty in motor planning and imitation (apraxia). A child with cerebral palsy asks, "Why can't I make my hand do what my eyes see?" This is but an extreme example of what we all experience. In drawing, for example, although we can see the object that we intend to draw (or paint, or sculpt), it is only those with special talent who can get their hands to accurately portray what the eyes see (Baroff, 1991a).

The visual modality also can present problems because of "figure-ground" confusion. We all are familiar with "hidden figures" in which objects to be found are camouflaged by their background and rendered relatively invisible. Not only are hidden figures more difficult for some children with cerebral palsy, but even recognition of shape, color, and size against normal backgrounds can be problematic. These figure-ground perceptual difficulties also are observed in the tactile (Dolphin & Cruickshank, 1951) and auditory spheres (Laraway, 1985).

In persons with spasticity, visual perceptual disorders are more frequent in those with either bilateral impairment or, at least, impairment of the left side (left hemiplegia) (Wedell, 1961). This is consistent with an understanding of the role of the right cerebral hemisphere in visual functions, a left hemiplegia or motor impairment meaning damage in the contralateral or right hemisphere (e.g., Gaddes & Edgell, 1994). In reproducing designs with blocks, for example, left-hemispheric damage and right-side motor impairment can lead to errors in detail, but the general form or *gestalt* of the design is preserved. With right-hemispheric damage (left-side motor impairment), however, there can be a total loss of the figure's general configuration. It is no longer recognizable as the design intended. The educational implication of these perceptual difficulties is to emphasize "figure" through color, size, or both.

In the tactile perceptual mode, there can be difficulty in recognizing objects only by touch (astereognosis). In those with spastic hemiplegia, the problem is limited to the impaired hand.

Health Problems.   The child with cerebral palsy is subject to a number of medical problems, notably seizures, orthopedic deformities, urinary infections, respiratory difficulties, eye abnormalities, and hearing loss (Menkes, 1995; Shapiro et al., 1983; Taft & Matthews, 1992). One of the most stressful aspects may be the need for repeated orthopedic surgery in childhood.

Treatment

Physical therapy, occupational therapy, speech therapy, and orthopedic surgery are the principal treatments in cerebral palsy. Physical therapy is intended to promote functional postures and movement and to prevent additional muscle tone–related deformities. Although the brain lesion does not change, its motor consequences can worsen. Despite physical therapy, about half of those with spasticity ultimately require some form of orthopedic intervention—often the just-mentioned multiple surgeries at ages 4 to 8 years. The surgery is designed to lengthen or release muscles and tendons. In adults, bone surgery is used to correct fixed deformities.

With reference to physical therapy, treatment beginning by age 2 years is generally desirable. In fact, so-called early-intervention programs are generally available in infancy and can involve a number of therapies—physical, occupational, speech, nursing, and education (Taft & Matthews, 1992).

Various drugs have been tried to ease spasticity or reduce involuntary movements, but they usually are ineffective (Menkes, 1995; Taft & Matthews, 1992). Drugs that produce muscle relaxation, for example, often cause a general state of sedation. In the case of a child with spastic quadriplegia, moreover, the benefits of physical therapy can be limited by the degree of mental retardation (Menkes, 1995).

Technology has a prominent role to play in this disorder. Assistive devices are widely used in helping the child compensate for movement limitations, and communication aids are much in vogue in providing an alternative for speech (Baroff, 1991a).

The Adult with Cerebral Palsy

In spite of the potential multiplicity of disabilities, the achievement of independence in adulthood is attainable for many persons with cerebral palsy, especially those with spastic hemiplegia and diplegia. And even those whose disabilities preclude a fairly independent existence can achieve varying degrees of self-management, including that of employment. Most now work in sheltered workshops, but with the advent of supported employment, the lowering of general physical barriers, and access to physically assistive devices, opportunities in regular employment will increase.

In recent years, severely physically disabled adults have been able to achieve more independent living arrangements through access to a personal attendant, an individual who can assist in self-care, household, and even vocational duties (Baroff, 1991a).

Epilepsy (Seizure Disorder)

A child with epilepsy:

It was Christmas; the children were about to open their presents. Suddenly, one of them said, "Something is wrong with Jonathan." He was sitting in his bed, quite still and with a fixed stare. Slowly his head turned to the left and his eyes moved laterally. His body stiffened and he began to slide to the floor. For seconds he got tighter and tighter; his face paled and then became a horrible blue. Small jerking movements began in his arms and legs. They were not violent, but they were forceful and not to be restrained. He grunted with each jerk as if it was a major effort. This seemed to last forever, but it could not have been more than 30 seconds, with his color steadily worsening.

Then it stopped, fairly quickly, and he lay there with his eyes turned up, motionless, not even seeming to breathe. I felt for his pulse; it was still there and as I held his wrist he took a few deep, gasping breaths. His color began to return and the blueness disappeared. He coughed, spit, and I wiped his lips because of the saliva. When his breathing was normal, he was carried to his bed where he slept for about 15 minutes. When he awoke, he was a bit tired and quiet, but he was soon back to normal and returned for more opening of presents. The entire episode lasted less than half an hour, but

those 30 minutes were to change our life. (Baroff [1991a], adapted from
Linnett [1982])

Clinical Features

Epilepsy or seizure disorder refers to an abnormality in the electrical activity of the brain that results in *recurrent* seizures (convulsions, fits). It
is their recurrent nature rather than their occurrence, per se, that war-
rants the designation *epilepsy* (Keranen, Sillinpaa, & Riekkinen, 1988).
Not regarded as epilepsy are fever-associated recurrent seizures in infancy
and early childhood—so-called febrile convulsions. Usually appearing between 9 and 18 months of age, they generally disappear by 5 years. They
can occur in children who are developing perfectly normally and leave no
residual effects. Indicating a genetic predisposition is the frequent finding
of a positive family history for febrile seizures (Abroms & Durbin, 1992).

In addition to their recurrent nature, epileptic seizures have a number
of other features in common. These are a sudden (paroxysmal) onset,
an altered state of consciousness, a similar time length for each type of
seizure, abnormal movements or a posture change, spontaneous cessation,
and a lapse of time before returning to the preseizure state. These elements
are evident in Jonathan's seizure. Although epilepsy includes a variety of
types of seizures, Jonathan's "tonic-clonic" or "grand mal" seizure is the
one most clearly associated with the disorder and is its most dramatic
representative.

Prevalence

Estimates of the prevalence of epilepsy vary tremendously. The most accurate data pertain to people under active treatment, about 5 per 1000 in
the United States (Hauser, 1978). It is chiefly a disease of the developmental years; in 75% seizures originate by age 18 years (Commission for the
Control of Epilepsy and its Consequences, 1977).

Causation

The distinction is commonly drawn between two types of causation: *symptomatic epilepsies*, those caused by a clear brain lesion (e.g., cerebral palsy
or brain tumor) or systemic disease (e.g., kidney failure); and *idiopathic
epilepsy*, seizures occurring in the absence of a structural brain abnormality
or disease. The various causes are shown in Table 4.5. It is arranged according to time of origin, from conception to postnatal life (Aird, Masland,
& Woodbury, 1984; Dreifuss, 1975; Marsden & Reynolds, 1982). Of all the
causes, brain infections are the most common.

TABLE 4.5. Causes of epilepsy

Conception
  Genetic: genetic susceptibility to abnormal brain waves (electrical activity); to idiopathic (cryptogenic) seizures in childhood, primarily tonic-clonic and absence; and to inherited disorders in which epilepsy is a symptom (e.g., phenylketonuria)
  Chromosomal: trisomy 13–15 (D) (Patau syndrome); fragile X (Musumeci et al., 1988)
Prenatal
  Infections: congenital rubella, syphilis, toxoplasmosis, and cytomegalovirus
Natal and perinatal
  Birth trauma
  Anoxia
  Bleeding into the brain
  Low blood sugar
  Maternal-fetal blood incompatibility
  Prematurity
Postnatal
  Brain infections: encephalitis and meningitis; abscess; fever
  Head injury: Closed or open
  Toxins: lead and mercury, alcohol, drugs (e.g., amphetamines), allergic factors, toxemia of pregnancy
  Metabolic and nutritional disorders: Imbalances of sodium, potassium, calcium, magnesium, and water; carbohydrate metabolism (e.g., hypoglycemia and diabetes); protein metabolism (e.g., phenylketonuria, porphyria); fat metabolism (e.g., lipid storage diseases); vitamin B6 deficiency; endocrine disorders (e.g., adrenal, thyroid, estrogens); kidney and liver failure
  Circulatory disease: Brain hemorrhage; stroke; arteriosclerosis; hypertensive encephalopathy; syncope
  Neoplasms: Brain tumor; blood vessel tumor; vascular malformations; familial and degenerative brain diseases

Types of Seizures

The current classification system for epilepsy, the International Classification of Epilepsy Seizures (Epilepsy Foundation of America, 1981), characterizes seizures in terms of two aspects—their symptoms and their site of origin in the brain's cerebral cortex. Two symptomatic forms are recognized: *generalized* seizures, those originating simultaneously in both cerebral hemispheres and affecting both sides of the body; and *partial* seizures, those originating in only one of the two cerebral hemispheres and affecting just one side of the body. Seizures also can originate in only one hemisphere and then spread to the other—*secondarily generalized* seizures.

TABLE 4.6. Epileptic seizures and their ages of onset

Type	Traditional Designation	Age of Onset
Simple (with elementary symptoms)	Focal	Any age
Complex (with altered consciousness)	Psychomotor, temporal lobe	Any Age
Partial seizures (secondary generalized)	Focal and/or grand mal	Any Age
Generalized		
Tonic-clonic	Grand mal	<1->20 years
Absence	Petit mal	3–15 years
Myoclonic		1–4 years
Atonic	Drop attack, minor motor	1–4 years
Infantile spasms	Jacknife, salaam, hypsarrhythmia	3–18 months

Table 4.6 lists the most common seizures and also includes their traditional designation and age of onset.

Partial Seizures

Simple Partial (Focal). These seizures originate as localized muscle or sensory symptoms, and there is no impairment of consciousness (Menkes & Sankar, 1995). The most common focal attack in children is the *versive* seizure. It typically consists of a turning of the eyes and head and also may involve the arm and hand on the same side toward which the head is turned. The child appears to be looking at a closed fist. These seizures are particularly common in hemiplegic children. Weakness often follows the seizure (Todd's paralysis) and can last for a day or more.

Simple partial seizures also may consist of the jerking of one arm or leg, tingling or numbness on one side of the body, seeing flashes of light, and experiencing strange odors (Hermann, Desai, & Whitman, 1988).

Complex Partial. Among the more frequent partial seizures in childhood (Menkes & Sankar, 1995) and the most common in adults (Hermann et al., 1988), it is not seen until about age 10 years. Its special quality is the occurrence of *apparently* purposeful behavior during what is, actually, a state of impaired consciousness. Often preceded by an *aura*, a somatic or sensory experience that alerts one to the imminence of an attack, the seizure usually begins with a drawing and jerking of the mouth and face. The eyes may stare in a searching manner, there may be "tonic" (muscle contraction) posturing (as in catatonic psychosis) or a desire to urinate. Most remarkable is the appearance of what appear to be intentional movements. Engaged in without awareness, these "automatisms" are performed in a repetitive and stereotyped manner and include clutching, fumbling with buttons, kicking, walking in circles, and a host of oral movements—swallowing, lip smacking, chewing, licking, and spitting. Less often seen are pill-rolling, athetoid, and flinging movements. Another striking feature is the presence of emotional behavior. Laughing, crying, and fear are frequent, and there also may be outbursts of aggression. These automatic behaviors are short-lived, usually lasting not more than 5 minutes. Following the seizure (the "postictal" period), there may be a period of drowsiness, and when wakefulness is fully recovered there is no memory of the episode.

Complex partial seizures are traceable to an abnormality in the temporal lobe but can also follow lesions in the frontal and occipital lobes. Apart from treatment with anticonvulsant drugs, it is this form of epilepsy that is treatable with surgery.

The possibility of complex partial seizures often is considered in the child with behavior problems *and* an abnormal electroencephalogram or in violent juveniles (e.g., Pritchard, Lombroso, & McIntyre, 1980).

Partial Seizures Secondarily Generalized. In a large proportion of children, an initial partial or focal seizure spreads to other parts of the body and becomes a "generalized" seizure with an accompanying loss of consciousness. On occasion, this seizure follows an orderly sequence as it spreads through the body, the so-called jacksonian march. This type of seizure generally is considered to be indicative of a structural lesion in the cerebral cortex (Menkes & Sankar, 1995).

Generalized Seizures

Tonic-Clonic (Grand Mal). This is the most common form of generalized seizure and the prototype of epilepsy. This was the seizure described in Jonathan at the beginning of this subsection.

The classic tonic-clonic seizure is sudden in onset, although it may be preceded by an aura. The seizure begins with a rolling of the eyes and loss of consciousness. If upright, one falls to the ground. The body muscles are initially rigid (tonic phase), and there is a fixed contraction of the diaphragm and chest muscles causing an expulsion of air and the "epileptic cry." Muscle rigidity also interferes with breathing, and a *temporary* loss of oxygen results in the bluish or cyanotic appearance of the face (Jonathan's "horrible blue"). The initial rigidity is followed in a few seconds by jerking (clonic) movements of the head, face, and limbs. These are the "convulsing" movements that we associate with the disorder. In the clonic phase there may be loss of bladder control, but breathing resumes although it is "snoring" in quality. As the episode ends, clonic movements slow and cease abruptly. Recall that Jonathan's mother noted that the jerking stopped "fairly quickly." The duration of the seizure can vary from just a few seconds to about 30 minutes; 1 to 3 minutes is typical. A seizure often is followed by a state of confusion, the person can be difficult to arouse and may sleep for several hours or awake with a headache and muscle soreness (Jonathan slept for about 15 minutes). Suggested first aid for a tonic-clonic seizure includes laying the person flat on the ground, turning the head to one side (allowing saliva to drain), and just waiting (Hermann et al., 1988). The most important thing to understand is that breathing does resume! Most tonic-clonic seizures require no medical intervention (Jonathan resumed opening presents!). If they are continuous, however, one seizure recurring before there is full recovery from the preceding one or "status epilecticus," immediate medical attention is in required. Although seizures are expressive of abnormal electrical activity in the brain, seizures that last for more than 1 hour themselves can damage the brain (Hermann et al., 1988). The most common cause of status epilepticus is the sudden withdrawal of anticonvulsants (Menkes & Sankar, 1995). Fortunately less than 4% of epileptic patients experience have episodes of status epilepticus (Maytal, Shinnar, Moshe, & Alvarez, 1989).

Tonic (Only) and Clonic (Only).   With the onset of the seizure and the loss of consciousness, there is only a single rather than an alternating state of muscular movement—either rigidity (tonic state) or clonic (jerking state).

Absence (Petit Mal).   This type of seizure consists of abrupt and brief lapses in consciousness manifested as vacant staring. Lasting only 5 to 10 seconds (Menkes & Sankar, 1995), it ends as abruptly as it began, and activity is resumed as if nothing has happened. If the seizure occurs while standing, there may be some swaying but usually not falling. There is also no postseizure difficulty. The seizure is often recognizable as a slow, rhythmical blinking of the eyes and rhythmical jerking of the head, arms, and trunk. Some absence episodes include automatisms—snapping of the fingers, patting, or walking in circles. Although automatisms are present in both absence and complex partial seizures, in other respects these two types of seizure are very different. Absence episodes are much briefer, lasting seconds rather than minutes, and there is immediate return to consciousness. The frequency of absence seizures can vary tremendously, from an occasional episode to more than 100 per day. If attacks are frequent, the child's cognitive functioning is slowed, and the first indication of the disorder may be a deterioration in school work and behavior

(Lennox, 1945). Indeed, the seizures may be confused with willful inattention (Herman et al., 1988). Originating in childhood, ages 5 to 9 years, and present in greater frequency in girls, absence seizures tend to decrease with time and, in about half of children, disappear by the late teens. In a considerable proportion of children, from one third to one half, absence and tonic-clonic seizures both are present, with absence usually appearing first.

Myoclonic. Myoclonic seizures consist of small, random, recurring twitches, largely in the fingers and hands (Menkes & Sankar, 1995). They occur on both sides of the body and can also can include the head (head bobbing) and trunk. Jerking may be rapidly repetitive or relatively isolated. Several types of nonepileptic myoclonus are found. They can be elicited by sensory stimuli, such as light, noise, or tapping on the face and chest.

Atonic (Akinetic, Drop Attack). This seizure is characterized by a sudden, momentary loss of posture or muscle tone. Legs give way and the child falls, sometimes violently (Menkes & Sankar, 1995). Consciousness is briefly lost, and the force of the fall can injure the face and head. Affected children wear headgear. The seizure usually lasts less than a minute, and there is quick recovery of alertness and muscle tone. Atonic episodes recur frequently during the day and are especially common in the morning and shortly after awakening.

Infantile Spasms (West Syndrome). With an onset in early infancy, from 3 to 8 months of age, and more frequent in males, infantile spasms consist of a series of muscular contractions causing the head to flex, the arms to extend, and the legs to draw up (Menkes & Sankar, 1995). This is the so-called bowing or salaam position. Lasting just seconds, these seizures can occur repeatedly and, if one occurs while standing, can result in a violent fall against which the child cannot protect himself or herself. As with atonic seizures, protective headgear is necessary. The majority of affected children have moderate to profound retardation. Infantile spasms are the type of seizure most often seen in tuberous sclerosis, the dominantly inherited retardation-related disorder described in Chapter 3.

Associated Disorders

Intelligence. Numerous studies indicate an average IQ reduction of 5 to 10 points in populations with epilepsy (Dodrill, 1982). This is especially true of chronic seizures; here there are higher rates of mental retardation (e.g., Bagley, 1971). Retardation is especially prominent in seizures arising in infancy and early childhood—infantile spasms, tonic-clonic, and myoclonic (Livingston, 1972). With infantile spasms one also may have impairment in physical development and head size together with deficits in vision and hearing (Abroms & Durbin, 1992).

The cause of the seizures much affects their intellectual impact. Those attributable to clear organic brain abnormality, symptomatic epilepsies, are more likely to produce cognitive impairment than those for which no physiological abnormality is evident (idiopathic epilepsy). Indeed one study found no difference in IQ between neurologically normal epileptic children and their unaffected siblings (Ellenberg, Hirtz, & Nelson, 1986).

The frequency of seizures themselves can affect intelligence (Dodrill, 1988; Trimble, 1988); reference is made to this elsewhere in connection with status epilepticus. Apart from status epilepticus, an effect of frequency of seizures on intelligence is seen in tonic-clonic and complex partial epilepsy.

The treatment of seizures itself can adversely affect cognitive function. The side effects of anticonvulsant medications, the chief form of seizure control, can weaken attention and concentration and, occasionally, even induce hyperactivity. Among the many anticonvulsants, two have been particularly problematic in persons with mental retardation—phenytoin (Dilantin) and phenobarbital. Both can lead to a progressive decline in an already impaired level of cognitive functioning (Trimble, Thompson, & Huppert, 1980). The drug carbamazepine (Tegratol) appears to produce less cognitive impairment (Andres, Bullen, Tomlinson, Elmes, & Reynolds, 1985).

Complex partial seizures, seizures usually caused by lesions in the left temporal lobe, the dominant area for language in most persons, can impair verbal memory and word finding apart from general intelligence. A comparable lesion in the right temporal lobe could affect memory for complex visual stimuli (e.g., Hermann, Wyler, Richey, & Rea, 1987).

Learning Problems.   Given the potentially adverse effects of seizures on intelligence, school learning problems are found (Seidenberg et al., 1986), often in reading and arithmetic.

Motor Functions.   Anticonvulsant medications also can affect motor behavior, producing either hyperactivity or slowing (Reynolds, 1981). They also can interfere with balance and gait.

Personality.   Epilepsy is associated with an increased risk of behavior problems in children and youth, and psychiatric disorders in adults. Attributable, in part, to the effect of a chronic illness, and one characterized by unpredictability, behavior disorders also can result from the medications taken to control seizures. In children one sees problems of irritability, hyperactivity, and aggressiveness (Kalachnik, Hanzel, Harder, Bauernfeind, & Engstrom, 1995; Trimble & Reynolds, 1976). In adults, epilepsy increases the risk of psychosis, especially in those with complex partial seizures (11% to 14%) (Aird, Masland, & Woodbury, 1984). As in the cognitive realm, behavior problems in children are more frequent in those with seizures originating in early childhood, although, if they are well controlled by adolescence, adult adjustment is grossly normal (Stores, 1978).

Personality effects in epilepsy are most apparent in those with complex partial seizures. In some adults, one encounters a pattern of behavior that consists of humorlessness, circumstantiality in speech and writing, religious or philosophical concerns, and disinterest in sex (Bear, Freeman, & Greenberg, 1984).

It also should be noted that the psychological problem tied to having a disorder that is both unpredictable and frightening itself creates major stress in the person's life. The disorder traditionally has raised the specter of social ostracism (Baroff, 1991a).

Treatment for epilepsy involves anticonvulsant medications. These result in either a major reduction in seizures or complete control, the latter being achieved in about half of affected persons. A lesser degree of control is attained in another third; about one fifth obtain no benefit at all (Aird, Masland, & Woodbury, 1984). Total elimination is a reasonable goal in absence and tonic-clonic seizures originating in childhood but not for infantile spasms, atonic, or myoclonic seizures. If seizures originate in either adolescence or adulthood, lifelong anticonvulsant therapy is likely. In the latter, the response to treatment in the first 2 years is a good predictor of future seizure control (Reynolds, 1987).

In the use of anticonvulsants, the goal is to achieve the greatest degree of seizure control with the fewest number of drugs, preferably only one— so-called monotherapy (Coulter, 1993). A combination of drugs sometimes is required, but multiple anticonvulsants ("polytherapy") increase the risk of unwanted side effects (Aird, Masland, & Woodbury, 1984). Recent studies of epilepsy in persons with retardation indicate that the great majority can be maintained on only one drug (Poindexter, Berglund, & Kolstoe, 1993). Contrary to a generally pessimistic view of the prospect for attaining good seizure control in persons with retardation, in one study (Marcus, 1993) it was the type of seizure rather than retardation or its severity that determined control. Virtually all can be controlled with not more than two drugs, and these should not include barbiturates (Coulter, 1993).

In the small proportion who do not achieve satisfactory seizure control, so-called refractory epilepsy, careful attention to seizure-inducing conditions, sensory, physical, and emotional, can be helpful (Aird, 1983). With regard to the anticonvulsants themselves, carbamazepine and valproic acid have been used increasingly in recent years (Coulter, 1993).

In preschool-aged children with refractory seizures, there may be a resort to a special diet, one high in fat and low in carbohydrates—the *ketogenic* diet (Menkes & Sankar, 1995).

Finally, as previously indicated, surgery is available to some individuals with complex partial seizures. This involves the removal of the anterior portion of the affected temporal lobe. If surgery is performed on the temporal lobe in the "dominant" cerebral hemisphere, care is taken to avoid excising areas related to language. The plasticity of the young brain with regard to recovery from major tissue loss is seen in children who are younger than 10 years old. If language areas require resection, language control can be transferred to the unaffected cerebral hemisphere (Menkes & Sankar, 1995).

☐ Summary

This is the second of the two chapters devoted to biological causes of mental retardation. In the first, the discussion was on the role of genetic factors; here the focus shifts forward time-wise to nongenetic adverse biological influences operating after conception and during the prenatal, perinatal, and postnatal periods. Considerable attention is paid to the prenatal period, as disorders are described that result from fetal exposure to infections, toxic substances, and maternal illness. Particular stress is placed on forms of retardation that are wholly preventable, the result of fetal exposure to "recreational" drugs and alcohol. The consequence of prolonged fetal exposure to alcohol, fetal alcohol syndrome, is described in detail. Recent research on the effects of nicotine (smoking) also is included.

During the perinatal period, the heightened risk for developmental abnormality is focused largely on low birth weight ("premature") infants but also includes health problems in the newborn that can damage cognitive development. During postnatal life, the child born healthy later can experience retardation as a result of exposure to infectious diseases, head injury, and such common environmental hazards as lead. The consequences of infantile and childhood exposure to lead are yet to be fully determined, especially the level of lead in the blood that poses no threat to cognitive development. Also receiving some detailed treatment is the effect of malnutrition on mental development. Primarily a problem in third-world countries, such as some Latin-American nations, this is also a form of developmental delay that is wholly preventable.

The final section of the chapter describes two neurological disorders often accompanied by mental retardation—cerebral palsy and epilepsy.

Possible Discussion Questions

Given the risks to which the fetus is exposed, how do we communicate to prospective mothers (and fathers) the need for exercising caution during pregnancy?

To try to prevent FAS in women with a history of chronic alcoholism and the prior birth of FAS children, some judges actually have incarcerated women during their pregnancy! Should adult and legally competent women be free to continue their drinking? Apart from attempts at "education," is society helpless in the face of such potentially destructive behavior? How are the "rights" of the high-risk woman to be reconciled with those of her unborn child? Does the unborn child have any rights?

To what degree are our local communities sensitive to the threat of lead exposure in young children? Are our local public-health departments actively seeking to minimize this exposure? What are they doing?

Epilepsy long has been a dreaded illness. Exposure to an individual experiencing a grand mal seizure can be frightening, especially if there is a brief cessation of breathing. But this is only a "phase" of the seizure and, with subsequent relaxation of the muscles, breathing resumes. Do you think that knowledge of the nature of the disease makes it less frightening to you? What are the implications for other feared conditions?

☐ Notes

1. Because the fetal period is four times longer than the embryonic one, future references are limited to the term "fetus."
2. A virus is the smallest living organism: about 1/25,000,000 of an inch. It reproduces only within living cells and causes a wide range of diseases in humans, plants, and animals.
3. Bacteria are one of the types of single-cell microorganisms that cause infections. Others are viruses (e.g., rubella), yeasts and fungi (ringworm and thrush), and protozoa (toxoplasmosis)
4. Inadequate care is defined as no medical examination in the first 13 weeks of pregnancy and fewer than five subsequent medical visits.
5. This term is later described in the section on cerebral palsy.
6. This term also is described in the section on cerebral palsy.

CHAPTER

Psychological Factors in Mental Retardation

☐ Overview

Having described the biological factors that can influence intellectual development, we now shift to "psychological" ones. By these are meant the caregiving environment to which the infant and young child is exposed. Related research is presented in terms of six general topics. They are the general relationship between certain kinds of childhood experiences and cognitive development, children raised under conditions of gross deprivation, children reared by parents who are themselves retarded, adopted and foster children, twin studies, and the prevention of mental retardation through early childhood education. Crocker (1992) attributes about 12% of mental retardation to nonbiological causes (e.g., deprivation), but if we add the environments of families in which both genetic and environmental factors are assumed to be operative (cultural-familial or psychosocial retardation), the environmental contribution is much greater.

☐ Psychological Experience and Intellectual Development

In this initial section of the chapter, research is cited that reveals at least *general* relationships between certain kinds of experience and cognitive development. The term "general" relationship is intended to convey the fact that although developmental research has been able to describe "normative" behavior throughout the life span, it has been unable to explain the *process* by which a child reaches, maintains, or diverges from such behavior. Growth in intelligence, that is, in increasing problem-solving capacity, can be viewed as the consequence of an interaction between a nervous system (the brain) and the child's experiences. One kind of experience that is thought to foster growth is confrontation with that which we do not understand. Our need for "structure," the need to make some sense of experience, compels us at the very least to *try* to understand. From this perspective growth is catalyzed by contradiction, by conflicting ideas. The young child watches water poured from a smaller but thicker container into one that is taller and thinner. Because the *height* of the water is necessarily elevated in the thinner receptacle, the child interprets the height difference as reflecting a change in the volume of the liquid. Confronted with the error of that conclusion, an error attributable to the young child's tendency to construe events in terms of only one dimension, the child may be able to recognize the *why* of his or her error and correctly solve similar problems in the future.

Whatever the cause of misunderstanding, the resolution of conflicting concepts requires exposure to potentially correcting experiences. The nature of these experiences is determined by the culture within which we live and the values that it communicates to parents, the actual nature of our childrearing experience, and our interactions with peers, teachers, and the wider society.

Culture plays a powerful role in our cognitive development. It specifies, in effect, the kinds of cognitive skills that are particularly valued. Rice farmers in Liberia, for example, excel at estimating quantities of rice (Gay & Cole, 1967), and children in Botswana, accustomed to story telling, have excellent memories for stories (Dube, 1982). Both of these groups outperform Americans on these tasks.

Schooling affects how we think. Classifying items into "categories" (e.g., putting animals in one group, food items in another, and implements in a third) is characteristic of adults in Western culture. Adults in other cultures tend to categorize according to "functional" groups, for example putting a hoe with a potato because it is used to dig up a potato. Functional groupings are more common in cultures with less formal schooling (Rogoff & Chavajay, 1995).

Our values and experience determine what catches our attention and what is ignored. They define for us what is relevant to our perceptual system and what is irrelevant, what we accept and what we reject. This perceptual "filter" constrains as well as broadens. Its constraining aspect, for example, is seen in the resistance of people who equate "knowing" only with direct experience to draw inferences. Thus a nonliterate Central

Asian farmer refused to draw an inference in a simple syllogism (Luria, 1976). The syllogism asserts that in the far north, where there is snow, all bears are white. The town of Novaya Zemlya is in the far north, and there is always snow there. Asked the color of the bears to be found there, respondents replied that they could only speak about that which they had directly experienced. The premise of the syllogism is ignored, as the respondent insists that if a man had *seen* a white bear and told about it, he could be believed. But the respondent had never seen one and hence could not say. His culture-specific way of thinking about the world rejects the very idea of a premise. Interestingly, a *younger* man volunteered, "Your words mean that the bears there are white." He was less bound by the cultural constraints. In general, being willing to reason on the basis of a premise that one cannot verify is characteristic of formal educational experience and literacy.

Although culture variations clearly affect *how* we think, and what we think about, the focus in this chapter is on the nature of the developmental experiences provided to children in contemporary Western societies. Can children be exposed to environments that could result in mental retardation although, as later evident, the potential for normal intellectual functioning was present? Unlike earlier chapters that deal with biologically based cognitive impairments, the concern here is with the child who enters the world with seemingly intact biological equipment. This is not to say that the biologically impaired child is not also vulnerable to potentially noxious psychological experiences. Indeed, the risk may even be greater for the child with a biologically limited growth potential. Such a child can face a dual risk—one attributable to brain impairment and the other to a "depriving" childhood experience.

In specifying childhood environments that appear to be associated with either good or bad intellectual outcomes, the reader is cautioned to not assume any simple and straightforward relationship between those environments and ultimate development. We cannot explain why children who have experienced apparently similar qualities of care have different developmental outcomes, or how children can emerge from either the most supportive or brutalizing of environments as equally competent (Sameroff & Chandler, 1975). It is clear that each child's experience even in the same family is unique—a uniqueness tied to such factors as gender, birth order, parental characteristics, and serendipity. Even in the most controlling of environments, life is largely an unplanned experience!

The complexity of the developmental process is evident in cases of children who were reared in the most abysmal of environments but were able to recover from the experience and progress developmentally (e.g., Koluchova, 1972). Together with studies of Guatemalan children

(Kagan, 1972) in which retarded development in infancy did not preclude normal adulthood, such "recovery" calls into question the presumed irreversibility of the experiences of infancy and early childhood and suggests a much longer period of growth potential than hitherto assumed. The studies to be presented illustrate the views of prominent theorists that there is greater malleability in the child than earlier psychoanalytic theory had proposed (Clarke & Clarke, 1986; Hunt, 1976; Wachs & Gruen, 1982).

☐ Conditions of Gross Deprivation

We begin to consider the complex nature of the impact of the psychological environment on intelligence by exploring, via case studies, what constitutes an unfavorable (or favorable) environment. Over the past 50 years there have been periodic descriptions in the psychological literature of children reared under the most abnormal conditions. Their experience suggests an extraordinary resilience in the developmental potential of preadolescent children (Clarke & Clarke, 1976; Skuse, 1984a,b).

In the second edition of this book, a pair of identical twins was described who were reared under conditions of isolation and brutality (Koluchova, 1972). This third edition permits us to update their status as well as to add several other children to this unfortunate grouping. Description is largely limited to children who appear to have been biologically intact when their plight was discovered—children free of sensory deficits and neurological abnormalities. Briefly included is a sibling of one of these children, a child with microcephaly.

PM and JM

First we consider the identical twins (Koluchova, 1972, 1976). Twin boys, PM and JM, were reared by a hostile stepmother under conditions of extreme isolation. Their situation was not detected until they were 6 years old, after which they were removed from parental custody and placed in group care and then in foster care. The stepmother was imprisoned and both she and the father lost parental rights.

For more than 5 years the twins lived under the most abnormal conditions. Some neighbors were unaware of their very existence! The father was once seen beating them with a rubber hose, but neighbors did not interfere because they feared conflict with the twins' stepmother.

The twins grew up in almost total isolation. They lived in a small, unheated closet and were not allowed in the rest of the house.

Following their discovery at age 7 years, they were admitted to a hospital. In the hospital kindergarten they were timid, mistrustful, and reclusive. They had to be brought to the kindergarten in wheelchairs, as they could barely walk! They had had little opportunity to use their legs. The condition of their experience had also affected their physical development!

The extraordinary degree of isolation from normal experiences was seen in their reaction to objects and activities commonplace to children. They showed surprise and horror at such things as moving mechanical toys, television, children doing physical exercises, and street traffic. These reactions gradually disappeared, and they began to explore their surroundings. Their shyness also diminished, and they began to respond positively to adults but in the kind of indiscriminate fashion seen in affection-deprived children.

Their speech was very poor, and they communicated through gestures. They tried to imitate adult speech but could only repeat fragments of sentences; words were poorly articulated.

Their spontaneous play was very primitive. Initially consisting only of object manipulation, imitative play soon appeared, but they did not join in the play of other children.

A remarkable finding was their lack of understanding of the meaning of pictures. To help them learn that pictures were representations of real objects, pictures initially were used that were identical in size and color to the objects portrayed. At the time of their rescue they were functioning developmentally at about the 3-year-old mental level. Although this was comparable to at least a moderate degree of retardation, it was assumed that their basic abilities were much higher and that, indeed, they were not really retarded.

Following hospitalization they were placed in a home for preschoolers where they made good progress. They began to relate to other children, interactions aided by the fact that their peers were younger. Their environmentally induced developmental delay (immaturity) made it easier for them to interact with younger children. Their motor skills improved; they learned to walk, run, jump, and ride a scooter. Progress was also seen in fine-motor skills.

At age 7 years, 7 months, their progress again was evaluated; their mental age had increased to 4 years. Although their mental development had exceeded expectations, their ultimate educability was uncertain. Not until age 9 years were they deemed ready for school, but continued impairment in speech and in fine-motor skills led to initial placement in a program for retarded children. At this time they moved from the children's home to a foster home. Their new foster parents were two unmarried, middle-aged sisters—intelligent, with wide interests, and capable of relating to children. One of the sisters earlier had adopted a baby girl who was now a normally developing 13-year-old. The other sister became the twins' actual foster mother.

Regarding their earlier experience, it was not until age 9 years that they had enough language to even roughly describe its nature. They referred to their stepmother as "that unkind lady," an apparent understatement! They recalled their hunger, their thirst, and being beaten on the head. Their scalps were badly scarred!

For a long time they dreaded the darkness. Perhaps it reminded them of their closet. They appreciated the physical warmth of their new home, the good food, and refuge from beatings. They sought reassurance that they would not be removed from their foster mother.

In a school with retarded children, the twins excelled. Their abilities to write, draw, and concentrate improved remarkably and, at 10 years old, they transferred to a second-grade class in a regular school. Their progress indicated that they could successfully complete their country's basic 9-year school program, although at 18 years old rather than at 15.

A summary of intelligence-test results shows that in the 25-month period from ages 7 to 9 years to 9 to 10 years their mental age scores increased by 36 months. A dramatic change in living conditions was able to effect mental growth even in children as "old" as 7 years. Beginning at age 8 years, 4 months, they were tested with the Wechsler Intelligence Scale for Children. Over a 3-year period, from ages 8 to 11 years, their full-scale IQs increased from 80 and 72 to 95 and 93, respectively. By 11 years old, their mental abilities were in the average range of intelligence. Some 5 years earlier they had been functioning in the range of moderate retardation! The greatest change was seen on the verbal scale, on which scores increased from IQs of 80 and 69 at 8 years, 4 months, to 97 and 96 at 11 years old. At age 22, the twins are described as socially and emotionally normal and above-average in intellectual competence (Clarke, 1984, via personal communication from Koluchova).

Louise and Mary

Louise and Mary, two sisters of four, were ages 3 and 2 years, respectively, when their plight was discovered. They also had an older stepsister and brother. Because of the wealth of the developmental data (Skuse, 1984a,b), our focus is on Louise and Mary. Living with a mother who appeared to be both mentally retarded and mentally ill, they were viewed as strange children who would scamper up and sniff strangers, making animal-like grunting and sniffing sounds. Both still sucked bottles and wore diapers; no attempt had been made to train them. If presented with toys, they made no attempt to play with them.

We have then two children with apparently intact vision and hearing whose primary way of interacting with the world was olfactory and tactile, the kinds of sensory preferences more appropriate to children with actual sensory deficit. Language was virtually nonexistent.

The children differed physically. Louise was normal in height, in sensory functions, and in head circumference. Mary, on the other hand, had a head circumference at less than the third percentile for her age; she was microcephalic, as was her mother.

The family all lived in one room, and social workers were horrified to discover that the children were kept *leashed* to a bedpost, apparently the mother's means of keeping her house "spotless."

They were allowed to remain in the custody of the mother and her partner Ruppert; the mother was encouraged to let the children attend a play group. Within a year, Louise had made great strides. Her motor skills were well developed, as were Mary's, and she formed a warm attachment to one of the female supervisors in the play group. Although already receiving speech therapy, language was still much delayed. Her speech consisted only of parroting what she heard (echolalia), but she enjoyed singing and understood gestures.

In contrast, Mary at age 3 years was "totally unresponsive," relating only to one of the workers and in a characteristically autistic manner. She would use the worker's hand to get things as if it were an extension of her own arm. Other autistic features consisted of a ritualistic return to her chair if she was removed from it and, if upset, rocking. Still olfactorily oriented, she would sniff at food. She vocalized like an infant but showed no understanding of words.

One year later, Louise, now 5 years old, was described as an active and happy child. The children had since been removed from the home and were living in a group home. Louise still was extremely deficient in language. Operating speech-wise at not more than the 15-month developmental level, she used only a few words, often incorrectly, and understood spoken language only if it was accompanied by gestures. Following a year of speech therapy, there was growth in language, although her speech still was occasionally echolalic. Her articulation was much improved; earlier she had vocalized in phrases that were normal in intonation but unintelligible in clarity. Nor was her lagging language development confined to the expressive domain. Her receptive language still was very deficient, and all of this with normal hearing. Over the next few years Louise continued to progress both socially and school-wise. Her final formal intellectual assessment was at age 10 years, when on the Wechsler Intelligence Scale she had a full-scale IQ of 83 with verbal and performance IQs of 77 and 80, respectively. Then functioning at the lower end of the "low average" intelligence range, her expressive and receptive language were at a 7- to 8-year-old level. Given that at age 4 years her development was at not more than the 2-year-old level, an IQ equivalent of about 50, she had come a long way. Mary never made the same progress as her sister. Burdened with both a smaller brain (microcephaly) and autism, at age 7 years she was placed in a setting for autistic children. Characteristic of autism was her continuing language impairment. At 8 years old her speech was only at the 2-year level and comprehension just a little better. Interestingly, she showed excellent ability in working visual puzzles. It is common in autism to see major differences between language and nonlanguage abilities, in favor of the latter. Eventually, in adolescence, her behavior deteriorated, and she was placed in a unit for retarded children at a psychiatric hospital.

Some Observations

Studies of children reared under extremely abnormal conditions indicate that, of our various abilities, it is *language* that is most likely to suffer. Motor skills seem to be preserved. The grossly deprived child tends to show extreme delays both in the understanding and use of speech. But what is also evident is that "recovery" is possible, and well beyond the years that earlier theory suggested. Children have been described who were functioning as "retarded" when first discovered but who, in middle childhood, with the attention of devoted caregivers, were able to largely overcome the effect of their earlier experiences. Caregivers' qualities that can make such a turnaround possible are the subject of the next section.

☐ Defining a "Favorable" Developmental Environment

Our shock at the brutalizing of these children provides at least an emotional cue as to the kinds of experiences to which neither children nor adults should be exposed. But let us move beyond a purely affective reaction and try to define the ingredients of a desirable developmental environment.

Early Development and Meeting of "Needs"

As a result of our own experience, each of us has some idea as to what constitutes a desirable developmental experience. There would be no disagreement as to the need for adequate nutrition and basic healthcare, but opinions might differ regarding the nature of a good parent (caregiver)–child relationship. Here, the application of the "need" personality model presented in Chapter 2 can offer guidance. Recall that those needs were survival, structure, self-esteem (intimacy, success, autonomy), and self-expression. Apart from survival (biological) needs, met at least minimally in the children we have described, we recognize that children need stimulation, guidance, limits, and direction (structure). They need love (intimacy), a sense of competence or "can do" (success), some control over their immediate environment, and freedom to explore it (autonomy). These are the elements that create our sense of worth (self-esteem). Finally, children need access to experiences that are a source of pleasure to them. These are embedded in the objects and playthings in the child's environment and in his or her interactions with loving parents.

Given the focus provided by our personality model, let us consider the relevant research. In a comprehensive review of the research literature pertaining to the cognitive and social development of the growing child (Wachs & Gruen, 1982), it is concluded that the most general characteristic of a healthy developmental environment is exposure to parents or caregivers who are responsive to the child's needs. Responsiveness involves sensitivity to the child's physical and psychological states and a readiness to respond to them. In considering the ultimate development of grossly deprived children, Skuse (1984b) suggests that what fosters development in the young child are parental or caregiver qualities of emotional availability, responsiveness, encouragement, and the provision of ample stimulation. How utterly removed from these qualities were the early experiences of the children we have described.

Parental "sensitivity" has been defined in terms of the ability to appropriately *interpret* and *respond* to the child's signals (Ainsworth & Bell, 1974). This is the role of the caregiver as a "verbal mediator." It is through language that we interpret the world to the child. As we see elsewhere, understanding what a child is communicating can be a problem for parents who are themselves mentally retarded (or mentally ill). Another important ingredient in fostering development is providing what is termed "contingent stimulation" (Bronfenbrenner, 1972). This refers to the child's need to produce some observable effect on its environment. This is commonly achieved through play with toys that "do something" in response to some action by the child. In terms of our personality model this behavior relates to our needs for success and autonomy, important ingredients of self-esteem.

Of Special Relevance to Cognitive Development

Apart from the ingredients just described, cognitive development in infancy is viewed as especially benefiting from homes offering organization, stimulation, and freedom to explore (Wachs, 1992). The last-mentioned brings to mind the virtual imprisonment of the twins who were kept in a closet and Louise and May, who were leashed to their bed.

In early childhood, the years from age 2 to 5, the child benefits from direct teaching in the cognitive area, much of which is transmitted through language. As reflected in our review elsewhere of early childhood education, much of the activity is organized around *verbal* exchange between child and teacher (parent). Although the bulk of the research on factors affecting cognitive development has been conducted with normal children, it should come as no surprise that these same ingredients work for children with disabilities. In a study of 60 mother-child pairs in which the great majority of the children (90%) had Down syndrome and the remainder had other organic syndromes associated with retardation, the young child's cognitive development was related to the mother's pleasure in interacting with the child in a play session and in her sensitivity to the child's emotional state, responsivity, and playfulness (Mahoney, Finger, and Powell, 1985). Interestingly, high levels of control, often a temptation for parents of retarded children, were associated with lower levels of child functioning. Mothers whose children had the highest developmental scores permitted the child to lead in the activity and participated by responding with enthusiasm to their child's play interests.

☐ Children Reared in Large Group-care Settings

Since at least the mid–20th century, there has been a strong bias toward the rearing of children in the family home in preference to placement in out-of-home settings, especially those of an "institutional" nature. Institutional placement of young children was seen as detrimental to social, emotional, and cognitive development, its adverse effects attributed to the absence of caring parents or caregivers, so-called maternal deprivation (e.g., Bowlby, 1951). In contrast to our emphasis on personal deficiencies in the caregiver child relationship, Casler (1961) saw the developmentally limiting factor as an environment barren of stimulation.

Apart from institutional care itself, the best known representative of large-group care was the orphanage. The suggestion of a prominent politician in 1996 that such placement could benefit children of women on public assistance created a storm of reaction and, at least briefly, revived discussion of the merits of out-of-home care. Shealy (1995) observed that the politician's model was the 1938 movie *Boy's Town,* featuring "the transformational benevolence" of its then director, Father Flanagan. Those horrified by the proposal pointed to the harsh conditions in *Oliver Twist,* Dickens's tale of a 19th-century orphanage. Neither image captures the typical picture of current forms of out-of-home residential care (Shealy,

1995). Indeed, it is the preferred form of placement for privileged children in Great Britain, *although not before age 8 years* (Tizard, 1975).

Concerns about orphanages and other large-group care settings with regard to the welfare of very young children pertain to the possible absence of the kind of warm, loving, responsive parenting to which we have referred. These same concerns apply to the large public institutions that formerly served mentally retarded children and adults. Indeed, it was the abuse seen in these institutions that led to the movement to depopulate them and to substitute for them smaller, more intimate, and more family-like settings. Moreover, these smaller residential settings could be located within the community rather than in the traditionally more remote locations of institutional ones.

The research on the effects of institutional care on mental development is instructive. Two studies are described. The first, conducted in the 1930s, is of the institutional care of young children thought to be mentally retarded. The second is of apparently normal children reared in a relatively modern residential program in England (Hodges and Tizard, 1989; Tizard, 1975).

In 1939, the attention of two psychologists was called to two infants who had been in an orphanage and whose lagging development at ages 13 and 16 months had led to placement in a mental retardation institution (Skeels and Dye, 1939). They were portrayed as "pitiful little creatures," emaciated, undersized (growth impairment), and lacking in muscle tone and responsiveness (Skeels, 1966). Their developmental levels were at less than half of those expected for their ages, although neither child had an apparent organic abnormality. The institution to which the children were admitted had no program for infants, and each was placed on a ward housing mildly retarded adolescent girls. The children came to be ward "pets," as each received a great deal of mothering from the older girls. Six months after admission striking changes were noted in their behavior. Retested, both showed huge developmental gains—from IQ of 46 to 87 in the younger child, and from IQ of 35 to 77 in the older one. Eventually adopted, some 2 years after admission, both children had IQs in the 90 to 100 range.

After observing these dramatic developmental changes, Skeels and Dye decided to try to repeat this "natural" experiment with other young children at the orphanage who were functioning at a retarded level. Thirteen infants, average age 19 months and mean IQ 64 (range 35 to 89—clearly some were not retarded) were transferred to the institution. Like their predecessors, free of apparent organic abnormality, they received the same kind of mothering and, 19 months later, their average IQ had risen to 92, an average gain of 28 points. Other studies mentioned elsewhere also show environmental effects of 20 to 30 IQ points. This study lacked a control group, but another group of low-functioning children who remained in the orphanage showed a decline in IQ. Their intellectual impairment appears to have been organic in origin. A follow-up study of the early-placed children in adulthood found them to be functioning normally (Skeels, 1966).

What was the nature of the orphanage experience that seemed to retard development in infancy—a retardation that could be reversed through intense mothering? Up to age 2 years, children in the orphanage were housed in a special hospital wing in which they were given basic physical and medical care but otherwise ignored. Interactions between infants and staff were tied to basic care needs. Play materials were scanty, and there was little interest in teaching the children how to use them. How stark the contrast with the children's later experience, in which they were lavished with attention and their developmental gains were celebrated by their caregivers. It is said that there was competition between wards to see which would have its child walking or talking first, and much time was devoted to "teaching" developmental tasks. In terms of our personality model, we can see how "intimacy" and "success" experiences were provided through intense cognitive and social stimulation. At least in early childhood, and with the supervision of normal adults, mildly retarded adolescents were capable of meeting crucial psychological needs.

We should not interpret the striking developmental gains of erstwhile "retarded" children as typifying the effects of residential placement in such centers. Indeed, in many states, such placement of very young children is no longer even possible, family care being the preferred mode. The study did reveal that a lack of personal attention and stimulation can seriously delay normal development, and that developmental lag, at least in early childhood, can be reversed by intense mothering and stimulation. Our earlier presentation of developmental gains in children reared in grossly aberrant environments indicated that such gains are also possible even after school age. Finally, the material presented thus far suggests that, at least for cognitive development, *where* a child is reared is less important than *how* he or she is reared.

Our second study (Hodges and Tizard, 1989) describes the development of a group of children separated from their parents but not delayed in their development. They had been reared in a residential nursery until at least 2 years of age and then adopted, placed in foster care, or restored to their biological parents. At follow-up at ages 8 and 16 years, the researchers were particularly interested in the children's language and cognitive development and in the depth of their emotional attachments to their caregivers. The question of their emotional attachment arose because of the very large number of caregivers they experienced while in institutional care.

They were raised in intimate family-like groups within small British childcare institutions; it was the intent of the setting to *discourage* deep emotional ties between children and care givers because it was expected that the children would eventually depart and come to live with one family—adoptive, foster, or biological. Although our main focus is on the effects of institutional or large-group care on intellectual functioning, the issue of emotional and general behavior cannot be ignored.

Within this group-care setting there was a generous staff-child ratio and much stimulation. The goal was to offer each child a family-like experience, although the "family" was all female and close emotional ties avoided. At follow-up study at ages 8 and 16 years the children were largely functioning in the normal IQ range. Indeed, at 16 years old the average IQ of a group of children who were adopted before age 4.5 years was 114 ("bright-normal" intelligence range); those adopted after 4.5 years old had a mean IQ of 102 ("average" intelligence range). It is not clear why these differences were related to the age of adoption. Perhaps more relevant to the group IQ difference is the suggestion that the higher functioning group had been adopted into higher socioeconomic families (Tizard and Hodges, 1978).

Adoptees, in every case, functioned at a somewhat higher level than those children who were restored to their natural families (mean IQ 97) and the few who remained at the nursery until school age (mean IQ 90). What is clear is that residence in this type of group-care setting from early infancy until at least age 2 years did not preclude grossly normal cognitive development.

But there is some evidence that a price was paid for such a childhood experience. In comparison to a non–nursery-reared control group, at age 16 years the nursery-reared group had more behavior problems. This was particularly true of the children restored to their natural parents. Unlike the adoptive parents who *wanted* the children, there appear to have been many natural parents with at least ambivalent feelings toward their children. Curiously, it was in these families that the child's emotional attachment seemed to be less adversely affected! The researchers concluded that there were undesirable social and emotional consequences of early experience in group care and that, wherever possible, children should be raised in families (natural, foster, or adoptive) and out-of-family placement, if necessary, should not be prolonged.

☐ Children Reared by Retarded Parents

General Concerns

Another group of children at risk for adverse developmental experiences are the children of parents who are themselves retarded. Despite the apparent benefits of at least short-term mothering by retarded adolescents, as in the supervised setting described in the Skeels and Dye (1939) study, there is general agreement that the risk for such problems as neglect and abuse is heightened (Feldman et al., 1985; Scally, 1973; Schilling, Schinke, Blythe, & Barth, 1982; Whitman & Accardo, 1990). Carol Ronai (1997) tells a graphic, painful, and poignant story about her experience as the daughter of a retarded mother.

Although lower socioeconomic status is related to the risk of neglect and abuse, and retarded parents are disproportionately poor, it is not economics alone that affects the developmental experiences of these children (Keltner, 1994). Studies of retarded parents, principally women in single parent families, reveal social, emotional, and cognitive difficulties that impact on their children. Tending to be socially isolated (e.g., Llewellyn, 1995), that is, to have few friends and often lack family support, they tend to resort to tight control and punitive measures in managing their child (Keltner, 1994). Lacking knowledge of normal child development, they may have inappropriate expectations for their child, for example, in eating and language (Accardo & Whitman, 1990). In sum, vulnerable to the multiple stresses associated with marginal income and lack of emotional support, the retarded parent can be overwhelmed by child care needs. This is especially likely in families with larger numbers of children (Accardo & Whitman, 1990). At least minimally adequate parenting care can deteriorate to neglect and abuse as family size increases and demands on the parent's limited cognitive and emotional resources are stretched. Studies suggest that, apart from lack of knowledge of what to expect in the infant and child, potential deficiencies are most likely in "responsiveness" and in emotional investment in the child (Feldman et al., 1985; Keltner, 1994).

All of these concerns intensify as the level of parental intelligence diminishes, particularly if IQs are below 60 (e.g., Borgman, 1990; Whitman & Accardo, 1990). Children in these homes are at special risk for conditions that can lead to their removal. These include inadequate supervision and inattention to safety and health care (Rolfe, 1990).

Withal, the kind of deprivation depicted previously is *not* typical of these homes. Rather than blatant rejection and seeming indifference to the child's welfare, parental limitations relate to inadequate parenting skills, poor management of the home, and unawareness of potentially helpful resources. The creation of "parent education" programs specifically targeted to this population is essential (Feldman et al., 1985; Whitman & Accardo, 1990).

Illustrating the loving and caring retarded parent is a letter from a mother whose children had been placed in a mental retardation institution (Fig. 5.1). It also graphically portrays her willingness to expose herself to physical abuse in order to retain her parental rights to the custody of

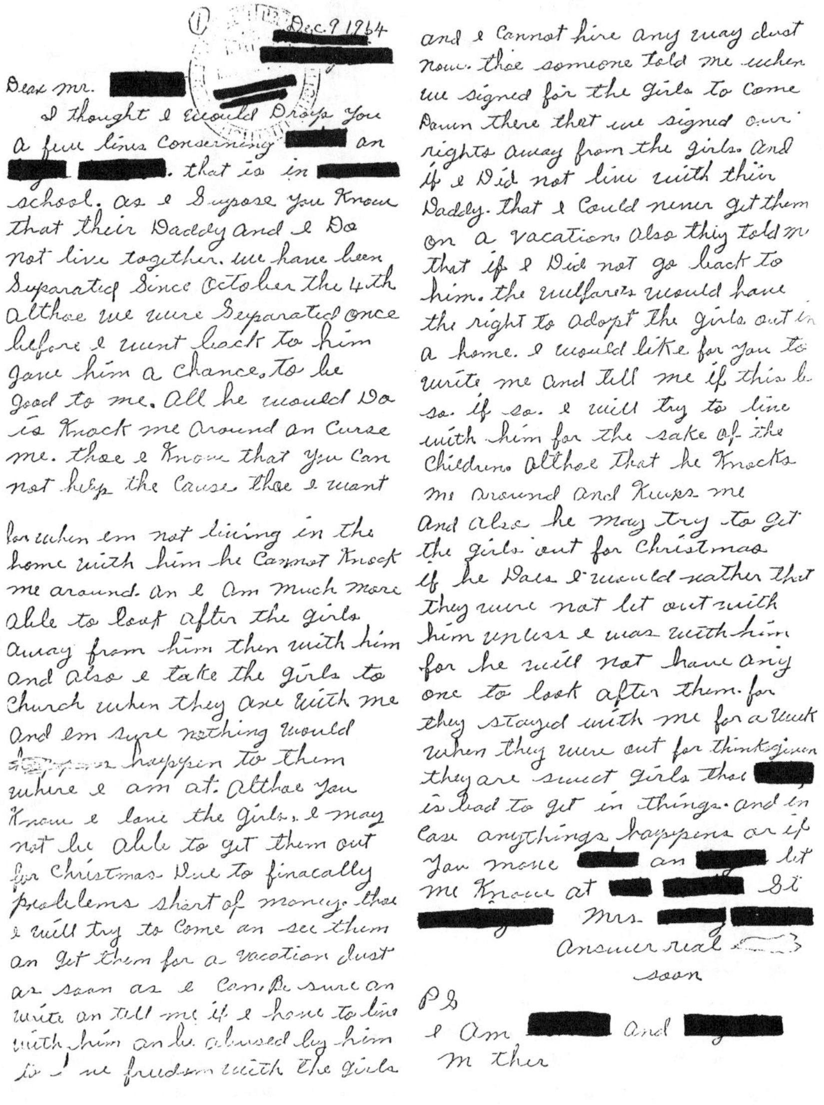

FIGURE 5.1. Letter from a mother with retardation to her then-institutionalized daughter.

her children. Her family consisted of three children, two girls and a boy. Both girls are retarded, as are the parents and grandparents. Amid mental subnormality, rural isolation, and paternal violence, one child, the boy, has managed to attain normal ability and to make a successful adult adjustment. Married to a teacher and employed as a laboratory technician, he recognizes the problems of his parents and siblings and has served as a liaison between them and the social agencies with which they have been involved. In this respect, the aforementioned Carol Ronai served from childhood as the intermediary between her mother and social agencies.

Increased Risk of Retarded Children in Families with a Retarded Parent or Parents

Given the role of genetic as well as environmental factors in intelligence, we can anticipate that the risk of retardation in children of retarded parents is increased relative to children of nonretarded parents.

Children of Two Retarded Parents

Based on family studies, more popular in the past than at present, the rates of retardation in children of whom both parents are retarded have varied from 39% to 61% (Birch et al., 1970; Halperin, 1945; Penrose, 1938; Reed & Reed, 1965; Scally, 1968). For purposes of estimate, roughly half of the children of two retarded parents, if reared in the parental house, also can be expected to be retarded. The next largest grouping, about one third, function in the borderline to low-average intelligence range (70 to 89 IQ); the remaining one sixth show normal intelligence. Although the focus of this chapter is on environmental influences, environment cannot be the sole determinant of intellectual development, because it would not explain those children who emerge from such families with normal intelligence.

Children in Families with Only One Retarded Parent

Suggestive of an environmental effect are the findings in families in which only one parent is retarded (Reed & Reed, 1965). If only the mother were retarded, the proportion of retarded children was more than twice as great, 19% versus 8%, as compared with families in which only the father was retarded. Because there is no evidence of a differential genetic contribution by either sex to the intelligence of the child, this maternal effect is presumed to be psychological (environmental) in nature and attributable to the mother's likely greater contact and influence on the child.

☐ Foster Children and Adopted Children

Another group of studies that offer evidence of an environmental effect on intellectual development is those of children early placed in foster or adoptive care. As will be seen, these indicate the apparent influence of *both* environmental and genetic factors on intelligence.

A number of earlier studies, conducted when this type of research was in vogue, show that the children of mothers with borderline or retarded intelligence display average to near-average intellectual development if reared in foster or adoptive homes of normal parents (e.g., Skeels & Harms, 1948; Skodak & Skeels, 1949). Moreover, the earlier the placement, preferably by age 2 years, the better the child is likely to do (Speer, 1940).

The impact of these findings on at least one set of researchers is evident in the following quote:

> Perusal of the child's social history . . . and comparison [of it] with the field agent's pre-placement evaluation of the adoptive home was disheartening. It did not seem possible that children with such meager possibilities *as projected from the intellectual, academic, and occupational attainments of their parents* could measure up to the demands of cultured, educated parents. Yet careful examination of one child after another showed none of the retardation or misplacement [regarding adoptive home] which might have been anticipated. (Skodak and Skeels, 1949; italics added)

This finding is all the more remarkable considering that the main criteria for matching the child to adoptive parents were religion, sex, and hair color!

The Skodak and Skeels study merits description because of its scope and the representativeness of its findings with regard to early adopted children, and because it appears to illustrate the influence of *both* heredity and the environment. One hundred children were studied, 60 boys and 40 girls, all of whom were adopted by age 6 months. Their intellectual development was assessed four times between ages 2 and 13 years, with their mean IQ usually falling in the "high average" range (110 to 119). For purposes of comparing the intelligence of the children with that of their biological mothers, the children's mean IQ at 13 years is used. (We know nothing about the father.) At that age, the children and their biological mothers were tested with the same intellectual measure, the earliest version of the Stanford-Binet intelligence test. The average IQ of the children was 107, in comparison with a mean IQ of 86 in their mothers, a difference of 21 points. The IQ range in the children was 65 to 144, with two thirds functioning in the average to high-average intelligence ranges. Although the information available precludes determination of the precise magnitude of the influence of the adoptive home on the children's IQs, had they been reared by their biological mothers, and assuming some regression to the general population mean, an average IQ of 95 is more probable than one of 107. Indeed, an analysis of that data based on a polygenic model of intelligence predicts an IQ of 94 (Jensen, 1973b). It is reasonable to propose that early placement in adoptive homes of parents of above-average educational and socioeconomic status increased the IQ of the children by at least 12 to 13 points. The greatest effects are seen in the children whose biological mothers were themselves retarded. There were 11 mothers with IQs below 70, their mean IQ being 63. The average IQ of their children was 96, exceeding the maternal mean by 33 points! Reared from infancy in advantaged adoptive homes, despite having retarded mothers, the majority of these children were of at least average intelligence.

A later French variant of the Skodak and Skeels study involved a comparison of siblings, full and half, one of whom was adopted while the other remained with a socioeconomically disadvantaged biological mother (Schiff et al., 1978). The adoptees all were raised in advantaged homes, and their mean IQ was 111 (high average). Their nonadopted siblings and halfsiblings had a mean IQ of 95.

Another very interesting study is one that examined the effects of "transracial" adoption (Scarr & Weinberg, 1976, 1978; Weinberg, Scarr, & Waldman, 1992). It also found cognitive benefits of early adoption. The subjects were black and interracial children adopted into advantaged white families. Their intellectual status was first studied at mean age 7 years and again at 17 years. At 7 years of age, the average IQ of the black and interracial adoptees was 107, exceeding by some 17 points the mean for nonadopted black and interracial children in this geographical area. The greatest benefit appeared to accrue to the children who were adopted by age 1 year. Interestingly, although functioning well above expectations, the adoptees themselves were outperformed by their stepsibs, the biological children of their adoptive parents. The mean IQ of their siblings was 116.

Follow-up again at 17 years old (Weinberg, Scarr, & Waldman, 1992) found a decline in IQ for adoptees and their stepsibs, a decline attributable to a difference in the test employed at the later age rather than to any real change in intelligence. The average IQ of the adoptees was now 97 as against 109 for their stepsibs. The benefits of early adoption were still evident at age 17 years, when the mean IQ of the early adoptees was 99 as against 92 for those adopted after age 1 year. The researchers view their findings as consistent with other adoption studies "in demonstrating strong effects of the rearing environment on IQ."

A Heredity-Environment Interaction

But these adoption studies reveal more than just an environmental effect on cognitive development. Let us further consider the findings of Skodak and Skeels (1949). Although the IQs of the adoptees typically surpassed those of their biological mothers, the children were not all alike. Their IQs ranged from 65 to 144, a spread that approximates the full range of IQs in the general population, from mentally retarded to gifted. Despite being reared in similar kinds of adoptive homes, they were no more alike than a random population of children reared in their natural family homes. Recognizing that the adoptive homes were much more homogeneous in their sociocultural makeup than would be true of a random sample of families, what could account for such IQ diversity? The answer cannot be the environment but rather lies in the meaning of a statistical relationship between the adopted child and his or her biological mother.

A correlation of .44 existed between the IQ of the biological mother and the child from whom she had been separated since early infancy. The correlation means that parent and child occupied relatively similar positions in the IQ distribution of their respective groups. Biological mothers whose IQs exceeded their group mean of 86 tended to have children whose IQs exceeded their group mean of 107. Similarly, biological mothers whose IQs fell below their group mean of 86 had children whose IQs tended to fall below their group mean of 107. This relationship is illustrated in Figure 5.2. The upper horizontal line shows the mean IQ of all of the adoptees (M') and of subgroups of eight children of the brighter biological mothers (A') and 11 children of the retarded biological mothers (B'). On the lower line is shown the corresponding mean IQs of the biological mothers—M, A, and B. The mean IQs at A' and A are 118 and 111; at B' and B, 96 and 63; and at M' and M, 107 and 86.

How can we explain a significant relationship between the intelligence of individuals who have been separated since infancy, a relationship that also was found in the transracial adoption study? In the latter the correlation between the biological mother was actually higher than that of the

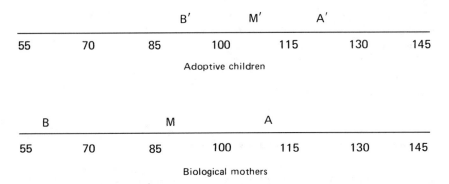

FIGURE 5.2. Mean IQs of biological mothers and of their children reared in adoptive homes.

adopted mother and child, .33 versus .21. As in the transracial study, the biological parents and children did not share a common childrearing experience although, as in the Skodak and Skeels study, some selective adoptive placement is said to have occurred with the children of mothers who were at the extremes of their distribution. What the biological mothers and adoptive children did share was not environment but heredity. Through heredity, through the genes, the biological mother (and father) are seen as influencing the child's capacity to use or benefit from the adoptive home. Biological parental influence was exercised through the kind of nervous system or biological equipment that their genes enabled the child to develop. Although an enriched environment in the adoptive home led to essentially normal intellectual development in the children of the retarded mothers, it is heredity that still left them well below the children of the brighter mothers. The effect of environmental enrichment was to elevate mental ability well beyond what might have been expected had they been reared by their own mothers, but this enhancement did not eliminate all differences among them. The differences persisted, but *at a higher IQ level*, and it is heredity that is viewed as contributing to the difference. Heredity acted to regulate the child's capacity to benefit from the enriched adoptive experience, to provide both "potential" and "limits."

☐ Twin Studies

Although studies of twins are prominently cited in describing the role of heredity in intelligence, and on personality as well, they also can reveal the influence of the environment. This is especially true in studies of identical twins who have been reared apart.

Identical (Monozygotic) Twins

Identical twins or identical triplets, quadruplets, quintuplets, and so on are the product of a single fertilized egg (a zygote) that either prior to or shortly after implantation divides by fission and creates two or more separate embryos that are genetically alike because they all derive from the same sperm cell and egg cell. Identical twins, and their larger multiple-birth counterparts, are unique in being the only examples of two or more persons sharing the same heredity. Recall that single-born siblings, on the average, share in common about one half of the parental chromosomes (and genes). In a sense, identical twins and their counterparts can be viewed as "pseudoclones." It is, of course, their genetic identicalness that accounts for their striking physical similarities; it is often difficult to tell them apart. Because gender, too, is determined by our genes, via the X and Y chromosomes, identical twins are necessarily of the same sex.

Fraternal (Dizygotic) Twins

Fraternal twins, and their multiple-birth counterparts, are the product of the simultaneous fertilization of two or more different egg cells by two or more different sperm cells. Genetically, such twins are no more alike than single-born siblings and may be either of the same sex or of opposite sexes.

Implications

The implications that flow from the two types of twins are themselves twofold. First, because identical twins are genetically alike, all differences between them must be nongenetic or "environmental" in origin. Further, and this is a sometimes overlooked aspect of twin research, the degree of *difference* between identical twins can reflect the range of variation that the environment can effect on a given genotype. The extent of this environmentally caused variation can be viewed as the "reaction range" for that genotype, a concept that is elaborated shortly.

Second, because fraternal twins are no more alike than single-born siblings, differences between them may be either genetic or environmental in origin. Twin studies typically compare identical and fraternal twins on some trait whose heritability is in question. If the identical twins are found to be significantly more similar, it can be concluded that the trait *may* have a genetic basis. The qualification is necessary because of an assumption that underlies the comparison of the two types of twins—that the environment of the identical twins was not more similar than that of the fraternal twins. Unless this can be shown, the greater similarity among the identical twins could be attributed to the environment rather than to heredity. Indeed, identical twins do seem to experience more similar environments than fraternal twins, as do fraternal twins relative to ordinary siblings (Bouchard, 1984). After all, unlike ordinary siblings, fraternal twins are of the same age.

The use in twin research of a third group for comparison, identical twins reared apart, helps to obviate this difficulty. They are assumed to have experienced less similar environments than identical twins reared in the same home. Because differences between them are necessarily environmental in origin, should they be less similar on some trait than identical twins reared together, this would indicate an environmental effect. Thus, of particular interest is a comparison of the degree of intellectual similarity between identical twins reared together and those reared apart, although our analysis also includes fraternal twins reared together.

Twin-Study Findings

The data on the degrees of similarity between the several types of twins is largely correlational in nature. There have been many studies of the IQ correlations in identical and fraternal twins reared together and, not unexpectedly, few of identical twins reared apart. The finding of such populations is daunting. In fact, there have been just six major studies of identical twins reared apart, but the accuracy of the data of one of them (Burt, 1966) has been called into serious question (Kamin, 1974), and it is not included here (Bouchard, Lykken, McGue, Segal, & Tellegen, 1990; Juel-Neilsen, 1965; Newman, Freeman, & Holzinger, 1937; Pedersen, Plomin, Nesselroade, & McLearn, 1992; Shields, 1962). In addition to the twin correlations, correlations also are shown for nontwin family relationships (Table 5.1) These provide a fuller perspective of the significance of those in twins.

Environmental Effect

The correlational and intrapair IQ differences show the influence of both genetic and environmental factors. If we look first at comparisons between children reared together and those reared apart, the former are consistently

TABLE 5.1. Familial resemblances in general intelligence

Family Relationship	Correlation
Twins	
Identical twins reared together	.86
Identical twins reared apart	.72
Fraternal twins reared together	.60
Fraternal twins reared apart	.33
Nontwins	
Siblings reared together	.48
Siblings reared apart	.24
Parent-child	
Single parent and child in same house	.42
Single parent and child with child in a different house	.24

more similar than the latter, an effect consonant with an environmental influence on intelligence. The influence of the environment is most evident in the comparisons between identical twins—those reared together and those reared apart. By correlation and median intrapair difference, the identical twins reared apart are less similar than those reared together. Although not shown in Table 5.1, the influence of the environment is also found in the range of differences found between identical twins reared apart. Although their median IQ difference was only 7 points, differences of up to 30 points have been found in such pairs (Bouchard et al., 1990). This apparent environmental effect is similar to that found in the previously mentioned studies of adopted children of retarded mothers. We would agree with Scarr-Salapatek (1975) that "a reasonable reaction range for most genotypes (neither severely retarded nor gifted) would include phenotypes in a 25-point IQ range." The term *reaction range* refers to the range of variation that could be found for a given genotype as a function of the environments to which it is exposed.

The remaining comparisons of children reared together and apart, fraternal twins and single-born siblings, show a similar picture. The children reared in the same home are, on the average, more similar in IQ than those reared in different homes. Admittedly, the effect is "modest" in the fraternal twin comparison.

A comment about the correlations between nonbiological siblings is in order. There is evidence that these correlations actually *decline* over time, although the children share the same home. By adolescence and adulthood, they are negligible. Whereas in infancy the correlation between stepsiblings may reach .30, by late adolescence it is essentially zero (Loehlin, Horn, & Willerman, 1989; Scarr & Weinberg, 1978). If the environment has an effect on intelligence, and it clearly has, how can these children reared in the same home become less similar over time? The answer lies in the other implication of these familial comparisons, the powerful role of heredity.

Genetic Effects

Although the environment clearly influences intellectual development, and the effect can be huge if children are reared in grossly aberrant homes, within the range of more "normal" environments heredity plays a not-inconsiderable role. If only the environment influenced mental development, then same-sex fraternal twins reared in the same home should be more similar than identical twins reared apart. But they are not. As evident in the correlations, identical twins reared apart are actually more similar than fraternal twins reared together. This is also strikingly seen in typical intrapair differences in IQ among twins. On the avergage, identical twins reared together differ by only about 5 IQ points. That difference increases to about 7 in identical twins reared apart, and to about 11 in fraternal twins reared together. This argues strongly for a genetic contribution to intelligence. In fact, based on these correlations, in adoption studies as well as those of twins, about one half of the variance in measures of general intelligence among the general population can be attributed to genetic factors (Plomin & Petrill, 1997). Conversely, apart from "error variance" inherent in psychometric measures of about 10%, the remaining 40% of variance in IQ scores can be attributed to environmental causes. It is their nature and magnitude that is addressed in this chapter. Genetic factors also are thought to account for decreasing similarity among siblings over time. This effect is depicted in Figure 5.3, which shows the role of genetic influences on intelligence over the life span as this has been revealed through studies of twins and siblings (Plomin & Petrill, 1997). How are we to understand the apparently increasing power of the genetic contribution after the earliest developmental years? It is to be understood as reflecting the effect of our unique individual biology or genotype on the "individualization" of experience. Although two children from the same home, in general, share a more similar environment than two children from different homes, the children in the same home do not, necessarily, have the *same* experiences. Within the family environment, each child responds to a potential *range* of

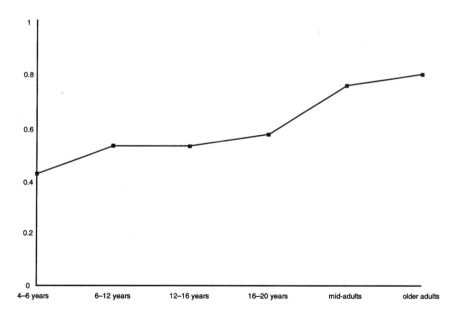

FIGURE 5.3. Genetic influences on IQ increase throughout the life span. (Reprinted with permission from ABLEX Publishing Corporation.)

experiences in terms of his or her own preferences, interests, and proclivities, and in the cognitive domain, those proclivities are much affected by
a gene-influenced central nervous system. With age, at least in the developmental years, we become increasingly *individualized*—creating as well
as responding to those aspects of the environment that are most congenial
to our personalities. Plomin and Petrill (1997) refer to this as a gravitation
to "niches" adapted to our own inherently unique characteristics. This
has been described as a process in which our genotype both creates and
maintains its own environment (Sears and McCartney, 1983). For Fuller
(1954), it reflects the essence of his conception of heredity—the capacity
to respond to an environment in a particular way.

☐ Prevention of Mental Retardation Through Early-childhood Education

In this section we review research that pertains to efforts to foster cognitive development and school achievement through educational activities
provided in the preschool years. Three types of programs are described:
Head Start, Follow Through, and "extremely early" intervention.

Head Start

Head Start is the national preschool program begun in 1965 with the
goal of strengthening the development of the economically disadvantaged child, mentally, emotionally, socially, and physically (Zigler & Styfco,
1994). The program also provided health services to children and supportive social services to parents. Certainly one of its major goals was to advance the academic achievement of the children, originally largely African
American youngsters from poor families.

Although not specifically directed toward the prevention of mental retardation, the Head Start population came from the kind of disadvantaged background in which the risk of retardation is much increased. This
risk is reflected in disproportionate numbers of children with relatively
poor school achievement; increased placement in programs for children
with learning problems, such as special education; and increased risk of
retention in grade rather than promotion. Accompanying poor educational progress is the heightened risk of a host of social problems—teenage
pregnancy, drug abuse, and delinquency (Campbell & Ramey, 1995).

Initiated as a summer program prior to entry into kindergarten, Head
Start quickly expanded to a year-long half-day effort for 4-year-olds. At
present, the typical program serves 3- and 4-year-olds. Ambitious in

conception, and with wide-ranging objectives, evaluations of its effectiveness have focused largely on cognitive development (IQ) and later school achievement.

There have been several major studies of Head Start (Bronfenbrenner, 1974; Cicirelli, 1969; Lazar, Darlington, Murray, Royce, & Snipper, 1982; McKey et al., 1985). In the cognitive sphere the finding has been of short-term gains in IQ (about 10 points) relative to non–Head Start control children. By age 7 years, however, there are no longer significant differences between the two populations. The IQs of the control children increase as they enter school, and there is some decline in the scores of Head Start youngsters. A similar picture emerges in the academic sphere, in which no lasting achievement benefits have been found.

Despite a general disappointment with its effect on IQ and academic achievement, some benefits of Head Start are found. A widely publicized and carefully researched Head Start effort, the Perry Preschool Program, has the largest follow-up history. Now in their late 20s, its graduates are more likely to have completed school and to be employed and less likely to have been involved in criminal activity (Schweinhart, Barnes, & Weikart, 1993). One of their findings is of particular interest as it relates to the prevention of mental retardation. They found that the greatest benefits of the preschool experience accrued to the most disadvantaged children. We are reminded of the previously mentioned findings on the intellectual development of adopted children of mentally retarded mothers. In the Perry Preschool Program, it was the children of mothers with the lowest educational levels who reaped the greatest benefits (Irvine, Flint, Hick, Horan, & Kikuk, 1982).

In spite of the absence of clear academic benefits, the Perry Preschool Program experience appears to have strengthened the children's general classroom adjustment. They were more likely to have completed school and to be employed as adults. As students they were less likely to have been in "special education" or to have been retained in grade. They also were less likely to have been involved in delinquent activity.

Although this characterization of the Perry Preschool graduates shows at least some benefits relative to children who did not have the preschool experience, in an absolute sense the overall adaptation of the former preschoolers leaves much to be desired. One third of them did not complete school, and nearly one third (30%) had been arrested at least once.

Interestingly, the first director of Head Start, Edward Zigler, sees its strongest impact in the health sphere (Zigler & Styfco, 1984). All children enrolled in Head Start are required to have medical screenings, immunizations, dental examinations, and corrective treatment, if needed. Additional benefits accrue from the nutritious meals served at each center along with nutritional counseling to parents.

In considering both the promise and disappointment of Head Start, Zigler and Styfco (1994) take the view that no preschool program can be expected to "inoculate" children against the ravages of poverty. Presumably they have reference to living conditions that foster values and ways of functioning that are maladaptive in the general society.

Follow-through

With clear evidence that the effects of Head Start were temporary and disappeared following entrance into school, it was logical to advocate for its extension as a means of preserving the gains that had been achieved. From this emerged Follow Through, another federal initiative, and one that involved supplemental educational support during the first three grades. Follow Through never attained the popularity of Head Start, but research has indicated some educational effects, especially in reading (Becker & Gersten, 1982; Fuerst & Fuerst, 1993).

In a study of a Chicago program, in comparison with the control group, children who had both Head Start and Follow Through achieved better reading skills and were more likely to have graduated from high school (Fuerst & Fuerst, 1993). Their high-school graduation rate was 62%, as against a 49% rate in the controls.

"Really Early" Intervention

Given the transient nature of Head Start effects and concerns about a family environment that is often lacking in the physical and psychological resources necessary to optimizing development, programs have been created to bridge the period *prior* to Head Start as well as the one after it. These are educational efforts that, literally, begin in infancy, in the first year of life, and carry through until kindergarten.

The first of these, the Milwaukee Project, was intended to try to prevent mental retardation. Its target was children of mothers with IQs of 75 or less, children who had earlier been identified as accounting for a disproportionate percent of the mildly retarded school population (Heber, Dever, & Conry, 1968). The Milwaukee Project generated much controversy; it was suggested that the extraordinarily high IQs obtained in the children resulted from "teaching to the test." Mean Stanford-Binet IQs in the 17 children who made up the treatment group varied from a high of 126 at age 4 years to a low of 119 at 6 years. In contrast, the children in the control group had IQs consistently in the 90 range, varying from 96 at 4 years to 87 at 6. Assessment with other tests and utilizing an IQ "correction" suggested by Flynn (1984) showed less dramatic differences. At age 14 years, an earlier reported approximate 20 point IQ difference

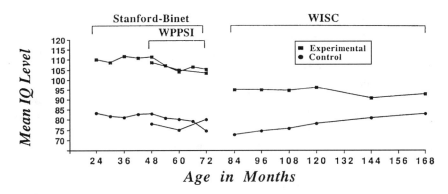

FIGURE 5.4. Differences over time between experimental and control children in the Milwaukee Project using "corrected" IQs. (Reprinted from Garber et al., 1991 with the permission of the publisher.)

between Project children and controls had diminished to 10 (Garber, Hodge, Rynders, Dever, & Velu, 1991).

Of interest is the project researchers' assumption that the preschool experience prevented an expected decline in IQ and eventual mental retardation in those children whose mothers were themselves retarded (Garber & Hodge, 1989). Figure 5.4 indicates little difference in developmental rates for experimental and control children. Indeed, after age 7 years the trend is of a steadily *rising* IQ in the controls from 73 at 8 years of age to 83 at 14. Even without the preschool experience only three eventually showed retardation (17%). The implication is that it is not only a maternal IQ in the retarded range that increases the risk for the child; other factors also must be operating. Presumably, these entail deficiencies in the childrearing environment.

Perhaps the most disappointing finding in the study was its apparent failure to translate the lengthy preschool experience into educational benefits. An earlier educational advantage to the children in the project relative to controls had disappeared by fourth grade. Like those in the Perry Project, however, the treatment children showed a lower rate of grade retention and less need for special services (Garber et al., 1991). We are reminded here again of Zigler and Styfco's caution regarding the limitations of a preschool experience in the face of poverty.

The Carolina Abecedarian[1] Project

Like the Milwaukee Project, the Abecedarian one began in infancy and provided a comprehensive "day" program until kindergarten. The average age at admission was 4 months. A special teaching curriculum was developed to enhance cognitive, language, perceptual-motor, and social development (Sparling & Lewis, 1981). In the later preschool years, emphasis was placed on language (Ramey, McGinness, Cross, Collier, & Barrie-Blackley, 1982). In addition to the educational program, the children also received comprehensive medical care, and there was much effort to involve the parents.

As in the Milwaukee Project, the children were drawn from low-income families (98% African American), but with a brighter group of mothers. Their average IQ was 85 (range 49 to 124), and their mean education level was 10.6 years. About one quarter of the children lived in two-parent families, with the majority dwelling in multigenerational households or extended families (Campbell & Ramey, 1994).

Via a rather complex experimental model and multiple cohorts of children, the Abecedarian Project offered two types of intervention—a 5-year preschool experience for the children and a 3-year school-aged program for parents. The latter was intended to help parents supplement the school experience. For each of the two forms of intervention, control groups were established. Thus the data reported at age 15 years and shown in the latest follow-up refer to four different groups. They are *EE* (8 years of intervention, 5 years preschool plus 3 years of family assistance, $N = 22$), *EC* (5 years preschool and no additional school-aged assistance, $N = 25$), *CE* (no preschool but 3 years of school-aged family assistance, $N = 22$), and *CC* (neither preschool nor school-aged assistance, $N = 22$).

In reviewing their findings, Campbell and Ramsey (1995) claim more lasting treatment effects in both IQ and academic scores than found in earlier studies. Although it is true that the children receiving the preschool experience (EE and EC) generally exceeded the mean IQ of control children (CE and CC) by an average of 7 points, at age 15 years the difference is less than 5 points and, indeed, does not meet the test of statistical significance. At 15 years old, the average IQ of the former preschoolers was approximately 95 (94.9) versus an average IQ of 90 (90.3) in the controls. There is also a pattern of declining IQ in all groups to at least age 12 years, and the rate of decline seems comparable for all.

Of interest was the absence of any IQ effects in the children who had the school-aged family educational supplement (CE). The EE (preschool and supplement) and EC (preschool and no supplement) children are alike IQ-wise at 15 years of age. A similar finding is reported for a related study of a family education supplement to Abecedarian children in the preschool years (Wasik, Ramey, Bryant, & Sparling, 1990). Whatever the role of the parents in influencing cognitive development, treatment benefits tied to the preschool years are directly related to services to the *children*.

In contrast to possibly waning differences in IQ between treatment and control groups, at least in the academic sphere benefits persist to at least age 15 years. The former preschoolers performed at a higher level in reading and math, an effect present throughout the school years. Interestingly,

TABLE 5.2. Mean IQs in adolescence of preschool graduates (Flynn "corrected" IQs are shown in parentheses)

Preschool Program	Length of Program	Preschool Treatment Group	Preschool Control Group
Perry	2 y	81(73)	81(73)
Abecedarian	5 y	95(87)	90(82)
Milwaukee	5 y	101(93)	91(83)

here the school-aged family follow-through program did have an effect. In spite of no IQ benefit, the children whose parents received the program achieved at a higher level academically. Of course, school achievement is only partly based on intellectual level; motivation and effort are also important contributors.

For comparative purposes, "uncorrected" and "corrected" IQs in adolescence are given in Table 5.2 for the children who participated in the three widely touted preschool programs. The Flynn "correction" shown in parentheses reduces all IQs by 8 points, an effect that may be more in keeping with the children's educational achievement.

Two differences are apparent in the effects of the preschool programs. In terms of overall cognitive development, adolescents who had participated in the 5-year programs are functioning IQ-wise at a significantly higher level than those who had only the 2-year one. Further, and perhaps more relevant in the long run, the Flynn corrected mean IQ in the Perry Preschool and control groups is perilously close to the retardation range, a range that precludes anything like normal school achievement. In contrast, the much larger Abecedarian Project and Milwaukee Project seem to have left their treatment groups somewhat better prepared to make some academic progress.

But apparent educational benefits cannot hide major educational problems even in the preschoolers. Although like their counterparts in the earlier studies there were fewer retentions in grade and placements in special education, almost one third of the preschoolers (31%) had been retained in grade. Of the control children, more than half were so retained (55%). In terms of special education, one quarter of the preschoolers had been so placed (25%), against nearly half (48%) of controls.

These educational differences between preschool and controls are also seen at eighth grade on the California Achievement Test. The preschoolers' measures were in the 39th percentile as against the 16th percentile for the controls—scores ranged between the 38th and 41st percentiles as against the 28th to 30th percentiles in the controls. In the Perry Project, even the preschooler California Achievement Test mean was only at the

16th percentile; the controls were below the 10th percentile (Personal communication of Schweinhart to Campbell and Ramey.)

On the brighter side, the Abecedarian Project, like the Milwaukee one, found that the greatest IQ benefits of the preschool experience accrued to the children at greatest disadvantage, those whose mothers had IQs in the retarded range. There were 13 such mothers and, at age 15 years IQ scores are available for 12 of their children (six preschoolers and six controls). The former preschoolers had an 11.7-point IQ advantage over their controls, a difference more than twice as great as the approximate 5-point difference between the total preschool and control groups. Moreover, their IQs averaged 32 points greater than their intellectually impaired mothers, a difference comparable with that of the adoptees in the previously described Skeels and Skodak (1949) study (Landesman & Ramey, 1989).

The Infant Health and Development Program

Undoubtedly the most ambitious research effort and by far the largest in magnitude, the Infant Health and Development Program (1990), studied the effects of an Abecedarian-like early intervention on low birth weight premature infants. These are children with birth weights of less than 2500 g (5.5 lb) and a gestation age of 37 weeks or less. In Chapter 4 we noted the dramatic increase in survival rates of low birth weight newborns, but there are concerns about their future health and development. These children are at greater risk for developmental delay and health problems than normal birth weight babies (Shapiro, McCormick, Starfield, & Krischner, & Bross, 1980). Low birth weight children tend to perform at a lower level cognitively (McBurney & Eaves, 1986) and are at a greater risk for academic and learning problems even with normal cognitive functioning (Klein, Hack, & Breslau, 1989). They also are more prone to behavior problems (e.g., Escalona, 1982). The risk for cognitive problems occurs throughout the spectrum of birth weights below 2500 g, increasing as birth weights diminish (Dunn, 1986).

Recognizing the apparent IQ benefits of early intervention with disadvantaged but normal birth weight children, such as demonstrated in the Abecedarian Project and in several studies of low birth weight infants (e.g., Ramey, Bryant, Sparling, & Wasik, 1984), a truly landmark study was undertaken involving no less than eight medical school sites throughout the United States. The Infant Health and Development Project (1990) is the first multi-site randomized clinical study of the efficacy of a combination of services designed to reduce developmental, behavioral, and health problems in low birth weight premature infants. The services provided were early childhood treatment à la Abecedarian, family support, and pediatric medical services.

Dividing their study population into two birth weight groups—*heavier* low birth weight infants (2001–2500 g) and *lighter* low birth weight infants (less than 2000 g), a total of 985 low birth weight infants (362 heavier and 623 lighter) were randomly assigned to either an *intervention* or a *follow-up* (control) group. During the first year of life, both child-development and family-support services were provided. There were weekly home visits, with the "home visitor" giving health and infant development information and implementing two teaching curricula. One focused on cognitive, linguistic, and social development through games and activities that involved the parents and child; the other was a systematic approach to problem-solving. Beginning at 12 months, parents also were offered bimonthly parent-group meetings that presented information on childrearing and health and safety, addressed general parental concerns, and provided some social support.

For the children, a 2-year daily program was provided at a child development center. Beginning at age 12 months and continuing to a prematurity-corrected age of 36 months, the center staff continued to implement the home-visitor curriculum, tailoring it to each child's needs. The teacher-child ratio was that of Abecedarian—1:3 for children ages 12 to 23 months and 1:4 for ages 24 to 36 months. Class size was six at 12 to 23 months and eight at 24 to 36. Children attended the program 5 days a week. Of special note was the care taken to ensure that the intervention and control groups were comparable on a host of variables that could have affected the response to the treatment, such as birth weight, gender, maternal education, and the primary language in the home.

Evaluations of the effect of the program were conducted first at 40 weeks of "conceptual age" and at the corrected conceptual ages of 4, 8, 12, 18, 24, 30, and 36 months. Importantly, those who conducted the evaluations—cognitive, behavioral, and medical—were "blind" as to whether the child was a treatment or control subject. Perhaps most significant is a lengthy follow-up study of these children at age 8 years (McCarton et al., 1997).

Findings at Age 3 Years.   The findings at age 3 years are unambiguous. For the total population, on the Stanford-Binet L-M intelligence test, at age 3 years the intervention children had a mean IQ of 94 (93.5) as against a mean IQ of 85 (84.5) in the controls. As might be expected, the magnitude of intervention benefit was related to birth weight. In the heavier birth weight children, 2001 to 2500 g, the intervention group exceeded the controls by 13.2 IQ points (98.0 versus 84.8). In contrast, there was a lesser but still significant difference between the lighter intervention children and their controls. The average difference here was 6.6 IQ points. The mean IQ of the lighter intervention children was 91.0 as compared with 84.4 in the controls. In view of the birth weight–related benefits of

TABLE 5.3. Percentages of low birth weight children with IQs below 70 at 36 months of age

	Lighter Birth Weights		Heavier Birth Weight (2001 to 2500 g)
	1500 g or less	1501 to 2000 g	
Intervention	26.8	7.9	4.8
Controls	28.7	18.8	18.2

the treatment program, it is surprising that the heavier and lighter *control* children were virtually identical in IQ; their overall mean IQ was 84.6.

Given the increased risk of developmental delay and retardation in this low birth weight population, of special interest is the intervention program's effect on rates of retardation. Table 5.3 shows the proportion of children with IQs below 70. For further analysis, they're divided into three low birth weight groups.

In each of the three birth-weight groups, there were fewer children with IQs below 70 among those who had had the early intervention program, although the difference is negligible in the smallest of the low birth weight groups. We also see the birth-weight effect itself. In the intervention children the frequency of retardation diminishes as birth weight rises. As in the case of IQ, in the controls, however, there is little difference between their retardation rates in the two heavier birth weight groups.

The impact of the program is especially evident in the proportion of children with IQs of at least 90 at age 3 years. Nearly two thirds of the intervention children (65.6%) had IQs of at least 90, as compared with less than 40% (38.9%) of the controls.

Findings at Age 8 Years. At age 8 years, the great majority of the difference found at age 3 years had dissipated. There was no longer a significant IQ difference between intervention and control children. The mean IQ for both groups was 91 (90.5). This score reflects a decline of about 4 IQ points for the intervention children and a rise of 6 points for the control. Once again we see an elevation in IQ in children following their entrance into school. This "schooling" or educational effect on intelligence has been noted both here and abroad (Ceci & Williams, 1997) and may account for as many as 8 IQ points by the end of high school.

As with intelligence, there were no differences between the total intervention and control children groups in school achievement. Nevertheless, like at the younger age, there were apparent yet modest benefits to the heavier low birth weight children. Their average IQ was 97 (96.5), 6.5 points greater than the total intervention group mean. Moreover, it significantly exceeded that of the lighter low birth weight children. The average IQ of the latter at age 8 years was 88.3. Interestingly, although the heavier low birth weight children's IQ exceeded that of their controls (96.5 versus 92.1), both the lighter intervention and lighter controls had average IQs of less than 90, 88.3 in the intervention children and 89.5 in the controls.

School-wise, there also were some modest benefits to the heavier low birth weight children. They exceeded their controls in math for the total intervention group. For the total intervention group, however, there was no significant difference relative to the controls in school achievement. Moreover, the intervention and control children were very similar in frequency of grade retention, 14% versus 16%, respectively. Parenthetically, the 16% grade retention rate for the controls also was found for the Abecedarian children. Even a 5-year preschool program did not seem to materially affect that index.

Summarizing the Effects of Early Intervention on Cognitive Development and on the Prevention of Mental Retardation

The studies that we have reviewed indicate that early intervention and education programs can produce significant although modest cognitive benefits if (a) they begin no later than age 1 year, (b) they provide an instructionally oriented day-care experience *throughout* the preschool years, and (c) they offer a program of support and encouragement to families. It must be emphasized, however, that although the family-support component can be helpful, it is the preschool experience itself that has the greatest impact (Campbell & Nabors, 1998). In contrast to the earlier early-intervention (Head Start) research, largely dealing with preschool programs of lesser length and intensity, durable treatment effects into adolescence are only found in the kind of comprehensive programs epitomized by the Abecedarian Project. Guralnick (1998) also has stressed the importance of length and intensity as keys to early childhood educational efforts. The benefits of the Infant Health and Development Project largely were lost with discontinuation at age 3 years.

On the Nature of the Specific Cognitive Benefits

In examining the effect of the Abecedarian preschool experience on specific aspects of cognition, as measured by the intelligence tests used in that research, it is clear that it is the verbal scale test items that were affected (Campbell & Nabors, 1998). A language-rich preschool experience can enhance functioning of disadvantaged children on such language-related cognitive functions as general knowledge (information) and word knowledge (vocabulary).

It also was their bedeviling finding that in spite of verbal scale IQ benefits, the developmental trend for *both* intervention and control children was a decline in verbal IQ. No such trend is evident in the nonlanguage performance scale. Indeed, it appears to have been little affected by the preschool experience.

Preventing Mental Retardation

Interestingly, the early intervention studies suggest that the greatest benefit of a lengthy and intensive preschool experience accrues to the children at greatest risk for mental retardation, those whose mothers are themselves quite limited intellectually, a conclusion also reached by early-intervention researchers (Ramey & Ramey, 1998). Moreover this reduced risk applies to low birth weight children as well as to those of normal birth weight.

Both the previously described adoption studies and the preschool data indicate that cultural-familial/psychosocial mental retardation is preventable. The most radical form of early intervention, adoption itself, can have an impact of as much as 25 IQ points. But even the less radical intervention of a comprehensive preschool experience can elevate the IQs of these high-risk children to a significant degree. Because only the latter form of intervention is widely possible in our society, the implication is that efforts must be maximized to reach the "high-risk" mother, offer her knowledge about child development and stimulation, provide comprehensive day care beginning by age 1 year, and continue to offer it throughout the preschool period. Indeed, such assistance probably is going to be necessary during the elementary-school years.

☐ Summary

This is the last of the three chapters devoted to the causes of mental retardation. In contrast to the first two, in which the focus was on "biological" determinants, here we seek to shed light on the "psychological" or psychosocial factors that affect intellectual development. In some respects, this is a more difficult task because we are not dealing with cognitive disorders whose basis can be traced readily to organic brain abnormalities. Rather we are dealing with grossly normal brains and trying to understand how they can be affected, positively and negatively, by nonbiological events. The effort to explicate the role of the "environment" involves presenting research that shows the effects of various kinds of early childhood experiences. These consist of children reared under conditions of gross deprivation and the implications for a "healthy" early childhood experience; children reared in large "group-care" settings, environments that can limit "individualized" child care; children reared by parents who are themselves retarded; and children reared in foster and adoptive homes.

Basic Rights

It was the civil rights movement of the 1950s and 1960s that created the climate within which people disadvantaged by disability, rather than by race or gender, could begin to claim these rights for themselves. At the international level, rights were asserted pertaining to education, work, place of residence, guardianship, and legal safeguards. In 1971, the United Nations adopted a Declaration of General and Special Rights of the Mentally Retarded and, in 1973, the then AAMD issued its own "rights" proclamation. AAMD later called attention to rights to habilitation, and to protection from both involuntary sterilization and so-called aversive treatment procedures, measures employed with some severe behavior disorders. The rights proclaimed by AAMD are quoted (Position Papers of the American Association on Mental Deficiency) along with an update on their current status.

The basic rights that a retarded person shares with his or her nonretarded peers include those implied in "life, liberty, and the pursuit of happiness."

The right to freedom of choice within the individual's capacity to make decisions. The decade of the 1990s has seen a stress on the "empowering" of both individuals with retardation and their families so as to give them greater influence on the decisions that affect them. The goal is to decrease dependency and increase autonomy or self-determination.

The right to live in the least restrictive individually appropriate environment. Nondisabled adults are free to choose their places of employment and residence. To the degree that adults with retardation can make such choices, those preferences should be honored. Here again, there is a stress on empowerment, choice, and autonomy.

The right to gainful employment and a fair day's pay. Among the disabled population in general, only about one third are regularly employed, a proportion that would be even further reduced among those with retardation. Major federal legislation since the 1970s, specifically the Rehabilitation Act of 1973 and its later amendments and the landmark Americans with Disabilities Act of 1988, have enhanced employment opportunities for persons with retardation, as has the development of "supported employment" as an alternative to traditional employment in sheltered workshops.

The right to be part of a family. Unlike the period prior to the 1960s, the institutional placement of young children with mental retardation is now a rarity. The earlier advice to new parents of an infant with a disorder associated with retardation, such as Down syndrome—"Place the child and then forget him"—has been replaced by an awareness that parents do want to care for *all* of their children and that there now exists a variety of community services to assist them in that function.

The right to marry and have a family. In an earlier societal climate that viewed retarded adults as a "reproductive menace," the large state institutions were seen as a means of containing the sexual appetites of individuals, largely mildly retarded, who could aspire to marriage and parenthood, and to sterilize those deemed capable of community return. Such control is no longer judicially possible, and the right to marriage and to parenthood can only be abrogated by formal legal procedures. In Chapter 5, concerns were expressed about the vulnerabilities of the retarded parent and possible adverse effects on their children; programs of "parenthood" training were urged.

Specific Extensions of Basic Rights

The right to a publicly supported and administered comprehensive and integrated set of habilitative programs and services designed to minimize handicap(s). Children, youth, and adults have the right, as in education, to publicly supported programs designed to meet their special habilitative needs. Of particular importance is the location of such programs within their home communities. Children should not have to leave home to receive such services. Moreover, these services should be available throughout the lifecycle, from those for infants and young children to those for older adults. If placement outside the family home becomes necessary, as is likely true in the case of retarded adults whose parents are no longer be able to provide care, such placement should be in the least restrictive setting relative to his or her competencies. Such a setting would be one in which the disabled person can exercise as much autonomy and decision making as his or her disability allows.

The right to a publicly supported and administered program of training and education including, but not restricted to, academic and interpersonal skills. The Federal legislation of the 1970s and 1990s has produced tremendous changes in educational access, including the provision of services in both the preschool and young adult years. With regard to education itself, there is now recognition of the need for a "functionally relevant" educational experience (e.g., Dever & Knapczyk, 1997), one that prepares the student for full participation in the post-school-age adult years. Further, the school must begin that preparation no later than age 16 years.

Rights of Special Concern

The Right to Life Itself: The Right to be Born

Nowhere is the stigma of mental retardation greater that in the medical arena. In the 1980s the nation's attention was drawn to the plight of an infant with Down syndrome following a parental decision to withhold treatment for an anatomical abnormality. The baby, then known as Baby Doe, was born with a blockage of the esophagus that prevented eating. Aware of the implications of Down syndrome for the infant's mental development, along with the special physical disabilities, the parents elected not to have the esophageal surgery performed. The baby died. Then President Reagan intervened asking that the Federal laws that protect persons with disabilities be applied to newborns. The "Baby Doe" rule followed; it forbade physicians from withholding treatment of newborns on the basis of the expected future "quality of life." Subsequent judicial review annulled the rule.

In response to the Baby Doe affair, hospitals developed guidelines for the care of infants when there is a question of withholding treatment. At our hospital in Chapel Hill, North Carolina, treatment generally is not withheld, irrespective of parent preference, on the basis of physical or mental impairments, present or anticipated. Treatment would be and traditionally has been withheld in the case of such extraordinary cognitive and physical impairment as anencephaly; the child being born, literally, without a brain. The decision not to treat is seen as "in the child's best interest," and death shortly ensues. Our hospital guidelines reject the implications of the child's future "productivity" or the current absence of community resources as grounds for withholding treatment. *The infant is not to be held hostage to societal conditions it cannot control.* If doubt exists as to the benefit of treatment, a presumption should exist in favor of it. But if the benefits of treatment are genuinely unclear the choice of the parents should be honored.

The Baby Doe affair and its aftermath confront us with questions on the "value" of human life, especially if that life will have qualities that we would not wish for ourselves and if lifelong major disability is anticipated. From a religious perspective, all lives have equal value, but it has been argued that in our more secular society, values that are not necessarily religiously based also should be recognized (Kuhse, 1985). Individual opinions on such issues necessarily are weighted by one's own experience. Not only is what we as parents or physicians view as a life not worth living necessarily subjective, but such a life may be viewed very differently from the perspective of one who is living it. The life of a slave as depicted by Frederick Douglass, in his remarkable autobiography, *My Bondage and My Freedom*, is one that involved exposure to unremitting cruelty and brutality. It might not seem worth living to modern eyes but, in the absence of any alternative, it was tolerated by its victims (Douglass, 1855, 1969).[2] Questions on the "value of life" affect our perceptions of "disability" itself. They led in Nazi Germany to the killing of persons with disabilities as well as of other "undesirables." Given that we humans are capable of the most extraordinary cruelty as well as angelic compassion, it behooves us to exercise the greatest caution if questions are raised of whose life is to be preserved. Eventually, the life that comes under scrutiny could be our very own!

The Right to Liberty

Life in our large state institutions, and in small group-care settings as well, necessarily involves restrictions of the fundamental right to liberty and those rights related to it—travel, free association, and privacy. Other rights also may be affected—the right to treatment itself, to sexual expression, and to protection from harm. It is the last-mentioned that stirred much of the concern about institutions; residents were not necessarily protected from each other or even from staff.

The most blatant infringement on liberty was the practice of *indefinite commitment* to an institution of a person charged with a crime but deemed incompetent to stand trial and be defended. The law does not proceed against a defendant who neither understands the nature or purpose of the proceedings against him nor is able to offer a rational defense. If mentally handicapped persons are found incompetent to stand trial, they are likely to be committed to psychiatric hospitals or to mental-retardation centers (depending on the crime), with the understanding that a trial would ensue if they were to become competent.

For persons with mental illness, recovery of competence is, at least, a reasonable supposition, but in the case of incompetency associated with retardation, such a change is less probable, and the commitment could be permanent. This issue was examined by the Supreme Court in 1972 (*Jackson v. Indiana*, 1972) in connection with a deaf-mute male with apparent mental retardation who had been charged with purse snatching and the theft of property worth $9. Virtually unable to communicate and found incompetent to stand trial, he was committed to a mental hospital, where he was to remain until becoming competent! Although the maximum sentence for the misdemeanor with which he was charged would have been 6 months, he already had been confined for 3 years and might have remained there for life if the Supreme Court had not decided to hear his case. The court ruled that a person charged with a criminal offense and committed to an institution by virtue of incapacity to stand trial cannot be held more than the reasonable period of time necessary to determine whether competency can be achieved. If this is not anticipated, then the person must be either civilly committed or released. Because the plaintiff had previously demonstrated his ability to live independently in the community and, at least on this basis, was not committable to an institution for the mentally retarded nor viewed as a danger to others, he was released.

The Right to Habilitation

But does civil commitment even if appropriate negate rights? This question arose out of the undesirable conditions often present in the large state institutions and to which we already have referred. A landmark case (*Wyatt v. Stickney*, 1972 addressed this issue. Originally initiated on behalf of psychiatric patients in a state mental hospital, the plaintiff group was broadened to include the residents of a sister mental retardation facility. The language of the federal court that heard the case is compelling and conveys a sense of the conditions that created public concern.

> The evidence ... has vividly and undisputedly portrayed [the institution] as a warehousing institution which because of its atmosphere of psychological and physical deprivation, is wholly incapable of furnishing habilitation to the mentally retarded and is conducive only to the deterioration and debilitation of the residents [like the conditions cited in Chapter 5]. The evidence has further reflected that safety and sanitary conditions ... are substandard to the point of endangering the health and lives of those residing there, that the wards are grossly understaffed, rendering even simple custodial care impossible, and that overcrowding remains a dangerous problem often leading to serious accidents, some of which have resulted in deaths of residents.

The *Wyatt v. Stickney* case was significant because, for the first time, a federal court held that retarded persons committed to a state institution had a constitutional right to habilitation. The right entailed a humane psychological and physical environment, an individual habilitation and training plan for each resident, and qualified professional and paraprofessional staff in sufficient numbers to deliver individualized habilitation and training.

Following the court decision, improvements occurred at the institution, but concerns were expressed about the adequacy of its services to those with the severest degree of cognitive impairment. In response, the institution raised the question as to what was appropriate treatment for those residents for whom future growth was questionable, those with profound retardation, and proposed a treatment plan based on "an enriched environment" as an alternative to one of "training and education." The court rejected the proposal but did not address the perhaps unanswerable question of whether continuous growth in abilities can be expected in those with the profoundest degree of cognitive impairment, or indeed for any of us. Assuming that there are, if nothing else, species-determined limitations on our growth potential, educational distinctions still can be drawn between training for *new* skills and *maintenance* of existing ones. The latter would allow for "horizontal" if not "vertical" growth, as one is offered new experiences at what appears to be the highest level of complexity attainable for that individual. In the teaching of reading, for example, to a retarded or learning-disabled adolescent who is reading at not more than the third-grade level, "graded" readers offer content of interest to an adolescent but at the student's reading level. Moreover, these experiences themselves may have the effect of increasing ability levels in the vertical sense.

The rulings of the court in *Wyatt* ultimately were codified in Federal legislation. They are found in laws pertaining to individuals with mental retardation and mental illness, such as the Protection and Advocacy for Mentally Ill Individuals Act of 1986. Establishing a "bill of rights" for mentally disabled persons, this act enumerates the right not to be discriminated against on the basis of handicap; the right to appropriate treatment in the least restrictive setting; the right to treatment based on an individual treatment plan and one subject to periodic review; the right to dignity, privacy, and confidentiality of personal records; and the right to a humane physical and psychological environment. The language of the *Wyatt* decision rings loud and clear! The inclusion of these rights in Federal legislation has had a profound influence on the nature of state and local services to individuals with mental retardation.

Least Restrictive Environment

The right to habilitation has come to include the right to receive it in settings that are least restrictive of personal freedom. The "least restrictive environment" is one that permits the greatest degree of independence consistent with one's decision-making capacity. The goal is to find the right balance between control and independence.

The concept of least restrictive environment also has included being served in settings in which there is ready contact with nondisabled people. This aspect is most often associated with school programs. The terms "mainstreaming" and, more recently, "inclusion" refer to the incorporation of disabled student as much as possible in the classroom experience of nondisabled peers.

The Right to Be Free from Harm

First enunciated in the previously mentioned Willowbrook case and spoken to in *Wyatt*, the concern is with exposure to environments that can threaten physical, mental, and emotional well-being. Interestingly, the legal challenge to such institutional conditions was based on the 8th Amendment to the Constitution, the amendment that prohibits "cruel and unusual punishment." Although typically applied to persons in prison, it came to be interpreted as referring to any individual for whom the state accepts the responsibility for providing custodial care (Friedman, 1976).

The Right to Education

Without doubt, the "right to education" has had the widest impact on children with mental retardation and with other developmental disabilities as well. The term *developmental disabilities* has come to be applied to disorders present at birth or arising in childhood that are chronic in nature and require similar habilitative services. Originally referring to mental retardation, cerebral palsy, epilepsy, and other neurological conditions arising in the "developmental" years prior to age 18, and later adding autism and severe dyslexia (reading disability), the term now encompasses all developmental disorders—sensory and physical as well as cognitive—that significantly affect major areas of daily living (Baroff, 1991a). Self-care, language, learning, and self-direction are some of the daily living areas involved.

Beginning with the enactment of the Education for All Handicapped Children Act of 1975 (Public Law 94-142), federal law established the right of every handicapped child to a "free appropriate education," and all states now have laws supporting this right. "Appropriateness" refers to the provision of an educational experience tailored to the child's individual needs (Smith & Luckasson, 1992). The more recent versions of this landmark legislation are the Individual with Disabilities Education Act of 1990 and its reauthorization as the Individual with Disabilities Act Amendments of 1997. Recognizing that more than half of handicapped children still were not receiving adequate services, the laws both broadened the population to be served and added new areas of emphasis. Highlights included the addition of autism and head injury (traumatic brain injury) to the disabilities needing special attention and a focus on "transition"—the preparation of students with disabilities for working and living in the general community in their post-school-age years.

The laws also continue the thrust of serving children in the least restrictive educational environment. We refer to this "right" elsewhere and here want to present the actual language of the 1990 legislation because it challenges the traditional way in which classes for "exceptional children" have been organized:

> To the extent appropriate, handicapped children, including children in public
> or private institutions or other care facilities, are educated with children who

are not handicapped, and ... special classes, separate schooling, or other removal of handicapped children from the regular education environment occurs only when the nature or severity of the handicap is such that education in regular classes with the use of supplementary aids and services cannot be achieved satisfactorily. (Individuals with Disabilities Education Act Ammendments of 1997)

This is the language of mainstreaming and inclusion. The related research is reviewed in the section on education itself.

Guardianship and Protectorship

The condition of "guardianship" is pertinent to the rights of individuals with retardation because it grants to one person, the guardian, the legal authority to make decisions for another, the ward. Guardianship brings into potential conflict two important social goals for retarded persons—the need for *protection* against injury and exploitation and the *obligation to foster maximum personal freedom and independence (autonomy)*. The principle of the least restrictive alternative allows for resolving the conflict. It holds that if one's decision-making ability is significantly impaired and restriction of that fundamental right is necessary, the degree of restriction should be no greater than that which is absolutely essential.

The least restrictive principle finds expression in the two types of guardianship—*general* and *limited*. General guardianship is the traditional form and is appropriate if the degree of cognitive impairment precludes the capacity for any complex decision-making. For example, in the care of an adult with severe and profound retardation, the capacity for giving "informed consent" to a surgical procedure likely would be absent. Informed consent requires the understanding of the procedure that is proposed and an awareness of alternatives and their relative risks. It requires a *weighing* of alternative courses of action and their respective consequences.

A lesser degree of external decision making is found in "limited guardianship" or "protectorship." It is a formalizing of the "benefactor" role described in Chapter 1. Appropriate to individuals with greater capacities for decision-making, it involves a partial rather than total delegation of personal control. Within limited guardianship a distinction is made between guardianship of the *estate* and guardianship of the *person*. The latter allows the guardian to make a wide range of decisions for the ward but *not* financial ones.

Interestingly, limits have been placed on the controls that a limited guardian can assume. A Wisconsin statute (S880.33, 1974) stipulates that guardianship of the person is tied to *specific court-determined* areas in which the ward is seen as lacking "competence."

No person shall be deprived of any legal rights, including the right to vote, to marry, to obtain a motor vehicle operator's license, to testify in any judicial or administrative proceedings, to make a will, to hold or convey property and to contract *except upon specific finding of the court. Such findings must be based on clear and convincing evidence of the need for such limitations.*

Our freedoms are not to be taken from us without due process of law.

In North Carolina, a guardianship program operates under the auspices of the longtime parent organization, the former Association for Retarded Citizens of North Carolina, now the Arc. Together with other public and private agencies, the Arc currently provides guardianship for over 200 protégés (wards) through a network of seven regional guardianship districts. Each regional district has either a fulltime or parttime "guardian specialist," who serves as the case manager for his or her region's protégés. Of interest, all major decisions about a protégé are made by one of two "protégé review committees." These committees meet monthly and are assisted in their work by a large number of consultants who offer their services at no cost.

For each protégé, the case manager tries to find at least one person who will serve as an "interested friend." This individual has no legal authority but is expected to keeps tabs on how the protégé is getting along.

Advocacy

In our discussion of guardianship, there was reference to the volunteer who enters into a friendship and supportive relationship with the disabled person. Such individuals can assume roles as advocates on behalf of the protégé in his or her interactions with the agencies that are providing services.

Another variant of advocacy is *legal* or *case* advocacy. It is this form of advocacy that has formally challenged the discrimination against and denial of rights to disabled persons and won for them new forms of judicial and legal protection. Every state now has a "protection and advocacy" agency whose role is to support and defend the rights of its retarded citizens and to train lawyers and other interested citizens to function as their advocates.

Self-advocacy

One of the dramatic developments in the field of disabilities has been the assertion by disabled individuals of the right to exercise some control over their lives. Especially prominent in retardation, we see an abandonment of the traditional stance of mute acceptance of whatever was offered and its replacement by demands for greater autonomy and self-determination (Dybwad, 1996). One example of this is the rejection of the labels that *others* have chosen for them, such as "retarded"; they now proudly wear the organizational title of "People First."

Originating in Oregon in the 1970s, a grass-roots effort had created as many as 37 state organizations by 1996 (Shoultz & Ward, 1996). At their 1991 Annual North American People First Conference, their cause was expressed in the following language:

> Self-advocacy is about independent groups of people with disabilities work-ing together for justice by helping each other take charge of their lives and fight discrimination. *It teaches us how to make decisions and choices that affect our lives so we can be more independent.* It teaches us about our rights, but along with learning about our rights, we learn about our responsibilities. [Rights and responsibilities can be likened to the two sides of a coin: You can't have one without the other.] The way we learn about advocating for ourselves is supporting each other and helping each other gain confidence in themselves to speak out for what they believe. (Dybwad, 1996, p. 2; italics added).

A perspective on the self-advocacy movement and its effect on the life of a disabled adult is found in the story of Bernard Carabello. Carabello, affected with cerebral palsy, had been a resident of the now infamous Willowbrook State School at the time of its exposé in 1972 (Perske, 1996). Interviewed by Geraldo Rivera, Carabello is described as writhing in his chair, his arms in constant motion (the athetoid form of cerebral palsy). It was doubted by Rivera that Carabello, then 21 years old and virtually a lifelong resident of Willowbrook, could respond verbally to his questions. But in struggling speech, Carabello told his story of life at Willowbrook. Rivera featured the Carabello story on the evening news and closed his report with the observation that Carabello's life at Willowbrook had been a "waste." He described him as just vegetating on one of the "stinking wards" (an accurate designation); as "rotting away" although with training he could have been a productive person. Subsequently Carabello was moved to the community and Willowbrook closed. But Rivera's relationship with Carabello apparently continues to the present. In 1981, Carabello was interviewed in his role as a self-advocate.

> I'm much better at helping others. I talk to people. I got SSI [federal financial assistance] for someone who really needed it. I got a home for someone else. That makes me feel really good [gratification of our need for "success"]. I try not to treat people "special." They don't need that. I have people come to me and talk down to me, as if I'm a child or hard of hearing. "How are you? You're a *good* boy!" I had a woman give me a dollar and tell me to buy myself some ice cream [note the childlike treatment of someone who is an adult]. One time a salesman knocked on the door, and he saw me and said, "Is anybody home?" I said "Who the hell do you think I am?" (Williams & Shoultz, 1982, p. 78)

In describing the pressures to close Willowbrook in 1972, Geraldo Rivera asserted, "If Willowbrook is ever closed ... it will be more because of Bernard Carabello than anyone else" (Carabello & Siegel, 1996). Today Willowbrook is closed, and Carabello lives in New York City where he works for the New York State Office of Developmental Disabilities.

Sexual Consent

We have referred to "consent" in conjunction with making an "informed" decision in the context of a proposed operation. No more controversial area exists than that related to the retarded person's "right" to consent to or to engage in sexual behavior. The issue here is the right to exercise sexual choice and to be able to distinguish between behavior that is consensual as opposed to coerced. The latter can be construed as "abuse" and as grounds for criminal action.

Decrying the lack of criteria that would permit determination of whether the retarded person's participation in sexual activity was truly consensual, Parker and Abrahamson (1995) note that observers tend to lean most heavily on the degree to which it appears to be "voluntary." Specific criteria have been proposed that allow for the distinction between "verbal" and "behavioral" consent. The latter applies to individuals who lack the verbal skills necessary to that means of communication (Ames & Samowitz, 1995). Verbal consent is communicated through verbally indicating an understanding of the nature of the proposed sexual activity and of choice with regard to participation; its possible consequences, including violation of criminal laws, such as those against pedophilia and rape, and exposure to sexually transmitted disease; the appropriate place and time; and how one could leave such a situation if the need arose.[1]

Clearly more difficult and controversial is judging consent if it cannot be communicated verbally and can only be shown in the nature of the behavior itself. Although all would agree that "actions speak louder than words," the notion of direct observation of such behavior is totally repugnant to our sensibilities. Yet there may be some merit in the approach; presumably it is, in fact, quietly exercised in residential settings in which consensual sexual behavior is sanctioned, at least informally.

☐ Normalization, Choice, and the "Quality of Life"

The terms in the title of this section, and their implications, represent the dominant values and beliefs of those who have most actively pursued change in our mental retardation service system, from one that was institutional to one that is now community-based. "Normalization" right-fully can be called the rallying cry that initiated the truly revolutionary changes in how persons with retardation and their families are served.

Normalization as a treatment concept was enunciated first in Scandinavia (Bank-Mikkelson, 1969; Nirje, 1969) and then elaborated with great vigor and intensity in the United States and Canada by Wolfensberger and his colleagues (Wolfensberger, 1972; Wolfensberger & Glenn, 1973, 1975). Its initial formulation spoke to creating patterns and rhythms of everyday life for individuals with retardation that would mirror as closely as possible those of the mainstream society. Broadened by Wolfenberger to apply to all human services, he first defined it as the utilization of treatment and habilitative *means* that are as culturally normative as possible in order to establish and maintain *personal behaviors* and *characteristics* that are as culturally normative as possible.

Normalization gives special attention to the *means* and *contexts* within which services are provided as well as to the services themselves. It seeks to reduce the "differentness" associated with disability and to promote personal competence such that the disabled individual can live a life that most nearly approximates that of his or her nondisabled counterpart. Its primary means of achieving this goal is through "integration"—that is, the *inclusion* of persons with disabilities *within* the general society in contrast to their earlier *exclusion*, as epitomized by life in large institutions and in separate schools and classes. Nor has the rallying cry of normalization been only rhetoric. Its language has found its way into state and Federal legislation.

The goals of normalization are reflected in proposals of the pioneering psychiatrist in mental retardation, Frank Menolascino. He insisted that programs and facilities should be physically and socially integrated into the community, there should be maximum contact with nonretarded individuals, and even severely retarded adults should have some opportunity to work (Menolascino, 1977).

Given the community thrust of current services, it is not surprising that integration features prominently in scales designed to evaluate the retarded person's "quality of life." In one recent measure of lifestyle outcomes (Newton, Ard, Horner, & Toews, 1996), two types of integration are assessed—*physical* activities in the community, not in the dwelling place; and *social* experiences with people *other* than the individuals with whom they live. This has particular relevance for adults living in "group homes," whose primary interactions with nonhandicapped people are the staff of these homes. Apart from integration, there is also attention to the retarded individual's degree of independence. It should be noted that with greater independence comes the opportunity to exercise greater *choice*, another of the major trends in current services. Indeed, choice is an important feature of the quality-of-life scale of a major accrediting agency (Gardner, Nudler, & Chapman, 1997).

Although the extraordinary influence of the normalization movement can be attributed in no small measure to its zealous advocacy by Wolfensberger and like-minded colleagues, as well as to national exposés of institutional abuses, there is also a body of research that supports its premises. In what can be considered a balanced review of the related research literature (Landesman & Butterfield, 1987), it is concluded, for example, that greater gains in adaptation result from movement from institutions to community group homes than from program improvements within institutional environments. Of interest, in light of the claim that institutions are the more appropriate setting for those with the severer degrees of retardation, individuals who constitute the large bulk of their present population (Lakin, Prouty, Braddock, & Anderson, 1997), there is evidence that even those with major health and behavior problems can progress in smaller and community-based environments. We return to this research literature in the next Chapter 7, when we examine in greater detail the effects of community versus institutional living on retarded adults.

But normalization is not without its critics; they see a continuing role for the large institutions (e.g., Crissey & Rosen, 1986), for example, as research centers in mental retardation. Wolfensberger became uncomfortable with the various interpretations given to the term and proposed a new one: "social role valorization" (Wolfensberger, 1983). Reflecting his conception of the highest goal of normalization, it calls for preparing retarded individuals to assume culturally valued social roles. The roles of "worker" and "friend" may lend themselves most readily to this objective. Recall that Menolascino in 1977 saw "work" as one of the important means of implementing normalization. Although social role valorization involves a valuing of the individual as well as of his or her social role, the term has not yet supplanted "normalization" in the national consciousness.

A Perspective on Services and Supports

In the language of the 1992 AAMR definition of mental retardation, many services to affected individuals and their families are characterized as "supports" (see Chapter 1).[2] Given the chronic nature of the disability associated with mental retardation, supports refer to services designed to maximize the individual's degree of personal competency and to meet those basic biological and psychological "needs" spelled out in Chapter 2. These are *survival, structure, self-esteem,* and *self-expression.* To the degree that these needs are met, the retarded individual will be free of physical and psychological discomfort, the same state that we would wish for ourselves.

Our biological and psychological needs are met through services that have both a horizontal and vertical dimension. "Horizontal" services refer to those that may be needed at any single point in life. Thus a preschooler with mental retardation might be living in a foster home (a residential service), attending a preschool program (an educational service), and receiving care for seizures (a health service) and physical therapy for cerebral palsy (another health service). "Vertical" services are those needed over time, the services necessary to each stage of development from infancy into old age. When this preschooler is of school age, there will be exposure to a wide range of services—some a continuation of earlier ones, such as education, and some relatively new ones, such as social, recreational, and vocational services. In the postschool adult years, there will be the need for employment or, at the very least, the opportunity to engage in some meaningful and satisfying daily activity (e.g., a vocational service). There will be need for social, sexual, and recreational outlets (social, educational, and recreational services) and, if there is at least a moderate degree of cognitive impairment, access to a community-living situation if, because of aging or death of parents, the family home no longer is available.

A New Model: Services Based on "Choice" and "Support"

In the section on normalization we describe the revolution in the field of mental retardation reflected in the shift from separate and essentially "segregated" services in our institutions and schools to services offered in the family home and local community. That shift meant the creation of programs and facilities in the local community. For example, in contrast to the single monolithic state institution as the chief out-of-home residential resource, a huge network of smaller residential settings in local communities has been established. The best-known example of these are "group homes." But now another fundamental shift has occurred in the way in which services are provided. Instead of now "assigning" people to an admittedly much wider array of existing programs and facilities, a literal "fitting" of the person into that which was available, there is now a concerted effort to build the service around the person's wishes (choice), so-called person-centered planning and services. With knowledge of those preferences and those of the family, the service system tries to respond by "supporting" those preferences. Support means not only honoring choices but *enabling* them. In the residential domain, for example, adults who wish to live in settings with only one or two other people, as in a regular apartment, but who need assistance in activities of everyday living, such as budgeting, cooking, or shopping, can obtain that assistance. The intent is to encourage a more normal type of living arrangement, an apartment in contrast to a group home, if this is the individual's wish, and to provide the support necessary to sustain it. This is to give the disabled individual as much freedom and responsibility as can be exercised and to "tailor" the resources and supports around that person's specific needs. The idea of the tailoring of services is conveyed in so-called wrap-around services for individuals with severe behavior problems (Burchard, Atkins, & Burchard, 1996).

Finally, the "person-centered" service model seeks to shift the emphasis away from the person's disabilities and toward their capabilities, at whatever their level. Disabilities become relevant if they are in conflict with the person's choices or aspirations (O'Brien, O'Brien, & Mount, 1997). Such conflicts are inevitable and require reconciliation so as to more nearly satisfy the disabled person's aspirations.

☐ Summary

This chapter serves as an introduction to the variety of services and supports provided to persons with mental retardation and their families. Its focus is on the philosophical values and beliefs that should underlie both the services themselves and the attitudes of those who provide them. The chapter begins with a consideration of the "right" to services, a legal consideration that has been addressed by the courts particularly in terms of public education. Federal legislation in the American with Disabilities Act has addressed such issues as physical access and employment. Another group of concerns, those arising from the earlier widespread practice of institutionalization, pertain to rights to liberty, rehabilitation, and freedom from harm. The assertion of these rights has involved "advocacy"—first by parents and professionals and, more recently, by disabled persons themselves.

In the philosophical or "values" realm, important treatment-relevant concepts are those of normalization (social role valorization), inclusion (community integration), and choice. Choice has been especially prominent recently and is reflected in what are now viewed as "person-" or "family-centered" services. Their focus is the creation of an array of services and supports that are based on the preferences of the disabled individual and his or her family. The goal is to increase the degree of control (autonomy) that the disabled individual and the family can exercise.

Possible Discussion Questions

What are the assumptions that underlie the granting of "rights" to persons with disabilities? If rights are never absolute, (e.g., the loss of freedom if persons are imprisoned), under what conditions may rights be curtailed?

How are rights to public education reflected in school programs? What has been the effect of federal legislation on such programs?

How do we feel about the right of retarded persons to engage in sexual activities? (This topic is addressed again in other chapters.). Can we imagine any conditions under which that "freedom" is constrained?

Does "normalization" mean "normal?" What is its intent? As efforts increase to create greater integration or interaction between disabled and nondisabled individuals, what becomes our responsibility as representatives of the nondisabled community?

How does the encouragement of employment of persons with mental retardation relate to "social-role valorization?"

☐ Notes

1. Discussed in greater detail in Chapter 8.
2. Our preference is for the traditional designation although both terms will be used.

CHAPTER

7

Services and Supports to Children and Youth

☐ Overview

In this chapter is described the variety of services and supports for children and youth with mental retardation. The topics presented are the prevention of mental retardation through biological and psychological means; services to the preschool-aged child—primarily diagnostic and educational, the latter including a review of the "efficacy" of early childhood intervention programs; services to school-aged children and youth, organized in terms of the "what," "where," and "how" of special education; leisure education; and noneducational services—recreational, family-support, and medical.

☐ Prevention

Biological

Our concern here is to enhance the likelihood of the conception and birth of healthy infants and then to provide them with access to health measures that minimize their exposure to future biological hazards.

This concern is not without basis. Each year more than 400,000 infants are born who, by age 4 years, will have a recognizable disability (Garwood, Fewell, & Neisworth, 1988). Each year more than 300,000 newborns have been exposed prenatally to drugs and alcohol (Stevens & Price, 1992). In Chapter 4 we dealt at length with the adverse effects of such exposure on development and such a possible outcome as "fetal alcohol syndrome." Finally, about 16% of all American children (3 to 4 million) are said to have blood lead levels in the neurotoxic range (Needleman, 1992).

Given this sorry litany, we can recognize that *prevention* entails such activities as the planning of pregnancies; awareness of genetic risk, if it exists; obtaining prenatal care; avoiding during pregnancy the consumption of substances that can damage the fetus; and availing oneself of prenatal diagnostic procedures—chorion biopsy or amniocentesis if risk of abnormality is increased, as in the older mother. At birth, prevention involves the recognition of high-risk babies, such as those who are premature and very small for their gestation age; screening for genetic metabolic abnormalities, such as phenylketonuria and galactosemia, and promptly commencing dietary and medical procedures. Thereafter, prevention entails supposedly "routine" health measures—immunization; a nutritious diet; avoidance of exposure to toxic substances, such as lead; and periodic medical examinations.

Psychological

Although we can be very specific about the kinds of physical health measures that reduce the risk of retardation, in the psychological realm we are on fuzzier ground. The research cited in Chapter 5 leaves no doubt about the importance of infancy and early childhood on mental development, but the kind of specificity of *what, how*, and *when* remains to be determined. It is clear that *stimulation* is important, and that exposure to a caring parent or caregiver who can encourage language development and serve as a "verbal mediator" is vital to cognitive development. The means by which psychological prevention is effected is "educational." It requires the incorporation of "family life" education in our schools; health education for prospective parents; availability to the at-risk child of early-childhood education, such as Head Start; and a teaching parent. With the tremendous increase in women in the workplace, national social policy should support the access of young children to loving and teaching parents, at least during the first 2 years of life. Thereafter, cognitively-oriented early childhood education can supplement what is available in the home.

☐ Services to Preschool-aged Children

In 1986, with the amending and reauthorization of the Education for all Handicapped Children Act of 1975 (Public Law 94-142) under its new name, the Individuals with Disabilities Education Act, (Public Law 101-476) the Federal government extended the rights and protection of the earlier legislation to preschoolers. Through access to federal funds, the states were encouraged to begin serving "infants and toddlers" (birth to 3 years) and required to serve 3- to 5-year-olds. States also were to provide programs of public awareness and "child finding" in order to identify children at risk for developmental delay. These are children who either are clearly lagging in development or have a physical or mental condition associated with such delay. Of special concern were the following developmental areas—physical, cognitive, speech and language, and self-help. The identification of such children was to be followed by services designed to meet the child's individual needs. States were encouraged to provide multidisciplinary evaluation of child and family needs; develop, on the basis of that evaluation, an individualized family services plan; and facilitate the implementation of the plan through a "case manager" or coordinator of services.

Establishing the Nature of the Child's Disability and Needs: A Family-Centered Model

Responding to the needs of child and family begins with an *evaluation*. Involving multiple disciplines, it is directed toward assessment of the child's developmental maturity and, in the older preschooler, includes social and play skills. Importantly, the evaluation gives greater attention to the parents than has been true in the past. This involves a consideration of the impact of the child's disability on the parents; the stresses, if any; and how the parents are coping. The breadth of the areas explored requires the participation in the assessment of a number of disciplines, including psychology, social work, special education, speech therapy, physical and occupational therapy for the motor-impaired child, psychiatry, medicine, nutrition, and dentistry.

The multidisciplinary evaluation describes the child's level of functioning in the major developmental areas and considers its impact on the family. Families differ tremendously in their responses to a child with disability. In part, this response reflects the "meaning" of the disability for them—a reflection of their values, the availability of services and general support, and their religious beliefs. For parents, the child's condition ultimately must be viewed through the prism of their expectations as parents, their self-esteem, their goals for themselves and their children, and their status in the community. Siblings too have concerns. These include self-esteem, possible loss of prior parent attention, and expectations with respect to sharing the parents' child-caring role. Much has been written about the impact of the retarded child on the family (e.g., Blacher, 1984;

Paul & Simeonsson, 1993; Rogers-Dulan & Blacher, 1995). In some instances there appears to be little or no effect, in some it is a source of painful stress, and in others a challenge and opportunity for growth. A major determinant seems to be the time that parents have for themselves, and this relates to the amount of care the child requires, the effect on the family routine, their financial resources, and their access to respite services (Gallimore, Coots, Weisner, Garnier, & Guthrie, 1996; Herman & Marcenko, 1997).

Given an assessment of both child and family, the diagnostic team specifies treatment goals, the means of their accomplishment, and their time frames and identifies the coordinating case manager. The diagnostic team is also expected to give some attention to the steps necessary to the child making the transition from one setting to another (e.g., from a home-based to a center-based preschool program).

Within this evaluation process, the really new element is to forge treatment recommendations that are reflective of *parents'* goals. Traditionally, professionals offered treatment recommendations to parents based only on *their* view of what the child needed. It was the job of the parents to follow through and implement those recommendations. With the new family-centered diagnostic procedure, this is no longer the case.

The rationale for a family-centered diagnostic approach lies in the recognition that it is the *family*, the parents, who ultimately have the responsibility for implementing recommendations for their child. The best treatment recommendations are useless if, for whatever reason, they do not fit into what the parents want or are willing to do. Thus, the goal of family-centered evaluation is to have the parents share in the process of deciding what treatment goals to set for their child. In an increasingly diverse society, it is recognized that the values, beliefs, and goals of the parents may be quite different from those of the professionals. For example, the parents might view their child's disability from a religious perspective. Although a religious perspective on the "why" of having a disabled child can provide a positive framework for parents (e.g., they have been chosen by God for a special mission as a parent), it also can create a negative one. Parents might view the child's disability as a form of divine punishment and actually view efforts to mitigate it as inappropriate. Parents also may assume that because the disability itself cannot be erased, efforts to reduce the degree of impairment are not worthwhile. Given more negative parental views of the child's condition, treatment recommendations that require their participation are not likely to be fulfilled. More often, especially in poorer families, it is the perceived need to give greater attention to meeting basic family survival needs that takes precedence over attempting to devote energies to meeting professional recommendations.

In sum, whatever the potential differences between parents and professionals, it is necessary to try to accommodate those of the parents within a framework that the parents can accept. In effect, the professionals must be prepared to fit their recommendations into the family's values and priorities.

Another of the goals of the family-centered approach is to "empower" the parents. By virtue of their participation in the development of treatment plans, they, no less than the professionals, can come to "own" the treatment goals chosen. As collaborators in the diagnostic and treatment process rather than as mere passive recipients of professional recommendations, the typical dependency of the parents on the professionals is reduced. The effect is to give the parents a greater sense of control over what is happening to their child and to position them to advocate on behalf of their own child and on behalf of other children, in concert with similarly situated parents.

Common Preschool Programs

Three types of preschool programs are provided to infants and young children with developmental delays. Typically defined by the setting in which they are offered, they are home-based, center-based, and home- and center-based. Of these, the center-based program is the most common.

Home-Based

Offered primarily to infants and toddlers are programs that are conducted in the home. Early childhood "interventionists"—often a teacher but also including other disciplines, such as physical and occupational therapists for the motor-impaired child, periodically visit the child's home, where they work with the parent in providing appropriate developmental activities for the child. A special home-based program has been created for severely impaired and medically fragile infants. Its goal is to foster positive interactions between parents and their babies. The baby's condition may limit its general responsiveness to parental stimulation, and the intent is to sensitize parents to the infant's necessarily more limited behavioral cues (Hedlund, 1989).

In addition to activities focused on the infant, programs for parents include counseling, access to child-services coordination (a case manager), and referral to other services.

In light of the large number of working mothers, such activities may need to be offered outside the home, for example at a day-care center, but the parents still are expected to be involved.

Center-Based

Center-based programs typically are delivered at day-care centers, as in a preschool (Heward & Orlansky, 1992). In settings that often include nonhandicapped youngsters as well, children attend for several hours a day and at least weekly, if not daily. Although these programs are conducted outside the home, parental involvement is always encouraged. Two center-based programs have been widely replicated. The first, the Model Preschool Center for Handicapped Children at the University of Washington at Seattle offers educational experiences for several groups of infants and toddlers with developmental delay. Programs are provided in infant learning as such, for children with communication disorders, for children in an integrated preschool (a mix of handicapped and nonhandicapped children), for children with Down syndrome, and for children with very severe impairment. Another model center-based program is the Carousel Preschool Program at the University of South Florida. Its special focus is on the older preschool child with severe behavior problems. As in the Seattle center, there is a mix of handicapped and nonhandicapped children, the expectation being that the nonhandicapped and developmentally more mature child can offer an appropriate behavioral model to the child with aberrant behaviors.

In general, center-based programs, typically serving older preschool children, provide a more intensive educational experience than is offered in the home (Fig. 7.1). They are the kind of program that is the essence of the early childhood experience provided to environmentally "at-risk" children described in Chapter 6.

Home- and Center-Based

Some preschool programs combine the home- and center-based experience. One of these, the Charlotte Circle Project, serves infants and toddlers with the most severe developmental delay. Again, as in the case of the previously described home-based version, it focuses on the child whose disability severely limits the child's behavioral repertoire and tries to maximize the child's responsiveness by encouraging in-home interactions between parent and child. Because of the severity of impairment, a center-based experience also is included, with attendance at the center for several hours per day, at least 3 days a week.

The Early Childhood Educational Experience

Developmental in its orientation, the early childhood educational experience consists of activities in the areas of sensorimotor development,

(a)

(b)

FIGURE 7.1. Practicing balance and cognitive activities in the preschool. (Courtesy of Kaplan, Lewisville, NC.)

language, social skills, and academic "readiness." The developmental orientation provides the basis for the sequence in which skills are taught. If the degree of developmental delay is more than moderate however, the program takes on a more "functional" quality, with a main goal of optimizing self-help skills (Bailey & Wolery, 1984). The effect is to move more directly toward teaching the desired self-help skills, such as dressing, rather than focusing on first teaching the developmental prerequisites, such as various grasping movements with the hands.

Early Education Benefits for Organically Impaired Children

Within the educational community perhaps no area has been more controversial than that of the effects of early-childhood education on the development of children with *biologically-based* developmental delays. In the previous chapter we reviewed a similar literature but one that focused on the biologically intact but economically disadvantaged child. We saw there that extensive efforts in infancy and in the preschool years, as in the Head Start program, could produce some cognitive and academic benefits, although these have to be viewed as modest relative to the effort expended.

With regard to the child whose developmental delay is assumed to be caused by some kind of aberration in brain development, the question is to what degree, if at all, can an already slower rate of development be accelerated. The findings from a raft of studies, none having the kind of experimental design and controls found in the Abecedarian and Infant Health and Development projects described in Chapter 5, are inconclusive. This stems, in part, from a service environment that does not allow children with clear developmental delays to be placed in studies only as "control" children. *All* such children are entitled to be in treatment programs.

Major reviews of the "effect" literature have been cautious in the conclusions drawn (e.g., Casto & Mastropieri, 1986; Guralnick & Bricker, 1987). This reflects both the inconclusiveness of the findings themselves and the desire to avoid discouraging efforts to help developmentally delayed children, a special concern given our societal history of general neglect and sometimes abuse of persons with disabilities. We are cautioned that the provision of such services should be based on "the least dangerous assumption" (Donellan, 1984; Strain & Smith, 1986). Lacking hard data pointing to clear acceleration in the rate of development of these children, policy makers should consider which option will do the least harm to children and their families. In effect, research notwithstanding, early-childhood programs for organically impaired children should be provided on the assumption that doing something is better than doing nothing.

In the absence of the kind of clarity indicated in the Abecedarian and Infant Health studies, what are the findings in which we can have some confidence? The first and perhaps most general conclusion is that major acceleration in the rate of development in biologically impaired infants is *not* to be found. Numerous studies report some gains following either a home- or center-based experience during the first two years of life, but their magnitude is not such as to reach statistical significance. In effect, the gains found could have occurred by chance rather than being attributed to the early childhood program. One set of researchers (Fewell and Glick, 1996) even have questioned the appropriateness of "accelerated development" as a criterion for evaluating intervention effects. Observing that our schools would regard as satisfactory at least the "maintenance" of age-expected school achievement, it is suggested that, perhaps, the same criterion should be applied to children whose disabilities preclude a normal rate of development. In effect, the "maintaining" of a stable rate of development, at whatever ability level, would be evidence of effectiveness. Of course, such a criterion implies the expectation of a decline in developmental rate in the absence of intervention. Such a decline is characteristic of Down syndrome and also may be found in other organically based disorders. For children with such disabilities, a loss in IQ of from 8 to 12 points appears to be common over the first 5 years of life (Guralnick, 1988, 1998).

But this criterion would be particularly relevant in Down syndrome, where a declining rate of development, a fall in IQ, *is* the norm. In a review of the effectiveness of early intervention with Down syndrome infants and young children, typically 1 to 3 years old, it is indicated that the cognitive decline (described in Chapter 3) could be either reduced or prevented, at least *during the period in which intervention services are being provided* (Guralnick & Bricker, 1987). A similar conclusion was drawn in an Australian study in which access to early childhood education was seen as *stabilizing* the developmental rate (no fall in IQ) in infants with Down syndrome and toddlers (Berry, Gunn, & Andrews, 1984). Again, as in the earlier discussion of Down syndrome, we should take care not to equate a falling or slowing developmental rate with a *loss* of previously acquired abilities; it is only that the rate of *new* skill acquisition diminishes. To what degree this phenomenon relates to the special delay in language development is an open question.

In contrast to Down syndrome, there is less evidence of influencing the developmental rate in children with other forms of developmental delay (Guralnick & Bricker, 1987). This population includes children with major physical and medical as well as cognitive disabilities. Especially in those with the greatest degrees of cognitive impairment, proportionately smaller developmental gains are found. Gains may occur, as in self-care skills, but these do not necessarily translate into measurable cognitive ones.

Early Intervention Programs and Parents

Whatever the effects of early childhood education on the developmentally delayed child, *parents* are clearly the most consistent benefactors. They receive assistance in learning how to care for a child whose development differs from the norm (Fig. 7.2) and they are offered exposure to parents who are in similar circumstances. The sense of aloneness, panic, and even helplessness that can confront new parents of children born with problems for which the parents are totally unprepared can be eased dramatically through contact with knowledgeable and caring professionals. The affected parents discover that they are not alone and that assistance is available to help them cope with an experience for which there is usually no preparation. Unquestionably, parental access to early childhood education and preschool programs is an important source of psychological support.

Let us listen to some parents—the mother of 6-year-old Walter and the father of Ira, a 4-year-old with Down syndrome:

FIGURE 7.2. A father utilizing preschool materials to interact with his child. (Courtesy of the Arc of Forsyth County, Winston-Salem, NC.)

Walter is very severely handicapped. He was extremely active as an infant and toddler and had to be carefully watched. He didn't recognize situations that were unsafe. There was a lot of stress on all of us, on me and on his brothers and sisters. It's hard to be patient and calm with such a child; you get angry and resentful.

The preschool program was a lifesaver. He's learning how to take care of himself—to feed and dress himself. He's a lot more independent. It's been good for me. I have a lot more free time and time to devote to my other children. I'm also doing a lot better with Walter; I'm much more patient [she is much less stressed].

[Ira's] birth was a shock [the classic reaction of unprepared parents]. I wanted to walk away and forget him [pretend it never happened].

Why did this happen to us? [Why me!] I was angry. I was jealous of our friends and resented their "normal" children. The program for kids like Ira helped us tremendously. My wife really got involved with the Center's program. When I saw progress in his development, I felt pride, just like any other father [from an initial desire to "throw Ira away," to a feeling of pride about him!]. Our outlook is now much more positive. Ira is a real person and we love him [an extraordinary parent turnaround].

"Integrated" or "Inclusive" Early Childhood Education

The concept of services to the handicapped child in the least restrictive environment is expressed in mainstreaming and inclusion at school age, but it also has its counterpart in the preschool, largely for 3- to 5-year-olds. The day care center may have a mix of handicapped and nonhandicapped children, but the achievement of the benefits of such a mix requires teacher effort. Research suggests, not surprisingly, that children tend to choose as playmates other youngsters who are at similar developmental levels. The effect of this is to potentially isolate the developmentally disabled age peer, because he or she necessarily is going to function at a lesser developmental age (the inherent "immaturity" tied to mental retardation) (Strain, 1984). If interactions between normally developing children and their disabled counterparts are encouraged, there appear to be social-skill benefits for the latter. For example, age-inappropriate or less mature play may be replaced by more mature play, presumably "modeled" by the nonhandicapped youngster (Guralnick & Groom, 1987).

To achieve these benefits, the normally developing child needs to adopt a *leadership* role in initiating interactions with his less mature peers. Opportunities for sharing play materials (Fig. 7.3) are good catalysts (Honig & McCarron, 1992). The nonhandicapped child becomes more comfortable around children who are "different" and develops an intimacy and familiarity that can reduce the likelihood of the development of undesirable stereotypes about "disability."

FIGURE 7.3. Children with and without disabilities interact in an "inclusive" day-care setting (Courtesy of the Arc of Forsyth County, Winstom-Salem, NC.)

Although our emphasis here is on the integration of the preschool child in activities with nondisabled peers, we also are reminded of the need to achieve that within the child's own family! This is especially relevant to the infant and toddler, the younger preschool child (McLean & Hanline, 1990). Given the potential obstacles to normal child-parent bonding, exemplified in Ira's father's response to having a Down syndrome child, and particularly if the degree of impairment is severe, the fostering of the parent-child relationship should take first priority.

☐ Services to School-aged Children and Youth

Of the Federal legislation, none has had a greater impact on the education of children with mental retardation than the Education for All Handicapped Children Act of 1975 (P.L. 94-142). Its truly revolutionary effect is epitomized in the observation that "the student is no longer required to fit the school, rather is the school expected to fit the student" (Turnbull, Turnbull, Summers, Brotherson, & Benson, 1986). Admittedly, establishing the "fit" has not always been easy, and our public schools, especially their teachers, continue to try to accommodate to a different set of expectations with reference to the classroom placement of children with mental retardation and other cognitive and physical disabilities.

But this act and its State equivalents have made a difference. Whereas prior to their enactment, schools generally were free to accept and exclude whomever they chose, the new law established the legal right of children with disabilities to a "free and appropriate education." The impact has been reflected in steady increases in the number of "exceptional" children served (Heward & Orlansky, 1992). Further, although in the past full-time self-contained special classes were the rule, now about two thirds of the children spend at least part of the school day in regular classes. Finally, whether in regular or in special classes, the public school is now accepted as *the* site for the education of children whose disabilities require special forms of educational intervention. Less than 10% now receive their education in other settings.

With the expansion of the population traditionally served by the public schools, an increase of almost 25% by 1990, there has also been a broadening of the educational services offered. As characterized by Heward and Orlansky (1992), the schools have become a more diversified resource, offering an array of services—medical, physical and occupational therapy, vocational training, parent counseling, recreation, and special transportation.

More importantly, it would appear that many disabled children, including those with mental retardation, are being educated *successfully* in the public schools and are winning some degree of social acceptance by their nondisabled schoolmates. Examples of effective integration, mainstreaming and inclusion[1] are found at all age levels, from preschool (e.g., Esposito & Reed, 1986) to high school (Warger, Aldinger, & Okun, 1983), and this includes children with disabilities ranging from mild (e.g., Algozzine & Korineek, 1985; Siperstein & Leffert, 1997) to severe (Brinker, 1985; Condon, York, Heal, & Fortschneider, 1986). In a large-scale study of integrated 12-year-old retarded children (Siperstein & Leffert), relatively popular with peers were youngsters who were seen by their classmates as "more friendly" in contrast to those who were "often sad or upset." Integrated retarded children generally exhibit relatively low rates of aggression, important in establishing satisfactory peer relations (Roberts, Pratt & Leach, 1991).

Specific educational and social benefits have been found, especially for the more able and mildly retarded student (Budoff & Gottlieb, 1976; Gottlieb, Alter, & Gottlieb, 1991). It is also clear that, as in the case of the integration of handicapped and nonhandicapped children in preschool programs, the potential benefits require teacher leadership and the provision of supportive social and educative experiences (Gottlieb, 1990).

Given the additional responsibilities explicit in the Education for All Handicapped Children Act, and with the schools themselves under much pressure in recent decades, we should not be surprised that its implementation has not been without problems. Administrators and teachers are wont to complain about inadequate resources, too much paperwork, and too little support (e.g., Chesley & Calaluce, 1997). Parents, too, may have concerns about integration, fearing the loss of special attention associated with special-class placement and the possible social isolation of their children in the integrated setting. Revolutions are never smooth in their transition; it takes time for the dust to settle, but the key is the establishment of a new reality to which *all* must adapt. Ignoring the educational needs of children with disabilities is no longer an option!

Curiously, within an expanded school population, of whom about 7% receive special education services (U.S. Department of Education, 1990), the proportion identified as "mentally retarded" actually has declined. Between 1977 and 1994 there was a 38% decline (a reduction of 335,000 children) in public-school students aged 6 to 21 years classified as "mentally retarded" (Annual Report to Congress on the Implementation of the Individuals with Disabilities Education Act [IDEA], U.S. Department of Education, 1995). Corresponding to this decline is a huge increase of 202% in children classified as learning disabled.

An interesting study of the process by which a group of children eligible for classification as mentally retarded ultimately were classified by the schools revealed that the diagnosis was primarily based on academic achievement and that intellectual functioning was given less weight (MacMillan et al., 1996). The desire was to avoid a classification of mental retardation because of its "pessimistic prognosis." Instead, children were more likely to be labeled learning disabled even though they did not meet their state's criterion of a major discrepancy between expected achievement based on cognition (IQ) and actual achievement. The effect is not only to substantially reduce the population designated as retarded but also to include in the learning-disabilities category children for whom the label was never intended. MacMillan et al. also note that because the traditional learning-disabled population is made up largely of pupils with IQs above 75, as these children move into later grades the difference in academic achievement between those who are truly learning disabled and those with retardation will increase, possibly requiring a reconsideration of their classification.

Finally, the average IQ of the children who were considered retarded was 62 against a mean of 68 in those considered learning disabled, a true shrinking of the population of children traditionally seen as mentally retarded.

The "elasticity" of diagnostic categories, as applied by the individual states, is revealed in the range of variation in the proportion of children classified as retarded. In the 1988–1989 school year, the overall rate was 1.2%, but the range varied from a low of 0.41% in California to 3.12% in Massachusetts, nearly an eight-fold variation (Smith & Luckasson, 1992)! It should be noted that the federal court in California has challenged the usual method of such classification, especially as it applies to minority populations. Nor was such variation limited to mental retardation. For "learning disabilities," the variation was three-fold—from 6.7% in Alaska to 2.1% in Georgia.

On a national scale, *within* the population of exceptional children, four conditions predominate. In order of frequency they are learning disabilities (48%), speech and language impairment (23%), mental retardation (14%), and emotional disturbance (9%) (Heward & Orlansky, 1992).

The "What" of Special Education

Traditionally, special education was either a "watered-down" version of the standard college preparatory academic curriculum—reading, writing, and arithmetic—and largely for mildly retarded (educable) children, or a nonacademic program focused on self-help and social skills for more severely handicapped, "trainable" children. With dropout rates of from 25% to 50%, the value of the traditional special education experience can be questioned (Sinclair, Christianson, Thurlow, & Evelo, 1994).

But with the new emphasis on the education of children with disabilities, including those with mental retardation, there has also been a shift in the *content*, that is, in the "what" of special education. The Education for All Handicapped Children Act called for an "appropriate" education. What should it be? Should it differ from the traditional special-education program?

In their excellent review of special education, Heward and Orlansky (1992) point out that a group of mildly retarded children might study a geography unit directed at teaching "capitals" of the 50 states or, as in my own state of North Carolina, the names of the 100 counties. Although such an exercise may nourish "trivia" buffs, its *value* as an educational experience can be challenged.

An example of questionable relevancy in education is found in the mocking description of the educational experience of 18-year-old Daryl as given by his brother (Lewis, 1994). Daryl had had 12 years of schooling, all of it in an elementary-school setting. His brother caustically notes that Daryl has had years of "individual instruction" and has learned to do a lot of things!

He can put pegs in a board but not coins in a vending machine.

He enjoys music but was never taught how to use a radio or a record player.

He can fold paper but he can't fold clothes.

He can roll Play Dough and make clay snakes but he can't roll bread dough and cut out biscuits.

He can string beads to a pattern but he can't tie his shoes.

He can name all the letters but he can't identify the "men's room."

Through pointing, he can identify picture cards but he can't order a hamburger by pointing to a picture of it.

He can walk a balance beam but he can't walk up the steps of a gym to see a basketball game.

He can put a cube in a box but he can't find the trash bin at McDonald's.

The issue of what retarded students should be learning is best addressed by considering what is needed in order to maximize personal competency, independence, and general functioning in the communities in which they live. Although some may be so severely impaired as to always require a carefully protected setting, the great majority, nearly 90%, can be expected to reach levels of functioning that allow essentially full participation in the life of their community. They will be living in the family home, attending neighborhood schools, playing and socializing with other children, moving into some form of employment after school, and, to varying degrees, fulfilling traditional adult roles. The school experience then can be viewed as preparing the child not only for maximum effectiveness as a student in the here and now but also preparing the child for the inevitable transition to postschool adult life (Brolin, 1991).

Given the certainty of change in role from student to adult, educators now are focusing on what is called a "functional curriculum," examples of which are Brolin's (1991) Life Centered Career Education and Dever's (1989) "taxonomy of essential community skills." The Life Centered Career Education curriculum is directed toward three sets of competencies—daily living, personal-social, and occupational—and appears to be geared toward students with not more than mild retardation. The Dever taxonomy of living skills has goals grouped into five domains—personal maintenance and development (self-care and health skills), homemaking and community life, vocational education, leisure, and travel. For each of these areas, the curriculum wisely calls attention to both the need for the social skills connected with that competency and how to cope with life's inevitable "glitches."

"Functional instruction" does not ignore academic concerns. Indeed, children with mild retardation, in particular, are beneficiaries of academics, as are some children with moderate impairment. The acquisition of at least some functional reading skill is especially useful, for reading a telephone book or food labels or filling out job applications. Similarly, some functional arithmetic skills are an obvious boon even if they are largely limited to simple money transactions, such as making change.

But what of the educational needs of children with more than mild retardation? Their educational experience even during the school years is going to include training in basic self-care skills, skills that are largely present in the normally developing child at beginning school age. Feeding, dressing, toileting, and grooming all became fundamental parts of the instructional effort. Heavily benefiting from behaviorally oriented instructional strategies described in the section on the "how" of special education, self-help training programs are portrayed that are applicable to children and also to adults. The adult beneficiaries are persons with severe and profound retardation, individuals who, as adults, have not achieved these skills because of the severity of their cognitive disability and the common presence of significant impairments in motor skills.

The "Where" of Special Education

The "where" of special education, that is, the context within which it occurs, also has changed dramatically and will change again as schools adopt instructional goals focused on maximizing skills necessary to broader community participation. With the enactment of the Education for All Handicapped Children Act, special education shifted away from special schools and from self-contained classes in regular schools to a greater involvement with the general student body. Education in "the least restrictive environment" came to mean that at least some children, notably those with mild retardation, would have some educational experiences in the "regular" classroom with their nonhandicapped peers. Although their primary *academic* instruction might occur in a small self-contained special class, a "resource" room, they could participate with regular-class students in other activities, such as home room, gym, and cafeteria. With the press for inclusion, at least some degree of integration now is sought for even the most severely retarded child.

The nature of the educational experience for the integrated child with more than mild retardation is illustrated by several students with moderate to severe retardation who were members of regular classes (McDonnell, Thorson, McQuivey, & Kiefer-O'Donnell, 1997). It should be understood however, that although they are in the same physical setting, the academic expectations for the students with retardation do not parallel those of nonhandicapped students. The academic goals in reading, writing, and arithmetic of normally developing third-graders, for example, cannot be the primary focus of the child who still is trying to master basic self-help and communication skills.

Alicia, a first-grader with moderate retardation (IQ 48), received the same instructional experience as her nonhandicapped classmates and received no special education assistance in the regular class. She did have, however, some individual time outside the classroom for one-on-one and small-group instruction. In contrast, Alexander, a fourth-grader with moderate to severe retardation (IQ 40), was supported in his regular class through individualized interaction in "peer partner" projects and by instructional materials developed by his regular class teacher. Although he, like Alicia, had no direct assistance from special education staff while in his regular class, he, also like her, had some individualized and small-group instruction in a separate "resource" class.

The child receiving the greatest assistance was Charles, a third-grader with severe retardation (IQ 39). Although he was a full-time member of a regular class, his participation was supported by an individual teaching assistant. She was present in the regular classroom to integrate the individual education plan's goals with the regular curriculum, to provide direct instruction, and to model for his nonhandicapped classmates appropriate teaching and behavioral strategies.

It is also of interest that these children spent about the same proportion of the day in instructional activities as their nondisabled classmates (McDonnell et al., 1997). Not only should a child be assigned to a regular class, that class should be appropriate to the child's age, and the child should move along grade-wise with nonhandicapped peers just as if the child had no disability (Meyer, 1994).

As noted previously, the nonhandicapped child may, in the long run, be the greater beneficiary of such interactions, learning something about people's "differences" but also about our common humanity. For my own college students who served as tutors with disabled children, it was the discovery that these children shared the same *emotions* as they that seemed to be an important bridge to accepting retarded children as fellow human beings.

For the most part, however, the question of where education of retarded children and youth should occur has been limited to the *physical* confines of the school itself. But it is pointed out that, even with fostering of contact with nonhandicapped peers, the traditional curriculum has failed to adequately prepare retarded students for adult life. For the retarded child, the academic benefits of mainstreaming and inclusion are thought to be greatest at elementary-school age and, again, for the less severely retarded pupil (Dever & Knapczyk, 1997). But many of these children begin to have major difficulties as they move into middle school or junior high school. Here they encounter a more rigidly academic curriculum, one ultimately geared toward preparation for college and inappropriate to the student with the major learning problems inherent in mental retardation. With the frustration that is likely to eventuate, high drop-out rates are not surprising.

To some degree the nature of the goals of a functional curriculum define where at least some instruction should occur. It should be in the setting in which the skills being taught can be most readily learned. Given that the classroom for even the normally developing child hardly constitutes the "real" world, its limitations as a teaching environment are even greater for those with significant learning problems. In particular, the student with retardation has special difficulty in transferring what has been taught in the classroom to the environment in which it is to be applied (Dever & Knapczyk, 1997). We deal here with the cognitive problem of "generalization." Although the "classroom store," for example, may try to simulate the real world store, the comparison pales, at best. To *acquire* skills that the retarded youth needs to function in the real world, there is the need for real-world instruction. This is also relevant to vocational preparation. Placement in actual work settings while still a student is bound to be more useful than performing simulated work.

An example of an educational experience that combines the classroom with the community is one described in the Fairfax, Virginia public schools (Wiggins & Behrman, 1992). Directed toward the moderately and severely retarded child, the youngster who has the greatest difficulty in transferring a classroom experience to its natural environment, at age 10 years children begin spending 1 day a week in the community, where instruction is provided in street crossing, use of public transportation, shopping in a grocery, eating in a restaurant, and general safety.

Such community-based instruction long has been a part of the educational experience of mildly retarded secondary students. Vocational preparation, for example, can begin through school relationships with stores, banks, and restaurants where an adolescent youth can learn something about the workaday world—its rhythms, disciplines, and expectations. The community becomes the laboratory in which the classroom experience is given reality.

The "How" of Special Education

The "how" of special education begins with the process by which a child is identified as in need of special assistance, usually initiated by a regular class teacher concerned with the child's behavior or academic progress. There ensues an evaluation that includes an assessment of the child's intelligence (a powerful predictor of school achievement), academic achievement, sensory status, learning style, and general behavior (Smith & Luckasson, 1992). It is through this process that the child's *eligibility* for special services is determined. Once eligibility has been established, work begins on the development of an educational plan.

Called the *individual education plan*, a requirement of the Education for All Handicapped Children Act, it specifies the information that must be obtained in planning the education of a child with disabilities. Also labeled the *individual program of instruction*, its key elements are descriptions of the child's current level of educational attainment, including academic (grade) achievement, social adaptation, prevocational and vocational skills, psychomotor status, and self-help skills; annual educational goals; short-term educational objectives relative to the longer-term annual goals; needs specific to the child's difficulties—physical, emotional, sensory, and so forth; transition services, beginning no later than age 16 years; the date of the commencement of services to be provided and their expected duration; and the requirement of at least an annual evaluation of progress toward the stated goals (Hallahan & Kauffman, 1991; Heward & Orlansky, 1992).

Classroom-relevant Cognitive Characteristics

Although all of our cognitive abilities are going to be applied in learning situations, some have particular relevance for the child with retardation. Special educators have been concerned particularly with such learning-relevant cognitive difficulties as a shorter attention span, limited memory—short-term and long-term—lack of the spontaneous use of "strategies" to help in learning, and a lesser likelihood of generalizing what is learned to other settings. To these are added both a personality dimension, a seeming diminished motivation to learn (Hallahan & Kauffman, 1992; Smith and Luckasson, 1992), and problems of language and communication.

Attention and Motivation.   Often, in the child with retardation, one finds a shorter attention span coupled with increased distractibility. In part, this may be a mental age–related phenomenon because younger children, too, have shorter attention spans. It also must be noted, however, that attention span is affected by the level of *interest* that a given topic holds for a child as well as prior *success* in dealing with it. With reference to the latter, previous experiences of success and failure influence our perception of our abilities. Recognizing that success on any task may result from a variety of causes, including "effort" or motivation, retarded children seem to be quicker to attribute their failures to their own deficiencies rather than to other equally plausible causes (Hale & Borkowski, 1991). Such beliefs clearly undermine readiness to undertake new learning, and "poor motivation" may be merely the child's way of protecting himself from facing another experience of expected failure. This behavior is not limited to children with retardation; for all of us, motivation to tackle a new task is affected by our expectation of success.

Memory and Strategizing. Our capacity to store experience in memory is equated with learning itself. Referred to in Chapter 1, as are all of the behaviors here described, the memory and learning difficulties seen in retardation reflect both a reduced memory store and a lessened awareness of how we can assist ourselves in learning, notably through the use of learning strategies (Hale & Borkowski, 1991).

Not unexpectedly, complexity of that which we seek to remember influences retention (Schultz, 1983). The largely sensory experience of seeing a book is more readily retained than its subject matter! The latter requires active engagement for its understanding, a "deeper" level of mental processing (Schultz, 1983). Our efforts to understand and remember the content of the book, as distinct from its cover, involve strategies. The most common in a straightforward memory task would be the simple repetition or "rehearsal" of that which is to be remembered. If the recall is not intended to be rote, the material might be organized into a more learnable form. For example, outlining the material reduces it to major topics, each of which in turn cues us to further detail. If we wish to remember a series of numbers, numbers lend themselves to grouping or clustering. Thus the four numbers 1, 9, 2, and 6 can be represented as 19, 26, two numbers rather than four, a literal reduction of the learning task by half. Although retarded youth can learn to utilize strategies, it is the absence of strategies without such instruction that marks the disability. Again, as in the case of a lesser attention span, the problem may be primarily "developmental" or mental age–related in nature. In normally developing children, the *spontaneous* use of strategies is not usually seen before age 8 or 9 years, and a mental age of 8 years appears necessary for its acquisition in the retarded child (e.g., Justice, 1987). Such a mental age or its developmental equivalent is going to be limited to youth with not more than mild retardation.

It is also the failure of retarded children to generalize or transfer a "taught" learning strategy that characterizes the disorder. Detterman (1993) offers the provocative notion that "transfer" neither exists nor can be taught. He suggests that people do not *spontaneously* apply what is known in one situation to others that are comparable. They need to be cued to apply previously learned strategies. For the senior author, age-related forgetting is a persistent problem, and there is recognition that some remedial measure is in order. The awareness that I can do something to help myself constitutes at least the cue for implementing a strategy to reduce forgetting. In mental retardation, the "strategy" research literature suggests that the failure to spontaneously apply procedures that would facilitate learning is traceable to the absence of a "concept" of a strategy. In studies of strategy, the distinction is made between the use and understanding of a *specific* strategy, such as rehearsal for memory, and the eventual acquisition of the more *general* understanding of the value of strategy itself (Pressley, Borkowski, & O'Sullivan, 1985; Hale & Borkowski, 1991). It is the latter stage of strategy understanding, an awareness that I can do things to ease the problem, that reflects the achievement of the concept of a strategy.

Language and Communication.   Difficulty in the understanding of language, its meaning or content, is inherent in mental retardation, but it is in the "expressive" or speech mode that the language disabilities can most interfere with the educational process. Because language is our primary means of signifying understanding, serious speech impediments create problems in the ordinary reciprocal speech behavior between teacher and pupil. Speech difficulties whose magnitude can block communication tend to be found at the severer degrees of cognitive impairment or in children with cerebral palsy. At the level of profound retardation, the child may be totally lacking in speech; at lesser levels of impairment, it may be the *intelligibility* of what the child articulates that obscures understanding.

Methods and devices that substitute for speech are in wide use. So-called *augmentative communication* systems offer a range of speech alternatives. Apart from simple gesture itself, they include the use of "communication boards" (Fig. 7.4), sign language, and technology-assisted communication. Possibly in no other area of disability has technology been of greater value than in the language domain. Children unable to articulate speech or even to gesture, as in cerebral palsy, may now be able to express themselves via computerized speech (Fig. 7.5).

In the language domain, technology also has been helpful to young children with Down syndrome (Meyers, 1990). In Chapter 3 much attention was given to the language problems of children with this disorder. In a study comparing the benefits of auditory and visual computer-generated language equivalents, it was found that toddlers with Down syndrome learned best if their computers generated a graphic as well as auditory representation of the word to be learned. It may be recalled that we have noted the distinct superiority of the visual modality as a means of understanding language in this disorder.

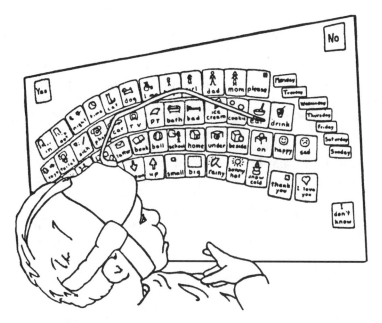

FIGURE 7.4. Sample communication board. Child with cerebral palsy using a head-pointer to communicate.

FIGURE 7.5. Computerized speech. (Courtesy of Crestwood Co., Milwaukee, WI.)

Of the language and communicative alternatives, one has been particularly controversial. Dubbed "facilitated language," and originally used with children with cerebral palsy in Australia, it has been applied to children (and adults) who seem unable to spontaneously communicate intelligibly either in spoken or written language. In the facilitated language procedure, the individual, purportedly, is helped to express himself or herself through typing on a computer keyboard *with the physical assistance of another person*, the "facilitator." Although the procedure makes perfectly good sense for the child who lacks the motor skills to use a keyboard and needs guidance to touch the right keys, facilitated communication also has come to be widely acclaimed for children with autism, youngsters who commonly have severe receptive as well as expressive deficits in language. Numerous studies seeking to replicate reported episodes of meaningful facilitated communication involving children or adults hitherto bereft of intelligible language generally have found that the message was not the creation of the child but rather the unconscious creation of the facilitator (e.g., Jacobson, Mulick, & Schwartz, 1995; Rimland & Greene, 1993; Shane, 1994).

Although there has been a flood of criticism directed at the procedure, there is at least *some* indication in carefully controlled studies that meaningful communication not engendered by the facilitator has occurred (e.g., Weiss, Wagner, & Bauman, 1996). These studies involve asking the child to respond to a question whose answer requires information unknown to the facilitator. Before we judge that it is all a fiction, special efforts should be made to affirm the validity of examples that seem to illustrate the phenomenon. At the very least, there is the indication that familiarity with the process itself by the language-disabled sender increases the probability of its occurrence.

Of particular interest was a carefully controlled study of a group of autistic and retarded youth, aged 11 to 22 years (Cardinal, Hanson, & Wakeham, 1996). The task for the sender was to type previously seen words not shown to the facilitator. Two sets of conditions were compared—typing the words without a facilitator and typing them with one. A little more than one quarter (26%) of the youth showed no facilitated communication but the remainder, almost three quarters, did. Moreover, successful communication increased with practice. The researchers suggest that in studies showing no facilitated communication there may have been insufficient practice between the child and the facilitator.

Behaviorally-Oriented Teaching Strategies

A psychological treatment approach widely applied to behavior disorders, and illustrated in the last two chapters of the book, also has proved effective in the classroom. *Applied behavior analysis* refers to the systematic arrangement of the environment to effect desired changes in behavior or learning. Its use in the diagnosis and treatment of behavioral problems is illustrated in the last section of the book.

As a teaching method, it is especially useful with students with the severer degrees of retardation (Hallahan & Kauffman, 1991). Its essentials can be represented in six steps (Wolery, Bailey, & Sugai, 1988). They are (1) teacher identification of an instructional goal, (2) determination of student status with regard to that goal prior to instruction (baseline), (3) breaking the teaching goal into its most elemental components or skills, (4) instruction in the specific skills along with rewards for encouraging achievement, (5) frequently monitoring student progress, and (6) monitoring overall progress relative to baseline status and modifying the program as appropriate.

Task Analysis.   The method by which a larger or more complex skill is broken down into more teachable subskills is called *task analysis*. The identification of the subskills and the sequence in which they are taught is the essence of the method. Subskills may be taught in the sequence in which they are performed, "forward chaining," or in reverse, "backward chaining." In teaching a dressing skill, for example, to a severely retarded or motor-impaired child, one could enhance motivation by teaching the child the last step first, such as pulling up a zipper in a jacket. The student has, initially, only to learn one step to complete the task and to be rewarded for its completion. As each skill in the sequence is taught, it is "chained" to the ones previously learned until the chain is complete and the child has learned the overall skill of putting on a jacket.

Self-help Skills.   The research literature on self-help training describes procedures for teaching toileting, dressing and grooming, eating and dining, and feminine hygiene (e.g., Reid, Wilson, & Faw, 1991). Toilet-training regimens have been developed for children and adults that include forward chaining for each of the steps involved in use of the toilet (Mahoney, Van Wagenen, & Meyerson, 1971; Van Wagenen, Meyerson, Kerr; & Mahoney, 1969); the use of automated devices that signal the onset of voiding (pants alarm); (Fig. 7.6) (Azrin, Bugle, & O'Brien, 1971); nighttime training incorporating both an automatic urine-alarm device and a mildly negative consequence if the bed is wet (Azrin, Sneed, & Foxx, 1973); and a method of "rapid" toilet training (Azrin & Foxx, 1971; Foxx & Azrin, 1974). Nighttime training is more difficult to achieve (Reid, Wilson, & Faw, 1991), and the use of a mild form of punishment can be helpful. For example, the trainee who has wet the bed can be required to change clothing or to wash both himself and his clothing.

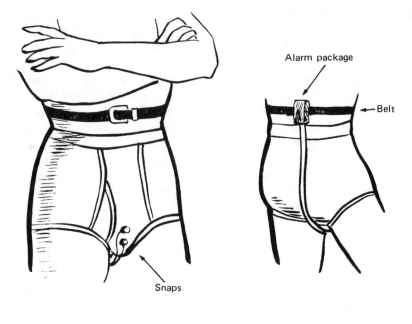

Front view   Rear view

FIGURE 7.6. Alarm pants apparatus. The pants are seen from front and back. Moisture-sensitive snaps are shown in front; the back shows wires leading to the "alarm package." Regular clothing is worn over the training pants, and a tone sounds when either urine or feces moisten the area between the snaps. (From Azrin and Foxx, 1971.)

An integration of the features of several programs has been proposed (Whitman, Scibak, & Reid, 1983). It is especially appropriate for the older child and youth, or even the adult, who has failed to achieve continence. It consists of a four-step regimen, the first step actually preceding direct elimination training. It begins with an auditory signal given by the teacher followed by instruction in each step involved in toileting except elimination itself—walking to the commode, removing clothing, sitting on the toilet, replacing clothing, and returning to the original setting. Once these prerequisites to independent toilet usage have been learned, toilet training itself begins.

In Step two, the goal is to achieve elimation in the toilet and, to speed the learning process, increased liquids are given. But caution is in order in encouraging high fluid intake, as overhydration can cause serious medical problems. A guide is offered that relates fluid intake to age and weight (Thompson & Manson, 1983). With the trainee wearing a pants-alarm automatic signal device (see Fig. 7.6), the onset of the signal becomes the cue to the wearer to go to the toilet. Toilet accidents are reduced by a combination of the alarm signal and an instructor reminding, "No, no, go to the toilet." Once some control has begun to be exercised, the third phase of training commences.

The third phase is identical to the second, except that urination (or defecation) in one's clothing is followed by a "cleanliness training procedure." As in nighttime training there is the requirement for both a change in clothing and the immediate washing of the soiled clothing. The intent is to create some kind of negative consequence for continued accidents.

The fourth and final step is undertaken when accidents have been reduced to a near-zero level. The signal device is removed, but the cleanliness training procedure still is employed (no free lunch!). A signaling device in the commode works similarly and permits prompt reinforcement. This makes continuous monitoring while on the toilet unnecessary and eliminates the need for visual inspection.

Rewards and Punishment. In the toilet training of young children, speed of acquisition can be hastened through the use of rewards. But although such rewards may increase toilet use, they may not necessarily end incontinence; the toilet may only be used more frequently! But the purpose of training is to limit excretory behavior to the toilet, and the addition of some modest penalties may help in that process. Penalties for children and adults have included delaying a change of wet clothing (assuming the clothes are uncomfortable to the wearer) (Smith, 1979), verbal reprimand (Smith et al., 1975), and denial of a preferred activity (Luiselli, 1977).

Dressing and Grooming Skills. Through the use of systematic instruction, a wide range of dressing and grooming skills have been taught to children and adults with severe cognitive impairment. Beyond the teaching of such basic skills as the removing and putting on of clothing (e.g., Watson & Uzzell, 1981), researchers have documented the transfer of skills from training to nontraining settings and with multiple caregivers (e.g., Nutter & Reid, 1978); the maintenance of skills, for example, via peer approval as a reinforcer (Matson, DiLorenzo, & Esuelto-Dawson, 1981); and even the teaching of the selection of clothing in terms of popular color standards (Reid, 1983).

Instructional Guidelines. Earlier in the chapter the use of chaining was referred to in connection with the "behavioral" teaching methodology. Following the analysis of a task into its most elemental components ("task analysis"), each component is taught repeatedly and then systematically linked or chained to its preceding one until the task is fully mastered (chained). Reference also was made to the possibility of teaching a complex skill in a sequence that is actually the reverse of the way that it is practiced—so-called backward chaining. This technique has proven particularly useful with children (and adults) who do not understand verbal directions (Watson & Uzzell, 1981). If the learner can follow verbal directions, the teaching of a task in its natural sequence is equally effective.

Whether used with backward or forward chaining, the technique of "graduated guidance" is commonly employed in teaching skills that require the physical guidance of the trainee. Beginning with direct hands-on guidance, the degree of guidance gradually is reduced, or it is replaced with verbal or gestural cues. Graduated guidance is illustrated in the eating and dressing program developed by Azrin and his colleagues (Azrin, Schaeffer, & Wesolowski, 1976). This program is also notable for their achievement of rapid learning through the use of massed trials.

Washing and Drying of Hands and Face. A group of 11 profoundly retarded girls, aged 10 to 20 years, were taught to wash and dry their hands and faces. They were able to follow simple verbal directions and had no motor impairments of hands and arms. The task was broken down into 11 steps (Table 7.1), and, prior to training, none of the girls could perform all steps without assistance. Training was conducted after

TABLE 7.1. Training steps in washing and drying face and hands

Training Steps (Backward Chaining)	Observations
1. Drying face 2. Drying hands 3. Rinsing soap from face 4. Rinsing soap from hands 5. Washing face with cloth and soap 6. Wetting face with cloth 7. Washing hands with cloth and soap 8. Wetting hands with cloth 9. Placing water in the sink 10. Placing the plug in the sink 11. Pointing to cold water tap on command	Steps 1–9 had to be broken down into smaller components. Step 9, for example, consisted of turning on the hot water tap, turning off the hot water tap, turning on the cold water tap, and turning off the cold water tap (forward chaining is appropriate in this step).

Note. From Treffry et al., 1970.

each meal with up to 15 minutes spent on each step. Learning was encouraged by the use of candy and praise as rewards. Inappropriate behavior led to a sharp "No!" and to 15 seconds of inattention to the girl ("time out"). Each new step was preceded by a verbal description of what was to be done, followed by physical guidance until the step was performed only with verbal prompts. The criterion for mastery was 10 consecutive correct responses. With the completion of each step it was chained to the previously mastered ones, with the reward now limited to completion of the total chain to that point. Gains were most rapid during the first 3 weeks and, by the 9th week, 7 of the 11 girls were able to completely wash and dry themselves when instructed to do so, although some needed occasional reminding.

Attention Span.   Teaching any task depends on gaining and holding the attention of the learner, and problems of attention span are particularly acute in those with profound (and severe) retardation. Before teaching dressing skills to this group of girls, including how to put on a sweater, they first were taught to pay attention, again using candy as a reward. Initially it was the candy itself to which attention was called. It was held in front of the trainees until it was attended to for 3 seconds, after which they were praised and given it. The period of attending and earning reinforcement was gradually lengthened to 15 seconds, after which training with clothing began. The garment was placed next to the candy and the trainee required to attend to both for 10 seconds and then to name the clothing. Some of the girls had speech; others could just point to it when it was named by the instructor.

Training typically involved only one garment at a time, for example, a sweater, with teaching periods of 15 to 30 minutes each. The training was conducted by direct-care staff members who had previously had a 30-hour course on "behavioral" instruction.

Feminine Hygiene.   In Chapter 6 there was reference to the management of menstrual hygiene in the section on sex education. Parental concern can lead to the medical suppression of menses by antihormone treatment (Depo-Provera) or even by hysterectomy.

Direct teaching of menstrual skills has been demonstrated in adult women with severe but not profound retardation (Richman, Reiss, Bauman, & Bailey, 1984). All of the women were ambulatory, able to self-toilet, and responsive to simple instruction. At the onset of training all of the women were dependent on direct-care staff for assistance during their menses.

Task analysis identified three skill areas, which were taught in the following sequence—(1) changing stained underwear, (2) changing a stained sanitary napkin, and (3) changing both. Training was conducted prior to, during, and after menses, with the use of food color to simulate menses blood during the nonmenses period. Each woman had a plastic-covered container available at all times that held a clean adhesive-stripped sanitary napkin, a paper bag for the disposal of the soiled one, and a plastic bag for the storing of soiled underwear until it could be laundered.

Of interest, the total amount of time to learn the three chains of behavior varied from only 1.5 to 4.5 hours. It is also noteworthy that the training was incorporated into the trainee's daily schedule; it did not require unusual amounts of staff time, and each training session itself did not exceed the usual 15-minute time period devoted to other training. The relatively brief training period can be explained by the fact that *all* of the women had basic toilet self-sufficiency at the beginning, so they all were experienced in relevant dressing and undressing skills. It was a matter of building on those skills rather than having to teach all new ones.

Other Grooming Skills.   Behaviorally-oriented training programs have been developed for a wide range of grooming skills. Examples include tooth brushing (Brody, Esslinger, Casselman, McGlinchey, & Mitala, 1975), showering (Girardeau & Spradzin, 1964), and bathing (Gray & Kasteler, 1969). In reviewing the studies reporting these programs, Whitman, Scibak, and Reid (1983) note their general lack of precision but also that such reports suggest that even severely and profoundly retarded individuals can, to varying degrees, acquire these skills.

Dining Skills.   In their review of the considerable research on dining skills, Reid, Wilson, and Faw (1991) note that much success has been achieved. Persons with severe impairments have been taught utensil use (Nelson, Cone, & Hanson, 1975), cafeteria line skills (Van Den Pol et al., 1981), and some cooking (Johnson & Cuvo, 1981). Self-feeding has been viewed as one of the easiest self-help skills to teach as long as there are no neuromuscular disabilities that could impair the needed movements—grasping, chewing, and swallowing (Whitman et al., 1983). Its special teachability lies in the fact that the behavior that one wants to teach involves something that is inherently reinforcing—food!

Of the various programs described for teaching appropriate eating and dining skills to profoundly retarded persons, the "rapid mealtime training" programs of Azrin and Armstrong (1973) have been of special interest. Within a period of 2 weeks, a group of profoundly retarded individuals were able to eat in a socially appropriate manner. The chief features of the training were "minimeals," graduated manual guidance, and overcorrection.[2] The training program is described in some detail because its techniques and strategies are applicable to all kinds of instructional settings.

Minimeals are regular meals divided into smaller portions that are served throughout the day. The effect is to increase the training periods beyond those ordinarily limited to meal time (O'Brien et al., 1972).

Graduated guidelines are as described in the section on rapid dressing training.

One utensil at a time One utensil is used during any one meal.

One hand in lap: The hand not being used is kept in the lap so as to prevent grabbing of food. A feeding trial does not begin until the hand is placed voluntarily in the lap and there is no resistance to the trainer's gentle restraint of that hand.

Incorrect behavior is prevented. Attempts to eat with fingers instead of the utensil are prevented.

No distractions are allowed. Training is conducted in the dining room but not during meal times.

Reinforcers include, in addition to the food itself, verbal praise and rubbing of the shoulders and back (tactile stimulation).

Correction of errors is required. Once reasonable proficiency has been demonstrated with the spoon, spilling errors are required to be cleaned up by the trainee ("restitutional overcorrection"). Similarly, the trainee must clean up any mess created by throwing food or utensils.

Positive practice is encouraged. Following correction for errors (e.g., spoon spilling because of overloading), the trainee is given several trials of loading only small amounts of food.

Multiple trainers are used, initially two trainers with each trainee. One trainer guides the utensil hand, and the other restrains the lap hand and controls head posture. Eventually just one trainer is able to manage the trainee.

Simple to complex: Training begins with relatively simple skills—using a spoon and drinking from a glass—and gradually progresses to the use of a fork and knife. Although each minimeal focuses on a single utensil, over the course of a day there is exposure to all utensils.

Eating skills were taught in the following sequence—napkin, glass, spoon, and fork. The trainee constantly was guided in the correct manner including wiping, drinking, scooping, and piercing. There also was instruction in using a knife to butter, and the process was aided by the use of precut bite-sized pieces of bread. The trainee first was taught to use a fork by piercing and immediately eating precut bite-sized pieces of meat with the fork tines facing down.

The criteria for successful completion of training were three consecutive correct performances of the skill being trained and not more than three errors in a standard test meal. The meal was a commercial TV dinner that was served at noon. The transfer of these skills and their maintenance in the regular dining room required some continued supervision and over-correction for inappropriate behavior.

Cooking Skills. Training in meal preparation generally has been lim-ited to individuals with not more than moderate retardation (Steed, 1974), although picture recipe cards have been developed for persons with even greater impairment (Robinson-Wilson, 1976). A pictorial approach to meal preparation has been described by Spellman et al. (1978); it uses pictures to teach meal planning, shopping, food preparation, and cooking.

Teaching Simple Problem-Solving Skills via Self-Ins-truction.

The teaching of problem-solving skills is uncommon in men-tal retardation and, certainly, rare with individuals who are more than mildly retarded. An interesting study is described that taught four persons with severe to profound retardation a problem-solving strategy for dealing with common household problems (Hughes, 1992). The problem-solving program was based on a *self-instructional* procedure in which the trainee was taught to guide his or her own behavior by verbalizing prompts. The self-prompts were intended to guide the individual throughout the problem-solving experience, a literal thinking out loud.

Self-instruction has been used to teach a variety of skills to retarded individuals, such as remaining on task (Hughes & Petersen, 1989), seek-ing assistance in a work setting if materials run out (e.g., Rusch, McKee, Chadsey-Rusch, & Renzaglia, 1988), and solving work-related problems (Hughes & Rusch, 1989).

The kinds of common household problems worked with in the Hughes (1992) study were unplugged electrical appliances, an empty soap dish, and a misplaced waste basket and toothbrush. Self-instruction consisted of statements that represent a *verbalization* of various aspects of the problem and its solution. In the case of an unplugged light fixture, for example, the self-instructions were stating the problem ("Light out"), stating the generic response ("Gotta fix it"), stating the specific response ("Plug in"), reporting the response ("Fixed it"), and self-reinforcing ("Good").

Training involved the verbalization and modeling of each response, with the trainees continually reminded to say these statements aloud through-out problem situations. Verbal praise was used as the reinforcer.

The study revealed that individuals with severe and profound retar-dation and who had some speech could generalize the strategy of self-instruction to solve both trained and untrained problems. Although the researchers could not be certain that self-instruction rather than model-ing or numerous examples were necessary for mastery of the task, high frequencies of correct responses were not produced or maintained until trainees verbalized all steps.

Educability and the Most Severely Disabled

A perennial issue in the teaching community is the "educability" of those with the greatest degree of cognitive impairment, persons with *profound retardation* (Orelove, 1991). Commonly grouped in the category of "severe disabilities," a grouping that could include moderate and severe retardation, they really represent a different population (Thompson & Guess, 1989). Often multidisabled with sensory, motor, and health and behavioral problems, in addition to cognitive impairment, these individuals need lifelong assistance, in some instances, for their very survival. They are likely to possess few or no formal communication skills; may be unable to control basic motor functions; lack self-care skills; exhibit large amounts of seemingly nonpurposeful (stereotypic) behavior, such as body rocking; and be relatively unresponsive to general stimulation.

A modest research literature relating to instructional effects has shown some gains in communication; in self-help skills, especially eating and toileting; in basic motor skills, such as head control, posture, and attaining a sitting position; and in reducing inappropriate behavior.

From a developmental perspective, gains following even intense educational efforts may seem minimal. Indeed, for the most part, skills achieved generally do not lead to full independence in any particular self-help skill and, for many, "partial participation" may be all that currently can be attained. Yet parents can take a very different view from teachers as to what constitutes a meaningful educational gain. Indeed, for these individuals, the parents' goals appear to be especially relevant (Orelove, 1991).

The mother of a severely handicapped daughter observes that parents of normally developing children can have no appreciation of the degree of satisfaction that parents of a severely disabled child can experience at even the most modest gains (Hawkins, 1984). For the parent of a child who has been almost totally dependent on others, the learning of flushing a toilet or pointing to food if another helping is wanted is almost monumental. In light of how "assistance technology" has altered dramatically the lives of persons with profound motor and communication deficits, as in severe cerebral palsy, we should be cautious about assuming that there is any child in whom an educational benefit cannot be achieved.

The language of Burton Blatt, a major advocate on behalf of persons with mental retardation, is still apt. He spoke to the importance of "attitude" on the part of those who attempt to produce change in such severely retarded individuals (Blatt, 1987):

The educability hypothesis [are they teachable?] has suffered both at hands of those who would not consider it (in spite of any evidence) and by those who insist on propagating it (in spite of a paucity of evidence). Like the ideas of normalization, deinstitutionalization, conservatism, or liberalism, the educability hypothesis is powered (or dismissed) by the conception one has of what human beings ought to be like and what opportunities they ought to have. Whether the educability hypothesis is true or not must await further and better examination. But what may be even more important is the idea that people should be treated—in schools, in developmental facilities, by their families, by society—*as if* they can change, *as if* careful systematic intervention on their behalf will make a difference. (p. 58)

Sex Education

It is ironic that those about whom society has the greatest ambivalence with respect to sex education have the greatest need for it. The retarded adolescent, likely excluded from the kind of "street" education that nondisabled adolescents freely acquire, simply has less opportunity to develop a realistic understanding of his or her sexual self. Our major textbooks in sex education, books intended for prospective teachers, are conspicuously silent on the topic.

Given our general discomfort with the subject and parental attitudes that commonly deny that retarded children are "sexual," the conspiracy of silence persists. Yet the reality of sexual behavior in retarded adolescents is documentable. In those with mild to moderate retardation, for example, secondary sexual development appears to proceed at its usual biological pace (Deisher, 1973). Such development also is found at severer levels of development, but at a slower rate.

Noteworthy is the finding in a study of young women with retardation who were served in a health clinic that at least one episode of sexual intercourse was experienced by 50% of those who were mildly retarded, 38% of the moderately retarded, and 9% of the severely retarded (Chamberlain, Rauth, Passer, McGrath, & Burkett, 1984). Of those who were sexually active, largely those with mild retardation, more than half had become pregnant, often after rape or long-term incest. Rapists usually were family members or acquaintances, and in only one instance was the assailant also retarded. There was recognition of the special need for birth-control measures for those who were sexually active and, of the various contraceptive methods, parents reported the greatest effectiveness for intrauterine devices. There was less satisfaction with oral contraceptives.

Parents also were concerned about menstrual hygiene, a special problem in those with more severe cognitive impairment, and about which a teaching program has been described.

With regard to sex education itself, a study of *mildly* retarded adolescents (Hall & Morris, 1976) found that these youth generally were knowledgeable about masturbation, menstruation, pregnancy, and intercourse but less informed about sexually transmitted diseases, planning of pregnancy, and birth control. Considering that this study was conducted prior to the onset of AIDS, the need for communicating such hazards has only intensified.

McClennen (1988) has noted the sex education needs of students with *moderate* retardation. Citing the availability of numerous commercial teaching materials, she sees the need for instructing youth on the nature of their bodies; comfort with their thoughts and feelings; the distinction between public and private behavior; various means of expressing affection; alternative ways of dealing with genital feelings, such as masturbation; and the understanding that one's body belongs to oneself.

The Teacher

A teacher comfortable with the topic is crucial (e.g., Johnson, 1973). The teacher must come to terms with the "language" of sex; teachers often fail to communicate because they use terms foreign to their students. Apart from the anatomy of sex, it is its behavioral aspect that is of special concern. An earlier well-known sex educator (Gordon, 1973) offered guidelines for teachers. Students should understand that masturbation is a normal or acceptable form of sexual expression, that genital behavior is always a private activity, and that sexual contact risks pregnancy. We would add that there is also the risk of sexually transmitted disease.

Effects of Sex Education

Data on the effects of sex education on retarded youth are meager. Students are freer to discuss their sexual feelings, and there may be some increase in masturbation (Kempton, 1978). Of particular interest was a long-term educational effort with a group of moderately and severely retarded adolescents, aged 12 to 18 years (Hamre-Nietupski & Williams, 1977). No behavioral data are reported, the emphasis being on general understanding. Virtually all were deemed able to grasp bodily distinctions, basic family relationships, and acceptable social behaviors. Concepts of personal hygiene were well understood, but not those related to reproduction.

Because parents are often unclear about their retarded child in "adult" roles and at least ambivalent about sex education for their child, the winning of their support is essential. In light of the prominent role of sexuality in our youth culture and the natural fears of parents of their children being exploited sexually, together with the spectre of AIDS as a heterosexual as well as homosexual concern, some parent support should be forthcoming.

In a monograph on sexuality in children (Gordon & Schroeder, 1995), there is a discussion of deviant sexual behavior in retarded adolescents. This refers to activities that vary from public standards: from nonaggressive violation of others, such as public masturbation or exposure of genitals, to those of a more aggressive nature—fondling and rape. In the senior author's forensic psychological practice, he occasionally has been asked to evaluate retarded persons charged with sexual offenses. Among youth, these offenses are likely to involve nonviolent sexual activity with children. Contributing to this behavior are such factors as a lack of social comfort with age peers, generally diminished social and recreational skills, and the vulnerability of the child-victim. Treatment services for the sex offender with retardation are woefully inadequate. They usually are targeted to nonretarded sex offenders and are likely to provide cognitive difficulties for those with retardation. In our own state, a special unit has been established in the adult correctional system for such individuals.

Fortunately, there is no indication of an increased frequency of sexual offenses in retarded youth relative to their nonhandicapped counterparts. Among all incarcerated youthful offenders, however, the proportion incarcerated for sexual offenses appears to exceed that incarcerated for other offenses. It is not that retarded offenders are more frequent perpetrators of sexual offenses but rather that the *range* of crimes for which they're imprisoned is probably narrower, necessarily increasing the respective proportions for those they do commit.

In Baroff's study (1996) of the North Carolina *adult* prison population, only about 2% of retarded adults were imprisoned for sexual offenses, the same rate as in the nonretarded prison population.

Leisure Education

Its General Significance

Within the realm of educational needs, recreation or leisure is likely to get short shrift. We tend to think of recreational activities as "spontaneous" and "untaught." Normally developing children spontaneously engage in "play" and, by school age, have developed interests, likes and dislikes, some sense of their own abilities, and how to play with others. Children with retardation tend to be delayed in the acquisition of play skills and, indeed, it is sometimes necessary to *teach* the child how to play! It is a matter of indicating how toys and materials are intended to be used and teaching the social rules that govern group play. Paradoxically, learning how to play is serious business. We all know how important it is to our lives, and it has very special significance for persons with retardation because constructive use of their leisure time can be a source of much difficulty. Parents bemoan their child's inactivity or inordinate tie to the television set, in part the consequence of the socially isolating effect of major disability and the failure to develop satisfying leisure alternatives.

Although we equate leisure and recreation with fun, they also can be a powerful medium for skill development and for enhancing feelings of self-worth (e.g., Wehman, 1977). The potential of using a purely recreational activity as an instructional tool is illustrated with the game of bingo. For children, bingo can be used to strengthen number recognition; we learn and play at the same time. Indeed, such an activity is the ideal teaching situation because the motivation to participate is "built in." The game itself is its own reward.

The focus here is to provide the kinds of recreational experiences that both enable the child to derive greater satisfaction from his present life and prepare him for the less structured and possibly more socially isolated life in the postschool years. In a sense this educational mission parallels the academic one. The latter prepares us for the serious business of work and adulthood, the former for, hopefully, its lighter side. Both are important; it is only that we take the recreational one for granted and never think about it as an activity requiring instruction.

Recreational Interests

Like yours and mine, the recreational interests of children and youth with retardation reflect the activities to which they have been exposed and their general levels of cognitive, motor, and social maturity. Activities enjoyed often represent those appropriate to developmental levels *intermediate* between the child's mental age and chronological age. This is especially true of those with mild retardation. A 16-year-old mildly retarded adolescent with a mental age of 10 years and an IQ of 60 is likely to have recreational interests that more nearly approximate those of a teenager than those of a preadolescent 10-year-old. As the degree of retardation increases, recreational interests come to more closely parallel mental age.

Encouraging Chronological Age-Appropriate Activities.   At the severer levels of retardation, recreational interests tend to be more typical of much younger children. But the immaturity imposed by the cognitive impairment does not *require* engaging in recreational activity enjoyed by normally developing children at that developmental or mental-age level. A major goal of normalization or social role valorization is to enhance the image of the culturally devalued person, and this can be done by providing recreational activities that are both within the individual's ken and not demeaning. Severely retarded teenagers rolling

balls across the floor at each other is incongruous, but similar physical activity can be offered in a more age-appropriate fashion through bowling. Wehman, Schleien, and Kiernan (1980) show how through the modification of standard recreational equipment, even severely physically handicapped youth can participate in age-appropriate recreation (e.g., bowling, picture taking, fishing, etc.).

Instructional Guidelines.   We have noted that there may not be spontaneous use of recreational materials. They may need to be introduced and their use demonstrated. Apart from encouraging participation, the recreator needs to recognize a shorter attention span and a need to vary what is presented; break up an activity into its simpler components; demonstrate precisely what is expected; practice each component with more than the usual frequency; encourage, praise, and reward at each step; and only gradually introduce more complex components.

Demonstrate.   Stress is placed on demonstration; retarded children, like the rest of us, learn best by doing—only more so! The advantage of demonstration over a purely verbal presentation is especially evident in Down syndrome in which learning by seeing is superior to learning by hearing.

Rules.   If physical or cognitive limitations affect the capacity to follow standard game rules, modification of the rules is in order. Rules have no intrinsic sanctity; they are merely a way of assuring "fair" participation and need to be adjusted in accordance with the players' level of understanding.

Skill Sequences.   As with respect to rules, there is no requirement that the steps in a recreational activity should be taught in the sequence with which they usually are performed. Reverse chaining has been suggested for picture taking. Whereas we take a picture by first raising the camera to eye level, sighting, and then depressing the shutter release; for children with problems of motor coordination, we might begin by initially teaching them to position their fingers on the release mechanism prior to raising the camera (Wehman et al., 1980). At least initially, we might waste some pictures!

Architectural Barriers.   Physical barriers to school and community recreational facilities are diminishing. Wheelchair ramps permitting access to public buildings are now common; other modifications include enlarged door knobs and extended handles on drinking fountains.

A Suggested Regimen. We want to expose the student to a variety of environments as well as activities because it expands the student's concept of the "where" as well as of the "what" of recreation. This becomes particularly important to the older student as a means of preparation for the postschool years. Educators are encouraged to include at least some such activity daily, provide activities that can be done alone as well as with others, and offer a mix of activities—those providing "active" as well as "passive" participation (Fine, 1988).

Recreational Content. Now presented are the kinds of recreational activities enjoyed by retarded children and youth—physical activities, arts and crafts, music, and camping.

Physical Activities: Motor Skills and Sports. Movements involving precision and speed commonly are impaired, especially if there is some organic basis for the retardation (Rarick, Dobbins, & Broadhead, 1976). This is especially true of females. Both sexes are likely to be overweight, in part, because of lesser participation in physical activities.

Physical educators recommend activities that develop strength (e.g., tumbling, gymnastics, and running), coordination (e.g., throwing, catching, and kicking), balance (e.g., balance beam and hopping), and flexibility (to improve the range of motion of spine and hip) and provide enough exercise to reduce tendencies to obesity.

These are gross-motor activities; fine-motor skills can be developed through arts and crafts. Within the limitation imposed by motor problems, retarded children and youth enjoy the usual range of popular sports—softball, skating, swimming, bowling, and so forth. Swimming is a particularly desirable recreational outlet.

Physical Activities and Those with Severe Handicaps. Even children and youth with severe and profound retardation can benefit from physical education. A variety of physical abnormalities often is seen, poor muscle tone and postural and spinal curvature being prominent. Activities are suggested that call for full extension of the trunk, head, neck, and limbs—activities that involve reaching, lifting of the chest, and upward stretching (Sherrill, 1980).

Children and Youth with Cerebral Palsy. Physical education here is directed toward increasing the interaction of impaired and unimpaired limbs, improving ambulation, sharpening hand-eye coordination, and strengthening laterality and directionality.

Bowling.   An extremely popular recreational outlet, participation can enhance social maturity, mobility, and independence. A large-scale program involving tournament play is described whose impact is best conveyed in the language of its initiator (Fitzsimmons, 1970):

> Any child living in a community has a chance to participate. We were not interested in only developing skills of bowling. It was everything that goes with it: proper dress, proper actions, expanding their world, motivating them . . .
>
> We were always told, they will learn to bowl in one bowling lane, and they will become highly confused [referring to cross-lane bowling]. We do cross-lane bowling. We are now teaching them to use foul lines which they said would really foul the whole thing up, but it doesn't. They do just as well [the old story of exceeding the expectations we set for them].
>
> They progress [in tournaments] from county to district. . . . They go on to state. But as they do this, they are learning to travel, learning to go by bus [increasing mobility]. They are learning to *plan* other things. If we are in the San Francisco area, they see the zoo; if we are in Los Angeles, they take in Disneyworld and Marineland. They are expanding their world. They have learned proper behavior in public. They have learned how to go to the bowling alley and order shoes for their size, watch for dangers at the ball returns, how to take turns at proper times.
>
> To begin with, we used college and high school students to help create enthusiasm for what they were doing. When we started you had to lead some of them up to the alley. They dropped the ball, turned around and went back and sat down. They did not know that the ball was even aimed at anything [these would be severely retarded persons]. Through the enthusiasm of the college and high school students working with them [an example of the use of volunteers], one girl who at first made no connection at all, finally found that her ball occasionally knocked down a pin. It did something when it got to the other end of the lane. This girl is now bowling over 100. This is just fantastic. I cannot do that—mine always go down the gutter. This was a girl who sat at home. Her mother was in a depressed state because she followed her around, or she whined all the time. The doctor contacted us because they were afraid the mother was going to commit suicide and kill the girl, too. Through bowling the girl became interested in other things. . . . She is now involved in a [sheltered] workshop sorting IBM cards. She has learned to iron.
>
> When they go bowling, these people also learn to order snacks [increasing independence]. This is introducing them to the community. When we first started bowling, some of the operators were a little reluctant about letting us bring groups in. When they saw how well behaved they are, they are now almost fighting to have us come.
>
> What we first became aware of is the fact that they could go as a group, but when they tried to go out individually, they were not accepted. We felt that as the program grew, it had to be something they could do alone [increasing independence], with their family, with a small group, or with a large group. It was something that those in institutions could participate

in when they came into the community and family-care homes. They were already familiar with a lane in the community and it was something they could do [building "bridges" from the old to the new—from the "structured" to the "unstructured"]. (pp. 50–52).

The parents became aware of their acceptance. Often parents would never go out and observe their children in public [shame and lowered self-esteem]. When they saw them accepted on a tournament basis . . . they became proud of their children [association with the children was no longer experienced as diminishing worth in the eyes of others]. The educable retarded persons in turn could take the trophies back to school and have them on display to show what their bowling team did. The trainable retarded persons have gained a great deal from bowling . . . it is something that they can participate in.

It is thrilling to watch a busload come up to the motels and now be able to handle their key [independence]. They can . . . match their key number to their room [using number skills], change into their swimming clothes and go swim [swimming *is* an excellent recreational outlet for persons with retardation], go back and get ready for the tournament. *The bowling tournament is just a vehicle for creating these experiences* [the essence of the habilitative or "therapeutic" aspect of recreation; emphasis added].

Competition is no . . . problem because they soon learn that first they are competing against themselves and then they learn to compete against one another [a principle that could be applied in other recreational settings]. Someone once said that *everyone* must have a trophy ["infantilizing" rather than "normalizing"]. So we let a state tournament chairman try this out one year. One boy, however, said to us, I do not know what you are giving me that for, I did not win!

The Fitzsimmons description epitomizes the educational benefits of a good recreational experience. These young people, apparently with all degrees of retardation, gained in self-confidence, mobility, maturity, and increased acceptance by others including their own parents. Truly such a program met needs for self-esteem and self-expression.

Arts and Crafts.   An important recreational outlet for retarded youth, arts and crafts can be enjoyed at all levels of complexity, from coloring a balloon to simple woodworking (Carlson & Ginglend, 1961). They furnish a medium for gaining a sense of achievement and an outlet for self-expression. Like other forms of recreation they lend themselves to learning. Materials have texture, color, weight, and odor and can be used in endless fashions. Drawing, cutting, posting, folding, and stitching all require some dexterity and can only strengthen fine-motor skills. Because the work that persons with retardation eventually perform is going to have a significant manual component, such activity can only contribute to future vocational potential. Arts and crafts enjoyed by retarded youth include construction (paper play), wire making, weaving and sewing, clay craft, and woodworking.

Music.   Both as a source of pleasure and as a teaching medium, music has much appeal. Songs, choral work, rhythms, musical games, and dances all have their appeal. The senior author has never forgotten how a good music teacher can take a group of retarded youth, none of whom had exceptional voices, and mold them into a fine chorus.

Water Play.   Water play, especially in a pool, provides both a recreational and therapeutic experience. The buoyant sensation in the water is especially appreciated by children (and adults) who have difficulties controlling their bodies. The child with cerebral palsy whose muscles need stretching, flexing, or just relaxing finds it easier to move his or her limbs in the water. It is also helpful to the overweight child or youth. Excess weight places a strain on the feet and the hips; floating relieves that stress and offers the opportunity of a comfortable and injury-free exercise (Letort, 1990).

Children who are nonambulatory can gain independence in the water. Steel wheelchairs, designed for water, can move down a ramp and directly into a pool.

We also should not forget the pool as a medium for teaching swimming itself. A valued activity for both its fun and its exercise, it can afford lifelong recreation and health benefits, especially to individuals whose lives tend to be sedentary.

Noneducational Services

Recreation

We have been describing recreational services as a component of the educational or school experience of the child or youth with retardation, but they also, and most often, are provided through our local parks and recreation departments. They may be offered on an after-school basis in afternoons, as in summer day-camp programs, and evenings.

An Integrated Camping Experience.   A study of an experimental integrated 2-week overnight camping experience found apparent benefits for both eight nondisabled children (aged 10 to 13 years) and three children with severe disabilities (aged 9 and 11 years) (Rynders, Schleien, & Mustonen, 1990). The latter group consisted of a nonverbal 9-year-old girl with autism, a 9-year-old boy with severe mental retardation and arrested hydrocephaly, and an 11-year-old girl with both deafness and severe retardation. The handicapped children showed significant gains in two targeted skill areas—clearing dishes after a meal and preparing to go swimming. Both goals were seen as having lifelong utility. The benefits for the nondisabled children were less specific. Undoubtedly they gained some understanding of what it means to be "disabled," that is to need assistance, and an increasing comfort around such youngsters. The integrated experience also was seen in a positive light by camp staff.

A quotation cited in the study merits presentation here. It refers to the mutual benefits of an integrated weekend camping experience for Boy Scouts (Peterson, 1987):

> Many of the special Scouts needed three minutes and a lot of helping hands to traverse the monkey bridge which able-bodied boys cross in 10 or 15 seconds.... But there was never a shortage of willing hands to help and there was no dearth of "Nice job!" from their buddies and instructors.
>
> It's hard to say whether the special Scouts or their buddies had more fun or learned more. For the nonhandicapped scouts, especially those who had never before had close contact with disabled people, it was an intense experience ... "What most of our boys seem to get out of it is a much greater understanding of handicapped people in general," said [an] Assistant Scoutmaster. (p. 31).

Special Olympics.   Begun in 1968 as an outgrowth of summer day-camp programs, Special Olympics involves retarded youth in sports activity and has achieved great prominence in America, if not worldwide. Some sense of its popularity is seen in the fact that Special Olympics games are conducted in no less that 25,000 communities and in all 50 states and 110 countries. Like the regular Olympics there are Winter and Summer games, and athletes compete in more than 20 individual and team events. A survey of attitudes toward the program elicited very positive views by both parents and mental-retardation professionals (Klein, Gilman, & Zigler, 1993). Although professionals tended to give greater value to its athletic nature, parents saw it more as a means of increasing their child's social experiences and providing a group with whom their child could identify. It generally was seen as enhancing self-esteem, and parents also noted that the travel involved increased independence. This is the same phenomenon noted earlier in connection with "bowling."

One of the goals of Special Olympics has been for the athletes to move into broader and integrated sports participation in their own communities. To help accomplish this, a program, Unified Sports, was created in 1989; it places athletes with and without retardation on the same team.

Some have complained about the "segregated" nature of Special Olympics, but in all competition there is grouping by ability to allow the opportunity to compete and win. Moreover, the athletes themselves appear to welcome the opportunity to mix with a peer group, one in which they do not feel different (Klein et al., 1993).

Family-Support Services

With the emphasis on the rearing of the retarded child in the family home, human services agencies have tried to provide to the family services designed to prevent or delay out-of-home placement. Offering either direct support or cash subsidies that enable families to finance their own support, such services include case management (coordination of services to the family), child assessment, respite care, parent counseling, out-of-home crisis placement, parent training, parent participation on advisory committees related to services for their child, and parent support groups (Herman & Hazel, 1991).

Respite Care.   Clearly one of the most popular services to parents and caregivers is "respite care." This is temporary and usually brief care for the retarded child, offered either in or out of the family home and enabling the family to take a break from the potential stresses of chronic care. Its specific benefits include a general relieving of family stress, improvement in overall family functioning, more positive parental attitudes toward the child, and a lessened sense of social isolation (Botuck & Winsberg, 1991).

Some Sources of Family Stress.   Apart from behavior problems, especially of an aggressive nature, it is the severity of retardation that bears most heavily on the child's residential status. Although out-of-home placement is virtually inevitable for all dependent retarded persons when their parents die, it is those with severe and profound retardation who are at greatest risk during the preadult years. In a study of the total developmentally disabled population receiving services in California in the early 1980's[3] (Meyers, Borthwick, & Eyman, 1985), by age 15 years less than half of those with severe retardation and less than a fifth of those who were profoundly retarded still were living in the family home. In contrast, the great majority of those with mild or moderate retardation, 70% to 80%, were still so placed. This study also found that by age 65 about 80% of all the dependent family members were in nonfamily residence. This study reminds us that, although continued deinstitutionalization and family-support services are increasing the number of retarded individuals remaining in the family home, out-of-home residence in whatever form becomes a likely reality with age. Hence the focus on developing community-based options to the family home.

In the segment of the total population younger than 18 years old with severe and profound retardation,[4] behavior problems were a prominent cause of out-of-home placement in those with severe retardation. For children and youth with the greatest degree of cognitive impairment, profound retardation, early out-of-home placement was associated with very limited self-help skills.

In addition to age, severity, and behavior, one's ethnic background also contributes to family attitudes toward parenting responsibilities. In particular, disadvantaged minority status often carries with it a stronger sense of a continuous responsibility to provide care. This is found in Asian families, is reinforced by religious values in Latinos, and also is seen in Blacks. To a greater degree than their middle-class White counterparts, these families keep their handicapped members in the family home (Myers, Borthwick, & Eyman, 1985).

Residential Services

Children and youth with retardation are served through a variety of residential treatment programs. Interestingly, it is young people who have chiefly benefited from the deinsitutionalization movement (Lakin, Braddock, & Smith, 1995). Between 1965 and 1985, the proportion of the population in the state institutions younger than 21 years old dropped 80%. In the decade between 1985 and 1994 there was a further decline, of 78%. In 1994, children and youth were less than 4% of the institutional population. In contrast, the adult population dropped only 7% in the 1965 to 1985 period, although in the later decade, 1985 to 1994, the drop increased to almost 39%. In 1996, the nationwide institutional population of 63,258 was virtually all adult, 95% against only 5% for children and youth (Lakin, Braddock, & Smith, 1996).

The current range of residential options for children and youth consist either of programs intended to avoid or delay out-of-home placement (the aforementioned family-support services) or out-of-home settings, as such, e.g. foster care.

Avoiding Out-of-Home Care. This so-called community alternatives program for children and youth with developmental disabilities is intended to support the continued in-home residence of individuals at risk of institutional placement. Through funds originally designated for institutional care, families are able to obtain a wide range of services that enable them to continue to care for their children in the family home. These include respite care, the purchase of health-related equipment, and personal assistance, for example helping in the basic care of the child—bathing, dressing, and so forth.

Specialized Foster Care. Specialized foster care is the preferred out-of-home placement option for children, youth, and older adults (Hayden, Lakin, Hill, Bruininks, & Chen, 1992) and was the most frequently used residential alternative in the just-described California study (Myers & Pueschel, 1985). The goal is to maintain the child as much as possible in a "family" rather than "group" care setting.

Group Care.   Group care for children, as distinct from adults, tends to be limited to those with more severe degrees of retardation and chronic health needs. Housed in facilities that provide access to 24-hour nursing care and to staff who can minister to basic self-care needs and, perhaps, to significant behavior problems, such programs are called *intermediate care facilities for individuals with mental retardation* (ICF-MRs).

Health Services

With deinstitutionalization, there has been greater pressure on the local medical, dental, and allied health communities to meet the sometimes complex health care needs of retarded children and youth. A statewide survey of physicians in Maine (Minihan, Dean, & Lyons, 1993) found that primary care physicians saw themselves as the appropriate resource for such care, although they recognized problems unique to the retarded population. These involve inadequate medical information regarding a patient, possible behavior problems in the doctor's office, and uncooperativeness during an examination, especially in relationship to gynecological examination. They also were concerned about what was seen as inadequate Medicaid reimbursement for their services.

Primary-care physicians often are asked how to manage behavior problems, and they tended to deal with these by advice, the use of psychotropic medications (discussed in the last portion of the book), and referral to mental-health specialists. Parenthetically, children with autism are disproportionately heavy users of medical outpatient services (Birenbaum, Guyot, & Cohen, 1990). Physicians were particularly interested in being made aware of other health practitioners (e.g., medical specialists and physical and occupational therapists) with knowledge about mental retardation. Referring to our earlier section on the rights of the retarded individuals and the giving of informed consent, they were particularly interested in receiving state guidelines on consent.

In addition to the concerns of individual medical providers, there has been recognition of the need for an adequate health care system to serve the retarded population at the local level. An adequate system would provide an identifiable primary care provider able to oversee medical care and possessing special knowledge of unique medical and social needs; linkage with medical subspecialists; mental-health and behavioral services; genetic counseling; rehabilitation services, including speech, occupational, and physical therapy; dental care; and a coordinator of the patient's health care (Crocker & Yankauer, 1987).

A medical program that seeks to be such a comprehensive resource is the Developmental Disabilities Center at Morristown Memorial Hospital in Morristown, New Jersey (Criscione, Kastner, O'Brien, & Nathanson, 1994). The center serves local, regional, and statewide populations and had more than 1700 patients under care in the 1990s. Available to anyone in New Jersey with mental retardation, its setting within a general hospital offers access to specialists and to inpatient as well as outpatient care. Its statewide reach is accomplished via a system of consultation and statewide training of health care providers.

In addition to basic medical care, the center offers programs that promote health and prevent disease, such as cholesterol screening and diet counseling, immunizations against influenza and hepatitis B, and awareness of seasonal problems, such as sunburn and Lyme disease. The Center also includes a mental health and behavioral team consisting of a psychologist, a developmental pediatrician, nurse practitioners, an educator, and a social worker. The center also provides dental services.

The heart of the program is its nurse practitioners. They function as the primary health providers and coordinators. The nurse practitioner works with patients in the community and is also is responsible for coordinating individual patient care with both the health staff at the center and the various community agencies providing nonhealth services to the patient.

The nurse practitioner is also the means by which the center can reach out to the broader health care community by providing technical support to local physicians serving retarded persons.

Together with the obvious benefits of a health care provider who can coordinate all health services, in this time of concerns about the cost of medical care, this system appears to have realized economic benefits in terms of less frequent patient hospital utilization and shorter stays if it is required (Criscione et al., 1994; Criscione, Walsh, & Kastner, 1995).

☐ Summary

This chapter describes the array of services provided to children, youth, and their families, organized in terms of those offered in the preschool- and school-aged years. The former includes a description of common early childhood educational programs and the kind of benefits they offer. At the school-age level, the content largely is organized in terms of "education"—its "what," "where," and "how." Particular attention is paid to the "how," as this is reflected in the use of "behavioral" psychological principles at the instructional level. These principles become especially important in the education and training of children and youth with the more severe degrees of intellectual disability. The chapter concludes with content on the recreational needs of children and youth, sex education—always a controversial topic—and "family support" and health services.

Possible Discussion Questions

With respect to the "prevention" of mental retardation, how has the material on biological and psychological mechanisms, highlighted in Chapters 3, 4, and 5, affected our own view of ourselves as prospective parents?

How does the current "family-centered" diagnostic process influence the kind of recommendations likely to be offered to parents? What kinds of services seem to be particularly valued by parents of infants and young children with mental retardation?

What appear to be the main benefits of "early childhood" education programs for children with mental retardation and for their parents?

In what way may normally developing young children benefit from an "integrated" preschool experience?

What are some of the issues pertaining to full "inclusion" of retarded and otherwise disabled children in "regular" classroom programs? Is there still a role for the "special" class? What kinds of combinations of regular- and special-class placements are currently in vogue?

What are fundamental principles underlying the "what," "where," and "how" of educational efforts with retarded children and youth?

What are some of the instruction-relevant cognitive characteristics of students with mental retardation, and how can these be addressed?

What are the chief features of behaviorally-oriented teaching strategies? Why do they have particular relevance for students with major learning difficulties?

How does the degree of cognitive impairment affect teaching content and the outcomes by which we measure educational gains?

What are some essential elements of an effective sex-education teaching program?

How do children with retardation differ from their nondisabled peers in their response to leisure and recreational materials? How do we introduce them to and encourage their participation in more "age-appropriate" recreational activities?

What appear to be some of the special benefits of bowling for youth with mental retardation?

What are some of the services and supports that families especially value and why?

What kind of nonfamily residential options are available to children and youth, and what are their apparent advantages and disadvantages?

How do we meet the health needs of children with mental retardation, many of whom, such as those with Down syndrome, have significant medical problems?

☐ Notes

1. "Inclusion" refers to the initial placement of a disabled child in a regular class, although some services may be provided in other settings. "Mainstreaming," on the other hand, involves a primary placement in a special class, with part-time participation in a regular one.
2. *Overcorrection* refers to restoring an environment to its condition before the accident.
3. Data were available for 59,000 of the 64,000 clients in the Developmental Disabilities (DD) system.
4. There were 6,087 individuals with severe and profound retardation, of whom data were available from 5,607. The latter represented about 10% of the developmentally disabled.

Services and Supports to Adults

☐ Overview

Chapter 8 provides an introduction to services and supports for adults and then characterizes them in terms of educational services, vocational and "day" services, recreational and leisure services, sexuality, residential needs, health needs, and the needs of older persons with mental retardation.

☐ Introduction to Adult Services and Supports

Recent decades reflect a shift in how we think about services to adults. From an earlier focus on their disability, there is now a concern with helping them to achieve the lifestyles they seek (e.g., Bellamy, 1991). The shift involves a recognition of the right of these individuals as *adults* to exercise greater control over their lives, to be free to participate as fully as possible in the life of their communities, and to be *part of* rather than *separated from* that community. To accomplish this, the recent emphasis has been on "support" services. Especially relevant to those with more severe impairment, from moderate to profound retardation, the intent is to provide supports—financial, physical, personal, and social—that would permit these persons to live in the ways that they desire. Instead of a service system that traditionally provided programs and settings to which the retarded adult had to accommodate, the intent now is to identify preferences, typically residential in nature, and then provide the assistance necessary to actualize those choices. And with greater involvement in the community, there is always the possibility of growth. The more complex the environment to which we are exposed, the greater the demand on our adaptive skills.

The story of Lizabeth, a 45-year-old woman with Down syndrome, illustrates the growth that can occur if we are *exposed* to the world, not just *protected* from it. Born to a large family in a mining community in West Virginia and severely delayed in her development, she initially was denied admission to the local school because she still lacked bladder control. By the time that she acquired it her mother chose not to send her. An older sister, Jean, explains: "My parents overprotected her. They were afraid that something might happen to her and so she just first stayed at home with my mother and colored or played with toys. *Basically she just existed to be taken care of.* She wasn't really a member of the family."

When Lizabeth was 29 years old, her mother became ill, and Lizabeth went to live with Jean. In her young adulthood she neither cared for her personal hygiene nor used speech. The lack of speech was puzzling; she had talked until she was 13 years old and then suddenly stopped. A possible cause was the shock of the sudden death of her father, to whom she was very attached. (Elsewhere in the book there is reference to a child with Down syndrome who had a catatonic psychotic episode following the death of a parent.)

Concerned about her sister's helpless state, Jean took her to a clinic in Charleston, saying, "I wanted more for her. I believed they could help her." The clinic recommended placement in a sheltered workshop, and there she remained until age 43. The death of another family member with whom she then was living required moving to still another community.

In the years of her attendance at the sheltered workshop, there was tremendous growth. She learned to care for all of her self-help needs as well as her personal hygiene. From a formerly vegetative existence, she became a contributing member of her family; she dusted, swept, used a vacuum, washed dishes and her clothes. Her supervisor at the workshop explains, "I taught her how to cash checks at the bank and how to shop. At the store she picks out the things she wants and goes through the checkout line to pay for them. Before she thought pennies were wonderful. Now she likes silver coins and dollar bills more!"

Her interests also changed. Jean notes "When Lizabeth first came to live with me, she liked toys. Whenever we'd go to the store, she'd head for the toy department. Now . . . she goes to the women's clothing department [much more age-appropriate]. Fond of jewelry and makeup, she enjoys buying things that other women of her age like. Her tastes . . . have dramatically changed. I'm just amazed that she's come this far."

Prior to the event that required her to move to another area, her supervisor thought that with the aid of a "job coach" she might eventually be placed in so-called supported employment. This form of employment is a work situation in regular work environment in which the disabled person learns the job with the tutorial assistance of a job coach (employment specialist). It is discussed later in the chapter in the section on vocational services. In fact, she did work as part of a "mobile crew," a group hired to perform janitorial duties. An impediment to more individualized employment was a very slow work rate and deficient social and communication skills.

Lizabeth's story speaks for itself. Unstimulated, left merely to exist, living in a family situation in which there were no expectations for her, she was much like a helpless infant. Moved into an environment in which people were learning and working, she, too, demonstrated a huge untapped potential. Although the severity of her disabilities set some limits on the level of independence that she ultimately achieved, there is no question that she had come a long way!

☐ Educational Needs in Adulthood

In some sense, educational services to the adult represent a continuation of those provided during the school years. This is most evident in those with the most severe degrees of retardation; their adult lives may find them still working on the kinds of basic self-care skills fully mastered by normally developing children prior to adolescence. In the material that follows, teaching goals are specified that can be achieved in near-normal fashion by adults with not more than mild retardation, and to a lesser degree if the level of impairment is greater. Although basic cognitive and motor skills, along with motivation, affect the ultimate level of skill attainment, it is in the education of people with major learning difficulties that creative ways of circumventing these difficulties are found. Illustrations are seen in teaching programs for individuals whose retardation is from moderate to severe in intensity (Dever & Knapczyk, 1997). We begin with a review of the kinds of competencies achievable in persons with mild retardation.

The Adult with Mild Mental Retardation

In Chapter 6, we refered to the Life Centered Career Education Curriculum. Its goals fall into three skill areas—daily living, personal-social, and occupational. Some degree of self-sufficiency and competency in each of these areas can be expected in adults with mild retardation, although difficulties will be encountered in skill areas that depend on academics. Wherever competencies require good reading ability or the understanding of arithmetic, such as budgeting and money management, difficulties will ensue. We also can expect that persons with retardation will not practice these skills with the same degree of understanding and judgment as their intellectually able counterparts. In the social skills domain, for example, although we can enhance abilities important to developing friendly relationships with strangers, we cannot teach the kind of judgment that permits the nonretarded person to assess quickly whether developing a friendship with this particular person is desirable!

Daily Living Skills

Reasonable teaching goals pertain to relatively independent management of a house and family, money, grooming and hygiene, domestic chores, shopping, recreation, community mobility, and citizenship. With reference to money management, a chronic concern, the problem is traceable to arithmetic achievement levels that usually do not exceed third grade (Bilsky, 1976). Dever and Knapczyk (1997) even have undertaken the daunting task of identifying all of the skills involved in budgeting and paying bills, specifying no fewer than 80 components!

An earlier study revealed that adults with mild retardation could learn the essentials of paying bills (LaCampagne & Cipani, 1987). Using a teaching methodology consisting of verbal instructions, modeling, practice, and feedback, and with the assistance of a calculator, all learned to write checks, record the check and the new balance in the checkbook, and pay bills by mail. Of particular interest is that the skills acquired in practice with "training bills" generalized to novel ones that were similar in format.

Personal-Social Skills

This curriculum is organized around interpersonal relations. It focuses on gaining self-awareness and self-confidence, on demonstrating socially responsible behavior, on problem-solving, on communication, and on functioning independently. As is seen subsequently in this chapter, the social skills area is a perennial concern. Intelligence has much to do with the quality of our social interactions. Appropriate social behavior requires judgment, sensitivity, subtlety, restraint, and above all, the ability to put ourselves in another person's shoes. All of these qualities are affected by retardation and can contribute to social isolation and chronic loneliness.

Occupational Guidance and Preparation

Addressed to the skills necessary for employability, occupational guidance is focused on understanding the nature of work, making realistic job choices, developing good work habits, and finding employment. Of these, the most essential to securing and maintaining employment is the development of the work habits necessary to job holding, such as punctuality, following directions, accepting supervision, and general reliability.

Adults with Moderate and Severe Retardation

Assuming prior educational experience in the public schools, and building on that curriculum, training activities are described that are deemed more appropriate to persons with moderate or severe retardation. Examples of such training are given as it might be conducted in a group home, for example, in the hope of moving the individual to more independent living (Dever & Knapczyk, 1997).

Two teaching programs are presented here—appropriate clothing selection and meal preparation. The former is more relevant to those with not more than moderate retardation, the latter to those with severe retardation. For each one, specific goals are set and their means of accomplishment shown. Notably, they illustrate how creativity in teaching can provide the kinds of cues that enable learners to circumvent their learning difficulties.

Dressing and Grooming: Appropriate Clothing Selection (Dever & Knapczyk, 1997)

Teaching materials: Clothing, television, calendar, umbrella, writing pad, pencil (at least some reading and writing skill is necessary), and a clothing selection chart.

Activity: Each evening the trainee locates the next day on the calendar and, from the television, notes the weather forecast on it. Referring to a "clothing selection chart" (Table 8.1), the trainee chooses appropriate dress based on temperature and weather. (For the nonreader, clothing can be represented pictorially.) Three rules are to be followed: Always carry an umbrella if there is a threat of rain; always carry a light jacket in the spring and fall; and do not wear sandals if the temperature is below 65°F.

Cooking and Meal Preparation: Cooking Scrambled Eggs and Preparing a Meal

A teaching procedure is offered for cooking scrambled eggs, and this is followed by a brief narrative summary of one for teaching meal preparation (Dever & Knapcyzk, 1997).

TABLE 8.1. Clothing selection chart

Temperature	Dry Weather	Wet Weather
<25 degrees	Long pants, long-sleeved shirt or turtleneck, winter coat, gloves, hat, scarf, ear protection	Long pants, long-sleeved shirt of turtleneck, winter coat, gloves, hat, scarf, ear protection, boots
25–45 degrees	Long pants, long-sleeved shirt, winter coat, gloves	Long pants, long-sleeved shirt, winter coat, scarf, boots
45–60 degrees	Long pants, long-sleeved shirt, light jacket	Long pants, long-sleeved shirt, heavy jacket
60–70 degrees	Long pants, short-sleeved shirt	Long pants, long-sleeved shirt, light jacket, umbrella
70–80 degrees	Long/short pants, short-sleeved shirt	Long/short pants, short-sleeved shirt, umbrella
>80 degrees	Short pants, short-sleeved shirt	Short pants, short-sleeved shirt, umbrella

Note. Reprinted from Dever & Knapczyk, 1997, with permission from Brown & Benchmark, Madison, WI.

Learners: Free of disabilities that would restrict the range of motion and with functional vision.

Major skill clusters (equivalent of task analysis):

1. Assemble relevant materials
2. Mix eggs and other materials
3. Cook (3 min)
4. Serve (1 min)
5. Clean up area (6 min)

Outcome: Learner will be able to prepare his or her own breakfast.

Standards: Eggs will be properly cooked, neither raw nor burnt; no liquids will run from eggs when placed on a plate; no shell fragments in eggs; eggs will be placed in center of plate and plate placed on the table at correct place setting; no spills will be evident; all dishes and utensils will be cleaned and in a dish drainer; the learner's hands will be dry. (Does this come from a military cookbook!)

Mastery criteria: Eight consecutive attempts without errors or assistance.

Tools and Materials: Electric range, frying pan, mixing bowl, dinner plate, spatula, table spoon measure, small whisk, church key–style can opener, condensed milk, eggs, butter, sink, sponge, dish drainer.

Preparing meals: Using a cookbook with a meal schedule, instructions are given for the preparation of entire meals. Appropriate for persons with few or no reading and number skills, directions are given in pictorial form. A chart is prepared that provides pictures of the foods to be cooked, their order of cooking, and their respective cooking times. Also shown are representations of cooking-time dials.

General Training Goals

As noted, the training areas in the life-centered curriculum are appropriate to virtually all levels of retardation, although the degree of mastery will be less than in those with moderate and severe impairment. Apart from the training areas already specified, continued development can be expected in feeding, dressing, grooming, and hygiene. Various household skills will be acquired, including the use of common appliances, such as a washer, dryer, vacuum, range, and microwave. There is training in the use of the telephone; in understanding postage; and in budgeting and money skills—learning the value of coins and currency, using coins in vending machines, and paying for public transportation. There is training in safety—in first aid and dealing with emergencies. Community skills are a particular emphasis—learning to use public transportation, safely crossing streets, shopping, and the use of recreational resources. And along with these go training in the social behavior appropriate to community settings.

Adults with Profound Mental Retardation: Special Learning Challenges

The special learning challenges of adults with profound retardation merit comment. At least three conditions are essential to maximizing the adaptive potential of this population. They are (a) the physical nature of their living and learning environments, (b) the use of systematic teaching procedures and meaningful learning incentives (appropriate reinforcers), and (c) conducting training when the individual is in an alert behavioral state.

Modifying the Physical Environment

The physical environment includes the tasks and objects to be mastered, for example utensils in eating, and the physical setting in which training occurs. Most of us cannot remember our own difficulties in acquiring basic self-care skills—feeding, dressing, and toileting—but this can be a formidable challenge if there is extreme cognitive impairment, especially combined with sensory or motor disabilities.

Simplifying the Task

Procedures that have been used to enhance the learning of self-care skills include color coding to aid in discrimination between different physical areas; alteration of clothing, such as making larger head and arm holes; and the modification of utensils (e.g., Roos, 1965).

A Humane Living Environment

The profoundly retarded person with sensory or motor impairments is at particular risk for exposure to adverse living conditions. Given the severity of the disability, a variable responsiveness to stimulation, and minimal or no communication skills, he or she is likely to evoke an attitude of hopelessness in caregivers and teachers. It was such dismal environments that sparked the Willowbrook exposé described in Chapter 6. Those environments typically consisted of a large day room housing sizable numbers of people whose days were marked by the absence of much planned activity and where various forms of stereotypic and self-injurious behaviors were the norm. By contrast, current group settings are likely to be characterized by specific "activity" areas, a much lower staff-to-resident ratio, and a variety of materials that can offer stimulation.

Teachable Behavior States

The term *behavior states* was first applied to behavioral and physiological states in the newborn (Wolff, 1959). Incorporated in the pediatrician Brazelton's (1973) Neonatal Behavior Assessment Scale, they have now been adapted and applied to behavior states seen in those with most severe disabilities (Guess et al., 1993). Eight behavior states are recognized—inactive sleep, active sleep, drowse, daze, awake inactive-alert, awake active-alert, awake active-alert with stereotypy, and crying/agitation (including self-injurious behavior). From a teaching standpoint, our interest is in the time that profoundly retarded individuals—children, youth, and adults—spend in these states. In a study of a school population of 66 students, aged 3 to 21 years, eight (12%) spent at least 75% of their time in the "educationally optimal" states—awake inactive-alert and awake active-alert (Guess, Roberts, Siegel-Causey, & Rues, 1995). There is some indication that stimulation can itself move the student (or adult) from a nonalert to an alert state.

Applying Systematic Instructional Procedures

The "behavioral" approach to teaching was described in the previous chapter. It has had particular application to children and adults with severe or profound retardation (e.g., Whitman et al., 1983). Research, as early as the 1960s, showed that through its application significant gains in self-care skills could be achieved even in profoundly retarded adults. The key to its successful use lies in first eliciting the desired behavior, or some approximation of it, typically through instructing, prompting, and modeling, and then reinforcing that behavior. With repetition, the behavior is gradually strengthened and rewards modified. Also widely used in the treatment of behavior problems (e.g., Matson & Mulick, 1991), its use in this area is illustrated in the succeeding chapters on behavior disorders in persons with mental retardation.

Social Skills Training

Impairment in social skills is one of the hallmarks of mental retardation and, necessarily, the focus of much training. An informal survey of a small group of adults living in the community (A. Amado, 1993a) found that their greatest concerns were "social" in nature—making friends and learning how to get along with people.

Jane Wells (1993) describes her long-term relationship as advocate, guardian, and friend of Mary Ann, a woman whom she helped to make the transition from institutional to community living. Her description suggests something of the social skills difficulties common to retardation, difficulties often magnified by lives that may be isolating and bereft of caring relationships.

Perhaps most revealing of Mary Ann's problems in establishing friendship was behavior characterized as "totally self-involved." She appeared to be unconcerned with the effect of her behavior on others. To Jane who was trying to be supportive, to be her friend, Mary Ann could react with uncontrolled anger, seemingly indifferent to its threat to their budding relationship. Her apparent unawareness or lack of sensitivity to the feelings of her would-be friend also was reflected in the absence of expressions of simple appreciation for things done for her, a little "thank you," or of regret for her actions and the offering of apologies.

But with the influence of Jane and other women who were determined to reach out to Mary Ann, to be her friends if she would let them, these behaviors changed. She began to express positive feelings for her friends: "You've got to stick up for them. You've got to be nice and good to them." She learned how to express appreciation and regret. Interestingly, so-called social skills training often has included the teaching of such common courtesies, but they are not likely to be developed and *practiced* except in the context of loving, caring relationships.

For many adults, whether living still in large residential centers or in small community-based homes, such caring relationships are absent. The

L'Arche program, described elsewhere, is a rare exception. The typical caregivers come and go; one may be moved from one set of caregivers to another, presumably in the interest of providing more independent living arrangements; and peers may be ill-prepared to provide the kinds of relationship adults seek. Certainly Mary Ann could not expect to develop friendships with peers with the kind of socially insensitive behaviors that characterized the early part of her relationship with Jane Wells. The price is a life devoid of genuine friendship and filled with loneliness (R. Amado, 1993). Although studies of the quality of life of adults with mental retardation suggest the benefits of living in the community, they show little evidence of change in the degree to which caring relationships exist there. At least one third of adults report no friends at all (e.g., Hill et al., 1989).

The importance of social skills to one's general adjustment is self-evident. They determine our acceptance by others and the extent and depth of our friendships (Matson & Hammer, 1996). They are fundamental to the quality of our lives because so much of our happiness, and unhappiness, is tied to experiences with other people. In terms of our personality model, they are the chief means through which we meet our need for "intimacy" and self-esteem.

The social-skills difficulties in mental retardation are reflected in how children and adults relate to other people—to peers, to older persons, to employers, to teachers. They are manifest in how people are greeted, addressed, paid attention to, talked with, and played with. They are evident in how emotions are governed and expressed. The rationale for "training" behavior that is acquired naturally in the normally developing child lies in the presumption that the lack of social skills reflects a deficiency of specific verbal and nonverbal social competencies rather than expression of the effect of delayed cognitive development on social and emotional development (Matson & Fee, 1991; Zigler & Harter, 1969).

It is the view here that these deficits are, in fact, tied to retarded mental development, that social behavior and general intelligence are closely related. The very concept of "social maturity" refers to developmental phenomena in which age and social and emotional behavior are linked and manifest in interpersonal behaviors that predictably vary with age and cognitive development. The kind of social interactions that we regard as age-appropriate or "mature" in a 4-year-old look very different from those of a 10-year-old!

But the social-skills deficits in mental retardation are not, seemingly, simply a reflection of a slower rate of growth in social and emotional maturity. They are not just childlike behaviors in an older person. Rather, do they have their own unique quality. Whether conveyed in greetings to one another, in conversation, in the exchange of pleasantries, or in the expression of common courtesies, the effects of retardation are striking. The disorder not only impinges on cognitive function, it also exacts a high price in social behavior. Let us now consider how social skills training programs seek to address these difficulties.

Social Skills Training Programs

Social skills training programs have been developed for children and adults (Matson & Fee, 1991). They are designed to increase assertiveness (e.g., Bregman, 1984), to strengthen "dating" (Foxx, McMorrow, Storey, & Rogers, 1984) and work-site behaviors (La Greca, Stone & Bell, 1983), to increase recognition of facial expressions of emotions (e.g., fear and surprise) (McAlpine, Singh, Ellis, Kendall, & Hampton, 1992), to enhance control of anger and teach more appropriate forms of its expression (Benson, 1992), and to generally improve interpersonal skills (e.g., Foxx, McMorrow, & Schloss, 1983). Of interest in relation to our view of their close tie to intelligence itself is the common finding of a lack of generalization of trained behavior to untrained settings (Castles & Glass, 1986; Matson & Fee, 1991). Social skills are a different order of behavior than learning to brush one's teeth or to add and subtract. They are skills that are called on in the flow of personal interaction; that are exquisitely sensitive to contingencies, both subtle and not so subtle, and to our feelings, hopes, and aspirations; and, above all, that reflect our *judgment* as to what is appropriate at any moment in time. In short, they indicate our *understanding* of a social situation, and only our cognitive capacities can provide that awareness.

In light of our view of "social behaviors" as manifestations of the application of cognitive skills to social situations, the study of Castles and Glass (1986) is instructive. Their goal was to improve social behaviors by teaching *problem-solving* skills. A group of mildly and moderately retarded adults were instructed in the *process* by which problems can be solved—generating alternatives with respect to how one might respond to a situation, considering the consequences of each alternative, selecting the apparent best outcome, and then implementing it. The last step, the actual behavior itself, was taught as a series of skills—maintaining eye contact with the person with whom you are interacting, being aware of the tone of your voice and its loudness, and being appropriate in your emotions and gestures. All of this has the quality of teaching actors how to deliver lines and is far removed from the generally spontaneous way in which we interact with each other. Interestingly, the greatest changes were in the social behaviors themselves, for example better eye contact, but there were no significant gains in problem-solving itself. This is not to say that problem-solving is unteachable. Examples were provided in the previous chapter, but they were tied to very specific, concrete kinds of problems, such as an unplugged electrical appliance, problems in which *judgment* is minimized as long as the initial learned response works (put the plug in). It is when that initial response is inadequate that the limitations of such problem solving become apparent.

Social skills training generally is conducted with groups. After all, the group provides a natural laboratory for the practice of the skills being taught, as participants must learn how to deal with one another. The teaching itself commonly consists of (1) describing the appropriate social response in a given situation, for example expressing gratitude or being complimented; (2) modeling the response for the trainees; (3) having the trainees perform it in role playing; and (4) providing appropriate feedback and reinforcement. An interesting side benefit is that the members of the group are encouraged to share feelings and concerns, to use the group therapeutically as well as instructionally.

Together with such group-oriented training, social skills board games also are employed. They have the appeal of "table games" and require less specially trained staff (e.g., Foxx, McMorrow, & Schloss, 1983). Some of the behaviors taught again convey the flavor of standard social-skills training—giving and receiving compliments, politeness, asking and answering questions, and responding to criticism.

Self-monitoring or self-control techniques also have been used (Matson & Fee, 1991). These require the trainee to monitor his or her own behavior. Even if the accuracy of recording is questionable, such a procedure tends to result in the reduction of unwanted behaviors. Presumably, the procedure necessarily *sensitizes* the person to his or her own behavior. By bringing the behavior into consciousness, one has a powerful means of controlling it.

Developing Friendships with Nondisabled People

Given the vulnerability of the adult with retardation to social isolation, a paucity of friends, and loneliness, efforts to develop friendships, especially with nondisabled persons, are a recent trend (A. Amado, 1993b). Apart from the sexual sphere, in which relationships with disabled partners would be more probable, there are clear advantages to having a non-retarded friend. Such a relationship offers a teaching model and can open doors to fuller community participation. Let us listen to one proponent of such relationships (Traustadottir, 1993):

> The goal of current reform efforts . . . is the full inclusion of people with disabilities into all aspects of community life . . . Despite almost two decades of efforts to establish community-based services, it appears that community programs have merely assisted people with disabilities to be *in* the community [but not] to become *part* of the community (Bogdan & Taylor, 1987) . . . Thus the emphasis on networks [e.g., a "circle of friends"] and personal relationships . . . is at the heart of current trends . . . The increasing awareness of the limitations of the service system in *connecting* people with

disabilities [typically mildly or moderately retarded] with ordinary community members has led to a call for *personal commitment* ... to establish relationships with people with disabilities. Implicit is the belief that such personal relationships and friendships [outside the "professional" sector] will ... serve as a basis for the supports necessary for people to participate fully in community life. (Schwier, 1993; pp. 121–122)

We earlier referred to the relationship between Jane Wells and Mary Ann. The great majority of these relationships involve women as the nondisabled partner (Traustadottir, 1993). Studies indicate that from childhood on, women tend to be more accepting of persons with disabilities and are more likely to become their friends. The senior author's class on "exceptional children" always had a large majority of female students. The adults active in encouraging friendships and community connectedness are chiefly women. Their orientation to relationships tends to be nurturing and caring; that of males tends to be focused around common interests and "doing." Nevertheless, friendships between men and retarded persons do exist (Schwier, 1993).

Francis, a 31-year-old with Down syndrome, would appear to have little in common with Rick, a university professor and father of three. What brought them together? Professional wrestling! They meet periodically at the McDonald's where Francis works, have a cheeseburger, talk about the latest dramas in the ring, and then attend a match. Francis loves wrestling and so does Rick. Says Francis, "He's a good guy all right. He gave me some wrestling magazines and he even showed up at McDonald's on my birthday as a surprise ... we got something great in common, that's for sure" (Schwier, 1993; pp. 161–162).

Friendships Between Persons with Disabilities

Commonly, the friendships of retarded adults are with peers. Jane, a 26-year-old woman with Down syndrome, lives with her parents. She has a friend, Irene, who was a former classmate and who occasionally visits Jane's home. Irene spends the night and they enjoy listening to music, eating pizza, and looking at magazines, some with a "teen" orientation.

Jane is also very interested in boys and may have had some sexual experiences at school. She is unduly forward in making her interests known, a forwardness that is not always reciprocated! Her view of male-female relationships is immature and a source of concern to her mother. (Sexuality is addressed elsewhere in this chapter.) What we see here is an example of inappropriate social behavior, a seeming lack of discretion. If it has not been learned by age 26, can you "teach" it?

Learning Reciprocity in Marriage

Dan and Brenda have experienced much stress in their marriage. They are parents of a 2-year-old boy, Trevor; who, on one occassion was removed from their custody and placed in a foster home. He since has been returned. Overall, the marriage seems strong. Behaviors are now described that resulted from Brenda's parents expecting too little from her, but which also show Brenda learning how to assume adult responsibilities. Let us listen first to Dan:

> I felt like I had to be strong for Brenda because she really needed me to be the man...My family didn't think we should get married...people said I was slower [a common form of self-description in retardation] and shouldn't get married...We met at the [sheltered] workshop...After we was married, we had to really have it out...about sharing the work...We had a few arguments...I told her she had to help me so it's not all left to one person to do the work. That's what marriage means is sharing of stuff.

The following are Brenda's words:

> Dan's family never wanted me around. They was always trying to break him and me up and they did lots of cruel things to run me off. I feel better about myself now that I know how to keep my house clean and cook and wash clothes. Dan and me share, but it took a long time to get over being lazy. *I never did anything at home with my mom* [no maternal expectations]. When the baby came along, I was still learning not to be spoiled and lazy. [Wanting to leave the hospital after giving birth, she doesn't explain her discomfort but then describes the following incident.] I told one of them [nurses] that I hit Trevor. I thought they'd get mad at me and send me home, but they took Trevor instead [illustrating poor judgment]. They watched us with him and we couldn't feed him or change him or dress him [presumably concerns about possible child abuse, an issue discussed in Chapter 5 in connection with parents who are retarded]. It felt like everyone was waiting, you know, for us to make a mistake so they could...say, "See, they aren't fit to have a baby." I sometimes felt scared about getting close to Trevor. He was living at the foster people's house, but sometimes we could see him if somebody watched us. I didn't want to love him a lot because what if they took him away in the end? [She *could* consider consequences.] He always used to go to Dan when he was little, until one day he came over to me and hugged my leg and held his arms up to me...I want to be a good mommy and we know we can call on people for help [aware of social resources]...The one person I can really count on during bad times is my husband, Dan. I think marrying him was one of my best ideas. (Schwier, 1993; pp. 159–160)

☐ Vocational and "Day" Services

On the Significance of Work

For many of us, our jobs become a powerful source of meeting psychological needs, at the minimum, structure and self-esteem. Although the significance of work has varied with social and economic conditions, it still has a powerful hold on our collective psyche. To a considerable extent, we are what we do. Beyond its role in meeting basic economic needs, it can provide us with culturally valued activities that can earn approval from those whose approval we seek—family, friends, employers, and coworkers (intimacy)—and a sense of our own competence (success). It can offer purpose, usefulness, and worth. Its contribution to our psychological health is no more apparent than in the emotional distress following prolonged unemployment or, in the case of older people, in enforced retirement.

Admittedly, attitudes toward work are not uniform. The cultural revolution of the 1960s probably weakened at least the traditional view of work. The extraordinary movement of women into the work force certainly has broadened our perspective on it, and people who largely have known multigenerational poverty probably would grant it a minor role in contributing to their self-esteem. But given its fundamental role in most of our lives, it behooves us to consider its impact on persons for whom we might have few expectations of employability, those with mental retardation.

We begin with an examination of the experience of several youth who were given the opportunity to work in a pet shop (Graham & Poling, 1963). Although this project was undertaken in the 1960s, its lessons are no less relevant today. It was begun by parents who had worked with retarded youth in a sheltered workshop; they believed that their children were insufficiently challenged in that setting, a complaint still commonly heard. They felt that some of the youth could work in regular jobs, "competitive employment," if they were given the proper training:

> In a store—under proper supervision—the kids are in the daily stream of life [integrated!]. And the constant challenge of new problems, new customers, different jobs...stretches their minds...instead of stagnating at lowest common denominator tasks [a potential problem at sheltered workshops], our kids are constantly stimulated—and they grow, amazingly. (Graham & Poling, 1963)

Johnny Rivas was 22 years old, unemployed, and except for the sheltered workshop, considered unemployable. Attending a private school until age 16 years, he returned home where for six years he had led a life of "intolerable emptiness." Shunned and teased by peers, he grew morose and hostile and spent his days locked in his room watching television.

His parents had rejected a possible sheltered workshop placement, seeing it as more of a recreational than vocational activity. He worked for a time at a riding academy where he cleaned stalls. He loved horses but lost the job when the academy closed. His parents had learned of the pet shop opportunity and, in concert with the parents of the other youth, helped get it started. His mother describes what happened:

> I still find it hard to believe. After years of heartbreak and despair, you gamble $50 on two people [originators of the pet shop] who you suspect are unpractical dreamers. And what happens...a small miracle. Our Johnny who had no life, now has a full and happy one. He has a job and a place to go every day [his life has *purpose*]. A place where he is needed [confirming self-worth], a place where he has puppies and people to love and be loved by [intimacy]. The change is unbelievable. Now he goes to the movies alone, eats by himself in restaurants, buys his own clothes, does everything he was afraid of before [extraordinary growth in autonomy and self-esteem]. And he laughs. So do his father and I. It's a welcome sound in a house that has heard none for years. (Graham & Poling, 1963)

The growth of Johnny and his peers into competent employees did not occur overnight. First given only simple tasks, success built on confidence and also indicated their interests. Once those interests were determined, "stretching" of their potential began. Danny, 27 years old and mildly retarded, was interested in handling money and was given the task of taking daily receipts to the bank. Then people in the shop began to pretend that they were too busy to prepare the deposit slip for him. Very slowly, Danny learned to count money (he could use a calculator now!), to enter it in the ledger, and to fill out a deposit slip. It took him an hour, but his confidence and self-esteem soared.

One of the youths was very frightened of the animals, and his continuation at the pet shop was in doubt. One morning he brought in a cake that he had baked for his coworkers. Recognizing an interest in cooking, he was assigned to preparing food for the animals. It involved mixing food in specified proportions for the different breeds of puppies. With obvious pride he began serving his "dishes" to animals that had earlier frightened him. In this case, as in Danny's, we see how creative use was made of their interests.

Initially supported through small contributions from the parents of the employers, pay schedules were impromptu. But with the progress of the youths, each was given a modest salary. Said one father, "That $5 meant more to my girl than a thousand dollars would have meant to me." Although having a regular salary clearly lifted self-esteem, even more important to self-worth was earning a key to the store. At the end of the first year, keys were given to the four young people who had shown the greatest initiative and responsibility. Thereafter, they were expected to open the store each morning. Earning a key and the status it signified became the greatest ambition of the youths. The manager commented that when the keys were first passed out he never dreamed they would become the store's equivalent of Phi Beta Kappa!

Apart from its inspirational aspect, this story also reveals the kinds of problems retarded youths can encounter in the "real world" and the need to prepare them educationally for the challenge. Danny's arithmetic or money problems were no surprise, given, as earlier noted, an average achievement level in arithmetic for those with even mild retardation of third grade (Bilskey, 1976). Let us now look at the vocational potential of individuals with mental retardation, their employability, the kinds of jobs they prefer, the skills that underlie these jobs, and typical work problems.

Vocational Potential in Mental Retardation

A wide range of employability exists, from those with minimal job skills to those who work in regular competitive employment (Fig. 8.1a). Employability is much affected by the level of cognitive functioning and, although competitive employment formerly was limited to those with mild retardation, with the advent of supported employment persons with moderate impairment are now so employable (Kregel, Hill, & Banks, 1988) (see Fig. 8.1b).

In addition to competitive employment, retarded adults are served in a variety of settings—adult day or day-activity programs, work-activity programs, and sheltered workshops. Each is briefly described.

Adult Day or Day Activity

These programs originated in the 1960s as a means of providing a community-based daily experience for adults who were not viewed as employable and who, in the absence of a structured day program, were at increased risk for institutionalization. The typical program is nonvocational in nature and consists of a mix of educational, recreational, and simulated work activities (e.g., sorting objects by shape or color). This is the most common day placement for adults with severe and profound retardation and, in the late 1980s, nearly half of all retarded adults (48%), some 175,000, were in such settings (Ellis & Rusch, 1991).

Work Activity

Work-activity programs commonly are housed in sheltered workshops and offer some limited remunerative work together with the educational,

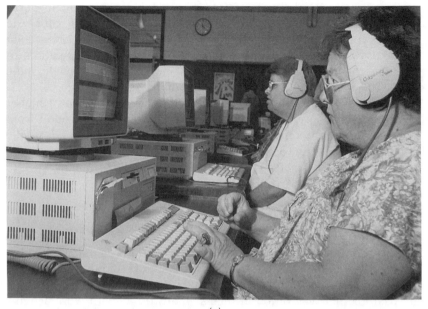

(a)

(b)

FIGURE 8.1. (a) Vocational training in computer skills. (b) A "supported employment" work setting. (Courtesy of Arc of Forsyth County, Winston-Salem, NC.)

social, and recreational activities found in the adult day program. In work-activity employment, the rates of work and pay are less than half of the standards for regular employment. Work activity programs are second only to day activity ones as day placements for the adult population. In the 1980s, they were serving about 160,000 individuals nationwide, some 44% of the adults who were in some kind of day program.

Although work activity has been viewed as preparation for a higher level of employability, such as the sheltered workshop, transition from the former to the latter has been very slow. In the late 1970s, for example, in California, the average retention in work activities was no less than 10 years, with only about 3% of participants annually moving up into "sheltered employment" (Ellis & Rusch, 1991)

Sheltered Employment

In the continuum of employability, this form of work is the last step before regular employment. The jobs often consist of repetitive assembly or packaging operations. Employees in this status earn at least half the wage rate paid for that type of job in regular industry. As with work activity, movement from the sheltered workshop into regular employment has been very slow, the average stay in sheltered employment in the late 1970s being about 9 years. About 11% moved into competitive employment annually (Ellis & Rusch, 1991).

Sheltered workshops have come under much criticism because their programs have been seen as inconsistent with efforts to stress placement of retarded persons in "regular" (integrated) job settings (e.g., Murphy & Rogan, 1995). Workshops typically have a nonintegrated quality in that, except for staff, all of the employees are disabled. The supported employment initiative of the 1980s was, in part, intended to increase placement in regular (nonsheltered) employment and to circumvent the movement bottleneck in the sheltered workshops. In fairness to the workshops, many of their disabled employees (and their families) resist movement into regular employment for social and economic reasons. Socially, there is the risk of losing valued friendships. Perhaps more than in competitive employment, the sheltered workshop can meet social relationship needs. At the economic level, there is risk of the loss of both dependency-related assured income and Medicaid health benefits in exchange for the uncertainties of low paying and often part-time employment in the unskilled job sector (e.g., Goldberg, McLean, LaVigne, Fratolillo, & Sullivan, 1990). Ironically, if employees are moved into regular jobs, the sheltered workshop is threatened because of the loss of those very employees on whom it depends to perform its job operations and sustain itself. The system neither works to promote maximum employability nor integration and some states, such as Virginia and Maryland, have begun to offer incentives to workshops to convert to a supported employment model (described in the next section).

Regular (Competitive) Employment

Numerous studies have shown that competitive employment is a realistic goal for a substantial portion of the retarded population. Although their unemployment rate at any one time probably exceeds 50% (e.g., Wehman, Kregel, & Seyfarth, 1985), this also reflects the personal, social, familial, and economic factors that encourage or discourage work. Reference has been made to some of these factors in connection with those individuals who prefer, for a variety of reasons, to remain in sheltered employment. In retardation, parental attitudes are especially influential, at least if the individual still resides in the family home and the parent may be resistive to change in the child's status. This can include those who have come to be financially dependent on their child's assured federal support as a "disabled and dependent adult!"

Jobs in the service domain have come to be the major source of employment for persons with disabilities. This is the fastest-growing employment sector and includes such work areas as hospitals, hotels and motels, restaurants, cafeterias, and nursing homes. In these settings, retarded and non-retarded unskilled workers are employed as aides, orderlies, kitchen workers, food servers, dishwashers, house cleaners, and janitorial aides. In the industrial domain, once the chief employer of unskilled workers, persons with retardation can be employed in warehouses, laundries, and simple assembly operations.

Supported (Competitive) Employment

As defined in the Developmental Disabilities Act of 1984, Public Law 98-527 *supported employment* refers to paid work for individuals who need some degree of support both to obtain competitive employment and to maintain that job. It requires that employment be in integrated work settings, those also peopled by persons without disabilities. The activities that are conducted to sustain employment include supervision, training, and transportation. Although supported employment primarily serves adults with mild and moderate retardation, some individuals with severe retardation also may be so employed (Mank, Cioffi, & Yovanoff, 1997). There are three forms of supported employment: individual job placement, mobile work crews, and enclaves.

Individual Job Placement.   In this placement, the disabled person works individually rather than as a member of a work group; this is the most widely used form of supported employment. More than three quarters of placements (79%) have been of this type (Wehman & Revell, 1996). Supported employment features the "job coach" or employment specialist, one who literally teaches the disabled employee on the job. The job coach not only functions as an instructor but, after the job is mastered, is available indefinitely to the supported employee on an as-needed basis. From working essentially full time with the supported employee during the early weeks of employment, one study found a rapid reduction in training time after the first 6 weeks. Thereafter, the job coach was present for an average of only about 1 hour a week (Kregel et al., 1988). Perhaps contributing to this reduction in job coach time is the assumption of some support activities by nondisabled coworkers, potential sources of "natural support." It may be that the use of natural supports as a substitute for the job coach, a recent initiative in the field, may prove more useful with the less cognitively impaired supported employee (Test & Wood, 1995).

A variant of the job coach is the "paid coworker." Most often paired with a physically disabled as well as retarded individual, the paid coworker complements the physically disabled person such that between the two of them the job is performed. The coworker is not paid by the empoyer but rather through other governmental, federal, and state resources.

Supported workers perform a wide array of jobs—assembly operations, warehouse stocking, child care, food service, office work, custodial work, and recycling or sorting. The typical supported employee, in one large study, worked about 20 hours per week, earned an average of $5.52 an hour, and $585 per month. We may ask whether these obvious economic benefits might have been offset by greater loneliness or social isolation in the work setting of regular employment as compared with the sheltered workshop or day-activity program? The modest research findings are conflicting (Chadsey-Rusch, DeStefano, O'Reilly, Gonzalez, & Collet-Klingenberg, 1992; McCaughrin, Ellis, Rusch, & Heal, 1983). Indeed, it is suggested that mildly retarded workers actually may feel lonelier in the nonintegrated work setting (Chadsey-Rusch et al.). Nevertheless, sensitivity to the possibility of social isolation and loneliness in the integrated setting, for adult and child, is an ever-present concern (Luftig, 1988; Chadsey-Rusch, Gonzalez, Tines, & Johnson, 1989).

Mobile Work Crew. This is a work setting in which one functions as a member of a small group of workers who perform custodial tasks under the guidance of an on-the-job supervisor. The mobile work crew may move from one job site to another.

Enclave. Another group-oriented work setting, an *enclave* refers to physical area within a business wherein a small group of disabled persons are employed and managed by a full-time supervisor.

In general, "group" supported employment settings serve as work sites for persons with the greatest degrees of cognitive impairment because they provide close worker supervision.

Obstacles to Supported Employment. Although a main objective of supported employment is to increase employment in the competitive work sector, Federal and state dollars, important sources of financial support to disability programs, continue to favor workshops. As noted earlier, some states, such as Virginia and Maryland, have sought to ease the transition from sheltered to competitive employment by offering financial incentives to workshops to encourage such placement. In spite of the obstacles, the greatest gain in the employment of retarded adults has been in the supported employment domain. Nonetheless, sheltered workshop and work activity programs still constitute, by far, the largest proportion of work settings serving this population (Kiernan, Butterworth, & McGaughey, 1995).

Desirable Job Characteristics

We have referred to a number of the jobs performed by persons with mental retardation. We want now to indicate briefly their major characteristics; it is these that must be considered in any type of job placement. Jobs that are performed well are *well defined, highly standardized*, and *fairly constantly paced* (Peterson & Jones, 1964). Falling within the "unskilled" area of employment, they are jobs that are highly predictable in their demands. The worker is not confronted daily with a new set of challenges. Unskilled jobs, by their very nature, do not require unusual abilities, and the skills necessary to their performance can be taught quickly. But another extremely important aspect of employability is the social skills and work habits inherent in employment. It is well-established that the most common reason for job termination among the largest group of retarded employees, those with mild retardation, relates to personal and interpersonal difficulties on the job rather than to an inability to perform the work (e.g., Greenspan & Shoultz, 1981). Examples of such behavior are excessive talking, ignoring directions, inappropriate interrupting, aggressiveness, lateness, and irregular attendance. Employability for any of us requires regular job attendance, punctuality, getting along with coworkers and supervisors, accepting directions and correction, maintaining an adequate work rate, and showing concern for the quality of our work. Encompassed by the term "dependability," if these behaviors are not initially present in the disabled (or nondisabled) employee, they can only be expected to be acquired over time. But the job is not the ideal setting for learning! They must be acquired prior to employment, and it is the responsibility of family, school, and vocational training settings to inculcate these "habits of employability."

☐ Recreational and Leisure Services

The recreational needs of adults, like those of children and youth, are met through activities that are sources of pleasure but, with age, considerations of health and wellness become increasingly relevant. The goal is to encourage a healthy lifestyle, one that calls attention to such dimensions as general health, physical fitness, nutrition, stress management, environmental safety, and personal responsibility (Hawkins, 1988).

Assessment of Relevant Lifestyle Measures

As in the development of individual education plans during the school years, the adult benefits from an analysis of recreational needs in terms of these lifestyle determinants. Such an analysis and subsequent programming, ideally, should involve the disciplines of therapeutic recreation, medicine, dietetics, and psychology.

General Health

The first step in the development of an individual recreation plan is the determination of the current state of health, because this affects the kinds of activities, especially vigorous ones, in which one can engage. The common problem of obesity is relevant here.

Physical Fitness

The assessment of "physical fitness" involves a determination of one's exercise history, flexibility, strength, balance and equilibrium, cardiopulmonary capacity, and contraindications to exercise. Physical fitness becomes an important tool in weight control in individuals prone to more sedentary lifestyles (e.g., Golden & Hatcher, 1997).

Nutrition

Of special relevance to the problem of obesity, especially in females, a nutritional and dietetic survey includes health history, food intake, eating problems, exercise—amount and intensity, one's personal and family situation, residential and work environment—and mechanisms for coping with stress.

Stress Coping

In relation to recreation, we need to identify the kinds of experiences that are stressful and how the stress is managed. Of course, one of recreation's great boons is to relieve stress, whatever its origin. Some strategies for coping with stress include learning relaxation techniques, such as deep breathing, nutritional and dietary modification, counseling, and alteration of one's activity schedule.

Assessment of Recreational Interests

A description of the individual's interests is an obvious cornerstone to the formulation of a recreational program. With input from those who know the person as well as the individual himself or herself, it should indicate interests, current activities, preferences, expectations, and the capacity to pursue these independently. This last-mentioned component deals with the person's ability to move about in the community without assistance, to utilize public facilities (e.g., restaurants), and to exercise caution when appropriate. Scales for the measurement of recreational and leisure skills are widely available (e.g., Schleien, Meyer, Heyne, & Brandt, 1995; Wehman & Schleien, 1981).

Desirable Recreational Activities

Chronological Age-appropriateness

Discussed in connection with recreational activities for children and youth, age-appropriateness becomes even more important in adulthood. The goal, at all ages, is to encourage activities that approximate one's chronological age, not mental age. But intellectual level cannot be ignored and can be expected to create at least some disparity between chronological age–and mental age–affected interests, a disparity that tends to increase with the level of retardation. Thus one may encounter adults who show preferences for more childlike activities or objects. Recall that Lizabeth, described in the first part of the chapter, in her 30s still enjoyed playing with children's toys while Jane and her friend Irene, in their 20s enjoyed looking at "teen" magazines. But as we also saw in the case of Lizabeth, exposure to a world outside the family home led to the development of much more age-appropriate interests, such as jewelry, make-up, and women's clothing. Apart from the possible maturing effects of exposure to a wider range of experience, the challenge is to identify activities that tap similar interests but are more appropriate to adults. In this regard, a group of 10 activities that can be enjoyed throughout life by disabled and nondisabled children, youth, and adults (Schleien et al., 1995). They are considered representative of the kinds of activities enjoyed by nondisabled individuals in such settings as the home, at school, and in the community. Detailed instructions are given for their teaching. The 10 activities are aerobic warm-ups, Connect Four, Jenga, Magic Mitts or Scotch, Nintendo, Game Boy, pinball, pottery, remote-control vehicles, Simon, and target games. Remote-control toys are enjoyed at all ages and can be adapted to varying skill levels and environments. Their novel movements excite interest at all levels of cognition. Pottery, too, can interest all age and ability groups and, as an activity, fosters creativeness, promotes manual dexterity, and teaches a sense of beauty. Aerobic warm-ups are to be especially encouraged in light of the previously mentioned fitness problems.

Choice

Fundamental to leisure and recreation is choice, the availability of a range of leisure options that allow for the exercise of preference. Hawkins (1988) notes that this can include a variety of types of activity—intentionally restful ones, such as lying down or napping; passive ones such as rocking or swinging; diversionary ones such as television, socializing, or hobbies; and more rigorous ones such as walking, jogging, gardening, or other fitness-promoting activities.

Community Recreational Resources

In addition to those activities that can be enjoyed at home, the community is, necessarily, the other setting in which recreation is pursued. This can include one's neighborhood and such activities as gardening, walking, and bicycling. In a less residential area, there may be shops, malls, theaters, and bowling alleys.

Parks are another community resource, and a local parks and recreation department is a useful ally. They ordinarily offer recreational programs for persons with disabilities and, in our community, provide dancing, swimming, arts and crafts, and field trips.

A common concern is *access* to recreational resources. For individuals who typically do not drive and have relatively little spending money, this can be a major barrier. It is important to teach adults, if they have not already learned, how to use local public transportation. This not only reduces dependence on caregivers but also immensely widens the range of possible choice. One can go *where* one wants to go *when* one wants to go and with *whom* one wants to go. One is not dependent on caregivers or the facility "van," and can move about at one's own pace, not having to adjust it to that of a group (Fig. 8.2a).

(*a*)

(*b*)

FIGURE 8.2. (*a*) Using a taxi for independent travel. (*b*) Enjoying dance. (*c*) Enjoying a chat on the porch of the group home. (Courtesy of the Arc of Forsyth County, Winstom-Salem, NC.)

(c)

FIGURE 8.2. *(Continued)*

Along with learning to use public transportation, there is the need for teaching safety, including areas to be avoided. This always creates a dilemma—the conflict between encouraging choice and maximal independence against the need to protect against possible disaster. Assuming that safety skills were not adequately acquired during the school years, they can be taught only by "graduated guidance," and the degree to which they can be acquired depends, in part, on the person's cognitive ability. Certainly, individuals with moderate retardation have been able to learn to use bus routes, for example, to travel safely from their homes to day programs.

Other Appropriate Activities

Hawkins (1998) sees a comprehensive recreational program as involving a number of major areas. Each is identified here, and examples are given (see Fig. 8.3*b,c*).

> *Sports and physical activity:* aerobics, jogging, swimming, bowling, or team games, such as soccer, horseshoes, Special Olympics
> *Creative experiences:* music, dance, theater, ceramics, pottery, woodworking

Amusements: movies, travel, county fairs, theme parks

Outdoor activities: gardening, picnics, camping

Social/cultural activities: holiday celebrations, parades, music festivals, social dancing, dining out, "hanging out," "malling"

With the exception of Special Olympics, all of these activities can be pursued in the same ways and in the same settings as those enjoyed by nondisabled people. Because Special Olympics is, by definition, a noninte-grated activity, should it be discouraged? In our view, no! Our recreational goal is to encourage and teach participation in age-appropriate and inte-grative activities, but not to deny or disallow choices that reflect either less mature interests or nonintegrative settings. After all, the essence of recreation is "free choice!" To allow less is not only to infringe on real choice but also to do it in such a way as to deny the effect that mental retardation *necessarily* has on maturity and interests.

☐ Sexuality

Treated previously in connection with the retarded adult as "parent" (Chapter 5) and in relation to the educational needs of adolescents (Chapter 6), the focus here is on adult sexuality and its various ramifications, especially as it relates to those persons living outside the family home. Although it is equally relevant to the individual residing in the family home, if nonfam-ily caregivers are legally responsible for a retarded adult's welfare, special precautions are in order.

Retarded Adults Have Sexual Needs

In considering how caregivers and parents (or family) respond to the sex-uality of their charges, we must begin with the recognition of the reality of sexual feelings, perhaps more evident in those with not more than mild retardation. They seek the same kind of gratification as you and I (Heshu-sius, 1982). As the degree of retardation intensifies, presumably because of greater biological abnormality, the level of drive may be diminished. The following excerpts are illustrative.

Enjoyment of Sex:

> When I try to hug him, he puts up his hands...and I get mad...like he didn't want to touch me...And when he's like that and when he tries to hug me, I do the same thing to him. Like I was telling him, "I got feelings too, like you got feelings!" (Henshel, 1972, p. 198)

Concerns About Sex:

> So one time I went out with the wrong company and I got pregnant. I never went out anymore. (Henshel, 1972, p. 70)

Sex and Marriage:

> Terry, a young woman, is talking to Linda, a residential staff person about visiting her boyfriend, Wayne, at his home: "Then he can't sleep with me since we're not married, can he?" Linda: "No, not until you are married." (Heshusius, 1982, p. 61)

Re: Sex and Pregnancy:

> Terry: "I thought I was prepared but I am not." Asked if she knows how you get pregnant, she replied, "When you make love?" and pointed to a picture of a man and woman kissing. (Heshusius, 1982, p. 64)

> They say when you first have intercourse . . . you can't get pregnant. Is that right? (Rostafinski, 1975, p. 12)

"If We're Sexual, Let Us Be Sexual"

In their discussion of this topic, Valenti-Hein and Dura (1996) share with us sexual "rights" as proclaimed by advocates of the Illinois Association for Retarded Citizens. Some of these must serve as the basis for addressing the sexuality of their charges by parents and caregivers:

> The right to dignity and respect as a total human being, which includes recognition as a sexual being
> The right to be allowed natural contacts with members of the opposite sex [and with the same sex?]
> The right to be given sexual information at every age level in a manner that can be understood
> The right to be protected from sexual exploitation
> The right to his or her feelings, be they anger, sexual, or other

I always have been impatient with those who would say, "You *shouldn't* have those feelings." It's not a matter of "should" or "shouldn't"—we just *have* feelings. As indicated in Chapter 2, they are tied directly to our needs. It is our emotional states that convey our level of need gratification. What we do have to learn is how to *express* our feelings in ways that are not destructive.

Of these, the right to be protected from exploitation epitomizes the complexity of the issue. On the one hand, there is the assertion of the right to "natural contacts with the opposite sex" and, on the other, the expectation of protection against would-be exploiters. It is the achievement of a balance between freedom and protection that becomes the goal of those involved in their supervision (e.g., Morris, Niederbuhl, & Mahr, 1993). In the view of one "advocate," this balance is most likely to be found if the individual has a "circle of friends," people with whom there are "caring" relationships (D. Shumway, personal communication).

A Policy Statement for Caregivers

In response to the dual reality of needs for gratification and for protection, caregivers look to "policy statements" for guidance. An example is found in one for residents of community programs in Australia (McCabe, 1993). In modified form, it reads as follows:

> A person with a disability has the right to develop relationships with others. Caregivers will ensure that residents have both opportunities and training in establishing and maintaining close relationships [same-sex as well as opposite sex?]. Residents will be informed about their sexuality, and about conception, contraception and sexually transmitted diseases so as to encourage appropriate sexual behavior. Where it is mutually desired by a resident and another person [mutual consent], they should be free to pursue an intimate relationship in privacy, including sexual intimacy if they so desire (p. 377, modified).

An official policy statement of a governmental agency supervising community residential programs, this represents a much more liberal view toward sexuality than is commonly expressed by the staff of residential programs. Martin, the young man described in Chapter 1 is heard to complain of the lack of privacy in the group home in which he lived prior to marriage. The staff would not allow him to be alone with a young woman and, if they were in the same room, the door had to be left open. He would be criticized if he held her hand or put his arms around her. His brother, commenting on the refusal of the staff to allow them to show some affection for each other, views this as forcing them to remain in a continued state of adolescence!

> "They wouldn't let us be alone together, and if we were in the same room, we had to leave the door open...House parents would criticize us if we held hands or if I put my arm around her [the woman he later married]." [Martin's] brother observes, "Their interest was affection, something that few people [in the 1970s] were as yet willing to grant them. *What they were granted was the right to remain in continuing adolescence* (p. 141, emphasis added).

Not only are caregivers uncomfortable with open physical expression of sexual feelings, but as we've seen this discomfort can extend to the precursors of sexual tenderness, affection and warmth as expressed in touch (Craft & Craft, 1978; McCabe, 1993).

Sexual Knowledge of Retarded Adults

The sexual knowledge possessed by retarded adults varies with their cognitive level, sex education, and range of experiences. Studies of mildly retarded individuals indicate a basic understanding of masturbation, menstruation, intercourse, and pregnancy. Commonly lacking is awareness of health aspects—sexually transmitted diseases, birth control, and planning of pregnancy (e.g., Edmondson, McCombs & Wish, 1979; Hall & Morris, 1976). At greater levels of retardation, understanding of sexuality is fragmentary at best (Edmonton & Wish, 1975). Among a group of moderately to severely retarded males living in an institution, only masturbation and intercourse were recognized with some frequency. Given the content of modern television, that level of understanding probably has increased!

Sex Education Programs

There have been a number of sex education programs for retarded adults (e.g., Green, 1983; Kempton, 1988). Of these, two have had at least some systematic evaluation—the Dating Skills Program (Valenti-Hein & Mueser, 1990) and Stacking the Deck (Foxx & McMorrow, 1983). Both of these, which are board games, are said to have produced some improvement in problem-solving in sociosexual situations.

Irrespective of format, educators agree that the context of sex education programs need to relate to sexual knowledge, preferences, hygiene, appropriate and inappropriate behavior, and protection from abuse. At the most basic level, it is assumed that virtually everyone can grasp the nature of privacy, at the minimum learning to close the bathroom door! At the most direct and concrete levels are programs that teach specific sexual behaviors—how to masturbate (Dura & Nunemaker, 1993), how to provide pleasure to a partner and to fantasize (Garwick, Jurkowski, & Valenti-Hein, 1993), and how to put on a condom (Samowitz, 1997, personal communication).

Consensual Sex and the Potential for Abuse

Retarded men, women, and children, are vulnerable to sexual exploitation and abuse. Periodically, our newspapers report episodes of normal adolescents taking advantage of young retarded women, sometimes brutalizing them in disgusting fashion. In Chapter 7, there was reference to the exposure of a mildly retarded young woman to long-term incest and rape by family members.

Sarah is a 15-year-old girl with severe cerebral palsy and profound retardation. Although neither toilet-trained nor able to feed herself, she became pregnant and had a son. No less than nine males, aged 14 to 63 years, including her 17-year-old *brother*, were charged with sexual abuse, a practice that appears to have persisted at least 2 years! At age 13 years, apparently in response to the onset of sexual abuse, there was a dramatic change in her behavior. Until then generally a happy youngster, she began to cry frequently and touch her genitals. She became fearful around males; her eyes would widen and her arms flail (Golden & Heckrotte, 1993). Totally lacking in formal communication skills, she appears to have been regarded as the "perfect victim." Imagine being regularly violated and unable to communicate with those who could help!

Given the vulnerability to exploitation and abuse, under what conditions can sexual intimacy between persons with retardation be regarded as truly consensual? This brings us to the legal concept of informed consent, a doctrine described in Chapter 6 in connection with issues of competency. It applies equally to the sexual sphere and involves three aspects: an understanding of the activity in which one wants to engage, an awareness of its consequences, and the absence of coercion (e.g., Abramson, Parker & Weisberg, 1988). Usually explored through questions and answers, in the common absence of clear criteria for determining both "understanding" and "awareness," weight has tended to be given to its "voluntary" aspect (Parker & Abramson, 1995).

We do have a study of the capacity to give consent as measured by a special scale, the Socio-Sexual Knowledge and Attitudes Test (Wish, McCombs, & Edmonson, 1980). It was concluded that persons with mild retardation could give valid consent. Those with mild retardation who were considered unable to give consent had psychiatric disorders in addition to their cognitive impairment (Morris & Niederbuhl, 1992). In keeping with the earlier research on sexual knowledge, males with moderate retardation usually were unable to give consent, as was true for all with severe and profound retardation. This finding accords with the position taken by Parker and Abramson (1995) that in cases of possible sexual abuse in those with severe or profound retardation, the individual should be deemed incapable of giving informed consent.

Of special interest and, perhaps, most controversial, is an approach to determining consent that would distinguish between verbally and nonverbally communicated consent (Ames & Samowitz, 1995). This approach has been in use with residents in programs operated by the Young Adult Institute in New York City. The authors report employing this method with some 70 clients in their residential programs, and at least in one instance a judge has viewed the nonverbal form as acceptable. They stress the importance of evaluating each case on an individual basis and, of course, obtaining family or guardian approval needed.

Each of the two forms of consent is described, and in some detail, so as to give potential users a feeling for their appropriateness.

Verbal Consent

The focus here is on one's understanding of the intended sexual act as this is communicated by the person through speech—the nature of the act; its possible consequences, such as health and legal; and participation in it as a free choice. This kind of consent, the traditional form, is assumed to be within the ken of those who are not more than mildly retarded. Five indices are offered as evidence of verbal consent. They are that the person:

1. Can describe the sexual act and understands that he or she is free either to engage or to abstain from it.
2. Understands that certain sexual acts are illegal and could result in punishment, such as public exposure, pedophilia, and sodomy.
3. Understands how to avoid both the transmission of sexual disease and pregnancy.
4. Understands that a given sexual situation could pose the threat of physical harm, abuse, or exploitation, and that one can remove oneself from it, if desired. (It is the view here that once in a sexual situation and in a state of arousal, it cannot be expected to be terminated with the same ease as turning off a flow of tap water!)

Nonverbal Consent

A seemingly much more subjective approach, "nonverbal consent" involves the making of a judgment of the ability to give consent through behavioral rather than verbal means. Considered appropriate for those who can neither communicate nor understand the indices for verbal consent, presumably persons with at least moderate and certainly severe and profound retardation, nonverbal consent would be based on prior sexual behavior as that behavior indicates a "practical understanding" of sexuality. Its application has been limited to individuals who are in residential settings in which there is full-time supervision and to sexual activities that would occur within that setting.

The indices are:

1. Voluntariness: Can the individuals make choices? Do they show by their past behavior the ability to choose or reject a particular partner?

2. Harm avoidance: Are the members of a pair "reasonably" protected from either physical harm or exposure to sexually transmitted disease? Are these likely outcomes of their relationship?
3. Avoidance of exploitation: Is one member of a pair exploiting the other? The exploiter ordinarily would be in a position of power over the person exploited. Any staff person (!) would be so regarded.
4. Avoidance of abuse: Is either member of a pair showing distress (the way Sarah did)?
5. Interrupting a scenario: Via either utterance or body language, is there the ability to communicate the desire to terminate the interaction?
6. Appropriateness of time and place: By their behavior, do they indicate an understanding of the proper time and place for intimate behavior or can they be prompted to go to an appropriate setting or wait for the appropriate time without resisting?

The attempt to "manage" the sexual lives of others is an extraordinarily difficult task in a society in which sex is a "private" activity and most of us are very uncomfortable with public displays of intimacy. This is to say nothing of religious and moral strictures that apply to the behavior. In spite of this, responsible caregivers and parents try to transcend the barriers that our culture imposes and look for positive ways in which their charges' feelings can be expressed. Would we want any less for ourselves?

☐ Residential Services

The Institutional Population

Out-of-home residential services have evolved from an institutionally oriented to a community-based system. There has been a decline of two-thirds in the number of people housed in public residential facilities (16 beds or more). From a peak population of 194,650 in 1967 (Lakin, White, Hill, Bruininks, & Wright, 1990), the number declined to 63,258 in 1996 (Lakin, Prouty, Smith, & Braddock, 1996). Correspondingly, there has been a huge increase in those served in small community settings (fewer than 16 beds). Indeed in 1995, for the first time, the majority of persons in nonfamily community settings resided in homes housing not more than six residents (Lakin, Braddock & Smith, 1996).

The reduction by two-thirds in the state institutional population has seen the closure of more than one-third (35%) of these facilities, from 348 in 1968 to 218 in 1996. By 1998, it was expected that closures would have increased to about 40%, and eight states would have closed all of their facilities (Lakin, Braddock, & Smith, 1996).

With the reduction in the institutional population, there also has been a change in its composition. The trend is increasingly to serve in the larger facilities individuals who are older and more functionally impaired. The proportion of institutional residents age 40 and older has increased from less than one-fourth (23%) to one-half (50%). Even more dramatic has been the decrease in the population of children and youth served in these centers—from 54,100 to 2937 (36% to only 5%). In effect, large institutional settings are no longer housing children and youth. If children are admitted to such centers, it tends to be at a later age (Lakin, Hill, Hauber, & Bruininks, 1982).

With regard to level of impairment, the *proportion* of persons with profound retardation in the large facilities has grown steadily although their absolute number has declined—from 69,000 to 30,000. These are individuals who need assistance in basic self-help skills—feeding, dressing, and toileting. But with the decline in their actual numbers in the large facilities, they, too, increasingly are being served in the smaller community settings.

The Rationale for Smaller and Community-Based Residential Settings

The issue of size has been one of the driving forces in the deinstitutionalization movement. Large congregate state institutions, often housing thousands of residents, were vulnerable to the kind of abuse and inhumane living conditions epitomized by Willowbrook, conditions described by Blatt (1970) and reported on television by Geraldo Rivera (see Chapter 6). Large size lends itself to impersonal treatment, a lack of "individualized" care. Whether in a large institution, a large college, or the military, for example, the management of large numbers of people necessarily constrains individualization. The goal of "institutional downsizing" was to allow people whose disabilities realistically required some kind of care and supervision to obtain that in more typical or "normal" kinds of living arrangements. Thus the movement from the large facility or institution to the much smaller "group home" and "family care" or foster homes. Such settings, smaller and located within the community rather than separated from it, could tailor their programs to individual needs and could be expected to offer their residents the opportunity to exercise greater responsibility and choice. They also would provide exposure to more normalizing peer models.

Admittedly, the research findings on the effects of size have been conflicting. Earlier studies in the 1970s and 1980s were likely to find desired effects only if comparisons were made between very large institutions and much smaller community ones (Stancliffe, 1997). More recent studies, focusing on community residences, have found smaller size associated with greater resident satisfaction and self-determination, and a better quality of life (Conroy, 1992; Schalock, 1994; Tossebro, 1995). In particular, a study by Stancliffe (1997) showed that as the number of residents diminished, the opportunities for choice (self-determination) increased. This benefit was evident in settings with a maximum of five and tended to disappear if the number was three or less. This finding is of special interest to the senior author, who conducted research on adult-resident satisfaction in community living arrangements in North Carolina. Concerned that with fewer people sharing the same home, there might be greater loneliness, it was clear that even those residing in homes with only one or two other residents still preferred a more private, environment.

Community Living and Behavioral Competency

In addition to generally greater resident satisfaction and increased autonomy in community rather than institutional settings, there is unambiguous evidence of gains in competency. Higher levels of adaptive functioning are associated with movement from institutions to the community (e.g., Conroy, Efthimiou, & Lemanowicz, 1982), with continued residence in the community (Aanes & Moen, 1976), and movement from larger to smaller units within the same setting (e.g., MacEachron, 1983). These findings parallel the finding of Stancliffe (1997) on greater choice. Within a picture of enhanced competence, several ability areas appear to have particularly benefited particularly—language, household skills, and socialization (Kleinberg & Galligan, 1983).

These benefits can be linked to "opportunity." Residents of small group homes or semi-independent apartments can learn a variety of cooking skills because the residence is feeding three or four people, not 300! Cooking takes place in a regular "family" kitchen; there is time to teach, to learn, to practice, to make mistakes. Caregivers are not operating under the kind of pressure that requires cooks in institutional settings to prepare meals for hundreds of persons. Moreover, shopping is done at neighborhood food stores where residents can accompany caregivers and participate in the selection and purchase of food. Residential programs serving large numbers of people do not purchase their groceries at the local supermarket; they have them trucked in!

Similarly, living *in* the community rather than being physically removed from it lends easier access to educational, vocational, and recreational resources. A study of community-based group homes found increases in residents' adaptive behavior associated with a location that was easily accessible and close to community services, a residence that fit well within the neighborhood (*residential* programs in *residential* neighborhoods), and a physically attractive and comfortable place in which to live (Eyman, Demaine, & Lei, 1979). Still another study found that location within the community was predictive of adaptive competence (Hull & Thompson, 1980). Convenience of access reduces the transportation problems of persons with mental retardation. A population with relatively little spending money and one unlikely to drive, in communities with limited public transit, tends to be very dependent on caregivers for getting about. Living in the community also enhances opportunity for interactions with nondisabled persons and for the kinds of "connections" or friendships referred to earlier in the chapter.

To the extent that the individual with mental retardation is exposed to opportunities for experiencing and coping with a wider range of environments, there is the possibility of change and growth. This is epitomized in the observation of Martin, the young man with mild retardation described in the first chapter, who noted, "People are retarded by what they don't know." Only through exposure can new learning occur and "what they don't know" diminish.

Typical Community-Based Residential Options

Within the community there is an array of out-of-family residential options. The two most commonly used have been *foster homes* and *group homes*. Most recently, there has been an emphasis on "supported" living settings—independent and semi-independent apartments and room-and-board arrangements (Hayden, Lakin, Hill, Bruininks, & Chen, 1992). Supported room-and-board settings have gained some prominence because they offer the greatest degree of choice, freedom, and autonomy to residents. Even into the 1990s, however, foster homes and group homes continue to be the most popular out-of-house placements. A nationwide survey offers a picture of the residents they serve (Hayden et al., 1992). Referred to in the previous chapter in connection with children's services, their nature and resident population is briefly described.

Foster Homes (Specialized Foster Care)

This is a family home that makes its dwelling available to one or more persons as a place in which they can live and be a part of the family. This is the principal residential setting for children and youth, ages 3 years and up, and for older adults. Foster homes serve individuals with all degrees of cognitive impairment, but the majority of their residents have either moderate or severe retardation. They are less likely than group homes to accept adults with major behavior problems.

Group Homes

Group homes have been a popular residential option. Providing a congregate living situation for generally five to six residents, ages 22 years and older, they serve all levels of retardation. Having a "training" as well as "residential" function, group homes seek to maximize independence and enable the resident, to move into more independent living. Unlike foster homes, in which the retarded resident lives with a family, the group home is staffed by employees of the facility.

Intermediate Care Facility

This is a residential setting for individuals with special needs—health needs, major behavior problems, or extensive personal-care needs. Chiefly serving adults in the 22- to 63-year-old age range, it also is likely to include persons older than 63 years. Intermediate care programs typically serve persons with the greatest degree of cognitive impairment and differ from group homes in having a higher proportion of those with severe and profound retardation.

Supported Independent and Semi-independent Living

Represented by one- or two-person apartments, these settings are appropriate for individuals needing less supervision than in the preceding ones. The extent of their supervision may be limited to periodic monitoring, for example, weekly, as the program seeks to offer as independent a living situation as possible by providing no more assistance than is necessary to sustain the degree of independence the resident desires. Assistance tends to be specific, centering, for example, around budgeting and bill paying, or provided if some special social or family-health issue arises. Technology has been especially helpful in enabling persons with major physical disabilities to live more independently:

> Preferring to live alone, Mary neither has nor wants a roommate. Both physically and cognitively disabled, she's confined to a wheelchair. A paging system worn around her neck permits her a fair degree of independence. Through it help is available 24 hours a day. Unable to lift herself from her wheelchair or her bed, physical assistance via the pager is always available.
>
> Technology allows the agency that uses the paging system to monitor homes even when there is no full-time on-site worker. A high tech speaker

telephone allows continuous contact with the disabled person. The paging and monitoring technology is the equivalent of the 911 emergency system. When Mary pushes her button, a screen full of information is presented to the on-call worker—her name and address, her doctor and guardian, and her medical status.

Nursing Homes

One of the controversial residential options has been nursing homes. Primarily intended for the generic older population with chronic health needs, nursing homes have housed a disproportionate representation of *younger* retarded adults (National Center for Health Statistics, 1979, 1987). Nursing homes have been regarded as "an expedient response to pressures for deinstitutionalization," and a statewide study in Illinois found that only one tenth of the retarded persons in their facilities actually warranted such placement. The remainder were free of medical problems. In response, federal legislation was enacted that restricts nursing home placement to retarded adults with medical needs. In response to the legislation, current nursing-home residents were to be moved to more appropriate facilities except for those who had been in a home for at least 2.5 years and wanted to remain there. A later national survey of nursing homes still found in them a picture of inappropriate placement of retarded individuals in them (Lakin, Hill, & Anderson, 1991). As implied, the inappropriate use of these facilities for retarded adults relates to age. Only 12% of the general residents of nursing homes were younger than age 65. In contrast, more than two thirds (68%) of their retarded residents were below that age. In addition to being younger than the nonretarded population, they were also less physically disabled. Retarded residents were, however, comparable to nonretarded patients in their self-care needs—feeding, bathing and dressing. Given the relatively small number of retarded individuals with health or mobility problems, only 20%, it was considered, as in the Illinois study, that the majority of them.

"Integrated" Communities

All of the residential programs described have been established specifically for persons with disabilities and are the options considered by service providers. But "integrated" communities are a very different kind of residential environment. These are residential communities, settings in which retarded and nonretarded persons share their lives—living, working, and playing together. Two examples of these are the international L'Arche and Camphill communities. The L'Arche communities, based on the work of Jean Vanier, first arose in France; now there are more than 100 of them, located in 16 countries, including the United States and Canada. The intent of L'Arche is to create a trusting and caring environment in which the person with retardation is valued for the emotional qualities he or she can bring to relationships. The goal of L'Arche's staff ("assistants") is to enter into the kind of mutually caring relationships with retarded individuals that tend to be rare among adults (Sumarah, 1987). Unlike caregivers whose function is to teach and supervise, L'Arche seeks neither to change nor modify the disabilities but only to enter into *relationships* with the person:

> We can give them drugs which may ameliorate their anguish (at the absence of truly loving and accepting relationships), we can rehabilitate them to certain social competencies. But the most important thing we can offer . . . is an assurance that we want them with us *as they are*. (Shearer, 1976, pp. 32–33, emphasis added)

To be valued for "qualities of the heart" rather than devalued for qualities of the mind reminds us of Wolfenberger's call to value the kinds of emotional qualities that we can encounter in retardation—trust and honesty, qualities that can become jaded in our more sophisticated development.

☐ Health Needs

Studies of the health of retarded persons, not surprisingly, find elevated rates of medical disorders (Beange, McElduff, & Baker, 1995). An entire issue of the journal *Mental Retardation* was devoted to the health needs of adults (Crocker & Yankauer, 1987) and, more recently, a comprehensive picture of how managed care will affect their health services is provided by Kastner, Walsh, and Caiscione (1997a), along with a description of some model managed care projects (Kastner et al., 1997b). The medical problems seen in adults include genetic diseases (Ziring, 1987); nutritional disorders—underweight and overweight (Simila & Niskanen, 1991); hearing and visual problems (Ellis, 1979; Reynolds & Reynolds, 1979); communicable diseases, such as hepatitis B (Zonia & Goff, 1986); and dental disease (Girgis, 1985). Some medical problems are characteristic of specific mental retardation syndromes, such as hypothyroidism in Down syndrome (Dinani & Carpenter, 1990).

Higher mortality rates than those of the general population are found at every age for retarded persons (Richards & Siddiqui, 1980). This is true irrespective of place of residence—institution or community (Miller & Eyman, 1978; Zaharia & O'Brien, 1997) or level of retardation (Fryers, 1984). Although place of residence may not affect survival, it can determine ease of access to medical care. Adults in institutional environments have ready access to medical services; this may be less true in the community (Beange et al., 1995; Rubin, 1987; Ziring, 1987).

Adults Living in the Community

With at least 90% of retarded adults residing in noninstitutional settings, there is growing interest in their status. In one study of a hospital catchment-area population younger than 50 that was served by a major medical center in Sydney, Australia (Beange et al., 1995), retarded adults, for example, differed from their nonretarded counterparts in a greater frequency of obesity—16% in males and 27% in females as compared with 8% and 9%, respectively, in the general population. On the positive side, although the retarded adults exercised less, they also smoked and drank less. Common medical problems were skin problems, often untreated; eye and hearing problems; seizures, sometimes poorly managed; and undiagnosed hypertension. Barriers to healthcare included problems of communication and mobility. Of particular concern were conditions such as skin disorders, easily recognized but untreated. A "team" approach to serve the retarded individuals in this medical catchment area was proposed. It would consist of a primary-care physician, a dentist, a dietitian, and a sports (exercise) physiologist. A similar team approach characterizes the previously described Developmental Disabilities Center at the Morristown Memorial Hospital in Morristown, New Jersey (Criscione, Walsh, & Kastner, 1995).

The most detailed characterization of the health status of adults is found in Rubin (1987), who reviewed studies of both institutional and community populations. Institutionalized adults had high frequencies of seizures, cerebral palsy, skin disorders, hearing and visual problems, and respiratory and gastrointestinal disease (Nelson & Crocker, 1978; Schafer, Ross, Schafer, & Houser, 1980). With deinstitutionalization, four patient populations were seen as having special needs—adults with Down syndrome, older adults (aged 60 or more years), adults with physical disabilities, and those with severe behavioral or psychiatric disorders. A more recent analysis indicates that young adults with severe and profound retardation, commonly including those with physical disabilities, have the highest rates of outpatient utilization of medical services (Birenbaum et al., 1990).

Down Syndrome

Of special concern for those with Down syndrome are the previously mentioned thyroid disorders as well as spinal abnormality (atlantoaxial subluxation), and Alzheimer's disease.

Older Adults: Geriatric Needs

With improved care retarded adults are now living longer (Carter & Jancar, 1983), but aging adds its own set of medical problems, such as Alzheimer's dementia in Down syndrome. This is referred to again in the last part of the chapter, dealing with the older or elderly adult.

Adults with Severe Physical Disabilities

The most medically-involved of the retarded population, adults with severe physical disabilities are disproportionately represented among persons with severe and profound retardation. Within the group, medical problems are of special note. They are seizures; multiple joint contractures, as in cerebral palsy; nutritional problems related to feeding difficulties, such as adults requiring tube feeding (gastrostomy); and recurrent respiratory problems. The last-mentioned is the most common cause of death in this group.

Adults with Severe Behavioral or Psychiatric Disorders

Because adults with major behavioral problems or psychiatric disorders commonly receive psychoactive medications, there has been longstanding concern about the simultaneous use of multiple psychoactive drugs (polypharmacy). This has led to more careful monitoring. With regard to persons with severe or profound retardation or those with major communication problems, it has been observed that disturbed behavior may be the only way in which a physically ill individual might convey distress!

Inadequate Care and Avoidable Death

Concerned about the quality of medical care received by children and adults living in the community, a study was conducted of the causes of death in the patient population served by the Morristown, New Jersey, medical program (Kastner, Nathanson, & Friedman, 1993). Data were obtained on 1400 individuals, aged 5 to 64 years, who had been seen over a 4-year period. These patients had been referred to the Developmental Disabilities Center at Morristown Memorial Hospital either because of a lack of services in their own communities or because of dissatisfaction with the care they were receiving. Over the 4 years, there were 14 deaths, an annual mortality rate of 4 per 1000. This is actually lower by more than half than the mortality rate in the general population, about 9 per 1000, and is attributed to the exclusion from their patient population of individuals served in the state institutions or in community-based intermediate care facilities. It is this latter group that is the most medically fragile.

More relevant was the finding that nearly half of the 14 deaths, six, were either clearly or potentially avoidable. Three deaths were clearly avoidable. They involved a 62-year-old woman who was not seen for medical evaluation until she was in late-stage cervical cancer. The other two were two 26-year-old women, one with cerebral palsy and one with Down syndrome, who died because of failure to treat infections illnesses—influenza and sepsis. The three potentially preventable deaths involved a 29-year-old man with Down syndrome who had cardiac symptoms but had failed to come in for treatment, a 36-year-old woman with cervical spinal cord compression whose parents refused surgical intervention, and a 10-year-old boy with Down syndrome and seizures who died of aspiration. The child with Down syndrome died shortly after movement to a new residential setting, a time of increased medical risk for all segments of the retarded population.

Possibly contributing to avoidable deaths and, certainly, complicating diagnoses, are individuals with a diminished sensitivity to pain. This appears to be a special problem in the particularly high-risk population, those with severe and profound retardation (Biersdorff, 1991). Here a nonmalignant gastrointestinal obstruction can lead to death because of a failure to report pain. The routine determination of pain sensitivity would appear to be an appropriate health precaution, especially in those whose lack of language interferes with the capacity to communicate discomfort.

☐ Family Support Services

Widely available to parents of children and youth, and referred to in Chapter 6, these services are also important to families of adults (Herman & Hazel, 1991). Deinstitutionalization has meant the *avoidance* of institutional care as well as the return of formerly institutionalized adults to their home communities, often into their natural homes. But the success of policies that encourage home care demand recognition of the special caregiving needs of families with a disabled adult member. Focusing on the entire family unit, as distinct from the retarded person alone, the intent of family support services is to assist the family in its role as primary caregiver and to prevent or delay out-of-home placement (Krauss, 1986).

As in the case of families with children and youth, *respite care* is one of the most requested services (Molaison, Black, Sachs, & Smull, 1995). This can entail both in-home and out-of-home care, the latter being short-term in nature. Families also benefit from *case managers*, persons who can assist in the management of their adult child's services and offer guidance to the family. Other prominent parent concerns are trying to balance their child's desire for greater independence and autonomy with safety considerations, and finding time for themselves away from caregiving responsibilities (Thorin, Yovanoff, & Irvin, 1996). Unlike the normal family, in which adulthood means the departure of the children from the home and an easing of caregiving responsibilities, there may be no lessening of these in the case of the dependent adult family member. Indeed, with adulthood and the loss of the school as a resource to the child, together with a possible lack of adult services in the local community, the family's caregiving duties actually may increase. Some sense of their nature is conveyed by the single mother of a 28-year-old daughter:

> I have been through schooling, waiting lists, family breakup, and placements in an adult family [foster] home and group home [possibly unsuccessful placements]. I have dealt with behavior changes, medical testing, dietary concerns, work-related issues, years of hands-on care and an ongoing concern and frustration about providing the best possible care . . . based on what resources were available to me . . . For a long time being her mother was most of my identity . . . Finding a way to have a life of my own and still assist [my daughter] to have a life involving being in the community, working and having other people in her life has been a real balancing act. (Thorin et al., 1996, p. 118)

It is important also to acknowledge that, apart from such stresses, for some parents the experience of rearing a child with serious disabilities is perceived as a challenge and an opportunity for personal growth (Turnbull, Guess, & Turnbull, 1988). Interestingly, at any given time such parents do not see themselves as under any special stress. Nonetheless, they are at greater risk for such problems as economic hardship (only one parent may be able to work), social isolation, sibling difficulties, and actual marital breakup (Singer & Irvin, 1991). In families with older parents, eventually there will be the need to surrender caregiving duties to others. If society wants families to continue their caregiving role into their child's adult years and they elect to do so, it is incumbent upon our communities to provide the kind of support that they need. They can provide care a lot better and more cheaply than the state!

☐ Older Persons with Mental Retardation

The aging of the general population has been one of the "stories" of the 20th century. Since 1960, the population of persons 65 years old and older has grown more than twice as fast as those under 65, and it is expected to triple by the early 2000s (Blake, 1981). Declining death rates from heart and cerebrovascular disease have contributed to greater longevity (National Center for Health Statistics, 1982), a benefit also accruing to those with retardation (Eyman, 1983), although, as reported in the section on health, their average life span remains shorter than that of the general population (Jacobson, Sutton, & Janicki, 1985). With the current emphasis on community-based services and retention in the family home into the adult years, awareness has grown of the elderly segment of the retarded population, less visible as a group during the institutional era, and its special needs.

Responding to the aging of our general population, a phenomenon shared with other industrialized nations (Grundy, 1983), Congress of 1965 (Public Law 89-73) enacted the Older Americans Act, and, in 1987, amended it to include recognition of a disabled older group, including those with mental retardation. A special feature of the 1987 Amendment was to encourage a linkage between existing community programs serving the general older population and those for people with disabilities. These generic aging programs consist of senior centers, nutritional centers, and social adult day care settings. The goal of linkage was to encourage access to these generic services for persons with disabilities and to find another vehicle for integrating disabled individuals into the societal mainstream.

Who is the Older Person with Mental Retardation?

As in the general aged population, there is a wide range of functioning in the retarded segment. Indeed, a distinction is drawn between "aging" and "elderly" retarded individuals, the former being in the 55- to 64-year age range (Jacobson et al., 1985). In terms of everyday functioning, three groups are recognized in the 55-or-older group. These are people who still have their usual zest and have no desire to slow down, individuals whose energies are beginning to flag and who seek a less work-oriented and more recreational lifestyle, and the "frail" elderly, those with major health problems.

Elderly Persons with Down Syndrome

Among older persons with Down syndrome the aging process appears to be accelerated. This was discussed in terms of premature aging in this disorder and its chromosomal connection to Alzheimer's disease. The great majority of individuals with Down syndrome, some 70%, are expected to live at least into their 50s (Mann, 1988); recent studies indicate an average life span of 56 years (Baird & Sadovnick, 1989), and there are documented cases of survival to at least age 83 (Chicoine & McGuire, 1997). By 60 years of age, however, about 40% will show symptoms of the Alzheimer's form of dementia (Schupf, Silverman, Sterling, & Zigman, 1989). Progressing more rapidly in Down syndrome, initial Alzheimer's changes include memory loss—both general and visual memory—and behavior changes (Wisniewski, Dalton, McLachlan, Wen, & Wishniewsky, 1985). Its middle stages are marked by a loss of social skills and decline in the ability to care for one's personal needs. Its later stages find impairments in mobility and gait, seizures, and incontinence.

Some General Characteristics of the Older Population

Several states have reported on the characteristics of the 55-and-older population, and their data have been reviewed by Jacobson, Sutton, & Janicki (1985).

Life Expectancy. Although life expectancy has increased for persons with mental retardation, it remains lower than that of the general population. But within the 55-and-older group, except for those with Down syndrome, life expectancy parallels that of the general population. Interestingly, the higher mortality rate among those younger than 55 years, and with severe and profound retardation, is less evident in the older segment.

Health Status. With advancing age, increasing health problems are inevitable. Visual, hearing, cardiovascular, and musculoskeletal problems are common but, in general, their health needs are similar to those of the general aged population. They do appear, however, to be less likely to practice preventative health measures (Anderson, 1998). Dental problems are prominent—there is less brushing and flossing of teeth, higher percentages still smoke, and women aged 40 years or more are less likely to have mammograms.

Residential Status. An especially comprehensive portrayal of the over-55 group is found in a study of nearly 2000 ($N = 1911$) such individuals then served by Massachusetts (Seltzer, 1988). Although incorporated in the research reviewed by Jacobson et al. (1985), the data on this population is presented separately here. Table 8.2 describes them in terms of age groups, gender, degree of retardation, and residential and day placement. Special attention is given to their residential and day settings.

Residential Status. Table 8.2 reveals that permanent residence in the family home is unlikely. Only 6% of older adults still lived with their family; another 5% apparently were living independently. Of the very great majority who were in some kind of supervised care (89%), more than

TABLE 8.2. Some characteristics of the 55-and-older population in Massachusetts

Characteristic	n	%
Age[a]		
55–60 years	759	40
61–69 years	679	36
70+ years	458	24
Unknown	15	1
Sex		
Male	965	50
Female	946	50
Level of mental retardation		
Mild/moderate	1142	60
Severe/profound	656	34
Unknown/not retarded	113	6
Residential placement[a]		
Public institutions	685	36
Nursing homes and other		
private institutions	402	21
Family	122	6
Group living arrangements[b]	580	30
Independent	101	5
Other	21	1
Day placements		
In public institutions	685	36
Noninstitutional		
Age-integrated programs	664	35
Specialized day programs	114	6
Generic aging day programs	143	7
At the residence	287	15
Other	18	1

Note. From Seltzer, 1998, and reprinted with permission of the American Association on Mental Retardation.
[a] Does not total to exactly 100% due to rounding errors.
[b] Includes group homes, foster homes, intermediate care facilities.

one third (36%) were in the state institutions; a little less than one third (30%) were in community-based settings—group homes, foster homes, and intermediate care facilities; and about one fifth (21%) were in nursing homes or other private care.

The high rate of out-of-home placement reflects the inevitable stress that aging places on older parents and the importance of planning for their adult child's future. Such planning, of course, includes financial and residential considerations (who will take care of my child?) but also reflects concern about meeting their social needs (Brubaker & Brubaker, 1993), needs heretofore met primarily through the family. Although they acknowledge the inevitability of eventual surrender of caregiving responsibility, as many as one third of aging parents have done no planning for it. Let us listen to a father who has planned for his child:

> Caregivers must plan for the future ... how to assure a continuing quality of life [for their child] ... I can't be sure ... that the agency which supports her will continue ... I can't rely on my children to stay close by.
> Things I have done that you might consider include:
>
> 1. Giving my daughter "a life of her own" today so that she is not physically and emotionally dependent on me now [acknowledging the reality of future separation].
> 2. Communicating with her siblings about her future and the options available.
> 3. Creating a financial plan.... Dying without a will or leaving a proportionate share ... directly to your child with disabilities may be the worst thing you can do.
> 4. Creating a plan for her future [with a case manager or other person who can assume a service coordination and advocacy role]. (Abbot, 1997, p. 2)

Nursing Homes.   More than a fifth of the older population was in nursing homes, possibly an appropriate setting for those with major health problems. As indicated previously, there have been longstanding concerns about the use of nursing homes as placements for retarded adults (e.g., Mitchell & Braddock, 1990). They appear to have been used indiscriminately, in that the majority of their retarded patients were of a younger age than their traditional patient group.

Day Programs.   The very great majority of the elderly population were served in typical day programs—adult activity centers and sheltered workshops. Only 14% were in "aging" programs—7% in generic ones and 6% in those specifically for persons with retardation.

Seltzer (1988) has described the types of day settings appropriate to elderly persons with retardation. The first, a so-called *age-integrated setting*, is the typical day program for adults of all ages, for example the sheltered workshop, and is appropriate for those who still desire a full day's activities. Such settings may yield a higher quality of social experiences and a more varied peer group. It is to such programs that one can expect to move if a less active lifestyle or retirement is desired. The second type, *specialized day programs*, are those specifically designed for older retarded persons. Such settings offer a less active day program, a necessarily narrower peer age range, but possibly greater opportunities for friendship with same-age peers. Note that only 6% were in such programs. The third type, the *generic aging day program*, is the one created for the general older population and with which the "linkage" effort is encouraged. Usually referring to "senior centers," it also includes nutritional programs and a "social adult day program." The senior centers, widely available in our local communities, are appropriate to higher functioning older retarded people. Their use of senior centers is also likely to be furthered by a relationship with a nondisabled volunteer senior companion. A fourth type of setting, the "social adult day program" is being designed for the "frail" elderly, those with physical and cognitive impairments. Examples of participation by retarded elders in each of these aging programs are found in the description of the integrative initiative in New York State (LePore & Janicki, 1990).

As an example, Jesse lives in a "developmental center" and, with the assistance of a nondisabled senior companion, attends a regular senior center three times a week. He is said now to be socializing for the first time; the response of the nondisabled participants at the center has been positive. It should be noted that negative attitudes of nondisabled seniors toward the inclusion of a retarded senior in their program can seriously restrict access. There also may be additional financial costs to the center (LePore & Janicki, 1990). In our county, careful preparation of the senior-center staff and of the seniors themselves has led to acceptance of those with retardation.

Resistance to seniors with retardation may be less evident in the social day program, because its participants are likely to be disabled, here from age-related cognitive and physical problems. Indeed, in this setting, the retarded elder is likely to be functioning at no lower or even at higher levels than his or her nonretarded peers and can assume "helping" relationships with them.

Mary, for example, resides in a community setting and also attends a senior center. Not more than mildly retarded, she has a group with whom she plays cards and joins in with other activities offered. Like Jesse, she also has a volunteer senior companion.

Lucille attends a social adult day program and, for the first time, finds herself assisting rather than receiving assistance. She looks after the clients with Alzheimer's disease because of their tendency to wander. She is helpful in many ways, including pushing wheelchairs of nonambulatory participants.

The role of "senior volunteer" or "senior companion" is not limited to nondisabled seniors. John is a retired senior volunteer who assists others in wheelchairs and helps the staff in decorating for parties, moving furniture, and cleaning up. Well-liked, he has become an integral part of the senior center.

Retirement Planning.   Prior to the 1980s, few retarded adults had the kind of work histories from which one could "retire." But with the tremendous growth of community vocational programs—sheltered work-shops and supported and nonsupported regular employment, retirement has become a meaningful prospect. But for the retarded worker, like his or her nonretarded counterpart, movement from a lifestyle dominated by work to one in which leisure predominates can be stressful. For the re-tarded employee, especially those in workshops, retirement may mean the loss of longtime social relationships, with staff as well as peers. Moreover, with the likelihood of a narrow range of interests, the older adult's identity may be tied closely to the role of "worker." Be that as it may, retirement is a reality and a major change in lifestyle for which one must prepare. Plan-ning for retirement involves first awareness of it as a reality; exploring, with assistance, the range of options, including part-time employment; and then exercising choice (Wadsworth, Harper, & McLeran, 1995). Just as the later school years can serve as preparation for the transition from student to worker, so should the planning process be viewed as facilitating transition from one lifestyle to another.

Apart from its possible economic consequences, the "social" effects of retirement also deserve attention. In the absence of planning, retirement may mean a solitary and sedentary life organized around the television set. With the loss of social relationships from one's day program, there may be loneliness and depression. In fact, complete disengagement from vocational activity is not the preferred choice for most retirees (Stroud & Sutton, 1988). They want to remain active but at a lesser level. For these, a mix of part-time employment and leisure activities becomes a desirable option (Stroud, Murphy, & Roberts, 1986). It also can include volunteering as in the case of John, the retired senior volunteer who assists at a senior center.

"Death" Education

By virtue of age, the older retarded adult is at heightened risk for experi-encing the loss of family members. Although an understanding of death is taken for granted in the general adult population, studies of retarded adults have found that many lack such understanding, especially of its per-manence (Lipe-Goodson & Goebel, 1983; Seltzer, 1989; Yanok & Beifus, 1993).

Chronological age seems to be most related to its understanding, ir-respective of disability. By about age 10 years, the normally develop-ing child has come to appreciate its two main features—universality and irreversibility. But substantial numbers of retarded adults lack this awareness and can benefit from educational efforts in this regard (Yanok & Beifus, 1993). The essential elements in the Yanok and Beifus curriculum are teaching (a) the distinction between the living and the inanimate; that all living things die; that death is permanent; that it happens, for example in fatal accidents and terminal illness; and (b) some of its "vocabulary," such as *funeral, cemetery, burial,* and *mourning.*

When should such training be offered? It is obviously appropriate following the death of a loved one; a more propitious time would be prior to such an event. Staff or caregivers could use the death of someone personally known to the individual or that of a famous person to introduce the topic. The intent is not to alarm but rather to use a death that may not represent a personal loss to explore this understanding. Discussion of the topic in a group also could serve to defuse alarm signals. By preparing for its eventuality, the retarded individual can better come to terms with loss, accept its permanence, and "move on" to other relationships, especially supportive ones.

The Elderly Caregiver

Reference has been made to older parents, especially the need to plan for the turning over of their child's care to someone else. A particularly comprehensive treatment of the needs of elderly parents is provided by Roberto (1993). Enabling elderly parents to continue caregiving responsibilities into their own senior years are such supports as respite care, home health aides, and recreational outlets for their adult child (Smith & Tobin, 1993). Although we note the services that older parents particularly value and the desirability of reducing the adult child's emotional dependency on now older parents, it also must be pointed out that if there are significant health problems in the parent, the dependency relationship may be reversed. The parent, for example, might become dependent on the child for physical assistance, a dependence that might lead to resistance to planning for the child's eventual out-of-home placement. Parents also value the assistance their child might provide with respect to household chores and, especially in old age, emotional support from loneliness following the loss of a spouse (Heller, Miller, & Factor, 1977). Moreover, the financial assistance tied to their child's disability may be valued as well.

Given the potential obstacles to planning, we should not be surprised that considerable numbers of retarded adults are left homeless each year because a surviving parent has died without making any plans for their future. But it is incumbent on case managers to acquaint elderly parents with this possibility.

☐ **Summary**

This chapter offers a characterization of the services and supports provided to adults with mental retardation. Introduced with a portrayal of Lizabeth, a woman with Down syndrome, it is intended to show the tremendous growth that is possible if individuals have access to meaningful developmental experiences, even if those experiences were not provided before the adult years. Chapter content is devoted to the educational needs of adults, those with both mild retardation and more severe degrees of impairment; appropriate vocational and day services, with particular attention to employment potential; recreational and leisure services—their assessment, "age-appropriateness," and choice, and the use of community resources; sexuality—a topic addressed in other chapters and dealt with here in greater depth, especially as it relates to the sexual activity of persons with more than mild retardation; residential services, with an emphasis on the range of community-based alternatives to the family home; family-support services, here to the older adult caregiver; and finally the needs and services available to the older adult with mental retardation.

Possible Discussion Questions

What does the life of Lizabeth tell us about the power of "expectations?"

In general, how might the adult with moderate to profound retardation differ in his or her "educational" needs in the postschool years?

What are some of the educational challenges posed by persons with profound retardation?

How does the relationship between Jane Wells and Mary Ann reveal something of Mary Ann's social skills difficulties? Are they potential contributors to purported higher rates of "loneliness" in adulthood? Would the senior author view the teaching of social skills as comparable to that of reading, for example? If not, how are they different? What are the implications for strengthening social skills in adults (and in children and youth)?

Are friendships between retarded and nonretarded adults possible? How about between two retarded adults?

What does the story of Johnny Rivas teach us about the importance of "work" in our culture? How is the experience of Johnny similar to that of Lizabeth? How do their stories reflect the importance of self-esteem and its ingredients?

Are persons with mental retardation capable of "regular" employment? What are some of the conditions necessary to achieving that outcome? How might "sheltered" employment constrain that possibility? How does "supported" employment circumvent the limited training opportunities in sheltered workshops? Within the range of job skills across the employment sector, what kind of job characteristics are most likely to fit the needs of workers with retardation?

Recreational activities are, by definition, self-initiated. Why then do we need to consider this aspect of life in persons with mental retardation? What is the relevance of "age-appropriateness" to the recreational and leisure interests of retarded adults? How do our local communities attempt to provide recreational services to persons with disabilities? Given the inherently nonintegrative nature of Special Olympics, how is its continuance justified?

What is your view of the policy statement regarding sexual behavior developed for community-based residential programs in Australia? What are some of the issues pertaining to protecting individuals with mental retardation from sexual exploitation and abuse? Is the "management" of the sexual life of another person possible? What qualities must be possessed by those who would undertake such a daunting task?

There has been a dramatic change in the settings chosen for out-of-home placement for persons with retardation. What was the rationale for the change? In what kinds of settings are adults currently being housed? What seem to be the benefits of residence in smaller and community-based settings? Are all nonintegrated residential programs undesirable? What about L'Arche?

How has the change in the institutional population and the comparable aging of the adult population affected access to health services? Apart from age, which segment of the retarded population has the highest health risk? Do we have evidence of grossly inadequate medical care? How can this be addressed most readily?

How does the transition of a retarded person from the role of "student" to that of "adult" pose potential stresses for caregivers? Given the popularity of respite care, is this an activity in which I would like to engage?

What kind of planning should be considered by aged caregivers?

As older retarded adults with a work or day-activity history reach retirement age, what kinds of transitional issues arise? What are alternatives to the "time-binding" nature of work in the older adult?

Why is there a need for death education in older adults? Should we wait until "old age" to explore their understanding of death?

CHAPTER

9

J. Gregory Olley

Maladaptive or "Challenging" Behavior: Its Nature and Treatment

☐ Overview

This is the first of two chapters on the most common severely maladaptive or "challenging" behaviors seen in mental retardation. With the exception of obsessive-compulsive disorder, the behavior problems presented in this chapter generally are not accorded formal psychiatric designations and, in this respect, differ from those to be presented in Chapter 10. Following a general introduction to the causes, diagnosis, and treatment of behavior problems in mental retardation, three groups of disorders are described—aggression, repetitive movement disorder (self-injurious and stereotyped behavior), and problematic sexual behavior. Each disorder is considered in terms of its nature, cause, and treatment.

☐ Behavior Problems and Mental Retardation

Maladaptive behavior is common in mental retardation. As indicated in Chapter 2, about one third of children, youth, and adults has behavioral difficulties that significantly affect their general adjustment.

Causes of Maladaptive Behavior

Current views of the causes of maladaptive behavior attribute it to at least three influences—biological, psychological, and social.

359

Biological

Biological causes generally exert their influence indirectly. They often are responsible for intellectual impairment that leaves the person with retardation more *vulnerable* to stress and less capable of dealing with it. Biology also can influence the nature of maladaptive behavior, as in the case of Lesch-Nyhan syndrome, a genetic disorder in which severe self-injury is a prominent feature.

Psychological

It is in this realm that the effects of mental retardation on personality are most evident. The personality model presented in Chapter 2 views individuals with mental retardation as having the same biological and psychological needs as the rest of us, and it is in the psychological domain that need gratification is most threatened. Driven both by our biology and experience, we seek *structure, self-esteem*, and *self-expression*. Self-esteem, in particular, is threatened by mental retardation. Threats to self-esteem, and to all other needs, evoke negative emotions, such as anxiety, fear, jealousy, anger, and depression, and it is in the "management" of these feelings that the disability of mental retardation exerts its influence. The mix of cognitive and personality characteristics associated with the disability leads to problems in the management of emotions that are expressed in behavioral difficulties. In effect, the behavior problems seen in retardation are expressions of immature and, hence, inappropriate ways of dealing with both the frustration of basic needs and the negative emotions it engenders. Exaggerated fears, extreme impulsiveness, and poorly controlled anger are all examples of how the disorder affects behavior. The ego mechanisms that we all apply to the control of our feelings are simply less effective in the individual with retardation. But problems are not limited solely to the "executive" or "control" aspects of behavior. At the "receptive" or "understanding" level, retardation can create difficulties by affecting our perception of the emotional intent of others (Rojahn, Rabold, & Schneider, 1985).

Social

It is the "social" domain that is a major contributor to the stresses created by mental retardation. Our culture values intelligence, success, beauty, athleticism, and talent. Individuals with disabilities commonly are hampered in their accomplishment of activities illustrative of these values. They are denigrated by our culture and are aware of how they are viewed.

The disability of mental retardation precludes normal school achievement and narrows the range of vocational choices. The child or youth with retardation, or other disabilities, is a target for teasing and bullying; the victim of such treatment recognizes the social rejection and reacts to it with the loss of self-esteem.

Mental retardation creates a greater likelihood of failing to meet the valued cultural roles in our society and thereby increases the risk of need frustration. In recent years, as indicated in previous chapters, major efforts have been undertaken to alter how we view persons with mental retardation (and other disabilities). Modification of societal attitudes toward disability will reduce the tensions that such attitudes produce on the disabled person and his or her family.

☐ Diagnosing Behavior Disorders

Severity of Cognitive Impairment and Behavior Disorders

The most common behavior disorders found in mental retardation are similar to those of the general population. Depression, for example, often is seen. At severer levels of retardation, however, we encounter behaviors that are relatively unusual: severe forms of aggression variously directed at the self (e.g., head banging), at others (e.g., hitting, kicking), and at objects (tearing of clothes, breaking windows). Such poorly controlled aggression is most prominent in persons with the more severe degrees of mental retardation, e.g. IQs below 50 (National Institutes of Health, 1991).

Overshadowing

Although the presence of mental health problems in mental retardation has long been recognized (Garfield, 1963), it was not until the 1980s that they were given much attention. Apart from the influence of retardation on the manifestation of behavior problems or psychiatric disorders, if both mental retardation and mental illness phenomena were present, it was the retardation that took diagnostic precedence. The psychiatric disorder or behavior problem was accorded less significance by mental health professionals because it was considered, *erroneously*, to be simply another manifestation of the cognitive disability. The effect of so-called "diagnostic overshadowing" (Reiss & Szyszko, 1983) was to slow the development of mental health services for a population now recognized as individuals with *both* mental retardation and psychiatric (behavioral) disorder—so-called dual diagnosis.

☐ Treatment Approaches

Three treatment approaches have had wide application—counseling and psychotherapy, behavioral treatment, and medical treatment.

Counseling and Psychotherapy

Among the "psychological" therapies, counseling has had greater application in retardation than psychotherapy. The latter traditionally has been associated with insight-based understanding, an understanding that requires good cognitive skills. Recalling the problems that persons with retardation have in generalizing, we can recognize that they would have difficulty in discerning *patterns* of behavior, that is, similar behavior in different contexts. Such recognition is one of the central features of psychotherapy. Counseling, as a therapeutic technique, is more direct in its nature and has been employed commonly in the educational and vocational spheres as well as to behavioral problems not generally regarded as "psychiatric" (Szymanski, 1980).

Reiss (1994b) has indicated the kinds of adaptations necessary to successful counseling in mental retardation. Emphasis is placed on clarity of language, structure and directiveness, mutually established realistic goals, a positive and supportive counselor stance, and counselor flexibility.

Clarification of the counselor's role vis-à-vis the client with retardation is of special concern. The counselor may be the client's greatest source of attention and support and may come to be viewed primarily as a "friend." Understanding by the client of the distinction between "counselor" and "friend" is probably limited to those with not more than mild retardation.

One of the special features of counseling persons with mental retardation is teaching them to be attentive to their own behaviors, that is, to learn to identify and describe their own emotional states. The counselor also wants to assist the client to gain a better understanding of his or her disability, the "cans" as well as the "cannots"; to improve communication skills; to teach decision-making and problem solving; and, above all, to help the client recognize that behavior has consequences for *oneself* as well as for others.

Counseling takes various forms, depending on the client's age and the severity of the disability. It may be in an individual or group format. In group counseling, for example, a combination of discussion and role playing can make issues concrete and understandable. The client can be encouraged to practice reporting events and emotions by recording daily experiences associated with feelings of happiness or unhappiness. This helps to generalize the counseling experience to daily life. For children, of course, play therapy offers a comfortable format.

Although research on the effectiveness of counseling in mental retardation is limited and evidence of its effectiveness modest, Reiss (1994b) views it as beneficial for some individuals. The research evidence indicates that it can be of assistance by providing a supportive environment in which to practice positive approaches to interpersonal relationships and problem solving.

Behavioral

A Rationale

Behavioral treatment, *applied behavior analysis*, is the most widely used strategy for behavior problems in mental retardation. As described in Chapter 6, it also has had wide application in the educational domain. An introduction to applied behavior analysis is now offered, to be followed by examples of its application to specific behavior problems.

Applied behavior analysis strategy rests on the assumption that *behavior is governed by its consequences*. Consequences may increase the future occurrence of a behavior (*reinforcing* consequences) or reduce it (*punishing* consequences). Consequences also may have no effect on a particular behavior. Applied behavior analysis strategy ultimately reflects an appreciation of our basic needs, that is, that we are governed by the wish to obtain pleasurable consequences (fulfill needs) and to avoid painful ones (not experience need frustration).

The motivating aspect of the pleasure-pain principle is well understood; rewards and penalties are its "coin." If we ask ourselves why we seek out some activities and avoid others, the answers lie in the pleasure-pain principle.

Implementing Applied Behavior Analysis

Although the principles of applied behavior analysis are self-evident, their implementation in treatment programs is more complex. As applied to educational or behavioral objectives, they require specifying the behavior to be increased or decreased in an objective or measurable manner, determining how changes in the target behavior will be measured, choosing potential reinforcers (consequences), specifying the conditions (contingencies) under which the desired behavior will be reinforced (rewarded) and the unwanted behavior punished (penalized), ensuring that these procedures are faithfully carried out (easier said than done!), determining whether the contingencies are affecting the target behavior, and revising contingencies of reinforcement and punishment as appropriate.

The Role of the Environment in Influencing Behavior

Apart from the effects of the systematic use of contingencies of reinforcement and punishment, the environment or physical context within which behavior occurs itself can affect behavior. Environmental factors that appear to trigger unwanted behavior are called *antecedents*. The institutional environments that scandalized the nation and led to the deinstitutionalization movement fostered all manner of aberrant behavior. Some sense of the environment in such settings prior to the changes in recent decades is conveyed in a description of a unit for girls aged 6 to 12 years with profound retardation.

> None of the girls could dress themselves . . . a few could feed themselves and were toilet trained. [They] manifested such behavior as: minimal response to stimuli, lying on the floor, . . . stereotypies, preoccupation with minutiae, smearing of feces, masturbation, overt aggression, and self-destructive biting, scratching, hair-pulling, and head banging. [The only omission is the smell!] (Gorton & Hollis, 1965, p. 16)

Applied Behavior Analysis as the "ABC" Approach

Applied behavior analysis often is dubbed the "ABC" approach because it considers antecedents, behavior, and consequences. It is *preventive* in that it tries to alter the antecedents of unwanted behavior, and it leads to a better understanding of the problem behavior because it seeks to understand its purpose or function. The unwanted behavior is presumed to serve some reinforcing function for its practitioner. The process of determining the purpose of an unwanted behavior is called the *functional analysis of behavior*.

Behavioral Consequences: Contingencies of Reinforcement

Positive Reinforcement.   Any consequence that strengthens a behavior is called a "reinforcer." "Positive reinforcement" refers to the strengthening of a behavior by linking its occurrence to a desired object or event (a reward). Positively reinforcing consequences fall into five categories—material reinforcers (e.g., object or food), activities (e.g., play or television), social reinforcers (e.g., praise and desired attention), information feedback (e.g., report cards, although they are not always reinforcing!), and symbolic reinforcers (e.g., gold stars or a trophy). Because reward preferences vary for each of us, individualizing reinforcers is crucial to their effectiveness.

Universality of Reward Systems. Applied behavior analysis is not unique in its stress on positive consequences to encourage desired ends. As we attempt to influence the behavior of others, we recognize that incentives (motivators) are a powerful ally. Behavioral programs are simply more explicit and systematic in their use. Some educational and human services workers may resist the use of rewards because they are perceived as "bribes." These workers may feel that "we were expected to work in school or follow parental instructions without the inducement of rewards, so everyone should be treated in that way." But even a cursory consideration of our own childhood, and of the personality model presented in Chapter 2, makes clear that our response to parents and teachers was not made in an incentive-free vacuum. The incentives *were* and *are* there, although not necessarily explicitly stated. The need for intimacy, for example, was both nurtured and fulfilled through parental love. Throughout our lives we continue to need experiences of intimacy, and we seek approval from those whose esteem we value—teachers, peers, employers, people in authority, and, always, our parents. Together with intimacy, experiences that fulfill our needs for success and autonomy all feed our extraordinary need for self-esteem. For the child, doing well in school can be a powerful means of winning parental and teacher approval (intimacy) as well as affirming a sense of personal competence (success). In our vocational lives, the possibility of job promotion and accompanying wage increases as well as greater prestige create strong incentives. We too, then, also are locked into a reward system.

But even the use of the word "bribe" in this context is inappropriate. A bribe is an incentive to do something we ought *not* to do. It is an inducement to *violate* some societal standard. But the use of rewards in applied behavior analysis is intended to provide an incentive to do what we *ought* to do. Admittedly, the conscious and conspicuous dispensing of rewards cannot be a permanent basis for maintaining desired behavior. Rather is it an *encouragement* to move in the desired direction. Whether the reinforced behavior is maintained depends on whether its "natural consequences" are strong enough to be ongoing reinforcers.

Negative Consequences (Punishment). In behavioral psychology, *punishment* refers to any consequence that has the effect of reducing the unwanted behavior. It is commonly associated with experiences that we would call painful or unpleasant. Nonetheless, if contingent consequences do not result in a reduction in the behavior, they are not regarded as punishment. If a child is paddled for breaking family rules but continues to do so in spite of the paddling, we can conclude that paddling is not viable deterrent *for this child*. If a jail sentence does not deter crime, it is not punishment *for that individual*.

Although a particular consequence, such as paddling or spanking, may weaken the unwanted behavior, the systematic use of punishment as a means of modifying behavior is fraught with difficulties. Punishment can create resentment and anger, especially if it is viewed as unjust, and can be expected to motivate its recipient to find ways of continuing the unwanted behavior without being punished. Positive methods of influencing behavior through the use of rewards are the foundation of modern treatment programs. Although punishment may be a necessary adjunct, its use must be judicious.

Two forms of punishment that have had general acceptance are "overcorrection" and "time out." *Overcorrection* is intended to be an "educative" consequence. If a child forgets to take the trash out of her room and her parents insist that she go back and do it, that is *correction*. If the child is required to remove trash from every room in the house, that is *overcorrection*! The procedure requires the individual to repeat the desired behavior several times (Foxx & Azrin, 1973). *Time out* is probably the most common form of punishment. It really refers to *a temporary loss of the opportunity for positive reinforcement*. Thus, if a child is playing and violates a rule, such as striking another child, the child's play activity may be instantly interrupted. The child is required to take "time out" from play. The key to the effectiveness of time out is that the activity interfered with is one that the child desires, one that is reinforcing. Too often, misbehavior occurs in settings that are not truly reinforcing, and their discontinuation may be viewed by the child as rewarding rather than punishing! This only leads to more misbehavior!

Negative Reinforcement.   Often confused with punishment because of the adjective "negative" (an unfortunate choice by early workers in the field), negative reinforcement actually refers to a desired contingency, the *termination* of an unpleasant state. Any consequence that frees us from an unwanted condition illustrates negative reinforcement, such as taking an aspirin to stop a headache. This behavioral mechanism is much in evidence in so-called "escape" behavior. The child with mental retardation who, for example, is experiencing much frustration in a learning situation may "act up" and, as a consequence, have the learning situation terminated. In effect, the child escapes from an unwanted experience by misbehaving. We do not want to reward children for misbehaving, but our response to such behavior may have that unintended effect!

Extinction.   Extinction refers to the deliberate ignoring of unwanted behavior and is most useful in settings in which "attention" is what the individual seeks. Bedtime disturbances in infancy are a common example of attention-getting behavior. Although the child has been put to sleep and the parents have retired, the infant does not immediately accept separation, and crying ensues. Crying brings *attention* from the parents, who then spend additional time with the child. In effect, the child's crying has been reinforced. But if parents adhere to a bedtime schedule, the crying eventually ceases because it does not produce the attention it sought. It is through such experiences that the child becomes "socialized." The child learns that needs cannot always be met on the child's terms. In the case of the child with retardation, or with any other disability, parents are likely to have more difficulty exercising such discipline because the child's disability evokes sympathy. But the disabled child, no less than the nondisabled one, needs to *learn* to defer need gratification. Parents who fail to teach this lesson become victims of the tyranny of their child's needs.

Because the effects of extinction are gradual rather than instant, as might be true of punishment, and the behavior lingers, extinction cannot be used with behavior that is dangerous. One cannot ignore aggression or fire setting, for example! In general, extinction is seldom used alone; rather it is part of a combined treatment approach in which unwanted behavior leads to extinction, and desired and adaptive behavior is reinforced.

Determining the Purpose or Function of a Given Behavior

Wishing to avoid the need for punishment and simultaneously seeking to encourage desired behavior, "positive" treatment approaches seek to discover the functions or purpose that the unwanted behavior serves. Thus the initial step in the behavioral approach is to determine the consequences or effects that the unwanted behavior typically evokes. If we know the consequence that strengthens or maintains (reinforces) the inappropriate behavior, a treatment program can be designed in which that consequence is offered only for appropriate or desired behavior (Iwata, Vollmer, Zarcone, & Rodgers, 1993). The following example illustrates the behavioral approach to maladaptive behavior, seeking to understand its cause in terms of both antecedents and consequences.

Susan often was restless and uncooperative in school in the afternoon. She refused to follow directions and sometimes threw violent temper tantrums. The teacher's response was to call Susan's mother and have her removed from the class and taken home. A behavioral analysis indicated that the tantrums (unwanted behavior) usually occurred in the afternoon when Susan was tired and when the teacher made requests that Susan found difficult to satisfy (antecedents).

The teacher's requests for removal allowed Susan to avoid the difficult task (consequence). Because the tantrums led to Susan's avoidance or escape from an unwanted situation, the tantrums were strengthened (reinforced).

An applied behavior analysis approach to this problem would focus on replacing the tantrums with appropriate classroom behavior. Susan would be instructed to communicate the need for a break if she gets tired in the afternoon. The teacher, for her part, might offer the break and, as appropriate, modify the classroom demands in the afternoon. If the tantrums were triggered by expected failure and frustration with math problems, for example, math might be offered at a time when Susan has more energy. It is not a matter of "surrendering" to Susan's whims but rather finding the conditions under which the teacher's educational goals can be achieved most readily. Numerous examples of this treatment approach are presented subsequently in the chapter as we consider specific behavior problems.

Medical Treatment

Psychotropic Drugs

The use of psychotropic drugs in the treatment of behavior disorders followed the discovery that they could reduce anxiety, alter moods, and modify psychotic symptoms. They were widely applied to behavior problems in mental retardation, initially in institutional settings and often as a substitute for adequate programming. Often employed only to suppress maladaptive behavior, in the absence of appropriate programming, they were viewed as "chemical straitjackets." Psychotropic drugs also frequently were used indiscriminately and without proper supervision. This came to be seen as a psychiatric scandal and, in recent years, has been much reduced (Aman, Sarphare, & Burrow, 1995; Hill, Balow, & Bruininks, 1985). A 1994 statewide study of all persons in the developmental-disabilities service system in Oklahoma found one third (33%) receiving psychotropic drugs. Antipsychotic drugs were the most commonly prescribed and were chiefly employed in intermediate care facilities and nursing homes, 43% and 33%, respectively, in contrast to much smaller rates of about 15% in group homes and in supported living settings. The higher rates in the intermediate care facilities and nursing homes may relate in part to the nature of the population they serve (Spreat, Conroy, & Jones, 1987). Ideally, psychotropic drugs should be just one component of a treatment program that offers the entire gamut of therapeutic approaches—behavioral, educational, social, and so forth. As a treatment adjunct, they can be extremely valuable and in certain disorders, such as major depression, essential. Let us now review the most commonly used psychotropic drugs and their application.

Antipsychotic Drugs

Also known as *neuroleptics* or "major tranquilizers," these antipsychotic drugs include chlorpromazine (Largactil, Thorazine), thioridazine (Mellaril), and haloperidol (Haldol, Serenace). Although effective against hallucinations and delusions in psychoses, in mental retardation they have been used chiefly to control such behavior as aggression, self-injury, property destruction, and overactivity. Studies of their effectiveness have shown mixed results (Aman, 1989; Aman & Singh, 1991).

Although the goal of treatment is to achieve greater participation in daily life, antipsychotic drugs may suppress *all* behavior, adaptive as well as maladaptive, producing states of general sedation or lethargy. Moreover, their long-term use can lead to serious neurological side effects, such as tardive dyskinesia, a movement disorder (Gualtieri & Hawk, 1980).

Antipsychotic drugs that affect the neurotransmitter dopamine have shown promise in the reduction of self-injury, one of the more serious maladaptive behaviors seen in retardation. They do, however, require close monitoring for side effects. These drugs include fluphenazine (Prolixin) (Gualtieri & Schroeder, 1989) and clozapine (Clozaril) (Hammock, Schroeder, & Levine, 1995).

Anticonvulsant Drugs

These are medications used in epilepsy, a neurological disorder present in about one third (35%) of persons with mental retardation (Aman & Singh, 1991) (see Chapter 4). In addition to controlling seizures, these drugs also can reduce some maladaptive behavior. Carbamazepine (Tegretol) and phenytoin (Dilantin), in particular, have been employed to control "explosive behavior" in adults (Aman & Singh, 1991; Evans, Aman, & Gualtieri, 1989). As with the use of antipsychotics to reduce behavior problems, research on their effectiveness is inconclusive.

Stimulant Drugs

These are medications widely used to treat problems of attention and hyperactivity in nonretarded children. Beneficial effects are found in improved attention (less distractibility), reduced motor restlessness, and greater participation in school activities. Commonly used are methylphenidate (Ritalin), dextroamphetamine (Dexedrine), amphetamine (Adderall), and magnesium pemoline (Cylert). They appear to be less effective in mental retardation, especially in those with more than mild impairment. They seldom are helpful in individuals with severe or profound retardation or as a treatment for stereotyped behavior (Aman, 1989).

Antidepressants and Mood Stabilizers

These mood-altering drugs appear to be equally effective in persons with and without mental retardation. The symptoms of depression—feelings of sadness and hopelessness, sleep difficulties, and weight change—also are seen in retardation. The most common antidepressants are the "tricyclic" group—imipramine (Tofranil), desipramine (Norpramin), nortriptyline (Pamelor), clomipramine (Anafranil), and selective serotonin reuptake inhibitors such as fluoxetine (Prozac) and paroxetine (Paxil).

Although research on antidepressants and mood stabilizers is limited, there has been dramatic increase in the use of Prozac and related drugs in mental retardation. Although classified as antidepressants, these drugs also have been effective in treating both repetitive movement and anxiety disorders in persons with retardation. One of the tricyclics, imipramine, has been useful in treating bed wetting in retardation, but its toxicity requires great caution (Gualtieri, 1989).

Lithium carbonate is another widely used drug. It is the preferred medication for bipolar disorder—formerly called *manic-depressive illness*. In persons with retardation it appears to be useful in the treatment of bipolar disorder and severe depression and also has been helpful in some instances of hyperactivity, aggression, and self-injury (Aman & Singh, 1991; Gualtieri, 1989).

Antianxiety Drugs

Antianxiety drugs (anxiolytics) are used to treat both anxiety and anxious-withdrawn behavior, the latter often coexisting with depression. Anxiety is treated with benzodiazepines, a group of drugs that include diazepam (Valium) and chlorodiazepoxide (Librium). These medications also are used for insomnia, as they have a calming effect and induce sleep. In mental retardation, they often are employed to ease agitated and disruptive behavior rather than for anxiety, as such (Fahs, 1989), but their usefulness is unproven and they may even worsen the behavior (Aman & Singh, 1991).

A newer type of antianxiety medication, buspirone (Buspar), may be more effective than the benzodiazepines and also have fewer side effects. There is some research showing its usefulness in reducing anxiety and aggression in individuals with mental retardation (Hillbrand, 1995).

☐ Severe Maladaptive or Challenging Behaviors and Their Treatment

The following sections offer descriptions of the most common forms of severe maladaptive behavior seen in mental retardation, their causes, and treatment. As is evident, a comprehensive treatment approach incorporates biological, psychological, and social elements.

Aggression

Nature

Aggression takes various forms. It may be expressed orally (threats, insults, swearing) or physically (hitting, biting, kicking). It may be directed toward the environment (property destruction) toward others or toward oneself. It is also a major feature of such psychiatric disorders as antisocial personality in adults and conduct disorder in children. Significant aggression cannot be ignored and results in restrictions of personal freedom. Indeed, aggression is the most common cause of removal from community residential settings and placement in institutional ones.

Major patterns of aggression are found in from 10% to 28% of individuals with retardation (Reid & Parsons, 1992). It is more prevalent in males, in adolescents and young adults rather than in children, and in those with severer degrees of retardation.

> Frank is a 28-year-old man who has lived in institutions and in highly restrictive settings most of his life. His parents have remained very involved in his care but because of his violent outbursts of aggression he has been unable to remain in the family home. His aggression consists of striking others with an open hand and doing it without warning. His behavior has limited all aspects of his life. It has affected where he lives, his friendships, his education, and his work. With extensive medical and behavioral assistance he is now being served in community settings, although safety concerns remain.

Causes

Within the personality framework presented in Chapter 2, aggression is viewed as a response to the frustration of basic needs, both biological and psychological. With unmet needs creating negative emotions, it is the emotion of anger that chiefly fuels aggression.

Biological factors themselves may contribute to aggression by heightening levels of irritability. Thus exposure to extreme temperatures, crowding, or noise can heighten irritability. Aggression may also be associated with physical pain, with seizures (as in temporal lobe or partial complex seizures), and as a side effect of medication.

In the psychological realm, aggression can result from chronic frustration of self-esteem and its chief ingredients—intimacy, success, and autonomy. Mental retardation appears to particularly threaten our need for intimacy, as individuals with this disability commonly experience rejection and social isolation. The need for social contact and affection figure prominently in personality research in retardation (Zigler & Burak, 1989).

Retardation also can be expected to jeopardize gratification of our need for success. All of us are discomforted by awareness of our inadequacies—it is inherent in being human. Experiences of failure are inevitable but with reasonably healthy resources (capacities); they're more than compensated for by experiences of success, of "can do." But disability of whatever kind impedes the capacity to be successful in at least some of the valued roles in our culture. Certainly, retardation renders the individual more vulnerable to the frustrations associated with mental and even physical challenges. The effect is heightened irritability and, if chronic, leads to both a withdrawal from situations in which failure is expected and a lack of willingness to persist at tasks at which some effort is required. The earlier description of Susan reveals a student who was frustrated by problems in math and who reacted with aggression in the form of temper tantrums.

The third ingredient of self-esteem, autonomy, also can be a source of frustration in retardation. We commonly hear of the adolescent with retardation who resents the freedom and autonomy granted to younger nondisabled siblings. More generally, adolescent rebellion, whether in the retarded or nonretarded child, illustrates a common reaction to the ambivalent status of youth in our society—neither child nor adult. Adolescent rebellion represents aggression in the service of achieving greater control of one's life, greater autonomy.

As frequently noted, the implication of the personality model is that chronic need deprivation leads to the persistent experience of unpleasant emotional states, and it is their forms of expression that constitute "maladaptive" forms of behavior. The management of aggression, as well as other behavior fueled by need frustration, begins with recognition of the necessity of providing experiences that meet basic needs.

Treatment

Medical. Biological or medical treatments may involve the relief of pain (e.g., dental, menstrual, constipation, medication side effects), preventive measures such as diet and exercise, and psychotropic drugs. As indicated earlier, antipsychotic drugs have been used widely in retardation to control aggression, but they also can create a general state of lethargy and, with long-term use, have serious neurological side effects (e.g., tardive dyskinesia). The biological realm also may cause aggressive episodes that occur without apparent provocation (antecedents). Aggression here may be manifestations of atypical seizures, of panic attacks (a type of anxiety disorder), and of posttraumatic stress disorder (also an anxiety disorder).

Behavioral.   Aggression, of course, can present genuine danger. Those who provide services to individuals with aggressive histories must have a strategy for immediate threats (a crisis plan) as well as a long-term plan for replacing the aggressive behavior with more adaptive ways of coping. A good example of a *crisis treatment program* is that of the Strong Center for Developmental Disabilities at the University of Rochester (Davidson et al., 1995). Available 24 hours a day, it offers behavioral intervention through a multidisciplinary team, inpatient services, training to service providers to prevent recurrence, respite care, and case management. The program offers a safe environment for the aggressive individual and a staff skilled in preventing future episodes.

But access to quality crisis care is not commonplace and, too often, the crisis leads to inappropriate placement in a state psychiatric hospital, a setting not designed to serve persons with retardation. The dearth of community-based crisis programs fosters needless institutionalization and an excessive reliance on psychotropic drugs. In several states, class action lawsuits have sought to require the creation of community-based mental health services for this population, including crisis intervention.

Assessment.   Assuming that a crisis can be safely managed, the next step in treatment is to carry out a *behavioral assessment*. (The remainder of this section provides a *strategy* for dealing with aggression). Assessment is designed to identify both causative factors and appropriate treatment. It is conducted through an analysis of the behavior problem—a consideration of each of the elements of the ABC treatment strategy—antecedents, behavior, and consequences.

Our first consideration is the nature of the aggression. What form does it take? Is it verbal or physical? Does it occur as a brief discrete event or is it continuous, as in a tantrum? If it is continuous, what is its duration, frequency, and severity?

The second step in assessment is identifying antecedents. Under what conditions is the aggression most likely to occur? Antecedents are infinite in possibility. They may include an activity, such as homework; a change in routine; a negative social experience; and so forth. An effective treatment program includes a daily schedule that seeks to maximize antecedents associated with desirable behavior and minimize those associated with aggression. Meaningful involvement of the individual in the planning of that daily routine is likely to further reduce the risk of aggression. This feeds the esteem-building ingredient—autonomy.

The third consideration in our behavioral analysis is consequences. What consequences typically follow the aggression? Susan's temper tantrums were reinforced by her getting what she wanted, avoidance of a painful class situation, an example of negative reinforcement. Aggression also may serve a communicative function. If retardation is severe or profound and the individual lacks the means of directly communicating his or her wants, aggression may accomplish that purpose.

Treatment Based on Behavioral Assessment. Based on a functional analysis of the aggression, a treatment program might involve changes (a) in antecedents (e.g., reducing crowding), (b) in the task itself during which aggression occurs (e.g., modifying the learning situation as in the case of Susan), and (c) in the consequences (in the case of Susan, rewarding appropriate classroom work and not its avoidance).

These three elements clearly are related. A treatment strategy incorporating antecedents requires changing them. Moreover, if aggression tends to occur during periods in which there are no planned activities, treatment might involve offering at that time activities that the individual prefers. And as in the case of Susan, aggression can occur if tasks are too difficult, too novel, or too familiar. Strategy b involves a change in the activity ongoing at the time of aggression.

If, after considering antecedents and activities, strategies a and b, further treatment is needed, strategy c comes into play. Are the typical consequences of aggression reinforcing (rewarding)? The functional analysis may reveal that the aggression led to escape or avoidance (e.g., Susan), or to attention. The treatment plan *must* involve a change in the consequences of aggression, and allow for the achievement of the same purpose or function through appropriate behavior. If, for example, hitting leads to attention, even in the form of a reprimand, a treatment strategy would involve limiting attention in response to aggression and offering it instead as a reward for appropriate behavior. The treatment plan might include a variety of activities that encourage desired behavior or its actual prompting, as a means of granting the sought-after attention. In the language domain, treatment may take the form of teaching an unambiguous form of communication such as nodding "yes" or "no" to requests for understanding.

If the aggression leads to escape and avoidance of activities or demands (negative reinforcement), treatment should teach adaptive ways of requesting a break from them. Some activities, of course, cannot be avoided or postponed for very long (e.g., hygiene and medical care). Here, the activity should be made as pleasant as possible, and some *choice* should be offered. If in reality there can be no choice, aspects of the activity could be modified to provide such opportunity (Dyer, Dunlap, & Winterling, 1990). Research has shown that people with retardation are more likely to undertake even unwanted activities if they are presented as *choices* (Vaughn & Horner, 1997). Choice, the exercise of autonomy, is a central element in current mental retardation services; this is stressed in Chapter 6. We take for granted our right, within limits, to exercise choice with regard to the food we eat, the clothing we wear, our activities, our companions, and how we spend our leisure hours. If the right of choice is granted to persons with retardation, it recognizes their dignity as human beings and their psychological need for autonomy.

In some cases, aggression may be unpredictable. Here, environmental factors may not be causative. Instead, the aggression may have a biological root, such as the previously mentioned seizures or the biological changes associated with illness. Under these circumstances coordination with a physician is important. The behavioral treatment component might involve an enrichment of the environment by providing preferred activities, offering reinforcing events during periods free of aggression, interrupting the aggression and safely redirecting the individual to another activity, or moving the person to an area designated for relaxation or "calming down" (Reid & Parsons, 1992). In connection with the last-mentioned, relaxation itself can be taught as a means of strengthening self-control and reducing aggression. Although requiring frequent practice, relaxation has been shown to be effective in reducing aggression as well as other impulsive and disruptive behavior (Baron, Groden & Cautela, 1988).

The issue of safety is, of course, always a concern with aggression, especially if it can be severe in nature. In addition to the use of crisis treatment programs, direct-care staff must be trained in methods of physical contact that assures safety for all.

We have described Frank as a 28-year-old male whose aggressive outbursts had led to long-term institutional placement. It will be recalled that he would strike with an open hand and without warning. Careful observation revealed that his hitting was not truly random. Moved to a new and attractive home, he would become upset in the basement recreation room. Review of his history revealed that the basement had been used in his previous residence as the place to which he was sent for punishment! His hitting diminished as opportunities for varied forms of reinforcement were increased and as his routine became more familiar (increased structure). He had wider opportunities to participate in community activities, and he was given greater choice in all aspects of his life.

Introducing choice was difficult; his behavior, obviously, had minimized such opportunities. He did not understand that he could control events in his life. He was severely retarded, and it took several months to teach him that his response to a question involving choice actually determined what happened. He loved coffee, and if offered the choice between coffee and something he disliked, he learned to request coffee. Eventually, choices became available in nearly all aspects of his life. His participation in a variety of activities increased, and his aggression slowly diminished.

Repetitive Movement Disorders

Commonly Seen Repetitive Movements

In addition to aggression, repetitive movement disorders are common in mental retardation, especially in those with severe and profound impairment. Repetitive movement disorders have been characterized as either "naturally occurring" or "drug-induced" (Rosenquist & Bodfish, 1997). The naturally occurring ones include stereotyped movements (stereotypies), self-injury, self-restraint, compulsions, and tics. The drug-induced ones are side effects of neuroleptic (antipsychotic) medication and include dyskinesia and akathisia (Table 9.1).

The Rosenquist-Bodfish classification system adds precision to the description of a variety of commonly seen behaviors, such as skin picking and eye rubbing, and recognizes physiological and behavioral concomitants. As many as half of those with mental retardation and with other developmental disabilities, as well, exhibit repetitive movement disorders (Rosenquist & Bodfish, 1997), and both their frequency and variety argue for distinguishing between those that interfere with adaptive behavior and those that do not. The former merit treatment; the latter can be viewed as simply odd or idiosyncratic in nature.

TABLE 9.1. Repetitive movement disorders

	Specific Features	Examples
Naturally occurring		
Self-injury	Directed toward the self and with the potential of causing physical injury	Head-banging, biting and scratching oneself
Stereotypy	Rhythmic and patterned movement	Body rocking, object manipulation
Self-restraint	Maintaining a particular body position to prevent self-injury	Hands and arms wrapped in clothing by the person
Compulsion	Follows rule, purposeful	Ordering, cleaning, closing, opening
Tic	Brief, rapid, sudden	Facial or shoulder twitch, grunt, spit
Drug-induced		
Dyskinesia	Nonrhythmic, slow or rapid	Generally mouth movements
Akathisia	Motor restlessness, fidgety	Marching in place, foot-to-foot rocking

The physiological link among these movement disorders, either naturally occurring or drug-induced, is a similar origin in the brain, specifically a dysfunction in the basal ganglia, a subortical structure involved in both movement and the regulation of emotions (Bodfish & Madison, 1993; Rapoport, 1991).

At the behavioral level, multiple forms of the disorder tend to occur in the same individual. In particular, stereotyped behavior, self-injury, and compulsive behavior commonly exist as a group (Bodfish et al., 1995).

We now describe in some detail each of these three repetitive movement disorders, their causes, and their treatment.

Self-injury

Certainly one of the most remarkable of the repetitive movement disorders, self-injurious behavior (SIB) refers to forms of self-harm that produce physical injury to the body (Tate & Baroff, 1966). SIB tends to be invariant in its expression, occurring the same way each time. It is this highly predictable pattern that distinguishes it from the self-mutilative and suicidal behaviors associated with mental illness.

Of the many forms of SIB, the most common are head banging, using the hand, the fist, or an object; striking other parts of the body; self-biting (typically hand biting; self-biting is a prominent feature of the genetic disorder Lesch-Nyhan syndrome; see Chapter 3); self-scratching or pinching; placing objects or fingers in body orifices (e.g., eye gouging); air swallowing (creating an extended abdomen—"aerophagia"); pulling out one's hair (trichotillomania); drinking extreme amounts of liquids (e.g., more than 3 L/d); and teeth grinding (bruxism) (Rojahn, Polster, Mulick, & Wisniewski, 1989). More than half of persons who engage in SIB exhibit multiple forms.

Some eating disorders also have been considered forms of self-injury— pica (mouthing and eating of inedibles) and self-induced vomiting and rumination (swallowing of regurgitated food). Self-injurious behavior can pose serious health hazards: Head banging can lead to retinal detachment and blindness; pica may cause serious digestive disorders.

Prevalence. Although often associated with mental retardation and autism, SIB is still a relatively rare disorder, found in only about 10% to 15% of the retarded population (Iwata & Rogers, 1992). Within mental retardation, SIB and all other forms of repetitive movement disorder occur with greater frequency at the severer levels of impairment. According to the degree of retardation, its prevalence is 2% in mild, 3% in moderate, 7% in severe, and 17% in profound (Jacobson, 1982). It also is observed more often in adolescents and young adults than in young children or in the elderly (Rojahn, 1995). SIB is especially prominent in persons whose retardation is associated also with autism, visual and hearing loss, little language ability, seizures, other movement disorders, and frank psychiatric illness (Nihira, Price-Williams, & White, 1988; Schroeder, 1991). Females show more varied forms and higher frequencies of biting and scratching than males. SIB in males, however, tends to be of greater concern because it is more likely to be expressed in head banging (Baumeister, 1991).

Some sense of the extraordinary nature of self-injury is found in the description of 18-year-old Susie (Baroff, 1986; Tate, 1972). She was admitted to an institution at age 11 years, battered and bruised; her injuries were attributed to head banging, and within hours of admission, she was restrained to protect her. During the next 7.5 *years*, she remained restrained in bed, although also receiving drug therapy, physical therapy, and concerned care. All treatment efforts were without avail. She was under 24-hour restraint with the exception of being briefly removed from the bed each day for a bath. Even this was hazardous, as she often had to be held by several attendants to prevent her from banging her head against the bathtub. Physically, Susie was normal in size, had good hearing, but was blind, possibly because of her head banging. She could say a few single words and hum portions of several tunes. She had an extensive repertoire of self-injury, seemingly only limited by her degree of physical freedom.

Behavioral treatment initially involved the freeing of one leg; she typically was restrained in bed, spread-eagle fashion on her back. If her leg was released from restraints, Susie kicked herself and any hard object in reach. She kicked the side of the bed, her other leg and foot, and her groin. During an initial 7-hour, 33-minute observation period during which her right leg was padded to minimize injury and her left leg was free, she kicked 5866 times!

Although kicking was a highly predictable behavior, its rate and topography varied. On some days, almost all kicks were heel to knee and at a steady rate. At other times, Susie kicked in bursts with pauses of several minutes. Some kicks were bone-jarring and produced bleeding, even if the kicked leg was padded with 4-inch-thick polyurethane foam!

Occasionally, the kicks were playfully light and accompanied by laughter. In a few instances, when she was restrained loosely and one leg was free, she would simultaneously move her head forward and her knee up, essentially "kneeing" her face and hand. Several hematomas were the consequence. If an arm was released from restraints, Susie hit her face and head repeatedly with her fist. One morning her right eye was closed by the swelling of the surrounding tissue, and blood oozed from cuts around the eye. She had worked her right hand free of the restraining cuffs during the night.

Even if fully restrained and with leather cuffs on her ankles and wrists, Susie was able to inflict damage. She bit the inside of her cheeks, cut her fingers with her fingernails, and banged her head against her shoulders. The shoulder damage was controlled by having her wear a 2-inch-thick polyurethane foam collar. The cutting and gouging of her fingers caused large open sores around her fingernails but could be managed by taping her fingers and by taping cotton gloves on her hands. Fortunately she did not often bite the inside of her cheeks; we never devised a method of controlling this activity. The biting had once been a serious problem and, when Susie was 14 years old, all of her teeth except her molars were removed as a last resort to stop self-biting. Before her teeth were extracted she had severely lacerated her shoulders and cut through her lower lip.

Clearly, Susie had a highly developed repertoire of self-injury. If her behavioral capacities included any normal behaviors besides the verbal ones, they were effectively masked by self-injury. If free to respond, Susie either injured herself or remained nearly motionless.

Biological Causes and Treatment of Self-Injury.

Except for the sex-linked recessive disorder Lesch-Nyhan syndrome, described in Chapter 3, no other organic disorder is particularly associated with self-injury, nor is the biological action leading to SIB understood. Recent research, however, has indicated two biochemical mechanisms that could explain it. These are *endorphins* and *neurotransmitters*.

Endorphins. In some instances, self-injury results in the release of brain chemicals (endorphins) that are associated with addiction and an elevated mood state (euphoria). These natural opiates have the effect of relieving pain and producing euphoria. It is hypothesized that self-injury leads to a state of addiction caused by the release of these natural opiates. In behavioral terms, self-injury is reinforced by endorphin release and the resulting "high" (Sandman & Hedrick, 1995; Thompson, Symons, Delaney, & England, 1995).

In support of this theory, the drug naltrexone, which blunts the effects of opiates, has in some studies produced substantial lessening of self-injury (reviewed by Sandman & Hedrick, 1995). Unlike typical addiction states, however, prevention of self-injury does not result in withdrawal symptoms, nor do those who engage in SIB appear to be in a state of elation. Nevertheless, an addiction-like etiology has been suggested.

Neurotransmitters. Neurotransmitters are brain chemicals that allow for the transmission of a nerve impulse from one cell to the next. Two of the neurotransmitters that have shown some effect on SIB and on other repetitive movement disorders as well are serotonin and dopamine.

The relevant serotonin research relates to a group of antidepressants, one of which, clomipramine (Anafranil) has shown significant reductions in both SIB (Lewis, Bodfish, Powell, Parker, & Golden, 1996) and stereotypy (Lewis, Bodfish, Powell, & Golden, 1995). Another of these drugs, fluoxetine (Prozac), has reduced compulsive behavior in mental retardation (Bodfish & Madison, 1993). These findings support the view that repetitive behaviors are a serotonin-related group of disorders associated with an abnormality in the basal ganglia. It also may be possible to treat several repetitive movement disorders with just one class of drugs.

Dopamine, the other neurotransmitter seemingly involved in these disorders, is affected by several antipsychotic drugs. Haloperidol (Haldol) has shown at least a modest effect in reducing both SIB (Baumeister, Todd, & Sevin, 1993) and stereotypy (Aman, Teehan, White, Turbott, & Vaithianathan, 1990). But haloperidol may have serious side effects (dyskinesia) and should be considered only after such serotonin-related drugs as clomipramine. The other two dopamine-related antipsychotic drugs are clozapine (Clozaril), a medication that has been useful in both self-injury and aggression (Hammock, Schroeder, & Levine, 1995), and fluphenazine (Prolixin), a drug that has reduced self-injury in some individuals (Gualtieri & Schroeder, 1989). On the basis of current research, however, it cannot be assumed that all neuroleptic drugs or those that affect dopamine will achieve similar benefits (Lewis, Aman, Gadow, Schroeder, & Thompson, 1996).

Another Potentially Useful Drug.   Elsewhere in the chapter there is reference to lithium carbonate, a drug used to treat bipolar illness. If bipolar disorder is accompanied by aggression or self-injury, the latter behaviors also may be improved by lithium carbonate (Aman & Singh, 1991; Gualtieri, 1989).

A Note of Caution.   None of the drugs described are effective in all cases of SIB or in other repetitive movement disorders. And even if they are beneficial the behavior is only reduced in frequency; it is not eliminated. But the self-injury may be reduced to manageable levels and, thus, lend itself to behavioral treatment. SIB is a good example of a disorder that benefits from the integration of biological and behavioral approaches.

SIB as a Compulsive Disorder.

It has been theorized that SIB is a form of compulsive behavior (King, 1993). Supporting this view is the finding that both self-injury and compulsions coexist to a significant degree in affected individuals (Bodfish et al., 1995). Interestingly, in Lesch-Nyhan syndrome, affected persons often indicate a wish to stop hurting themselves but report an inability to do so. Indeed, apparent attempts at self-restraint reveal its noxious nature for its victims.

Environmental or Behavioral Causes of Self-Injury.

In the environmental sphere, speculation as to the cause of SIB has included viewing it as a kind of early developmental *stress* response (Kraemer, 1992). In this respect, it should be noted that SIB has a "normal" developmental counterpart. Mild head banging, presumably in the service of tactile stimulation, is seen in about 10% to 15% of normally developing infants (Thompson, Axtell, & Schaal, 1993). Benign in this context, it commonly disappears in early childhood, although it may persist and intensify in children with severe intellectual impairments. We speculate that its disappearance in the normally developing child relates to the growing power of *visual* and *auditory* experience as sources of sensory reinforcement, with a corresponding decline in the reinforcing power of *tactile* and *kinesthetic* experience. In this view, SIB begins as a form of sensory (tactile) reinforcement, although it can be maintained later by social factors. In the social or interpersonal realm, self-injury can be perpetuated either as a means of obtaining positive reinforcement, such as attention (it's hard to ignore it!), desired food, or favorite toys or by negative reinforcement, such as escape from demands or other undesired situations. Understanding the utility of self-injury to the child, in which social factors are relevant, is essential to its treatment. Self-injury, like tantrums, can be so intimidating that caregivers give way to the child's demands. And once established as a powerful means of influencing caregivers, it is not going to be eliminated easily!

Behavioral Treatment of Self-injury.

DRO and DRI.   Of the various behavioral treatment strategies, differential reinforcement of other behavior (DRO) has been most widely used. Its goal is to reinforce any behavior *other* than SIB and assumes that the non-SIB behaviors will be strengthened. One of its two limitations is that if non-SIB but *other* maladaptive behavior occurs during a designated time, it too is reinforced, albeit inadvertently. DRO alone has been used with only limited effectiveness in SIB. A review of 35 studies in which DRO was the only strategy found that in only 10 (29%) of them was there a significant reduction in SIB (Carr, Taylor, Carlson, & Robinson, 1991). The power of DRO can be increased if it is employed in conjunction with the teaching of an adaptive behavioral alternative that is incompatible with SIB. That is, both behaviors cannot be manifested at the same time. Called *differential reinforcement of incompatible behavior* (DRI), its use with SIB in which the person strikes himself with his hand would involve reinforcing

TABLE 9.2. Potential reinforcers of self-injury

Form of Reinforcement	Reinforcing Consequences: Socially Mediated and Automatic
Positive	Attention and/or desired sensations
Negative	Avoidance of demands and/or pain/tension relief

some adaptive behavior involving the use of the hands, such as assembling objects in a work setting. But even with the use of both DRO and DRI, in only 30% of the published instances have they been effective (Carr et al., 1991).

Reinforcement in the Context of a Functional Analysis of SIB. SIB, like other behavior, exists both because it serves some function in terms of the person's needs and because it is maintained by its reinforcing consequences. Reinforcing consequences may be "socially mediated," that is, delivered by a person, or "automatic," a natural consequence of the behavior itself (Iwata, Zarcone, Vollmer, & Smith, 1994). Table 9.2 illustrates the possible combinations of reinforcement that can maintain SIB.

Among the socially mediated consequences maintaining SIB, attention and avoidance of unwanted situations are prominent. If SIB appears to be primarily meeting the need for attention, treatment calls for providing attention only in the *absence* of SIB. The reinforcer here is under the control of the therapist. On the other hand, "automatic" reinforcers, are by their nature, more difficult to control because the act itself provides the reinforcer. Severe self-scratching, for example, may relieve itching, an example of negative reinforcement. A treatment plan might rely on a combination of the prevention of scratching and a reinforcer that serves the same function as scratching. With that person's hands blocked from scratching, the individual might be taught to use a hand signal to request medication that would relieve itching. If scratching also seems to have an attention-getting component, attention would be added to the treatment strategy as a reinforcer contingent on periods of reduced or no scratching. Indeed, attention can be provided when the anti-itch medication is applied—soothing for the soul and soothing for the skin!

Many problem behaviors serve the function of automatic negative reinforcement because they lead to reduction in stress. Treatment here, as with itching, must focus on teaching adaptive forms of stress relief. Relief of tension, for example, can be achieved through learning relaxation techniques, such as deep breathing or progressive muscle relaxation, or by involvement in such activities as taking a walk, listening to music, lying down for a few minutes, or taking a warm bath. Although they take time to teach, they eventually can offer the same reinforcement as the maladaptive behavior—relief of tension. A program has been described in which children and adults with mental retardation and autism acquired relaxation skills and greater self-control (Baron, Groden, & Cautela, 1988).

Let us now consider socially mediated negative reinforcement. Self-injury that leads to escape from teacher demands is a common example. In this situation a teacher's demand is followed by SIB. Concerned about possible physical injury, the demand is withdrawn. By the removal of the demand, self-hitting is reinforced. It works! The teacher can address this behavior by designing a program that does not allow escape or by providing a respite following appropriate behavior, for example after completing an assignment.

SIB as a Form of Communication. For people with severe and profound retardation, individuals who typically lack functional communicative skills, SIB may serve as a form of nonverbal communication. There is reference to this in the section on aggression. SIB also may be a means of communicating physical discomfort or pain in persons suffering from undiagnosed medical disorders, such as otitis media, esophagitis, duodenal ulcers, constipation, and dysphagia with aspiration (Bosch, Van Dyke, Smith, & Poulton, 1997).

SIB and a Functional Analysis of Behavior. Given the variety of conditions that might evoke and reinforce SIB, a functional analysis of the behavior provides a rational strategy for its treatment. The following questions serve as a basis for such an approach.

The Behavior Itself. What is the exact form of the SIB, its frequency, duration, and severity? Does it occur in isolation or in conjunction with other unwanted behavior? Is it accompanied by an emotional or physical state, such as anger, fear, hyperactivity, sweating, or seizure-like activity?

Antecedents. Under what conditions is the SIB most likely to occur? Is there a pattern to the time, location, or type of activity that typically precedes it? Does it tend to be associated with particular individuals or activities such as a change in activity or the absence of planned activity? If it appears to be connected with a particular activity, is that activity new or one that previously has been mastered? Are there conditions under which it rarely or never occurs, an obviously important consideration?

Relevant Reinforcers (Consequences).   What is the source of the reinforcement that is maintaining the SIB? Is it positive or negative reinforcement? Is it socially mediated and thus more amenable to change or automatically mediated and more difficult to prevent? Is the reinforcement social, sensory, or material; is it escape from demands or relief from pain, crowding, noise, heat, and so forth? Is it an attempt to exert some control over one's life?

Modifiability of Reinforcers.   Is it feasible to remove the source of reinforcement, for example to ignore SIB so as to remove "attention" as a reinforcer? This can be done only if the behavior is physically noninjurious or, seemingly, conscious in its attention-getting intent.

The Individual's Preferred Activities.   What does the individual enjoy? Is there adequate access to these reinforcing experiences during a typical day? Could these activities and experiences be increased?

Substituting Adaptive Behavior for SIB.   What adaptive behavior might we teach that would serve the same function as the SIB? This can be done only if the behavior is physically noninjurious.

The means of conducting such a functional analysis in community-service settings have been described in detail (Groden, Stevenson, & Groden, 1993). Other guides to functional analysis in community settings are provided by Crawford, Brockel, Schauss, & Miltenberger (1992) and Sturmey (1994).

Common Findings in the Functional Analysis of SIB.   The most common function of SIB is *escape from demands* (Iwata et al., 1994). This can include nothing more demanding than complying with requests for cooperation in daily routines. Especially subject to SIB are tasks that are novel, lengthy, and presented rapidly. In developing a treatment strategy, a *schedule* itself is therapeutic. Individuals prone to SIB generally respond well to routine, to predictability, to "structure."

Extinction and SIB.   Given the universal power of attention as a reinforcer, if it is the reinforcer in SIB, the ideal treatment would be to withhold attention for SIB; that is, simply ignore it. But as indicated, our ability to ignore it depends on its severity. We cannot ignore the likelihood of real injury. Further, if attention is withheld now after it was given before, the behavior can be expected to intensify, at least initially, as its practitioner applies a principle learned earlier. This intensification of SIB or of any behavior immediately upon our ignoring it is called an *extinction burst,* and this requires even greater monitoring because of possible

injury. Clearly, there are practical problems in implementing an *exclusive* "extinction" strategy with SIB, and this has rendered it less useful than treatments that *combine* removal of reinforcement for SIB (extinction) with teaching and reinforcement of desired behavior. Of the various approaches to the reduction of SIB, as well as aggression and other serious behavior problems, those that focus on *teaching adaptive skills* are the most effective (Carr et al., 1991). The acquisition of adaptive skills not only reduces SIB, it enhances adaptation in all aspects of community living.

Behavioral Prevention of Self-injury.

The prevention of SIB, as with any problem behavior, requires identifying its triggers, its antecedents. Good medical care can reduce the frequency of biological antecedents—infections, menstrual pain, sleeplessness, drug side effects, and so forth. Careful classroom structure makes the environment more predictable and reinforcers more easily scheduled (Olley & Reeve, 1997). Given the pernicious nature of SIB, it is not surprising that modifying antecedents is almost as effective as skill acquisition in reducing it (Carr et al., 1991). In general, treatment approaches that combine modifying antecedents, removal of reinforcement for the unwanted behavior, and the teaching and reinforcement of desired behavior are more effective than any one approach.

Noncontingent Reinforcement in the Treatment of SIB.

Although the essence of the behavioral approach, whether in education or behavior management, is *contingent reinforcement*, that is, providing reinforcement contingent upon the desired response, there is evidence that some consequences can reduce SIB even if not presented contingently. If, for example, SIB has been reinforced by attention, increasing the availability of attention can reduce SIB even if it is not offered contingently (Vollmer, Iwata, Zarcone, Smith, & Mazaleski, 1993). An extension of this finding was that SIB could be reduced through noncontingent access to "escape" (Vollmer, Marcus, & Ringdahl, 1995) and to a tangible reinforcer (Marcus & Vollmer, 1996). Similarly, offering a noncontingent schedule of preferred consequences, such as food, that were shown to not reinforce SIB reduced it (Fischer, Iwata & Mazaleski, 1997).

While behavioral research continues to seek a mechanism for understanding noncontingent effects, they are comprehensible in terms of our personality need model. Our needs, biological and psychological, are not quantitatively infinite. We require some *optimal* degree of satisfaction of them, and if they are being gratified in one domain, their absence in another is less painful. This is not to imply that all potential sources of gratification carry equal weight. Clearly they do not. Disappointment in love, or in a job promotion, is not going to be erased by seeing a good movie, but to the degree that one is afforded a rich range of other potential reinforcers, the disappointment, at least, is eased. Put in more positive terms, if the basic needs of survival, structure, self-esteem, and self-expression are being met, positive emotional states rather than negative ones predominate. There is a greater level of "comfort" than tension and a lesser proneness to problem behavior.

Self-restraint in SIB.   Persons who engage in SIB often appear to be seeking to restrain themselves. This can take the form of wrapping their arms or legs in clothing, assuming body postures that immobilize the limbs, or even requesting mechanical restraints, such as splints or restraining jackets. Although the presumed basis for self-restraint is to prevent discomfort or pain associated with self-hitting, the behavior also may be maintained because it can reduce external demands. Direct-care providers tend to leave people alone if they self-restrain both because this behavior is preferable to SIB and because its practitioners protest if their self-restraint is removed.

Self-restraint also may be a source of positive reinforcement. The experience of being restrained can provide positive sensory stimulation (Fisher & Iwata, 1996). A woman with autism enjoyed placing herself in a box that provided tactile pressure on her body, a "squeeze box" (Grandin & Scariano, 1986). Also illustrative of the potentially reinforcing quality of restraint is a laboratory study that found that SIB increased if it was followed by access to self-restraint (Smith, Lerman, & Iwata, 1996). If access to self-restraint is actually a reinforcer for some people, it can be used as a treatment.

Treatment of Self-restraint.   Although self-restraint is clearly preferable to self-injury, it is not necessarily a wholly benign behavior. Not only does it limit opportunities to participate in activities, but it can lead to muscle atrophy and other medical problems.

Another rationale for treatment of self-restraint lies in its seemingly "compulsive" nature. We have noted the association of SIB and compulsions in adults with retardation (Bodfish et al., 1995) and, interestingly, in one study more than half of persons (57%) who manifested SIB and self-restraint also exhibited compulsions. Among those with SIB and no self-restraint, significantly fewer (33%) had compulsions (Powell, Bodfish, Parker, Crawford, & Lewis, 1996).

The compulsive quality of self-restraint is reflected by its persistence and in negative reactions to its interruption (Powell et al., 1996). This is evident in Harry, who is described elsewhere in this section. People with SIB appear to react to interference with self-restraint in the same way as those whose compulsions are blocked. But in contrast to compulsive behavior in the nonretarded population, self-restraint seems to be a compulsion that lacks any accompanying *obsessional thought*. Although SIB and self-restraint are more common in persons without functional language, even those who have useful speech do not indicate obsessional thinking. Parenthetically, even individuals with Lesch-Nyhan syndrome who have speech cannot do more to explain their self-injury than to communicate the sense that they are *compelled* to do this and cannot stop themselves.

Illustrating the curiously complex nature of self-restraint as a potential reinforcer in its own right is a study in which the reduction of SIB associated with the drug clomipramine (Anafranil) was followed by *increased* self-restraint! (Lewis, Bodfish, Powell, Parker, & Golden, 1996)

With respect to behavioral treatment, nearly continuous enthusiastic praise and positive touching (noncontingent attention) have affected almost complete elimination of both SIB and self-restraint if attention appeared to be the primary reinforcer (Derby, Fisher, & Piazza, 1996). Although providing continuous attention may not be a very practical form of treatment, it does reveal that both SIB and self-restraint are amenable to change through positive methods.

A more practical treatment strategy is to offer access to self-restraint contingent upon periods of no SIB. The best-known example of this treatment approach is that of Harry, who at the onset of treatment was 22 years old and presumed to be severely retarded. He had engaged in SIB since infancy.

> Restraints had been used . . . to control his self-injurious behavior. Over the years restraints became reinforcing since Harry asked for them, appeared to be quite relaxed when wearing them, became highly agitated and self-injurious when they were removed, would help put them on, and attempted to restrain himself in his clothing or by holding on to others when his restraints were removed. (Foxx, 1990, p. 68)

Treatment of Harry's SIB began with a functional analysis that revealed that self-injury was triggered by demands. When he hit himself, the demands ceased, thus negatively reinforcing SIB. But the SIB also was positively reinforced by access to restraint. Treatment included teaching Harry adaptive skills such as tolerance for demands, with access to his restraints (hinged arm splints and a face mask) employed as a reinforcer for increasing periods of abstinence from SIB. Harry has made remarkable progress. Now in his 40s, he lives in a group home, works, and has reduced the severity of his SIB to an insignificant level. Harry's dependence on his restraints was treated by gradually reducing their size.

Stereotyped Behavior

Rhythmic repetitive behavior that is invariant in form is called *stereotyped behavior*. The most common repetitive movement disorder in mental retardation, it often coexists with self-injury but differs from SIB in being physically noninjurious and without apparent "external" purpose.

The most frequently seen stereotypies are body rocking, swaying, hand waving, and finger movements. Although regarded as aberrant, stereotypy is seen in all infants, normal and delayed, with its greatest prominence in the period just preceding the establishing of control of the involved body part (Thelen, 1996). Thus stereotyped leg kicking and rocking are most evident just prior to crawling, stereotyped arm waving prior to reaching, fist banging prior to good hand control, and swaying prior to standing. Occurring most often if the infant is excited or fussy, these movements eventually are incorporated in play, exploration, and social communication. As motor skills increase, stereotypies ultimately vanish.

Why, in some individuals, do these behaviors persist, even to adulthood? Although Thelen attributes their persistence to failure to acquire good motor skills, a kind of permanent motor immaturity, in our view their continued presence lies in the disproportionate prominence in the severely delayed child of tactile and kinesthetic sensation in the child's sensory repertoire. It will be recalled that head banging also is seen in some normally developing infants, a behavior thought to reflect the desire for mild tactile stimulation. As cognitive development proceeds, the visual and auditory sensory modalities assume increasing prominence in our interactions with our environment, with the role of the other senses diminishing in importance although never disappearing. We enjoy the experience of rocking in a rocking chair, and tactile stimulation in the form of massage is much in vogue. For the individual whose cognitive development is greatly impaired, the sensory experiences of touch, taste, movement, and smell can be appreciated *directly*. Unlike much visual and auditory sensation, which requires *interpretation* or perceptual processing in order to be meaningful, the other sensory modes can be more directly enjoyed. And if the child is reared in an environment devoid of enriching sensory experience, as is the case of the deprived children described in Chapters 2 and 5, the child can create his or her own sensory experience by producing these sensations, so-called self-stimulation. It is the *continued* existence of such behavior after infancy that gives it its "peculiar" quality.

Jarrod: Stereotyped Dirt Kicking.

Jarrod is a 10-year-old boy with severe mental retardation, seizures, autism, and few communication skills. He has never shown interest in games or in activities involving others, including his parents or other children, and if approached he pushes them away. Jarrod's lack of play skills and insensitivity to social cues results in rejection of him as a playmate. Although he enjoys being outside, he avoids other children and walks about with his head lowered until he finds dirt to kick. He persists in kicking dirt for up to 2 hours or until redirected to another activity. He becomes so disturbed if his dirt kicking is interrupted, his parents allow him to continue at it for as long as he wishes, but they are concerned that it interferes with opportunities for acquiring needed social and communication skills, and rightfully so!

Much more common than SIB, stereotypic behavior is found widely in other populations as well as in those with mental retardation—especially in persons with autism and blindness. As many as two thirds of the latter groups show some form of stereotypy (called "blindisms" in those with visual impairment). And in the retarded population, as with SIB, stereotypy is more prevalent at the more severe levels of cognitive impairment.

Biological Causes and Treatment of Stereotypies. As

with SIB, recent biological research sheds light on the cause of stereotypy, and on other repetitive behavior. As indicated previously, these disorders may be associated with abnormalities in the basal ganglia, a brain structure important to movement, and the neurotransmitters, dopamine and serotonin (Lewis, Gluck, Bodfish, Beauchamp, & Mailman, 1996).

A biological basis for stereotypy and other repetitive behavior is indicated by the effects of medication. In a controlled study of 10 severely retarded adults, six showed clinically significant improvement in their stereotypies when administered clomipramine (Anafranil) (Lewis et al., 1995). Clomipramine, a psychotropic drug that affects serotonin, also reduced hyperactivity and irritability, as well as other repetitive movements.

Environmental or Behavioral Causes and Treatment.

Associated with conditions of diminished sensory stimulation (environmental deprivation), stereotypies are assumed to be practiced for their sensory effects. Although such stereotypies as rocking, spinning, visual stimulation, and rubbing provide a variety of self-induced sensory experiences, functional analyses typically reveal multiple reinforcers. One study of 12 adults who engaged in chronic hand mouthing found that in 10 of them it was the sensory experience that maintained the behavior; in the other two, attention and access to desired materials was the reinforcer (Goh et al., 1995).

Stereotypies can be contrasted with obsessive-compulsive disorder with respect to relevant reinforcers. Whereas stereotypies are maintained by such positive reinforcers as sensory experience and attention, obsessive-compulsive disorder features repetitive behavior that reduces tension or anxiety, an example of negative reinforcement.

The functional analysis of hand mouthing in each individual allowed for the discovery of an appropriate treatment. If sensory stimulation was the reinforcer, the individuals were offered desired objects that they could handle (tactile stimulation). When hand mouthing occurred, either the desired materials were removed or mittens were placed on the hands. In either case, hand mouthing disappeared and object manipulation increased.

Trichotillomania

This tongue twister refers to the habit of literally pulling out one's hair and, unsurprisingly, results in noticeable hair loss. It is seen in both normally developing young children and those with mental retardation. Hair may be removed from all parts of the body. The persistence of this behavior can be regarded as a "habit disorder" or as a disorder of impulse control (discussed in Chapter 10).

Given the common nature of repetitive behavior in normal as well as abnormal development, such as tapping with a pencil or hair twirling, it is important to decide to what degree they require intervention. Certainly our criterion should be whether the activity interferes with the development of age-appropriate behavior. Autistic children, for example, often persist in repetitive activities to the exclusion of age-appropriate play and protest if their stereotyped activity is interrupted. Unlike the normal child, such behaviors may form the *predominant* activity in those with autism or severe mental retardation.

Dyskinesia and Akathesia

Dyskinesia. Stereotypies resemble the dyskinetic movements of tardive dyskinesia, a side effect of long-term treatment with neuroleptic drugs (antipsychotic medications). Although stereotypies tend to involve the whole body and be voluntary in nature, those in tardive dyskinesia are involuntary, less rhythmical, and chiefly *orofacial* in character, for example, grimacing, tongue tremors or thrusts, and lip smacking. Less frequent are wrist-arm movements and "pill rolling" (the hand movement seen in the neurological disease parkinsonism). The presence of stereotypy appears to increase the risk of tardive dyskinesia (Bodfish et al., 1996).

Dyskinesias also can occur in the absence of neuroleptic medications. We referred to them in regard to cerebral palsy, and they also are seen in epilepsy, rheumatic fever, and Huntington's disease (Rosenquist & Bodfish, 1997).

Akathesia. As noted in the introduction to repetitive movement disorders, this is a group of movements characterized by restlessness or fidgeting, "marching in place," and foot-to-foot rocking. Found in about 16%

of individuals with severe and profound retardation, they are slightly less prominent then those attributed to dyskinesia (Rosenquist & Bodfish, 1997).

Treatment. These disorders are associated chiefly with antipsychotic medication; treatment involves finding drugs that are less likely to cause these movements, such as clozapine (Clozaril), risperidone (Risperdal), and olanzapine (Zyprexa). But change from one antipsychotic medication to another demands caution. There is little research on or clinical experience with the effects of the newer drugs on individuals with retardation. Removal of *all* neuroleptic drugs can be expected to ease dyskinetic movements, although it must be done gradually and carefully monitored (Rosenquist & Bodfish, 1997).

Obsessive-Compulsive Disorder

Nature. Obsessive-compulsive disorder (OCD) refers to obsessive *thoughts*, compulsive or "driven" *actions*, or both. Obsessive thoughts influence compulsive actions. Obsessive thoughts about being unclean, for example, trigger compulsive cleaning (Lady MacBeth's hand washing is Shakespeare's contribution to OCD). In mental retardation, the verbal limitations, especially in those with more than "mild" impairment, limit our knowledge of their possible obsessional thoughts, in contrast to their observable compulsive behavior.

As noted in the earlier discussions of both SIB and stereotypy, the presence of these repetitive movement disorders is associated with an increased risk of OCD (Bodfish et al., 1995).

OCD is particularly conspicuous in adults with severe or profound retardation (Bodfish et al., 1995) and is a feature of the chromosomal eating disorder Prader-Willi syndrome (Dykens & Kasari, 1997). Whereas only about 3% of the nonretarded population exhibit OCD, as many as 40% of those with the more severe degrees of cognitive impairment are so affected (Bodfish et al., 1995). Usually arising in adolescence, its development is gradual rather than sudden, and affected persons generally have multiple obsessions or compulsions (Crawford & Bodfish, 1992).

Bodfish (1996) characterized *compulsions* as "repetitive," "ritualistic" behaviors in the service of preventing or reducing anxiety or distress. Various forms of compulsive behavior are found. They involve ordering or arranging objects or activities in a certain place or sequence; completeness— opening or closing doors, repeatedly removing items from their places and replacing them; cleaning—completing hygiene steps in a fixed sequence, excessive cleaning of a body part (e.g., Lady MacBeth); checking or touching—touching or tapping something repeatedly, unusual sniffing; and grooming—repeated cutting or pulling of hair, picking at a body part. These are the categories found on the Compulsive Behavior Checklist for Clients with Mental Retardation (Gedye, 1992), a useful tool for identifying OCD behaviors.

Although compulsions may be associated with obsessive thoughts, for example compulsive cleaning because of a fear of germs, the affected person cannot explain why the actions are so necessary and becomes disturbed if they are interrupted. Despite their intensity, however, they typically wax and wane.

Treatment: Biological and Behavioral. OCD currently is viewed as a biologically based disorder related to a dysfunction in the basal ganglia (Crawford & Bodfish, 1992) and treatments of OCD are both pharmacological and behavioral. As noted previously, pharmacological treatment has focused on antidepressant drugs that affect the neurotransmitter serotonin, particularly clomipramine (Anafranil), fluvoxamine (Luvox), and fluoxetine (Prozac). In one study of ten individuals with compulsions and retardation, seven showed significant reduction after treatment with fluoxetine (Bodfish & Madison, 1993).

Apart from trying to control the antecedents that may intensify symptoms, the most successful approach to treatment in nonretarded individuals has been to expose them to the stimulus that triggers the compulsive act and then prevent its expression. Although this procedure, "exposure and response prevention," initially increases anxiety, eventually the anxiety and compulsions subside. This approach can be combined with medication to reduce the anxiety associated with the intervention.

The use of exposure and response prevention in retardation has been controversial because it involves the creation of at least an initial period of intense anxiety, and professionals are reluctant to expose persons to this who may not understand what is to happen. If truly informed consent cannot be given, alternative approaches are necessary.

Few accounts of behavioral treatment are currently available. Matson (1982) treated three men with mild retardation whose OCD behaviors included clothes and body checking. Treatment included differential reinforcement of other behavior, response prevention, modeling, and verbal feedback. Compulsive behavior was reduced or eliminated, along with the accompanying anxiety.

Current practice calls for a combination of treatment procedures—medication, the avoidance of stressful conditions, and exposure and response prevention. Research suggests that the complete elimination of OCD is improbable and that the appropriate treatment goal is improved tolerance for stress and reduced problem behavior (Crawford & Bodfish, 1992).

Problematic Sexual Behavior

Nature

In Chapters 6 and 7 there is a relatively detailed discussion of the sexual needs of persons with mental retardation. Sexual expression is related to the degree of retardation and to the setting in which one lives and socializes (Gordon & Schroeder, 1995). Those with mild retardation who live either relatively independently or with only occasional support have greater opportunity to engage in all types of community and social activities and can be expected to have more experience with dating and sexual behavior. Adolescent girls with mild retardation are thought to be sexually active with about the same or slightly less frequency than nonretarded youth. If retardation is at least moderate in degree, however, the level of sexual activity appears to diminish (Gordon & Schroeder, 1995).

Common problems in this population are unintended pregnancy, sexually transmitted disease, and vulnerability to sexual abuse (such as incest and rape, e.g., Sarah, the 18-year-old girl with cerebral palsy described in Chapter 8). One also sees a variety of inappropriate behaviors, including public masturbation, exposure of genitals, and inappropriate verbal expressions or touching. Some of this behavior may be because of restricted opportunities for normal sexual experiences as well as the effects of social isolation and reduced social skills and judgment (Gordon & Schroeder, 1995). The senior author, an unlikely candidate for sexual targeting, found himself being assaulted by a moderately retarded male adolescent during the administration of an intelligence test. He literally had to get assistance to free himself from the young man's attempted "embrace." This adolescent had a history of aggressive homosexual behavior, although his targets usually were younger children. Once the youth was settled again in his chair, the examination was resumed without incident! Undoubtedly, many of the sexual behaviors of retarded youth are tied to their cognitive and social immaturity. Interestingly, in light of this experience, it is reported that the most common cause for arrest in retarded individuals is for a sexual act (Gordon & Schroeder, 1995).

Treatment

The treatment of sexual problems in retardation is largely *educational* in nature, and in other chapters there is reference to such programs. The educational effort must be concerned with the learning characteristics of persons with retardation. Information must be made concrete and desired behavior rewarded. In order to assure that appropriate behavior is reinforced, coordination is necessary among service providers, family, and teachers (Valenti-Hein & Dura, 1996). The preferred treatment format is "group" in nature; here participants can actively respond to questions, solve problems, and practice socially appropriate behavior. The discussion of this topic in Chapter 6 also includes reference to board games developed to teach such behavior.

With regard to the initiation of sexually inappropriate behavior (as in the experience described previously), it is noted that these individuals themselves may have been victims of sexual abuse (Gordon & Schroeder, 1995; Valenti-Hein & Dura, 1996). Perpetrators of violent crimes typically come from family backgrounds in which they themselves were victimized by physically abusive parents, generally fathers. There also may be the need for the treatment of a post–traumatic stress disorder resulting from such earlier abuse. We can assume that the exposure to unfamiliar young men of Sarah, the physically helpless victim described in the previous chapter, would create a good deal of anxiety. Finally, the inappropriate behavior itself must be addressed. There is no short-term treatment here. Victims of sexual abuse, too, may require lengthy support and structured opportunities in order to learn adaptive sexual functioning.

☐ Summary

The first of two chapters devoted to significant behavior disorders in mental retardation, this chapter is introduced by a discussion of the various causes of these behaviors, their diagnoses, and treatment. With regard to treatment, special emphasis is given to the "behavioral" approach, with its rationale and essential ingredients highlighted. The remainder of the chapter consists of descriptions of three groups of disorders—aggression; repetitive movement disorder, such as SIB and stereotypy; and problematic sexual behaviors. For each of these disorders, the nature of the behavior is specified and treatment suggestions offered. With respect to treatment, the behavioral approach commonly is combined with a pharmacological one. Indeed, the chapter provides much information on the use of psychotropic drugs in these disorders.

Possible Discussion Questions

If we think in terms of the personality need model spelled out in Chapter 2, how does it help us understand the relatively high frequency of behavior disorders in persons with mental retardation? What has contributed to a tendency to underdiagnose behavior problems in this population?

What contribution can the therapeutic technique of counseling make to the management of behavior problems? Among individuals with retardation, who are most likely to benefit from this form of treatment and why?

Can the rationale for the behavioral approach be understood in terms of the fundamental motivation suggested by the personality model? How would various reinforcing consequences relate to need gratification?

What are the essential elements of the "ABC" approach in the analysis of a behavior problem? What is the distinction between "implicit" and "explicit" reward systems? What are the various contingencies that the ABC approach applies to behavior problems? What is the reason for trying to understand the *purpose* of a given maladaptive behavior?

Under what conditions do psychotropic drugs have a role in the management of behavior problems in retardation?

Discuss the causes and treatment of aggression, the repetitive-movement disorders, and problematic sexual behavior.

10

CHAPTER

J. Gregory Olley
George S. Baroff

Psychiatric Disorders in Mental Retardation

☐ Overview

In contrast to the preceding chapter, which is devoted to a description of behavior problems not necessarily accorded a formal psychiatric diagnosis, this chapter is concerned with behavior seen in retardation that is classifiable in terms of formal psychiatric syndromes. The topics presented are the identification of psychiatric disorders in persons with retardation; their specific nature, presumed causes, and current treatment; and the description of two "developmental" disorders that share with mental retardation significant learning difficulties—autism and the "developmental learning disorders" ("learning disabilities"). Although there is no question about the "psychiatric" nature of autism—emotional and social difficulties are ever-present—the developmental learning disorders refer only to *academic* learning problems and have no implication for any significant emotional disturbance. The justification for their inclusion lies in their presence, along with retardation, in the general category of "developmental disorders" as found in the *Diagnostic and Statistical Manual of Mental Disorders*, 4th edition (DSM-IV; American Psychiatric Association, 1994).

☐ Identifying Psychiatric Disorders in Mental Retardation

In the previous chapter there is reference to diagnostic "overshadowing," the tendency to view emotional and behavioral problems in retardation as inherent in the disorder rather than as separate phenomena. The effect is to underdiagnose psychiatric conditions in this population. In addition to diagnostic overshadowing, there are four factors that are relevant to our consideration of these disorders as seen in persons with mental retardation (Sovner 1986; Sovner & Pary, 1993).

Intellectual Distortion

Impairments in cognitive and communicative skills can interfere with the accurate reporting of symptoms and emotional states. This can render suspect diagnosis based on clinical interviews.

Baseline Exaggeration or Aggravation of Existing Behavior

Existing maladaptive behavior, such as inappropriate anger or irrational thought, can be expected to worsen under stress. If a psychiatric disorder is present, its symptoms may represent an intensification of previous maladaptive behavior or a mix of old and new features.

Psychosocial Masking

The cognitive impairment and narrowed range of personal experience associated with mental retardation can alter psychiatric symptoms. In psychoses, for example, the symptoms are less complex and elaborated than those seen in nonretarded individuals.

Cognitive Disintegration

Retardation leaves the individual at a high risk for even greater impairment in cognitive functioning in the face of emotional stress. The further impairment or "disintegration" can occur even with low stress and is expressed in unusually concrete or immature ways of coping, behavior that may be mistaken for mental illness.

It is the emotional domain that is the usual source of our behavioral difficulties—managing the emotions created by the frustration of our basic needs. Mental retardation complicates the already difficult task of governing our feelings by adding cognitive impediment to our capacity to recognize specific emotional states in ourselves and others and link specific events to the emotions they arouse. Another major problem is impairment in the ability to *think* about our feelings and to consider the *consequences* of acting upon them. Given these difficulties, we should not be surprised at the high prevalence of emotional disturbance in mental retardation. Within the broad category of emotional or psychiatric disorders, we now focus on those most frequently observed.

☐ Major Psychiatric Disoders in Mental Retardation

Anxiety Disorders

Generalized Anxiety Disorder

The risk of anxiety in persons with retardation is greater than that in the general population. It also appears to have an earlier onset in those with severer levels of cognitive impairment (Ollendick, Oswald, & Ollendick, 1993), although its manifestations as "anxiety" may not be obvious. With reference to specific syndromes, children with the chromosomal condition Williams syndrome commonly show anxiety disorders, and also hyperactivity and attention deficit (Einfeld, Tonge, & Florio, 1997). Elderly persons with retardation are also at increased risk (Pary, 1996), some of it undoubtedly because of side effects of medication or medical disorders themselves associated with aging. The elderly population requires particular attention if retardation is severe, because the individual may have difficulty in describing what he or she is experiencing.

Although anxiety is a normal reaction to any event that threatens basic biological and psychological needs, in retardation it commonly is stirred by pressures to achieve; by confrontation with tasks perceived as difficult (thereby risking failure and frustration of the self-esteem–related subneed "success"); and by crowding, noise, or unfamiliar people or situations (too little "structure"). The last-mentioned factor is particularly prominent in adults (Levine, 1985).

Although some degree of anxiety can elevate our performance on tasks relevant to self-esteem, and a *little* test anxiety is probably preferable to none at all, it appears to be more debilitating to people with retardation. This was evident in a study that compared effects of anxiety on the athletic performance of retarded and nonretarded adults (Levine & Langness, 1983).

The debilitating effects of anxiety are seen in Barbara, who is in her 20s and is mildly retarded. Residing in a group home since age 14 years, she attended special-education classes and later a sheltered workshop. Her work skills were good and, with "supported employment," she was offered a position. Despite her many strengths, she struggled through several jobs, often returning to the sheltered workshop after being fired from what had appeared to be an ideal situation. She had particular difficulty coping with changes in her job routine. (In the discussion of the vocational needs of persons with retardation in Chapter 8, we stressed the need for jobs that are well defined, highly routinized, and consistently paced. Barbara's job did *not* fit that mode). If she was asked to speed up (change her pace), to stop what she was doing and help another worker, or to do the job in a different way (not "routinized"), she felt anxious. She began to dread going to work and to feel anxious both in her job and elsewhere. Eventually, she began to have headaches and would call in sick instead of going to work. She established a pattern of frequenting a walk-in health clinic where she would report that she was having an anxiety attack and then obtain a medical excuse to remain out of work. As the number of missed days increased, she was fired, a consequence that only further increased her anxiety and lowered her self-esteem. Behavioral difficulties on the job were paralleled by emotional difficulties elsewhere. Although she was outgoing and friendly, her feelings were hurt easily and she gave free vent her emotions. Teased by a coworker about her weight, she lashed out with verbal abuse and threats.

Barbara's anxiety can be viewed as an exaggerated version of what we all experience, although generally we handle these stresses without letting them interfere with our daily functioning. But this is only possible if we actively try to manage the situations that distress us and control the feelings they evoke. It is this "governing" or "controlling" function that is threatened by the cognitive deficits associated with mental retardation. In the information-processing models of intellectual functioning in mental retardation, much attention is given to this domain—so-called executive functions.

With comprehensive services, including counseling, antianxiety medication, and community support, Barbara has been functioning well in recent years. She has lost weight, maintained a job, and moved to a more independent living arrangement.

Panic Attack

Panic attacks are sudden, unexpected, and brief states of intense fear. They are accompanied by such physical symptoms as shortness of breath, trembling, and heart palpitations. Victims may think that they are going to die. Panic attacks can coexist with other anxiety disorders and with abnormalities of mood. Little is known of their frequency in mental retardation, but it is speculated that they are found only in individuals with not more than mild retardation (McNally, 1991). Nevertheless, sudden and apparently unprovoked outbursts in those with greater degrees of cognitive impairment may be panic attacks. They also can reflect atypical seizures or post-traumatic stress reactions.

Panic attacks can lead to *agoraphobia*, the fear of places or situations from which escape might be difficult or in which help might not be available in the event of an attack. For persons with agoraphobia, the range of activity can become extremely constricted, with fear even of leaving one's home for a trip to the neighborhood grocery.

Phobias

In contrast to the more pervasive and amorphous quality of generalized anxiety states, *phobias* refer to anxiety disorders tied to specific objects or events, such as snakes, spiders, heights, and closed-in spaces. Although all of us experience some discomfort in one or more such situations, it is the extreme intensity of the fear that marks it as a phobia. The intensity of the reaction seems out of proportion to the thing feared and results in rigid avoidance of the source of dread.

The sources of fear in retardation appear related to cognitive maturity (McNally, 1991). Given that the mental ages of persons with retardation do not exceed 12 years, one finds that their fears are similar to those of children of the same mental age. For examples, fears of the dark, animals, dental procedures (not limited to children!), and storms are common in normally developing children and in retarded adults. Interestingly, children with mental retardation do not appear to have a wider range of fears than nonretarded youngsters, but their reactions to them tend to be more intense (Ramirez & Kratochwill, 1997). The intensity of their reactions can escalate to the level of a phobia.

Anxiety may be induced by social situations, such as meeting strangers or being observed by others. We all can be made uncomfortable by such situations; public speaking is notoriously anxiety-producing. Again, it is if such a normal fear becomes so intense as to frighten us away from participating in such experiences that it acquires a phobic quality. We fear being embarrassed, viewed as inadequate, or even humiliated. There is also the fear of rejection in social situations, an experience common in retardation. People may be rejected socially because they are "retarded" or because of undeveloped social skills. Repeated experiences of such rejection or exposure to conditions of humiliation can create "social phobias," that is, the fear of future exposure to such settings.

Obsessive-Compulsive Disorder

Discussed at length in the previous chapter in relation to repetitive movement disorders, in the formal psychiatric nomenclature (DSM-IV) it is classified as an anxiety disorder because obsessive thoughts are associated with anxiety, anxiety that the compulsive acts seek to dispel.

Post traumatic Stress Disorder

Exposure to an extremely traumatic (fear-producing) event can lead to a chronic reexperiencing of its painful emotions. Attended by such symptoms as nightmares, flashbacks, and intrusive thoughts, these symptoms may be difficult to document in persons with limited language. Nonetheless, given the vulnerability of retarded persons to various forms of abuse and neglect (Sobsey, 1994), the disorder may account for some of the fearfulness, anxiety, hyperarousal, and general oversensitivity seen in retardation. It also could be responsible for outbursts of emotion that cannot be linked to current environmental events.

Treatment of Anxiety Disorders

Biological.   The biological or medical treatment of anxiety disorders begins with careful consideration of the medical conditions that can produce such symptoms, such as hyperthyroidism and heart disease. Anxiety also may be a side effect of medication. Conversely, odd movements possibly attributed to anxiety may have a neurological origin, such as akathisias caused by neuroleptic medication.

The efficacy of medications for anxiety in persons with retardation has been widely studied. As indicated earlier, the benzodiazepines (e.g., Valium, Librium) have been employed commonly, although evidence for their effectiveness is lacking (Aman & Singh, 1991). Buspirone (Buspar) appears to be more effective and has fewer side effects (Hillbrand, 1995). Medications for phobias have shown little effectiveness in retardation (Sevin & Matson, 1992), although such drugs as Prozac still are used. Panic attacks commonly benefit from treatment with a combination of medication and behavioral methods. Alprazolam (Xanax) acts quickly to block both panic attacks and the generalized fearfulness that attends them. Because Xanax can be addictive, long-term management may be achieved with the antidepressant imipramine (Tofranil) (McNally, 1991). Post–traumatic stress disorder has been little studied in retardation, but Prozac and similar antidepressants offer promise. However, some but antipsychotic medications may worsen the condition (Ryan, 1996).

Behavioral.   There are two elements essential to long-term success in behavioral treatment of anxiety. They are learning to manage the immediate anxiety or fear, and acquiring adaptive skills that will prevent such reactions in the future. Behavioral treatment and medication may be offered simultaneously, but unless there is an urgent need for relief, as in frequent panic attacks, behavioral treatment should precede the more intrusive approach of medication.

Controlling Immediate Fear: "Stress Management."   The most widely used and effective approach to controlling unwanted emotion is *systematic desensitization* (Wolpe, 1958). The procedure has two components—learning to relax, a response that is incompatible with anxiety (Cautela & Groden, 1978), and then being gradually exposed to the source of anxiety. For example, treatment of fear of dogs would involve first teaching the skill of relaxing. Once in a relaxed state, actual exposure to dogs would begin and be done in small steps. These could include first listening to someone talking about a dog or looking at a picture of one; watching someone pet a dog; moving physically closer to a dog in the presence of a trusted person; and, eventually, touching the animal. The essential element is *graduated* exposure under conditions of relaxation.

Skill Acquisition as a Means of Reducing Anxiety.   Especially relevant to the interpersonal situations that evoke anxiety (in all of us), the preceding method of relaxation and desensitization is combined with "problem solving" (Benson, 1995; Olley, Paraschiv, Jacob & Allison, 1998). Problem solving teaches simple steps that are applied first in familiar nonthreatening situations and then transferred to more challenging ones. These techniques also are very useful to disabled individuals who aspire to leadership roles as, for example, the self-advocate, described in Chapter 6.

Mood Disorders

These are affective states characterized by both extremes of mood and associated changes in thought, behavior, and physical functioning. They may consist of states of elation, depression, or both. We now review the mood disorders most often found in mental retardation and how cognitive impairment affects their expression.

Four types of mood disorders are seen—depressive, bipolar, those associated with a medical condition, and those that are substance-induced. Each of these is distinguished by a combination of self-description of one's mood state; observed behavior, whether depressed or elated; and physical symptoms.

Depressive Disorder

Depression is characterized by diminished interest or pleasure in most things, feelings of worthlessness (low self-esteem) and helplessness, and such physical symptoms as loss of appetite, difficulty in sleeping, and fatigue.

There may be accompanying thoughts of death or suicide. Depression tends to wax and wane; there can be periods of complete freedom (remission) from symptoms, a lengthy depressed state (*major depressive disorder*), and a milder but chronic depressed mood that may last for years (*dysthymic disorder*). Some forms of anxiety, such as panic attacks, also may include depression.

Bipolar Disorder

This disorder consists of *cycles* of altered mood, mania, or depression that alternate with periods of normal emotional functioning. Mania is characterized by overactivity and an exaggerated energy level. In mania, there may be very little desire to sleep, speech is rapid, and thoughts skip from one to another. There can be euphoria or irritability, and judgment may be impaired and behavior irresponsible, for example, spending sprees or poorly planned travel.

Mood Disorder Related to a Medical Condition

Depressed or euphoric mood states may be induced by purely medical disorders. Depression, for example, can be a reaction to chronic, incurable, and painful diseases, such as cancer, AIDS, end-stage renal disease, or head- or spinal-cord injury.

Substance-Abuse Mood Disorder

Mood disorders can arise from the abuse of medications, alcohol (and its withdrawal), and the use of illegal drugs. Some prescription drugs can alter mood as a side effect, a risk that increases if two or more medications are combined. This is one of the reasons for the declining use of multiple medications, especially psychotropic ones, in mental retardation.

Diagnosis of Mood Disorders in Mental Retardation

The diagnosis of mood disorder, typically depression, is based on several considerations. First, given possible retardation-related difficulties in self-description, the diagnosis necessarily relies more heavily on observed behavior and physical signs. Second, behaviors such as withdrawal and reduced activity may be missed by service providers, who are likely to be more disturbed by aggressive and disruptive behavior! Third, cognitive signs of depression such as difficulty in concentrating and poor motivation are common in mental retardation and may be falsely attributed to the intellectual impairment rather than to depression.

Difficulties in the diagnosis of depression call for systematic observation over time, reports from people who know the individual well, the use of rating scales adapted for retardation, and careful interview. With this kind of information the behavioral and physical signs can be recognized (Sevin & Matson, 1992). Reported prevalence rates in retardation vary from 1% to 3% (Sovner & Pary, 1993). Although diagnostic limitations may render these rates artificially low, an increased risk of depression is found in Down syndrome (Collacott, Cooper, & McGrother, 1992), and in Chapter 3 there was discussion of depression's potentially confounding aspect in the diagnosis of Alzheimer's disease in this population.

Causes of Mood Disorders

Like other maladaptive behaviors, the causes of mood disorders may be biological, environmental, or a combination of both. Genetic and neuro-biological determinants are widely recognized in depression, and recent advances in psychotropic drug treatment relate to their effects on brain chemistry, for example, serotonin.

We all experience mood changes. Grieving, for example, shows that experience can affect mood. Mental retardation, as a disabling condition, engenders more probable exposure to situations that can depress mood. The personality model predicts that repeated experiences of failure at tasks in which success is sought would lead to a decrease in motivation with regard to those tasks, avoidance of them if possible, and anger or despair at one's condition. Despair or depression is likely to be followed by apathy and a turning to other activities as possible vehicles for achieving some gratification. Self-esteem is bound to be lowered by frustration in activities in which success is sought.

Of the ingredients of self-esteem, intimacy needs are also likely to be adversely affected by retardation; we have discussed the loneliness often found in retarded adults. This loneliness can lead to depression (Reiss & Benson, 1985).

Apart from social causes of depression, the disorder also can be triggered by movement from a familiar to an unfamiliar setting; such moves are certain to threaten existing social relationships and supports. Depression is, of course, also a likely response to the death of a loved one, and the reaction to such an event may be even more intense in retardation (Sovner & Pary, 1993). In Chapter 8, the discussion of death education relates to helping individuals with retardation to be emotionally and cognitively prepared for such loss.

Treatment of Mood Disorders

Biological. As noted previously, psychotropic drugs regularly are used to treat mood disorders in mental retardation. Lithium generally is effective with bipolar disorders. More recently, anticonvulsants such as valproic acid (Depakene) or divalproex (Depakote) and carbamazepine (Tegretol) have offered effective and sometimes safer treatment for bipolar disorder.

Behavioral.   The range of behavioral treatments include attempting to modify depressive behaviors themselves, counseling, and inculcating more adaptive social behavior. In fact, most behavioral approaches focus on the teaching of social skills, because depression commonly is associated with social-skills deficit (Benson, Reiss, Smith, & Lamina, 1985). Counseling, of course, can offer personal and emotional support. Recent approaches particularly encourage the use of natural community supports to help children and adults enhance social skills and coping strategies (Koegel, Koegel, & Dunlap, 1996), for example, a "circle of friends."

Behavioral treatment may focus on encouraging positive rather than negative self-statements ("I can handle this" rather than "It's too much for me") or learning how to use friends or preferred activities to break depressive cycles. In a series of studies summarized by Sevin and Matson (1992), reinforcement procedures were targeted at depressive behaviors related to eye contact, grooming, flattening of affect, and somatic complaints.

Schizophrenia

Schizophrenia, the best known of the psychoses, can coexist with mental retardation and in these individuals shows a symptom picture comparable to that of the general population. The symptoms most often found are delusions—false beliefs that are firmly held; hallucinations—false sensory perceptions; disorganized speech, often incoherent; abnormal motor behavior, such as catatonia; and "negative" symptoms (American Psychiatric Association, 1994). Although no one of the symptoms is required for the diagnosis, hallucinations and delusions are commonly present.

A distinction between so-called positive and negative symptoms as manifested in schizophrenia is relevant to mental retardation. Positive symptoms are *excesses* of behavior, behaviors not normally present in individuals functioning adaptively, such as delusions, hallucinations, and bizarre speech. Negative symptoms reflect a narrowing or constriction of the range of behavior, such as flattening of affect, impoverishment of speech or thought productivity, diminished motivation, a lessened sense of self, and social withdrawal. Because some of these negative symptoms may be viewed as manifestations of mental retardation itself, the diagnosis tends to rely on positive symptoms, although problems can arise in self-report because of language limitations.

The possible confusion of symptoms between mental retardation and schizophrenia is illustrated in a study that found that the great majority of adults with Down syndrome (81%) engaged in "self-talk," a behavior that could be interpreted as a hallucinating conversation (McGuire, Chicoine, & Greenbaum, 1997). In fact, this self-talk is a form of "thinking out loud" and is helpful in problem solving. Verbalizing our thoughts may give them greater clarity!

The diagnosis of schizophrenia generally follows a change in the person's usual behavior pattern, a change that takes the form of *regression* to less mature ways of functioning, such as loss of grooming skills and good hygiene, changes in attention, and diminishing problem-solving skills. Typically arising in adolescence or in early adulthood, schizophrenia also can occur later in life. The prevalence of schizophrenia in mental retardation appears to be about the same as in the general population, about 1% (Reiss, 1994b).

In earlier years, the diagnosis of "childhood schizophrenia" commonly was applied to children displaying unusual cognitive, emotional, and motor behaviors. These youngsters are now viewed as autistic, with the diagnosis of schizophrenia reserved for at least school-aged children.

Causes of Schizophrenia

Earlier attributed to disturbed interpersonal relationships, as in the case of other mental disorders, schizophrenia now is regarded as a biological disorder, and one with a strong genetic component. Although only 1% of the general population is at risk for the condition, that risk is increased to 10% in biological first-degree relatives of affected individuals (parents, children, and siblings). A child of schizophrenic parents has a 40% risk; the risk of an identical twin of a schizophrenic individual is from 30% to 50%. In contrast, the fraternal-twin risk rate is much lower, from 10% to 15% (*The Harvard Mental Health Letter*, 1995). The neurophysiology of the disorder is yet to be clarified; no laboratory findings are diagnostic of schizophrenia, although recent studies are indicative of both atrophy in the brain areas related to emotions and memory (the limbic system) and a smaller-than-average thalamus (the relay station between the cortex and the rest of the brain).

As in other psychiatric disorders, schizophrenia has been associated with abnormal neurotransmitter functions in the brain, notably dopamine (Romanczyk, Lockshin, & Harrison, 1993). The effectiveness of medications that affect dopamine, such as haloperidol, reveal this relationship.

Although resting on a biological base, vulnerability to the disorder also is influenced by environmental factors, such as stress. Difficult early life experiences may cause an earlier onset of the disorder or increase its severity.

Numerous characteristics associated with mental retardation affect prognoses for individuals with both conditions. Poorer outcomes are found if problems in adaptive behavior preceded the symptoms, if negative symptoms predominate, and if there are signs of neuropsychological impairment (e.g., poor attention and slower reaction time).

Treatment of Schizophrenia

Effective treatment of the disorder began in the 1950s with the introduction of the drug chlorpromazine (Thorazine). Earlier therapies consisted largely of sedative drugs, occasional psychosurgery (lobotomy), and hospitalization. As in the general population, persons with retardation benefit from antipsychotic drugs, such as thioridazine (Mellaril), haloperidol (Haldol), molindone (Moban), and chlorpromazine. The use of these antipsychotic medications has been less helpful if targeted to behavior problems, such as aggression and SIB, rather then to schizophrenia. They also carry the risk of neurological side effects such as tardive dyskinesia and akathisia.

Newer drugs such as clozapine (Clozaril), risperidone (Risperdal), and olanzapine (Zyprexa) have the benefit of fewer side effects and are as effective in treating positive symptoms and even more so with respect to negative ones. These drugs, however, are not risk-free. The use of clozapine, for example, requires weekly white blood cell counts to monitor for a possibly fatal blood-pressure disorder. Little research on these newer drugs is available in retardation.

Although medication diminishes symptoms, successful community living also requires support in employment, in one's residence, and in interpersonal relations. Community services for those with both schizophrenia and mental retardation have been woefully lacking, primarily because of the administrative separation that commonly exists between state mental-retardation and mental health services. The so-called dually diagnosed individual needs both.

In rare instances, crisis services (described previously) are available, but the inadequacy of state psychiatric hospitals and community programs for this population has been so great that in several states appropriate services only followed the pressure of class-action lawsuits. For individuals with both disorders, life in the community is possible if there is adequate daily structure and access to meaningful activity. The latter can "crowd out" problem behavior (Risley, 1996).

Although medication, structure, and meaningful activity may enable community participation, behavioral treatment procedures also can be helpful. The unusual speech of adults with retardation and schizophrenia has been treated through educational procedures, such as instruction, modeling, rehearsal, and reinforcement (Stephens, Matson, Westmoreland, & Kulpa, 1981). These have been effective in reducing a variety of language problems, such as nonsense phrases, perseverative discussion of past problems, inappropriate changing of the subject of a conversation, and using inappropriate words. Adaptive behavior also has been increased.

Psychotic Disorder Not Otherwise Specified

This diagnosis, "atypical psychosis," often is used if either behavioral history or symptom description is very limited. Intended as a temporary diagnosis, to be updated with more complete information, it appears to be used more frequently in mental retardation than in the general population. Moreover, once rendered, the diagnosis tends to remain rather than being updated.

A study of adults with mental retardation who had been in state psychiatric hospitals, found that more than one quarter (29%) had such a diagnosis (Antonacci & Ulzen, 1997). Reexamined by researchers knowledgeable about retardation *and* psychiatric disorders, the majority could be classified according to standard diagnoses. Most were seen as having a mood disorder; others were diagnosed as schizophrenic. Less than one quarter retained their "atypical" diagnosis; a similar number were found to have no formal psychiatric disorder.

The diagnosis of psychotic disorder not otherwise specified seems to be commonly a classification of expediency whose main purpose is either to secure hospital services or to allow for some kind of diagnosis if the clinician is unfamiliar with mental retardation.

Tourette Syndrome

Tourette syndrome is a neurologically based repetitive movement disorder that also includes psychiatric features. The repetitive movement is called a *tic*. Tics are involuntary, nonrhythmical, sudden, quick, stereotyped movements or vocalizations. They may occur frequently over the course of a day, typically in the form of episodes or "bouts."

Intellectual functioning usually is not impaired. The neurologist-author Oliver Sachs (1995) described tics in an accomplished surgeon and amateur pilot, and they also are present in a professional basketball player (Mahmoud Abdul-Rauf, formerly Chris Jackson). The urge to express a tic has been compared to sneezing. It can be postponed but eventually will occur. Tics also can coexist with other repetitive movement disorders, such as obsessive-compulsive disorder and self-restraint.

So-called simple motor tics usually involve the face and head (e.g., eye blinking, nose twitching, grimacing, sniffing) but also may include the trunk and limbs (e.g., arm thrusting, shoulder shrugging, and kicking). More complex motor tics include touching, smelling, squatting, hopping, clapping, or twirling about.

Vocal Tics

Vocal tics may involve repetition of one's words or phrases, such as "Oh boy" (so-called palilalia), but more often are sounds such as clicks, barks, snorts, throat clearing, and coughs. Its most unusual manifestation is in the form of seemingly involuntary profanity, the uttering of threats or racial epithets, and other inappropriate vocalizations (so-called coprolalia). Perhaps one third of persons with tics show this curious behavior, with a greater frequency in adolescents and in those with more severe forms of the disorder.

Social Aspects

Because tics are very difficult to suppress and appear odd, the disorder can cause much embarrassment and interference in one's work and social life. Moreover, these problems may be exacerbated by the common presence of such other difficulties as obsessive-compulsive disorder, hyperactivity, distractibility, and impulsiveness. Such a condition leads to self-consciousness, likely rejection by others, and reduced self-esteem.

Cause

Tourette syndrome is a genetically based neurological disorder inherited as an autosomal dominant. In families with an affected parent, the risk of inheriting the condition is 1 in 2 for each child. As with other dominantly inherited disorders, there is wide variability in how it manifests itself in affected persons. Like other repetitive movement disorders, Tourette appears to be associated with abnormalities in such brain neurotransmitters as dopamine, noradrenaline, and serotonin and with impairment in the basal ganglia (Rapoport, 1988).

Treatment

Biological. Most of the symptoms of Tourette syndrome are relatively mild and actually may not be targeted for treatment. If treatment is undertaken, the most common medication has been the neuroleptic drug haloperidol (Haldol), although many individuals prefer the symptoms to the drug's side effects! Other frequently used neuroleptics are pimozide (Orap) and fluphenazine (Proxilin). Tourette syndrome also has been treated with the antianxiety drug clonazepam (Klonopin) and the high blood-pressure medication clonidine (Catapres) (Rosenquist & Bodfish, 1997). Because young children with the syndrome may show hyperactivity and attention deficit prior to the onset of tics, stimulant medication, such as methylphenidate (Ritalin), may be initiated, but this actually can induce tics or worsen those already present. It is important, therefore, to determine whether tics, or a family history of tics, are present before using stimulant medication in a child with hyperactivity!

Behavioral.   Behavioral treatments, to date, have been limited to non-retarded individuals. In the few published studies, the most common strategy is "habit reversal" (Peterson & Azrin, 1993). This approach treats tics as if they were forms of common "nervous habits"—nail biting, hair pulling, or thumb sucking. Given that tics are biological in origin, they may be more difficult to control than everyday nervous habits, although some treatment success is reported. Treatment consists of a "package" of techniques that relate to both habits and tics. With respect to the "habit" aspect, one attempt to sensitize the person to the behavior tries to replace it with something less aberrant, seeks to increase motivation to refrain, and seeks to generalize benefits. With respect to tics, treatment also includes increased self-monitoring, progressive muscle relaxation, relaxed breathing, visual imagery, and relaxing self-statements (Azrin & Peterson, 1988, 1990). Interestingly, rapid and lasting reductions have been attained with motor tics but not with vocal ones. Application of these procedures to persons with mental retardation would require some adaptation.

Personality Disorders

Personality traits refer to *enduring* patterns of behavior, our characteristic ways of perceiving and responding to events and thinking about ourselves. It is only if these personality traits cause either impairment in adaptive functioning or subjective distress that they are viewed as disorders. Many of the behavioral features of personality disorders are seen with greater intensity in the major psychiatric syndromes. Personality disorders typically are diagnosed in early adulthood, although some characteristics may be present in adolescence.

Personality disorders are common in mental retardation and a prominent cause of out-of-home placement (Reiss, 1994b). We now describe those frequently seen.

Anxiety-Induced Personality Disorders

Avoidant Personality Disorder.   Like the rest of us, most people with retardation are very responsive to attention, praise, approval, and other forms of positive social contact. They also share with us negative responses to criticism or disapproval. But in retardation such reactions tend to be intensified. Avoidant personality disorder is diagnosed if one eschews virtually all social situations because of feelings of inadequacy and fear of criticism or rejection. Parenthetically, nothing is so damaging to our self-esteem as "criticism." It is not surprising that it commonly evokes anger and counterattack. This is our way of protecting our self-esteem, of rejecting the validity of anything that would lower it. In this respect, all "defensive" behavior can be viewed as behavior intended to maintain or "shore up" our self-image. The more fragile the self-image, the greater the sensitivity to criticism and the more defensive our response to it. Given the disabilities associated with retardation in a culture that values intelligence, independence, and general competence, it is not surprising that persons with retardation find themselves experiencing more than their share of general criticism. Of all the personality disorders in mental retardation, avoidant is the most common (Reiss, 1990).

Dependent Personality Disorder. This personality disorder is characterized by an excessive need to be cared for, an unusual fear of separation, and engagement in submissive and clinging behavior. Individuals with this disorder tend to have very close relationships with one or two others (e.g., a family member or a direct caregiver) and intense fears of their loss. This behavior pattern is more common in females (American Psychiatric Association, 1994).

"Acting-Out" Personality Disorders

Antisocial Personality Disorder. The presence of various forms of aggression (e.g., verbal and physical assault, property destruction, stealing, and lying) in the absence of remorse is characterized as antisocial personality disorder. Primarily absent in adult males, persons with this personality pattern frequently become involved in criminal behavior. To the degree that antisocial personality is equated with "psychopathic" or "sociopathic" behavior, this aspect is typically absent in persons with retardation because the intellectual impairment reduces their capacity to engage in deliberate manipulation of others. The typical "con man" is bright and applies his knowledge of human behavior to criminal ends.

   In the absence of remorse for one's misbehavior, opportunities for treatment are very limited and largely tied to "punishment" and to the need to protect society from such individuals.

Childhood Precursors of Antisocial Personality Disorder: Oppositional Defiant Disorder and Conduct Disorder. Although the diagnosis of antisocial personality disorder is not applied to children, there are two childhood conditions that resemble antisocial personality disorder and commonly lead to that diagnosis in adulthood. Referring to a pattern of hostile and defiant behavior present

in the child before age 8 years and that persists for at least 6 months, *oppositional defiant disorder* is characterized by outbursts of anger; arguments with parents, teachers, and caregivers; refusal to comply with requests; and a high level of irritability. Other features involve some cognitive sophistication and are less evident in children with more severe levels of retardation. These include spitefulness or vindictiveness, blaming others, and deliberate attempts to annoy.

The other disorder in this category, *conduct disorder*, includes the key elements of oppositional defiant disorder but also involves more serious violations of the law. Although young children may be regarded as "oppositional defiant," it is the older child, typically the adolescent, whose antisocial behavior can assume a criminal character, for example breaking into houses, theft, assault, rape, and use of a weapon.

Each of the three types of acting-out personality disorders has the common element of aggression, along with such other behavior problems as disorders of mood, hyperactivity, attention deficit, poor school and work histories, impaired peer relations, communication difficulties, and vulnerability to substance abuse. Although aggression is found at all levels of cognitive impairment, its manifestation in the form of adult antisocial behavior is largely limited to persons with mild retardation.

Causes of Aggression in Personality Disorders

A general discussion of the causes of aggression is presented in the preceding chapter. With respect to antisocial behavior, there is, curiously, some evidence for a genetic vulnerability. Apart from the obvious influence of parental behavior on that of children, there is indication that the risk is increased even if children of parents with such behavior are raised in adoptive homes (Yancy, 1999). Environmental factors are important in families that rely heavily on coercion, threats, and punishment as the chief means of influencing their children's behavior and such families can undermine the development of prosocial behavior (Patterson, 1982). More to the point, in the scenario that the senior author commonly encounters in people convicted of first-degree murder, the murderer himself has been the target of physically abusive behavior by his father during childhood. Violence is learned and mimicked!

Treatment

Although the conditions that often accompany antisocial behavior (e.g., depression and hyperactivity) may respond to medication, no drug inculcates prosocial skills. Happily, behavioral treatment has been effective in engendering adaptive social behavior and is a standard part of most early-education curricula for children from backgrounds that place them at risk for developing antisocial behavior (Meisels & Shonkoff, 1990). Admittedly, exposure to families that "model" aggression and to antisocial peers makes treatment more difficult as the child grows older, but even in adolescence treatment can be effective. An example of such treatment is the "teaching-family model" first demonstrated at Achievement Place in Kansas City, Kansas. It is a model that combines a residential setting with the encouragement of prosocial behavior (Bernfeld, Blave, & Fixen, 1990).

In contrast to residential treatment programs that literally move the child into a less aggressive environment, as in Achievement Place, other therapies have been less effective. Modifying patterns of antisocial behavior is a difficult task. It requires exposure to nonaggressive adult and peer models, role playing (Matson & Stephens, 1978), and participation in activities specifically designed to teach more socially adaptive behavior (Edmonson & Han, 1983). Unfortunately, the immediate influences of peer and neighborhood values are often more powerful than the effects of nonresidential treatment. The ultimate consequence of such a failure is a future pattern of law violation and imprisonment.

Borderline Personality Disorder

The hallmarks of this disorder are chronic volatility of interpersonal relationships and affect, manipulation of others, and poor impulse control. Other characteristics are inappropriate interpersonal (e.g., touching and standing too close) and emotional boundaries (e.g., asking questions that are too personal). These individuals also are very demanding and frequently in crisis. They often display intense anger, threaten suicide, and express fear of abandonment. Although seen as manipulative, they are not subtle in their attempts to influence others. Rather they feel manipulated by forces beyond their control, and their extreme acts (e.g., threats of suicide) are undisguised cries for help (Linehan, 1993).

Although the disorder has only been accorded formal diagnostic status since about 1980, it now represents one of the largest groups of patients in the general psychiatric population (Linehan, 1993). Including people with mental retardation (Gabriel, 1997), these individuals typically come to attention because of episodes of self-injury and attempts at suicide. The type of self-injury found in borderline personality disorder differs from that seen in persons with severe and profound retardation both in intent and form. Individuals with borderline personality disorder are more likely to inflict self-injuries that involve deliberate cutting or scratching of oneself or burning oneself with a cigarette. More extreme behaviors include overdosing with drugs, self-stabbing, and self-asphyxiation (Linehan, 1993).

In contrast to that seen in retardation, self-injury in the borderline personality appears to be more purposeful and manipulative.

More common in women, borderline personality disorder may coexist with other forms of mental illness, chiefly mood disorders and acute psychotic states. Sexual abuse in childhood frequently is present in these women, a vulnerability particularly shared with retarded women (reported in Chapter 6).

As with other personality disorders, treatment is difficult. Medication has been helpful with some symptoms, such as mood problems; psychotic episodes may respond to antipsychotic drugs (Gabriel, 1997). Angry outbursts have been treated with the anticonvulsant carbamazepine (Tegretol). In the use of medication with these individuals, however, one needs to be aware of their potential to abuse medications and overdose (Linehan, 1993).

The only behavioral treatment that has shown effectiveness is "dialectical behavior therapy" (Linehan, 1993). This procedure requires a close relationship with the therapist in individual and group treatment and requires long-term *consistency* as a key element. Dialectical behavior therapy views the disorder as a deficiency in the capacity to modulate biological states, such as arousal.

Some of its success is attributable to its consistent adherence to agreed-on rules of behavior (structure), setting limits for individuals who had difficulty in setting their own.

Disorders of Impulse Control

Impulsive Acting-Out Behavior

Although not a formal diagnostic classification, "impulsiveness" is a feature of many of the behavior disorders described; it is the intense acting out of emotions or feelings. Common in mental retardation in general, it is also prominent in psychiatric disorders as the behavioral expression of emotionally driven impulses. Impulsiveness increases with the intensity of emotions and can lead to actions that reflect little or no concern for their consequences.

Much maladaptive behavior in retardation occurs impulsively, such as aggression, self-injury, and property destruction. We should not be surprised that impulsiveness is a feature of mental retardation; our capacity to control or inhibit emotionally driven impulses is tied to our abilities to consider the consequences of acting out our feelings. It is precisely in the kind of language-based cognitive functions that affect our ability to "self-talk," "think," or consider consequences that the person with retardation is at a disadvantage. A deficit in the capacity for *verbal mediation* has been seen as a central feature of mental retardation (Milgram, 1973).

Among the psychiatric disorders, impulsiveness is seen in schizophrenia, in the sexual disorders, in borderline personality, and in substance abuse. It is also an aspect of the previously described stereotypies trichotillomania and bruxism.

Intermittent Explosive Disorder

Acting out aggressively without apparent provocation or where the behavior is clearly disproportionate to the provocation illustrates this impulse disorder. A formal psychiatric diagnostic clarification, it fits much aggression seen in retardation. Such explosive episodes typically are followed by expressions of regret or remorse, at least in persons with not more than mild retardation. Individuals who show this behavior tend to be impulsive in many aspects of their lives.

Treatment commonly involves the kind of psychotropic medications described in the section on aggression in the previous chapter. A functional analysis of this disorder is difficult, because it occurs so suddenly and its antecedents may be obscure. The presence of such outbursts should alert one to the possibility that they may be symptoms of atypical seizures, post traumatic stress disorder, or panic attack.

Eating Disorders

The most common eating disorders in mental retardation are pica and rumination. Also seen as transient behaviors in normally developing infants, in retardation they are likely to be later in onset and to persist throughout life. Pica also is observed sometimes in Prader-Willi syndrome, the genetic disorder of uncontrolled eating described in Chapter 3.

Pica

Pica is a disorder characterized by the consumption of nonfood substances. It may include the eating of cigarette butts, paper, clothing, dirt, leaves, or paint chips and even such dangerous objects as rocks, razor blades, and safety pins. Even feces may be consumed (coprophagy). Because of the objects consumed, pica can pose immediate health risks, such as the swallowing of sharp objects or poisonous materials. There also can be long-term risks tied to the consumption of such substances as leaded paint. (The health hazards posed by lead consumption were described in Chapter 4). Other medical complications include parasitic infections, peritonitis, asphyxiation, intestinal blockage, vomiting, constipation, and malnutrition (McCuller, 1992b). Pica also may be a part of a chain of behavior that begins with "scavenging" and progresses from pica to rectal digging, feces smearing, and coprophagy (Schroeder, 1989b). In such a chain, the material consumed may cause constipation or discomfort at elimination, and these lead to rectal digging and the rest of the chain.

Although observed in about one half of all infants by age 1 year, pica is found in less than 10% of children by age 4 years. In contrast, the rate of pica in institutionalized adults with retardation has been reported as 26% with greater frequency and severity among those with severe or profound retardation (Danford & Huber, 1982).

Although the range of ingestibles is huge, practitioners of pica tend to focus on a particular nonedible. The range of their food choices indicates that the behavior cannot be attributable to a simple failure to *discriminate* between edibles and inedibles; practitioners of pica know what they want!

Considering the hazards of pica, treatment emphasizes prevention. This means keeping the individual's environment free of ingestibles, a daunting task given the rank of potential edibles. Unfortunately, it also means limiting the individual's access to the wider community.

Behavioral approaches focus on the nature of the reinforcement in pica. If attention appears to be at least maintaining the behavior, and pica does get our attention! treatment may involve withholding attention (extinction) and offering it for appropriate eating (differential reinforcement of incompatible behavior). If it is maintained by sensory consequences (positive reinforcement), other oral sensory experiences should be offered, such as popcorn, rice cakes, or chewing gum. If pica is maintained by escape from demands or other unwanted experiences (negative reinforcement), demands may be reduced as the individual is taught more appropriate means of avoiding them. Interestingly, some forms of pica, notably the consumption of coffee grounds or cigarettes, may reflect a genuine addiction, the individual having developed a chemical dependency on caffeine and nicotine. Here, the chemical dependency can be treated as the individual is offered a safer way of attaining the desired substances (McCuller, 1992). Although research exists on the use of punishment to reduce pica, treatment programs typically stress the engaging of the individual in preferred but adaptive activities.

Rumination

This eating disorder consists of self-induced vomiting of food just consumed, chewing of the vomitus (rumination), and then swallowing it. Observed in the normally developing infant between 3 and 10 months of age, it frequently follows a period of feeding difficulty that may include vomiting (Friedman & Daum, 1992). Happily rare, it can be life-threatening but usually resolves itself in less than a year. Rumination in retardation does not appear to be simply a prolongation of the condition as it appears in normally developing infants. Rather it tends to have a later onset and to persist throughout life (Rast, 1992; Schroeder, 1989c).

Regurgitation and rumination typically occur within 15 minutes after the completion of nearly every meal and are pursued in a consistent pattern that lasts from 20 to 60 minutes (Rast, 1992). Hopefully, improved nutritional practices may be reducing its frequency (Rast, 1992).

Although seldom life-threatening, like pica it can pose serious health threats—choking, weight loss (or even malnutrition), dehydration, or infection (e.g., pneumonia). Retention of food in the mouth also increases the risk of gum disease, tooth decay, and bad breath. Not surprisingly, the odor, appearance, and repugnant nature of the behavior leads to the social isolation of its practitioners and severely limits opportunities for greater independence and community integration (Rast, 1992; Schroeder, 1989c).

The diagnosis of rumination requires careful medical, psychological, and nutritional assessment in order to rule out other conditions that cause vomiting (e.g., pyloric stenosis and "operant" vomiting). Operant vomiting can be distinguished through a functional analysis of behavior that also provides important treatment information. In operant vomiting, the behavior typically is directed toward attaining attention (another "good" attention getter!) or toward escape from demands or an unwanted situation. In such cases, the vomitus is expelled, sometimes at another person!

Although operant vomiting clearly is maintained by its effects on other people and, thus, lends itself to treatment, rumination is more often reinforced by *sensory* stimulation—chewing, taste, and the feeling of fullness.

It has been difficult to treat the disorder. Mild punishment has been effective if consistently implemented (e.g., lemon juice, mouthwash, or other aversive-tasting substances in the mouth). More positive approaches seek to make the meal and the time after it more satisfying (Rast, 1992). These include offering foods that require more chewing, gradually increasing the time between bites to prevent gorging, providing oral stimulation immediately after the meal (e.g., coffee or chewing gum), and offering bigger and bulkier meals (e.g., peanut butter). The intent is to create the feeling of satiation. Satiation and its accompanying feeling of "fullness" can be achieved with healthy, low-calorie foods (Lobato, Carlson, & Barrera, 1986) and may reduce not only rumination but also other forms of self-stimulation (Clauser & Scibak, 1990).

Finally, the nonmealtime experience must be enriched while socially mediated reinforcement (i.e., attention or escape) is denied (Rast, 1992). This treatment strategy illustrates the importance of considering multiple determinants in the management of maladaptive behavior in lower functioning individuals.

A Summary Thought

It is difficult to write about the behaviors associated with pica and rumination. We are confronted with the jarring reality of behavior that is utterly repugnant. But such behavior is not limited to mental retardation. It also is seen in serious mental illness where the smearing of feces is a common psychotic symptom. These behaviors are manifestations of altered brain functioning. Although their origin may lie outside our understanding, it is essential to recognize that we, too, have the capacity to engage in such aberrant activity. At least as important, these behaviors can be modified.

Alcohol and Substance Abuse

Prior to the 1980s, there was little attention to alcohol and substance abuse in retardation. Although the rate of drug abuse appears to be lower than that in the general population (Christian & Poling, 1997), a study comparing special and regular education students found very similar rates. One quarter of the special-education students had used marijuana in the prior year as compared with the 28% of regular class students. In both groups there was much less use of harder drugs, averaging about 6% in special-education youth and about 11% in "regular" students (Gress & Boss, 1996). A study of nearly 600 retarded adults living semi-independently in the community found that 56% drank alcohol and 3% smoked marijuana. Given current trends, it can be assumed that these rates are now higher. In particular, abuse of drugs and alcohol seems to be especially prevalent among those with both mental retardation and mental illness (Longo, 1997). Why is this happening?

Cause of Alcohol and Substance Abuse

As a first consideration we must recognize that many of the behaviors and medical conditions found in persons with substance abuse also are common in retardation. These include impulsiveness; poor judgment and planning, especially under stress; low self-esteem; inadequate social support from friends; and chronic physical discomfort (Moore & Polsgrove, 1991). Anxiety or the fear of becoming anxious also may lead to self-medication with drugs (Reiss, 1994b).

A second explanation of increased substance abuse lies in the much greater freedom and community access now available to youth and adults with retardation. They now are subject to the same temptations as the rest of us!

Treatment

The study of the problem of alcoholism and drug addiction in retardation is so new that little is known about its treatment. Earlier methods that relied on punishment or restriction are challenged in an era of emphasis on self-determination and individual rights. Contemporary programs providing residential and other community services must balance the person's "right to choose" and to free movement in the community with the need to protect people who may be particularly vulnerable to addictive exposure.

This dilemma also exists in relation to presumably less lethal addicting substances, such as nicotine and caffeine. Although there would be universal agreement that one should discontinue smoking after a diagnosis of emphysema, many nonretarded adults choose to ignore their doctors' advice. Should people with retardation have the same option? Many people with retardation have family members who drink to excess or use marijuana. Should retardation be a basis for preventing the individual from engaging in the same behavior? Apart from legal considerations, it would appear that our best approach is to apply the same criteria used to obtain informed consent. We only can insist on conveying awareness of the risks of these behaviors and, in the absence of unnatural levels of supervision, hope that the message "takes." To the degree that adults are involved in programs providing some level of support, their readiness to accept the advice of caregivers is tied to the quality of their relationships with them. Like the child or adolescent in a family, you want to please those with whom you have caring relationships. Parenthetically, all noncoercive relationships that seek to influence the behavior of another ultimately depend on a base of trust and caring.

A Closing Thought on Behavior Disorders

The failure to fulfill basic human needs in the person with mental retardation, as with us all, places that individual at increased risk for maladaptive behavior and psychiatric disorders. As noted previously, apart from conditions that are primarily biological in origin, such as Lesch-Nyhan syndrome, maladaptive behavior is the outward expression of the chronic frustration of basic psychological needs. Our understanding of the nature, cause, and treatment of such behavior has grown. We now recognize the presence of a wide variety of such disorders in mental retardation—in children, youth, and adults. Treatment has improved significantly and, as a result, more people with mental retardation are now leading full and meaningful lives in their communities.

☐ Related Developmental Disorders

In this final section are presented two developmental disorders that share with mental retardation significant learning difficulties—*autism* and *developmental learning disorders* ("learning disabilities"). Although retardation is a common feature of autism and in this respect contributes to its learning problems, the developmental learning disorders are distinguished by the presence of *specific* academic learning difficulties that are not explicable in terms of "general intelligence."

Autism

General Features

The greatest area of overlap between mental retardation and other developmental disorders is found in autism. First described in 1943 by the American child psychiatrist Leo Kanner (1993), the term "early infantile autism" was applied to a small group of children whose chief characteristics were extreme aloofness and uninterest in people, impairment in language, an intense need for sameness ("structure"), and a fascination with objects rather than people.

This behavioral picture has been confirmed by later researchers (e.g., Schopler, 1983) and is reflected in the current diagnostic criteria of DSM-IV. With an onset by age 3 years, autism is seen as adversely affecting social behavior, communication, and one's range of interests and activities.

The severity of the social and communication abnormalities together with much odd and seemingly bizarre behavior led people to view autistic children as "psychotic" and to regard the disorder as a childhood form of schizophrenia (Goldfarb, 1961). Subsequent research has not indicated any relationship between autism and schizophrenia. Unlike schizophrenia, autistic children rarely develop delusions and hallucinations (Rutter, 1970). In the current psychiatric nomenclature, autism is classified as a "pervasive developmental disorder" rather than as a psychosis.

Apart from issue of psychosis, there has been much confusion between autism and mental retardation. The majority of autistic children also are mentally retarded (e.g., Lincoln, Courchesne, Kilman, Elmasian, & Allen, 1988) and both groups include children who show odd, stereotyped movements, e.g., body rocking and hand and arm waving. Particularly prominent in nonautistic children with severe or profound retardation

(Baumeister, 1978), these movements also are found in blind children, presumably a form of self-initiated sensory stimulation. Although all three disability groups show stereotypy, it is only the autistic child who is unable to develop normal affectionate relationships. It is the social distance of the autistic child that sets him apart.

Each of the major features of autism now is illustrated.

Social (Interpersonal) Abnormalities

Here is one mother's description of her son, Peter, as an infant:

> More troubling was the fact that Peter didn't look at us, or smile [autistic children tend to avoid looking at faces, so-called gaze aversion].... While he didn't cry, he rarely laughed, and when he did, it was at things that didn't seem funny to us [inappropriate affect]. He didn't cuddle but sat upright in my lap even when I rocked him [avoidance of touching is common, although some enjoy roughhouse play]. Peter's uncle visits him when he's eight months old and notes, "That kid has no social instincts whatever" [an extremely insightful observation about the autistic child]. Although Peter was a first child, he was not isolated. I frequently put him in his playpen in front of the house where the school children stopped to play with him as they passed. The children showed interest in him; he didn't respond. (Eberhardy, 1967, p. 258)

Another feature of the autistic child, social and emotional distance, characterizes the interaction when the child is involved with people. People, including parents, may be treated, quite literally, as if they were inanimate objects rather than feeling human beings. If the child wants the parent to get something that is out of reach, the child will take the parent's wrist, not hand, and move it to the desired object as if the hand were a tool. There is also little or no reaction to the distress of others. The children seem to lack normal feelings of compassion or identification with other people (Hobson, 1989).

The unresponsiveness to normal parental affection is devastating to parents. Parental needs for intimacy are frustrated by a child who seems to have little interest or desire for parental affection. In terms of our personality model, the classic autistic child is unique in the lack of the need for intimacy.

Communication (Language) Abnormalities

Language difficulties exist in both the understanding of speech and its use (e.g., Baron-Cohen, 1988; Schopler & Mesibov, 1985). Speech may not develop at all and "language" may consist only of inarticulate grunts and sounds sporadically punctuated by clearly expressed words that have no relevance to the situation in which they occur. Indeed, the very imitation of speech or speech sounds can be difficult (Yoder & Layton, 1988). About one half of individuals with autism never develop functional speech (Paul, 1987), in spite of normal hearing. Some autistic children seem so indifferent to speech, and to other sounds as well, as to cause their parents to suspect a hearing loss (Rutter, 1972). It is the child's "selective" response to sounds that reveals the general intactness of hearing.

Of those who acquire speech, the majority have a lengthy period of *echolalia*, the immediate or delayed parroting of words or phrases used by others (Rutter, 1972). Interestingly, echoed speech may mimic accurately that of its originator, evidence of normal hearing for speech sounds, but the spontaneous speech of the same child will be much poorer in intelligibility. Together with echolalia, there frequently are reversals of pronouns; the child referring to himself as "you" rather than as "I." In asking for a cookie, for example, the child might say, "You want a cookie," instead of, "I want a cookie." It is as though the child were a tape recorder literally playing back what it hears. After all, the parent might pose the question to the child, "Do you want a cookie?" It is as if there is no appreciation that the "you" referred to is "I."

Words are commonly interpreted literally. A child who always referred to her dog's dinner plate as a "dish" was completely confused when asked to put something in the dog's "bowl." In autism, things have only one label; the concept of a synonym is alien. The word is not understood as a label for an object that can have many designations; it is as if the word-label and the object were one. A more bizarre example is the child who instead of saying "no" would say, "Don't throw it out of the window" (Wing, 1985). Parents had shouted the latter phrase to him in the act of trying to prevent a household disaster, and he had come to connect that event with the idea of "no." Remarkably, children may never acquire such words as "yes" and "no."

In spite of these difficulties, by about age 5 years, many children are able to understand at least single brief expressions, such as, "Put your hat on," and show improvements in functional speech. Nevertheless, their spontaneous language tends to be telegraphic in quality. As in the very young child, connective words are not used, and even speech order may be confused. And even if speech is generally normal in sentence length and structure, its sound quality is odd. It may lack normal variations in tone and have a monotonous or robot-like quality.

But language problems are not limited to speech itself. There is a fundamental impairment in the understanding of language. It is as if the child were hearing a foreign language. Not only are the words not understood but there is little sensitivity to the meaning of the facial expressions and gestures that accompany them (Baron-Cohen, 1988).

In autism there is a fundamental difficulty in understanding and using the most basic aspects of communication. Indeed, the child seems unaware of the very *idea* of communication and may not even use simple gestures. If attempts to communicate occur in children without functional language, they tend to be indirect, expressed in crying, temper tantrums, self-hitting, or even echolalic speech. With reference to echolalia, studies suggest that it can serve as an indirect way of communicating requests, protest, and affirmation (Prizant & Rydell, 1984). Remarkably, direct expressions of what one wants or does not want are simply not present or are limited to requests for objects or actions. Autistic children do not use speech to request information or to comment on what others have said (Wetherby & Prutting, 1984).

And even if speech is acquired, its use is aberrant. What passes for a verbal exchange or "conversation" tends to be a monologue. The child may persist in repeating questions for which the intent does not seem to be eliciting an answer. The content of speech may be of little or no interest to the listener, but the listener's reaction has no influence on the child. The normal reciprocity or "give and take" of a verbal exchange is absent. Speech and language simply are not used in their usual fashion, a so-called pragmatic difficulty. Presumably, this reflects the child's *social* insensitivity.

The mother of an autistic child describes her daughter's early language development:

> Lagging far behind even this slow expansion of social responses was speech, the prime instrument of social interchange. The few isolated words she had spoken up to age 4 had no social meaning; she gave no sign of comprehension when we spoke the very same words to her. Jessy's few words did not include a sound for greeting, or a sound for mother or father, or the names of any of the family. Even when at five she began to retain the names of people and objects, she did not use them for communication of any kind, least of all shared and sharable intentions. [Language is not really used for "communication," per se.] She was 6 before she used a word to request something; it was years (she's now a grown woman) before she used a name to call one of us to her. (Park, 1986, p. 84)

Activities and Interests

In autism there is an extraordinary constriction of interests. Whereas the normally developing child seeks a blend of the novel and the familiar, the child with autism craves sameness. Novelty is not the spice of life in autism. In relentless fashion the child pursues activities that are repetitive, compulsive, indeed ritualistic in quality. Whatever is engaged is done in a rigid and unchanging fashion. A sense of the lengths to which the need for sameness can go is seen in a child who insisted that the wood that was used to build a fire in the fireplace always be laid out in exactly the same manner (Wing, 1985)! In the obsessional pursuit of interests, the child may spend hours lining up objects on the floor or playing the same record, or only parts of it, repeatedly.

Although change is upsetting, a radical change may cause no distress. Thus one child reacted calmly to a move to a new house but became frantic when given a new bedcover. Another responded with a tantrum to any new clothes.

In adolescence, one finds odd interests. There may be fascination with travel schedules or telephone numbers. One child insisted on being read to from the telephone book! Their preoccupation with an activity or topic may lead to endless questions. As indicated, these questions are not really intended to obtain information; rather, they seem intended to evoke a standard answer.

Autistic youth tend to be collectors, but their collections are not usually of the things people generally collect or even value. Leaves, string, empty containers, even pieces of concrete may be collected and prized with the same intensity as valued stamps or coins.

Another idiosyncratic quality is their use of toys (Wing, 1985). A toy is not played with in the way intended, for example, *pulling* a toy wagon. Rather it may be enjoyed for its sensory properties. The child may like the smooth texture of its surface or enjoy watching the spinning of its wheels. There appears to be a special interest in watching things spin, and these children enjoy whirling themselves around, seemingly without getting dizzy. Another striking feature of their play is the apparent lack of fantasy or "pretend" quality. The children do not play games in which one pretends to be someone or something.

Cognitive Functioning

The prominence of mental retardation in autism has been noted. Kanner (1943) recognized the frequent presence of intellectual impairment, but he assumed that their basic intellect was intact, only disguised by the disorder. He noted that the children's facial expression appeared "intelligent" in contrast to the stigmatic appearance of some retarded children, and that they often showed unusual rote memory ability. It also has been observed that, in contrast to their language difficulties, some children showed normal functioning in such nonlanguage areas as assembling a puzzle.

The presumption of an underlying normal cognitive capacity could have been confirmed if dramatic changes in mental ability were common. This is not the case. Although the degree of impairment often lessens by school age, the majority of those affected still function in the retarded range.

At least as significant is the degree of cognitive impairment. The majority of autistic children (50% to 67%) function in the below-50 IQ range (Schopler, 1983). The more severe levels of retardation tend to be found in children who have the poorest prognosis for major changes in general adjustment (Carr, 1976).

Although there is clear overlap between mental retardation and autism, the pattern of cognitive functioning between the two populations does differ. The extraordinary concreteness or literalness of the autistic child has no parallel in retardation, nor does one see the same kind of language peculiarities in retardation. Especially distinguishing the autistic child are so-called splinter skills or islets of intelligence. These splinter skills, if present, include such phenomena as relatively normal or even superior ability in rote memory, visual tasks such as jigsaw puzzles, and their previously described calendar calculating.

Finally, it should be noted that a fraction of the autistic population is not retarded at all and some, such as Temple Grandin, have achieved at a high level academically (Grandin & Scariano, 1986). In such persons, however, autism is likely to affect their social relationships. Indeed, the Internet has given some opportunities for autistic adults to communicate with people by computer and thus avoid the discomfort of actual face-to-face contact!

Other Common Findings

In addition to the features described thus far, one also sees in autism a variety of odd behaviors. Like children with severe and profound retardation, autistic children commonly exhibit stereotypic movements and engage in self-injurious behavior. They may show unusual fears, dramatic changes in emotional states, and unusual sensory reactions, and they are at high risk for seizures, especially in adolescence.

Patterns of Behavior in Children, Youth, and Adults

Much variability is seen in the behavior of individuals who show the basic characteristics of autism. Within the total population, three subgroups have been distinguished, largely on the basis of their interpersonal behavior. They are *aloof, passive,* and *active but odd* (Wing & Attwood, 1987). The "aloof" child approximates the classical picture of autism as described by Kanner. The "passive" child is less withdrawn and, although not initiating social exchange, is more accepting of it. The passive child can be encouraged to participate in activities. The "active but odd" child, unlike the other two groups, initiates interaction, but in a peculiar, naive, and one-sided manner, such as insistence on listening to a reading of the telephone book. The most verbal of the three groups, these children talk *at* a person rather than engaging in a reciprocal verbal exchange.

Prevalence, Cause, and Treatment

A rare disorder, autism is found in about 1 in 2000 of the general population, with males much more likely to be affected. The ratio of males to females is about 4:1. Earlier workers in the field tended to attribute autism to inadequate parenting, but subsequent studies found no parental characteristics that distinguished parents of autistic children from parents of nonautistic children (e.g., DeMyer et al., 1974). In contrast to the earlier view of parents as "pathogenic," Schopler (1983) regards parents as allies and potential cotherapists in the treatment of their children. Current workers tend to view the disorder as caused by some kind of organic brain abnormality, but a specific locus has yet to be defined. Brain areas that appear to be involved include the arousal and alertness center in the brain stem; the limbic system—the system that controls emotional and motivational aspects of behavior; and the cerebellum.

Although a wide variety of treatment programs have had their advocates, the most consistently effective ones have been "behavioral" and "educational" in nature (Lovars, 1987; McEachlin, Smith, & Lovars, 1993; Schopler, 1976; Wing, 1985). Accepting the reality of the disability, educationally oriented treatment is designed to maximize the child's skills and to prepare him to function as adaptively as possible within the limits of the disability. In this endeavor, parents are key agents.

In addition to a highly structured educational experience, the child may benefit from medications used to treat various associated behavior disorders. We are cautioned that pharmacological treatment should never be the sole therapeutic modality. Rather, it should be viewed as a part of a comprehensive and individualized treatment program (Campbell, Schopler, Mesibov, & Sanchez, 1995).

Developmental Learning Disorders

General Characteristics

Treated in depth in books on learning disabilities, these are disorders of learning that are *not* attributable to impairment in general intelligence or in sensory skills. Further, they are present in *spite* of exposure to learning environments in which these abilities would normally be expected to develop. The central feature of these disorders is the failure to acquire these skills at the level commensurate with the child's basic intellectual and sensory capacities. At school age these skill deficits are commonly characterized as "learning disabilities," and in the psychiatric literature, they have been termed *academic skills disorders* (DSM III-R; American Psychiatric Association, 1987) or, more recently, as simply "learning disorders" (DSM-IV; American Psychiatric Association, 1994). The latter designation is consistent with the classification system proposed in Chapter 1, wherein these disorders would be characterized as *specific academic disorders of learning*. The description here focuses on the areas of major academic difficulty but also includes those of language and motor development.

With respect to language, problems with receptive language, that is, failure to understand spoken language, can be confused with mental retardation. Demoralization, low self-esteem, and poor social skills often accompany learning disorders. Children with these problems are much more likely to drop out of school and, for adults, these conditions can adversely affect employment and social adjustment (American Psychiatric Association, 1994). Although general intelligence is not grossly affected, there may be underlying problems in such cognitive processes as visual perception, attention, memory, and cognitive processes related to language. Although commonly found in association with such medical conditions as lead poisoning, fragile X syndrome, and fetal alcohol syndrome, the typical picture is one that is *free* of clear organic abnormality.

Developmental Arithmetic Disorder

This is a disorder marked by an impairment in the development of arithmetic skills that is not explicable in terms of sensory deficits (e.g., vision), inadequate schooling, or general intelligence. Usually evident by third grade, it may affect a variety of related cognitive abilities. These include linguistic skills, such as understanding or naming mathematical terms, operations, and concepts and translating written problems into mathematical symbols; perceptual skills, such as reading numerical symbols and clustering objects in groups; "attention" skills—copying figures correctly, remembering to add "carried" numbers, and observing operational signs; and common arithmetic skills—counting objects, learning multiplication tables, and following sequences of mathematical steps.

Developmental Expressive Writing Disorder

In this disorder, the child shows extreme difficulty in composing written material, perhaps the most complex of the language skills. The *written* product may be marred by errors of organization, grammar and punctuation, and spelling. In severe cases, the condition is evident by age 7 (2nd grade); in milder forms, it may not be apparent until age 10 (5th grade) or later.

Developmental Reading Disorder

Probably the most common of the developmental academic disorders, its main feature is impairment in word recognition and reading comprehension. As in the other developmental learning disorders, the condition exists in spite of grossly normal intelligence, intact vision, and adequate educational opportunity. Also referred to as "dyslexia," the disorder usually is manifest by age 7 years (second grade).

Developmental Language and Speech Disorder

Although disorders of language at both the "expressive" and "receptive" levels are common in mental retardation, these conditions can arise in the presence of normal intellectual functioning, intact hearing and a physically normal speech mechanism.

Developmental Articulation Disorder. In the presence of apparently normal cognitive and physical abilities, the child fails to articulate speech sounds at the level expected for his age. The condition is reflected in frequent misarticulation and the substitution or omission of speech sounds. This gives the child's speech a "babyish" quality.

The sounds most frequently misarticulated are those arising later in development—*r, sh, th, f, z, l,* and *ch.* In more severe cases or in younger children, there may be mispronunciation of such sounds as *b, m, t, d, n,* and *h.* One or more speech sounds may be affected, but these are limited to consonants. Vowel sounds are not affected.

With speech therapy there usually is complete mastery of these sounds and, in milder cases, sounds may be mastered before age 8 years.

Developmental Expressive Language (Speech) Disorder. The linguistic features of this speech disorder are varied, depending on its severity and the age of the child. Nonlanguage functioning is usually perfectly normal. Its common manifestations are a difficulty in learning new words and a very narrow vocabulary; imprecise speech, for example verbal circumlocution; shortened sentences; simplified grammatical structures, such as verb forms; unusual word order; omission of critical parts of sentences; and a generally slow rate of speech development.

Severe forms are usually evident before age 3 years. Less severe ones may not be apparent until adolescence.

The prognosis for the eventual development of relatively normal speech is very good if the disorder is mild in severity. About half of children with this disorder spontaneously catch up in their language by school age and do not require further assistance. And even in more severe cases, normal language usually is acquired by late adolescence as long as there is no accompanying "receptive language" disorder. If a receptive (understanding of language) disorder is present, there is always an expressive one accompanying it.

Developmental Receptive Language Disorder. This is a disorder in which there is a marked impairment in the ability to understand spoken language that, as in the other developmental disorders, it is not explicable in terms of mental retardation, hearing impairment, or unfamiliarity with the language itself. In mild cases there may be only difficulties in understanding specific types of words, such as spatial forms, or such complexities as "if-then" statements. With greater severity there may be multiple deficits including an inability to understand simple words or sentences and problems in auditory processing. The latter could include poor discrimination of speech sounds and impairments in verbal learning, memory, and sequencing. With severe receptive language deficit, as noted, one also can expect an expressive language disorder as well.

Developmental Coordination (Motor Skills) Disorder

Noncognitive in nature, this disorder is marked by impairment in motor coordination. Children exhibit clumsiness and delays in developmental motor milestones including tying shoelaces, buttoning shirts, and zipping pants. The children have difficulty with the motor aspects of puzzle assembly, model building, athletics, and handwriting.

☐ Summary

The second of two chapters on behavior problems in mental retardation, this chapter describes disorders that have formal psychiatric designations. After a brief review of issues pertaining to psychopathology in persons with retardation, the remainder of the chapter, with the exception of the final section, is devoted to a presentation of the most commonly seen disorders. The conditions covered are anxiety and mood disorders, schizophrenia, Tourette syndrome, personality disorders, panic attack, phobias, obsessive-compulsive disorder, post traumatic stress disorder, impulsive disorders, and eating disorders. The last section of the chapter deals with two developmental disorders—autism and the developmental learning disorders (learning disabilities). Both conditions involves significant learning problems, although only autism overlaps with mental retardation. Autism, of course, also includes major emotional and social difficulties.

Possible Discussion Questions

In what ways can mental retardation affect our recognition of psychiatric disorders in affected individuals?

How did the need for "structure" manifest itself in Barbara, the young woman with "generalized anxiety disorder?"

How does the cognitive immaturity associated with mental retardation affect the kinds of fears experienced?

What two "behavioral" elements are necessary to the management of anxiety?

What factors can hinder the recognition of depression in retardation? Which one of the ingredients of self-esteem is most likely to be a contributor to depression in adults?

Why are so-called positive symptoms of schizophrenia generally more relevant to its diagnosis in retardation? Do individuals with retardation benefit from the use of psychotropic drugs in the treatment of this disorder?

What are the likely contributions of the retarded child's developmental experience to the fostering of antisocial behavior? What can "structure" or "setting limits" contribute to the management of such behavior in children and adults?

How does self-injury in persons with borderline personality disorder differ from that in individuals with severe and profound retardation?

What is a "cognitive" feature of mental retardation that contributes to impulsivity?

How does an eating disorder such as pica contribute to health problems?

In a society in which consumption of alcohol and drugs is widely practiced, how can we help individuals with retardation avoid their abuse? As a young person, how would you communicate this concern to a peer with retardation? How do we help persons with significant cognitive impairment make "responsible" decisions? What is our responsibility to those whose levels of retardation may preclude genuine understanding of the risks of alcohol and drugs? Can we formulate a policy comparable to that developed for managing the sexual needs of residents of community programs in Australia?

What are the main features of autism? How do its manifestations overlap with those of retardation? In what ways do children with autism differ from those with mental retardation? Given its gender distribution, if we speculated about a possible chromosomal or genetic origin, where would we look? Why? In which one of the recessively inherited forms of retardation do we find children who may show autistic symptoms?

The "developmental learning disorders" do not imply the presence of any significant behavioral or emotional difficulties. But, like retardation, they are associated with significant learning problems, although these tend to be primarily school-related in nature. How do the two populations differ with respect to the role of "intelligence" in their respective disorders? What are common developmental learning disorders?

REFERENCES

Aanes, D., & Moen, M. (1976). Adaptive behavioral changes of group home residents. *Mental Retardation, 14,* 36–40.

Abbot, Q. (1997). Thoughts on caregiving. *The Arc Today, 46*(2), 2.

Abel, E. L., & Sokol, R. J. (1991). A revised conservative estimate of the incidence of FAS and its economic impact. *Alcoholism, Clinical and Experimental Research, 15,* 514–524.

Abramson, P. R., Parker, T., & Wenberg, S. (1988). Sexual expression of mentally retarded people: Educational and legal implications. *American Journal on Mental Retardation, 93,* 328–334.

Abroms, I. F., & Durbin, Jr., W. A. (1992). Central nervous system afflictions. In M. D. Levine, W. B. Carey, & A. C. Crocker (Eds.), *Developmental-behavioral pediatrics* (pp. 254–270). Philadelphia: W. B. Saunders.

Accardo, P. J., & Whitman, B. Y. (1990). Children of parents with mental retardation. In B. Y. Whitman & P. J. Accardo (Eds.), *When a parent is mentally retarded* (pp. 123–131). Baltimore: Brookes.

Addis, B. (1968). *Resistance to parsimony: The evaluation of a system for explaining the calendar calculating abilities of idiot savant twins.* Paper presented at the Southwestern Psychological Association, New Orleans.

Ainsworth, M. D. S., & Bell, S. M. (1974). Mother-infant interaction and the development of competence. In K. J. Connolly & J. S. Bruner (Eds.), *The growth of competence.* (pp. 97–118). New York: Academic Press.

Aird, R. B. (1983). The importance of seizure-inducing factors in the control of refractory forms of epilepsy. *Epilepsia, 24,* 567–583.

Aird, R. B., Masland, R. L., & Woodbury, D. M. (1984). *The epilepsies: A critical review.* New York: Raven Press.

Alderfer, C. P. (1972). *Existence, relatedness, and growth.* New York: Free Press.

Alexander, M. A., & Bauer, R. E. (1988). Cerebral palsy. In V. B. Van Hasselt, P. S. Strain, & M. Hersen (Eds.), *Handbook of developmental disabilities* (pp. 215–226). New York: Pergamon.

Alexander, D., Ehrhardt, A. A., & Money, J. (1966). Defective figure drawing, geometric and human, in Turner's syndrome. *Journal of Nervous and Mental Disorders, 142,* 161–167.

Alexander, D., & Money, J. (1965). Reading ability, object constancy, and Turner's syndrome. *Perceptual and Motor Skills, 20,* 981–984.

Algozzine, B., & Korinek, L. (1985). Where is special education for students with high prevalence handicaps going? *Exceptional Children, 51,* 388–394.

Amado, A. N. (Ed.). (1993a). *Friendships and community connections between people with and without developmental disabilities.* Baltimore: Brookes.

Amado, A. N. (1993b). Working on friendships. In A. N. Amado (Ed.), *Friendships and community connections between people with and without developmental disabilities* (pp. 279–298). Baltimore: Brookes.

Amado, R. S. (1993). Loneliness: Effects and complications. In A. N. Amado (Ed.), *Friendships and community connections between people with and without developmental disabilities* (pp. 67–84). Baltimore: Brookes.

Aman, M. (1989a). Neuroleptics. In T. B. Karasu (Ed.), *Treatments of Psychiatric Disorder*. (Vol 1, pp. 71–77). Washington, D.C.: American Psychiatric Association.

Aman, M., Sarphare, G., & Burrow, W. (1995). Psychotropic drugs in group homes: Prevalance and relation to demographic/psychiatric variables. *American Journal on Mental Retardation, 99*, 500–509.

Aman, M. G., & Singh, N. N. (1991). Pharmacological intervention. In J. L. Matson & J. A. Mulick (Eds.), *Handbook of mental retardation* (2nd ed., pp. 347–372). New York: Pergamon.

Aman, M. G., Teehan, C. J., White, A. J., Turbott, S. H., & Vaithianathan, C. (1989). Haloperidol treatment with chronically medicated residents: Dose effects on clinical behavior and reinforcement contingencies. *American Journal on Mental Retardation, 93*, 452–460.

American Association on Mental Retardation. (1992). *Mental retardation: Definition, classification and system of supports*. Washington, DC: Author.

American Association on Mental Deficiency (1973). Position paper.

American Psychiatric Association. (1987). *Diagnostic and statistical manual of mental disorders* (3rd ed. rev.). Washington, DC: Author.

American Psychiatric Association (1994). *Diagnostic and statistical manual of mental disorders* (4th ed.). Washington, DC: Author.

Americans with Disabilities Act of 1990. (Public Law 101-336).

Ames, M. D., Plotkin, S. A., Winchester, R. A., & Atkins, T. E. (1970). Central auditory imperception: A significant factor in congenital rubella deafness. *Journal of the American Medical Association, 213*, 419–421.

Ames, T.-R., & Samowitz, P. (1995). Inclusionary standard for determining sexual consent for individuals with developmental disabilities. *Mental Retardation, 33*, 264–268.

Amin-Zari, L., Majeed, M. A., Clarkson, T. W., & Greenwood, M. R. (1978). Methymercury poisoning in Iraqi children: Clinical observations over 2 years. *British Medical Journal, 1*, 613–616.

Anderson, D. J. (1998). Older adults with mental retardation living at home: Health issues. *Advantage* (A newsletter of the Rehabilitative Research and Training Center on Aging with Mental Retardation, University of Illinois at Chicago), *9*(2), 14–16.

Anderson, L. T., Ernst, M., & Davis, J. V. (1992). Cognitive abilities of patients with Lesch-Nyhan Syndrome. *Journal of Autism and Developmental Disorders, 22*, 189–203.

Andres, D. G., Bullen, J. G., Tomlinson, L., Elmes, R. D. C., & Reynolds, E. H. (1985). A comparative study of the cognitive effects of Phenytoin and Carbamazepine in new referrals with epilepsy. *Epilepsia, 26*, 268–278.

Andron, L., & Tymchuk, A. (1987). Parents who are mentally retarded. In A. Craft (Ed.), *Mental handicap and sexuality: Issues and perspectives*. Turnbridge Wells: Costello.

Annest, J. L. (1983). Trends in the blood lead levels of the VS population. In M. Rutter & R. R. Jones (Eds.), *Lead versus health* (pp. 33–58). New York: John Wiley & Sons.

Antonacci, D. J., & Ulzen, T. P. M. (1997). "Atypical psychosis" in the mentally retarded: Challenges to diagnosis and treatment. *The NADD Newsletter, 14*(1), 1–4.

Antonarakis, S. E., & the Down Syndrome Collaborative Group. (1991). Parental origins of the extra chromosome in trisomy 21 as indicated by analysis of DNA polymorphisms. *New England Journal of Medicine, 348*, 872–876.

Assadi, F. K., & Zai, M. (1986). Zinc status of infants with fetal alcohol syndrome. *Pediatric Research, 20*, 551–554.

Atkinson, J. W. (1964). *An introduction to motivation*. Princeton: Van Nostrand.

Autti-Ramo, I., Gaily, E., & Granstrom, M.-L. (1992). Dsysmorphic features in offspring of alcoholic mothers. *Archives of Diseases in Childhood, 67,* 712–716.

Aylward, G. P., Pfeiffer, S. I., Wright, A., & Verholst, S. J. (1989). Outcome studies of low birth weight infants published in the last decade: A meta-analysis. *Journal of Pediatrics, 115,* 515–520.

Azrin, N. H., & Armstrong, P. M. (1973). The "mini-meal"– A method for teaching eating skills to the profoundly retarded. *Mental Retardation, 11,* 9–13.

Azrin, N. H., Bugle, C., & O'Brien, F. (1971). Behavioral engineering: Two apparatuses for toilet training retarded children. *Journal of Applied Behavior Analysis, 4,* 249–253.

Azrin, N. H., & Foxx, R. M. (1971). A rapid method of toilet training the institutionalized retarded. *Journal of Applied Behavior Analysis, 4,* 89–99.

Azrin, N. H., & Peterson, A. L. (1988). Habit reversal for the treatment of Tourette syndrome. *Behaviour Research and Therapy, 26,* 347–351.

Azrin, N. H., Schaeffer, R. M., & Wesolowski, M. D. (1976). A rapid method of teaching profoundly retarded persons to doss by a reinforcement-guidance method. *Mental Retardation, 14,* 29–33.

Azrin, N. H., Sneed, T. J., & Foxx, R. M. (1973). Dry bed: A rapid method of eliminating bedwetting (enuresis) of the retarded. *Behavior Research and Therapy, 11,* 427–434.

Bagley, C. (1971). *The social psychology of the epileptic child.* Coral Gables, FL: University of Miami Press.

Bailey, D. B., & Wolery, M. (1984). *Teaching infants and preschoolers with handicaps.* Columbus: Merrill.

Bailey, J. S., & Pyles, D. A. M. (1989). Behavioral diagnostics. In E. Cipani (Ed.), *The treatment of severe behavior disorders: Behavior analysis approaches* (pp. 85–107). Washington, DC: American Association on Mental Retardation.

Baird, P. A., & Sadovnick, A. D. (1987). Life expectancy in Down syndrome. *Journal of Pediatrics, 110,* 849–854.

Bak, J. J., & Siperstein, G. N. (1987). Effects of mentally retarded children's behavioral competence on nonretarded peers' behavior and attitudes: Toward establishing ecological validity in attitude research. *American Journal of Mental Deficiency, 92,* 31–39.

Baker, D., Telfer, M. A., Richardson, C. E., & Clark, G. R. (1970). Chromosome errors in men with antisocial behavior. *Journal of the American Medical Association, 214,* 869–878.

Baller, W., Charles, D., & Miller, E. (1966). *Midlife attainment of the mentally retarded:* A longitudinal study. Lincoln: University of Nebraska Press.

Bandura, A. (1977). Self-efficacy: Toward a unifying theory of behavioral change. *Psychological Review, 84,* 191–215.

Bank-Mikkelsen, N. E. (1969). A metropolitan area in Denmark: Copenhagen. In R. Kugel & W. Wolfensberger (Eds.), *Changing patterns in residential services for the mentally retarded* (pp. 229–254). Washington, DC: President's Committee on Mental Retardation.

Barclay, A. G., Drotar, D. D., Favell, J. F., Foxx, R. M., Gardner, W. I., Iwata, B. A., Jacobson, J. W., Matson, J. L., Mulick, J. A., Ramey, S. L., Routh, D. K., Schroeder, S. R., Sprague, R. L., Switzky, H. N., & Thompson, T. (1996). Definition of mental retardation. In J. W. Jacobson & J. A. Mulick (Eds.), *Manual of diagnosis and professional practice in mental retardation* (pp. 13–54). Washington, DC: American Psychological Association.

Barkley, R. A. (1981). *Hyperactive children.* New York: Guilford Press.

Baroff, G. S. (1999). General learning disorder: A new designation for mental retardation. *Mental Retardation, 37,* 68–70.

Baroff, G. S. (1982). Predicting the prevalence of mental retardation in individual catchment areas. *Mental Retardation, 20,* 133–135.

Baroff, G. S. (1986). *Mental Retardation: Nature, Cause, and Management* (2nd ed. pp. 446–447). Washington, D.C.: Hemisphere.

Baroff, G. S. (1991a). *Developmental disabilities: Psychosocial aspects*. Austin, TX: PRO-ED.

Baroff, G. S. (1974). *Mental Retardation: Nature, Cause, and Management* (1st ed. p. 348). Washington, D.C.: Hemisphere.

Baroff, G. S. (1958). Current theories on the etiology of monolism. *Eugenics Quarterly, 5*, 212–215.

Baroff, G. S. (1991b). Establishing mental retardation in capital cases: A potential matter of life and death. *Mental Retardation, 29*, 343–349.

Baroff, G. S. (1996). The mentally retarded offender. In J. W. Jacobson & J. A. Mulick (Eds.), *Manual of diagnosis and professional practice in mental retardation* (pp. 311–322). Washington, DC: American Psychological Association.

Baroff, G. S., & Freedman, S. C. (1988). Mental retardation and Miranda. *The Champion, 12*(3), 6–9.

Baroff, G. S., & Tate, B. G. (1968). The use of aversive stimulation in the treatment of chronic self-injurious behavior. *Journal of the American Academy of Child Psychiatry, 7*, 454–470.

Baron-Cohen, S. (1988). Social and pragmatic deficits in autism: Cognitive or affective? *Journal of Autism and Developmental Disabilities, 18*, 379–402.

Baron, M. G., Groden, J., & Cautela, J. R. (1988). Behavioral programming: Expanding our clinical repertoire. In G. Groden & M. G. Baron (Eds.), *Autism: Strategies for change* (pp. 49–73). New York: Gardner.

Battle, J. (1979). Self-esteem of students in regular and special classes. *Psychological Reports, 44*, 212–214.

Baumeister, A. A. (1978). Origins and control of stereotyped movements. In C. E. Meyers (Ed.), *Quality of life in severely and profoundly mentally retarded people: Research foundation for improvement* (pp. 353–384). Washington, DC: American Association for Mental Deficiency.

Baumeister, A. A. (1991). Etiologies of self-injurious and destructive behavior. In *National Institutes of Health treatment of destructive behaviors in persons with developmental disabilities* (pp. 32–37). Washington, DC: U.S. Department of Health and Human Services, Public Health Service, National Institutes of Health.

Baumeister, A. A., Todd, M. E., & Sevin, J. A. (1993). Efficacy and specificity of pharmacological therapies for behavioral disorders in persons with mental retardation. *Clinical Neuropharmacology, 16*, 271–294.

Bayley, N. (1969). *Manual for the Bayley Scales of Infant Development*. New York: Psychological Corp.

Bayley, N. (1970). Development of mental abilities. In P. M. Mussen (Ed.), *Carmichael's manual of child psychology* (3rd ed., vol. I, pp. 1163–1210). New York: Wiley.

Beange, H., McElduff, A., & Baker, W. (1995). Medical disorders of adults with mental retardation: A population study. *American Journal on Mental Retardation, 99*, 595–604.

Bear, D., Freeman, R., & Greenberg, M. (1984). Behavioral alterations in patients with temporal lobe epilepsy. In D. Blumer (Ed.), *Psychiatric aspects of epilepsy* (pp. 197–228). Washington, DC: American Psychiatric Press.

Beck, M. A., Roblee, K., & Hanson, J. (1981). Special education/regular education: A comparison of self-concept. *Education, 102*, 272–279.

Becker, W. C., & Gersten, R. A. (1982). A follow-up of Follow Through: The later effects of the direct instruction model on children in fifth and sixth grades. *American Education Research Journal, 19*, 75–92.

Bednar, R. L., Wells, M. G., & Peterson, S. R. (1989). Self-esteem: Paradoxes and innovations in clinical theory and practice. Washington, DC: American Psychological Association.

Bell, N. J. (1976). IQ as a factor in community lifestyle of previously institutionalized retardates. *Mental Retardation, 14*, 29–33.

Bellamy, G. T., Peterson, L., & Close, A. (1975). Habilitation of the severly and profoundly retarded: Illustrations of competence. *Education and Training of the Mentally Retarded, 10,* 174–186.

Belman, A. L., Diamond, G., Dickson, D., Horoupian, D., Llena, J., Lantos, G., & Rubinstein, A. (1988). Pediatric acquired immunodeficiency syndrome: Neurological syndromes. *American Journal of Diseases of Children, 142,* 29–35.

Belmont, J. M., & Burkowski, J. G. (1994). Prudence, indeed, will dictate ... [Review of *Mental retardation: Definition, classification, and systems of supports* (9th ed.)]. *Contemporary Psychology, 39,* 495–496.

Benda, C. E. (1954). Psychopathology of childhood. In L. Carmichael (Ed.), *Manual of child psychology* (2nd ed., pp. 1115–1161). New York: Wiley.

Benke, P. J. (1984). The isotretinoin terntogen syndrome. *Journal of the American Medical Association, 251,* 3267–3269.

Bennett, F. C., LaVeck, B., & Sells, C. J. (1978). The Williams Elfin Facies Syndrome: The psychological profile as an aid in syndrome identification. *Pediatrics, 61,* 303–305.

Benson, B. A. (1992). *Teaching anger management to persons with mental retardation.* Cleveland, OH: International Diagnostic Systems.

Benson, B. A., Reiss, S., Smith, D. C., & Laman, D. S. (1985). Psychosocial correlates of depression in mentally retarded adults: II. Poor social skills. *American Journal of Mental Deficiency, 89,* 657–659.

Bergman, I., Hirsch, R. P., Fria, T. J., Shapiro, S. M., Holzman, I., & Painter, M. J. (1985). Cause of hearing loss in the high-risk premature infant. *Journal of Pediatrics, 106,* 95–101.

Bernfeld, G. A., Blase, K. A., & Fixen, D. L. (1990). Towards a unified perspective on human service delivery systems: Application of the teaching-family model. In R. J. McMahon & R. DeV. Peters (Eds.), *Behavior disorders of adolescence: Research, intervention, and policy in clinical and school settings* (pp. 191–205). New York: Plenum.

Berry, P., Gunn, V. P., & Andrews, R. J. (1984). Development of Down's syndrome children from birth to five years. In J. M. Berg (Ed.), *Perspectives and progress in mental retardation: Vol. I. Social, psychological, and educational aspects* (pp. 167–180). Baltimore: University Park Press.

Berry, H. K., O'Grady, D. J., Perlmutter, L. J., & Botinger, M. K. (1979). Intellectual development and academic achievement of children treated early for phenylketonuria. *Developmental Medicine and Child Neurology, 21,* 311–320.

Bialer, I. (1961). Conceptualization of success and failure in mentally retarded and normal children. *Journal of Personality, 29,* 303–320.

Biersdorff, K. K. (1991). Pain insensitivity and indifference: Alternative explanation for some medical catastrophes. *Mental Retardation, 29,* 359–362.

Bilsky, L. H. (1976). Transfer of categorical clustering set in mildly retarded adolescents. *American Journal of Mental Deficiency, 80,* 588–594.

Birch, H. G., & Cravioto, J. (1966). Infection, nutrition and environment in mental development. In H. V. Eichenwald (Ed.), *The prevention of mental retardation through the control of infectious disease* (Public Health Service Publication No. 1692). Washington, DC: U.S. Government Printing Office.

Birch, H. G., Pinuro, C., Atcalde, E., Toca, T., G., & Cravioto, J. (1971). Relation of Kwashiorkor in early childhood to intelligence at school age. *Pediatric Research, 5,* 579–585.

Birch, H. G., Richardson, S. A., Baird, D., Horobin, G., & Illsley, R. (1970). *Mental subnormality in the community: A clinical and epidemiological study.* Baltimore: Williams & Wilkins.

Birenbaum, A., Guyot, D., & Cohen, H. J. (1990). *Health care financing for severe developmental disabilities.* Washington, DC: American Association on Mental Retardation.

Blacher, J. (1984). Sequential stages of parental adjustment to the birth of a handicapped child: Fact or artifact. *Mental Retardation, 22,* 55–68.

Blake, R. (1981). Disabled older persons: A demographic analysis. *Journal of Rehabilitation, 47*(4), 19–27.

Blank, C. E. (1960). Apert's syndrome (a type of acrocephalosyndaetyly) observations on a British series of thirty-nine cases. *Annals of Human Genetics, 24,* 4–32.

Blatt, B. (1970). *Exodus from pandemonium: Human abuse and a reformation of public policy.* Boston: Allyn & Bacon.

Blatt, B. (1987). *The conquest of mental retardation.* Austin, TX: PRO-ED.

Blatt, B., & Kaplan, F. (1966). *Christmas in purgatory: A photographic essay on mental retardation.* Boston: Allyn and Bacon.

Blunden, R. (1988). Program features of quality services. In M. P. Janicki, M. M. Krauss, & M. Seltzer (Eds.), *Community residences for persons with developmental disabilities: Here to stay* (pp. 117–122). Baltimore: Brookes.

Bodfish, J. W. (1996, October). *Behavioral and psychiatric disorders associated with mental retardation and developmental disabilities.* Paper presented at the Cornwell Lectures, Morganton, NC.

Bodfish, J. W., Crawford, T. W., Powell, S. B., Parker, D. E., Golden, R. N., & Lewis, M. H. (1995). Compulsions in adults with mental retardation: Prevalence, phenomenology, and comorbidity with stereotypy and self-injury. *American Journal on Mental Retardation, 100,* 183–192.

Bodfish, J. W., & Madison, J. T. (1993). Diagnosis and fluoxetine treatment of compulsive behavior disorder of adults with mental retardation. *American Journal on Mental Retardation, 98,* 360–367.

Bodfish, J. W., Newell, K. M., Sprague, R. L., Harper, V. N., & Lewis, M. H. (1996). Dyskinetic movement disorder among adults with mental retardation: Phenomenology and co-occurrence with stereotypy. *American Journal on Mental Retardation, 101,* 118–129.

Bogdan, R., & Taylor, S. J. (1987). Conclusion: The next wave. In S. J. Taylor, D. Birklen, & J. Knoll (Eds.), *Community integration for people with severe disabilities* (pp. 209–220). New York: Teacher's College Press.

Bonthius, D. J., & West, J. R. (1990). Alcohol-induced neuronal loss in developing rats: Increased brain damage with binge exposure. *Alcoholism: Clinical and Experimental Research, 14,* 102–118.

Borberg, A. (1951). Clinical and genetic investigations into tuberous sclerosis and Recklinghausen's neurofibromatosis. *Acta Psychiatrica et Neurologica, 71,* 239.

Borgman, R. D. (1990). Intelligence and maternal inadequacy. *Child Welfare, 48,* 301–304.

Borthwick-Duffy, S. (1993). [Review of *Mental retardation: Definition, classification, and systems of supports* (9th ed.)]. *American Journal on Mental Retardation, 98,* 541–544.

Borthwick-Duffy, S. A. (1994). Epidemiology and prevalence of psychopathology in people with mental retardation. *Journal of Consulting and Clinical Psychology, 62,* 17–27.

Bosch, J., Van Dyke, D. C., Smith, S. M., & Poulton, S. (1997). Role of medical conditions in the exacerbation of self-injurious behavior: An exploratory study. *Mental Retardation, 35,* 124–130.

Botuck, S., & Winsberg, B. G. (1991). Effects of respite on mothers of school-age and adult children with severe disabilities. *Mental Retardation, 29,* 43–47.

Bouchard, T. J., Jr. (1984). Twins reared together and apart: What they tell us about human diversity. In S. W. Fox (Ed.), *Individualism and determinism* (pp. 147–184). New York: Plenum.

Bouchard, T. J., Lykken, D. T., McGue, M., Segal, N. L., & Tellegen, A. (1990). Sources of human psychological differences: The Minnesota study of twins reared apart. *Science, 250,* 223–228.

Bouchard, T. J., & McGue, M. (1981). Familial Studies of intelligence: A review. *Science, 212,* 1055–1059.

Brazelton, T. B. (1973). *Neonatal behavioral assessment scale*. Philadelphia: Lippincott.

Bregman, S. (1984). Assertiveness training for mentally retarded adults. *Mental Retardation, 22*, 12–16.

Brinker, R. P. (1985). Interactions between severely mentally retarded students and other students in integrated and segregated public school settings. *American Journal of Mental Deficiency, 89*, 587–594.

Brinker, R. P., & Thorpe, M. E. (1986). Features of integrated educational ecologies that predict social behavior among severely mentally retarded and nonretarded students. *American Journal of Mental Deficiency, 91*, 150–159.

Brody, J. F., Esslinger, S., Casselman, G., McGlinchey, M., & Mitala, R. (1975). The itinerant training team: Variations on a familiar concept. *Mental Retardation, 13*, 38–42.

Brolin, D. E. (1991). *Life centered career education: A competency based approach* (3rd ed.). Reston, VA: The Council for Exceptional Children.

Bronfenbrenner, U. (1972). The roots of alienation. In U. Bronfenbrenner (Ed.), *Influences on human development* (pp. 658–677). Hinsdale, IL: Dryden.

Bronfenbrenner, U. (1974). Is early intervention effective? In M. Gutentag & E. L. Strevening (Eds.), *Handbook of evaluation research* (vol. 2, pp. 519–605). Beverly Hills, CA: Sage.

Brown, B. S., & Courtless, T. F. (1967). *The mentally retarded offender*. Washington, DC: The President's Commission on Law Enforcement and Administration of Justice.

Brubaker, E., & Brubaker, T. H. (1993). Caring for adult children with mental retardation. In K. A. Roberto (Ed.), *The elderly caregiver: Caring for adults with developmental disabilities* (pp. 51–60). Newbury Park, CA: Sage.

Brudnell, M. (1989). Diabetic pregnancy. In A. Turnbull & G. Chamberlain (Eds.), *Obstetrics*. Edinburgh: Churchill Livingstone.

Bruno, P., Loveman, E., & Pfadt, A. (1993). Prader-Willi syndrome. *News and Notes* (A publication of the American Association on Mental Retardation), *6*, 4–5.

Budoff, M., & Gottlieb, J. (1976). Special class EMR children mainstreamed: A study of an aptitude (learning potential) × treatment interaction. *American Journal of Mental Deficiency, 81*, 1–11.

Budoff, M., & Siperstein, G. N. (1978). Low income children's attitudes toward the mentally retarded: Effects of labeling and academic behavior. *American Journal of Mental Deficiency, 82*, 474–478.

Brunner, R. L., Jordan, M. K., & Berry, J. K. (1983). Early-treated PKU: Neuropsychological consequences. *Journal of Pediatrics, 102*, 381–385.

Burchard, J. D., Atkins, M., & Burchard, S. N. (1996). Wraparound services. In J. Jacobson & J. A. Mulick (Eds.), *Manual of diagnosis and professional practice in mental retardation* (pp. 403–412). Washington, DC: American Psychological Association.

Burd, L., Martsolf, J. T., & Randall, T. (1990). A prevalence study of Rett Syndrome in an institutionalized population. *American Journal of Medical Genetics, 36*, 33–36.

Bureau of Labor Statistics, U.S. Department of Labor. (1993). Employment and Earnings, *40*(4), 29.

Burt, C. (1966). The genetic determination of differences in intelligence: A study of monozogotic twins reared together and apart. *British Journal of Psychology, 57*, 137–153.

Byers, R. K., Paine, R. S., & Crothers, B. (1955). Extrapyramidal cerebral palsy with hearing loss following erythrohlastosis. *Pediatrics, 15*, 248–254.

Byrnes, M. M., & Spitz, H. H. (1977). Performance of retarded adolescents and nonretarded children on the Tower of Hanoi problem. *American Journal of Mental Deficiency, 81*, 561–569.

Calhoun, G. C., & Elliot, R. N. (1977). Self-concept and academic achievement of educable retarded and emotionally disturbed pupils. *Exceptional Children, 43*, 379–380.

Campbell, F. A., & Nabors, L. (1998). A longitudinal study of factors associated with Wechsler verbal and performance IQ scores in students from low-income African American families. In W. Tomic & J. Kingma (Eds.), *Conceptual issues in intelligence research* (pp. 77–162). Greenwich, CT: J.A.I. Press.

Campbell, F. A., & Ramey, C. T. (1994). Effects of early intervention on intellectual and academic achievement: A follow-up study of children from low-income families. *Child Development, 65,* 684–698.

Campbell, F. A., & Ramey, C. T. (1995). Cognitive and school outcomes for high risk African American students at middle adolescence: Positive effects of early intervention. *American Educational Research Journal, 32,* 743–772.

Carabello, B. J., & Siegel, J. F. (1996). Self-advocacy at the crossroads. In G. Dybwad & H. Bersami, Jr. (Eds.), *New voices: Self-advocacy by people with disabilities* (pp. 237–239). Cambridge, MA: Brookline.

Cardinal, D. N., Hanson, D., & Wakeham, J. (1996). An investigation of authorship in facilitated communication. *Mental Retardation, 34,* 231–242.

Carpenter, W. V. (1851). *Use and abuse of alcohol liquors.* Boston: Crosby & Nichols.

Carr, J. (1970). Mental and motor development in young mongol children. *Journal of Mental Deficiency Research, 14,* 205–220.

Carr, J. (1976). The severely retarded autistic child. In L. Wing (Ed.), *Early Childhood Autism.* (pp. 247–270). New York: Pergamon.

Carr, J. (1988). Six weeks to twenty-one years old: A longitudinal study of children with Down syndrome and their families. *Journal of Child Psychology and Psychiatry, 29,* 407–431.

Carr, E. G., Taylor, J. C., Carlson, J. I., & Robinson, S. (1991). Reinforcement and stimulus-based treatments for severe behavior problems in developmental disabilities. In *National Institutes of Health: Treatment of destructive behaviors in persons with developmental disabilities* (pp. 173–229). Washington, DC: U.S. Department of Health and Human Services, Public Health Service, National Institutes of Health.

Carroll, J. B. (1993). *Human cognitive abilities.* Cambridge, MA: Cambridge University Press.

Carroll, J. B. (1997). Psychometrics, intelligence and public perception. *Intelligence, 24,* 25–52.

Casler, L. (1961). Maternal deprivation: A critical review of the literature. *Monographs of the Society for Research in Child Development, 26*(2).

Cassidy, S. B. (1984). Prader-Willi syndrome. *Current Problems in Pedatrics, 15,* 1–53.

Castles, E. E., & Glass, C. R. (1986). Training in social and interpersonal problem-solving skills for mildly and moderately mentally retarded adults. *American Journal of Mental Deficiency, 91,* 35–42.

Casto, G., & Mastropieri, M. A. (1986). The efficacy of early intervention programs: A meta-analysis. *Exceptional Children, 52,* 417–424.

Cautela, J. R., & Groden, J. (1978). *Relaxation: A comprehensive manual for adults, children, and children with special needs.* Champaign, IL: Research Press.

Ceci, S. J., & Williams, W. M. (1997). Schooling, intelligence, and income. *American Psychologist, 52,* 1051–1058.

Cepeda, E. E., Lee, M. I., & Mehdizadeh, B. (1987). Decreased incidence of intraventicular hemorrhage in infants of opiate dependent mothers. *Acta Paediatrica Scandinavica, 76,* 16–18.

Chadsey-Rusch, J., DeStefano, L., O'Reilly, M., Gonzalez, P., & Collet-Klingenberg, L. (1992). Assessing the loneliness of workers with mental retardation. *Mental Retardation, 30,* 85–92.

Chadsey-Rusch, J., Gonzalez, P., Tines, J., & Johnson, J. R. (1989). Social ecology of the workplace: An examination of cotextual variables affecting the social interactions of employees with and without mental retardation. *American Journal on Mental Retardation, 94,* 141–151.

Chamberlain, A., Rauth, J., Passer, A., McGrath, M., & Burket, R. (1984). Issues in fertility control for mentally retarded female adolescents: I. Sexual activity, sexual abuse and contraception. *Pediatrics, 73*, 445–450.

Charness, N., Clifton, J., & MacDonald, L. (1988). Case-study of a musical "mono-savant:" A cognitive-psychological focus. In L. K. Obler & D. Fein (Eds.), *The exceptional brain* (pp. 277–293). New York: Guilford Press.

Chelsey, G. M., & Calaluce, Jr., P. D. (1997). The deception of inclusion. *Mental Retardation, 35*, 488–490.

Chess, S., Korn, S., & Fernandez, P. B. (1971). *Psychiatric Disorders in Children with Rubella*. New York: Brunner/Mazel.

Chicoine, B., & McGuire, D. (1997). Longevity of a woman with Down syndrome: A case study. *Mental Retardation, 35*, 477–479.

Christian, L., & Poling, A. (1997). Drug abuse in persons with mental retardation: A review. *American Journal on Mental Retardation, 102*, 126–136.

Cicirelli, V. G. (1969). *The impact of Head Start: An evaluation of the effects of Head Start on children's cognitive and affective development*. Athens, OH: Westinghouse Learning Corp.

Civitello, L. A. (1991–1992). Neurologic complications of HIV infection of children. *Pediatric Neurosurgery, 17*, 104–122.

Clarke, A. D. B., Clarke, A. M., & Reiman, S. (1958). Cognitive and social changes on the feebleminded: Three further studies. *British Journal of Psychology, 49*, 144–157.

Clarke, A. M. (1984). Early experience and cognitive development. In E. W. Gordon (Ed.), *Review of research in education* (pp. 125–160). Washington, DC: American Educational Research Association.

Clarke, A. M., & Clarke, A. D. B. (1974). *Mental deficiency: The changing outlook* (3rd ed.). New York: The Free Press.

Clarke, A. M., & Clarke, A. D. B. (1976). *Early experience: Myth and evidence*. London: Open Books.

Clarke, A. M., & Clarke, A. D. B. (1986). Thirty years of child psychology: A selective review. *Journal of Child Psychology and Psychiatry, 27*, 719–759.

Clauser, B., & Scibak, J. W. (1990). Direct and generalized effects of food satiation in reducing rumination. *Research in Developmental Disabilities, 11*, 23–36.

Clayton-Smith, J. (1992). Angelman syndrome in the adolescent and young adult. In S. B. Cassidy (Ed.), *Prader-Willi syndrome and other chromosome 15q deletion disorders* (pp. 233–236). New York: Springer-Verlag.

Cobb, H. V. (1972). *The forecast of fulfillment*. New York: Teacher's College Press.

Cofer, C. N., & Appley, M. H. (1967). *Motivation: Theory and research*. New York: Wiley.

Cohen, S., & Warren, R. D. (1987). Preliminary survey of family abuse of children served by the United Cerebral Palsy centers. *Developmental Medicine and Child Neurology, 29*, 12–18.

Coleman, J. (1990). Parents learning together III. In B. Y. Whitman & P. J. Accardo (Eds.), *When a parent is mentally retarded* (pp. 111–120). Baltimore: Brookes.

Coles, C. D., Brown, R. T., Smith, I. E., Platzman, K. A., Erickson, S., & Falek, A. (1991). Effects of prenatal alcohol exposure at school age. I. Physical and cognitive development. *Neurotoxicology and Teratology, 13*, 357–367.

Collacott, R. A., Cooper, S. A., & McGrother, C. (1992). Differential rates of psychiatric disorders in adults with Down syndrome compared with other mentally handicapped adults. *British Journal of Psychiatry, 161*, 671–674.

Collin, M. F., Halsey, C. L., & Anderson, C. L. (1991). Emerging developmental sequel as in the 'normal' extremely low birthweight infant. *Pediatrics, 88*, 115–120.

Columbo, J. (1993). *Infant cognition: Predicting later intellectual functioning*. Newbury Park, CA: Sage.

Comings, D. E. (1986). The genetics of Rett syndrome: The consequence of a disorder where every case is a new mutation. *American Journal of Human Genetics, 50*, 278–287.

Commission for the control of epilepsy and its consequences (1997).

Condon, M. E., York, R., Neal, L. W., & Fortschneider, J. (1986). Acceptance of severely handicapped students by nonhandicapped peers. *The Journal of the Association for Persons with Severe Handicaps, 11*, 216–219.

Conley, R. W., Luckasson, R., & Bouthilet, G. N. (1992). *The criminal justice system and mental retardation*. Baltimore: Paul N. Brookes.

Conroy, J. W. (1992). *Size and quality in residential programs for people with developmental disabilities*. Unpublished doctoral dissertation, Temple University, Philadelphia.

Conroy, J., Efthimou, J., & Lemanowicz, J. (1982). A matched conjunction of the developmental growth of institutionalized and de-institutionalized mentally retarded clients. *American Journal of Mental Deficiency, 68*, 581–587.

Cooke, N. L., Heron, T. E., Heward, W. L., & Test, D. W. (1982). Integrating a Down's syndrome child in a classwide peer tutoring system: A case report. *Mental Retardation, 20*, 22–25.

Cooper, L. Z. (1968). Rubella: A preventable cause of birth defects. *Birth Defects*. Original Article Series, *4*, 23–25.

Cooper, L. Z. (1977). Rubella. In A. M. Rudolph (Ed.), *Pediatrics* (16th ed.). New York: Appleton-Century. Crofts.

Coopersmith, S. (1967). *The Antecedents of Self-Esteem*. San Francisco: W. H. Freeman.

Cornwell, A. C., & Birch, H. G. (1969). Psychological and social development in home-reared children with Down's syndrome (mongolism). *American Journal of Mental Deficiency, 74*, 341–350.

Coulter, D. L. (1993). Epilepsy and mental retardation: An overview. *American Journal on Mental Retardation, 98*(supplement), 1–11.

Craft, A., & Craft, M. (1978). *Sex and the mentally handicapped*. London: Routledge & Kegan Paul.

Crawford, T. W., & Bodfish, J. W. (1992). Obsessive-compulsive disorder. In E. A. Konarski, J. E. Favell, & J. E. Favell (Eds.), Manual for the assessment and treatment of the behavior disorders of people with mental retardation (Tab BD7, pp. 1–13). Morganton, NC: Western Carolina Center Foundation.

Crawford, J., Brockel, B., Schauss, S., & Miltenberger, R. G. (1992). A comparison of methods for the functional assessment of stereotypic behavior. *Journal of the Association for Persons with Severe Handicaps, 17*, 77–86.

Criscione, T., Kastner, T. A., O'Brien, D., & Nathanson, R. (1994). Replication of a managed health care initiative for people with mental retardation living in the community. *Mental Retardation, 32*, 43–52.

Criscione, T., Walsh, K. K., & Kastner, T. A. (1995). An evaluation of care coordination in controlling impatient hospital utilization of people with developmental disabilities. *Mental Retardation, 33*, 364–373.

Crissey, M. S., & Rosen, M., Eds. (1986). *Institutions for the mentally retarded: A changing role in changing times*. Austin, TX: PRO-ED.

Crnic, K. A., Friedrich, W. N., & Greenberg, M. T. (1983). Adaptation of families with mentally retarded children: A model of stress, coping, and family ecology. *American Journal of Mental Deficiency, 88*, 125–138.

Crocker, A. C. (1992). Human immunodeficiency virus. In M. D. Levine, W. B. Carey, & A. C. Crocker (Eds.), *Developmental-behavioral pediatrics* (pp. 271–275). Philadelphia: W.B. Saunders.

Crocker, A. C., & Yankauer, A. (Eds.). (1987). Sterling D. Garrard Memorial Symposium: Community health care services for adults with mental retardation. *Mental Retardation, 25*(4).

Crothers, B. & Paine, R. S. (1959). *The Natural History of Cerebral Palsy*. Cambridge, MA: Harvard University Press.

Crowe, F. W., Schull, W. J., & Neel, J. V. (1956). *A clinical, pathological and genetic study of multiple neurofibromatosis.* Springfield, IL: Charles C. Thomas.

Cruickshank, W. M., Bice, H. F., & Wallen, N. E. (1957). *Perception and Cerebral Palsy* (2nd ed.). Syracuse: Syracuse University Press.

Cullen, S. M., Cronk, C. E., Pueschel, S. M., Schnell, R. R., & Reed, R. B. (1981). Social development and feeding milestones of young Down syndrome children. *American Journal of Mental Deficiency, 85,* 410–415.

Cummins, S. K., Nelson, K. B., & Grether, J. K. (1993). Cerebral palsy in four northern California counties, births 1983 through 1985. *Journal of Pediatrics, 123,* 230–237.

Curfs, L. M. G. (1997). Psychological profile and behavioral characteristics in the Prader-Willi syndrome. In S. B. Cassidy (Ed.), *Prader-Willi syndrome and other chromosome 15q deletion disorders* (pp. 211–222). New York: Springer-Verlag.

Curfs, L. M. G., & Fryns, J. P. (1992). Prader-Willi syndrome: A review with special attention to the cognitive and behavior profile. *Birth Defects: Original Article Series, 28*(1), 99–104.

Danford, D. E., & Huber, A. M. (1982). Pica among mentally retarded adults. *American Journal of Mental Deficiency, 87,* 141–146.

Das, J. P., Naglieri, J. A., & Kirby, J. R. (1994). *Assessment of cognitive processes: The PASS theory of intelligence.* Needham Heights, MA: Allyn & Bacon.

Dattilo, J., & Schleien, S. J. (1994). Understanding leisure services for individuals with mental retardation. *Mental Retardation, 32,* 53–59.

Davidson, P. W., Cain, N. N., Sloan-Reeves, J. E., Giesow, V. E., Quijano, L. E., Van Heyningen, J., & Shoham, I. (1995). Crisis intervention for community-based individuals with developmental disabilities and behavioral and psychiatric disorders. *Mental Retardation, 33,* 21–30.

Day, N. L., Goldschmidt, L., Robles, N., Richardson, G., Taylor, P., Geva, D., & Stoffer, D. (1991). Prenatal alcohol exposure and offspring growth at 18 months of age: The predictive validity of two measures of drinking. *Alcoholism: Clinical and Experimental Research, 15,* 914–918.

Day, N. L., & Richardson, G. A. (1991). Prenatal alcohol exposure: A continuum of effects. *Seminars in Perinatology, 15,* 271–279.

de la Cruz, F. F. (1985). Fragile X syndrome. *American Journal of Mental Deficiency, 90,* 119–123.

de La Cruz, F. F., & LaVeck, G. (1962). Tuberous sclerosis: A review and report of eight cases. *American Journal of Mental Deficiency, 67,* 369–380.

Deary, I. J., & Stough, C. (1996). Intelligence and inspection time. *American Psychologist, 51,* 599–608.

Deci, E. L., & Ryan, R. M. (1990). A motivational approach to self: Integration in personality. In R. Dienstbier (Ed.), *Nebraska symposium on motivation: Vol. 38, Perspectives on motivation* (pp. 237–288). Lincoln: University of Nebraska Press.

Deisher, R. W. (1973). Sexual behavior of retarded in institutions. In F. F. De La Cruz & G. D. LaVeck (Eds.), *Human sexuality and the mentally retarded* (pp. 145–152). New York: Brunner/Mazel.

Dekaban, A. (1968). Abnormalities in children exposed to x-radiation during various stages of gestation: Tentative timetable of radiation injury to the human fetus, part I. *Journal of Nuclear Medicine, 9,* 471–477.

Delgado-Escueta, A. V., & Janz, D. (1992). Consensus guidelines: Preconception counseling, management, and care of the pregnant woman with epilepsy. *Neurology, 42*(suppl. 5), 149–160.

DeMyer, M. K., Barton, S., Alpern, G. D., Kimberlin, C., Allen, J., Yang, E., & Steele, R. (1974). The measured intelligence of autistic children. *Journal of Autism and Childhood Schizophrenia, 4,* 42–60.

Denhoff, E. (1976). Medical aspects. In W. M. Cruickshank (Ed.), *Cerebral palsy: A developmental disability* (3rd ed.) (pp. 29–72). Syracuse, NY: Syracuse University Press.

Denkowski, G. C., & Denkowski, K. M. (1985). The mentally retarded offender in the state prison system: Identification, prevalence, adjustment and rehabilitation. *Criminal Justice and Behavior, 12*, 55–70.

Derby, K. M., Fisher, W. W., & Piazza, C. C. (1996). The effects of contingent and noncontingent attention on self-injury and self-restraint. *Journal of Applied Behavior Analysis, 29*, 107–110.

Detterman, D. K. (1993). The case for the prosecution: Transfer as an epiphenomenon. In D. K. Detterman & R. J. Sternberg (Eds.), *Transfer on trial: Intelligence, cognition, and instruction* (pp. 1–24). Norwood, NJ: Ablex.

Dever, R. B. (1989). A taxonomy of community living skills. *Exceptional Children, 55*, 395–404.

Dever, R. B., & Knapczyk, D. R. (1997). *Teaching persons with mental retardation*. Madison, WI: Brown & Benchmark.

Diamond, A., Prevor, M. B., Callender, G., & Druin, D. P. (1997). Prefrontal cortex longitudinal deficits in children treated early and continuously for PKU. *Monographs of the Society for Research in Child Development, 62*, i–v, 1–208.

Diamond, G. W. (1989). Developmental problems in children with HIV infection. *Mental Retardation, 27*, 213–217.

Diamond, G. W., Kaufman, J., Belman, A. L., Cohen, L., Cohen, H. J., & Rubinstein, A. (1987). Characterization of cognitive functioning in a subgroup of children with congenital HIV infection. *Archives of Clinical Neuropsychology, 21*, 245–256.

Dicks-Mireaux, M. J. (1972). Mental development of infants with Down's syndrome. *American Journal of Mental Deficiency, 77*, 26–32.

Dinani, S., & Carpenter, S. (1990). Down's syndrome and thyroid disorder. *Journal of Mental Deficiency Research, 34*, 187–193.

Dobson, J. C., Kushida, E., Williamson, M., & Friedman, G. (1977). Intellectual assessment of 111 four-year-old children with phenylketonuria. *Pediatrics, 60*, 822–827.

Dobzhansey, T. (1982). *Mankind Evolving*. New Haven: Yale University Press.

Dodrill, C. B. (1982). Psychological assessment in epilepsy. In H. Sands (Ed.), *Epilepsy: A handbook for the mental health professional* (pp. 111–134). New York: Brunner/Mazel.

Dodrill, C. B. (1988). Correlates of generalized tonic-clonic seizures with intelligence, neuropsychological, emotional, and social functioning in patients. *Epilepsia, 27*, 399–411.

Doll, E. A. (1941). The essentials of an inclusive concept of mental deficiency. *American Journal of Mental Deficiency, 46*, 214–219.

Doll, E. A. (1964). *Vineland scale of social maturity*. Minneapolis, MN: American Guidance Service.

Dolphin, J., & Cruickshank, W. M. (1951). The figure-background relationship. *Journal of Clinical Psychology, 7*, 228–232.

Donnellan, A. (1984). The criterion of the least dangerous assumption. *Behavioral Disorders, 9*, 141–150.

Douglas, F. (1855, 1969). *My bondage and my freedom*. New York: Dover.

Dreifuss, F. E. (1975). The nature of epilepsy. In G. N. Wright (Ed.), *Epilepsy rehabilitation* (pp. 8–27). Boston: Little, Brown.

DSM-III-R (1987). *Diagnostic and Statistical Manual of Mental Disorders*. (3rd ed., Revised). Washington, DC: American Psychiatric Association.

DSM-IV-R (1994). *Diagnostic and Statistical Manual of Mental Disorders*. (4th ed., Revised). Washington, DC: American Psychiatric Association.

Dube, E. F. (1982). Literacy, cultural familiarity, and "intelligence" as determinants of story recall. In U. Neisser (Ed.), *Memory observed: Remembering in natural contexts* (pp. 274–298). San Francisco: Freeman.

Duffner, P. K., & Cohen, M. E. (1991). The long-term effects of central nervous system therapy on children with brain tumors. *Neurologic Clinics, 9*, 479–495.

Duffner, P. K., Horowitz, M. E., Krischer, J. P., Friedman, S. H., Burger, P. C., Cohen, M. E., Sanford, R. A., Mulhern, R. K., James, H. E., Freeman, C. R., et al. (1993). Postoperational chemotherapy and delayed radiation in children less than three years of age with malignant brain tumors. *New England Journal of Medicine, 328*, 1725–1731.

Dunn, H. G. (1986). Neurological, psychological and ophthamological sequelae of low birthweight. In H. G. Dunn (Ed.), *Sequelae of low birthweight: The Vancouver study* (pp. 1–23). Philadelphia: Lippincott.

Dunst, C. J., & Paget, K. (1991). Parent-professional partnerships and family empowerment. In M. Fine (Ed.), *Collaboration with parents of exceptional children* (pp. 25–44). Brandon, VT: Clinical Psychology Publishing.

Dura, J., & Nunemaker, H. (1993). *Masturbation instruction for men who have developmental disabilities.* Bowling Green, OH: Practical Programming Group.

Dybwad, G. (1996). Setting the stage historically. In G. Dybwad & H. Bersani Jr. (Eds.), *New voices: Self-advocacy by people with disabilities* (pp. 1–17). Cambridge, MA: Brookline.

Dyer, K., Dunlap, G., & Winterling, V. (1990). Effects of choice making on the serious problem behaviors of students with severe handicaps. *Journal of Applied Behavior Analysis, 23*, 515–524.

Dykeman, K. J., & Levy, I. S. (1991). The study and teaching of ethics for persons with mental retardation. *Mental Retardation, 29*, iii–iv.

Dykens, E. M., & Kasari, C. (1997). Maladaptive behavior in children with Prader-Willi syndrome, Down syndrome, and nonspecific mental retardation. *American Journal on Mental Retardation, 102*, 228–237.

Dykens, E. M., Goff, B. J., Hodapp, R. M., Davis, L., Devanzo, P., Moss, F., Halliday, J., Bhavik, S., State, M., & King, B. (1997). Eating themselves to death: Have "personal rights" gone too far in treating people with Prader-Willi syndrome. *Mental Retardation, 35*, 312–314.

Dykens, E. M., Hodapp, R. M., & Evans, D. W. (1994). Profiles and development of adaptive behavior in children with Down syndrome. *American Journal on Mental Retardation, 98*, 580–587.

Dykens, E. M., Hodapp, R. M., & Leckman, J. F. (1987). Strengths and weaknesses in the intellectual functioning of males with Fragile X syndrome. *American Journal of Mental Deficiency, 92*, 234–236.

Dykens, E. M., Hodapp. R. M., Ort, S. I., Finucane, B., Shapiro, L. R., & Leckman, J. F. (1989). The trajectory of cognitive development in males with fragile X syndrome. *Journal of the American Academy of Child and Adolescent Psychiatry, 28*, 422–426.

Dykens, E. M., Hodapp, R. M., Ort, S. I., & Leckman, J. F. (1993). Trajectory of adaptive behavior in males with fragile X syndrome. *Journal of Autism and Developmental Disabilities, 23*, 135–145.

Dykens, E. M., Hodapp, R. M., Walsh, K., & Nash, L. J. (1992). Adaptive and maladaptive behavior in Prader-Willi syndrome. *Journal of the American Academy of Child and Adolescent Psychiatry, 31*, 1131–1136.

Dykens, E. M., & Kasari, C. (1997). Maladaptive behavior in children with Prader-Willi syndrome, Down syndrome, and nonspecific retardation. *American Journal of Mental Retardation, 102*, 228–237.

Dynon, L. L. (1991). Families of young children with handicaps: Prenatal stress and family functioning. *American Journal on Mental Retardation, 95*, 623–629.

Eberhardy, F. (1967). the view from the couch. *Journal of Child Psychology and Psychiatry, 8*, 257–263.

Edgerton, R. (1962). *The cloak of competence: Stigma in the lives of the mentally retarded.* Berkeley: University of California Press.

Edgerton, R. B., & Bercovici, S. M. (1976). The cloak of competence: Years later. *American Journal of Mental Deficiency, 80,* 485–497.

Edgerton, R. B., Bollinger, M., & Herr, B. (1984). The cloak of competence: After two decades. *American Journal of Mental Deficiency, 88,* 345–351.

Edmonson, B., & Han, S. (1983). Effects of socialization games on proximity and prosocial behavior of aggressive mentally retarded institutionalized women. *American Journal of Mental Deficiency, 85,* 473–477.

Edmondson, B., McCombs, K., & Wish, J. (1979). What retarded adults believe about sex. *American Journal of Mental Deficiency, 84,* 11–18.

Edmondson, B., & Wish, J. (1975). Sex knowledge and attitudes of moderately retarded males. *American Journal of Mental Deficiency, 80,* 172–179.

Education for All Handicapped Children Act of 1975 (Public Law 94-142).

Edwards, J. H., Harnden, D. G., Cameron, A. H., Crosse, V. M., & Wolff, O. H. (1960). New trisomic syndrome. *Lancet, i,* 787–790.

Einfield, S. L., Tonge, B. J., & Florio, T. (1997). Behavioral and emotional disturbance in individuals with Williams syndrome. *American Journal on Mental Retardation, 102,* 45–53.

Ellenberg, J. H., Hirtz, D. G., & Nelson, K. B. (1986). Do seizures in children cause intellectual deterioration? *New England Journal of Medicine, 314,* 1085–1088.

Elliott, D., Weeks, D. J., & Elliott, C. L. (1987). Cerebral specialization in individuals with Down syndrome. *American Journal on Mental Retardation, 92,* 263–271.

Elliott, D., Weeks, D. J., & Gray, S. (1990). Manual and oral praxis in adults with Down syndrome. *Neuropsychologica, 28,* 1307–1315.

Ellis, D. (1979). Visual handicaps of mentally handicapped people. *American Journal of Mental Deficiency, 83,* 497–511.

Ellis, N. R. (1970). Memory processes in retardates and normals. In N. R. Ellis (Ed.), *International review of research in mental retardation* (vol. 4, pp. 1–32). New York: Academic Press.

Ellis, W. R., & Rusch, F. R. (1991). Supported employment: Current practices and future directions. In J. L. Mation & J. A. Mulick (Eds.), *Handbook of Mental Retardation* (2nd ed., pp. 479–488). New York: Pergamon.

Ellis, N. R., Woodley-Zanthos, P., Dulaney, C. L., & Palmer, R. L. (1989). Automatic-effortful processing and cognitive inertia in persons with mental retardation. *American Journal of Mental Retardation, 93,* 412–423.

Elwes, R. D. C., Johnson, A. L., Shorvon, S. D., & Reynolds, E. H. (1984). The prognosis for seizure control in newly diagnosed epilepsy patients. *New England Journal of Medicine, 311,* 944–947.

Epilepsy Foundation of America, 1981.

Epstein, S. (1973). The self-concept revisited: On a theory of a theory. *American Psychologist, 28,* 404–416.

Epstein, L. G., Sharer, L. R., Oleske, J. M., Cannon, E. M., Goudsmit, J., Bagdon, L., Robert-Guroff, M., & Koenigsberger, M. R. (1986). Neurological manifestations of HIV infection in children. *Pediatrics, 78,* 678–687.

Ericcson, K. A., & Faivre, I. A. (1988). What's exceptional about exceptional abilities? In L. K. Obler & D. Fein (Eds.), *The exceptional brain* (pp. 436–473). New York: Guilford Press.

Erickson, M., & Upshur, C. C. (1989). Caretaking burden and social support: Comparison of mothers of infants with and without disabilities. *American Journal on Mental Retardation, 94,* 250–258.

Ernhart, C. B., Sokol, R. J., Ager, J. W., Morrow-Tlucak, M., & Martier, J. (1989). Alcohol-related birth defects: Assessing the risk. *Annals of the New York Academy of Sciences, 562,* 159–172.

Escalona, S. K. (1982). Babies at double hazard: Early development of infants at biologic and social risk. *Pediatrics, 70,* 670–676.

Esposito, B. G., & Reed, T. M. (1986). The effects of handicapped persons on young children's attitudes. *Exceptional Children, 54,* 224–229.

Evans, R. W., Aman, M. G., & Gualtieri, C. T. (1989). Anticonvulsant drugs. In T. B. Karasu (Ed.), *Treatment of Psychiatric Disorders* (Vol. 1, pp. 94–99). Washington, DC: American Psychiatric Association.

Eyman, R. K. (1983). On the survival and development of the mentally retarded. *Psychology in Mental Retardation, 9,* 1–2.

Eyman, R. K., Demaine, G. C., & Lei, T. (1979). Relationship between community environments and resident changes in adaptive behavior: A path model. *American Journal of Mental Deficiency, 83,* 330–338.

Fahs, J. J. (1989). Antianxiety and sedative-hypnotic agents. In T. B. Karasu (Ed.). *Treatments of Psychiatric Disorders.* (Vol. 1, pp. 58–91). Washington, DC: American Psychiatric Association.

Farquhar, J. (1974). Offspring of PKU mothers. *Archives of Disease in Childhood, 49,* 205–208.

Farriaux, J. P., Dhondt, J. L., & Lebecq, M. F. (1988). Intellectual outcomes in hypothyroid children screened at birth. In F. Delange, D. A. Fisher, & D. Glinoer (Eds.), *Research in congenital hypothyroidism* (pp. 253–264). New York: Plenum.

Feldman, M. A., Case, L., Towns, F., & Betel, J. (1985). Parent education project I: Development and nurturance of children of mentally retarded parents. *American Journal of Mental Deficiency, 90,* 253–258.

Fernald, W. E. (1919). After-care study of the patients discharged from Waverly for a period of twenty-five years. *Ungraded, 5,* 25–31.

Fessard, C. (1968). Cerebral tumors in infancy: 66 clinicoanatomical case studies. *American Journal of Diseases of Children, 115,* 302–308.

Festinger, L., & Bramel, D. (1962). The reaction of humans to cognitive dissonance. In A. J. Bachrach (Ed.), *Experimental Foundations of Clinical Psychology* (pp. 254–279). New York: Basic Books.

Fewell, R. R., & Glick, M. P. (1996). Program evaluation findings of an intensive early intervention program. *American Journal on Mental Retardation, 101,* 233–243.

Finberg, L. (1977). Syphilis. In A. M. Rudulph (Ed.). *Pediatrics.* New York: Appleton-Century-Crofts.

Fine, A. N. (1988). The goal of leisure with the schools. In A. M. Fine and N. M. Fine (Eds.), *Therapeutic recreation for exceptional children* (pp. 255–281). Springfield, IL: Thomas.

Fischer, S. M., Iwata, B. A., & Mazaleski, J. L. (1997). Noncontingent delivery of arbitrary reinforcers as treatment for self-injurious behavior. *Journal of Applied Behavioral Analysis 30,* 239–249.

Fisher, W. W., & Iwata, B. A. (1996). On the function of self-restraint and its relationship to self-injury. *Journal of Applied Behavior Analysis, 29,* 93–98.

Fishler, K., Donnell, G. N., & Wenz, E. (1980). Developmental aspects of galactosemia from infancy to childhood. *Clinical Pediatrics, 29,* 38–44.

Fishler, K., & Koch, R. (1991). Mental development in Down syndrome mosaicism. *American Journal on Mental Retardation, 96,* 345–351.

Fitzjimmons, M. (1970). Bowling. In L. L. Neal (Ed.), *Recreation's role in the rehabilitation of the mentally retarded* (pp. 50–52). Eugene, OR: University of Oregon, Rehabilitation Research and Training Center in Mental Retardation.

Fletcher, J. M., Francis, D. J., Pequegnat, W., Raudenbush, S. W., Bornstein, M. H., Schmitt, F., Brouwers, P., & Stover, E. (1991). Neurobehavioral outcomes in diseases of childhood. *American Psychologist, 46,* 1267–1277.

Flynn, J. R. (1985). Wechsler intelligence tests: Do we really have a criterion of mental retardation? *American Journal of Mental Deficiency, 90,* 236–244.

Fontanesi, J. & Haas, R. H. (1988). Cognitive profile of Rett syndrome. *Journal of Child Neurology,* 3 Suppl: S20-S24.

Ford, A., Schnorr, R., Meyer, L., Davern, L., Black, J., & Dempsey, P. (1989). *The Syracuse community-referenced curriculum guide.* Baltimore: Brookes.

Ford, C. E., & Hamerton, J. L. (1956). The chromosomes of man. *Nature, 178,* 1020–1023.

Forrest, F., & du V. Florey, C. (1991). The relation between maternal alcohol consumption and child development: The epidemiological evidence. *Journal of Public Health Medicine, 13,* 247–255.

Fowler, A. E. (1988). Determinants of rate of language growth with Down syndrome. In L. Nadel (Ed.), *The psychobiology of Down syndrome* (pp. 218–245). Cambridge, MA: MIT Press.

Fowler, A., Gelman, R., & Gleitman, L. (1980). *A comparison of normal and retardate language equated on MLV.* Paper presented at 5th Annual Boston University Conference on Child Language Development.

Foxx, R. M. (1996, September). *Managing challenging behavior.* Paper presented at the meeting or the North Carolina chapter of the American Association on Mental Retardation, Raleigh.

Foxx, R. M., & Azrin, N.H. (1973). The elimination of autistic self-stimulatory behavior by overcorrection. *Journal of Applied Behavior Analysis, 6,* 1–14.

Foxx, R. M., & Azrin, N. H. (1974). *Toilet training the retarded: A rapid program for day and nighttime independent toileting.* Champaign, IL: Research Press.

Foxx, R. M., & McMorrow, M. J. (1983). *Stacking the deck.* Champaign, IL: Research Press.

Foxx, R. M., McMorrow, M. J., & Schloss, C. N. (1983). Stacking the deck: Teaching social skills to retarded adults with a modified table game. *Journal of Applied Behavior Analysis, 16,* 157–170.

Foxx, R. M., McMorrow, M. J., Storey, K., & Rogers, B. M. (1984). Teaching social/sexual skills to mentally retarded adults. *American Journal of Mental Deficiency, 89,* 9–15.

Frank, J. L. (1975). Normalization: "Marc. A young man I'll never forget." *Mental Retardation, 13*(3), 25.

Fraser, J., & Mitchell, A. (1876). Kalmuc idiocy: Report of a case with autopsy with nodes on 62 cases. *Journal of Mental Science, 22,* 161.

Fried, P. A., & O'Connell, C. M. (1987). A comparison of the effects of prenatal exposure to tobacco, alcohol, cannabis and caffeine on birth size and subsequent growth. *Neurotoxicology and Technology, 9,* 79–85.

Fried, P. A., & Watkinson, B. (1988). 12 and 24 month neurobehavioral follow-up of children prenatally exposed to marijuana, cigarettes, and alcohol. *Neurobehavioral Toxicology and Teratology, 10,* 305–313.

Friedman, P. R. (1976). *The rights of mentally retarded persons.* New York: Avon.

Friedman, S. B., & Daum, F. (1992). The gastrointestinal tract: Psychosocial considerations. In M. D. Levine, W. B. Carey, & A. C. Crocker (Eds.), *Developmental-behavioral pediatrics* (2nd ed., pp. 322–326). Philadelphia: W.B. Saunders.

Fryers, T. (1984). *The epidemiology of severe intellectual impairment: The dynamics of prevalence.* London: Academic Press.

Fuerst, J. S., & Fuerst, D. (1993). Chicago experience with an early childhood program: The special case of the Child-Parent Center program. *Urban Education, 28,* 69–96.

Fuhrmann, K., Reiher, H., Semmler, K., Fincher, F., & Glockner, E. (1983). Prevention of cognitive malformation in infants of insulin-dependent diabetic mothers. *Diabetic Care, 6,* 219–223.

Fuller, J. L. (1954). *Nature and nurture: A modern synthesis.* New York: Doubleday.

Gabriel, S. (1997). The borderline: Borderline personality disorders in persons with mental retardation. *National Association for the Dually Diagnosed Newsletter, 14*(1), 5–9.

Gaddes, W. H., & Edgell, D. (1994). *Learning disabilities and brain function.* New York: Springer Verlag.

Gaily, E., & Granstrom, M. L. (1988). Minor anomalies in offspring of epileptic mothers. *Journal of Pediatrics, 112,* 520–529.

Gal, P., & Sharpless, M. K. (1984). Fetal drug exposure: Behavioral teratogenesis. *Drug Intelligence and Clinical Pharmacy, 18,* 186–201.

Gallimore, R., Coots, J., Weisner, T., Garnier, H., & Guthrie, D. (1996). Family response to children with early development delays II: Accommodation intensity and activity in early and middle childhood. *American Journal on Mental Retardation, 101,* 215–232.

Gampel, D. H., Gottlief, J., & Harrison, R. H. (1974). A comparison of the classroom behavior of special class EMR, integrated EMR, low IQ, and non-retarded children. *American Journal of Mental Deficiency, 79,* 16–21.

Garber, H. L. (1988). *The Milwaukee Project: Preventing mental retardation in children at risk.* Washington, DC: The American Association on Mental Retardation.

Garber, H. L., & Hodge, J. D. (1989). Risk for deceleration in the rate of mental development. *Developmental Review, 91,* 259–300.

Garber, H. L., Hodge, J. D., Rynders, J., Dever, R., & Velu, R. (1991). The Milwaukee Project: Setting the record straight. *American Journal on Mental Retardation, 95,* 493–525.

Gardner, D. L., & Cowdry, R. W. (1986). Positive effects of carbamazepine on behavioral dyscontrol in borderline personality disorder. *American Journal of Psychiatry, 143,* 519–522.

Gardner, J. F., Nudler, S., & Chapman, M. S. (1997). Personal outcomes as measures of equality. *Mental Retardation, 35,* 295–305.

Garfield, S. L. (1963). Abnormal behavior and mental deficiency. In N. R. Ellis (Ed.), *Handbook of mental deficiency* (pp. 574–601). New York: McGraw-Hill.

Garwick, G., Jurkowski, E., & Valenti-Hein, D. (1993). Full normalization: Goal based romance, sensuality, and friendship skill-building for people with developmental disabilities. Paper presented at the annual conference of the American Association on Mental Retardation, Washington, DC.

Garwood, S. G., Fewell, R. R., & Neisworth, J. T. (1988). Public Law 94–142: You can get there from here! *Topics in Early Childhood Special Education, 8*(1), 1–11.

Gath, A., & Gumley, D. (1986). Behavior problems in retarded children with special references to Down's syndrome. *British Journal of Psychiatry, 149,* 151–161.

Gay, J. & Cole, M. (1967). *The New Mathematics and an Old Culture: A Study of Learning among the Kpelle of Liberia.* New York: Holt, Rhinehart, & Winston.

Gedye, A. (1992). Recognizing obsessive-compulsive disorder in clients with developmental disabilities. *Habilitative Mental Healthcare Newsletter, 11,* 73–77.

Gibbs, M. V., & Thorpe, J. G. (1983). Personality stereotype of noninstitutionalized Down syndrome children. *American Journal of Mental Deficiency, 87,* 601–605.

Gibson, D. (1966). Early developmental staging as a prophesy index in Down syndrome. *American Journal of Mental Deficiency, 70,* 825–828.

Girardeau, F. L., & Spradzin, J. E. (1964). Token rewards in college program. *Mental Retardation, 2,* 345–351.

Girgis, S. S. (1985, November–December). Dental health of persons with severe mentally handicapping conditions. *Special Care in Dentistry,* 246–249.

Glidden, L. M., & Pursley, J. T. (1989). Longitudinal comparisons of families who have adopted children with mental retardation. *American Journal of Mental Retardation, 94,* 272–277.

Glorieux, J. (1988). Mental development of patients with congenital hypothyroidism detected at screening: Quebec experience. In F. Delange, D. A. Fisher, & D. Glinoer (Eds.), *Research in congenital hypothyroidism* (pp. 281–290). New York: Plenum.

Gorton, C. E. & Hollis, J. H. (1965). Redesigning a college unit for better programming and research for the severely retarded. *Mental Retardation, 3,* 16–21.

Goddard, H. H. (1912). The *Kallikak family: A study in the heredity of feeblemindedness.* New York: MacMillan.

Goh, H., Iwata, B. A., Shore, B. A., DeLeon, I. G., Lerman, D. C., Ulrich, S. M., & Smith, R. G. (1995). An analysis of the reinforcing properties of hand mouthing. *Journal of Applied Behavior Analysis, 28,* 269–283.

Golbus, M. S. (1980). Teratology for the obstetrician: Current status. *Obstetrics and Gynecology, 55,* 269–277.

Gold, A. P., Hammill, J. F., & Carter, S. (1977). Cerebrovascular diseases. In A. M. Rudolph (Ed.), *Pediatrics* (16th ed.). New York: Appleton-Century-Croft.

Golden, E., & Hatcher, J. (1997). Nutrition knowledge and obesity in community residences. *Mental Retardation, 35,* 177–184.

Goldberg, R. T., McLean, M. M., LaVigne, R., Fratolillo, J., & Sullivan, F. T. (1990). Transition of persons with developmental disability from extended sheltered employment to competitive employment. *Mental Retardation, 28,* 299–304.

Golden, J. A., & Heckrotte, M. L. (1993). Sexual abuse of disabled persons: A case history. *The Journal (North Carolina Crime Prevention), 1*(1), 6–7.

Goldfarb, W. (1901). *Childhood Schizophrenia.* Cambridge, MA: Harvard University Press.

Goldman, J. J. (1988). Prader-Willi syndrome in two institutionalized older adults. *Mental Retardation, 26,* 97–102.

Goldstein, H., Moss, J. W., & Jordan, L. J. (1965). The efficacy of special class training on the development of mentally retarded children (U.S. Office of Educational Cooperative Project No. 619). Urbana, IL: University of Illinois.

Gomez, M. (1988). Neurologic and psychiatric features. In M. Gomez (Ed.), *Tuberous sclerosis* (pp. 85–94). New York: Raven.

Gordon, S. (1973). Telling it like it is. In K. Thaller & B. Thaller (Eds.), *Sexuality and the mentally retarded.* Washington, DC: Office of Economic Opportunity.

Gordon, B. N., & Schroeder, C. S. (1995). *Sexuality. A developmental approach to problems.* New York: Plenum.

Gorton, C. E., & Hollis, J. H. (1965). Redesigning a cottage unit for better programming and research for the severely retarded. *Mental Retardation, 3*(3), 16–21.

Gosch, A., & Pankau, R. (1994). Social-emotional and behavioral adjustment in children with Williams-Bevren syndrome. *American Journal of Medical Genetics, 53,* 335–339.

Gottlieb, J. C. (1974). Attitudes toward retarded children: Effect of labeling and academic performance. *American Journal of Mental Deficiency, 79,* 268–273.

Gottlieb, J. (1990). Mainstreaming and quality of education. *American Journal of Mental Retardation, 95,* 16–17.

Gottlieb, J., Alter, M., & Gottlieb, B. (1991). Mainstreaming mentally retarded children. In J. L. Matson & J. A. Mulick (Eds.), *Handbook of Mental Retardation* (2nd ed., pp. 63–73). New York: Pergamon.

Gottlieb, J., & Budoff, M. (1972). Attitudes toward school by segregated and integrated retarded children. *Proceedings of the American Psychological Association, 7,* 713–714.

Gozali, J. (1972). Perception of the EMR special class by former students. *Mental Retardation, 10,* 34–35.

Graham, Jr., J. M. (1992). Congenital anomalies. In M. D. Levine, W. B. Carey, A. C. Crocker, & R. T. Gross (Eds.), *Developmental-behavioral pediatrics* (pp. 229–243). Philadelphia: W.B. Saunders.

Graham, J., & Poling, J. (1963). Help is a warm puppy. *Ladies Home Journal, 80,* 28.

Grandin, T., & Scariano, M. M. (1986). *Emergence labeled autism*. Navato, CA: Arena Press.

Grantham-McGregor, S. M., Powell, C. A., Walker, S. P., & Himes, J. H. (1991). Nutritional supplementation, psychological stimulation and development of stunted children; the Jamacia study. *Lancet, 338,* 1–5.

Gravel, R. A., Clarke, J. T. R., Kaback, M. M., Mahuran, D., Sandhoff, K., & Suzuki, K. (1995). The Gm2 gangliosidoses. In C. R. Scriver, A. L. Beaudet, W. S. Sly, & D. Valle (Eds.), *The metabolic and molecular basis of inherited disease* (vol. II, pp. 2839–2882). New York: McGraw-Hill.

Gray, R. M., & Kasteler, J. M. (1969). The effects of social reinforcement and training on institutionalized mentally retarded children. *American Journal of Mental Deficiency, 74,* 50–56.

Green, D. T. (1983). A human sexuality program for developmentally disabled women in a sheltered workshop setting. *Sexuality and Disability, 6,* 20–24.

Green, T., Ernhart, C. B., Sokol, R., Martier, S., Marler, M. R., Boyd, T. A., & Ager, J. (1991). Prenatal alcohol exposure and preschool physical growth: A longitudinal analysis. *Alcoholism: Clinical and Experimental Research, 15,* 905–913.

Greenspan, S., & Granfield, J. M. (1992). Reconsidering the construct of mental retardation: Implications of a model of social competence. *American Journal of Mental Retardation, 96,* 442–453.

Greenspan, S., & Shoultz, B. (1981). Why mentally retarded adults lose their jobs: Social competence as a factor in work adjustment. *Applied Research in Mental Retardation, 2,* 23–38.

Greenspan, S., Switzky, H. N., & Granfield, J. M. (1996). Everyday intelligence and adaptive behavior: A theoretical framework. In J. W. Jacobson & J. A. Mulick (Eds.), *Manual of diagnosis and professional practice in mental retardation* (pp. 127–136). Washington, DC: American Psychological Association.

Greenswag, L. (1987). Adults with Prader-Willi syndrome: A survey of 232 cases. *Developmental Medicine and Child Neurology, 29,* 145–152.

Gresham, F. M., MacMillan, D. L., & Siperstein, G. N. (1995). Critical analysis of the 1992 AAMR definition. *School Psychology Quarterly, 10,* 1–19.

Gress, J. R., & Boss, M. S. (1996). Substance abuse differences among students receiving special education school services. *Child Psychiatry and Human Development, 26,* 235–246.

Grether, J. K., Cummins, S. K., & Nelson, K. B. (1992). The California cerebral palsy project. *Pediatric and Perinatal Epidemiology, 6,* 339–351.

Griffiths, P., Smith, C., & Harvie, A. (1997). Transitory Hyperphenylalaniniemia in children with continuously treated Phenlylketonvaia. *American Journal of Mental Retardation, 102,* 27–36.

Groden, G., Stevenson, S., & Groden. J. (1993). *Understanding challenging behavior: A step-by-step behavior analysis guide*. Providence, RI: Manisses Communications Group.

Grossman, F. D. (1972). *Brothers and sisters of retarded children: An exploratory study*. Syracuse, NY: Syracuse University Press.

Grossman, H. J. (1973). Manual on terminology and classification in mental retardation (rev.). Washington, DC: American Association on Mental Deficiency.

Grossman, H. J. (1983). *Classification in mental retardation*. Washington, DC: American Association on Mental Deficiency.

Grossman, H. J. (Ed.), (1997). *Manual on Terminology and Classification in Mental Retardation*. Washington, DC: American Association on Mental Deficiency.

Grundy, E. (1983). Demography and old age. *Journal of the American Geriatrics Society, 31,* 325–332.

Gualtheria, C. T. (1989). Antidepressant drugs and lithium. In T. B. Karasu (Ed.). *Treatments of Psychiatric Disorders* (Vol. I, pp. 77–85). Washington, DC: American Psychiatric Association.

Gualtieri, C. T., & Hawk, B. (1980). Tardive dysenesia and other drug-induced movement disorders among handicapped children and youth. *Applied Research in Mental Retardation, 1*, 55–69.

Guerina, N. G., Hsu, H.-W., & Meisaner, H. C. (1994). Neonatal serologic screening and early treatment for Toxoplasma Gondii infection. *New England Journal of Medicine, 330*, 858–863.

Guess, D., Roberts, S., Siegel-Causey, E., Ault, M., Guy, B., Thompson, B., & Rues, J. (1993). An analysis of behavior state conditions and associated environmental variables among students with profound handicaps. *American Journal of Mental Retardation, 97*, 634–653.

Guess, D., Roberts, S., Siegel-Causey, E., & Rues, J. (1995). Replication and extended analysis of behavior state, environmental events, and related variables among individuals with profound disabilities. *American Journal of Mental Retardation, 100*, 36–50.

Guilford, J. P. (1967). *The nature of human intelligence*. New York: McGraw-Hill.

Gunn, P., & Berry, P. (1985). Down's syndrome temperament and maternal response to descriptions of child behavior. *Developmental Psychology, 21*, 842–847.

Guralnick, M. J. (1988). Efficacy research in early childhood intervention programs. In S. L. Odom & M. B. Barnes (Eds.), *Early intervention for infants and children with handicaps. An empirical case* (pp. 75–88). Baltimore: Brookes.

Guralnick, M. J. (1998). Effectiveness of early intervention for vulnerable children: A developmental perspective. *American Journal on Mental Retardation, 102*, 319–345.

Guralnick, M. J., & Bricker, D. (1987). The effectiveness of early intervention for children with cognitive and general developmental delays. In M. Guralnick & F. C. Bennett (Eds.), *The effectiveness of early intervention for at-risk and handicapped children* (pp. 115–174). Orlando, FL: Academic Press.

Guralnick, M. J., & Groom, J. M. (1987). The peer relations of mildly delayed and non-handicapped preschool children in mainstreamed play groups. *Child Development, 58*, 1556–1572.

Hagberg, G. (1980). *Infantile autistic dementia and loss of hand use. A report of 16 Swedish girl patients*. Paper presented at the Research Session of the European Federation of Child Neurology Societies. Manchester, England.

Hagberg, G. (1985). Rett syndrome: Swedish approach to analysis of prevalence and cause. *Brain and Development, 7*, 277–280.

Hagberg, G. & Wit-Engerstrom, I. (1986). Rett syndrome: A suggested staging system for describing the impairment profile with increasing age toward adolescence. *American Journal of Medical Genetics, 24*, (Suppl. 1), 47–59.

Hagberg, G., Aicardi, J., Dias, K., & Ramos, O. (1983). A progressive syndrome of autism, dementia, ataxia, and loss of purposeful hand use in girls: Rett's syndrome. Reports of 35 cases. *Annals of Neurology, 14*, 471–479.

Hagerman, R. J. (1992). Chromosomal disorders. In M. D. Levine, W. B. Carey, & A. C. Crocker (Eds.), *Developmental-behavioral pediatrics* (pp. 213–220). Philadelphia: W.B. Saunders.

Hale, C. A., & Borkowsky, J. G. (1991). Attention, memory, and cognition. In J. L. Matson & J. A. Mulick (Eds.), *Handbook of mental retardation* (2nd ed., pp. 505–528). New York: Pergamon Press.

Hall, J. E., & Morris, H. L. (1976). Sexual knowledge and attitudes of institutionalized and noninstitutionalized retarded adolescents. *American Journal of Mental Deficiency, 80*, 382–387.

Hall, J. G., Pauli, I., & Wilson, K. M. (1980). Maternal and fetal sequalae of anticoagulation during pregnancy. *American Journal of Medicine, 68*, 122–140.

Hallahan, D. P., & Kauffman, J. M. (1991). *Exceptional children: Introduction to special education* (5th ed.). Englewood Cliffs, NJ: Prentice-Hall.

Halperin, S. L. (1945). A clinico-genetical study of mental defects. *American Journal of Mental Deficiency, 50,* 8–25.

Hammock, R. G., Schroeder, S. R., & Levine, W. R. (1995). The effect of clozapine on self-injurious behavior. *Journal of Autism and Developmental Disorders, 25,* 611–626.

Hamre-Nietupski, S., & Williams, W. (1977). Implementation of selected sex education and social skills to severely handicapped students. *Education and Training of the Mentally Retarded, 12,* 364–372.

Hanson, J. W., Myriathopoulos, N. C., Harvey, M. A. S., & Smith, D. W. (1976). Risks to the offspring of women treated with hydantoin anti-convulsants, with emphasis on the fetal hydantoin syndrome. *Journal of Pediatrics, 89,* 662–668.

Hanson, J. W., Streissguth, A. P., & Smith, D. W. (1978). Effects of moderate alcohol consumption during pregnancy on fetal growth and morphogenesis. *Journal of Pediatrics, 92,* 457–460.

Harris, S. L., Alessandri, M., & Gill, M. J. (1991). Training parents of developmentally disabled children. In J. L. Matson & J. A. Mulick (Eds.), *Handbook of mental retardation* (pp. 373–381). New York: Pergamon.

Harris, V. S., & McHale, S. M. (1989). Family life problems, daily caregiving activities, and psychological well-being of mothers of mentally retarded children. *American Journal on Mental Retardation, 94,* 231–239.

Hawk, B. A., Schroeder, S. R., Robinson, G., Otto, D., Mushak, P., Kleinbaum, D., & Dawson, G. (1986). Relation of lead and social factors to IQ of low-SES children: A partial replication. *American Journal of Mental Deficiency, 91,* 178–183.

Hawkins, B. A. (1988). Leisure and recreational programming. In M. P. Janicki, M. W. Krauss, & M. M. Seltzer (Eds.), *Community residences for persons developmental disabilities* (pp. 217–230). Baltimore: Brookes.

Hawkins, R. P. (1984). What is "meaningful" behavior change in a severely/profoundly retarded learner? The view of a behavior analytic parent. In W. L. Heward, T. E. Heron, D. S. Hill, & J. Trap-Porter (Eds.), *Focus on behavior analysis in education* (pp. 282–286). Columbus, OH: Merrill.

Hayden, M. F., Lakin, K. C., Hill, B. K., Bruininks, R. H., & Chen, T. H. (1992). Placement practices in specialized foster homes and small group homes for persons with mental retardation. *Mental Retardation, 30,* 53–61.

Heber, R. F. (1957). *Expectancy and expectancy changes in normal and mentally retarded boys.* Unpublished doctoral dissertation, George Peabody College for Teachers, Nashville, TN.

Heber, R. F. (1959). A manual on terminology and classification in mental retardation. *American Journal on Mental Deficiency, 64,* Monograph Supplement, (Rev. Ed.), 1961.

Heber, R. F. (1964). Personality. In H. A. Stevens & R. Heber (Eds.). *Mental Retardation: A review of Research.* Chicago: University of Chicago Press.

Heber, R. F., & Dever, R. B. (1970). Research on education and habilitation of the mentally retarded. In H. C. Haywood (Ed.), *Social-cultural aspects of mental retardation* (pp. 395–427). New York: Appleton-Century-Crofts.

Heber, R. F., Dever, R. B., & Conry, J. (1968). The influence of environmental and genetic variables on intellectual development. In H. J. Prehm, L. A. Hamerlynck, & J. E. Crossen (Eds.), *Behavioral research in mental retardation.* Eugene, OR: University of Oregon Press.

Hecht, F., Bryant, B. K., Gruber, D., & Townes, P. L. (1964). The nonrandomness of chromosomal abnormalities: Association of trisomy 18 and Down's syndrome. *New England Journal of Medicine, 271,* 1081–1086.

Hecht, F., & MacFarlane, J. P. (1969). Mosaicism in Turner's syndrome reflects the lethality of XO. *Lancet, ii,* 1197.

Hedlund, R. (1989). Fostering positive social interactions between parents and infants. *Teaching Exceptional Children, 21,* 45–48.

Heifetz, L. J. (1987). Integrating religious and secular perspectives in the design and delivery of disability services. *Mental Retardation, 25,* 127–131.

Heller, T., Miller, A. B., & Factor, A. (1997). Adults with mental retardation as supports to their parents: Effects on parental caregiving appraisal. *Mental Retardation, 35,* 338–346.

Helm, D. T., Miranda, S., & Chedd, N. A. (1998). Prenatal diagnosis of Down syndrome: Mother's reflections on supports needed from diagnosis to birth. *Mental Retardation, 36,* 55–61.

Hemmer, R., & Boehm, B. (1976). Once a shunt, always a shunt? *Developmental Medicine and Child Neurology, 18*(suppl. 37), 69–73.

Hendrick, E. B. (1993). Results of treatment in infants and children. In P. H. Schurr, & C. E. Polkey (Eds.), *Hydrocephalus.* Oxford: Oxford University Press.

Henretig, F. (1992). Toxins. In M. D. Levine, W. B. Carey, & A. C. Crocker (Eds.), *Developmental-behavioral pediatrics* (pp. 285–292). Philadelphia: W.B. Saunders.

Henshel, A. M. (1972). *The forgotten ones: A sociological study of angla and chicano retardates.* Austin, TX: University of Texas Press.

Herman, S. E., & Hazel, K. L. (1991). Evaluation of family support services: Changes in availability and accessibility. *Mental Retardation, 29,* 351–357.

Herman, S. E., & Marcenko, M. O. (1997). Perceptions of services and resources as mediators of depression among parents of children with developmental disabilities. *Mental Retardation, 35,* 458–467.

Hermann, B. P., Desai, B. T., & Whitman, S. (1988). Epilepsy. In V. B. Van Hasselt, P. S. Strain, & M. Hersen (Eds.), *Handbook of developmental and physical disabilities* (pp. 247–270). Elmsford, NY: Pergamon.

Hermann, B. P., Wyler, A. R., Richey, E. T., & Rea, J. M. (1987). Memory function and verbal learning ability in patients with complex partial seizures of temporal lobe origin. *Epilepsia, 28,* 547–554.

Herrnstein, R. (1994). *The Bell Curve: Intelligence and Class Structure in America.* New York: Free Press.

Herzberg, F., Mausner, B., & Snyderman, B. (1959). *The motivation to work.* New York: Wiley.

Heshusius, L. (1982). Sexuality, intimacy, and persons we label mentally retarded: What they think—what we think. *Mental Retardation, 20,* 164–168.

Heward, W. L., & Orlansky, M. D. (1992). *Exceptional children: An introductory survey of special education* (4th ed.). New York: MacMillan.

Hill, A. L. (1974). Idiot savants: A categorization of abilities. *Mental Retardation, 12,* 12–13.

Hill, B. K., Balow, E. A., & Bruininks, R. N. (1985). A national study of prescribed drugs in institutions and community residential facilities for mentally retarded people. *Psychpharmacology Bulletin, 21,* 279–284.

Hill, B. K., Lakin, K. C., Bruininks, R. H., Amado, A. N., Anderson, D. J., & Copher, J. I. (1989). *Living in the community: A comparative study of foster homes and small group homes for people with mental retardation* (Report No. 28). Minneapolis: University of Minnesota, Center for Residential and Community Services.

Hillbrand, M. (1995). The use of buspirone with aggressive behavior. *Journal of Autism of Developmental Disorders, 25,* 663–664.

Hobson, R. P. (1989). Beyond cognition: A theory of autism. In G. Dawson (Ed.). *Autism: New Perspecives on Diagnosis, Nature, and Treatment.* (pp.22–48). New York: Guilford.

Hodapp, R. M. (1997). Direct and indirect behavioral effects of different genetic disorders of mental retardation. *American Journal on Mental Retardation, 102,* 67–79.

Hodapp, R. M., & Dykens, E. M. (1994). Mental retardation's two cultures of behavioral research. *American Journal of Mental Retardation, 98,* 675–687.

Hodapp, R. M., Leckman, J. F., Dykens, E. M., Sparrow, S. J., Zelinsky, D. G., & Ort, S. I.

(1992). K-ABC profiles in children with fragile X syndrome, Down syndrome, and non-specific mental retardation. *American Journal on Mental Retardation, 97,* 39–46.

Hodges, J., & Tizard, B. (1989). IQ and behavioral adjustment of ex-institutional adolescents. *Journal of Child Psychology and Psychiatry, 30,* 53–75.

Holden, R. H. (1972). Prediction of mental retardation in infancy. *Mental Retardation, 10,* 28–30.

Holm, V. A. (1981). The diagnosis of Prader-Willi syndrome. In V. A. Holm, S. J. Sulzbacher, & P. L. Pipes (Eds.), *The Prader-Willi syndrome* (pp. 27–44). Baltimore: University Park Press.

Holm, V. A., Sulzbacher, S. J., & Pipes, P. L. (Eds.). (1981). *The Prader-Willi syndrome.* Baltimore: University Park Press.

Holton, J. B. (1991). Galactosemia. In J. Schaub, F. V. Hoof, and H. L. Vis (Eds.), *Inborn errors of metabolism.* New York: Raven.

Holtzman, N. A., Kronmal, R. A., Van Doornick, W., Azen, C., & Koch, R. (1986). Effect of age at loss of dietary control on an intellectual performance and behavior of children. *New England Journal of Medicine, 314,* 593–598.

Honig, A. J., & McCarron, P. A. (1992). Prosocial behaviors of handicapped and typical peers in an integrated preschool. In K. F. Freiberg (Ed.), *Educating exceptional children* (6th ed., pp. 32–37). Guilford, CT: Duskin:

Hook, E. W. (1973). Behavioral implications of the human xyy genotype. *Science, 179,* 139–150.

Hopkins, T., Bice, H. V., & Colton, K. C. (1954). *Evaluation and education of the cerebral palsied child: New Jersey study.* Washington, DC: International Council for Exceptional Children.

Horn, J. L. (1968). Organization of abilities and the development of intelligence. *Psychological Review, 75,* 242–259.

Howard-Teplansky, R. B. (1992). Nutrition and development. In M. D. Levine, W. B. Carey, & A.C. Crocker (Eds.), *Developmental-behavioral pediatrics* (pp. 276–284). Philadelphia: W.B. Saunders.

Hughes, C. (1992). Teaching self-instruction utilizing multiple exemplars to produce generalized problem-solving among individuals with severe mental retardation. *American Journal of Mental Retardation, 97,* 302–314.

Hughes, C., & Petersen, D. L. (1989). Utilizing a self-instructional training package to increase on-task behavior and work performance. *Education and Training in Mental Retardation, 24,* 114–120.

Hughes, C., & Rusch, F. R. (1989). Teaching supported employees with severe mental retardation to solve problems. *Journal of Applied Behavior Analysis, 22,* 365–372.

Hull, J. T., & Thompson, J. C. (1980). Predicting adaptive functioning of mentally retarded persons in community settings. *American Journal of Mental Deficiency, 85,* 253–261.

Hunt, A., & Dennis, J. (1987). Psychiatric disorders in children with tuberous sclerosis. *Developmental Medicine and Child Neurology, 29,* 190–198.

Hunt, E. (1976). Varieties of cognitive power. In L. B. Resnick (Ed.), *The nature of intelligence* (pp. 237–260). Hillsdale, NJ: Erlbaum.

Hunt, N. (1967). *The world of Nigel Hunt.* Beaconfield, UK: Darwen Finlayson.

Hurlock, E. G. (1964). *Child development* (4th ed.). New York: McGraw-Hill.

Hyman, S. L. (1996). A transdisplinary approach to self-injurious behavior. In A. J. Capute & P. J. Accardo (Eds.), *Developmental Disabilities in Infancy and Childhood: The Spectrum of Developmental Disabilties* (2nd ed., vol. II, p. 319). Baltimore, MD: Brookes.

Individuals with Diabilities Education Act of 1990, Pub. L. No. 101-476.

Individuals with Disabilities Education Act Amendament of 1997, Pub. L. No. 105-17.

Infant Health and Development Program. (1990). Enhancing the outcomes of low-birth-weight, premature infants. *The Journal of the American Medical Association, 263,* 3035–3042.

Inge, K. J. (1992). Cerebral palsy. In P. J. McLaughlin & P. Wehman (Eds.), *Developmental disabilities*. Boston: Andover Medical Publishers.

Ingram, T. T. S. (1964). *Pediatric Asects of Cerebral Palsy*. Edinburgh: Edinburgh Press.

Inwood, S. (1986). *Food and the Prader-Willi child in school*. Unpublished manuscript.

Irvine, D. J., Flint, D. L., Hick, T. L., Horan, M. D., & Kikuk, S. E. (1982). *Evaluation of the NY State experimental preschool program: Final report*. Albany: State Education Department.

Irwin, O. (1972). *Communication variables of cerebral palsied and mentally retarded children*. Springfield, IL: Charles C. Thomas.

Iwata, B. A., Pace, G. M., Dorsey, M. F., Zarcone, J. R., Vollmer, T. R., Smith, R. G., Rogers, T. A., Lerman, D. C., Shore, B. A., Mazeleski, J. L., Goh, H., Cowdery, G. E., Kalsher, M. J., McKosh, K. C., & Willis, K. D. (1994). The function of self-injurious behavior: An experimental-epidemiological analysis. *Journal of Applied Behavior Analysis, 27*, 215–240.

Iwata, B. A., & Rogers, T. A. (1992). Self-injurious behavior. In E. A. Konarski, J. E. Favell, & J. E. Favell (Eds.), *Manual for the assessment and treatment of the behavior disorders of people with mental retardation* (pp. 1–18). Morganton, NC: Western Carolina Center Foundation.

Iwata, B. A., Zarcone, J. B., Vollmer, T. R., & Smith, R. G. (1994). Assessment and treatment of self-injurious behavior. In E. Schopler & G. B. Mesibov (Eds.), *Behavioral issues in autism* (pp. 131–159). New York: Plenum.

Jackson V. Indiana, 406 U.S. 715(1972).

Jacobson, J. (1982). Problem behavior and psychiatric impairment within a developmentally disabled population I: Behavior severity. *Applied Research in Mental Retardation, 3*, 121–139.

Jacobson, J. W., Mulick, J. A., & Schwartz, A. A. (1995). A history of facilitated communication: Science, pseudoscience, and antiscience. *American Psychologist, 50*, 750–765.

Jacobson, J. W., & Schwartz, A. A. (1991). Evaluating living situations of people with developmental disabilities. In J. L. Matson & J. A. Mulick (Eds.), *Handbook of Mental Retardation* (pp. 35–62). New York: Pergamon.

Jacobson, J. W., Sutton, M. S., & Janicki, M. P. (1985). Demography and characteristics of aging and aged mentally retarded persons. In M. P. Janicki & H. M. Wisniewski (Eds.), *Aging and developmental disabilities: Issues and approaches* (pp. 115–142). Baltimore: Brookes.

Janicki, M. P. (1991). *Building the future: Planning and community development in aging and developmental disabilities*. Albany: New York State Office of Mental Retardation and Developmental Disabilities.

Jennett, B., Teasdale, G., Braakman, R., Minderhoud, J., Heiden, J., & Kurze, T. (1979). Prognosis in a series of patients with severe head injury. *Neurosurgery, 4*, 283–289.

Jensen, A. R. (1973a). *Educability and group differences*. New York: Harper & Row.

Jensen, A. R. (1973b). Let's understand Skodak and Skeels, finally. *Educational Psychologist, 10*, 10–35.

Jensen, A. R. (1990). Speed of information processing in a calculating prodigy. *Intelligence, 14*, 259–274.

Johnson, B. F., & Cuvo, A. J. (1981). Teaching mentally retarded adults to cook. *Behavior Modification, 5*, 187–202.

Johnson, W. R. (1973). Sex education of the mentally retarded. In F. F. De La Cruz & G. D. LaVeck (Eds.), *Human sexuality and the mentally retarded* (pp. 57–66). New York: Brunner/Mazel.

Jones, H. E. (1926). Phenomenal memorizing as a special ability. *Journal of Applied Psychology, 10*, 367–377.

Jones, K. L., Smith, D. W., & Ulleland, C. N. (1973). Pattern of malformation in offspring of chronic alcoholic mothers. *Lancet, i*, 1267–1271.

Jordan, T. E., & DeCharms, R. (1959). The achievement motive in normal and mentally retarded children. *American Journal of Mental Deficiency, 64*, 457–466.

Juel-Neilsen, N. (1965). Individual and environment: A psychiatric-psychological investigation of monozygous twins reared apart. *Acta Psychiatrica Neurologica Scandinavica Monograph*, 183(Suppl.)

Justice, E. M. (1987). Metamemory development in the mentally retarded: Research and implications. In N. R. Ellis (Ed.), *International review of research in mental retardation* (vol. 13, pp. 79–108). New York: Academic Press.

Kagan, J. (1966). Reflection-impulsivity: The generality of conceptual tempo. *Journal of Abnormal Psychology, 71*, 17–24.

Kagan, J. (1972, December). *Cross-cultural perspectives on early development.* Paper presented at the Meeting of the American Association for the Advancement of Science, Washington, DC.

Kagan, J. (1981). Temperamental contributions to social behavior. *American Psychologist, 44*, 668–674.

Kail, R. (1992). General slowing of information-processing by persons with mental retardation. *American Journal of Mental Retardation, 97*, 333–341.

Kaiser, A. P., Alpert, C. L., & Warren, S. F. (1988). Language and communication disorders. In V. B. Van Hasselt, P. S. Strain, & M. Hersen (Eds.), *Handbook of developmental and physical disabilities* (pp. 395–422). New York: Pergamon Press.

Kalachnik, J. E., Hanzel, T. E., Harder, S. R., Bavernfeind, J. D., & Engstrom, E. E. (1995). Antiepileptic drug behavioral side effects in individuals with mental retardation and the use of behavioral measurement techniques. *Mental Retardation, 33*, 374–382.

Kaltenbach, K., & Finnegan, L. P. (1987). Perinatal and developmental outcome of infants exposed to methadone in utero. *Neurotoxicology and Teratology, 9*, 311–313.

Kamin, L. J. (1974). *The science and politics of IQ.* New York: Halsfed Press.

Kamphaus, R. W. (1987). Conceptual and psychometric issues in the assessment of adaptive behavior. *Journal of Special Education, 21*, 27–35.

Kanner, L. (1964). *A history of the care and study of the mentally retarded.* Springfield, IL: Charles C. Thomas.

Kanner, L. (1973). Autistic disturbances of affective contact. *The Neuron Child, 2*, 217–250.

Kaplan, F. (1969). Siblings of the retarded. In S. B. Sarason & J. Doris (Eds.), *Psychological problems in mental deficiency* (4th ed., pp. 186–208). New York: Harper & Row.

Kassari, C., Mundy, P., Yirmiya, N., & Sigman, M. (1990). Affect and attention in children with Down syndrome. *American Journal on Mental Retardation, 95*, 55–67.

Kastner, T., Nathanson, R., & Friedman, D. L. (1993). Mortality among individuals with mental retardation living in the community. *American Journal on Mental Retardation, 98*, 285–292.

Kastner, T. A., Walsh, K. K., & Caiscione, T. (1997a). Overview and implications of Medicaid managed care for people with developmental disabilities. *Mental Retardation, 35*, 257–269.

Kastner, T. A., Walsh, K. K., & Caiscione, T. (1997b). Technical elements, demonstration projects and lived models in Medicaid managed care for people with developmental disabilities. *Mental Retardation, 35*, 270–285.

Katz, S., & Kravetz, S. (1989). Facial plastic surgery for persons with Down syndrome: Research findings and their professional and social implications. American Journal of *Mental Retardation, 94*, 101–110, 119–120.

Kaufman, A. J., & Kaufman, N. L. (1990). *Kaufurou Brief Intelligence Test (K-BIT).* Circle Pines, MN: American Guidance Service.

Keltner, B. (1994). Home environments of mothers with mental retardation. *Mental Retardation, 32*, 123–127.

Kemper, M., Hagerman, R., & Altshul-Stark, D. (1988). Cognitive profiles of boys with fragile X syndrome. *American Journal of Medical Genetics, 30*, 191–200.

Kempton, W. (1978). Sex education for the mentally handicapped. *Sexuality and Disability, 1*, 137–145.

Kempton, W. (1988). *Life horizons*. Philadelphia: Planned Parenthood.

Kennedy, R. A. (1966). *A Connecticut community revisited: A study of the social adjustment of a group of mentally deficient adults in 1948 and 1960*. Hartford: Connecticut State Department of Health, Office of Mental Retardation.

Keranen, T., Silinpaa, M., & Riekkinen, P. J. (1988). Distribution of seizure types in an epileptic population. *Epilepsia, 29*, 1–7.

Kesaree, N., & Wooley, P. V. (1963). A phenotypic female with 49 chromosomes, presumably XXXXX: A case report. *Journal of Pediatrics, 63*, 1099–1103.

Kiernan, W. E., Butterworth, J., & McGaughey, M. (1995). Treads and Milestones: Movement from segregated to integrated services in the United States. *Mental Retardation, 33*, 64.

Kinsbourne, M. (1995). Disorders of mental development. In J. H. Menkes (Ed.), *Textbook of child neurology* (pp. 924–964). Baltimore: Williams & Wilkins.

Kirk, S. A. (1968). *Educating exceptional children*. Boston: Houghton-Mifflin.

Klapper, Z. J., & Birch, H. G. (1967). A fourteen year follow-up study of cerebral palsy: Intellectual change and stability. *American Journal of Orthopsychiatry, 37*, 540–547.

Klees, M. (1988). Intellectual and neuropsychological assessment of children with congenital hypothyroidism. In F. Delange, D. A. Fisher, & D.Glinoer (Eds.), *Research in congenital hypothyroidism* (pp. 265–280). New York: Plenum.

Klein, N. K., Hack, M., & Breslau, N. (1989). Children who had very low birthweight: Development and academic achievement at nine years of age. *Journal of Developmental and Behavioral Pediatrics, 10*, 32–37.

Klein, T., Gilman, E., & Zigler, E. (1993). Special Olympics: An evaluation by professionals and parents. *Mental Retardation, 31*, 15–23.

Kleinberg, J., & Galligan, B. (1983). Efforts of deinstitutionalization on adaptive behavior of mentally retarded adults. *American Journal of Mental Deficiency, 88*, 21–27.

Koch R., Azen, C., Friedman, E. G., & Williamson, M. L. (1984). Paired comparisons between early treated PKU children and their matched sibling controls on intelligence and school achievement test results at eight years of age. *Journal of Inherited Metabolic Diseases, 7*, 86–90.

Koller, H., Richardson, S. A., Katz, M., & McLaren, J. (1983). Behavior disturbance since childhod in a five-year birth Cohort of all mentally retarded adults in a city. *American Journal of Mental Deficiency, 87*, 386–395.

Koluchova, J. (1972). Severe deprivation in twins: A case study. *Journal of Child Psychology and Psychiatry, 13*, 107–114.

Koluchova, J. (1976). The further development of twins after severe and prolonged deprivation: A second report. *Journal of Child Psychology and Psychiatry, 17*, 181–188.

Komrower, G. M., & Lee, D.H. (1970). Long-term follow-up of galactosemia. *Archive of Diseases of Childhood, 45*, 367–373.

Kopp, C. B., Baker, B. L., & Brown, K. W. (1992). Social skills and their correlates: Preschoolers with developmental delays. *American Journal of Mental Retardation, 96*, 357–366.

Kostir, M. S. (1916). *The family of Sam Sixty* (Ohio Board of Administration Press Publication No. 8). Ohio State Reformatory.

Kott, M. G. (1968). Estimating the number of retarded in New Jersey. *Mental Retardation, 6*, 28–31.

Kraemer, G. W. (1992). A psychobiological theory of attachment. *Behavioral and Brain Sciences, 15*, 493–541.

Kramer, L. D., Locke, G. E., Ogunyemi, A., & Nelson, L. (1990). Neonatal cocaine-related seizures. *Journal of Child Neurology, 5*, 60–64.

Krause, W. L., Helminski, M., McDonald, L., Dembure, P., Salvo, R., Friedes, D., & Elsas, L. J. (1985). Biochemical and neuropsychological effects of elevated plasma phenylalanine in patients with treated phenylketoneuria. *Journal of Clinical Investigation, 75*, 40–48.

Krauss, M. W. (1986). Patterns and trends in public services to families with a mentally retarded member. In J. J. Gallagher & P. M. Vietze (Eds.), Families of handicapped persons: Research programs and policy issues (pp. 237–250). Baltimore: Brookes.

Kregel, J., Hill, M., & Banks, P. D. (1988). Analysis of employment specialist intervention time in supported competitive employment. *American Journal on Mental Retardation, 93,* 200–208.

Krick, J. A., & Remington, J. S. (1978). Current concepts in parasitology: Toxoplasmosis in the adult—overview. *New England Journal of Medicine, 298,* 550–553.

Krywawych, S., Haseler, M., & Brenton, D. P. (1991). Theoretical and practical aspects of preventing fetal damage in women with phenylketonuria. In J. Schaub, F. Van Hoof, & H. L. Vis (Eds.), *Inborn errors of metabolism* (pp. 125–136) (Nestle, Nutrition Workshop Series, Vol. 24). New York: Vevey/Raven Press.

Kurland, L. T., Faro, S. N., & Seidler, H. (1960). Minimata disease. *World Neurology, 1,* 370–395.

Kyllerman, M., Bager, B., Bensch, J., Bille, B., Olow, I., & Voss, H. (1982). Dyskinetic cerebral palsy I: Clinical categories, associated neurologic abnormalities and incidence. *Acta Paediatrica Scandinavica, 71,* 543–550.

LaCampagne, J., & Cipani, E. (1987). Training adults with mental retardation to pay bills. *Mental Retardation, 25,* 293–303.

Lachiewicz, A. M., Gullion, C. M., Spiridigliozzi, G. A., & Aylsworth, A. S. (1987). Declining IQs of young males with fragile X syndrome. *American Journal of Mental Retardation, 92,* 272–278.

Lachiewicz, A., Harrison, C., Spiridigliozzi, G., Callanan, N. P., & Livermore, J. (1988). What is the fragile X syndrome? *North Carolina Medical Journal, 49*(4), 203–208.

Lachiewicz, A. M., Spiridigliozzi, G. A., Gullion, C. M., Ransford, S. N., & Rao, K. (1994). Aberrant behaviors of young boys with fragile X syndrome. *American Journal on Mental Retardation, 98,* 567–579.

Lafora, G. R. (1934). Estudio psicologico de una debil mental calculadora del calendario. *Archivos de Neurobiologia, y Psiquiatria, 14,* 45–70.

LaGreca, A. M., Stone, W. L., & Bell, C. R. (1983). Facilitating the vocational-interpersonal skills of mentally retarded individuals. *American Journal of Mental Deficiency, 88,* 270–277.

Laird, C. D. (1987). Proposed mechanism of inheritance and expression of the human fragile-X syndrome of mental retardation. *Genetics, 117,* 587–599.

Lakin, K. C., Anderson, L., Prouty, R., & Polister, B. (1999). State institution populations less than one third of 197, residents older with more impairments. *Mental Retardation, 37,* 85–86.

Lakin, K. C., Braddock, D., & Smith, G. (1995). Children and youth in state MR/DD institutions. *Mental Retardation, 33,* 203.

Lakin, K. C., Hill, B. K., Hauber, F. A., & Bruininks, R. H. (1982). Changes in age at first admission to residential care of mentally retarded people. *Mental Retardation, 20,* 216–219.

Lakin, C., Prouty, B. Braddock, D., & Anderson, L. (1997). State institution populations smaller, older, more impaired. *Mental Retardation, 35,* 231–232.

Lakin, K. C., Prouty, B., Smith, G., & Braddock, D. (1996). Nixon goal surpassed: Two-fold. *Mental Retardation, 34,* 67.

Lakin, K. C., White, C. C., Hill, B. K., Bruininks, R. H., & Wright, E. A. (1990). Longitudinal change and interstate variability in the size of residential facilities for persons with mental retardation. *Mental Retardation, 28,* 343–351.

Landesman, S., & Butterfield, E. C. (1987). Normalization and deinstitutionalization of mentally retarded individuals. *American Psychologist, 42,* 809–816.

Landesman, S., & Ramey, C. T. (1989). Developmental psychology and mental retardation: Integrating scientific principles with treatment procedures. *American Psychologist, 44,* 409–415.

Lane, V. W., & Samples, J. M. (1984). Tuberous sclerosis: Case study of early seizure control and subsequent normal development. *Journal of Autism and Developmental Disorders, 14,* 423–427.

Laraway, L. A. (1985). Auditory selective attentin in cerebral-palsied individuals. *Language, Speech, Hearing Services in Schools, 16,* 260–266.

Laurence, K. M. (1993). Causes, incidence, and genetics of hydrocephalus. In P. H. Schurr & C.E. Pickey (Eds.), *Hydrocephalus* (pp. 1–18). Oxford: Oxford University Press.

Lazar, I., Darlington, R., Murray, H., Royce, J., & Snipper, A. (1982). Lasting effects of early education: A report from the Consortium for Longitudinal Studies. *Monographs of the Society for Research in Child Development, 47* (2–3, Serial No. 195).

Lazarus, R. (1991). Progress on a cognitive-motivational-relational theory of emotion. *American Psychologist, 46,* 819–834.

Lead-Base Painting Act of 1971, Pub. L. No. 91-695.

Lenke, R. L., & Levy, H. L. (1980). Maternal phenylketonuria and hyperphenylalaninemia. *New England Journal of Medicine, 303,* 1202–1208.

Lennox, W. G. (1945). The petit mal epilepsies: Their treatment with Tridione. *Journal of the American Medical Association, 129,* 1069–1074.

Leonard, M. F., Landy, G., Riddle, F. H., & Lubs, H. A. (1974). Early development of children with abnormalities of the sex chromosomes: A prospective study. *Pediatrics, 54,* 208–212.

LePore, P., & Janicki, M. P. (1990). *The Wit town: How to integrate older persons with developmental disabilities into community aging programs.* Albany: New York State Office for the Aging.

Leppert, M., & Hofman, K. (1996). Fetal alcohol syndrome. In A. J. Capute & P. J. Accardo (Eds.), *Developmental disabilities in infancy and childhood* (2nd ed., vol. II, pp. 281–287). Baltimore, MD: Brookes.

Lerner, J. W. (1995). *Children with learning disabilities: Theories, diagnosis and teaching strategies.* Boston: Houghton-Mifflin.

Leroy, J. G. (1983). Heredity, development, and behavior. In M. D. Levine, W. B. Carey, A. C. Crocker, & R. T. Gross (Eds.), *Developmental-behavioral pediatrics* (pp. 195–212). Philadelphia: W.B. Saunders.

Lesny, I. A. (1979). Follow-up study of hypotonic form of cerebral palsy. *Brain Development, 1,* 87–90.

Letort, M. (1990, Winter). Pools and people are a year-round combination. *The Promise* (A publication of the South Mississippi Retardation Center, Long Beach, MS).

Levine, H. G. (1985). Situational anxiety and everyday life experiences of mildly mentally retarded adults. *American Journal of Mental Deficiency, 90,* 27–33.

Levine, H. G., & Langness, L. L. (1983). Context, ability, and performance: Comparison of competitive athletics among mildly mentally retarded and nonretarded adults. *American Journal of Mental Deficiency, 87,* 528–538.

Levitt, S. (1982). *Treatment of cerebral palsy and motor delay* (2nd ed.). Oxford: Blackwell.

Lewin, K. (1935). *A dynamic theory of personality.* New York: McGraw-Hill.

Lewis, M. H., Bodfish, J. W., Powell, S. B., & Golden, R. N. (1995). Clomipramine treatment for stereotypy and related repetitive movement disorders associated with mental retardation. *American Journal on Mental Retardation, 100,* 299–312.

Lewis, M. H., Bodfish, J. W., Powell, S. B., Parker, D. E., & Golden, R. N. (1996). Clomipramine treatment for self-injurious behavior in mental retardation: A double-blind comparison with placebo. *American Journal on Mental Retardation, 100,* 654–665.

Lewis, M. H., Gluck, J. P., Bodfish, J. W., Beauchamp, A. J., & Mailman, R. B. (1996). Neurobiological basis of stereotyped movement disorder. In R. L. Sprague & K. M. Newell (Eds.), *Stereotyped movements: Brain and behavior relationships* (pp. 37–67). Washington, DC: American Psychological Association.

Lewis, P. (1994, Winter). My other brother Daryl. Reprinted in the Newsletter of the Exceptional Children Assistance Center, Davidson, NC, p. 3.

Lewontin, R. C. (1975). Genetic aspect of intelligence. *Annual Review of Genetics, 9,* 387–405.

Lincoln, A. J., Courchesne, E., Kilman, B. A., Elmasian, R., & Allen, M. (1988). A study of intellectual abilities in higher functioning people with autism. *Journal of Autism and Developmental Abilities, 18,* 505–524.

Linden, M. B., Bender, B. G., Harmon, R. J., Mrazek, D. A., & Robinson, A. (1988). 47 XXX: What is the prognosis? *Pediatrics, 82,* 619–630.

Linehan, M. M. (1993). *Cognitive-behavioral treatment of borderline personality disorder.* New York: Guilford.

Linnett, M. J. (1982). People with epilepsy: The burden of epilepsy. In J. Laidlaw & A. Richens (Eds.), *A textbook of epilepsy* (2nd ed., pp. 1–15). Edinburgh: Churchill-Livingstone.

Lipe-Goodson, P. S., & Goebel, B. L. (1983), Perception of age and death in mentally retarded adults. *Mental Retardation, 21,* 68–75.

Liveneh, H. (1988). A dimensional perspective on the origin of negative attitudes towards persons with disabilities. In H. Yuker (Ed.), *Attitudes toward persons with disabilities* (pp. 254–274). New York: Springer.

Livingston, S. (1972). *Comprehensive management of epilepsy in infancy, childhood and adolescence.* Springfield, IL: Thomas.

Llewellyn, G. (1995). Relationship and social support: Views of parents with mental retardation/intellectual disability. *Mental Retardation, 33,* 349–363.

Lobato, D. Carlson, E. I., & Barrera, R. D. (1986). Modified satiation reduced ruminative vomiting without excessive weight gain. *Applied Research in Mental Retardation, 7,* 337–347.

Loehlin, J. C., Horn, J. M., & Willerman, L. (1989). Modeling I2 change: Evidence from The Texas Adoption Project. *Child Development, 60,* 993–1004.

Longo, L. P. (1997). Alcohol abuse in persons with developmental disabilities. *The Habilitative Mental Healthcare Newsletter, 16,* 61–64.

Lovaas, O. I. (1987). Behavior treatment and normal eduactional and intellectual functioning in young austistic children. *Journal of Consulting and Clinical Psychology, 55,* 3–9.

Loveland, K. A., & Kelley, M. L. (1988). Development of adaptive behavior in adolescents and young adults with autism and down syndrome. *American Journal of Mental Retardation, 93,* 84–92.

Loveland, K. A., & Kelley, M. L. (1991). Development of adaptive behavior in preschoolers wtih autism or Down syndrome. *American Journal on Mental Retardation, 96,* 13–20.

Lubetsky, M. J., Mueller, L., Madden, K., Walker, R., & Len, D. (1995). Family-centered/interdisciplinary team approach to working with families of children who have mental retardation. *Mental Retardation, 33,* 251–256.

Luckasson, R., Coulter, D. L., Polloway, E. A., Reiss, S., Schalock, R. L., Snell, M. E., Spitalnik, D. M., & Stark, J. A. (1992). *Mental retardation: Definition, classification, and system of supports* (9th ed.). Washington, DC: American Association of Mental Retardation.

Luckey, R. E., & Neman, R. (1976). Practices in estimating mental retardation prevalence. *Mental Retardation, 14*(1), 16–18.

Luiselli, J. (1977). Case report: An attendant administered contingency management program for the treatment of toilet phobia. *Journal of Mental Deficiency Research, 21,* 283–288.

Luftig, R. L. (1988). Assessment of the perceived school loneliness and isolation of mentally retarded and nonretarded students. *American Journal on Mental Retardation, 92,* 472–475.

Lupi, M. & Porcella, J. (1985). *Prader-Willi syndrome: A fact sheet for teachers and other school personnel.* (Available from Dr. M. H. Lupi, Hunter College, 695 Park Ave., New York, NY 10021.)

Lupi, M. & Porcella, J. (1987). Some considerations in the education and management of the child with Prader-Willi syndrome in the special education classroom. *Techniques, 3,* 230–235.

Lupi, M. H. (1988). Education of the child with Prader-Willi sundrome. In L. R. Greenswag

& R. C. Alexander (Eds.), *Management of Prader-Willi syndrome* (pp. 113–123). New York: Springer-Verlag.

Luria, A. R. (1976). *Cognitive development: Its cultural and social foundations.* Cambridge, MA: Harvard University Press.

Lutzer, V. D., & Brubaker, T. N. (1988). Differential respite needs of aging parents of individuals with mental retardation. *Mental Retardation, 26,* 13–15.

Lynch, M. P., Oller, D. K., Steffens, M. L., Levine, S. L., Basinger, D. H., & Umbel, V. (1995). Onset of speech-like vocalizations in infants with Down syndrome. *American Journal on Mental Retardation, 100,* 68–86.

MacEachron, A. E. (1983). Institutional reform and adaptive functioning of mentally retarded persons: A field experiment. *American Journal of Mental Deficiency, 88,* 2–12.

MacMillan, D. L. (1977). *Mental retardation in school and society.* Boston: Little, Brown.

MacMillan, D. L., Gresham, F. M., & Siperstein, G. N. (1995). Heightened concerns over the 1992 AAMR definition: Advocacy versus precision. *American Journal on Mental Retardation, 100,* 87–97.

MacMillan, D. L., Gresham, F. M., Siperstein, G. N., & Bolian, K. M. (1996). The labyrinth of IDEA: School decisions on referred students with subaverage general intelligence. *American Journal on Mental Retardation, 101,* 161–174.

MacMillan, D. L., Siperstein, G. N., & Gresham, F. M. (1996). A challenge to the viability of mild mental retardation as a diagnostic category. *Exception Children, 50,* 356–371.

Mahoney, G., Finger, I., & Powell, A. (1985). Relationship of maternal behavioral style to the development of organically impaired mentally retarded infants. *American Journal of Mental Deficiency, 90,* 296–302.

Mahoney, K., Van Wagenen, R., & Meyerson, L. (1972). Toilet training of normal and retarded children. *Journal of Applied Behavior Analysis, 4,* 173–181.

Maloney, M. P., & Ward, M. P. (1979). *Mental retardation and modern society.* New York: Oxford University Press.

Mandoki, M., Sumner, G. S., Hoffman, R. P., & Riconda, D. L. (1991). A review of Klinefelter's syndrome in children and adolescents. *Journal of the American Academy of Child and Adolescent Psychiatry, 30,* 167–172.

Mank, D., Cioffi, A., & Yovanoff, P. (1997). Analysis of the typicalness of supported employment jobs, natural supports, and wage and integration outcomes. *Mental Retardation, 35,* 185–197.

Mann, D. (1988). Alzheimer's disease and Down syndrome. *Histopathology, 13,* 125–137.

Marcus, B. A., & Vollmer, T. R. (1996). Combining noncontingent reinforcement and differential reinforcement schedules as treatment for aberrant behavior. *Journal of Applied Behavior Analysis, 29,* 43–51.

Marcus, J. C. (1993). Control of epilepsy in a mentally retarded population: Lack of correlation with IQ, neurological status, and electroencephalogram. *American Journal on Mental Retardation, 98*(suppl.), 47–51.

Marsden, C. D., & Reynolds, E. H. (1982). Neurology, part I. In J. Laidlaw & A. Richens (Eds.), *A textbook of epilepsy* (pp. 90–131). Edinburgh: Churchill-Livinstone.

Martin, H. P. (1970). Microcephaly and mental retardation. *American Journal of Diseases of Children, 119,* 128–131.

Masland, R. L. (1958). The prevention of mental subnormality. In R. L. Masland, S. B. Sarason, & T. Gladwin (Eds.), *Mental subnormality* (pp. 11–144). New York: Basic Books.

Maslow, A. H. (1954). *Motivation and personality.* New York: Harper.

Matson, J. L. (1982). Treating obsessive-compulsive behavior in mentally retarded adults. *Behavior Modification, 6,* 551–567.

Matson, J. L. (1982). treating obsessive-compulsive behavior in mentally retarded adults. *Behavior Modification, 6,* 551–567.

Matson, J. L. (1995). Comments on Gresham, MacMillan, & Siperstein's paper "Critical analysis of the 1992 AAMR definition: Implications for school psychology." *School Psychology Quarterly, 10*, 20–23.

Matson, J. L., DiLorenzo, T. M., & Esuelto-Dawson, K. (1981). Independence training as a method of enhancing self-help skills acquisition of the mentally reatarded. *Behaviour Research and Therapy, 19*, 399–405.

Matson, J. L., & Fee, V. E. (1991). Social skills difficulties among persons with mental retardation. In J. L. Matson & J. A. Mulick (Eds.), *Handbook of mental retardation* (2nd ed., pp. 468–478). New York: Pergamon.

Matson, J. L., & Hammer, D. (1996). Assessment of social functioning. In J. W. Jacobson & J. A. Mulick (Eds.), *Manual of diagnosis and professional practice in mental retardation.* (pp. 157–164). Washington, DC: American Psychological Association.

Matson, J. L., & Mulick, J. A. (1991). *Handbook of mental retardation.* New York: Pergamon.

Matson, J. L., & Stephens, R. M. (1978). Increasing appropriate behavior of explosive chronic psychiatric patients with a social skills training package. *Behavior Modification, 2*, 61–76.

May, D. C., & Turnbull, N. (1992). Plastic surgeons' opinions of facial surgey for individuals with Down Syndrome, *Mental Retardation, 30*, 29–33.

May, P. A., Hymbaugh, K. J., Aase, J. M., & Samet, J. M. (1989). Epidemiology of fetal alcohol among American Indians of the Southwest. *Journal of Studies on Alcohol, 50*, 508–518.

Mayer, C. L. (1966). The relationship of early special class placement and the self-concepts of mentally handicapped children. *Exceptional Children, 33*, 77–81.

Maytal, J., Shinnar, S., Moshe, S. L., & Alvarez, L. (1989). Low morbidity and mortality of status epilepticus in children. *Pediatrics, 83*, 323–331.

McAfee, J. (1988). Retardation: Occupational, economic, and community living issues. In P. J. Schloss, C. A. Hughes, & M. A. Smith (Eds.), *Mental retardation: Community transition* (pp. 163–206). Boston: College Hill Press.

McAlpine, C., Singh, N., Ellin, C., Kendall, K., & Hampton, C. (1992). Enhancing the ability of adults with mental retardation to recognize facial expressions of emotion. *Behavior Modification, 16*, 559–573.

McBurney, A. K., & Eaves, L. C. (1986). Evolution of developmental and psychological test scores. In H. G. Dunn (Ed.), *Sequelae of low birthweight: The Vancouver study* (pp. 54–67). Philadelphia: Lippincott.

McCabe, M. P. (1993). Sex education programs for people with mental retardation. *Mental Retardation, 31*, 377–387.

McCarton, C. M., Brooks-Gunn, J., Wallace, I. F., Bauer, C. R., Bennett, F. C., Bernbaum, J. C., Broyles, R., S. Casey, P. H., McCormick, M. C., Scott, D. T., Tyson, J., Tonaseia, J., & Meinert, C. L. (1997). Results at age 8 years of early intervention for

McCaughrin, W. B., Ellis, W. K., Rusch, F. R., & Heal, L. W. (1993). Cost-effectiveness of supported employment. *Mental Retardation, 31*, 41–48.

McClelland, D. (1961). *The achieving society.* Princeton, NJ: Van Nostrand.

McClennen, S. (1988, Summer). Sexuality and students with mental retardation. *Teaching Exceptional Children*, 59–61.

McCuller, W. R. (1992). Pica. In E. A. Konarski, J. E. Favell, & J. E. Favell (Eds.), *Manual for the assessment and treatment of the behavior disorders of people with mental retardation* (pp. 1–8). Morganton, NC: Western Carolina Center Foundation.

McDevitt, S. C., Smith, P. M., Schmidt, D. W., & Rosen, M. (1978). The deinstitutionalized citizen: Adjustment and quality of life. *Mental Retardation, 16*(1), 22–24.

McDonnell, J., Thorson, N., McQuivey, C., & Kiefer-O'Donnell, R. (1997). Academic engaged time of students with low-incidence disabilities in general education classes. *Mental Retardation, 35*, 18–26.

McEachin, J. J., Smith, T., & Lovaas, O. I. (1995). Long-term outcome for children with autism who received early intensive behavioral treatment. *American Journal on Mental Retardation, 97,* 359–372.

McGaughey, M. J., Kiernan, W. E., McNally, L. C., & Gilmore, D. S. (1995). A peaceful co-existence? State MR/DD Agency trends in integrated employment and facility-based services. *Mental Retardation, 33,* 170–180.

McGuire, D., Chicoine, B. A., & Greenbaum, E. (1997, July–August). "Self-talk" in adults with Down syndrome. *Disability Solutions, 2*(2), 1, 3–5.

McIvor, W. B. (1972). Evaluation of a strategy-oriented training program on the verbal abstraction performance of EMRs. *American Journal of Mental Deficiency, 76,* 652–657.

McKey, R. H., Cowdelli, L., Ganson, H., Barrett, B. J., McConkey, C., & Plantz, M. C. (1985). *The impact of Head Start on children, families, and communities* (U.S. Department of Health and Human Services Publication No. OHDS 90-31193). Washington, DC: U.S. Government Printing Office.

McKosick, V. A. (1990). *Mendelian inheritance in man. Catalogs of autsomal dominant, autosomal recessive, and x-linked phenotypes* (9th ed.). Baltimore, MD: Johns Hopkins University Press.

McLaren, J., & Bryson, S. E. (1987). Review of recent epidemiological studies of mental retardation: Prevalence, associated disorders, and etiology. *American Journal of Mental Retardation, 92,* 243–254.

McLean, M., & Hanline, M. F. (1990). Providing early intervention services in integrated environments: Challenges and opportunities for the future. *Topics in Early Childhood Special Education, 10*(2), 62–77.

McNally, R. J. (1991). Anxiety and phobias. In J. L. Matson & J. A. Mulick (Eds.), *Handbook of mental retardation* (2nd ed., pp. 413–423). New York: Pergamon.

McRae, R., & Costa, Jr., P. T. (1986). Comment: Clinical assessment can benefit from recent advances in personality psychology. *American Psychologist, 41,* 1001–1003.

Meisels, S., & Schonkoff, J. P. (Eds.) (1990). *Handbook of early childhood intervention.* New York: Cambridge University Press.

Melyn, M. A., & Grossman, H. J. (1976). Neurophysiological correlates. In W. M. Cruickshank (Ed.), *Cerebral palsy: A developmental disability* (3rd ed., pp. 73–94). Syracuse, NY: Syracuse University Press.

Melyn, M. A., & White, D. T. (1973). Mental and developmental milestones of noninstitutional Down's syndrome children. *Pediatrics, 52,* 542–545.

Mengreli, C., & Pantalakis, S. (1988). Epidemiologic study of transient hyperthyrotropinemia. In F. Delange, D. A. Fisher, & D. Glinoer (Eds.), *Research in cogenital hypothyroidism* (p. 330). New York: Plenum.

Menkes, J. H. (1995). *Textbook of child neurology.* Baltimore: Williams & Wilkins.

Menkes, J. H., & Sankar, R. (1995). Paroxysmal disorders. In J. H. Menkes, *Textbook of child neurology* (5th ed., pp. 725–814). Baltimore: Williams and Wilkins.

Menkes, J. H., & Till, K. (1995). Tumors of the nervous system. In J. H. Menkes, *Textbook of child neurology* (pp. 635–701). Baltimore: Williams & Wilkins.

Menolascino, F. J. (1977). *Challenge in mental retardation: Progressive ideology and services.* New York: Human Sciences Press.

Mercer, J. R. (1973). *Labeling the mentally retarded.* Berkeley: University of California Press.

Merrill, E. C., & Jackson, T. S. (1992). Sentence processing by adolescents with and without mental retardation. *American Journal of Mental Retardation, 97,* 342–350.

Meyer, L. A. (1994). Quality inclusive schooling: How to know it when you see it. *Newsletter (The Association for Persons with Severe Handicaps), 20,* 18–22.

Meyerowitz, J. H. (1962). Self-derogations in young retardates and special class placement. *Child Development, 33,* 443–451.

Meyers, B. A., & Pueschel, S. M. (1991). Psychiatric disorders in persons with Down syndrome. *The Journal of Nervous and Mental Disease, 179,* 609–613.

Meyers, L. F. (1990). Technology: A powerful tool for children learning language. *OSERS News in Print, III*(2), 2–7.

Milar, C. R., & Schroeder, S. R. (1983). The effects of lead on retardation of cognitive and adaptive behavior. In J. L. Matson & F. Andrasik (Eds.), *Treatment issues and innovations in mental retardation* (pp. 129–158). New York: Plenum.

Milgram, N. A. (1973). Cognition and language in mental retardation: Dsfunctions and implications. In D. K. Routh (Ed.), *The experimental psychology of mental retardation* (pp. 157–230). London: Crosby Lockwood Staples.

Miller, C., & Eyman, R. (1978). Hospital and community mortality rates among the retarded. *Journal of Mental Deficiency Research, 22,* 137–145.

Miller, E., Craddock-Watson, J. E., & Pollock, T. M. (1982). Consequences of confirmed maternal rubella at successive stages of pregnancy. *Lancet, i,* 781–784.

Miller, L. K. (1987). Developmentally delayed musical savant's sensitivity to tonal structure. *American Journal of Mental Deficiency, 91,* 467–471.

Miller, L. K. (1991). Assessment of musical aptitude in people with mental disabilities. *Mental Retardation, 29,* 175–183.

Miller, R. M. (1967). Prenatal origins of mental retardation. *Journal of Pediatrics, 71,* 455–458.

Miller, R. W., & Blot, W. J. (1972). Small head after "in utero" exposure to atomic radiation. *Lancet, ii,* 784–787.

Millman, R. B., & Botwin, G. J. (1992). Substance use, abuse, and dependence. In M. D. Levine, W. B. Carey, & A. C. Crocker (Eds.), *Developmental-behavioral pediatrics* (pp. 451–467). Philadelphia: W.B. Saunders.

Milunsky, A. (1975). *The prevention of genetic disease and mental retardation.* Philadelphia: W.B. Saunders.

Minihan, P. M., Dean, D. H., & Lyons, C. M. (1993). Managing the care of patients with mental retardation: A survey of physicians. *Mental Retardation, 31,* 239–246.

Mintzer, D., Als, H., Tronick, E. Z., & Brazelton, T. B. (1984). Parenting an infant with a birth defect: The regulation of self-esteem. *Psychoanalytic Study of the Child, 39,* 561–589.

Molaison, V. A., Black, M. M., Sachs, M. L., & Smull, M. W. (1995). Services for adult family members with mental retardation: Perceptions of accessibility and satisfaction. *Mental Retardation, 33,* 181–185.

Monckberg, F. (1968). Effect of early merasmic malnutrition on subsequent physical and psychological development. In N. S. Scrimshaw & J. E. Gordon (Eds.), *Malnutrition, learning and behavior* (pp. 269–277). Cambridge, MA: MIT Press.

Moore, D., & Polsgrove, L. (1991). Disabilities, developmental handicaps, and substance misuse: A review. *International Journal of the Addictions, 26,* 65–90.

Moore, M. L. (1977). *The developing human. Clinically oriented embryology* (2nd ed.). Philadelphia: W.B. Saunders.

Morgan, S. B. (1979). Developmental distribution of intellectual an adaptive skills in Down syndrome children: Implications for early intervention. *Mental Retardation, 17,* 247–249.

Morishima, A., & Brown, L. F. (1976). An idiot savant case report: A retrospective view. *Mental Retardation, 14,* 46–47.

Morishima, A., & Brown, L. F. (1977). A case report on the artistic talent of an autistic idiot savant. *Mental Retardation, 15,* 33–36.

Morris, C. D., & Niederbuhl, J. M. (1992). *Sexual knowledge of dually diagnosed and the capability to consent to sexual contact.* Paper presented at meeting of the National Association on Dual Diagnosis, Toronto.

Morris, C. D., Niederbuhl, J. M., & Mahr, J. M. (1993). Determining the capability of individuals with mental retardation to give informed consent. *American Journal of Mental Retardation, 98,* 263–272.

Morrow-Tiucak, M., Ernhart, C. B., Sokol, R. J., Martier, S., & Ager, J. (1989). Underreporting of alcohol use in pregnancy: Relationship to alcohol problem history. *Alcoholism: Clinical and Experimental Research, 13,* 399–401.

Moss, J. W. (1958). *Failure-avoiding and success-striving behavior in mentally retarded and normal children.* Unpublished doctoral dissertation, George Peabody College for Teachers, Nashville, TN.

Mowatt, M. H. (1970). Group therapy approach to emotional conflicts of the mentally retarded and their parents. In F. J. Menolascino (Ed.), *Psychiatric approaches to mental retardation* (pp. 422–434). New York: Basic Books.

Mulick, J. A., Hammer, D., & Dura, J. R. (1991). Assessment and management of antisocial and hyperactive behavior. In J. L. Matson & J. A. Mulick (Eds.), *Handbook of Mental Retardation* (2nd ed., pp. 397–412). New York: Pergamon.

Murphy, S. T., & Rogan, P. M. (1995). *Closing the shop: Conversion from sheltered to integrated work.* Baltimore: Brookes.

Murray, H. A. (1938). *Exploration in personality.* New York: Oxford University Press.

Myers, B. A., & Pueschel, S. M. (1995). Major depression in a small group of adults with Down syndrome. *Research in Developmental Disabilities, 16*(4), 285–299.

Myers, D. G. (1989). *Psychology.* New York: Worth.

Najenson, T. L., Mendelson, L., Schechster, I., David, C., Mintz, N., & Groswasser, Z. (1978). Rehabilitation after severe head injury. *Scandinavian Journal of Rehabilitation Medicine, 6,* 5–14.

National Center for Health Statistics (1979). *The national nursing home survey: 1977 summary for the United States.* Hyattsville, MD: Author.

National Center for Health Statistics. (1982). Advance report on final mortality statistics, 1979. *NCHS Monthly, 31*(6, suppl.).

National Center for Health Statistics (1987). *Nursing home characteristics: Preliminary data from the 1985 National Nursing Home Survey* (Advance data No. 131). Hyattsville, MD: Author.

National Institute of Child Health and Human Development. (1976). *Malnutrition, learning and behavior* (H. E. W. Publication No. 76–1036). Washington, DC: U.S. Department of Health, Education, and Welfare.

National Institutes of Health. (1991). *Treatment of destructive behaviors in persons with developmental disabilities.* Washington, DC: U.S. Dept. of Health & Human Services, Public Health Service, National Institutes of Health.

National Institute on Alcohol Abuse and Alcoholism. (1991, July). Fetal alcohol syndrome. *Alcohol Alert,* no. 13, 297.

Needleman, H. L. (1992). Childhood exposure to lead: A common cause of school failure. *Phi Delta Kappan, 74,* 35–37.

Needleman, H. L., Schell, A., Bellinger, D., Leviton, A., & Allred, E. N. (1990). The long-term effects of exposure to low doses of lead in childhood. *New England Journal of Medicine, 322,* 83–88.

Neisser, V. (1979). The concept of intelligence. *Intelligence, 3,* 217–227.

Nelson, G. L., Cone, J. D., & Hanson, C. R. (1975). Training correct utensil use in retarded children: Modeling vs. physical guidance. *American Journal of Mental Deficiency, 80,* 114–122.

Nelson, L., Lott, I., Touchette, P., Satz, P., & D'Elia, L. (1995). Detection of Alzheimer Disease in individuals with Down syndrome. *American Journal of Mental Retardation, 99,* 616–622.

Nelson, R. P., & Crocker, A. C. (1978). The medical care of mentally retarded persons in public residential facilities. *New England Journal of Medicine, 299,* 1039–1044.

Nelson, R. P., & Crocker, A. C. (1992). The child with multiple disabilities. In M. Levine, W. B. Carey, & A. C. Crocker (Eds.), *Developmental-behavioral pediatrics* (pp. 543–551). Philadelphia: W.B. Saunders.

Newman, H. H., Freeman, F. N., & Holzinger, K. J. (1937). *Twins: A study of heredity and environment.* Chicago: University of Chicago Press.

Newton, J. S., Ard, Jr., W. R., Horner, R. H., & Toews, J. D. (1996). Focusing on values and lifestyle outcomes in an effort to improve the quality of residential services in Oregon. *Mental Retardation, 34,* 1–12.

Newton, J. S., Horner, R. H., Ard, Jr., W. R., LeBaron, N., & Sappington, G. (1994). A conceptual model for improving the social life of individuals with mental retardation. *Mental Retardation, 32,* 393–402.

Nielsen, J. (1970). Criminality among patients with Klinefelter's syndrome and XYY syndrome. *British Journal of Psychiatry, 117,* 365–369.

Nihira, K., Price-Williams, D. R., & White, J. F. (1988). Social competence and maladaptive behavior of people with dual diagnosis. *Journal of the Multihandicapped Person, 1,* 185–199.

Nirje, B. (1969). The normalization principle and its human management implications. In R. Kugel & W. Wolfensberger (Eds.), *Changing patterns in residential services for the mentally retarded* (pp. 179–196). Washington, DC: President's Committee on Mental Retardation.

Noble, Jr., J. H., & Conley, R. W. (1992). Toward an epidemiology of relevant attributes. In R. W. Conley, R. Lockasson, & G. N. Bouthilet (Eds.), *The criminal justice system and mental retardation* (pp. 17–54). Baltimore: Brookes.

Noel, B., Duport, J. P., Revil, D., Dussuyer, I., & Quach, B. (1974). *Clinical Genetics, 5,* 387–394.

Nozyce, M., Diamond, G., Belman, A., Cabot, T., Douglas, C., Hopkins, K., Cohen, N., Rubenstein, A., & Willoughby, A. (1989). Neurodevelopmental impairments during infancy in offspring of IVDA and HIV seropositive mothers [abstract]. *Pediatric Research, 25*(4/2), 359A.

Nugent, P. M., & Mosley, J. L. (1987). Mentally retarded and nonretarded individuals' attention allocation and capacity. *American Journal of Mental Deficiency, 91,* 598–605.

Nutter, D., & Reid, D. H. (1978). Teaching retarded women a clothing selection skill using community norms. *Journal of Applied Behavior Analysis, 11,* 114–122.

Nyhan, W. L. (1994). The Lesch-Nyhan disease. In T. Thompson & D. B. Gray (Eds.), *Destructive behavior in developmental disabilities: Diagnosis and treatment* (pp. 181–197). Thousand Oaks, CA: Sage.

Nyhan, W. L., & Sakati, N. O. (1976). *Genetic and malformation syndromes in clinical medicine.* Chicago: Yearbook Medical Publishers.

O'Brien, C. L., O'Brien, J., & Mount, B. (1997). Person-centered planning has arrived . . . or has it? *Mental Retardation, 35,* 480–484.

O'Brien, F., Bugle, C., & Azrin, N. H. (1972). Teaching correct eating to the mentally retarded: Reinforcement and extinction. *Journal of Applied Behavior Analysis, 5,* 67–72.

O'Brien, J. (1987). A guide to life-style planning: Using The Activities Catalog to integrate services and natural support systems. In G. T. Bellamy & B. Wilcox (Eds.), *A comprehensive guide to the activities catalog: An alternative curriculum for youth and adults with severe disabilities* (pp. 175–190). Baltimore: Brookes.

O'Brien, J. (1994). Down stairs that are never your own: Supporting people with developmental disabilities in their own homes. *Mental Retardation, 32,* 1–7.

Ohr, P. S., & Fagen, J. W. (1991). Conditioning and long-term memory in three-month-old infants with Down syndrome. *American Journal on Mental Retardation, 96,* 151–162.

Older Americans Act of 1965, Pub. L. No. 89-73.

Older Americans Act of 1987, Pub. Law. No. 100-175.

Ollendick, T. H., Oswald, D. P., & Ollendick, D. G. (1993). Anxiety disorders in mentally retarded persons. In J. L. Matson & R. P. Barrett (Eds.), *Psychopathology in the mentally retarded* (2nd ed., pp. 41–85). Boston: Allyn and Bacon.

Olley, J. G., & Reeve, C. E. (1997). Issues of curriculum and classroom structure. In D. J. Cohen & F. R. Volkmar (Eds.), *Handbook of autism and pervasive developmental disorders* (2nd. ed., pp. 484–508). New York: Wiley.

Olley, J. G., Paraschiv, I., Jacob, A. V., & Allison, J. (1997). *Problem solving for life.* Chapel Hill,

NC: University of North Carolina, Clinical Center for the Study of Development and Learning.

Orelove, F. P. (1991). Educating all students: The future is now. In L. H. Meyer, C. A. Peck, & L. Brown (Eds.), *Critical issues in the lives of people with severe disabilities* (pp. 67–88). Baltimore: Brookes.

Orr, R. R., Cameron, S. J., Dobson, L. A., & May, D. M. (1993). Age-related changes in stress experienced by families with a child who has developmental delays. *Mental Retardation, 31,* 171–176.

Paine, R. S. (1964). The evolution of infantile postural reflexes in the presence of chronic brain syndrome. *Developmental Medicine and Child Neurology, 6,* 345–361.

Parke, C. C. (1986). Social growth in autism. In E. Schopler & G. B. Mesibov (Eds.), *Social behavior in autism* (pp. 81–99). New York: Plenum.

Parker, T., & Abramson, P. R. (1995). The law hath not been dead: Protecting adults with mental retardation from sexual abuse and violation of their sexual freedom. *Mental Retardation, 33,* 257–263.

Pary, R. J. (1996). Anxiety disorders in elderly persons with mental retardation. In A. Poindexter (Ed.), *Assessment and treatment of anxiety disorders in persons with mental retardation* (pp. 21–29). Kingston, NY: National Association for the Dually Diagnosed.

Patterson, G. R. (1982). *A social learning approach: Vol. 3. Coercive family process.* Eugene, OR: Castalia.

Paul, J. L., & Simeonssen, R. J. (1993). *Children with special needs: Family, culture, and society.* New York: Harcourt, Brace, Jovanovich.

Paul, R. (1987). Communication. In D. J. Cohen, A. M. Donellan, & R. Paul (Eds.), *Handbook of autism and pervasive developmental disorders* (pp. 61–84). New York: Wiley.

Payne, J. S. (1971). Prevalence survey of severely mentally retarded. *Wyandotte, County, Kansas, Training School Bulletin, 67,* 220–227.

Pedersen, N. L., Plomin, R., Nesselroade, J. R., & McLearn, G. E. (1992). A quantitative genetic analysis of cognitive abilities during the second half of the life span. *Psychological Science, 3,* 346–353.

Pendler, B. (1979). My daughter is leaving home: What do I do now? *Exceptional Parent, 9,* 14–16.

Pennington, B. F., van Doornick, W. J., McCabe, L. L., & McCabe, E. R. B. (1985). Neuropsychological deficits in early treated phenylketonuric children. *American Journal of Mental Deficiency, 89,* 467–474.

Penrose, L. S. (1938). *A clinical and genetic study of 1,280 cases of mental defect.* London: Medical Research Council.

Perske, R. (1996). Self-advocates on the move: A journalist's view. In G. Dybwad & H. Bersani, Jr. (Eds.), *New voices: Self-advocacy by people with disabilities* (pp. 18–36). Cambridge, MA: Brookline.

Peterson, A. L., & Azrin, N. H. (1993). Behavioral and pharmacological treatments for Tourette syndrome: A review. *Applied and Preventive Psychology, 2,* 231–242.

Peterson, R. (1987, March–April). Scouting together: A lesson in brotherhood. *Scouting, 31–34,* 54.

Peterson, R. D., & Jones, E. M. (1964). *Guide to jobs for the mentally retarded.* Pittsburgh: American Institute for Research.

Pfadt, A., & Anguco, M. (1991). *Biosynthetic growth hormone as a laptogenic agent: Applications in treating obesity associated with Prader-Willi syndrome.* Paper presented at annual Prader-Willi syndrome conference, Chicago.

Pipes, P. L. (1981). Nutritional management of children with Prader-Willi syndrome. In V. A. Holm, S. Sulzbacher, & P. L. Pipes (Eds.), *The Prader-Willi syndrome* (pp. 91–104). Baltimore: University Park Press.

Plomin, R., & Petrill, S. (1997). Genetics and intelligence: What's new? *Intelligence, 24,* 53–77.

Pober, B. R. (1996). Williams syndrome. In A. J. Capute & P. J. Accardo (Eds.), *Developmental disabilities in infancy and childhood* (2nd ed., vol. II, pp. 271–279). Baltimore, MD: Brookes.

Poindexter, A. R., Berglund, J. A., & Kolstoe, P. D. (1993). Changes in antiepileptic drug prescribing patterns in large institutions: Preliminary results of a five-year experience. *American Journal on Mental Retardation, 98*(suppl.), 34–40.

Pollitt, E. (1994). Poverty and child development: Relevance of research in developing countries to the United States. *Child Development, 65*, 283–295.

Pollitt, E., Gorman, K., Engle, P. L., Martorell, R., & Rivera, J. (1993). Early supplementary feeding and cognition. *Monograph of the Society for Research in Child Development, 58*(7), 1–99, discussion 111–118.

Popcock, S., Ashby, D., & Smith, M. A. (1987). Lead exposure and children's intellectual performance. *International Journal of Epidemiology, 16*, 57–67.

Powell, S. B., Bodfish, J. W., Parker, D., Crawford, T. W., & Lewis, M. H. (1996). Self-restraint and self-injury: Occurrence and motivational significance. *American Journal on Mental Retardation, 101*, 41–48.

Prasher, V. P., & Krivhnan, V. H. R. (1993). Age of onset and duration of dementia in people with Down syndrome: A study of 98 cases. *International Journal of Geriatric Psychiatry, 8*, 915–922.

Pressley, M., Borkowski, J. G., & O'Sullivan, J. T. (1985). Memory strategy instruction is made of this: Metamemory and durable strategy use. *Educational Psychologist, 19*, 94–107.

Pritchard, P. B., Lombroso, C. T., & McIntyre, M. (1980). Psychological complications of temporal late epilepsy. *Neurology, 30*, 227–232.

Prizant, B. M., & Rydell, P. (1984). Analysis of the functions of delayed echolalia in autistic children. *Journal of Speech and Hearing Research, 27*, 185–192.

Prouty, R. W., Lakin, K. C., & Smith, G. A. (1996). Growth in residential settings of 6 or fewer individuals with MR/DD. *Mental Retardation, 34*, 130.

Pueschel, S. M. (1992). The child with Down syndrome. In M. D. Levine, W. B. Carey, & A. C. Crocker (Eds.), *Developmental-behavioral pediatrics* (pp. 221–228). Philadelphia: W.B. Saunders.

Pueschel, S., & Thuline, A. C. (1991). Chromosome disorders. In J. L. Matson and J. A. Mulick (Eds.), *Handbook of mental retardation* (pp. 115–138). New York: Pergamon Press.

Putnam, J. W., & Rynders, J. E. (1982). Advancing the development of independence in adults with Down syndrome. In S. M. Pueschel & J. E. Rynders (Eds.), *Down syndrome: Advances in biomedicine and the behavioral sciences* (pp. 453–482). Cambridge, MA: Ware Press.

Ramey, C. T., McGuiness, G., Cross, L., Collier, A., & Barrie-Blackley, S. (1982). The Abecedarian approach to social competence–Cognitive and linguistic intervention in disadvantaged preschoolers. In K. Borman (Ed.), *The social life of children in a changing society* (pp. 145–174). Hillsdale, NJ: Erlbaum.

Ramey, C. T., & Ramey, S. L. (1998). Early intervention and early experience. *American Psychologist, 53*, 109–120.

Ramirez, S. Z., & Kratochwill, T. R. (1997). Self-reported fears in children with and without mental retardation. *Mental Retardation, 35*, 83–92.

Rapoport, J. L. (1988). The neurobiology of obsessive-compulsive disorder (clinical conference). *Journal of the American Medical Association, 260*, 2888–2890.

Rapoport, J. L. (1991). Basal ganglia dysfunction as a proposed cause of obsessive-compulsive disorder. In B. J. Carroll & J. E. Barrett (Eds.), *Psychopathology and the brain* (pp. 77–95). New York: Raven.

Rapport, M. D. (1989). Hyperactivity and attention deficit disorders. In V. B. Van Hasselt, P. S. Strain, & M. Hersen (Eds.), *Handbook of developmental and physical disabilities* (pp. 295–315). New York: Pergamon.

Rarick, G. L., Dobbins, D. A., & Broadhead, G. D. (1976). *The motor domain and its correlates in educationally handicapped children.* Englewood Cliffs, NJ: Prentice-Hall.

Rast, J. (1992). Rumination. In E. A. Konarski, Favell, J. E., & Favell, J. (Eds.), *Manual for the assessment and treatment of behavior disorders of people with mental retardation* (pp. 1–9). Morgantown, NC: Western Carolina Foundation.

Redman, C. W. G. (1989). Hypertension in pregnancy. In A. Turnbull & G. Chamberlain (Eds.), *Obstetrics* (pp. 515–542). Edinburgh: Churchill Livingstone.

Reed, E. W., & Reed, S. C. (1965). *Mental retardation: A family study.* Philadelphia: W.B. Saunders.

Rees, L. M., Spreen, O., & Harnadek, M. (1991). Do attitudes toward persons with handicaps really shift over time? Comparison between 1975 and 1988. *Mental Retardation, 29,* 81–86.

Rehabilitation Act Amendment of 1992, Pub. L. No. 102-569.

Reid, D. A. (1983). Trends and issues in behavioral research on training feedback and dressing skills. In J. L. Matson & F. Andrasik (Eds.), *Treatment issues and innovations in mental retardation* (pp. 213–240). New York: Plenum Press.

Reid, D. A., Wilson, P. G., & Faw, G. D. (1991). Teaching self-help skills. In J. L. Matson & J. A. Mucick (Eds.), *Handbook of mental retardation* (2nd ed., pp. 436–450). New York: Pergamon.

Reid, D. H., & Parsons, M. B. (1992). Aggression. In E. A. Konarski, J. E. Favell, & J. E. Favell (Eds.), *Manual for the assessment and treatment of the behavior disorders of people with mental retardation* (pp. 1–7). Morganton, NC: Western Carolina Center Foundation.

Reid, D. H., Wilson, P. G., & Faw, G. D. (1991). Teaching self-help skills. In J. L. Matson & J. A. Mulick (Eds.), *Handbook of mental retardation* (pp. 436–450). New York: Pergamon.

Reiss, S. (1990). Prevalence of dual diagnosis in community-based day programs in the Chicago metropolitan area. *American Journal on Mental Retardation, 94,* 578–585.

Reiss, S. (1994a). *Handbook of challenging behavior: Mental health aspects of mental retardation.* Worthington, OH: IDS.

Reiss, S. (1994b). Issues in defining mental retardation. *American Journal on Mental Retardation, 99,* 1–7.

Reiss, S., & Benson, B. A. (1985). Psychosocial correlates of depression in mentally retarded adults: I. Minimal social support and stigmatization. *American Journal of Mental Deficiency, 89,* 331–337.

Reiss, S., & Szyszko, J. (1983). Diagnostic overshadowing and professional experience with retarded persons. *American Journal of Mental Deficiency, 7,* 396–402.

Reschly, D. J., & Jipson, F. J. (1976). Ethnicity, geographic locale, age, sex, and urban-rural residence as variables in the prevalence of mild retardation. *American Journal of Mental Deficiency, 81,* 154–161.

Rett, A. (1966). On an until now unknown disease of a cogenital metabolic disorder (German). *Krankenschwester, 19,* 121–122.

Reynolds, E. H. (1981). Biological factors in psychological disorders associated with epilepsy. In E.H. Reynolds & M.R. Trimble (Eds.), *Epilepsy and psychiatry* (pp. 264–290). Edinburgh: Churchill-Livingstone.

Reynolds, E. H. (1987). Early treatment and prognosis of epilepsy. *Epilepsia, 28,* 97–106.

Reynolds, W. M., & Reynolds, S. (1979). Prevalence of speech and hearing impairment of noninstitutionalized mentally retarded adults. *American Journal of Mental Deficiency, 84,* 68–86.

Ricciuti, H. N. (1993). Nutrition and mental development. *Current Directions in Psychological Science, 2,* 43–46.

Richards, B. W., & Siddiqui, A. Q. (1980). Age and mortality trends in residents of an institution for the mentally handicapped. *Journal of Mental Deficiency Research, 24,* 99–105.

Richardson, S. A. (1978). Careers of mentally retarded young persons: Services, jobs, and interpersonal relations. *American Journal of Mental Deficiency, 82,* 349–358.

Richardson, S. A., Katz, M., & Koller, H. (1993). Patterns of leisure activities of young adults with mild mental retardation. *American Journal on Mental Retardation, 97,* 431–442.

Richman, G. S., Ponticar, Y., Epps, S., & Page, T. J. (1986). Simulation procedures for teaching independent menstrual care to mentally retarded persons. *Applied Research in Mental Retardation, 7,* 21–35.

Richman, G. S., Reiss, M. L., Bauman, K. E., & Bailey, J. S. (1984). Teaching menstrual care to mentally retarded women: Acquisition, generalization and maintenance. *Journal of Applied Behavior Analysis, 17,* 441–451.

Rimland, B., & Fein, D. (1988). Special talents of autistic savants. In L. K. Obler & D. Fein (Eds.), *The exceptional brain* (pp. 474–482). New York: Guilford.

Rimland, B., & Green, G. (1993). Controlled evaluations of facilitated communication. *Autism Research Review International, 7,* 7.

Risley, T. (1996). Get a life! Positive behavioral interventions for challenging behavior through life arrangement and life coaching. In L. K. Koegel, R. L. Koegel, & G. Dunlap (Eds.), *Positive behavioral support: Including people with difficult behavior in the community* (pp. 425–437). Baltimore: Paul H. Brookes.

Roberto, K. A. (Ed.). (1993). *The elderly caregiver.* Newbury Park, CA: Sage.

Roberts, C., Pratt, C., & Leach, D. (1991). Classroom and playground interaction of students with and without disabilities. *Exceptional Children, 57,* 212–224.

Robinson, G. C., Conry, J. L., & Conry, R. F. (1987). Clinical profile and prevalence of fetal alcohol syndrome in an isolated community in British Columbia. *Canadian Medical Association Journal, 137,* 203–207.

Robinson, H. B., & Robinson, N. M. (1976). *The mentally retarded child.* New York: McGraw-Hill.

Robinson-Wilson, M. A. (1976). Picture recipe cards as an approach to teaching severely retarded adults to cook. In G. T. Bellamy (Ed.), *Habilitation of the severely and profoundly retarded: Report from the specialized training program* (pp. 99–108). Eugene, OR: University of Oregon Press.

Rogers, C. R. (1951). *Client-centered therapy.* Boston: Houghton-Mifflin.

Rogers, R. C., & Simensen, R. J. (1987). Fragile X syndrome: A common etiology of mental retardation. *American Journal of Mental Deficiency, 91,* 445–449.

Rogers-Dulan, J., & Blacher, J. (1995). African American families, religion, and disability: A conceptual framework. *Mental Retardation, 33,* 226–238.

Rogoff, B., & Chavajay, P. (1995). What's become of research on the cultural basis of cognitive development. *American Psychologist, 50,* 859–877.

Roizen, N. J., & Johnson, D. (1996). Cogenital infections. In A. J. Capute & P. J. Accardo (Eds.), *developmental disabilities in infancy and childhood* (2nd ed., pp. 175–193). Baltimore, MD: Brookes.

Rojahn, J. (1995). Epidemiology and topographic taxonomy of self-injurious behavior. In T. Thompson & D. B. Gray (Eds.), *Destructive behavior in developmental disabilities: Diagnosis and treatment* (pp. 49–67). Thousand Oaks, CA: Sage.

Rojahn, J., Polster, L. M., Mulick, J. A., & Wisniewski, J. J. (1989). Reliability of the Behavior Problems Inventory. *Journal of the Multihandicapped Person, 2,* 283–293.

Rojahn, J., Rabold, D. E., & Schneider, F. (1995). Emotion specificity in mental retardation. *American Journal on Mental Retardation, 99,* 477–486.

Romanczyk, R. G., Lockshin, S., & Harrison, K. (1993). Schizophrenia and autism. In J. L. Matson & R. P. Barrett (Eds.), *Psychopathology in the mentally retarded* (2nd ed., pp. 149–178). Boston: Allyn and Bacon.

Ronai, C. R. (1987). On loving and hating my mentally retarded mother. *Mental Retardation, 35*, 417–432.

Roos, P. (1963). Psychological counseling with parents of retarded children. *Mental Retardation, 1*, 345–350.

Roos, P. (1965). Development of an intensive habit-training unit of Austin State School. *Mental Retardation, 3*, 12–15.

Roper, W. L., Houk, V. N., Falk, H., & Binder, S. (1991). *Preventing lead poisoning in children.* Washington, DC: Centers for Disease Control and Prevention, Public Health Service, U.S. Department of Health and Human Services.

Rosenquist, P. B., & Bodfish, J. W. (1997). Neuropsychiatric movement disorders in those with mental retardation or developmental disability. *Psychiatric Annals, 27*, 213–218.

Rosett, H. L., Quelette, E. M., Weiner, L., & Owens, E. (1978). Therapy of heavy drinking during pregnancy. *Obstetrics and Gynecology, 51*, 41–46.

Ross, R. T., Begab, M. J., Dondis, E. H., Giampiccolo, Jr., J. S., & Meyers, C. E. (1985). *Lives of the mentally retarded: A forty-year follow-up study.* Stanford, CA: Stanford University Press.

Rotholz, D. A., & Massey, P. S. (1996). Comparison of states' utilization of large residential settings for persons with mental retardation. *Mental Retardation, 34*, 303–311.

Rousey, A. B., Blacher, J. B., & Hanneman, R. A. (1990). Predictors of out-of-home placement of children with severe handicaps: A cross-sectional analysis. *American Journal on Mental Retardation, 94*, 522–531.

Rubin, I. L. (1987). Health care needs of adults with mental retardation. *Mental Retardation, 25*, 201–206.

Rubin, I. L. (1992). Perinatal stresses. In M. D. Levine, W. B. Carey, & A. C. Crocker (Eds.), *Developmental behavioral pediatrics* (pp. 244–253). Philadelphia: W.B. Saunders.

Rubin, K., & Cassidy, S. B. (1988). Hypogonadism and osteoporosis. In L. R. Greenswag & R. C. Alexander (Eds.), *Management of Prader-Willi syndrome* (pp. 23–33). New York: Springer-Verlag.

Rubin, S. E., & Rosseler, R. T. (1994). *Foundations of the vocational rehabilitation process* (5th ed.). Austin, TX: PRO-ED.

Rubinstein, J. H. (1968). The broad thumbs syndrome. Progress report 1968. In D. Bergsms (Ed.), *The clinical delineation of birth defects* (pp. 25–41). New York: Liss, For the National Foundation–March of Dimes. Birth Defects: Original Article Series.

Rugh, R. (1958). X-irradiation effects on the human fetus. *Journal of Pediatrics, 52*, 531–538.

Rusch, F. R., McKee, M., Chadsey-Rusch, J., & Renzaglia, A. (1988). Teaching a student with severe handicaps to self-instruct: A brief report. *Education and Training in Mental Retardation, 23*, 51–58.

Russell, M., & Skinner, J. B. (1988). Early measures of maternal alcohol misuse as predictors of adverse pregnancy outcomes. *Alcoholism: Clinical and Experimental Research, 12*, 824–830.

Rutter, M. J. (1970). Autistic children: Infancy to adulthood. *Seminars in Psychiatry, 2*, 435.

Rutter, M. J. (1972). Psychiatric causes of language retardation. In M. Rutter & J. A. Martin (Eds.), *The child with delayed speech.* London: Heinemann.

Ryan, R. (1996). Post-traumatic stress disorder in persons with developmental disabilities. In A. Poindexter (Ed.), *Assessment and treatment of anxiety disorders in persons with mental retardation* (pp. 41–52). Kingston, NY: National Association for the Dually Diagnosed.

Ryckman, D. B., & Henderson, R. A. (1965). The meaning of a retarded child for his parents: A focus for counselors. *Mental Retardation, 3*, 4–7.

Rynders, J. E., & Horrobin, J. M. (1990). Always trainable? Never educable? Updating educational expectations concerning children with Down syndrome. *American Journal on Mental Retardation, 95*, 77–83.

Rynders, J. E., Schleien, S. J., & Mustonen, T. (1990). Integrating children with severe disabilities for intensified outdoor education: Focus on feasibility. *Mental Retardation, 28,* 7–14.

Sachs, O. (1995). *An anthropologist on Mars.* New York: Vintage.

Salbenblatt, J. A., Meyers, D. C., Bender, B. G., Linden, M. G., & Robinson, A. (1987). Gross and fine motor development in 47 XXY and 47 XYY males. *Pediatrics, 80,* 240–244.

Sameroff, A. J., & Chandler, M. J. (1975). Reproductive risk and the continuum of caretaking casualty. In F. D. Horowitz (Ed.), *Review of child development research* (vol. 4, pp. 187–244). Chicago: University of Chicago Press.

Sampson, P. D., Bookstein, F. L., Barr, H. M., & Streissguta, A. P. (1994). Prenatal alcohol exposure, birth weight and measures of child size from birth to age 14 years. *American Journal of Public Health, 89,* 1421–1428.

Sandman, C. A., & Hedrick, W. P. (1995). Opiate mechanisms in self-injury. *Mental Retardation and Developmental Disabilities Research Reviews, 1,* 130–136.

Sarnat, H. (1992). *Cerebral dysgenesis.* New York: Oxford University Press.

Sattler, J. M. (1974). *Assessment of children's intelligence.* Philadelphia: W.B. Saunders.

Scally, B. G. (1968). The offspring of mental defectives. In D. H. Woolham (Ed.), *Advances in teratology* (vol. 3, pp. 65–84). London: Logos Press.

Scally, B. G. (1973). Marriage and mental handicap: Some observations in Northern Ireland. In F. F. De La Cruz & G. D. LaVeck (Eds.), *Human sexuality and the mentally retarded* (pp. 186–194). New York: Brunner/Mazel.

Scarr-Salapatek, S. (1975). Genetics and the development of intelligence. In F. D. Horowitz (Ed.), *Review of child development research* (Vol. 4, pp. 1–58). Chicago: University of Chicago Press.

Scarr, S., & Weinberg, R. (1976). IQ test performance of black children adopted by white families. *American Psychologist, 31,* 726–739.

Scarr, S., & Weinberg, R. (1978). The influence of "family background" on intellectual attainment. *American Sociological Review, 43,* 674–682.

Scarr, S., & Weinberg, R. (1983). The Minnesota Adoption Studies: Genetic differences and malleability. *Child Development, 54,* 260–267.

Schalock, R. L. (1994). The concept of quality of life and its current applications in the field of mental retardation/developmental disabilities. In D. Goode (Ed.), *Quality of life for persons with disabilities: International perspectives and issues* (pp. 266–284). Cambridge, MA: Brookline Books.

Schalock, R. L., & Kiernan, W. E. (1990). *Habilitation planning for adults with developmental disabilities.* New York: Springer-Verlag.

Schalock, R. L., Stark, J. A., Snell, M. E., Coulter, D. L., Polloway, E. A., Luckasson, R., Reiss, S., & Spitalnik, D. (1994). The changing conception of mental retardation: Implications for the field. *Mental Retardation, 32,* 181–193.

Schiff, M., Duyme, M., Dumaret, A., Stewart, J., Tomkeiwicz, S., & Feingold, J. (1978). Intellectual status of working-class children adopted early into upper-middle-class families. *Science, 200,* 1503–1504.

Schild, S. (1971). Social work services. In R. Koch & J. C. Dobson (Eds.), *The mentally retarded child and his family: A multidisciplinary handbook* (pp. 205–213). New York: Brunner/Mazel.

Schilling, R. F., Schinke, P., Blythe, B. J., & Barth, R. P. (1982). Child maltreatment and mentally retarded parents: Is there a relationship? *Mental Retardation, 20,* 201–209.

Schleien, S. J., Meyer, L. H., Heyne, L. A., & Brandt, B. B. (1995). *Lifelong leisure skills and life styles for persons with developmental disabilities.* Baltimore: Brookes.

Schmidt, A., Mahle, M., Michel, U., & Pietz, J. (1987). Continuation versus discontinuation of low-phenylalanine diet in PKV adolescents. *European Journal of Pediatrics, 146*(suppl. 1), A17–19.

Schopler, E. (1976). Towards reducing behavior problems in autustic children. In L. Wing (Ed.), *Early childhood autism* (pp. 221–245).

Schopler, E. (1983). New developments in the definition and diagnosis of autism. In B. B. Laney & A. E. Kazdin (eds.), *Advances in clinical child psychology* (vol. 6, pp. 93–127). New York: Plenum.

Schopler, E., & Mesibov, G. B. (Eds.). (1986). *Social behavior in autism*. New York: Plenum.

Schroeder, S. R. (1989a). Pica in the mentally retarded. In T. B. Karasu (Ed.), *Treatments of psychiatric disorders* (vol. 1, pp. 51–53). Washington, DC: American Psychiatric Association.

Schroeder, S. R. (1989b). Rectal digging, feces, smearing, and coprophagy. In T. B. Karasu (Ed.), *Treatments of psychiatric disorders* (vol. 1, pp. 43–44). Washington, DC: American Psychiatric Association.

Schroeder, S. R. (1989c). Rumination. In T. B. Karasu (Ed.), *Treatments of psychiatric disorders* (vol. 1, pp. 53–55). Washington, DC: American Psychiatric Association.

Schroeder, S. R. (1991). Self-injury and stereotypy. In J. L. Matson & J. A. Mulick (Eds.), *Handbook of mental retardation* (2nd ed., pp. 382–396). New York: Pergamon.

Schultz, E. E., Jr. (1983). Depth of processing by mentally retarded and MA-matched non-retarded individuals. *American Journal of Mental Deficiency, 88,* 307–313.

Schupf, N. Silverman, W. P., Sterling, R. C., & Zigman, W. B. (1989). Down syndrome, terminal illness and risk for dementia of the Alzheimer's type. *Brain Development, 2,* 181–188.

Schweinhart, L. J., Barnes, H. V., & Weikart, D. P. (1993). Significant benefits: The High Scope/Perry Preschool Study through age 27 (Monographs of the High/Scope Educational Research Foundation, number 10). Ypsilanti, MI: The High Scope Press.

Schweitzer, S., Shin, Y., Jakobs, C., & Brodehl, J. (1993). Long-term outcome in 134 patients with galactosemia. *European Journal of Pediatrics, 152,* 36–43.

Schwier, K. M. (1993). Ordinary miracles: Testimonies of friendship. In A. N. Amado (Ed.), *Friendships and community connections between people with and without developmental disabilities* (pp. 155–168). Baltimore: Brookes.

Scola, P. S. (1982). Genitourinary system. In S. Pueschel & J. E. Rynders (Eds.), *Down syndrome: Advances in biodmedicine and the behavioral sciences* (pp. 210–212). Cambridge, MA: Ware Press.

Scriver, C. R., Kaufman, S., Eisensmith, R., & Woo, S. (1995). The hyperphenylalaninemias. In C. R. Scriver, A. L. Beaudet, W. S. Sly, & D. Valle (Eds.), *The metabolic and molecular bases of inherited disease* (vol. I, pp. 1015–1076). New York: McGraw-Hill.

Segal, S., & Berry, G. T. (1995). Disorders of galactose metabolism. In C. R. Scriver, A. L. Baudet, W. S. Sly, & D. Valle (Eds.), *The metabolic and molecular bases of inherited diseases* (vol. I, 7th ed., pp. 967–1000). New York: McGraw-Hill.

Seidenberg, M., Beck, N., Geiser, M., Giordani, B., Sackellares, J. C., Berent, S., Dreifuss, F. E., & Boll, T. J. (1986). Academic acheivement of children with epilepsy. *Epilepsia, 27,* 753–759.

Selkoe, D. J. (1991). Amyloid protein and Alzheimer's disease. *Scientific American, 265,* 68–78.

Sells, C. J., & Bennett, F. C. (1977). Prevention of mental retardation: The role of medicine. *American Journal of Mental Deficiency, 82,* 117–129.

Seltzer, M. M. (1988). Structure and patterns of service utilization by elderly persons with mental retardation. *Mental Retardation, 26,* 181–185.

Severy, L. J., Brigham, J. C., & Schlenker, B. R. (1976). *A contemporary introduction to social psychology.* New York: McGraw-Hill.

Sevin, J. A., & Matson, J. L. (1992). Mood disorders. In E. A. Konarski, J. E. Favell, & J. E. Favell (Eds.), *Manual for the assessment and treatment of the behavior disorders of people with mental retardation* (pp. 1–10). Morganton, NC: Western Carolina Center Foundation.

Shane, H. C. (Ed.) (1994). *Facilitated communication: The clinical and social phenomenon*. San Diego: Singular Press.

Shapiro, B. K., Palmer, F. B., Wachtel, R. C., & Capute, A. J. (1983). Associated dysfunctions. In G. H. Thompson, I. L. Rubin, & R. M. Bilenker (Eds.), *Comprehensive management of cerebral palsy*. New York: Grune & Stratton.

Shapiro, S., McCormick, M. C., Starfield, B. H., Krischer, J. P., & Bross, D. (1980). Relevance of correlates of infant deaths for significant morbidity at 1 year of age. *American Journal of Obstetrics and Gynecology, 136*, 363–373.

Sharav, T., & Shlomo, L. (1986). Stimulation of infants with Down syndrome: Long-term effects. *Mental Retardation, 24*, 81–86.

Share, J. B. (1975). Developmental progress in Down's syndrome. In R. Koch & F. F. De La Cruz (Eds.), *Down's syndrome (mongolism): Research, prevention, and management* (pp. 78–86). New York: Brunner/Mazel.

Shea, V., & Gordon, B. N. (1991). *Growing up: A social and sexual education picture book for young people with mental retardation* (2nd ed.). Chapel Hill, NC: Clinical Center for the Study of Development and Learning.

Shealy, C. N. (1995). From Boys' Town to Oliver Twist: Separating fact from fiction in welfare reform and out-of-home placement of children and youth. *American Psychologist, 50*, 565–580.

Shearer, A. (1976). *L'Arche*. Toronto: Daybreak Publication.

Sheehan, C. M., & Matuozzi, R. T. (1996). Investigation of the validity of facilitated communication through the disclosure of unknown information. *Mental Retardation, 34*, 94–107.

Sherman, J. A., Sheldon, J. B., Harchik, A. E., Edwards, K., & Quinn, J. M. (1992). Social evaluation of behaviors comprising three social skills and a comparison of the performance of people with and without mental retardation. *American Journal of Mental Retardation, 96*, 94–107.

Sherrill, C. (1980). Posture training as a means of normalization. *Mental Retardation, 18*, 135–138.

Shields, J. (1962). *Monozygotic twins brought up apart and brought up together*. London: Oxford University Press.

Shipe, D., Reisman, L. E., Chung, C., Darnell, A., & Kelly, S. (1968). The relationship between cytogenetic constitution, physical stigmata, and the intelligence in Down's syndrome. *American Journal of Mental Deficiency, 72*, 789–797.

Shoultz, B., & Ward, N. (1996). Self-advocates becoming empowered: The birth of a national organization in the U.S. In G. Dybwad & H. Bersani, Jr. (Eds.), *New voices: Self-advocacy by people with disabilities* (pp. 216–236). Cambridge, MA: Brookline.

Silon, E. L., & Harter, S. (1985). Assessment of perceived competence, motivational orientation, and anxiety in segregated and mainstreamed educable mentally retarded children. *Journal of Educational Psychology, 77*, 217–230.

Silverstein, A. B., Herbs, D., Miller, T. J., Nasuta, R., D'Nyce, L. W., & White, J. F. (1988). Effects of age on the adaptive behavior of institutionalized and noninstitutionalized individuals with Down syndrome. *American Journal on Mental Retardation, 92*, 455–460.

Simila, S., & Niskanen, P. (1991). Underweight and overweight cases among the mentally retarded. *Journal of Mental Deficiency Research, 35*, 160–164.

Simpson, D., & Hemmer, R. (1993). Social aspects of hydrocephalus. In P. H. Schurr & C. E. Polkey (Eds.), *Hydrocephalus* (pp. 223–246). Oxford: Oxford University Press.

Sinclair, M., Christianson, S., Thurlow, M., & Evelo, D. (1994). *Are we pushing students in special education to drop out of school?* (Policy Research Brief No. 6, Vol. 1). University of Minnesota Center on Residential Services and Community Integration.

Singer, C. (1997). Tourette syndrome: Coprolalia and other coprophenomena. *Neurologic Clinics, 15*, 299–308.

Singer, G. H. S., & Irvin, C. K. (1991). Supporting families of persons with severe disabilities. In L. H. Meyer, C. A. Peck, & L. Brown (Eds.), *Critical issues in the lives of people with severe disabilities* (pp. 271–312). Baltimore: Brookes.

Siperstein, G. N., & Bak, J. J. (1985). Social behavior: How it affects children's attitudes toward mildly and moderately retarded peers. *American Journal of Mental Deficiency, 90,* 319–327.

Siperstein, G. N., & Leffert, J. S. (1997). Comparison of socially accepted and rejected children with mental retardation. *American Journal on Mental Retardation, 101,* 339–351.

Skeels, H. M. (1966). Adult status of children with contrasting life experiences. *Monographs of the Society for Research in Child Development, 31*(3), No. 105.

Skeels, H. M., & Dye, H. B. (1939). A study of the effects of differential stimulation on mentally retarded children. *Proceedings of the American Association on Mental Deficiency, 44,* 114–130.

Skeels, H. M., & Harms, I. (1948). Children with inferior social histories: Their mental development in adoptive homes. *Journal of Genetic Psychology, 72,* 283–294.

Skodak, M., & Skeels, H. M. (1949). A final follow-up study of one hundred adopted children. *Journal of Genetic Psychology, 75,* 85–125.

Skuse, D. (1984a). Extreme deprivation in early childhood: I. Diverse outcomes for three siblings from an extraordinary family. *Journal of Child Psychology and Psychiatry, 25,* 523–541.

Skuse, D. (1984b). Extreme deprivation in early childhood: II. Theoretical issues and a comparative review. *Journal of Child Psychology and Psychiatry, 25,* 543–572.

Smith, D. D., & Luckasson, R. (1992). *Introduction to special education.* Boston: Allyn & Bacon.

Smith, D. W. (1982). *Recognizable patterns of human malformation.* Philadelphia: W.B. Saunders.

Smith, G. C., & Tobin, S. S. (1993). Case managers' perceptions of practice with older parents with developmental disabilities. In K. A. Roberto (Ed.), *The elderly caregiver* (pp. 146–172). Newbury Park, CA: Sage.

Smith, P. (1979). A comparison of different methods of toilet training the mentally handicapped. *Behavior Research and Therapy, 17,* 33–43.

Smith, R. G., Lerman, D. C., & Iwata, B. A. (1996). Self-restraint as positive reinforcement for self-injurious behavior. *Journal of Applied Behavior Analysis, 29,* 99–102.

Smith, R. S., Britton, P. G., Johnson, M., & Thoman, D. (1975). Problems involved in toilet training of institutionalized mentally retarded individuals. *Behavior Research and Therapy, 3,* 301–302.

Smith, S. B. (1988). Calculating prodigies. In L. K. Obler & D. Fein (Eds.), *The exceptional brain* (pp. 19–47). New York: Guilford Press.

Smith, T., Klevstrand, M. & Lovaas, O. I. (1995). Behavioral treatment of Rett's disorder: Ineffectiveness in three cases. *American Journal of Mental Reatardation, 100,* 317–322.

Sobsey, D. (1994). *Violence and abuse in the lives of people with developmental disabilities: The end of silent acceptance?* Baltimore: Brookes.

Sovner, R. (1986). Limiting factors in the use of DSM-III criteria with mentally ill/mentally retarded persons. *Psychopharmacology Bulletin, 22,* 1055–1059.

Sovner, R., & Pary, R. J. (1993). Affective disorders in developmentally disabled persons. In J. L. Matson & R. P. Barrett (Eds.), *Psychopathology in the mentally retarded* (2nd ed., pp. 87–147). Boston: Allyn and Bacon.

Sparing, J. J., & Lewis, I. (1981). *Learning games for the first three years: A guide to parent-child play.* New York: Walker.

Sparrow, S., Balla, P., & Cicchetti, D. (1984). *The Vineland Adaptive Behavior Scales: Interview edition, survey form.* Circle Pines, MN: American Guidance Service.

Spearman, C. (1923). *The nature of "intelligence" and the principles of cognition.* London: MacMillan.

Spearman, C. E. (1927). *The abilities of man.* New York: MacMillan.

Speer, G. S. (1940). The intelligence of foster children. *Journal of Genetic Psychology, 57,* 49–55.

Spellman, C., DeBreiere, T., Jarboe, D., Campbell, S., & Harris, C. (1978). Pictorial instruction: Training dailing living skills. In M. E. Snell (Ed.), *Systematic instruction of the moderately and severly retarded.* Columbus, OH: Merrill.

Spitz, H. H. (1986). Disparities in mentally retarded persons' IQ derived from different intelligence tests. *American Journal of Mental Deficiency, 90,* 588–591.

Spitz, H. H., & DeRisi, D. T. (1978). Porteus maze test performance of retarded young adults and nonretarded children. *American Journal of Mental Deficiency, 83,* 40–43.

Spock, B. (1961). *On being a parent of a handicapped child.* Chicago: National Society for Crippled Children and Adults.

Spohr, H.-L., & Steinhausen, M.-C. (1984). Clinical, psychopathological and developmental aspects in children with the fetal alcohol syndrome: A four-year follow-up study. In *Mechanisms of alcohol damage "in utero"* (CIBA Foundation symposium 105) (pp. 197–217). London: Pitman.

Spreat, S., Conroy, J. W., & Jones, J. C. (1997). Use of psychotropic medication in Oklahoma: A statewide study. *American Journal on Mental Retardation, 102,* 80–85.

Stainback, J., & Stainback, W. (1992). *Curriculum considerations in inclusive classrooms: Facilitating learning for all students.* Baltimore: Brookes.

Stancliffe, R. J. (1997). Community living: Unit size, staff presence, and residents' choice-making. *Mental Retardation, 35,* 1–9.

Stanfield, J. S. (1973). Graduation: What happens to the retarded child when he grows up? *Exceptional Children, 39,* 548–552.

Stanovich, K. E. (1978). Information processing in mentally retarded individuals. In N. R. Ellis (Ed.), *International review of research in mental retardation* (vol. 9, pp. 29–60). New York: Academic Press.

Steed, F. R. C. (1974). *A special picture cook book.* Lawrence, KS: H & H Enterprises.

Stein, Z., Susser, M., Saenger, G., & Marolla, F. (1975). *Famine and human development: The Dutch hunger winter of 1944–45.* New York: Oxford University Press.

Stephen, E., & Hawks, G. (1974). Cerebral palsy and mental subnormality. In A. M. Clarke & A. D. B. Clarke (Eds.), *Mental deficiency: The changing outlook* (3rd ed., pp. 482–526). New York: Free Press.

Stephens, R. M., Matson, J. L., Westmoreland, & Kulpa, J. (1981). Modification of psychotic speech with mentally retarded patients. *Journal of Mental Deficiency Research, 25,* 187–197.

Sternberg, R. J. (1981). The nature of intelligence. *New York University Education Quarterly, 12,* 10–17.

Sternberg, R. J., Conway, B. E., Ketron, J. L., & Bernstein, M. (1981). People's conceptions of intelligence. *Journal of Personality and Social Psychology, 41,* 37–55.

Sternberg, R. J., Wagner, R. K., William, W. M., & Horvath, J. A. (1995). Testing common sense. *American Psychologist, 50,* 912–926.

Stevens, C. A., Carey, J. C., & Blackburn, B. L. (1990). Rubinstein-Taybu syndrome–A natural history study. *American Journal of Medical Genetics Supplement, 6,* 30–37.

Stevens, C. A., Hennekam, R. C. M., & Blackburn, B. L. (1990). Growth in Rubinstein-Taybi syndrome. *American Journal of Medical Genetics Supplement, 6,* 51–55.

Stevens, L. J., & Price, M. (1992). Meeting the challenge of educating children at risk. *Phi Delta Kappan, 74,* 18–23.

Stevenson, R. E., Goodman, H. O., Schwartz, C. E., Simensen, R. J., McLean, Jr., W. T., & Herndon, C. N. (1990). Allan-Herndon syndrome I: Clinical studies. *American Journal of Human Genetics, 47,* 446–453.

Stores, G. (1978). School children with epilepsy at risk for learning and behavior problems. *Developmental Medicine and Child Neurology, 20,* 502–508.

Strain, P. S. (1984). Social behavior patterns of nonhandicapped and nonhandicapped-developmentally disabled friend pairs in mainstreamed preschools. *Analysis and Intervention in Developmental Disabilities, 4*(1), 15–28.

Strain, P. S., & Smith, B. J. (1986). A counter-interpretation of early intervention effects. A response to Casto and Mastropieri. *Exceptional Children, 53*, 260–265.

Streissguth, A. P., Aase, J. M., Clarren, S. K., Randels, S. P., LaDue, R. A., & Smith, D. F. (1991). Fetal alcohol syndrome in adolescents and adults. *The Journal of the American Medical Association, 265*, 1961–1967.

Streissguth, A. P., Barr, H. M., & Martin, D. C. (1984). Alcohol exposure in utero and functional deficits in children during the first four years of life. In *Mechanisms of alcohol damage "in utero"* (CIBA Foundation symposium 105) (pp. 176–196). London: Pitman.

Streissguth, A. P., Barr, H. M., Martin, D. C., & Herman, C. S. (1980). Effects of maternal alcohol, nicotine, and caffeine use during pregnancy on infant mental and motor development at eight months. *Alcoholism: Clinical and Experimental Research, 4*, 152–164.

Streissguth, A. P., Barr, H. M., Olson, N. C., Sampson, P. D., Bookstein, F. L., & Burgess, D. M. (1994). Drinking during pregnancy decreases word attack and arithmetic scores on standardized tests: Adolescent data from a population-based prospective study. *Alcoholism: Clinical and Experimental Research, 18*, 248–254.

Streissguth, A. P., Barr, H. M., & Sampson, P. D. (1990). Moderated prenatal alcohol exposure: Effects on child IQ and learning problems at age 7 1/2 years. *Alcoholism: Clinical and Experimental Research, 14*, 662–669.

Streissguth, A. P., Moon-Jordan, A., & Clarren, S. (1995). Alcoholism in four patients with Fetal Alcohol Syndrome. *Alcoholism Treatment Quarterly, 13*, 89–103.

Streissguth, A. P., Randels, M. S. N., & Smith, D. F. (1991). A test-retest study of intelligence in patients with fetal alcohol syndrome: Implications for care. *Journal of the American Academy of Child and Adolescent Psychiatry, 30*, 584–587.

Stroud, M., & Sutton, E. (1988). *Expanding options for older adults with developmental disabilities.* Baltimore: Paul H. Brookes.

Sturmey, P. (1994). Assessing the functions of aberrant behaviors: A review of psychometric instruments. *Journal of Autism and Developmental Disorders, 24*, 293–304.

Sulzbacher, J. (1988). Psychological and behavioral management. In L. R. Greenswag & R. C. Alexander (Eds.), *Management of Prader-Willi syndrome* (pp. 99–112). New York: Springer-Verlag.

Sumarah, J. (1987). L'Arche: Philosophy and ideology. *Mental Retardation, 25*, 165–169.

Sundram, C. J. (1992). Plain talk about sex and mental retardation. *Quality of Care* (Newsletter of N.Y. State Commission on Quality of Care for the Mentally Disabled), No. 54.

Swaab, D. F., Puarba, J. S., & Hofman, M. A. (1995). Alterations in the hypothalamic paraventricular nucleus and its oxytocin neuron (putative satiety cells) in Prader-Willi syndrome: A study of five cases. *Journal of Clinical Endocrinology and Metabolism, 80*, 573–579.

Szymanski, L. S. (1980). Individual psychotherapy with retarded persons. In L. S. Szymanski & P. E. Tanguay (Eds.), *Emotional disorders of mentally retarded persons: Assessment, treatment, and consultation* (pp. 131–147). Baltimore: University Park Press.

Taft, L. J., & Matthews, W. S. (1992). Cerebral Palsy. In M. D. Levine, W. B. Carey, & A. C. Crocker (Eds.), *Developmental-behavioral pediatrics* (pp. 527–533). Philadelphia: W. B. Saunders.

Tarjan, G., Wright, S. W., Eyman, R. K., & Keeran, C. V. (1973). Natural history of retardation: Some aspects of epidemiology. *American Journal of Mental Deficiency, 77*, 369–379.

Tate, B. G. (1972). Case study: Control of chronic self-injurious behavior by conditionaing procedures. *Research and Bahvior Therapy, 4*, 281–287.

Tate, B. G., & Baroff, G. S. (1966). Aversive control of self-injurious behavior in a psychotic boy. *Behaviour Research and Therapy, 4*, 281–287.

Terman, L. M., & Merrill, M. A. (1960). *Stanford-Binet intelligence scale.* Boston: Houghton Mifflin.

Terman, L. M., & Merrill, M. A. (1973). The Stanford-Binet Intelligence Scale (3rd rev., form L-M). Boston: Houghton-Mifflin.

Test, D., & Wood, W. (1995). Natural supports: Separating fact from fiction. Presentation at the meeting of the Association for Persons in Supported Employment, Denver, CO.

Thase, M. E. (1988). The relationship between Down syndrome and Alzheimer's disease. In L. Nadel (Ed.), *The psychobiology of Down syndrome* (pp. 345–368). Cambridge, MA: MIT Press.

Thelen, E. (1996). Normal infant stereotypies: A dynamic systems approach. In R. L. Sprague & K. M. Newell (Eds.), *Stereotyped movements: Brain and behavior relationships* (pp. 139–165). Washington, DC: American Psychological Association.

Thomas, A., & Chess, S. (1977). *Temperament and development*. New York: Brunner/Mazel.

Thomas, A., & Chess, S. (1986). The New York Longitudinal Study: From infancy to early adult life. In R. Plomin & J. Dunn (Eds.), *The study of temperament: Changes, continuities, and challenges*. Hillsdale, NJ: Erlbaum.

Thompson, B., & Guess, D. (1989). Students who experience the most profound disabilities. In F. Brown, D. H. Lehr, et al. (Eds.), *Persons with profound disabilities: Issues and practices* (pp. 3–41). Baltimore, MD: Brookes.

Thompson, D. G., Greenswag, L. R., & Eleazer, R. (1988). Residential programs for individuals with Prader-Willi syndrome. In L. R. Greenswag & R. C. Alexander (Eds.), *Management of Prader-Willi syndrome* (pp. 205–222). New York: Springer Verlag.

Thompson, T., Axtell, S., & Schaal, D. (1993). Self-injurious behavior: Mechanisms and intervention. In J. L. Matson & R. P. Barrett (Eds.), *Psychopathology in the mentally retarded* (2nd ed., pp. 179–211). Boston: Allyn and Bacon.

Thompson, T., & Manson, R. (1983). Overhydration: Precautions when treating urinary incontinence. *Mental Retardation, 21*, 139–143.

Thompson, T., Symons, F., Delaney, D., & England, C. (1995). Self-injurious behavior as endogenous neurochemical self-administration. *Mental Retardation and Developmental Disabilities Research Reviews, 1*, 137–148.

Thompson, W. R., & Grusec, J. E. (1970). Studies of early experience. In P. H. Mussen (Ed.), *Carmichael's manual of child psychology* (vol. 1, p. 606). New York: Wiley.

Thorin, E., Yovanoff, P., & Irvin, L. (1996). Dilemmas faced by families during their young adults' transitions to adulthood: A brief report. *Mental Retardation, 34*, 117–120.

Thorndike, R. L., Hagen, E. P., & Sattler, J. M. (1986). *The Stanford-Binet intelligence scale* (4th ed.). Chicago: Riverside.

Thurstone, L. L., & Thurstone, T. G. (1941). *Factorial studies of intelligence*. Chicago: University of Chicago Press.

Tizard, B. (1975). Varieties of residential nursery experience. In J. Tizard, I. Sinclair, & R. V. G. Clarke (Eds.), *Varieties of residential experience* (pp. 102–121). London: Routledge and Kegan Paul.

Tores, C. P., Vandenberg, B. J., Oechsli, F. W., & Cummins, S. (1990). Prenatal and perinatal factors in the etiology of cerebral palsy. *Journal of Pediatrics, 116*, 615–619.

Tossebro, J. (1995). Impact of size revisited: Relation of number of residents to self-determination and deprivatization. *American Journal on Mental Retardation, 100*, 59–67.

Traustadottir, R. (1993). The gendered context of friendships. In A. N. Amado (Ed.), *Friendships and community connections between people with and without developmental disabilities* (pp. 109–128). Baltimore: Brookes.

Tredgold, A. F. (1937). *A textbook of mental deficiency* (6th ed.). Baltimore: Wood.

Trimble, M. R. (1988). Cognitive hazards of seizure disorders. *Epilepsia, 29*(suppl. 2), 519–524.

Trimble, M. R., & Reynolds, E. H. (1976). Anticonvulsant drugs and mental symptoms: A review. *Psychological Medicine, 6*, 169–178.

Turnbull, A. P., Guess, D., & Turnbull, A. (1988). Vox populi and Baby Doe. *Mental Retardation, 26*, 127–132.

Turnbull, A. P., Turnbull, H. R., Summers, J. A., Brotherson, M. J., & Benson, H. A. (1986). *Families, professionals and exceptionality: A special partnership*. Columbus, OH: Merrill.

Tymchuk, A. J., & Andron, L. (1992). Project Parenting: Child interactional training with mothers who are mentally handicapped. *Mental Handicap Research, 5*, 4–32.

Tymchuk, A. J., Andron, L., & Rahbar, B. (1988). Effective decision-making problem-solving training with mothers who have mental retardation. *American Journal on Mental Retardation, 92*, 510–516.

Udwin, O., & Yule, W. (1991). A cognitive and behavioral phenotype in Williams syndrome. *Journal of Clinical and Experimental Neuropsychology, 13*, 232–244.

United Nations. (1971). Declaration of general and special rights of the mentally retarded.

Update on Alzheimer's disease: Part II. (1995). *Harvard Mental Health Newsletter, 11*(9), 1–5.

U. S. Department of Education (1995). Annual report to Congress on the implementation of the Individuals with Disabilities Education Act.

U.S. Department of Health and Human Services. (1993). Effects of alcohol on fetal and postnatal development. In *Alcohol and Health*. Eight special report to the U.S. Congress, 203–232.

Valenti-Hein, D., & Dura, J. R. (1996). Sexuality and sexual development. In J. W. Jacobson & J. A. Mulick (Eds.), *Manual of diagnosis and professional practice in mental retardation* (pp. 301–310). Washington, DC: American Psychological Association.

Valenti-Hein, D., & Mueser, K. T. (1990). *The dating skills program: Teaching social/sexual skills to adults with mental retardation*. Worthington, OH: International Diagnostic Systems.

Van Den Pol, R. A., Iwata, B. A., Ivancic, M. T., Page, T. J., Neef, N. A., & Whitley, F. P. (1981). Teaching the handicapped to eat in public places: Acquisition, generalization, and maintenance of restaurant skills. *Journal of Applied Behavior Analysis, 14*, 61–69.

Van Osdol, B. M. (1972). Art education for the MR. *Mental Retardation, 10*, 51–53.

Van Osdol, B. M., & Carlson, L. (1972). A study of developmental hyperactivity. *Mental Retardation, 10*, 18–23.

Van Wegenen, R. K., Meyerson, L., Kerr, N. J., & Mahoney, K. (1969). Field trials of a new procedure for toilet training. *Journal of Experimental Child Psychology, 8*, 47–159.

Vargas, G. C., Pildes, R. S., Vidyasagar, M. R., & Keith, L. G. (1975). Effect of maternal heroin addiction on 67 liveborn neonates. *Clinical Pediatrics, 14*, 751–753.

Vaughn, B. J., & Horner, R. H. (1997). Identifying instructional tasks that occasion problem behaviors and assessing the effects of student versus teacher choice among these tasks. *Journal of Applied Behavior Analysis, 30*, 299–312.

Vernon, P. E. (1950). *The structure of human abilities*. New York: Wiley.

Vig, S., & Jedrysek, E. (1996). Application of the 1992 AAMR Definition: Issues for preschool children. *Mental Retardation, 34*, 244–246.

Villee, D. B. (1975). *Human endocrinology: A developmental approach. Philadelphia*: Saunders.

Vollmer, T. R., Iwata, B. A., Zarcone, J. R., Smith, R. G., & Mazaleski, J. L. (1993). The role of attention in the treatment of attention-maintained self-injurious behavior: Noncontingent reinforcement (NCR) and differential reinforcement of other behavior (DRO). *Journal of Applied Behavior Analysis, 26*, 9–26.

Vollmer, T. R., Marcus, B. A., & Ringdahl, J. E. (1995). Noncontingent escape as treatment for self-injurious behavior maintained by negative reinforcement. *Journal of Applied Behavior Analysis, 28*, 15–26.

Wachs, T. D., & Gruen, G. E. (1982). *Early experience and human development*. New York: Plenum Press.

Wacker, D. P., Harding, J., Cooper, L. J., Derby, K. M., Peck, S., Asmus, J., Berg, W. K., & Brown, K. A. (1996). The effects of meal schedule and quantity on problematic behavior. *Journal of Applied Behavior Analysis, 29*, 79–87.

Wadsworth, J. S., Harper, D. C., & McLeran, H. E. (1995). The transition from work to retirement among adults with mental retardation. *Journal of Applied Rehabilitation Counseling, 26*(3), 42–48.

Waggoner, D. D., Buist, N. R. M., & Donnell, G. N. (1990). Long-term prognoses in treated galactosemics: Results of a survey of 350 cases. *Journal of Inherited Metabolic Diseases, 13,* 802–818.

Waisbren, S. E., & Levy, H. L. (1991). Agoraphobia in phenylketonuria. *Journal of Inherited Metabolic Disease, 14,* 755–764.

Waisbren, S. E., Schnell, R. R., & Levy, H. L. (1980). Diet termination in children with phenylketonuria: a review of psychological assessments used to determine outcome. *Journal of Inherited Metabolic Disorders, 3,* 149–153.

Warger, C. L., Aldinger, L. E., & Okun, K. A. (1983). *Mainstreaming in the secondary school: The role of the regular teacher.* Bloomington, IN: Phi Delta Kappa Educational Foundation.

Warkany, J. (1971). *Congenital malformations: Notes and comments.* Chicago: Yearbook Medical Publishers.

Warner, F., Thrapp, R., & Walsh, S. (1973). Attitudes of children toward their special class placement. *Journal of Exceptional Children, 40,* 37–38.

Wasik, B. H., Ramey, C. T., Bryant, D. M., & Sparling, J. J. (1990). A longitudinal study of two early intervention strategies: Project CARE. *Child Development, 61,* 1682–1696.

Waterhouse, L. (1988). Extraordinary visual memory and pattern perception in an autistic boy. In L. K. Obler & D. Fein (Eds.), *The exceptional brain* (pp. 325–340). New York: Guilford Press.

Watson, L. S., Jr., & Uzzell, R. (1981). Teaching self-help skills to the mentally retarded. In J. L. Matson & J. R. McCartney (Eds.), *Handbook of behavior modification with the mentally retarded* (pp. 151–210). New York: Plenum Press.

Wechsler, D. (1981). *WAIS-R manual. Wechsler adult intelligence scale-revised.* New York: Harcourt Brace.

Wedell, K. (1961). Follow-up study of perceptual ability in children with hemiplegia. In *Hemiplegic cerebral palsy in children and adults.* London: Spastics Society/Heinemann.

Wehman, P. (1977). *Helping the mentally retarded acquire play skills.* Springfield, IL: Thomas.

Wehman, P., & Revell, W. G. (1996). Supported employment: A national program that works. *Focus on Autism and Other Developmental Disabilities, 11,* 235–243.

Wehman, P., & Schleien, S. (1979). *Leisure skills curriculum for developmentally disabled persons.* Richmond: Virginia Commonwealth University.

Wehman, P., & Schleien, S. (1981). *Leisure programs for handicapped persons: Adaptations, techniques, and curriculum.* Austin, TX: Pro-Ed.

Wehman, P., Schleien, S., & Kiernan, J. (1980). Age appropriate recreation programs for severely handicapped youth and adults. *Journal of the Association for the Severely Handicapped, 5,* 395–407.

Weinberg, R., Scarr, S., & Waldman, I. D. (1992). The Minnesota Transracial Adoption Study: A follow-up of IQ test performance at adolescence. *Intelligence, 16,* 117–135.

Weisberg, H. F. (1982). *Water, electrolyte, and acid-base balance.* Baltimore: Williams and Wilkins.

Weiss, M. J. S., Wagner, S. H., & Bauman, M. L. (1996). A validated case study of facilitated communication. *Mental Retardation, 34,* 220–230.

Wells, J. (1993). Making it up as we go along: A story about friendship. In A. N. Amado (Ed.), *Friendships and community connections between people with and without developmental disabilities* (pp. 197–212). Baltimore: Brookes.

Wetherby, A. M., & Prutting, C. A. (1984). Profiles of communicative and cognitive-social abilities in autistic children. *Journal of Speech and Hearing Research, 27,* 364–377.

Whitman, B. Y., & Accardo, P., Eds. (1990). *When a parent is mentally retarded.* Baltimore: Brookes.

Whitman, T. L., Scibak, J. W., & Reid, D. H. (1983). *Behavior modification with the severely and profoundly retarded: Research and application.* New York: Academic Press.

Widaman, K. F., Gibbs, K. W., & Geary, D. C. (1987). Structure of adoptive behavior, I:

Replication across fourteen samples of nonprofoundly retarded people. *American Journal of Mental Deficiency, 91,* 348–360.

Widaman, K. F., MacMillan, D. L., Helmsley, F. D., & Balow, I. H. D. (1992). Differences in adolescents self-concept as a function of academic level, ethnicity, and gender. *American Journal on Mental Retardation, 96,* 387–403.

Widaman, K. F., & McGrew, K. S. (1996). The structure of adaptive behavior. In J. W. Jacobson & J. A. Mulick (Eds.), *Manual of diagnosis and professional practice in mental retardation* (pp. 97–112). Washington, DC: American Psychological Association.

Wiggins, S. B., & Behrmann, M. M. (1992). Increasing independence through community learning. In K. L. Freiberg (Ed.), *Educating exceptional children* (6th ed., pp. 98–103). Guilford, CT: Duskin.

Williams, P., & Shoultz, B. (1982). *We can speak for ourselves: Self-advocacy by mentally handicapped people.* Bloomington, IN: Indiana University Press.

Wilson, G. S., McCreary, R., Kean, J., & Baxter, J. C. (1979). The development of preschool children of heroin-addicted mothers: A controlled study. *Pediatrics, 63,* 135–141.

Wing, L. (1985). *Autistic children* (2nd ed.). New York: Brunner/Mazel.

Wing, L., & Attwood, A. (1987). Syndromes of autism and atypical development. In D. J. Cohen, A. M. Donellan, & R. Paul (Eds.), *Handbook of autism and pervasive developmental disabilities* (pp. 3–19). Silver Spring, MD: Winston.

Wise, P. A., Kotelchyck, M., Wilson, M. L., & Mills, M. A. (1985). Racial and socioeconomic disparities in childhood mortality in Boston. *New England Journal of Medicine, 313,* 360–366.

Wish, J., McCombs, K., & Edmonson, B. (1980). *The socio-sexual knowledge and attitudes test.* Chicago: Stoelting.

Wisniewski, K. E., & Silverman , W. (1996). Alzheimer's disease neuropathology and dementia in Down syndrome. In J. A. Rondal, L. Nadel, & J. Perkera (Eds.), *Down syndrome, psychological, psychobiological, and socioeducational perspectives* (pp. 43–50). London: Cholin Whurr.

Wisniewski, K. E., Dalton, A., McLachlan, C., Wen, G., & Wishniewsky, H. M. (1985). Alzheimer's disease in Down syndrome: Clinicopathological studies. *Neurology, 35,* 957–961.

Wolery, M., Bailey, D. B., & Sugai, G. M. (1988). *Effective teaching: Principles and procedures of applied behavior analysis with exceptional students* (p. 24). Boston: Allyn & Bacon.

Wolfensberger, W. (1972). *The principle of normalization in human services.* Toronto: National Institute on Mental Retardation.

Wolfensberger, W. (1983). Social role valorization: A proposed new term for the principle of normalization. *Mental Retardation, 21,* 243–239.

Wolfensberger, W., & Glenn, L. (1973). *PASS (Program analysis of service systems: A method for the quantitative evaluation of human services.* Toronto: National Institute on Mental Retardation.

Wolfensberger, W., & Glenn, L. (1975). *PASS 3: A method for the quantitative evaluation of human services.* Toronto: National Institute on Mental Retardation.

Wolfensberger, W., & Kurtz, R. A., Eds. (1969). *Management of the family of the mentally retarded.* Chicago: Follett.

Wolff, P. H. (1959). Observations on newborn infants. In L. J. Stone, H. T. Smith, & L. B. Murphy (Eds.), *The competent infant* (pp. 257–268). New York: Basic Books.

Wolpe, J. (1958). *Psychotherapy by reciprocal inhibition.* Stanford, CA: Stanford University Press.

Wood, J. W., Johnson, K. G., & Omori, Y. (1967). In utero exposure to the Hiroshima atomic bomb: An evaluation of head size and mental retardation 20 years later. *Pediatrics, 39,* 385–392.

Woodcock, R. W., & Johnson, M. B. (1989). *Woodcock-Johnson psycho-educational battery: Revised.* Allen, TX: DLM Teaching Resources.

Yancy, W. S. (1999). Aggressive behavior and delinquency. In M. D. Levine, W. B. Carey, & A. O. Crocker (Eds.), *Developmental-behavioral pediatrics* (3rd ed., pp. 421–476). Philadelphia: Saunders.

Yanok, J., & Beifus, J. (1993). Communicating about loss and mourning: Death education for individuals with retardation. *Mental Retardation, 31*, 144–147.

Yoder, D. E., & Miller, J. F. (1972). What we may know and what we can do: Input toward a system. In J. E. McLean, D. E. Yoder, & R. L. Schiefelbusch (Eds.), *Language intervention with the retarded* (pp. 89–110). Baltimore: University Park Press.

Yoder, P. J., & Layton, T. L. (1988). Speech following sign language training in autistic children. *Journal of Autism and Developmental Disorders, 18*, 217–229.

Young, R. L., & Nettelbeck, T. (1994). The "intelligence" of calendrical calculators. *American Journal of Mental Retardation, 99*, 186–200.

Zaharia, E. S., & O'Brien, K. (1997). Mortality: An individual or aggregate variable. *American Journal of Mental Retardation, 101*, 424–429.

Zelson, C., Rubio, E., & Wasserman, E. (1971). Neonatal narcotic addiction: 10 year observation. *Pediatrics, 48*, 178–189.

Zetlin, A. G., & Murtaugh, M. (1988). Friendship patterns of mildly learning handicapped and nonhandicapped high school students. *American Journal on Mental Retardation, 92*, 447–454.

Zigler, E. (1966). Research on personality structure in the retardate. In N. R. Ellis (Ed.), *International review of research in mental retardation* (vol. 1, pp. 77–108). New York: Academic Press.

Zigler, E., Balla, D., & Hodajpp, R. (1984). On the definition and classification of mental retardation. *American Journal of Mental Deficiency, 89*, 215–230.

Zigler, E., & Burack, J. A. (1989). Personality development and the dually diagnosed person. *Research in Developmental Disabilities, 10*, 225–240.

Zigler, E., & Butterfield, E. C. (1968). Motivational aspects of changes in IQ test performance of culturally deprived nursery school children. *Child Development, 39*, 1–14.

Zigler, E. F., & Harter, S. (1969). The socialization of the mentally retarded. In D. A. Goslin (Ed.), *Handbook of socialization theory and research* (pp. 1065–1102). Chicago: Rand McNally.

Zigler, E., & Styfco, S. J. (1994). Head Start: Criticisms in a constructive context. *American Psychologist, 49*, 127–132.

Zigman, W., Seltzer, G., & Silverman, W. P. (1994). Physical, behavioral, and mental health changes associated with aging. In G. B. Seltzer, M. W. Krauss, & M. Janicki (Eds.), *Life course perspective on adulthood and old age* (pp. 67–91). Washington, DC: American Association on Mental Retardation Monograph Series.

Zigman, W. B., Schupf, N., Lubin, R. A., & Silverman, W. P. (1987). Premature regression of adults with Down syndrome. *American Journal of Mental Deficiency, 92*, 161–168.

Ziring, P. R. (1987). A program that works. *Mental Retardation, 25*, 207–210.

Zonia, S. C., & Goff, G. A. (1986). Communicable illnesses in the mentally retarded and nonretarded populations of three Michigan counties. *American Journal of Mental Deficiency, 90*, 453–456.

Zuckerman, B., & Bresnahan, K. (1991). Developmental and behavioral consequences of prenatal drug and alcohol exposure. *The Pediatric Clinics of North America, 38*, 1387–1406.

INDEX